HENRY JAMES

LETTERS

Volume III
1883–1895

Henry James in the 1890s, from a photograph by Elliott and Fry

HENRY JAMES

LETTERS

Edited by

Leon Edel

Volume III

1883–1895

The Belknap Press
of
Harvard University Press
Cambridge, Massachusetts

1980

Printed in the United States of America

Library of Congress Cataloging in Publication Data

James, Henry, 1843–1916.

Letters.

Includes index.

CONTENTS: v. 1. 1843–1875. — v. 2. 1875–1883. — v. 3. 1883–1895.

1. James, Henry, 1843–1916—Correspondence. 2. Novelists, American—19th century—Correspondence.

PS2123.A42 1974 813′.4 [B] 74–77181

ISBN 0–674–38782–1

Acknowledgments

As in the earlier volumes, the letters collected here come from many sources, institutions as well as private owners, and I want to express my thanks to them, as well as to the individuals in the libraries and records offices who facilitated my work. My first thanks go to Alexander R. James, the present head of the James family, who generously renewed my priorities in the materials accorded me long ago by the sons of William James, Henry and William, and renewed by his grandsons.

I owe a great debt to the President and Fellows of Harvard College and to the librarians and officers of the Houghton Library, where I spent so many of my working days when I was writing the life of Henry James. My debt to these preservers of our literary heritage has been fully acknowledged in my *Life of Henry James* (1953–1972) as well as in the *Bibliography of Henry James* (1957), which I compiled in collaboration with Dan H. Lawrence. I owe a particular debt to C. Waller Barrett, whose collection of American literature is to be found in the Alderman Library at the University of Virginia, which now also houses my manuscripts and other materials that went into my biography of James. I wish to record also my gratitude to the late Clare Benedict, niece of Constance Fenimore Woolson, for permission to use the Woolson material I have included in this volume.

As before, Ts stands for typescript and Ms for holograph in the designations at the head of each letter. The institutions and collections whose documents I use are the following:

Arents—George Arents Research Library, Syracuse, New York
Barrett—C. Waller Barrett Collection, University of Virginia
Berg—Henry W. and Albert A. Berg Collection of English and American Literature, New York Public Library, Astor, Lenox and Tilden Foundations
British Library—formerly British Museum

Brown—John Hay Library, Brown University
Chester—Chester Public Records Office, England
Colby—Colby College Library
Congress—Library of Congress, Washington
Dartmouth—Baker Library, Dartmouth College
Gardner—Isabella Stewart Gardner Museum, Boston
Glasgow—University of Glasgow Library
Harvard—Houghton Library, Harvard College
Huntington—Henry E. Huntington Library, San Marino, California
Imperial College—Imperial College Library, London
Leeds—Brotherton Library, University of Leeds
Mass. Historical—Massachusetts Historical Society, Boston
Morgan—Trustees of the Morgan Library, New York
NYPL—Manuscript Division, New York Public Library, Astor, Lenox and Tilden Foundations
Pembroke—Pembroke College, Oxford
Penn—University of Pennsylvania, Philadelphia
Rochester—Rush Rhees Library, University of Rochester
Scotland—National Library of Scotland
Texas—Humanities Research Center, University of Texas at Austin
Yale—Beinecke Rare Book and Manuscript Library, Yale University

"Ms Unknown" signifies that the only copy of a given letter I have seen has been a transcript made from a holograph whose whereabouts are now unknown to me. Some of these I made myself long ago, and I now have no knowledge of the fate of the manuscripts; others were communicated to me by friends who had access to the originals.

For manuscripts designated as "Ms Private" I am indebted to Reg. Gadney and S. Gorley Putt, Dr. and Mrs. Henry D. Janowitz (Adeline Tintner), Count Bernardo Rucellai and the Marchesa Fossi, the late Jeannette Gilder, the late Ethel Sands and Lt. Col. M. C. Sands, and Katie Lewis, daughter of Sir George Lewis. For assistance with some of the material in this volume I wish to acknowledge the help of Mrs. Tamie Cole, Daphne du Maurier, Dr. Wendy Baron, Mrs. Stanley Hawks (for the material relating to her father, Dr. Baldwin), Alan S. Bell of the National Library of Scotland, Herbert Cahoon of the Morgan Library, the late Donald G. Brien, Marjorie Wynne of the Beinecke Library (for particular help with the Stevenson letters), and Lola L. Szladits, curator of the Berg Collection. Professor Kathleen Falvey of the University of Hawaii generously helped me with HJ's Italian, and Louise Hazlett gave me considerable research assistance and helped in particular with the editing of Miss Woolson's letters.

L.E.

Contents

Illustrations

Introduction

The letters in this volume, selected from Henry James's general correspondence, show the novelist's extended relations with art and society in the old cities of Europe during the waning years of the nineteenth century. The two earlier volumes were devoted in large measure to the novelist-son's correspondence with "family." After the death of his parents at the beginning of the 1880s, the Quincy Street home in Cambridge disappears from Henry James's life. His sister Alice joins him in England; his expatriation is complete. His closest connection with America is his brother William, just beginning his career at Harvard, to whom he writes at intervals; and he has retained his earlier American friends, William Dean Howells, Charles Eliot Norton, and Norton's sister Grace. To Grace he furnishes an entertaining summary record of his movements and his life in the Victorian world, his travels to Continental centers, and his increasingly prolonged visits to Italy.

The novelty of European travel has worn off. James no longer writes long letters about his adventures among paintings and artifacts in galleries and museums; the "picturesque" of the Old World has faded; he is now much more concerned with personal relations. His letters rarely speak of his work save when he writes to publishers—and usually he writes to them for money. He goes to France to resume his old connections with the Flaubert group—although Flaubert is now dead. James is linked to this group by memories of that beloved writer and of Ivan Turgenev. In Italy he finds his old circle of friends: in Venice, Katherine De Kay Bronson in her Casa Alvisi on the Grand Canal and the Daniel Curtises in their Palazzo Barbaro; in Florence, the Boott circle in the Villa Castellani on Bellosguardo, and Constance Fenimore Woolson. By now the novelist has tired of English country visits and London dining-out. He prefers to spend his summers on the Channel, usually at Dover, and he is much preoccupied with his ailing sister, whom he visits first at Bournemouth, later at Leamington, and finally in the invalidical home she makes for herself in London with her loyal companion, Katharine Loring.

The modern literary traveler in Europe is struck by the life of ease and grandeur James created for himself in the margin of his days at his writing table—frescoed palazzos, Palladian villas, private gondoliers, endlessly available servants, great estates, the glories and ostentations of Mentmore among the Rothschilds and Lord Rosebery, the brown and purple moors of Scotland, indeed the as yet unviolated landscapes of England and the Continent. He lived and enjoyed the life he wrote about; but to see him entirely in the lap of luxury is to forget that James also moved in London's bohemia, haunted the cafés of Paris with journalist friends, and could be quite as comfortable with the lower middle class. His letters, as he moves into his many worlds, reflect his commitment to the social scene and the dilemma of the humans within. During this period he writes *The Bostonians, The Princess Casamassima, The Tragic Muse,* some thirty-five of his finest tales, a brilliant series of essays, and half a dozen mediocre plays. His genius falters when he approaches the stage.

James's literary and personal friendships multiply: the busy and intimate-gossipy friendship with Edmund Gosse; the devotion to Robert Louis Stevenson, who very soon departs for the South Seas; the formal literary relation with the British bluestocking Mrs. Humphry Ward; the modest suburban ties in Hampstead with George du Maurier, where James goes on Sunday evenings with Jusserand, the French literary diplomat, to eat cold roast beef; the exchanges with Vernon Lee; the discipleship of Paul Bourget, whose novels James detests but whose conversation he enjoys. These letters introduce us into literary and social London and Paris in the century's late afternoon. And the letters take us finally into the rough-and-tumble of the British theatre of the nineties.

James's general correspondence reveals a different persona from the dutiful son and brother of his earlier years. The worldly social animal remains committed to the truths of art and his total aestheticism—since for him all the arts are one; but he also practices the deceits of society, its duplicities and persiflage. He can tell civilized lies in the interest of preserving civilized myths, and he flatters at times to the point of embarrassment—but always with a touch of humor, a kind of contract with his correspondents that "this is the way we play the game, but we really know what it's all about." He can be ingenuous, hypocritical, grandiose, and certainly at moments paranoid, especially in the midst of the frustrations of his play-writing. The grand style is there, the amusement at the vanities of this world, the insistence that the great ones of the earth lack the imagination he is called upon to supply; and then his boundless affection and empathy for those who have shown him warmth and feeling. He is never more touching than when he stands beside the graves of his friends and puts into words his elegiac feelings; he celebrates old Fanny Kemble and Mrs. Procter, who have finally at great age dropped out of his London life; he is equally touching when he mourns the young dead, those who have been robbed of their future. The handwriting becomes larger, more regal, more indecipherable; and he splashes about his French and Italian phrases so that his letters become polyglot—as if expatriation required a special language.

Beneath the humor and the irony and his moments of euphoria, we can discern—in the very midst of his social alembications—loneliness and melancholy. In writing of his sister's death he admits to a kind of chronic depression—"she contributed constantly, infinitely, to the interest, the consolation, as it were, in disappointment and depression, of my own existence." During a goodly part of the 1880s he is still struggling with his mourning for his parents; and in the 1890s there are new losses and new disappointments: yet we must look closely, for his depression is hidden behind a facade in which he is the pet of hostesses, the charmer of the tea table, and the bearer of an ever-greater eminence—which his royalty checks belie. To be an artistic and social success and yet a financial failure, so that he had constantly to be writing for the magazines, was a burden James found humiliating—as we can see from his letters to his publishers. Howells becomes the recipient of his articulated woe, and at times it descends on his brother. His novels were in the periodicals, but in book form they didn't sell: that was the long and the short of it. They were esteemed but not even intelligently criticized. His tales were found entertaining; gathered into a volume they might appear in editions of five hundred or a thousand copies. He had currency in the lending libraries, hardly a source of income. He could not sit back and live on accumulated royalties—as Howells was doing in America and as the prodigy Rudyard Kipling did within two or three years of his leap to fame. James desperately needed this kind of success for himself. The thought of gold flowing into theatrical box offices turned him to the drama. "C'est la soif de l'or qui me pousse dans cette voie déshonorante," he wrote to his young French friend Urbain Mengin. In later life, in the gilded salons of the Gilded Age, he would remark, "I can stand a great deal of gold."

His five years of frenetic play-writing are documented in his letters. And his "dramatic years" end with the debacle of *Guy Domville;* his play was booed; he was cast out of the theatre. The letters in this volume, selected from among many hundreds, end on a note of defeat and despair. He had gone through "the most horrible experience of my life." He would never again allow himself to be led into "traps, abysses and heart break." At fifty-two James pronounced himself a public failure. His audience had rejected him, and he had only the solace of private success and the encouragement of the artistic elite. But he could not, as he put it, take the measure of "the great flat foot" of the public; or as he expressed it another way, it was impossible for him to turn a silk purse into a sow's ear. Readers of James's stories will recognize the sources of the wry humor in "The Next Time," "The Lesson of the Master," "The Death of the Lion," "The Figure in the Carpet"—his tales of creative spirits cheapened by the marketplace. He was telling himself that he was "too good" for a public that did not perceive quality—his kind of finished art—even when quality was placed right before its eyes.

There is another story to be read between the lines of these letters. It is that of his strange friendship with Constance Fenimore Woolson, the grandniece of James Fenimore Cooper. I have devoted certain chapters to it in my *Life of Henry James,* and we may perceive in the letters—in those brief and peripheral allusions to the middle-aged authoress—an attachment or symbiosis, a game of gallantry and misplaced social charm, for which he paid a painful price. Miss Woolson had come to Europe half in love with James from her close reading of his works. She was a somewhat deaf spinster, trim, compulsive, and meticulous, who wrote popular fiction for the women's magazines. James found her interested and interesting, and he turned on her the forceful charm of which he was capable: it was flattering to his ego to have so "devoted" a reader. A "virtuous" attachment grew up between them, filled with reticences and avoidances and with certain falsities on James's part—that is, a failure to recognize the effect he was having on a woman for whom he had the loyalty and affection of friendship but not a shred of romantic love. He was a little like the narrator in "The Aspern Papers" who trifles with the niece of the great Juliana; but the narrator's motives are predatory, and James had no motives beyond the gratifications of male gallantry. Miss Woolson was intelligent, and often sarcastic and aggressive; she placed herself in a bitter situation which is documented for us in the four long letters printed for the first time in the appendix to this volume. It would be too much to say that James's aloof discretions led to her ultimate suicide. She had a history of depression. She had led a lonely self-contained life. However, James responded to her death with so much pain that we can read a strong element of guilt and bewilderment in his letters, and, even more, in those extraordinary tales of the next half-dozen years, "The Altar of the Dead" and "The Beast in the Jungle," the one filled with desolation and the other with confession. Life's unpremeditated crudities gave to these tales a superior eeriness and magic—but above all a deep anguish—which reflected James's decision not to attend Miss Woolson's funeral in Rome when he learned that she had died not of natural causes but by her own hand.

When, years ago, I first decided to describe as "dramatic" the period James devoted to the writing of plays, I had in mind simply his "siege" of the theatre. But James's "dramatic years" show themselves to have been filled with drama in many more ways, indeed to have been the most dramatic of his life. He set out to write plays in the belief that he had mastered the art by assiduous theatre-going, above all to the Théâtre Français, where he had absorbed the tradition of Molière. He had studied the acting of a great school, from the flamboyance of Sarah Bernhardt to the more measured and highly skilled techniques of Coquelin, Got, Mounet-Sully, Bartet, Febvre, and others. He had sought out Bartet, in her *loge,* in Paris; he had visited the green room; he had talked to old Parisian theatrical hands and to the veteran critics. James brought the method of Sardou, and the stimulus of Ibsen, to a London still addicted to the actor-manager and the overdressed play. He expected the tough managers to respond to the same niceties as existed in France, such as the eager author's reading and explaining his script to the players, attending all the rehearsals, and so to speak crawling about on all fours to show how everything should be done. When the American producer Augustin Daly chose to have the actors try the first reading, and insisted that James sit quietly and listen, the novelist-turned-playwright imagined a "plot" against himself. He called it a mock rehearsal. He accused Daly of trying to get him to withdraw the play—even though Daly had already invested money in designs for the sets and the costumes, as his account books show. The letter of withdrawal to Daly is James at the height of his anxious play-fever; and I know of no letter in his entire epistolarium written with more elaborate, dull politeness over many pages, scrawled and hedged with so many clichés of good manners, behind which James scarcely conceals a rage that only the most rigid courtesy could control.

In the midst of these exasperations there came the sudden deaths —the young Balestier, of typhoid, in Dresden; Stevenson on his faraway island; and, a year before *Guy Domville,* the unbelievable death of Miss Woolson in Venice. Her family said she had fallen from a narrow casement window into the *calle* below. Press dispatches said she had jumped. These unscheduled dramatic events in James's calculated dramatic years threw his life into upheaval. Nothing was going according to plan. He had been in mourning for his sister—but that had been a private loss, an expected termination. The others belonged to the stuff of the stage—they were *coups de théâtre.* And when a few months later the final *coup* came, and the audience booed his delicate comedy, James knew that he was, as he repeatedly said, on the edge of an abyss.

We can begin to glimpse in these letters another side of Henry James, a side that foreshadows the breakdown in his egotism and his opening himself up to homoerotic love. It is still a mere hint, but the tone of his later affections for Hendrik Andersen, Jocelyn Persse, and Hugh Walpole may be read in some of his gestures to the journalist Morton Fullerton. "You write me in mystic mazes of wit and grace which tell me nothing whatever about yourself, your life, your occupations or impressions"; "Your sympathy enters into the soul of a man singularly accessible to affection"—these are but signals of a much greater openness to come. Unfortunately we have no letters to the young Balestier; but from Balestier's own letters to Howells we may judge that he and James had a great affection for each other. The anniversary of Balestier's death was honored each year by a letter to the young man's mother; and James would speculate on what might have been had he lived.

Along with his increasing candor of feeling, we have in these letters the elegances of his style, the irresistible charm of a writer who turned all that he touched into literature (save when he wrote to actor-managers). "What is more delicate than the extinction of delicacy?"—thus he eulogizes Walter Pater; or again, "He reminds me, in the disturbed midnight of our actual literature, of one of those lucent matchboxes which you place, on going to bed, near the candle to show you in darkness, where you can strike a light: he shines in the uneasy gloom—vaguely, and has a phosphorescence, not a flame." Or again—and the subject once more is death—he thanks Fullerton for the news of Maupassant's end, "when the indignity that life had heaped upon [him] found itself stayed." He accepts from Stevenson "the tragic statement of your permanent secession" and complains to him that he doesn't describe sufficiently "people, things, objects, faces, bodies, costumes, feathers, gestures, manners, the introductory, the *personal* paintertouch." This touch is constantly present in James's letters; and we may come to consider them among the last and greatest of the letter-writing era, before the electronic devices of our time substituted the verbosity of dictation for the economy of the pen. Even James would capitulate to the typewriter and a form of dictation—and his later letters, as we shall see, underwent a change in which the medium may indeed have become the message.

A final word needs to be said about the epistolary "absences" in these volumes beyond those created by selectivity. There are letters we know to have perished—those to John Singer Sargent, to Miss Woolson, to Jonathan Sturges; there are others that still lie hidden in family archives or unknown attics. Where are the letters to Mrs. Clifford? We have only the copies Percy Lubbock made. I have never found the letters to some of the painters—to Abbey, for example—and somewhere there must linger at least one letter to Charles Darwin or to Ruskin, and certainly a few to George Meredith. For some of these, as for the letters to Zola, I have searched without success. Time will ultimately unearth certain of the missing documents; others leave us with minor mysteries to remind us that in researching such a long and full career there remain inevitable unlighted corners, unilluminated chapters. In the Woolson letters there is a passage that suggests the kind of letter James wrote to her—and the kind she destroyed. "I should always bear in mind the fact, that when I have written to you many sheets, I have received a short note in reply, beginning with some such sentence as this: 'Dear Miss Woolson. One doesn't answer your letters. One can't. One only reads them and is grateful'; and this followed up by three very small pages (in a very big hand) in which no allusion is made to anything I have said, the 'faithfully' of the signature occupying the room of several of my sentences. Then, when I have written you a short note myself, I have received from you a charming letter in reply, eight pages long, and not such a very big hand either, and the 'faithfully' even put across the top or side of the first page instead of being relied upon to fill the last half of the last."

Thanks to Miss Woolson we at least glimpse this much of a correspondence otherwise gone. There are other examples, in other letters, of the flourish, the tongue-in-cheek, the playing of a social role. We have, however, such abundance that when there are gaps we are able to extrapolate—as James himself advised when he told young novelists that there was such a thing as deducing the unknown from the known, including the complexities of human relations.

Brief Chronology

1883: Resumes life in London. Death of Turgenev. Searches for a house but decides to remain in Bolton Street. Death of brother Garth Wilkinson. Serializes *The Bostonians.*

1884: To Paris in February for a month; renews friendship with Daudet, Zola, Edmond de Goncourt. Spends August at Dover and finishes *Bostonians.* Publishes series of tales, among them "Lady Barberina" and "The Author of Beltraffio." Publishes "The Art of Fiction," a manifesto on the art of the novel. Paul Bourget becomes a disciple. Alice James comes from Boston to visit her brother and remains in England in invalidical state.

1885: Starts work on *The Princess Casamassima.* Cultivates friendship with Robert Louis Stevenson. Returns to Dover for August and spends autumn in Paris.

1886: Moves from Bolton Street into Kensington flat, at No. 34 De Vere Gardens. Spends summer in England finishing *Princess* and in December goes for holiday to Italy.

1887: In Florence, stays in rooms rented from Constance Fenimore Woolson in Villa Brichieri, then in Hotel du Sud. Enjoys polyglot social life of Florence. In March, guest of Mrs. Bronson in Venice. Contracts jaundice; returns to Florence and convalesces in Villa Brichieri, in independent rooms adjoining Miss Woolson's apartment. Writes "The Aspern Papers." Returns to Venice as guest of Daniel Curtises. In England at end of summer visits Broadway painters' group (Sargent, Millet, Abbey, Parsons) and settles to writing *The Tragic Muse.*

1888: In London until October. Goes to Geneva for rendezvous (in separate hotels) with Miss Woolson. Brief visit to Monte Carlo and Genoa. Magazine publication of the tales written during his Italian months.

1889: During long serialization of *Muse,* decides to become a dramatist. Spends September at Dover and goes briefly to Paris to discuss theatre and play-writing with his French confrères.

1890: Dramatizes his novel *The American* for the Compton Comedy Company. To Italy to stay with Curtises in June. Visits Dr. W. W. Baldwin in Florence in July and stays also at Vallombrosa. Visits Siena, and goes on brief walking tour in Tuscany with Baldwin and his friend Taccini. The *Atlantic Monthly* rejects his story "The Pupil." Begins to write series of comedies for the theatre. Meets Rudyard Kipling.

1891: *The American* is produced at Southport and tours provinces. Visits Miss Woolson at Cheltenham. Circulates plays (*Mrs. Vibert,* later called *Tenants,* and *Mrs. Jasper,* later *Disengaged*) but managers are noncommittal. In Ireland in July, recuperating from flu. Death of James Russell Lowell. *The American* brought to London by Compton; runs seventy nights. Wolcott Balestier dies in Dresden, and HJ goes to funeral.

1892: Death of Alice James in March. Goes to Siena in June to spend a month with Bourgets. Visits Curtises in Venice. Augustin Daly agrees to produce *Mrs. Jasper* as vehicle for Ada Rehan. HJ becomes enthusiastic Ibsenite.

1893: Death of Fanny Kemble. In Paris in spring, sketches *Guy Domville* for Comptons. Spends summer at Ramsgate writing first act and scenario for rest of play. George Alexander agrees to produce it. Daly stages first rehearsal of *Mrs. Jasper.* HJ withdraws play, claiming rehearsal a mockery.

1894: At end of January learns Miss Woolson has committed suicide in Venice. In spring goes to Venice and assists Miss Woolson's sister in winding up the dead woman's affairs and recovers his letters to her. Late in year begins rehearsals of *Guy Domville.* Death of Robert Louis Stevenson.

1895: *Guy Domville* produced by Alexander at the St. James's on 5 January. HJ booed when he comes out to take a bow.

1
Search for an Anchorage

1883–1886

1
Search for an Anchorage

Henry James returned to London during the midsummer of 1883 in a pronounced state of melancholy. He had wound up his father's affairs after the elder James's death in 1882. The family home in Cambridge had been sold following his mother's death earlier that year. All his ties to what had been "home" were cut; and he distinctly felt himself "orphaned" and adrift. This feeling was reinforced by the death of his beloved friend, and in a sense his literary mentor, Ivan Turgenev. His first act in London was to seek a house; he did not like returning to his dingy rooms in Bolton Street. He would make himself a new home. He found a fine dwelling in St. John's Wood—a studio, a garden, and much light and space, very suitable for a sedentary bachelor. His friends began to inquire whether he planned to marry. After a while he realized that he was well enough off in his Piccadilly lodgings, that in St. John's Wood he would be out of the center of things; and he abandoned all thought of a change in his mode of life.

The house hunt was a symptom of his malaise. And so were the two novels he now wrote—*The Bostonians,* which deals with his lost American home, and *The Princess Casamassima,* whose hero is an aesthetic young man, early orphaned and adrift in an indifferent London. The next three or four years were for Henry James years of endless labor as he wrote out his depressed feelings and laid his personal Cambridge and Boston ghosts. In quest of his earlier years, he went to Paris in 1884 in search of Turgenev's friends, seeking out Daudet and Zola and old Edmond de Goncourt, to whom he had been introduced by the Russian at Flaubert's. Like himself, they had achieved success; and he discussed the art of fiction and "naturalism" with them. The ensuing letters show how he absorbed some of Zola's ideas, notably in the *Princess,* in which he emphasized the heredity and environment of his young hero. This novel was also his first exclusively English subject: no Americans are in it. Its theme is revolution: the unrest among Britain's workers and the white-collar class. "You see, I am quite the Naturalist," he writes to T. S. Perry after visiting Millbank Prison to collect fictional "atmosphere." He is prescient in foreshadowing our own times, in which young revolutionaries blow themselves up with their own dynamite, and equally so in *The Bostonians,* where he chooses feminism as a salient issue in American life. The inner statement in these novels is personal: he pictures loneliness, an inability to make peace with Boston, and his sense of being an "outsider" in London.

In the midst of such profound crises of feeling, his sister comes abroad, bringing her personal crisis with her. She is also adrift; she has been lonely in her Beacon Hill home. She is ill and has to be carried off the ship. For her, as for many Victorian spinsters, illness has become a way of life—her way of demanding that the world take notice of her and take care of her. Financially independent (James has made over to her his income from the family estate), she can live apart from her brother, but for the remaining eight years of her life she is a source of intermittent anxiety to him, as the letters show.

He now begins, in his search for an anchorage, to correspond with English writers and artists. A notable correspondence is that with Robert Louis Stevenson—two stylists showing off their virtuosity to each other. There are his gossipy letters to Edmund Gosse and his admirable letter-lectures to Mrs. Humphry Ward correcting her novels and mentally rewriting them. He enjoys the growing esteem of the London social and artistic world. His melancholy is submerged in constant action. At the end of his four years of writing he is ready to go to Italy, the country in which he has always felt the greatest personal freedom.

To Theodore E. Child

Ms Barrett

[Tillypronie, Aberdeen]
Oct. 1*st* [1883]

Dear Child.[1]

I wonder whether you can do me a little service?

I returned from America, where I had been for the last nine

months, on September 1st, and shortly after my arrival in London, received a note from Alphonse Daudet, thanking me for a little article I had published about him in the *Century*,[2] and asking me a question, for which he begged a prompt answer, about another article (of his own) which is to appear there and which I have translated.[3] I immediately replied to his note and his inquiry, but as he had given me no address whatever (his letter hadn't even a date) my missive has been returned on my hands (opened, to ascertain my address) by the French post office. He was in Provence when he wrote, but he said "écrivez-moi à Paris, et on fera suivre." I addressed him simply *Paris,* trusting to his renown to convey the letter to his house; but as I say, his renown simply shirks the whole business. I should still like him to get the letter, to show that I immediately acknowledged his courtesy, and as I know you know him well, I appeal to your *obligeance* to forward it. Will you very kindly do so, and place me in your debt to the amount of a postage stamp? If at the same time you would send him a line to let him know why my epistle is a fortnight old, you would add greatly to my indebtedness. I am writing to you too in the dark, for though I know you are always in Paris, I don't know that you are always Rue de Constantinople. May heaven direct this communication. I wrote a second time to Daudet (in the same way) adding a word about the information he had asked of me; and that letter has not yet been returned—but doubtless it will be. Perhaps I shall send it to you as well.

I am in Scotland, in the wilds of Aberdeenshire, but go back to London in a day or two. I am always at my old quarters (3 Bolton Street, Piccadilly, W.), where I shall be very glad to hear from you if this safely reaches you. I am settled again in the British Babylon (which I am as fond of as you are of Paris); but have the prospect of occasional absences the very next of which is to be *de votre côté.* As soon as I arrive there I shall let you know. I hope you are well and happy—you must at least be by this time *archi-parisien.* All that seems far from Tillypronie! I greet the honourable Huntington,[4] with whom I hope you still consort. Excuse my importunity and believe me

Very truly yours,
H. James

Excuse my stamped envelope—the only one I can put my hand on *here.*

1. HJ had maintained his friendship with the British journalist since their meeting in 1875. As Paris correspondent for various London journals, Child had made many friends in French literary circles. See *Letters* II, 86, 88.

2. HJ's essay on Daudet appeared in the *Century,* XXVI (August 1883), 498–509.

3. Daudet's memoir of Turgenev appeared in the *Century,* XXVII (November 1883), 49–53, entitled "Tourguénieff in Paris: Reminiscences by Daudet." The anonymous translator was HJ. The manuscript of the translation, in the Barrett Collection, is in HJ's hand.

4. W. H. Huntington, one of the New York *Tribune*'s Paris correspondents. See *Letters* II, 11–12.

To Theodore E. Child

Ms Barrett

3 Bolton St. Piccadilly
Oct. 10*th* [1883]

My dear Child.

What a dear little note from Alphonse, and how I thank you for so fully transmitting it! My heart warms to him and I am most grateful to him for the rank he assigns me in the animal kingdom.[1] It seemed to me that in all these be-Britished years my French had become quite that of Stratford-atte-Bowe. I found your other note but last night on my return from Scotland, and the second came in this A.M. Thank you kindly; I shall be delighted to go to break bread with you somewhere, *aussitôt l'arrivée* in the city of sense, if not of the soul. My dream is to go over to Paris about Christmas time, and I anticipate the greatest pleasure from seeing Daudet, as I beg you to tell him, with many thanks. How charmingly he says whatever he has to say—*craquelé comme une figure*[2] is the happiest possible description of sunburn. I value you his compliment, but it is a terrible thing to have to live up to!—your account of Huntington is very interesting—there is something very humorous in the idea of his moving, after thirty years, five doors off! I am only very sorry to hear of his illness—I suppose you mean that he has one of the miserable incidents of an honoured old age, an affection of the vessie[3] or thereabouts. I hope the doctor will ease him off. Can't his friend Clemenceau[4] do something for him; or is Clemenceau occupied exclusively with the national bladder? Give Huntington many good wishes from me, and tell him that I hope he not only collects the Great but recollects the small. I trust he will be still *dans son quartier* (not in Florence, I mean, if he still goes there) at Christmastide. I am sorry to have missed you when you were in this place—I only got back from America, where I had been since last December, on September 1st. I appreciate fully what you say about one's always remaining a foreigner and outsider in Paris; and it is because one is so much less so here that I cling to my London. Apropos of Paris and the foreign, how beautifully the French are conducting their relations with their neighbours! If only nothing will happen before Christmas.

Ever yours,
Henry James

1. In accordance with HJ's request in the previous letter, Child transmitted HJ's note, and Daudet replied: "Remerciez Henry James de sa charmante et affectueuse lettre. S'il se tire de sa langue comme de la nôtre, c'est un rude lapin. J'aimerais bien le connaître. Amenez-le moi, je vous en prie, à son premier voyage; que nous déjeunions longuement et affectueusement."

2. Literally "crackle like a face."

3. The bladder.

4. Georges Clemenceau (1841–1929), a friend of Daudet and Zola, later premier of France, called "The Tiger" during the First World War.

To Elizabeth Boott
Ms Harvard

3 Bolton St. Piccadilly
Oct. 14*th* 1883

My dear Lizzie.

It is little to my honour that I should not long before this have responded to the gracious note from Sharon which came to me before I sailed and which lies before me now, bearing the reproachful date of August 12th. During those last days at home I was so pressed with occupations and so knocked up by the violent heat that I intentionally postponed writing to you till I should begin to possess my soul—and body—again, in this land of constitutional freedom. It would seem from my further delay—that this result has only just occurred. The truth is that I found an accumulation of letters as high as my head awaiting me here; and I have had to attend to them before doing anything else. Heaven forbid I should stand on ceremony with *lei*[1]—and I don't; witness the fact that I send you herewith the most familiar and most affectionate greetings. I have been back here six weeks now, and have become re-naturalized as completely as if I had never been away. I like London as much as ever, and find here in a quarter of an hour a greater impression of *life* than I had in Boston in the whole nine months I spent there. I have indeed at present a good many sad and anxious thoughts; but they come from America and not from London. My last letter gave an account of poor Wilky's[2] rapid decline, and the very last of all was a note from William telling me that he was about to start for Milwaukee immediately. I am therefore in painful suspense—though my foremost feeling is an earnest wish to hear that Wilky has laid down forever the burden of all his troubles. All the last news of him is a record of unmitigated suffering, and he was long ago ready to go. I have before me now a little pencil-drawing that William made of him, years ago, after he was brought home wounded from Fort Wagner and when he thought he was dying. It was taken at a moment when he looked as if everything was over, and is a most touching, vivid little picture. I say to myself as I look at it that it probably represents the dear boy now. Peace be to his spirit—one of the gentlest and kindest I have ever known!—I am settled here for the winter, and except for a week or two in Paris during some part of it, shall indulge this year in no going-abroad. I have work enough and to spare, in this place: and I hope, by the time the Season comes, to be "located" in a quieter part of the town, where I shall be out of the reach of the bustle and clatter of this quarter, pervaded by the predatory American. I am in treaty for a small house in St. John's Wood.[3] The matter drags a good deal, but I shall probably get it in the end, and if I do, I shall get into it about March—not before. I have been to Scotland for a week of bad weather, which made my visit there rather a failure; but returning to London I lingered along and saw half a dozen cathedrals in a row. I had seen most of them before, but I enjoyed the revision, to which lovely days contributed. Won't you come over and see a few? I will show you them all *de ma main*. London, as yet, of course, is very quiet—but never too quiet for me. My taste, as I grow older, is made more sedentary. I saw Burne-

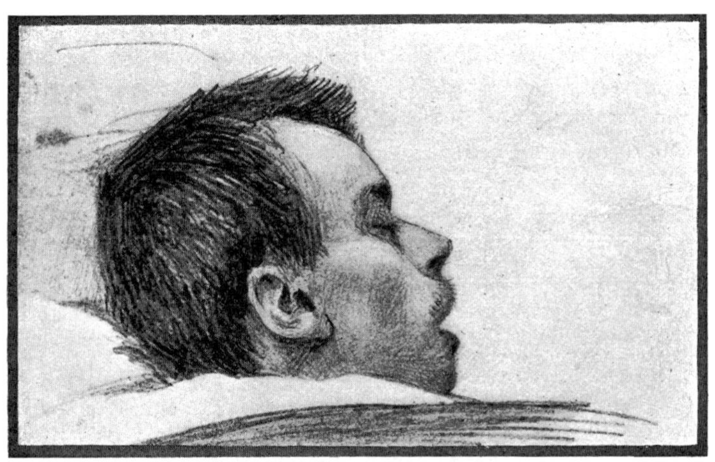

Sketch by William James of Garth Wilkinson (Wilky) James brought home wounded from the assault on Fort Wagner

Jones[4] yesterday and am to dine with him tomorrow. He is a wonderfully nice creature, and with all the limitations of his art, it has a great deal of beauty. His talent, weak, in some ways, and queer as it is, is one of the most individual there is today. I met Mrs. Boit[5] several times since at the Sturgis's[6] and she gave me a famous account of Sargent,[7] whom she constantly sees. She says he is *de plus en plus fort*—but I don't know that she is a judge. Du Maurier[8] I was to have seen yesterday, but it came on to rain hard and prevented my pilgrimage to Hampstead. I hear with great distress that he has been having another alarm about his sight, which I believe, however, has passed away. The terrible thing is that it all depends now on one eye. Don't repeat this—please; I have such a horror in the U.S.A. of everything getting into the papers. Of course you have long ago left Sharon—but you will scarcely be back in the rear of your Palazzo della Signoria as yet. You are probably with the genial Annie [Dixwell] on the top of her mountain, from which I trust by this time the mosquitoes have descended. That Annie should have remained so genial through the annual épreuve speaks volumes as to her nature. Tell me about your work, your prospects. Remember that I can make a place for you whenever you will come over here—in spite of the fact that Costanza has just arrived in South Kensington, and that the Rensellina[9] is due in Half Moon Street—round the corner. Much love to your Father, and believe me ever

your very faithful friend
H. James

1. HJ always mixed Italian and French words with English in his letters to the Continentalized Miss Boott. In this case *lei* = you.

2. Garth Wilkinson James (1845–1883), HJ's younger brother, had been in ill health since his service in the Civil War, during which he was seriously wounded.

3. The house was in Elm Tree Road and had a studio and a garden.

4. Edward Burne-Jones (1833–1898), the painter, whom James had known from the time of his first independent journey abroad in 1869.

5. Mary Louisa (Cushing) Boit, wife of Edward Darley Boit, the American painter. See *Letters* I, 356.

6. Russell Sturgis (b. 1805), American banker, senior partner in Baring Brothers until 1882. See *Letters* II, 224, 301. See also Julian Sturgis, *From Books and Papers of Russell Sturgis,* privately printed (Oxford, at the University Press, n.d.).

7. John Singer Sargent, the American painter, was coming to the fore and would become famous within a few months on showing his portrait of Madame Gautreau in the Paris salon.

8. George du Maurier, by now a close friend of HJ's. See *Letters* II, 113.

9. The Costanza may have been HJ's friend the novelist Constance Fenimore Woolson; the Rensellina was probably Mrs. Philip Livingstone Van Rensselaer, an American expatriate he had known in Rome and later met socially in London.

To Grace Norton
Ms Harvard

3 Bolton St. Piccadilly
Oct. 29*th* [1883]

My dear Grace.

Let me say once for all that when I let *weeks* elapse before answering a letter of yours, I must ask you to believe that I have a very good reason. My reason now is that these last three (since I received your excellent and most welcome remarks on my *French Poets and Novelists*) have been a time of pressing occupation (I mean painfully pressing) and has brought with it the need of constantly writing home on family matters, which have left me weary of the pen, and unfit for communion with one who handles it so easily as you. My prolonged stay in America (the summer especially) put me back so in my work that I have had more than I can do to "catch up"—have not caught up yet and [am] accordingly bothered. It was most kind and wise of you to make all those suggestions about a new edition of my "Poet" book—but alas, my dear Grace, they came six months too late. The new edition is nothing but the Tauchnitz edition (published for the first time last winter) and simply re-issued here in exactly the same form by the Macmillans, who have bought the Tauchnitz stereotype plates.[1] Therefore the pleasure of your emendations can only be for me alone, and not for the public, of whom they are so worthy. It is true that to one or two of them I don't exactly agree. I don't think you understand Mérimée. He was a cynic of cynics, his *sécheresse* WAS voluntary as well as real, and I haven't any particular pity for him in his old age. He had a very good time, and had always had it. He was an ADMIRABLE writer and I admire him, and his Inconnue[2] may have been a brute (I suspect she was); but I haven't much other sentiment about him, for I am pretty sure he never gave himself away, and accordingly didn't suffer. I didn't mean that George Sand's marriage was made by her mother—and—grandmother-relatives; but by some other people under whose care she was (more or less) when she met Dudevant. But perhaps I was wrong in this, and the book is so full of faults and errors that this one perhaps is not one of the worst. I am just about to publish another, called *Portraits of Places*[3] (all collected things, of course) which I will send you.—I think of you, my dear Grace, very frequently and very tenderly, and wonder what the particular texture of your days may be now. That of mine is of a fair London sort. This place has repossessed me, and I have repossessed myself of it. I have been a week in Scotland (at Tillypronie) with the Clarks—so delicate a topic!—but good people—; but otherwise have stuck to London and shall stick all the rest of the winter. I haven't yet taken a house—I have too much work on hand—but am more and more conscious of the necessity of doing so. If I should take one by Christmas, however, I should not get into it before March; so think of me as for the winter, between these much-tested walls. London is waking up and I see people—a little. A little, for London, that is; it would [be] a multitude for Boston (as I saw Boston). You asked me once *why* (in a word) I like this place so much and wished to come back. Put my answer into a word: because I have here in an hour a greater feeling of *life* than *là-bas* in six months!—I am getting sad news from home—but of which the sadness was to be expected. My poor brother Wilky is slowly, painfully sinking to his end, and his condition, as you probably know, is such that one must fervently pray it may be near. I hear almost nothing from Alice—she can write so little; and am haunted by fears and anxieties about her—having (as you know—or perhaps even don't) an unlimited capacity for imagining and apprehending that things are going, or will go, badly. But I try and keep this disposition in check, and it is worthwhile. She has not yet come back to town and taken possession of her lonely house; and it will not be till then that I shall know how she gets on.—Charles and Eliot,[4] as you will know, were with me for a week before they sailed. Charles was *charming,* and Eliot remarkably pleasant. That Charles was better was not, to me, striking; but you will have judged of this for yourself. He was most genial, pleasant company, and full of impressions of what he had seen. As for Eliot, he *feels* his father too much for his happiness—and no wonder! It is rather absurd, however, my giving you information about the tenants of Shady Hill! Lawrence Godkin[5] was also with me for a week, and was a comfortable but not a thrilling companion. He is a very nice intelligent fellow and easy—perfectly—to live with. But he is not appreciative, and he has no tastes, not an interesting youthful mind. He is too preoccupied, also, with the artificial view of things.—I see no new people here, but my old friends are turning up one by one. Mahlon Sands has just (as I write) come in to ask me to dine (not that he is an old friend!). If Matthew Arnold[6] lectures in Boston, *do* go and hear him—not because he will lecture well; but because I want him to succeed!—I have just got a letter from Mrs. Lee Childe,[7] which is mainly a long diatribe against her aunt Mme de Triqueti, lately defunct, on account of the condition in which she has left the estate which Mrs. C. inherits and in which Mme de T. had a life-interest. Mrs. C. says she has been despoiled! The attack is a violent one—for a charming woman to make; but Mme de T. cut down £35,000 worth of trees!—Nothing has given me more pleasure in a long time than your telling me that you can lose yourself more and more in reading. Bravo, my dear Grace—your words delight me. Lose yourself as much as possible—for it is a great world—the world of all the past and a great part of the present and future. I shall send you some readabilities; but you must give me time. I hope your autumn glows a little, and that your days are not too heavy. It is odious to be so transatlanticked from you; and all I can say is that if you will come over to my side I will introduce you to every one I know. I think of Cambridge at about 9 P.M.; and recommend you to keep as much of your reading as possible for that hour. I am very well—only *haunted* to a certain extent with family contingencies and remembrances. This however probably does me good, and does no one else harm! Lowell[8] is in Paris with his wife, but soon returns. I dined the other day with Burne-Jones, who is sympathetic and charming, but weak. Also with Du Maurier who is ditto, ditto, but very nervous about his eyesight, which is precarious. Be sure, dear Grace, I am with you whenever you think of me—and that of an evening I am not so absent from your parlour as might seem. I am ever your most faithful

H. James

1. *French Poets and Novelists* was published originally in England in 1878 in a small edition by Macmillan. There was no separate American edition. Tauchnitz reprinted it on the Continent in 1883 in its "Collection of British Authors," and Macmillan reissued it from the Tauchnitz plates in 1884.

2. Prosper Mérimée's *Lettres à une inconnue* (1873) written to Mlle Jenny Daquin from 1831 until a few hours before his death in 1870.

3. *Portraits of Places* was published 18 December 1883 in England and 29 January 1884 in the United States.

4. Miss Norton's brother Charles Eliot Norton and her nephew Eliot.

5. Son of E. L. Godkin, editor of the *Nation*.

6. Arnold was then at the start of his much-publicized American tour.

7. For HJ's friendship with the Childes and Mme de Triqueti see *Letters* II, 61–62.

8. James Russell Lowell, American minister to the Court of St. James's.

To Thomas Sergeant Perry

Ms Colby

3 Bolton St. W.
Nov. 25*th* [1883]

Dear Tom.

Oddly enough I bought the two volumes, (*Madame d'Épinay, Jeunesse et Dernières Années*)[1] three or four days since, but haven't had time to read them *yet*. The curse of London (or at least *my*

London) is that I have so little time to read. Her Memoirs I read years ago: they are full of the period and the *moeurs*—also of the lubricity that M[atthew] A[rnold] deplores. I am very sorry you didn't like poor dear old Mat. I like him—love him rather—as I do my old portfolio, my old shoe-horn: with an affection that is proof against anything he may say or do today, and proof also against taking him too seriously. And, after all, Zola *is* lubric. Vide, for my sentiments on Mat, a charming article in Macmillan's new (illustrated) Magazine for January next, in which I have expressed nothing but tenderness and in a manner absolutely fulsome.[2] Or rather, don't look at it, as it will probably excite your disgust.—I have just been reading the two last (sixth and seventh) volumes of Mme de Rémusat,[3] just out—her correspondence with her son—and finding them interesting and *very* (as they say in Marlborough Street) high civilised. Yes, I have read Trollope's autobiography and regard it as one of the most curious and amazing books in all literature, for its density, blockishness and general thickness and soddenness. Not a voice has been lifted to say so. But I must do it, sometime and somewhere.[4] Oh, England!—and oh, America! I envy you your heroic *lectures*—your thirty-six volumes of *Mémoires secrètes.* I have just sent about a hundred volumes (mostly French) to the binders—but I haven't read every one even of those! I shall thank you for the *Senilia*—though I have been reading them all in German, and have also received (but not yet read) *Klara Milich,*[5] in the same tongue. What is it, and what the degree of its interest? Why don't you translate it? I bought the other day at a railway book stall an English copy of your version of *Virgin Soil,*[6] with a brilliant picture on the cover.—You will have heard, days ago, of poor Wilky's liberation—which is a blessing unspeakable. But it was a dark end for such a gentle, genial, sociable soul for whom the world should have been easy, as he was easy (too easy) for it and for everything. Love to Madame. Ever yours

Henry

1. Louise-Florence d'Épinay (1726–1783), friend of Rousseau and Diderot. HJ had just purchased C. A. L. Herpins's newly published two-volume biography of d'Épinay.

2. Perry had attended Arnold's Boston lecture. HJ's article on Arnold appeared in the *English Illustrated Magazine,* I (January 1884), 241–246.

3. The Countess Claire-Elisabeth de Rémusat (1780–1821) was lady-in-waiting to the Empress Josephine. Her letters (1804–1814) to her son, published in 1881,

were in James's library. The volumes contain a picture of Napoleon's court life from the time of the Consulate to just before his divorce from Josephine.

4. Trollope's autobiography was published posthumously in two volumes in 1883. James's essay on the novelist appeared in the *Century*, XXVI (July 1883), 384–395.

5. Turgenev's *Senilia* and *Klara Milich* appeared in German translations in 1883.

6. HJ had obtained permission from Turgenev for Perry to translate *Virgin Soil*. Since Perry knew no Russian, his version was taken from the French and German translations.

To William James
Ms Harvard

3 Bolton St. W.
Nov. 24*th* [1883]

Dear William.

I return without delay Bob's letter enclosed to me this A.M. I rejoice in his apparently reasonable state of mind, and hope the trusteeship can be settled satisfactorily. It seems to me a hundred times better that you shouldn't be saddled with it. At the same time it must be also arranged that *you* do not have to send elaborate monthly reports—a burden under which you will perish if it be kept up. Never, I again beg you, take the trouble to tell *me* anything at all about my Syracuse dividend. I have made my income entirely over to Alice and take no further interest in it.—A telegram from Carrie about poor Wilky's blessed liberation came to me two hours before yours, which arrived at 2.30 A.M. I instantly wrote to Carrie, and afterwards to Alice, who will have forwarded you my letter. It is a great weight off my spirit—not to see him lying there in that interminable suffering. Meanwhile your letter comes to me, forwarding Carrie's and Bob's notes and speaking of the days before his death—just as they came to you here, last winter, after you had heard that Father had gone. You will, I hope, have had news to send me about his last hours. May they have been easy—I suppose they were unconscious. I like to think that somewhere in the mysterious infinite of the universe, Father and Mother may exist together as pure, individual spirits—and that poor Wilky, lightened of all his woes, may come to them and tell them of us, their poor *empêtrés* children on earth.—This post brings me also a letter from Katharine Loring from which I gather, though she tries to dissimulate it, that on the whole, since I have been away, Alice has been pretty poorly. I try to hope, however, that now she is in her own house, independent and surrounded with her own arrangements, she may pull herself together, if she doesn't languish from loneliness. I am very sorry to hear of Miss Webb's condition—and fear it must make a sad house in Garden Street. Much love to your Alice.—You will have received my letter expressing my anxious hope for an *early* execution of the division.[1]

Ever your
Henry

P.S.—As I must always worry about something, I worry now, as regards Wilky, about his burial-place. It would be a great regret to me if he doesn't lie beside Father and Mother, where we must all lie.[2] I hope, at any rate, you have had no trouble—that is no discussion and no excessive correspondence or fatigue about it—and above all no expense. I have sent Carrie £42, to contribute to Wilky's funeral (and other expenses).

Yours ever
H. J.

1. Of their father's estate.

2. Wilky was not buried in the James family plot in Cambridge Cemetery, his widow preferring burial in Milwaukee, where she and Wilky had lived for a number of years.

To Elizabeth Boott
Ms Harvard

3 Bolton St. Piccadilly
Dec. 11*th* [1883]

Dear Lizzie.

I must thank you tenderly for your copious and charming letter which came in this morning. The promptness of my answer must be the measure of my appreciation. Excuse me if I am rather brief—my correspondence, coming on top with my other scribbling, and always keeping pace with it, is so large and exacting. It is especially valuable to me to get news of Alice from one who sees her frequently—even though that news is condemned to be but indifferently good. She writes to me whenever she can, but I think I have no illusions about her condition. Her loneliness is of course a drawback; she is very fond of her independence and that is in itself an advantage to her. There are few people she would care to live with or to have live with her. It is my belief that in the course of time her health will mend; but I am prepared for many more delays and obstacles. She fortunately has great pluck, and in certain ways much freedom. I do not wonder she should not wish to come abroad while she is still so great an invalid; yet I confess I tremble when I think of Katharine Loring's absence. But time will help us all. It helped poor Wilky at last, and his death, which was an unmitigated release, lifts a great load off my mind. I am completely re-domiciled here—though not in St. John's Wood—having at the last moment changed my mind about that move and given up the house. It was a perfect little residence, with a pretty garden and a most commodious and agreeable interior—it had once belonged to a painter and the studio had become the dining room, a really noble apartment; but the place was too far from the centre of things and it was revealed to me in a dream that I should spend half the time on the roads. So that, *per ora,* having resisted that temptation I shall remain in these after all very comfortable and central rooms. They have many advantages. Sooner or later, I suppose, I shall take a house, but there is no hurry, and when I do a conjugal Mrs. H. is not among the articles of furniture that I shall put into it. I think, my dear Lizzie, that the human race is going crazy and am sorry to see that the madness has touched your gentle and luminous brain as well. Twenty people have spoken to me of late about renouncing my happy state—all save three or four taking upon themselves to urge it. Those three or four—the only wiseheads—have remarked "Don't—don't—for heavens sake!" and I never shall, my dear Lizzie, for I find life quite interesting enough as it is, without such complicated and complicating appendages. What strikes me most in the affaire is the want of application on the part of society of the useful, beneficent, and civilizing part played in it by the occasional unmarried man of a certain age. He keeps up the tone of humanity—he stands for a thousand agreeable and delightful things. People ought really to be ashamed not to feel better than that what one is doing for it. *Dunque, cara Lisa, non mi sposarò mai—mai!* The Rensellina is much improved—writes no more notes, cultivates reserve and discretion etc.; but even for this —*mai, mai.* The lady just mentioned is here still, having many social ties now, apparently in England. She has always her German maid and her little dog; but she has not as yet anything else. I heard the other day that she was engaged to Hamilton Aïdé: but the tale is not confirmed.—The Littératrice is also here, and is really an angel of quiet virtue; *ma non prenderò neppure lei!*[1] These ladies don't meet, fortunately, and both are behaving very well. Their stay in the British capital appears to be of indefinite duration.— I hope you won't doubt of my sincerity if I remark even in a sentence immediately following the above statement that I wish you were here too! I do indeed, for I think you would enjoy the artistic world of London, and find it intelligent, and cultivated—find it, that is, above all, sociable and entertaining. I went only last night to a pleasant artistic function: to see Leighton,[2] as president of the R[oyal] A[cademy], deliver the annual prizes to the students of that Institution. Boughton took me, who is a very good fellow, if a weak painter, and before it we dined together with dear little Abbey, the American, and Alfred Parsons,[3] the landscapist, his *fidus achates.* Leighton is wonderful for such an occasion as that— he *represents* admirably—and the thing was interesting. I often see Tadema,[4] and also Du Maurier, who has something in him singularly intelligent and sympathetic and satisfactory and whom I like exceedingly. Burne-Jones I have become quite intimate with, and he sends me photos of his works, marked with assurances of his "affection." A few days hence I dine with Richmond, the younger, and also with Frank Dicey; so you see that, if you come, I am prepared to show you round among the British studios, despise them though you will, and Philistine though they be. Burne-Jones is really interesting, and is (privately) a most delightful caricaturist and pencil-satirist, little as you might suspect it. I hear with interest of your own exhibits and of your life and manners this winter. Give this to your father and tell him to read between the lines how I cherish and remember him. I shall write to him ultimately—or rather, I mean, proximately. I fear Lady Rose's[5] death will have checked your Newport visit. Poor Aunt Mary will feel it much. Ever dear Lizzie very faithfully yours

H. James

1. HJ is indulging here in considerable private wit concerning the rumors of his planning to marry. In coupling the bouncing "Rensellina" (see 14 October 1883, n. 9) with Charles Hamilton Aïdé, the inveterate party-goer and aesthete of London society, HJ is creating a highly incongruous couple. As for the "Littératrice" who is a "quiet one," and a "costanza"—constancy—HJ affirms in his Italian phrase "but I will take not even her."

2. Frederick, later Lord Leighton (1830–1896), neoclassical painter of immense prestige in his day. He had served as president of the Royal Academy since 1878. See *Letters* II, 241.

3. George Henry Boughton (1833–1905) and Edwin Austin Abbey (1852–1911) were American painters residing in London; Alfred Parsons (1847–1920) was a British landscape painter and book illustrator.

4. Lawrence Alma-Tadema (1836–1912), Dutch painter of the neoclassical school, who had settled in England. He was at this time at the height of his fame.

5. Lady Rose, an aunt of HJ's Temple cousins. See *Letters* II, 7.

To Edmund Gosse
Ms Leeds

3 Bolton St. Piccadilly W.
Dec. 26*th* [1883]

My dear Gosse.[1]

Your note of yesterday—or rather, I should say, your copious and friendly letter—gives me real pleasure. It is very good of you to say to me all those ingenious and appreciative things. I appreciate them, in my turn, heartily, and am your debtor for that sort of sympathy that does one good, and which, in fact, when one meets it, is one of the best things of life.

I am glad you find the paper on Turgénieff something of a picture.[2] He was a noble, a really inspiring model, and I almost feel as if what I had *not* managed to say in my article was the most essential and characteristic thing. But if it has an aroma of admiration and tenderness, it has some justification. He was a pure, beautiful, delightful mind; and I have never known any one who made upon me the same kind of impression. The thing, alas, is full of errors, from my having seen no proof; e.g. Mme Pauline *Pierdot!*—for Viardot. Yes, I too like what I read the better when I know (and like) the author. That is partly why I have read your letter with so much pleasure. I shall look you up again some proximate Sunday. Noël, Noël! Ever faithfully yours

Henry James

1. HJ had met Edmund Gosse (1849–1928) in 1879; but with his absences in America their friendship of good-natured gossip and literary criticism did not ripen until around 1883. Gosse was then translator for the Board of Trade.

2. HJ's memorial essay appeared in the *Atlantic Monthly*, LIII (January), 42–55, and was reprinted in *Partial Portraits* (1888).

To Grace Norton
Ms Harvard

3 Bolton St. W.
Jan. 19*th* [1884]

My dear Grace.

I have before me (as I believe the well-regulated write), your letter of December 6th, which is mainly about Matthew Arnold and his womankind. I won't descant on this topic in response to it, as we all by this time must have ceased to be conscious of an Arnold-hunger. I am sorry not to have heard his lecture on Emerson, but perhaps he will re-deliver (as he will certainly print) it here. Oddly enough, I can't make out whether he is a *success* in the U. S. or not, and as that question is instantly asked me here, as if as an American I had some intuitive knowledge on the subject, quite independent of experience, my darkness is rather a social drawback. Katharine Loring writes me that he delights in Ben Butler;[1] and that I think is a form of victory.—What shall I tell you? The most beautiful winter I have known in England—fogless and frostless—pursues its rapid course; and the way it *melts* out of one's fingers is only an item of my constant consciousness of today being already tomorrow and tomorrow next month, while work, and plans and fruits of every kind are halting behind in the unrecoverable regions of yesterday. It is not the hurry of the social train that brings this about, for I have had a less worldly winter than usual. It is, I think, simply the native spite of time against those who are growing old. —I think of going to Paris a week hence, to spend a fortnight; and the sentiment with which I do so reminds me afresh of the way in which with my extreme affection for London is mingled a peculiar relish of occasional, homesick absence from it. It is *too much;* that is its only fault. Be thankful, dear Grace, that Cambridge is not too much.—This is a lovely Sunday morning, the sun discreetly traverses my astonished window-pane, and I am in better form than might be expected of a littérateur who went to *supper* in St. John's Wood last night at exactly the witching hour (midnight) and afterwards walked home through the sleeping town at 2.30 A.M. The affair took place at the house of my hospitable (if not otherwise remunerative) publisher, Frederick Macmillan, and was pleasant enough, with six or seven persons "connected with literature and art." I don't often take my food so irregularly. I go to lunch half an hour hence with a nice Mrs. Pakenham,[2] *née* American, (though your subtlety would perhaps contest the epithet) in order to meet Julian Sturgis[3] and his wife—the latter a little obscure Irish maid (of the race of Beresford), whom a short time since (all in a day or two) he took as his comfortable bride. I dined a week ago with the Lowells, who have moved into a big "smart" house, and bored myself a little, though the dinner was also big and smart. Mrs. L. is now a very good ministress, with London conversation and long tails of her gowns, and *him* I have never seen more happy and hearty. I see Mrs. Kemble pretty regularly once a week. She shows the marks of time more or less—lives on her old *fonds*—and is somewhat out of tune with the present world; but that I suppose is what most people of advanced age (though not all, for I know striking cases of the opposite), are condemned to. She has periodical cataclysms in her material and social relations, and has just passed through one (material) which has landed her for a year (to come) in a house of her own—a relief to me, who have her various lodgings and migrations a good deal on my mind. The incongruity of this hotel-life for a person of her ripe habits is almost grotesque. She remains to me a most interesting and valuable friend (one of the very best, after you).—I have written various things of late, and you will see them in *The Century* etc.) and not care for them any more than I do. But I am just beginning a shortish novel (also for the *Century*), which you *will* care for, as I do, and which is to mark a new era in my career, and usher in a series of works of superior value to any I have yet produced. These last things are the mechanical working off of an old, unprofitable contract.—I have much better news of Alice, and am sure she is learning to live alone and to get better. K[atharine] L[oring]'s departure for Europe will help her, for herself, much more than hinder her.—Get from the University Library the *Mémoires* du Comte Beugnot,[4] a book not new but delightful. I ask you no questions, dear Grace; you will speak and relate, as occasion assists you. I envelop you with affection, and am ever your faithfulest—

Henry James

1. Benjamin Franklin Butler (1818–1893), a civil war soldier and political figure who became the standard bearer of the "People's Party" against Cleveland and was a flamboyant advocate of the rights of workers, women, and blacks.

2. The former Elizabeth Staples Clark of New York, wife of the naval captain (later admiral) William Christopher Pakenham. See *Letters* II, 102, 324.

3. Julian Russell Sturgis (1848–1904), a Boston-born novelist, son of Russell Sturgis, the American banker.

4. Count Jacques-Claude Beugnot (1761–1835) denounced Marat during the French revolution. His memoirs were published in 1866.

To Frederick Macmillan
Ms British Library

3 Bolton St. W.
Jan. 29*th* [1884]

My dear Macmillan.

The last time I saw you in Bedford Street I was interrupted by the arrival of visitors before I had discharged the latter portion of my errand; and last night was of course not an occasion for talking of business. But before I leave town, as I expect to do for some little time on Friday or Saturday, I want to repair my omission.

It is only within a few days past that I have looked over the statement of account you sent me a number of weeks ago, and taken home to myself its melancholy results. I postponed the contemplation of it, as I am apt to do disagreeable things, because I expected the said results would be small, but I now perceive them to be virtually *nil*. The balance owing me is £2.17.6!—for a year's sale of some seven or eight books. The sale is depressingly small;—it appears however to have amounted to some 500 copies for all the books, without counting a quantity of sheets of one of them sent to America. I feel that for the future I must make some arrangement that shall be more fruitful, and such as I made a year ago in America. Even my *old* American arrangement, which still holds with regard to most of my volumes there, yields me an appreciable yearly profit. It is not, however, of this I wish to speak to you now, as there will be time for that before I publish something new. What moves me today is the sense of being rather in want of money, owing to having (among other things) expected from the source which has yielded me £2.17.6, a sum less insubstantial, though, as I said just now, not large. It occurs to me to ask you whether the sale of the little books in a box[1]—or that of the *Portraits of Places* —or the two sales together—may be such as to warrant your sending me a cheque on account. In the natural course you would not, I suppose, do so for another year; but I should be glad if the process might be anticipated. In any case, please debit me with the sum I owe for the printing of my American tale the other day, in the manner most convenient. I had supposed that my share of the profits of my old books would at least cover that. I am trying to leave town on Friday.

Yours very faithfully,
Henry James

1. The "little books in a box" were the pocket-size 1883 collective edition of HJ's novels and tales published in fourteen volumes. See Edel and Laurence, *A Bibliography of Henry James* (1961), 58–60.

To Richard Watson Gilder
Ms Private

3 Bolton St. W
Feb. 1*st* [1884]

My dear Gilder.[1]

I am very glad you like *Lady B.*;[2] and your expression of the fact gives me pleasure. I am sorry you are to publish it as *three*; the interest is not calculated for that. This, however, reassures me a little in one way, as the process of writing a very short story becomes constantly more difficult to me. As one grows older, and sees and learns more, it becomes harder to squeeze this enlarged matter into brevity of form, and I find I *must* take elbow-room. I say this partly to prepare you for the fact that if you are to print *Lady B.* as three you will probably print my third tale, which (now being copied by a type-writer), is on the point of going to you, as two. If you are obliged to do this I hope that you will not rage at my betrayal—for I promised to make this No. 3 proper for being printed at once and entire. It is called "A New England Winter," and it is all about Boston; where it probably (though most *lacteal* in its satire) won't be liked. I shall add in a p.s. two or three corrections for Lady B. one of which you yourself ask about.—I go to Paris tomorrow for ten days; otherwise I am having a very quiet London winter. The *Century* flourishes here hugely, and the *Breadwinners* (which I have received but not yet read—I mean to) is spoken of with London assurance as J. Hay's.[3] Mrs. Procter[4] is younger than ever, H. Aïdé more of a patron of everything and everyone; and Literature rather low. My twenty-four hours at Marion[5] look iridescent and exotic out of this time and place. *Bien des choses* to your wife from yours faithfully ever

H. James

1. Gilder was assistant editor of *Scribner's Monthly* after 1870 and when it was succeeded by *The Century* (1881) remained as editor until his death.

2. HJ contracted to write three tales for *The Century*. They became "The Impressions of a Cousin," XXVII (November-December 1883), 116–129, 257–275; "Lady Barberina," XXVIII (May-June 1884), 18–31, 222–234, 336–350; and "A New England Winter," XXVIII (August-September 1884), 573–587, 733–743. The three tales were collected in 1884 and titled *Tales of Three Cities*, the cities being London, New York, and Boston.

3. James's informants were accurate. John Hay (1838–1905) was the anonymous author of *The Breadwinners* (1884), one of the earliest fictions in America dealing with trade unions.

4. Anne Benson Procter, widow of Bryan Waller Procter, was then in her eighties. See *Letters* II, 208.

5. HJ, while in the United States in 1883, had visited the Gilders at their summer home in Marion, Massachusetts, near Cape Cod. He would use this setting in *The Bostonians*.

To Thomas Bailey Aldrich

Ms Harvard

Paris, Feb. 13*th* [1884]
Hôtel de Hollande

My dear Aldrich.

It is all right about poor H. Aïdé. My application to you was purely perfunctory and I sacrificed you without scruple to a social tie! You will already have received my note asking you to please send back his MS. to *Queen Anne's (Garden) Mansions, St. James's Park, London, S.W.* and this is the end of that.

Yes—I think I should like to do you a serial to begin in 1865 [*sic*].[1] Only I don't think I should be able to begin it in January. It would suit me better to open, as the theatrical papers say, in July. I gather, from the way you express yourself, that this would not be inconsistent with your plan. I have in my head, and have had for a year or two, a very good *sujet de roman* of which I should make use. What I desire is that you should give me twelve monthly instalments of twenty-five pages each: that my novel should in other words run exactly a year. Please let me hear from you in regard to this matter of beginning in July 1865, and as to when in this case you should desire the first batch of copy. I think too that for a work beginning upwards of a year and a half from now there would probably be something to be said about terms: pregnant word! Between this and that the *Century* is to publish, *de moi,* 1/ a story in three parts. 2/ a story in two parts. 3/ a story in six parts.[2] And three or four short tales, from my turning hand, are to appear (this is a profound secret)—have been, in a word, secured, *à prix d'or* in—*je vous en donne en mille*—the New York Sunday *Sun!!*[3] This last fact, I repeat, is really as yet *a complete and sacred secret.* Please bury it in oblivion and burn my letter. I mention it, with the preceding items, simply to denote that by July 1865 I expect to be in the enjoyment of a popularity which will require me to ask $500 a number for the successive instalments of *The Princess Casamassima*[4] (which will probably be the name of my novel, though on this I am not yet fixed). I should like also to say that it will probably be a good thing for all of us that I should send you between this and the end of the year three or four short critical articles which I have in my head, and which crave to be written. Besides relieving my mind of thoughts that ferment in it, they will do to complete a volume of essays which I desire to put forth by the end of the year and which will probably represent the last of this sort of work which I shall do for a long time to come.—This latter is a reason which says more of course to me than to you; but I leave it in its naiveté: one learns to be so naif in Paris.—I have been here (for that and other advantages) for the last fortnight and shall remain to the end of the month. Paris is charming; bright, mild and a little dull, and "naturalism" is in possession *sur toute la ligne.* I spent last evening at Alph. Daudet's, and was much impressed with the intense seriousness of that little group—himself,

Zola, Goncourt, etc.[5] About Daudet's intensity of effort there is something tragical, and his wasted, worn, extraordinarily beautiful and refined little face expresses it in a way which almost brings tears to my eyes. The torment of style, the high standard of it, the effort to say something perfectly in a language in which *everything* has been said and re-said,—so that there are certain things, certain cases, which can never again be attempted—all this seems to me to be wearing them all out, so that they have the look of galley-slaves tied to a ball and chain, rather than of happy producers. Daudet tells me that the act of production, and execution, for him, is nothing but effort and suffering—the only joy (and that he admits is great) is that of conception, of planning and arranging. This all proves, what one always feels, that (in their narrow circle) terrible are the subtleties they attempt. Daudet spoke of his envy and admiration of the "serenity of production" of Turgénieff—working in a field and a language where the white snow had as yet so few foot-prints. In French, he said, it is all one trampled slosh—one has to look, forever, to see where one can put down his step. And he wished to know how it was in English. What do you think I ought to have told him?—Your account of your work gives me yearnings even in the Rue de la Paix. But you will probably see me here (that is in London) before I see you in your savoury halls. I am very sorry to hear of Howells's visitation. Give him my love, and tell him that I am always, theoretically and platonically, writing him letters. Some day before long he shall have a direct sign from me. I thank Mrs. Aldrich very kindly for her attention to the volume of *Portraits*[6] and am very faithfully yours

Henry James

1. For a discussion of this and subsequent slips of the pen in this letter see Edel, *Henry James: The Untried Years, 1843–1867* (1953), the chapter entitled "Heroine of the Scene."

2. See preceding letter to Gilder. The story in six parts was *The Bostonians.*

3. The stories in the *Sun* were "Pandora," 1, 8 June 1884 and "Georgina's Reasons," 20, 27 July and 3 August 1884.

4. *The Princess Casamassima* ran in the *Atlantic Monthly* from September 1885 to October 1886.

5. An anonymous account of this evening's conversation was published in the *Atlantic* "Contributors' Club" columns, LIII (May 1884), 724–727. This was written by Theodore E. Child, who had accompanied HJ to Daudet's. See Edel, *Henry James: The Middle Years, 1882–1895* (1962), the chapter entitled "The Besotted Mandarins." See also ensuing letter to Howells.

6. *Portraits of Places* (1883).

To William Dean Howells

Ms Harvard

Paris, Hôtel de Hollande
Feb. 21*st*, 1884

My dear Howells.

Your letter of the 2d last gives me great pleasure. A frozen Atlantic seemed to stretch between us, and I had had no news of you to speak of save an allusion, in a late letter of T. B. A[ldrich], to your having infant-disease in your house. You give me a good account of this, and I hope your tax is paid this year at least. These are not things to make a hardened bachelor mend his ways.—Hardened as I am, however, I am not proof against being delighted to hear that my Barberina tale entertained you. I am not prepared even to resent the malignity of your remark that the last third is not the best. It isn't; the Ameri[can] part is squeezed together and *écourté*. It is always the fault of my things that the head and trunk are too big and the legs too short. I spread myself always, at first, from a nervous fear that I shall not have enough of my peculiar tap to "go round." But I always (or generally) have, and therefore, at the end, have to fill one of the cups to overflowing. My tendency to this disproportion remains incorrigible. I begin short tales as if they were to be long novels. Apropos of which, ask Osgood to show you also the sheets of another thing I lately sent him—"A New England Winter." It is not very good—on the contrary; but it will perhaps seem to you to put into form a certain impression of Boston.—What you tell me of the success of Crawford's[1] last novel sickens and almost paralyses me. It seems to me (the book) so contemptibly bad and ignoble that the idea of people reading it in such numbers makes one return upon one's self and ask what is the use of trying to write anything decent or serious for a public so absolutely idiotic. It must be totally wasted. I would rather have produced the basest experiment in the "naturalistic" that is being practised here than such a piece of sixpenny humbug. Work so shamelessly bad seems to me to dishonour the novelist's art to a degree that is absolutely not to be forgiven; just as its success dishonours the people for whom one supposes one's self to write. Excuse my ferocity, which (more discreetly and philosophically) I think you must share; and don't mention it, please, to any one, as it will be set down to green-eyed jealousy.

I came to this place three weeks since—on the principle that anything is quieter than London; but I return to the British scramble in a few days. Paris speaks to me, always, for about such a time as this, with many voices; but at the end of a month I have learned all it has to say. I have been seeing something of Daudet, Goncourt and Zola;[2] and there is nothing more interesting to me now than the effort and experiment of this little group, with its truly infernal intelligence of art, form, manner—its intense artistic life. They do the only kind of work, today, that I respect; and in spite of their ferocious pessimism and their handling of unclean things, they are at least serious and honest. The floods of tepid soap and water which under the name of novels are being vomited forth in England, seem to me, by contrast, to do little honour to our race. I say this to you, because I regard you as the great American naturalist. I don't think you go far enough, and you are haunted with romantic phantoms and a tendency to factitious glosses; but you are in the right path, and I wish you repeated triumphs there—beginning with your Americo-Venetian—though I slightly fear, from what you tell me, that he will have a certain "gloss." It isn't for me to reproach you with that, however, the said gloss being a constant defect of *my* characters; they have too much of it—too damnably much. But I am a failure!—comparatively. Read Zola's last thing: *La Joie de Vivre.* This title of course has a desperate irony: but the work is admirably solid and serious.—I haven't much London news for you. I see the genial Gosse occasionally, and the square-headed Tadema, whose d's and t's are so mixed; and they frequently ask about you. Miss Fenimore Woolson[3] is spending the winter there; I see her at discreet intervals and we talk of you and Mrs. *you.* She is a very intelligent woman, and understands when she is spoken to; a peculiarity I prize, as I find it more and more rare.—I am very happy as to what you tell me of [T. S.] Perry's having a large piece of work to do; and I pray it may yield him some profit and comfort. Sad indeed has been hitherto the history of his career, and the cynical indifference of the public to so good a production (in spite of weakness of form) as his *Eighteenth Century*[4] makes me blush for it. As you see I am blushing a good deal for the public now. Give Perry my love, please, when you see him next, and tell him I am acutely conscious of owing him, and indeed his wife, a letter; they shall really have it soon. *Addio*—

stia bene. I wish you could send me anything you have in the way of advance-sheets. It is rather hard that as you are the only English novelist I read (except Miss Woolson), I shouldn't have more comfort with you. Give my love to Winny: I am sure she will dance herself well. Why doesn't Mrs. Howells try it too? *Tout à vous*,

Henry James

1. Francis Marion Crawford (1854–1909) had just published *To Leeward* for the Christmas trade of 1883 and was currently serializing *The Roman Singer* in the *Atlantic Monthly*.

2. See preceding letter to Aldrich.

3. HJ had met Constance Fenimore Woolson (1840–1894) in Florence in 1880, and the American regionalist had become his admirer and disciple. She alternately lived in Italy and in England. See *Letters* II, 289.

4. Thomas Sergeant Perry's *English Literature of the Eighteenth Century* (1883).

To John Addington Symonds
Ts Lubbock

Paris
Jan. [Feb.] 22*nd* 1884

My dear J. A. Symonds.

Your good letter came to me just as I was leaving London (for a month in this place—to return there in a few days,) and the distractions and interruptions incidental to a short stay in Paris must account for my not having immediately answered it, as the spirit moved me to do. I thank you for it very kindly, and am much touched by your telling me that a communication from me should in any degree, and for a moment, have lighted up the horizon of the Alpine crevice in which I can well believe you find it hard, and even cruel, to be condemned to pass your life. To condole with you on a fate so stern must seem at the best but a hollow business; I will therefore only wish you a continuance of the courage of which your abundant and delightful work gives such evidence, and take pleasure in thinking that there may be entertainment for you in any of my small effusions.—I *did* send you the *Century* more than a year ago, with my paper on Venice,[1] not having then the prevision of my reprinting it with some other things. I sent it you because it was a constructive way of expressing the good will I felt for you in consequence of what you have written about the land of Italy—and of intimating to you, somewhat dumbly, that I am an attentive and sympathetic reader. I nourish for the said Italy an unspeakably tender passion, and your pages always seemed to say to me that you were one of a small number of people who love it as much as I do—in addition to your knowing it immeasurably better. I wanted to recognize this (to your knowledge); for it seemed to me that the victims of a common passion should sometimes exchange a look, and I sent you off the magazine at a venture, in spite of its containing an article (*à mon adresse*) of painfully overcharged appreciation from my dear friend Howells and a horrible effigy of my countenance; to neither of which did I wish to give circulation. I spent last winter in the United States and while I was there another old and excellent friend of mine, Sergeant Perry, the most lettered American almost, and [the] most unsuccessful writer that I know, read me a portion of a note he had had from you, in which you were so good as to speak (in a friendly—very friendly way) of the little paper in the *Century*. The memory of this led me, when *Portraits of Places* came out, to wish to put you in possession of the article in a more decent form. I thank you very sincerely for the good-natured things you say of its companions. It is all very light work indeed, and the only merit I should dream of any one finding in it would be that it is "prettily turned." I thank you still further for your offer to send me the Tauchnitz volumes of your Italian local sketches. I know them already well, as I have said, and possess them in the English issue; but I shall welcome them warmly, directly from you—especially as I gather that they have occasional retouchings.

I lately spent a number of months in America, after a long absence, but I live in London and have put my constant address at the top of my letter. I imagine that it is scarcely ever in your power to come to England, but do take note of my whereabouts, for this happy (and possibly, to you, ideal) contingency. I should like very much to see you—but I go little, nowadays, to Switzerland in summer (though at one time I was there a good deal). I think it possible moreover that at that season you get out of your Alps. I certainly should, in your place, for the Alps are easily too many for me.—I can well imagine the innumerable things you miss at Davos—year after year—and (I will say it) I think of you with exceeding sympathy. As a sign of that I shall send you everything I publish.[2]

I shake hands with me [you], and am very truly yours

Henry James

1. "Venice" appeared in the *Century*, XXV (November 1882), 3–23, and was reprinted in *Portraits of Places* (1883) and in *Italian Hours* (1909).

2. This is apparently the only extant letter from HJ to Symonds. See *Letters* II, 99. It is not known whether HJ kept his word: he may have learned that Symonds was not one of his admirers. On his side, HJ had in his library nearly all of Symonds's writings.

To Grace Norton
Ms Harvard

Paris, Feb. 23*d* 1884

My dear Grace.

I lose no time in thanking you for your charming letter of the 7th, as it came to me only yesterday. I had been thinking of you the day before, as Mrs. Strong[1] then mentioned to me the death of Mrs. Swift. What you say about it is in agreement with what I supposed you would feel, and I can't but greatly grieve to hear of your losing a friend. Besides, anything sad that happens to you always seems to me sadder than the same thing happening to any one else—I don't know, indeed, that I can explain the sense in which I mean that; I shrink, instinctively, my sympathy when I hear of your receiving another *indentation*.—I congratulate you on having Shakespeare to take you out of these and other current realities. He is indeed a world, by himself, and there is no world of the mind in which one can lose one's self more, and feel more beguilement and fascination—more infinite suggestion and illumination. There is no one who, literally, transports us more.—I came to Paris three weeks ago, and I return to Bolton Street at the end of my month. If you ask me why I came, I don't know that I can tell you more than that it is a part of my present plan of existence to get six weeks of the year in this place, and that (not having been here for a year and a half) the present month of February seemed a good moment to take out a part of my time. It has broken the back of the London winter. I always like Paris for a fortnight—

but ought to take only a fortnight at once. However it always gives me a certain sort of intellectual stimulus, and speaks to me on the whole with many voices. Those of certain old friends belonging to the little American group are doubtless among the number; though as a general thing, if I may say it without disloyalty, to you, they are not the most eloquent. That is a very contracted and monotonous set, three or four of whose members were meant for better things. Poor Mrs. Strong I have seen several times—and can only say of her—poor Mrs. Strong!—flitting with weary eagerness from one exhausted little Paris pastime to another, and completely destitute of domestic or internal resources. She is really a warning. (These remarks, by the way, are very indiscreet, and you had better burn my letter.) The only Franco-American product of importance here strikes me as young John Sargent the painter, who has high talent, a charming nature, artistic and personal, and is civilized to his finger-tips.[2] He is perhaps spoilable—though I don't think he is spoiled. But I hope not, for I like him extremely; and the best of his work seems to me to have in it something exquisite. The Lee Childes[3] are just now back from three months in Algeria and Tunis, and I have seen them, familiarly, three or four times; am indeed to breakfast with them tomorrow, Sunday: the only day I ever commit that matutinal crime. He seems to me worn and weary and bored, and she very intelligent, even brilliant, and very agreeable in the superficial commerce of life; but quite destitute of moral sense. (Burn, decidedly; burn!) I greatly miss Turgénieff, and see how much his presence here has been for me in all these last visits of mine to Paris. I saw yesterday an old Russian friend of mine, the Princess Ouroussoff,[4] who told me some very interesting (and sad) things about his condition in the last year of his life, and also gave me some impressions (very sad also) of a late visit of hers to Russia after a long absence. "C'est un pays perdu—il faut y être ou laquais ou nihiliste." I have been working about as usual since I have been here, and am pouring various works of fiction into the capacious bosom of the *Century,* which will come to the front when the *Century* pleases. I have likewise agreed to publish a long novel in the *Atlantic* (to run a twelve month) next year. Finish up Shakespeare, therefore, to have an unbiased mind for H.J.—I thank you tenderly for your good words about the *Portraits of Places.* Yes, I reflect too much—or not enough; I don't know which.

I ought, that is, to go either much further, or not so far. But they belong to a class of composition which I have left behind me today; they are very slight and thin, and I don't take enough interest in them to judge them. Wait for my future productions.—I hear on the whole good news of Alice; that is in the sense that I feel quite warranted in ceasing to worry about her. She is evidently able to stand on her own feet, and her "loneliness" gives her much more comfort than distress. It presents itself to her in the form of independence and absolute freedom, and her appreciation of these things is, from the cast of her character, very high. Therefore she is, I am happy to say, a good deal "off my mind"; a fortunate circumstance, as she has already been much disgusted when she suspected she was *on* it.—Wilky's children are, I believe, doing well enough (in their odious circumstances); but his poor wife much less so, inasmuch as she wrote me the other day that it would be, to her thinking, a "glorious thing" if she and they could lie down together and die. She is desolate, feeble in health, and poor; but during the trials of her last six months has shown great courage, feeling and discretion; "come out" more than I expected her to. It is my belief that she will not live long. Then we shall be confronted with the question of her children—but sufficient unto the day!—I got a pleasant letter the other day from Howells—whose simplicity of mind—in artistic and literary questions—seems to me—especially in the midst of a Parisian contagion—inexpressible. I have been seeing a little of the propagators of that contagion—Daudet, Goncourt etc. and should tell you about them if we could really talk. Daudet is a dear little man, extraordinarily beautiful, but very sad, and looking to me exhausted with all the brilliant ingenuities he has dug out of his heart. He and two or three others here interest me much; they have gone so far in the art of expression. But they are the children of a decadence, I think (a brilliant one—unlike ours: that is, the English) and they are strangely corrupt and prodigiously ignorant. In spite of all this they represent a great deal of truth. I don't want my last word to be about French novels;—but it is no fiction, dear Grace that I am ever your *tout dévoué*

Henry James

1. Mrs. Charles Strong, the former Eleanor Fearing. See *Letters* II, 43.

2. HJ had just met John Singer Sargent and had begun his successful campaign to induce him to settle in London.

3. Edward Lee Childe and his wife. See *Letters* II, 61–62.

4. Princess Marie Ourousov, daughter of the Russian industrialist Maltzov, lived a cosmopolitan life and was a friend of the leading Russian and French writers of her time. See *Letters* II, 45–46.

To Alice James
Ms Harvard

3 Bolton St. W.
Feb. 29*th* [1884]

Dearest Sister.

I seem to myself to be constantly letting longer intervals elapse between my letters to you; but I suppose that is inevitable in a prolonged correspondence. I will try and not let silence get too much ahead of speech. I wrote you last just after I had gone over to Paris; from which place I returned, after a stay of some three weeks, two days ago. I am very glad to relapse into Bolton Street as I always am, after any absence, however pleasant, and I say this without detriment to Paris, which, for short periods, is always charming to me. Nothing very particular happened to me there, but I saw my old friends and the new plays and had some excellent food. I greatly missed Turgénieff, but I saw the Princess Ouroussoff, whom I used to see a great deal of old, and who is a most clever and curious woman, and she told me various things about the last year of his life. I am much horrified to learn that since his death Mme Viardot[1] complains of him—of his having impoverished them; whereas he ruined himself for her and her children. But these are odious discussions. While I was in Paris I heard from Aunt Kate of your intending to go on to N.Y. to try an electrician;[2] and therefore suppose that you have achieved it and that you even now are lodged behind some brownstone front of your native city. This sounds to me like a big attempt, and I hope it will be a big success. The drama of your separation from Katharine[3] is well over now, I suppose; and I will not indulge in vain conjectures as to how you bear your bereavement. I pray that whatever it may be, it is at least not worse than you—or she—supposed. I am writing her a word of greeting, here, through the Barings, and she probably will send me a line—describing you, as she left you—when she arrives in Italy.—We are having the first cold of the winter and

Mrs. Duncan Stewart[4] is dead. But the cold is bright and wholesome and Mrs. Stewart had become a kind of talking melancholy ghost. She was a charming old being, however, and I shall miss her much. Someday I shall put her into a book. I have already seen Mrs. Kemble and find her constantly a little more and a little more broken and, as it were, indented. I shall never put *her* into a book. —Salvini made his first appearance here, last night, in *Othello*,[5] and I went to see him; but to my surprise and distress he gave all the climax of the play much less finely than when I saw him a year ago in Boston, and I was proportionately taken aback, having puffed him so to some of my friends who were there. It was as if he had toned it down and weakened it deliberately, and I don't understand the mystery. I shall try and see him, and inquire.—A note just comes in from William, accompanying some papers for me to sign in which he speaks definitely of your going to N.Y. on the 14th. I hope Mary will be an efficient (and effective) soubrette. I don't think I have any news that will interest you. Miss Motley (a supposedly hopeless old maid, plain and not moneyed) is to marry Colonel Mildmay. There is a sign of cheer for you—having the advantages that she lacks. Mrs. Lombard was still seriously ill when I left Paris, and I took upon myself to write to her son. She ought to come home unless she has some one with her more powerful than Fanny.—I hear every now and then from Carrie, but it is difficult to write to her, for want of topics. But I do what I can. I shall send this to Aunt Kate to give you. Bob's quietude seems almost too good to be true. Ever your affectionate

Henry

1. Michelle Pauline Garcia Viardot (1821–1910), the famous singer, was followed by Turgenev wherever she traveled until she accepted him into her household.

2. An "electrician" at the time was one who administered electric therapy. See letter to William James, 2 January 1885.

3. Katharine Loring.

4. Mrs. Duncan Stewart, wife of a Liverpool merchant, who moved in high London society and was reputed to have been the natural daughter of an earl. Leigh Hunt and Disraeli were among her friends. She was the original of Lady Davenant in HJ's "A London Life."

5. Tommaso Salvini (1829–1916), a celebrated Italian actor who scored in Shakespearean roles. HJ had reviewed his performances in Boston in March 1883 in the *Atlantic Monthly*, LI, 377–386.

To Theodore E. Child
Ms Barrett

3 Bolton St. W.
March 8*th* [1884]

Dear Child.

I thank you cordially for your letter and the various primeurs you enclose. Goncourt's preface I immediately return, no other human eye having beheld it. It is interesting, and I agree with much of it. But there is something indefinitely disagreeable to me in what that man writes, something hard and irritated, not sympathetic. Why also should the note of egotism, of vanity, of the claims he makes for himself, be condemned to sound in every Frenchman's utterance, sooner or later? However, I am for the *roman d'analyse, sans intrigue et sans ficelle, tant qu'il voudra,* and also, *Dieu sait!* for writing exquisitely and resisting reportage. And why the devil will he make me wait twenty years for those wonderful Memoirs!—and thirty years after his death too.[1] In your place, with your opportunities, I should secretly poison him tomorrow, so that the twenty years may commence to run. *Mlle Tantale* must be a sweet thing, and I confess there are moments when such emanations seem to me to sound the *glaise* of a literature. Nevertheless, I am sorry that the divine Daudet is going to virtuefy his *souillon. Puisque souillon il y a,* I should say let her be a real one. The said Daudet, however, cannot put three words together, that I don't more or less adore them. I enter into your divided feelings about Paris—though fortunately, for myself, I have worked into quiet waters; I find life *possible* in London (on condition of swearing at it) and the ideally arranged existence (by the year) for me would be five months of London, five of Italy (mainly Rome), a month for Paris and a month for the *imprévu.* I have settled down again into this Indian village and the matutinal tea and toast, the British coal scuttle, the dark back-bedroom, the dim front sitting-room, the *Times,* the hansom cab, the London dinner, the extension of the franchise, *partagent* my existence. This place *is* hideously political, and there don't seem to me to be three people in it who care for questions of art, or form, or taste. I am lonely and speechless. Everything around me is woolly, stuffy, literal, unspeakably Philistine. I went, however, to see Salvini[2] last night, and he is the greatest of the great. Stick to your bright little Parisian *cinquième*, to the light and easy civilization of the Gauls. Don't rashly make an exchange which is like refusing a *riz de veau à la jardinière* for a dish of tripe and onions!

Yours ever, cynically,
Henry James

1. The Goncourt journals contained allusions to living persons and could not be integrally published. Excerpts were brought out in 1888 and reviewed by HJ in the *Fortnightly Review*, (October), 501–520; the review was included in *Essays in London and Elsewhere* (1893). The complete journal has been published in modern times.

2. HJ wrote "A Study of Salvini," which appeared in the *Pall Mall Gazette*, 27 March 1884.

To Thomas Bailey Aldrich
Ms Harvard

3 Bolton St. Piccadilly
March 19*th* 1884

My dear Aldrich.

I have had your note of February 27*th* for a week, meaning every day to answer it; but putting this off because I was a little embarrassed as to my best mode of doing so. The matter is after all, very simple, however—and I will defer no longer, as I wish to get this off before the arrival of your second letter, which the above-mentioned leads me to expect.

I am not surprised that £100 a number, during twelve months, for my novel strikes you as an exceptionally high price; it produces the same effect on myself, and I must agree that I was inconsiderate to demand it; inasmuch as I do not believe—have no reason to believe—that I should receive it from an English periodical. To tell the truth, I had forgotten, till I received your letter, that in speaking of terms in mine from Paris, I *had* demanded it! This was not a deliberate and mature proceeding, but comes back to me now as an off-hand and indigested proposal. I wrote back to you the same morning your letter came, and if I had taken time to consider the question of price should have written differently. I had in mind the simple fact that for my last long novel I received £100 a number, and that I must not receive less for a prospective one; but I did not sufficiently weigh the circumstance that the said £100 came to me from two different magazines (*Macmillan* as well as the *Atlantic*). I tell you all this in order that I may not appear to have been over-reaching, and to have "two prices." The proposal from Paris dropped from my pen as I wrote, and I didn't write afterwards to modify it simply because I had forgotten what I said. My view of the matter now (that your letter brings my full attention to it) is still however that I ought to receive more for a novel to begin in 1885 (it's only the shape of my eights)[1] than I did, from the *Atlantic*, for the *Portrait of a Lady*. I shall be very well satisfied if you pay me at the same rate as for my various recent things. This, kept up for a year, may not suit you; but I ought to say that it is, this time, my deliberate and digested estimate of the *Princess*. If it does not meet the idea of the publishers, we will hang her up on her peg again.—I ought to add that I can't undertake to handle her in less than about twenty-five pages at a time.—Does all this suit you, and suit Messrs. Houghton and Mifflin? You will tell me at your convenience.—I should like to be able to keep up the standard of £100 if it would (as you say) operate to bring you out. But apparently I must see you on cheaper terms! Let them not, however, be too ruinous to yours always

Henry James

1. HJ seems to be alluding to his slips of the pen in his letter of 13 February 1884 to Aldrich. It should be added that HJ's eights are distinctly sixes in the holograph.

To Lord Rosebery
Ms Scotland

The Durdans, Epsom
April 14 [1884]

My dear Rosebery.

Don't be alarmed at a note from me—it is only to give you good news of all the valuable lives that you have left in my care: [those] of your wife and children, and of the prime-minister of your country[1] and *his* lady and daughter. I give them all my time and attention, and a certain good effect is already perceptible. When Lady Rosebery suggested to me just now to send you a line that you might know that I am *à la hauteur de la situation* I immediately seized my—I mean your—that is, one of your—pens—in spite of the fact that I am to take Miss Gladstone out for her walk and that she is fretting (very naturally) at my delay. The sublime old man was in the drawing room last night after dinner and talked about bookbinding and the vulgarity of the son of a Tory Duke having talked about "pooh-poohing" something or other in the House of Commons: a vile new verb, unworthy of that high assembly. Today he lunched downstairs and discoursed about the new version of the Scriptures and the advisability of having at Oxford both a lay and a clerical professor of Hebrew! So you see I keep up the tone of the conversation. Sir A. Clarke, arriving from London, interrupted the meal, inspected the statesman, admired the children, reassured Mrs. Gladstone and gave every sanction to the party leaving for Hornbury tomorrow. Granville, Leveson-Gower etc. are I believe coming over to lunch and to take them back. I am nervous about dinner this evening and should like to read up beforehand—but a walk with Miss Gladstone is I suppose a liberal education, and that I must no longer shrink from. I shall take her to the Downs, but we won't discuss those topics I discussed with you the last time we went there: Byron, Carlyle etc.—Excuse my indecent haste. I ought to mention that Sybil[2] has at last accepted me—without a *dot*: but it won't come out till I go. *Bien à vous*

H. James

1. Gladstone.
2. Sybil, Rosebery's eldest daughter, was then four.

To William James
Ms Harvard

3 Bolton St. W.
April 21*st* [1884]

Dear William

I received a note from you of 9th, to which, though it doesn't demand any particular answer I will dash off a few lines of response before taking up the pen of imagination. You enclose an extract from a newspaper purporting to be an article of Matt.

Arnold's about Chicago society, and seem to believe it is his! It doesn't, I must confess, appear to me even a good hoax—full of phrases ("intelligent gentleman," "cultured people," "owner of a large grocery-business" etc.) which he is incapable of using. Nor would he talk about "Chicago-society." It seems to me poor as a parody—and it marks the (geographical) gulf that separates Appian Way from Bolton Street!—that this writer should have appeared to you to catch the tone in which a London man of M.A.'s stamp would express himself. The thing, of course, never appeared in the P[all] M[all] G[azette]. Excuse the invidious style of my acceptance of your offering.

I too am "excited" about the prospect of your getting into John Gray's house. It is a charming idea, but I should fear you would find it an expensive place to live in; as you would have to have a man for the grounds.—But I shall hear with great interest of the sequel. As you don't dwell on the character of Aunt Kate's convalescence, besides saying it is slow, I suppose there is nothing particular to hope or fear in regard to it, and nothing to be done for the poor dear woman but to write to her when one can, which I do.—I got your enclosure of Bob's note, a few days since, with news of his curatorship. I hope he may keep it, and make it grow. Have you any idea that he has himself this winter advanced in the practice of art? As regards your child's name I am glad the appendage has not yet been fastened. I am afraid *all* "selected" names appear to you "tawdry." If I had a child I would call him (very probably) *Roland!* "Roland James" is very good. If this doesn't suit you—nor Godfrey, nor Gautier, nor any name of chivalry, take something out of Shakespeare: a capital source to name a child from: Sebastian, Prosper[o], Valentine (I like Valentine though not sure I'd give it), Adrian, *Lancelot,* Bernard, *Justin,* Benedick, or Benedict, *Bertram,* Conrad, Felix, Leonard, etc. Putting Hagen apart, I like *Herman.*[1] But I don't exactly understand the obligation you seem to feel under to provide Dr. Hagen with a namesake—"because he was never in America"—and has failed to make the provision himself. Did I tell you in my last that I spent at Easter nearly three days at the Durdans (Rosebery's) with Gladstone, and only two or three others? *Haec olim meminisse jubavit,*[2] I suppose; but in the present, Gladstone's mind doesn't interest me much: it appears to have no preferences, to care equally for all subjects—which is tiresome! Look in the *Academy* of April 19th for a notice of your last article in *Mind.* I would send you the paper, were it not so difficult, and out-of-the-way (time-taking), to buy. I have attacked your two *Mind* articles, with admiration, but been defeated. I can't give them just now the necessary time. I lunched the other day with Arthur Balfour, and lunch tomorrow (elsewhere) to meet Pasteur, returning from the Edinburgh tricentenary. I am anxious to hear your impressions of Alice on her return from N.Y. Love to your own.

Ever
H. James

1. The child, William's third, received among other names that of Herman, by which he was called.
2. Virgil, "to remember these things hereafter will be a pleasure."

To Elizabeth Boott
Ms Harvard

3 Bolton St. W.
Whitmonday [2 June] 1884

My dear Lizzie.[1]

Your postcard revives all my remorse, already constantly felt, at having so long neglected your delightful and welcome letter of—weeks ago. It lies before me now, in all its generous length—but I won't mention the date of it, hoping you may have forgotten. With it came the beautiful photo of your mother and child which I ought long since to have thanked you for in a manner commensurate with my admiration. I expressed this sentiment however (to myself and the public) by having it immediately mounted and framed, in the highest style of art, and it now forms one of the principal ornaments of my sitting-room. It is very good and complete and of a beautiful tone, and would be, I think, the best thing you have done, if it were not for the charming little girl in white you send me today, which strikes me as even more brilliantly successful. She is most delicate and exquisite, and marks a great jump in your development. Is it a portrait (to be paid for)—or an order—or an idea of your own? In any case *tous mes compliments.*—I have just come back from spending yesterday (Whitsunday) with some friends near Godalming, and though today is Bank Holiday and London is supposed to be both dreary and empty, I resisted all temptations to remain over till tomorrow (at a lovely place) and have returned to work—and to you! My work awaits me (I have a great deal on hand and am, as usual, behind with it) but I *must* have ten minutes' chat with you before I can have my mind free for other lucubrations. This Whitsuntide period is one of those occasions when all London empties itself (socially speaking) for a week—precious moments of rest and relief in its perpetual rush and scramble. I am not dining out once this week—which is an eloquent proof of there being "nothing going on." I should like to give you some news of the art-world—but the art-world here doesn't produce any valuable incidents. The one that most concerns me is that Sargent was lately here for three weeks and is to come back, in a day or two, for the month of June, to paint three or four English portraits, among others that of little Lady Playfair,[2] whom you know. I saw and shall probably see again a great deal of him; I was able, I think, to make things pleasant and easy for him. I like him extremely (he is more intelligent about artistic things than all the painters here rolled together) and in short we are excellent friends. He has had this year both a success (here) and a failure, and in Paris a failure which I judge to be pretty bad. His big portrait of Mrs. Henry White, at the Academy here, (she belongs to our Legation) is splendid and delightful. She is at full length (a very big canvas), in white satin and white lace, with a vague, pinkish, pearly background. It is a masterpiece (*selon moi*) of style and tone, and has had, among the artists, immense success. In the Grosvenor he has another portrait, far less good, of a certain English Mrs. Legh, in yellow satin, with a startled face and a long disconnected-looking neck. It is a rather reckless and ill-considered thing (though full of life and skill), and has, I fear, damaged him here as much as the Mrs. White has helped him. I want him to come here to live and work—there being such a field in London for a *real* painter of women, and such magnificent subjects, of both sexes. He is afraid but he inclines, I think, this way, and will probably end by coming. He has got all, and more than all—that Paris can give him—and he can *apply* it here, I believe, as nowhere. His Madame Gautreau (at the *Salon*) has produced a kind of scandal—a full length of a so-called French beauty (*femme du monde*), half-stripped and covered with paint—blue, green, white, black. I saw it in his studio in the winter and only half liked it. Sargent strikes me as being in rather a bad place now—which is probably, only, transitory—and has, at any rate, a certain sort of *excess* of cleverness: too much chic and not enough naïveté. His character is charmingly naïf, but not his talent. But I take a great interest in him, and am very desirous to witness his future. He is intelligent *en diable.* I wish he would paint a picture. I took him one day to Burne-Jones's studio (having first made B.J. dine with him) to see his big thing for this year's Grosvenor, "King Cophetua and the Beggar Maid." Burne-Jones is always adorable, and we had a charming hour. Sargent enjoys and appreciates his things in the highest degree—but I am afraid poor dear, lovely, but slightly narrow B.J. suffers from a constitutional incapacity to enjoy Sargent's—finding in them "such a want of finish." His great devotee, George Howard, said to me in front of Sargent's portrait of Mrs. White that it must be only patriotism that would make me care for such a work as that! Burne-Jones's Cophetua, however—all this doesn't prevent it from being his finest thing, and very beautiful and interesting. I spent a charming day in the country with him the other week; that is we went down to visit a common friend at Esher. I enclose you, for local colour's sake, a note of his which alludes to the project. Also one of Du Maurier's. Please keep them both and some day I shall perhaps ask you for them again. Also one from Sargent, to complete the trio—and add to the spell I try to work, *de vous attirer* here. I *did* sit to Du Maurier—for *five* hours! and the result is a pretty little head. But the picture (not the water-colours), I grieve to say, is pale and weak, and I fear he is too late in the day to begin to paint successfully. Whenever I see him it is with affection and pleasure, but Hampstead[3] interposes long intervals. The exhibitions this year are rather more *débile* than usual. The Academy full of poor stuff, and the Grosvenor no better. The best thing at the latter—putting Sargent's Mrs. Legh apart—is an adorable big Whistler, a portrait of Lady Archibald Campbell. It is almost as good as the portrait of his Mother. Julian Story has a *very* clever and skillful big subject, *Aesop telling fables,* and portrait (less good) of Cardinal Howard. He has a real talent but rather an uninteresting one, and carries even further (with far less ability) Sargent's danger—that of seeing the *ugliness* of things.—

What shall I tell you *di me?* I am working pretty steadily and am having various things, long and short, appearing and to appear. I think of going abroad early this summer—in July—and making for some quiet salubrious place in the southern Alps or the Tyrol. I haven't lain on the grass for ten years, and am dying to do so. The Realist[4] is three or four doors off. She "located" first in Half Moon Street, two streets off: then moved up to Clarges Street, the next; and now, these several weeks, has been in Bolton Street itself! The nearer she comes the less I see of her, and have seen very little all winter. She has a whirl of society here, is taken up by the aristocracy etc. and is a great social success, in spite of—of everything! The Costanza[5] is handy, in Sloan Street, and is to remain, I believe, till August. But she is a most excellent reasonable woman, absorbed in her work, upon whom I have not a single reflection to make. I like and esteem her exceedingly. They never meet! I am delighted with your account of Alice—her dinners, etc. I feel sadly eliminated, and by my own fault, from your dear Father but shall prove to him yet that I am his, as I am yours, ever affectionately

Henry James

1. The Italianate Miss Boott apparently was in America at the time. See *Letters* I and II for HJ's earlier correspondence with her and her father, Francis Boott. Their home was in a villa on Bellosguardo, in Florence.

2. Lady Playfair, American-born wife of the first baron, Lyon Playfair, British scientist and reformer.

3. George du Maurier lived in Hampstead, then distinctly suburban and reachable by horse-drawn omnibus.

4. It is difficult to identify "The Realist," although her social activities could be ascribed to Violet Paget (1856–1935), who wrote under the name Vernon Lee: but Miss Lee usually stayed with friends when she was in London.

5. See letter to Elizabeth Boott, 14 October 1883, n. 9.

To Alphonse Daudet
Ms Harvard

3 Bolton St. Piccadilly W.
London. 19 juin [1884]

Mon cher Alphonse Daudet.

J'aurais dû déjà vous remercier de tout le plaisir que vous m'avez fait en m'envoyant *Sapho.*[1] Je vous suis très reconnaissant de cette bonne et amicale pensée, qui s'ajoutera désormais, pour moi, au souvenir du livre. Je n'avais pas attendu l'arrivée de votre volume pour le lire—mais cela m'a donné l'occasion de m'y remettre encore et de tirer un peu au clair les diverses impressions que tant d'admirables pages m'ont laissées. Je n'essaierai pas de vous rapporter ces impressions dans leur plénitude—dans la crainte de ne réussir qu'à déformer ma pensée—tout autant que la vôtre. Un nouveau livre de vous me fait passer par l'esprit une foule de telles idées, que je vous confierais de vive voix—et de grand coeur—si j'avais le bonheur de vous voir plus souvent. Pour le moment je vous dirai seulement que tout ce qui vient de vous compte, pour moi, comme un grand événement, une jouissance rare et fructueuse. Je vous aime mieux dans certaines pages que dans d'autres, mais vous me charmez, vous m'enlevez toujours, et votre manière me pénètre plus qu'aucune autre. Je trouve dans *Sapho* énormément de vérité et de vie. Ce n'est pas du roman, c'est de l'histoire, et de la plus complète et de la mieux éclairée. Lorsqu'on a fait un livre aussi solide et aussi sérieux que celui-là, on n'a besoin d'être rassuré par personne; ce n'est donc que pour m'encourager moi-même que je constate dans *Sapho* encore une preuve—à ajouter à celles que vous avez déjà données—de tout ce que le roman peut accomplir comme révélation de la vie et du drôle de mélange que nous sommes. La fille est étudiée avec une patience merveilleuse—c'est un de ces portraits qui épuisent un type. Je vous avouerai que je trouve le jeune homme un peu sacrifié—comme étude et comme recherche—sa figure me paraissant moins éclairée—en comparaison de celle de la femme—qu'il ne le faudrait pour l'intérêt moral—la valeur tragique. J'aurais voulu que vous nous eussiez fait voir d'avantage par où il a passé—en matière d'expérience plus personnelle et plus intime encore que les coucheries avec Fanny—en matière de ramollissement de volonté et de relâchement d'âme. En un mot, le drame ne se passe peut-être pas assez dans l'âme et dans la conscience de Jean Gauvin. C'est à mesure que nous touchons à son caractère même que la situation devient intéressante—de ce caractère, vous me faites l'effet de l'avoir un peu négligé. Vous me diriez que voici un jugement bien anglais, et que nous inventons des *abstractions,* comme nous disons, afin de nous dispenser de toucher aux grosses réalités. J'estime pourtant qu'il n'y a rien de plus réel, de plus positif, de plus à peindre, qu'un caractère; c'est là qu'on trouve bien la couleur et la forme. Vous l'avez bien prouvé, du reste, dans chacun de vos livres, et en vous disant que vous avez laissé l'amant de Sapho un peu trop en blanc, ce n'est qu'avec vous-même que je vous compare. Mais je ne voulais que vous remercier et répondre à votre envoi. Je vous souhaite tout le repos qu'il vous faudra pour recommencer encore! Je garde de cette soirée que j'ai passée chez vous au mois de février une impression toute colorée. Je vous prie de me rappeler au souvenir bienveillant de Madame Daudet, je vous serre la main et suis votre bien dévoué confrère.

Henry James

1. *Sapho,* Daudet's novel about the relations of a young man from Provence with a Parisian model, had just appeared in France. The copy Daudet sent to James survives and is inscribed simply "à Henry James Alph. Daudet."

To Lawrence Barrett

Ms Private

3 Bolton St. Piccadilly W.
July 18*th* [1884]

Dear Lawrence Barrett.[1]

Your view of my "Portrait"[2] as a possible play is very friendly and favourable; but I may as well say concisely that I think you are mistaken in seeing a drama in it. I don't myself, even with the utmost rearrangement that I can conceive myself willing to subject the story to. I apprehend, I think, to the full, and yet do not exaggerate, the difference of nature between a novel and a play, and in the light of this discrimination the *Portrait* seems to me to belong essentially to the former class and to be inconvertible into any thing different. I feel sure that an attempt to convert it into a drama would despoil the story of such merits as it possesses and not give it sufficient others in their place. The book is before all things a study of character—descriptive, analytic, psychological, concerned with fine shades, emotions, etc. These are elements which, to become popular with any English-speaking audience, a drama must possess—as you are no doubt still better aware than I—only in a barely perceptible degree. In a word, I don't think the *action* of the "Portrait" vivid enough to keep a play on its legs, even if bolstered up by numerous changes. It would be simpler and easier for me to invent a new story altogether. I have not forgotten the talk we had about these matters; and though various considerations have combined to drain away the very earnest desire I formerly had to do something for the stage, that ambition, I think, is not incapable of reviving in the presence of any prospect of (to put the matter in its homely crudity) pecuniary gain! Without swagger, I believe I could write a more successful comedy (of a serious kind) than any transmogrification of the *Portrait* would be. Have you by chance ever read a novel of mine entitled the *American*? Three or four years ago I conceived the idea of writing a play, in four acts, founded upon it, and following it with tolerable closeness, with this exception, that a happy dénouement was substituted for the tragical one of the story. I wrote the first act, and then was interrupted by more pressing duties; after which I laid it aside, and haven't touched the thing since.[3] I should be willing to take it up again, if on a perusal of the story it should seem to you that you would believe in, or care for, a play extracted from it. I think I see, myself, a strong and successful one. I ought to add that should I undertake this business I shouldn't be able to do so for some months. I have lately begun a long novel (for the *Atlantic*)[4] and must get it off my hands before I attack anything else, and I work slowly.

The Season, thank God, is nearly at an end, and I haven't had much complaint to make of it this year, as I have spent it mainly in the country. I congratulate you on your well-earned rest, and am with kind remembrances, very faithfully yours

Henry James

1. HJ had met Lawrence Barrett (1838–1891), an American actor noted for his Shakespearean roles, during his recent visit to the United States.

2. *The Portrait of a Lady* (1881).

3. No trace of this early version has been found among HJ's papers. In 1891 the British actor-manager Edward Compton produced HJ's four-act play based on *The American*.

4. *The Princess Casamassima*.

To Francis Parkman

Ms Mass. Historical

(3 Bolton St. Piccadilly W.)
15 Esplanade
Dover
August 24*th* [1884]

My dear Parkman.

This is only three lines, because I cannot hold my hand from telling you, as other people must have done to your final weariness, with what high appreciation and genuine gratitude I have been reading your Wolfe and Montcalm. (You see I am still so overturned by emotion that I can't even write the name straight.)[1] I have found the right time to read it only during the last fortnight, and it has fascinated me from the first page to the last. You know, of course, much better than any one else how good it is, but it may not be absolutely intolerable to you to learn how good still another reader thinks it. The manner in which you have treated the prodigious theme is worthy of the theme itself, and that says everything.[2] It is truly a noble book, my dear Parkman, and you must let me congratulate you, with the heartiest friendliness, on having given it to the world. Do be as proud as possible of being the author of it, and let your friends be almost as proud of possessing his acquaintance. Reading it here by the summer-smooth channel, with the gleaming French coast, from my windows, looking on some clear days only five miles distant, and the guns of old England pointed seaward, from the rumbling, historic castle perched above me on the downs; reading it, as I say, among these influences, it has stirred all sorts of feelings—none of them, however, incompatible with the great satisfaction that the American land should have the credit of a production so solid and so artistic. There was three or four days ago a review of it in the *Times*, very complimentary, but without evidence of the writer's knowing much of the subject, as the article was a mere mechanical evisceration of the book. I didn't send it to you, because I thought it wouldn't strike you as valuable—but I will do so, after all, by this same post; though it is very likely you will have seen this already.

I am spending the month of August at this rather dingy and cockneyfied resort—or rather no-resort—where I find white cliffs and a very amusing sea (crowded with all the sails of the channel), leisure for work and a blessed immunity from any social encounters. In a week or two I shall cross to Paris, there to spend the greater part of the autumn. I hope, wherever this finds you, that it will descend upon a happy scene. The scene I figure is that delightful back verandah of yours at Jamaica Plain, from which the world seems all festooned with wisteria. I have been disappointed, this year, of a general expectation and hope that in London, the summer would bring you forth. Aren't you coming soon again, and haven't you any more papers or cabinets to dive into? I shall be very glad when there are signs of your reappearance. This will be a very interesting autumn for dwellers on these shores—thanks to the spectacle of a general election, with a new and immensely democratized electorate. Neither party seems to me rich in ideas just now, but the Tories are pitifully poor, and poorer still in men. They must transform themselves or perish, and it will be curious to see their contortions, in the effort. The Liberals have only one word to conjure with: Gladstone, and they use it to satiety. It is still tolerably potent, but it won't last forever, and we shall see. Come and see too! unless you are too fascinated by the spectacle of Cleveland.[3] Do give my kindest remembrance to your sisters and believe in the personal gratitude of yours ever very faithfully

H. James

1. Francis Parkman (1823–1893), the American historian, published during this year his *Montcalm and Wolfe* in his series depicting the conflict for domination of the New World.

2. The "prodigious" theme was also HJ's—the contrasts and similarities of the Old and New Worlds.

3. Grover Cleveland loomed as the Democrat likely to upset twenty-three years of Republican power in the United States. He was elected President in the autumn of 1884.

To Violet Paget (Vernon Lee)

Ms Colby

3 Bolton St. W.
Oct. 21*st* [1884]

Dear Miss Paget.

The kindness of your note, and of Miss Abby-Williams's, makes me regret passionately the necessity I have been under of returning that fair editress an answer so much less gracious than your accomplished selves. I am literally up to my neck in engagements already formed to supply fiction to periodicals with which I have been long in intercourse (the *Atlantic, Century, Harper,* etc.); and I don't see my way to any prospect of depositing my footprints on the sands of *Time.* But I can feel none the less the honour of your recommendation, and the amiable words with which it is accompanied, as well as of your friend's appeal. I am sadly afraid she will find the market over-stocked with the particular commodity that she seeks to send to it, and that dead *Cornhills* are not to be revived. Excuse these sinister remarks: I have just been reading the new instalment (conclusion) of Froude's Carlyle and am tinged with pessimism in consequence. This does not, however, prevent me from giving my blessing to the new magazine. I am greatly interested in the coming advent of *Miss Brown,*[1] and shall give her, and the valuable portrait, my most sympathetic attention. But to tell the truth it frightens me a little that you should attach to me the honour of an invocation, however casual; it is an honour I am really not *de taille* to carry. I have been reading your *Euphorion*[2] and I find it such a prodigious young performance, so full of intellectual power, knowledge, brilliancy, the air of being *comme chez vous* at the dizziest heights of the Idea—that dedications should come to you not from you. Please hint that you offer me *Miss Brown* only to encourage me! I dined two days since with the plastic John,[3] who was in town from Petworth where he is painting the portrait of a lady whose merits as a model require all his airy manipulation to be expressed (in speech). I trust it is a happy effort and will bring him fame and shekels here. I see poor Hillebrand's[4] death in the newspapers and grieve for the event and for that poor devoted woman, devoted for so many years. I am afraid she has passed some very sad months during the last few, and wonder what will be left to her in her deaf old age. Hillebrand was a brilliant intelligence and had good reasons for living yet. He had been very friendly to me of old and I liked him much. Of what use then to dwell by the Arno, to have given years to Italy the lovely and literature the delusion, if the commonest ills must overtake you? May *you* live to a hundred, and always by the Arno except when you are on Kensington leads. I shall write to Madame Hillebrand as soon as I dare.—Bourget[5] has returned to his Parisian element, to cultivate homesickness (for England) as a place of culture and a quality of high civilization. Miss Robinson[6] I have not again seen, but it is a pleasure I shall give myself soon, as a definite sign that the season of fireside joys has set in. If you can put your hand on the two last volumes of Froude's Carlyle,[7] don't fail to read them; they are deeply entertaining. He (Carlyle) appears to me to have been no more of a *thinker* than my blotting paper, but absorbent (like that), to a tremendous degree, of life; a prodigious *feeler* and painter; as a painter indeed, one of the very first of all. I wish you, dear Miss Paget, the freest and happiest exercise [of] your admirable mind and am ever faithfully yours

Henry James

1. HJ had encouraged Miss Lee in her fictional undertaking. Her *Miss Brown* appeared in 1884 and was dedicated to HJ.
2. A volume of Miss Lee's essays just published.
3. Sargent was an old Florentine friend of Miss Lee and painted her portrait, now in the Tate.
4. Karl Hillebrand, the German writer, who lived in Florence and whom HJ had known since 1869.
5. HJ had recently met Paul Bourget (1852–1935), then at the beginning of his career as a novelist. He also dedicated his first novel to James.
6. Mary A. F. Robinson (1857–1944), poet, essayist, and biographer, later wife of James Darmesteter, the French orientalist, and on his death of the French scientist Pierre Emile Duclaux.
7. James Anthony Froude (1818–1894), Carlyle's chief disciple and literary executor, issued between 1881 and 1884, in a series of volumes, papers and memorabilia of Carlyle and his wife. Froude's frankness about the Carlyles astonished and shocked late Victorian England. See succeeding letter to Grace Norton.

To Grace Norton

Ms Harvard

3 Bolton St. W.
Nov. 3*d* 1884

My dear Grace.

I have more letters to thank you for than I (or even you) can count—following each other with a liberality of which each outpouring caused my cheek to mantle with the blush of shame (at my own silence). "Answer" *them* all I can't,—but I can at least in some sort answer *you;* and I shall do so before another hour of dumbness has added to my facial crimson. Your letters contain everything—

and above all they contain yourself. I wish they did in very fact and that the postman could hand you in, in the flesh, bag and baggage. I would pay, without a murmur, the heaviest postage for the parcel. Let me say, just in general, *yes* to everything, and then in particular, *no, no,* to some of your items. Let me above all, both thank you and reassure you as regards to what you wrote me about Alice's coming out. It was an act of true friendship and I understand perfectly the emotion that prompted it: but my dear Grace it was at the same time a proof of your rare faculty of taking the world tragically. I have a large dose of the same talent, and yet (I am almost proud to announce it), I have quite escaped, as yet, being alarmed by Alice's now impending advent. I *may* be wrong, and it *may* wreck and blight my existence, but it will have to exert itself tremendously to do so. She is not coming in any special sense, at all, "to me"; she is simply coming to Europe, and apparently will not even alight at my door when she arrives to spend the first week or two (which will perhaps be all) of her present stay in London with me. There is no question of her living with me. She is unspeakably un-dependent and independent, she *clings* no more than a bowsprit, has her own plans, purposes, preferences, practices, pursuits, more than any one I know, has also amply sufficient means etc. and, in short, even putting her possible failure to improve in health at the worst, will be very unlikely to tinge or modify my existence in any uncomfortable way. My belief is that *at the end of six months,* she *will* mend physically in European conditions and after that will be no preoccupation to me at all. I go to Liverpool to meet her next week, and am hiring a maid to take to her—so I needn't even wait to bring her to town if she wishes to stop and rest. All this, dear anxious—too-anxious friend—for your comfort and mine. I came back this A.M. from a Sunday at Oxford, spent at Merton with the renowned and peculiar George Brodrick[1] ("Curius Dentatus"), whom you doubtless remember, and who is now Warden of that college, where he exercises a liberal hospitality. There were in the house, John Bright, Lady Sarah Spencer, the Charles Roundells etc. and at lunch and dinner various lights of the Oxford world. Humanly it was heavy, tainted with that Oxford priggery which is not one of the things I enjoy most; but the place is always divinely delicious to me, and the college is quite the oldest and one of the most romantic: window embrasures six feet thick; rooms of the thirteenth century, dear old garden etc. John Bright[2] is *to me* one of the least interesting types in England, and is moreover today quite a spent volcano, fallen into the prattling, rather boring, mildly senile stage. I sat up with him last night an hour after the others had gone to bed, and he described to me beautiful American poems that I sent to him from the U.S., and a splendid novel by General Lew Wallace[3]—of which he related the plot at extraordinary length. His "culture" is so narrow, his taste so bad, and what remains of his intellect so weak, that I wondered greatly that a "great statesman" should have coexisted with such limitations. It made me think that great statesmen may sometimes be very measurable creatures. However, J.B. was never, and never pretended to be, that: he was simply a great orator, with a special gift of speaking which, having died out, has left him childlike and bland, and rather bare. I have read with much enjoyment your various articles—enjoyment of them in themselves and also of the fact that you do them. I can't sufficiently recommend you to launch yourself in literature, for which you have an excellent faculty. Make this now your occupation and diversion, and you will have a very honourable and profitable career. I welcome any allusions you may make to me, and all you may quote or not quote, from me; and I thank you particularly for your long letter about my article in *Longman*.[4] I think we are at bottom abundantly agreed about the art of fiction, and where you think you differ from me it is (I believe) simply that you don't understand me! And yet I can't explain myself here; I am too pressed with many duties. But I mean (as soon as I can find a moment free from other writing) to publish another article on the subject—for the [one] in *Longman* was only about half even of the essence of what I have to say. Meanwhile I am also writing a novel[5] (to appear in the *Century* early in the ensuing year), which I think will practically answer in some degree, perhaps, some of your objections or at least illustrate some of my own artistic convictions. I congratulate you on your present intimacy with Balzac. I have a great affection, a kind of reverence for him, as for the founder and father of our modern effort, and on the whole the greatest genius in his line. He is an immense comfort to me, and I even like (or rather care for—I don't *like*) him personally.

I wish you hadn't said in the *Nation* that his people are "puppets." The failures yes, but the others *live,* it seems to me, with all the life an artist can impart. The winter, socially speaking, has fairly begun here; parliament is launched upon an autumn session and one begins to be asked out to dinner. The days continue splendid; it has been a year, more than a year, of positively unexampled brilliancy, and still they continue. Poor old London doesn't know itself, has never been so exposed to the garish light of day, feels its natural modesty and coquetry almost violated. I have not moved; but contrary to Charles's report of me after his return (which strikes me as almost cruelly meager), I *do* mean to—generally—as soon as I can find time. Meanwhile it doesn't press, I am comfortable enough, and I have the very best situation in London; so I won't till exactly the right place offers itself; for when I move again it will be *forever.* Thank you kindly, dear Grace, for setting me up in matrimony with the British female. I shall never take that liberty with her and shall to a dead certainty never change my free unhoused condition. I can't see why you should wish me to: it seems to me you pass there from the tragic view of life to the *comic!* At any rate, I shall never marry; I regard that now as an established fact, and on the whole a very respectable one; I am both happy enough and miserable enough, as it is, and don't wish to add to either side of the account. Singleness consorts much better with my whole view of existence (of my own and of that of the human race), my habits, occupations, prospects, tastes, means, situation "in Europe," and absence of desire to have children—fond as I am of the infant race. I give you here the results, simply, of much meditation, but can't narrate the process. But I may say that since definitely and *positively* (from a merely negative state) making up my mind not to marry, I feel that I have advanced in happiness and power to *do* something in the world. There are all sorts of things to be said about it; mainly this, that if marriage is *perfectly* successful it is the highest human state; and that if it fails of this it is an awful grind, an ignoble, unworthy condition. I have never regarded it as a necessity, but only as the last and highest luxury. I don't think all the world has a right to it any more than I think all the world has a right to vote.—The greatest pleasure I have lately had has been the perusal of the two last volumes of Froude's Carlyle. They are of the deepest interest and entertainment. Decidedly Carlyle was a brute, a man of a jealous, grudging, sinister, contemptuous, ungenerous, most invidious soul; and one who, with all his violence of feeling, felt life, as a whole, most incompletely (calls Keats a "dead dog," "venal of hell," etc., sneers at "art" in a way which shows that all *that* salutary world was closed to him). But what a genius, painter, humourist, what a literary figure, what a faculty of expression. These things put him in the front rank, though not in the highest place in it, I think; for I am convinced that he will be a curiosity for future people rather than a teacher. He and his wife, at all events, were a most original and entrancing pair, and their Chelsea-history is as fascinating as a fairy-tale. Nine-tenths of Carlyle's contempt—the brutal mockery he poured over all human things—seem to me perfectly barren and verbose, and his crude, stiff remedies (shootings, prisons etc.) not to meet the difficulties of human cases at all—in which you will probably agree with me.—I must close, my dear Grace—to go and see the Bootts, who have telegraphed me an hour to meet them here on their stoppage of but twelve [hours] between Boston and Paris. Their apparition surprises me altogether, it being the first I have heard of their coming. I shall try and let fewer *months* elapse before I write again; if I can't send you ten pages I will send you four. I see you in your winter-parlour, and could almost get up to shut the door! I pray you are well and that things keep tolerably straight around you. Don't let literature make you too impersonal—at least when you write to your very faithful friend

Henry James

1. George Charles Brodrick (1831–1903), a son of Lord Midleton, was warden of Merton College from 1881. He made several unsuccessful efforts to enter Parliament as a liberal and as opponent of Gladstone's Irish policy.

2. The statesman and prototype of Victorian radicalism (1811–1889). See *Letters* II, 318.

3. Lewis Wallace (1827–1905),whose *Ben-Hur* (1880) sold two million copies.

4. This was HJ's essay "The Art of Fiction," *Longman's Magazine,* IV (September 1884), 502–521, reprinted in *Partial Portraits* (1888). Although HJ promised a second article on the subject, he never wrote it.

5. *The Bostonians.*

To Francis Boott
Ms Harvard

Adelphi Hotel
Liverpool
Nov. 13*th* [1884]

My dear Francis.

As I wrote on Tuesday to Lizzie you will know of my being for the moment in durance here. Alice was so extenuated by her voyage that she is resting here till Saturday or Sunday. K. P. Loring[1] has gone to Bournemouth and Alice will go there next week. I sympathise with your discomfiture and uncertainty in Paris, and can imagine that you should look about you and think of another *séjour*. But, my dear Francis, I cannot advise you on the subject of coming to London, beyond saying that I should be very glad to see you there. Lizzie would like it, and you wouldn't—that is my impression—and Lizzie's liking would depend upon her remaining there long enough to settle down to some regular life and interest. I am afraid that as a simple transient even she would not get into the proper swing, swim or rhythm. We shall of course have the cholera there too—but I somehow don't dread it much in this "tubbing" country. I know of course nothing about the letting of studios. There are many in London, and I have no doubt that Pennington could give her much information about them. I should be happy—delighted—I needn't say—to help you in any way in my power. Clarges Street and Half Moon Street are *full* of apartments—and all the streets about Hanover Square, etc., Cavendish Square, etc. I know of no special ones, as having had my own quarters the last eight years, I have had no need of going elsewhere. I recommend you, if you come to London, to come first to an hotel and look about you for rooms. All the places have the notice, in the door or window, of "apartments." E. Jackson probably goes to 40 Clarges Street, where I have known many people to stay and be happy. Thank you for hoping I shall see him; I hope I shall not! He is a bore and I don't care about him. It is exactly against such people, in London, that one must defend one's life and one's time. I hope you won't—after a little—find sufficient ground for leaving Paris; I shrink from the responsibility of positively drawing you to London. *You* might give me some bad moments if I were to be the cause of your being miserable there. Here is a table: for and against a London winter.

AGAINST	FOR
Darkness.	Good fires.
Fog—bad climate etc.	Good lodgings.
Necessity of being sometime in the place to get going.	Good cabs.
Absence of foreign and American customs.	Chance of seeing people if you stay long enough.
General fact that Italians hate it, and most strangers who are there (in winter) on a mere temporary footing.	General interest and richness of the biggest city in the world.
Presence of H. James etc.	Good service—the best—good prices!
	Presence of H. James.

Give my love to Lizzie and tell her I pray your path may be lighted. Ever yours affectionately

H. James

1. See *Letters* II, 172–173. Katharine Loring would remain loyal to Alice James to the end. Illness now made HJ's sister a permanent expatriate, as Grace Norton (3 November 1884) had foreseen.

To Robert Louis Stevenson
Ms Yale

3 Bolton St. Piccadilly
Dec. 5*th* [1884]

My dear Robert Louis Stevenson

I read only last night your paper in the December *Longman's* in genial rejoinder to my article in the same periodical on Besant's lecture, and the result of that charming half-hour is a friendly desire to send you three words.[1] Not words of discussion, dissent, retort or remonstrance, but of hearty sympathy, charged with the assurance of my enjoyment of everything you write. It's a luxury, in this immoral age, to encounter some one who *does* write—who is really acquainted with that lovely art. It wouldn't be fair to contend with you here; besides, we agree, I think, much more than we disagree, and though there are points as to which a more irrepressible spirit than mine would like to try a fall—that is not what I want to say—but on the contrary, to thank you for so much that is suggestive and felicitous in your remarks—justly felt and brilliantly said. They are full of these things, and the current of your admirable style floats pearls and diamonds. Excellent are your closing words, and no one can assent more than I to your proposition that all art is a simplification. It is a pleasure to see that truth so neatly uttered. My pages, in Longman, were simply a plea for liberty: they were only half of what I had to say, and some day I shall try and express the remainder. Then I shall tickle you a little affectionately as I pass. You will say that my "liberty" is an obese divinity, requiring extra measures; but after one more go I shall hold my tongue. The native *gaiety* of all that you write is delightful to me, and when I reflect that it proceeds from a man whom life has laid much of the time on his back (as I understand it) I find you a genius indeed. There must be pleasure in it for you too. I ask Colvin about you whenever I see him, and I shall have to send him this to forward to you. I hope the present season is using you tenderly, and I am with innumerable good wishes yours very faithfully,

Henry James

1. HJ's first letter to Robert Louis Stevenson marks the beginning of an important friendship. The Scot had written a reply in *Longman's* (December 1884) to HJ's "The Art of Fiction" (*Longman's*, September 1884), entitling it "A Humble Remonstrance." He took as excuse HJ's allusion in his essay to *Treasure Island*. Stevenson argued against HJ's "realism," writing that life is "monstrous, infinite, illogical, abrupt and poignant," whereas a work of art is "neat, finite, self-contained, rational, flowing and emasculate."

To Mrs. Humphry Ward

Ms Barrett

3 Bolton Street West
Dec. 9*th* [1884]

Dear Mrs. Ward.

There was more I wanted to say about *Miss Bretherton*.[1] I read it with much interest and pleasure—it is very refined and *senti* (on your part) and contains a great deal of charming, suggestive writing. Very charming indeed is the scene between Isabel and Kendal on the Oxford excursion, and very touching and human many other passages—especially the description of Mme de C's death. The whole thing is delicate and distinguished, and the reader has the pleasure and security of feeling that he is with a woman (distinctly with a woman!) who knows how (rare bird!) to write. I think your idea, your situation interesting in a high degree, and I further think that you have drawn many of the notes of its meaning, its beauty. The private history of the public woman (so to speak), the drama of her feelings, heart, soul, personal relations, and the shock, conflict, complication between those things and her publicity, her career, ambition, artistic life—this has always seemed to me a tempting, challenging subject. It seems to me, however, that, as I said, you have rather limited yourself—you have seen that concussion too simply, refused perhaps even to face it. I am afraid I have a certain reputation for being censorious and cynical: let me therefore profit by it with you and insist on one or two points in which I should have liked your story to be a little different; or at least upon *one*. I am capable of wishing that the actress might have been carried away from Kendal altogether, carried away by the current of her artistic life, the sudden growth of her power, and the excitement, the ferocity and egotism (those of the artist realizing success, I mean; I allude merely to the natural normal dose of those elements) which the effort to create, to "arrive" (once one had had a glimpse of her possible successes) would have brought with it. (Excuse that abominable sentence.) Isabel, the Isabel you describe, has too much to spare for Kendal—Kendal being what he is; and one doesn't feel her, see her, enough, as the pushing actress, the *cabotine*. She lapses toward him as if she were a failure, whereas you make her out a great success. No, she wouldn't have thought so much of him, at such a time as that—though very possibly she would have come back to him later. You have endeavoured to make us feel her "respectability" at the same time as her talent, her artistic nature, but in taking care to preserve the former, you have rather sacrificed the latter. Then granting that she cared to marry Kendal, you overlook too much, I think (but this I said to you), the problem of a union between two such opposed lives, and how her blaze etc., with all its vulgarities, would appear to him, keep him off. Also how the concessions she would have to make to his tone and his *type* would alarm her, hungry for more fame and success. I should have made her pass away from him—with hopes (on his part perhaps) of catching up with her later. I think your end has a little too much of the conventional love-story: though granted your view it is very pretty indeed. Mme de C. is charming—but your French people are too English! They take Isabel too seriously, too philanthropically, and Mme de C. wouldn't, I fear, in reality, have contributed so tenderly and candidly to her brother's suit with Miss B. Also M. de C., paternal to Miss B. after his wife's death for *his* sake, and that Miss B. may not vanish from Kendal's horizon: I think that mixes slightly incongruous things a little more than they would have been mixed in life. But excuse my hasty harshness:—I didn't want merely to murmur compliments. These, however, you deserve for the grace and ease, the pleasant colour and discreet form of your story. Excellent is the description of the first night of *Gloire;* and charming the picture of Kendal in Surrey, reading his foreign letters on the common. Yours very faithfully,

H. James

1. HJ's friendship with the British bluestocking and best-selling novelist was maintained during the rest of his life. He took a particular interest in *Miss Bretherton* (1884) because it dealt with an actress. Five years later he would write on a similar subject in *The Tragic Muse.* He was also at this moment writing "the private history of the public woman" in *The Bostonians.*

To Thomas Sergeant Perry
Ms Colby

3 Bolton St. W.
Dec. 12*th* [1884]

Dear Tommy.

Yours of Thanksgiving Day dropped in three or four days ago (Boston letters are incredibly slow), and this is but a word to thank you and give you good morrow. I kept that national festival by dining at Lowell's, in company with other homeless and puddingless Americans, and I suspect I ate almost half as much turkey as you did in the intenser Brookline. A propos of Lowell, I lie awake now o' nights, with the fear (for which there is ample ground) of his being recalled by Cleveland. He is much attached, and very justly, to his work and position here, he is in all ways an ornament to the country, his presence is a distinct satisfaction to all who wear the American name etc. etc.—and it is horrible to me to think of his being swept away to make room for some Democratic vulgarian or Philistine. The change for him (to relapse into American obscurity) will be immense, as you would feel if you had my observation of his position and career here. But why this tirade? you can't avert his doom, my poor Tommy, or I am sure you would. I have been all the morning at Millbank prison (horrible place) collecting notes for a fiction scene. You see I am quite the Naturalist. Look out for the same—a year hence.[1] A propos of fiction scenes Vernon Lee's *Miss Brown* has appeared. As I told you, my modest name is on the dedication-page, and my tongue is therefore tied in speaking of it—at least generally. But I may whisper in your ear that as it is her first attempt at a novel, so it is to be hoped it may be her last. It is very bad, *strangely* inferior to her other writing, and (to me at least) painfully disagreeable in tone. It is in three thick volumes; so I can't send it to you; but it will probably be reprinted by some one in the U. S., and then you will look at it and recognize what I mean. It is violently satirical, but the satire is strangely without delicacy or fineness, and the whole thing without form as art. It is in short a rather deplorable mistake—to be repented of. But I am afraid she won't repent—it's not her line. Don't betray this very private opinion of mine. I am sadly put to it to know what to write to *her*. I think I shall be brave and tell her what I think—or at least a little of it. The whole would never do. Commend me to your good lady and believe me ever yours

Henry James

1. The first chapter of *The Princess Casamassima* is partly set in a prison.

To William James
Ms Harvard

3 Bolton St. Piccadilly
Jan. 2*d* 1885

Dear William.

I must give some response, however brief, to your letter of December 21st, enclosing the project of your house and a long letter from R[obert] Temple.[1] Three days ago, too, came the two copies of Father's (and your) book, which have given me great filial and fraternal joy.[2] All I have had time to read as yet is the introduction—your part of which seems to me admirable, perfect. It must have been very difficult to do, and you couldn't have done it better. And how beautiful and extraordinarily individual (some of them magnificent) are the extracts from Father's writings which you have selected so happily. It comes over me as I read them (more than ever before), how intensely original and personal his whole system was, and how indispensable it is that those who go in for religion should take some heed of it. I can't enter into it (much) myself—I can't be so theological nor grant his extraordinary premises, nor through [throw] myself into conceptions of heavens and hells, nor be sure that the keynote of nature is humanity etc. But I can enjoy greatly the spirit, the feeling and the manner of the whole thing (full as this last is of things that *dis*please me too,) and feel really that poor Father, struggling so alone all his life, and so destitute of every worldly or literary ambition, was yet a great writer. At any rate your task is beautifully and honourably done. May it be as great—or even half as great—a service as it deserves to be, to his memory! The book came at a bad time for Alice, as she has had an upset which I will tell you of; but though she has been able to have it in her hand but for a moment it evidently gives her great pleasure. She burst into tears when I gave it to her, exclaiming "How beautiful it is that William should have done it! isn't it, isn't it beautiful? And how good William is, how good, how good!" And we talked of poor Father's fading away into silence and darkness, the waves of the world closing over this System which he tried to offer it, and of how we were touched by this act of yours which will (I am sure) do so much to rescue him from oblivion. I have received no notice from Trübner of the arrival of the other volumes, and shall write to him in a day or two if I don't hear. But I am rather embarrassed as to what to do with so many—wishing only to dispose of them in a manner which will entail some prospect of decent consideration and courtesy. I can give away five or six copies to persons who will probably have some attention and care for them (e.g. Frederick Harrison, Stopford Brooke, Burne-Jones, Mrs. Orr, etc.). But the newspapers and reviews are so grim and philistine and impenetrable, and stupid that I can scarcely think of any to which it isn't almost an act of untenderness to send it. But I will go into the matter with Trübner.—Alice's upset was a sudden illness on Sunday night last (this is Friday) which gave her great distress of *heart* etc., and made her think she was dying. I needn't go into the details of it, as she is already much better, and will be quite so, probably, a fortnight hence. The thing was so strange and unaccountable in its nature that Garrod looked for some special and extraordinary cause, and found it (apparently to his complete satisfaction) in the fact that she had, the last thing before going to bed, with her maid's help, applied Galvanism[3] (to relieve a headache) to the base of her neck, behind—top of her spine. He says she had struck the pneumo-gastric (?) nerve, and what she had induced was an approach to a paralytic stroke! He has seen just the same effect from the same cause, has treated her beautifully and she is now another creature. K. Loring came to her, from Bournemouth, on Tuesday, and will stay till the 5th or 6th. Of course she will never touch Galvanism, at least in that way, again; but never surely was a creature born to worse luck or more grievous accidents. She had been remarkably well for ten days before this sudden catastrophe, out of a clear sky. Don't do more than allude to it in the lightest way, if you write, for by the time your letter comes it will belong quite to the past, and of course don't breathe the word *paralysis!* Garrod has now seen her several times, she likes him extremely and finds his thoroughness, minuteness and general first-rateness superior to anything (medical) she has ever known. He has not gratified her very much in her theory of *gout*, and thinks that her trouble in her legs arises from a functional weakness of the lower part of the spine which is perfectly treatable and not permanently dangerous. The treatment he was giving her had already helped her very much when this accident occurred; but he regards the way in which she has already thrown off the attack (most serious) of Sunday night as a sign that there is in her condition nothing profoundly bad. I have had two talks with him, and he gives on the whole a distinctly favourable account of Alice. He says she has no organic malady of any kind, and that there is no reason why a person in so many respects so sound should not get very much better, and at last really well. He is a charming little old man, of a gentlemanly-Punchinello type, very polite and conscientious, and Alice (fortunately) quite adores him!

—I have read the letter from Robert Temple which you enclose and I return, and have received various very similar ones from him myself. He now begs *me* to pay the $250 to get him out of prison, entreats me very hard and even piteously. As he makes no acknowledgement of any kind of, and no allusion to, the $35 including that $10 from you on my behalf, I sent him in November, he is not encouraging, though possibly he had not had time to receive these when he wrote. I am much perplexed, and at any rate find it impossible to hand out £50 to him on the spot, as he appears to expect. It goes hard, when one has so many poor relations, to give one's earnings to a being so degraded, nevertheless and shameless. I have just sent a Christmas (or rather New Year's) present to Carrie, and have all my 1st January annual bills to pay. But I will think of the matter (his definite appeal came only last night) and answer him in two or three days. The project for your house is charming—very big, it looks, and of a most pleasant type. Love to all. Ever your

Henry

1. Robert Emmet Temple (b. 1840), eldest brother of HJ's beloved cousin Minny Temple. See *Letters* I, 218–223.

2. *The Literary Remains of the Late Henry James.*

3. Mild electrical treatment using a battery, then fashionable in handling of various nervous disorders.

To Grace Norton
Ms Harvard

3 Bolton St. W.
Jan. 24*th* [1885]

My dear Grace.

You are so accustomed by this time to my long silences that I won't unduly call your attention to my reticence for so many weeks past. These unamiable pauses have always, on my part, in my circumstances, plenty of justification, and I know that you know it and that everything is always all right. It is a feature of life in this place that the longer it lasts the more one's liabilities, of every kind, accumulate—the more things there are to be done, every hour of the day. I have so many to do that I am thinking of inventing some new day, with forty or fifty hours—or else some newer one still, with only half a dozen, as that would simplify a large proportion of one's diurnal duties out of existence. Since I last wrote I have your most amusing little Gosse-letter, and before that (how much before I won't say) came another long one, which I thanked you for, I think (but which I never can *answer!*) when I wrote you my little request in regard to the said Gosses.[1] Apropos of whom, by the way, it strikes me that he took Charles's faux pas altogether too tragically. There was nothing involved in the anecdote save that Mrs. Tadema had pretty black hair and was the daughter of a cocoa-vendor. I don't suppose that Gosse would contest either fact, and he oughtn't to have been so lacerated, for if this were inevitable, he oughtn't to have let Charles go on. I dined with Burne-Jones the other day at the Athenaeum (who remarked, by the way, that Charles—he had just had a letter from him,—was a "dear warm-hearted old thing!") but of course I didn't regale him with the anecdote. In the way of friends of yours I have only seen, lately, the excellent Reay,[2] whom I spent a day or two in company with in the country, and who looks white and invalidical (though I don't know that he is so) to go forth as the satrap of an immense Asiatic province. Lady Reay, however, will make a good satrap*ess*—and is to have four *houses* to live in, in Bombay, which will suit her very well.—All this while I haven't thanked you for your little Christmas photos. I blessed you, at the time, for the kindly thought and I think you must have heard the appreciative murmur. It will at any rate waft toward you a little etching which I shall send to-morrow.—Alice has gone to Bournemouth, after spending several weeks of close confinement near me (in Clarges Street) here. She was so completely knocked up by her voyage out that she is only now, I think, beginning to get over the deadly effects. She will probably stay at B. for the next three months, and after that I know not. She is too invalidical to plan ahead. I am very, very busy, as *The Bostonians* which you may have looked at in the *Century,* and which, by the way, contains two or three vile misprints ("single old maid" for "signal old maid," etc.) is no sooner off my hands than I push on with another and a longer production. I have also lately been revamping and almost rewriting various old and early (short) tales, which I have dug out of dusty periodicals and half a dozen of which are to be published, with three or four recent ones (Beltraffio etc.) in three volumes by Macmillan. They will be re-published, later, in America.[3] Apropos of publications, everyone is waiting here for John Cross's book about George Eliot, and I have promised to write an article upon it in the *Atlantic,* to which I refer you.[4] It comes out in a couple of days, and is to consist, I believe, almost exclusively of letters. I am certain, in advance, to praise it. Has the fame of the unfortunate "Miss Brown" reached the U.S.A.? Such is the title of a disagreeable and really very unpleasant novel dedicated to me, by Vernon Lee, which appeared here a couple of months since, and about which I haven't even yet been able to bring myself to write to the authoress, though my delay, in view of the dedication, and the first copy being sent me, is scandalous.[5] You probably know that Vernon Lee is the pen-name of a certain astounding young woman named Violet Paget, who lives in Florence, spends part of her time here, and has written two or three very imperfect but very able and interesting books on the Italian Renaissance—*Belcaro, Euphorion* etc. She has not the kind of ability that a novel requires, and *Miss Brown* is a rather serious mistake (I think); still, with an awful want of taste and of tact, you will say of *decency*—it yet has *du bon,* and is an interesting failure, if an unsavoury one. I tell you this however, not that you should read it if it is republished in America, but that you shouldn't! I am having a "quieter" winter than I have had for some years (in London) and have seen very few new people and not even many old friends. My quietness (comparative of course) is my solemn choice, and means that I have been dining much less than at most former times, for the sacred purpose of getting my evenings to myself. I have been sitting at the festive British board for so many years now that I feel as if I had earned the right to give it up save in really seductive cases. You can guess the proportion of these! It is the only way to find any time to read—and my reading was going to the dogs. Therefore I propose to become henceforth an occasional and not a regular diner, with the well-founded hope that my mind, body, spirits, temper and general view of the human understanding and of the conversational powers of the English race, will be the gainers by it. Moreover, there is very little "going on"—the country is gloomy, anxious, and London reflects its gloom. Westminster Hall and the Tower were half blown up two days ago by Irish Dynamiters, there is a catastrophe to the little British force in Soudan in the air (rather an ominous want of news since Gen. Stewart's victory at Aboukir a week ago), and a general sense of rocks ahead in the foreign relations of the country—combined with an exceeding want of confidence—indeed a deep disgust—with the present ministry in regard to such relations. I find such a situation as this extremely interesting and it makes me feel how much I am attached to this country and, on the whole, to its sometimes exasperating people. The possible *malheurs,* reverses, dangers, embarrassments, the "decline," in a word, of old England, go to my heart, and I can imagine no spectacle more touching, more thrilling and even dramatic, than to see this great precarious, artificial empire, on behalf of which, nevertheless, so much of the strongest and finest stuff of the greatest race (for such they are) has been expended, struggling with forces which, perhaps, in the long run will prove too many for it. If she only will struggle, and not collapse and surrender, and give up a part, which, looking at Europe as it is to-day, still may be great, the drama will be well worth watching from such a good, near standpoint as I have here. But I didn't mean to be so beastly political. Another drama interesting to me is the question of poor dear J. R. Lowell's possible recall after Cleveland mounts the throne. This, to me, is tragic, pathetic. His position here is in the highest degree honourable, useful, agreeable—in short perfect; and to give it all up to return, from one day to another, to John Holmes and the Brattle Street horsecar (which is very much what it amounts to—save when he goes to see you,) seems to me to be the sport of a cruel, a barbaric, fortune. I didn't know H. Wild but a little—Lady Harcourt told me the other day he was dead, and I was interested and touched by your mention of him in your last. Good-bye, dear Grace for this time. I haven't asked you about yourself—the complexion of your winter, etc. But there are some things I know sufficiently without asking. So do you—as that I am always praying for you (though I don't pray, in general, and don't understand it, I make this brilliant exception for *you*!).

Your very faithful friend,
Henry James

P.S. Go on, go on, with the *Nation*; your things—for which I always thank you—are full of "literary feeling."

1. HJ had written to the Nortons introducing Edmund Gosse and his wife, who were traveling in the United States. Gosse delivered a number of very successful lectures while in America.

2. Donald James Mackay, eleventh Baron Reay (1839–1921), had just been appointed governor of Bombay, a post he held until 1890.

3. The three-decker *Stories Revived* (1885) was never republished in the United States.

4. The article appeared in the *Atlantic Monthly*, LV (May 1885), 668–678, as "George Eliot's Life" and was reprinted as "The Life of George Eliot" in *Partial Portraits* (1888).

5. See letter to Violet Paget, 21 October 1884.

To William James
Ms Harvard

3 Bolton St. W.
Feb. 14*th* [1885]

Dear William.

I am quite appalled by your note of the 2d, in which you assault me on the subject of my having painted a "portrait from life" of Miss Peabody![1] I was in some measure prepared for it by Lowell's (as I found the other day) taking for granted that she had been my model, and an allusion to the same effect in a note from Aunt Kate. Still, I didn't expect the charge to come from you. I hold, that I have done nothing to deserve it, and think your tone on the subject singularly harsh and unfair. I care not a straw what people in general may say about Miss Birdseye—they can say nothing more idiotic and insulting than they have already said about all my books in which there has been any attempt to represent things or persons in America; but I should be very sorry—in fact deadly sick, or fatally ill—if I thought Miss Peabody *herself* supposed I intended to represent her. I absolutely had no shadow of such an intention. I have not seen Miss Peabody for twenty years, I never had but the most casual observation of her, I didn't know whether she was alive or dead, and she was not in the smallest degree my starting-point or example. Miss Birdseye was evolved entirely from my moral consciousness, like every person I have ever drawn, and originated in my desire to make a figure who should embody in a sympathetic, pathetic, picturesque, and at the same time grotesque way, the humanitary and *ci-devant* transcendental tendencies which I thought it highly probable I should be accused of treating in a contemptuous manner in so far as they were otherwise represented in the tale. I wished to make this figure a woman, because so it would be more touching, and an old, weary, battered and simple-minded woman because that deepened the same effect. I elaborated her in my mind's eye—and after I had got going reminded myself that my creation would perhaps be identified with Miss Peabody—*that* I freely admit. So I bore in mind the need of being careful, at the same time that I didn't see what I could do but go my way, according to my own fancy, and make my image as living as I saw it. The one definite thing about which I had a scruple was some touch about Miss Birdseye's spectacles—I remembered that Miss P.'s were always in the wrong place; but I didn't see, really, why I should deprive myself of an effect (as regards this point) which is common to a thousand old people. So I thought no more about Miss Peabody *at all,* but simply strove to realize my vision. If I have made my old woman *live* it is my misfortune, and the thing is doubtless a rendering—a vivid rendering, of my idea. If it is at the same time a rendering of Miss Peabody I am absolutely irresponsible—and extremely sorry for the accident. If there is any chance of its being represented to *her* that I have undertaken to reproduce her in a novel I will immediately write to her, in the most respectful manner, to say that I have done nothing of the kind, that an old survivor of the New England Reform period was an indispensable personage in my story, that my paucity of data and not my repletion is the faulty side of the whole picture, that, as I went, I had no sight or thought of her, but only of an imaginary figure which was much nearer to me, and that in short I have the vanity to claim that Miss Birdseye is a creation. You may think I protest too much: but I am alarmed by the sentence in your letter—"It is really a pretty bad business," and haunted by the idea that this may apply to some rumour you have heard of Miss Peabody's feeling *atteinte.* I can imagine no other reason why you should call the picture of Miss Birdseye a "bad business," or indeed any business at all. I would write to Miss P. on this chance—only I don't like to *assume* that she feels touched, when it is possible that she may not, and know nothing about the matter. If you can ascertain whether or no she does and will let me know, I will, should there be need or fitness, immediately write to her. Miss Birdseye is a subordinate figure in the *Bostonians,* and after appearing in the first and second numbers, vanishes till toward the end, where she re-enters, briefly, and pathetically and honourably dies. But though subordinate, she is, I think, the best figure in the book, she is treated with respect throughout, and every virtue of heroism and disinterestedness is attributed to her. She is represented as the embodiment of pure, the purest philanthropy. The story is, I think, the best fiction I have written, and I expected you, if you said anything about it, would intimate that you thought as much—so that I find this charge on the subject of Miss P. a very cold douche indeed.—

I shall be very willing to let little Howard James have $25,[2] to be taken by you out [of] the money you say you owe me—by which I think you mean the money you had *prélevé* (or borrowed) from my share of the Syracuse rents to pay for Father's book (that is, for your half of the costs). I'm writing to B. Temple to tell him I withheld the $100, I enclosed him a ten dollar greenback.—About Alice I have written to Aunt Kate two or three times quite lately, and there ought to be an agreement between you that she always forwards you my notes. I sent her a word this A.M. with a very short note of Alice's, and one of K. Loring's, both just received by me from Bournemouth enclosed. Alice is evidently now rather stationary, but not *bad.* She has been a month at Bournemouth but has not yet left her room. Her *legs* seem always a serious question. K. Loring and Louisa will probably remain at B. till the end of April, and then go elsewhere. I shall then go to Alice, who, however, may subsequently rejoin the Lorings in the place they go to. They spend the summer in Europe. I don't think the climate has anything at all to do with Alice's state. She isn't in the least in touch with it, always indoors, with the same profuse fires, never reached by the outer air. I am sorry—very—for your botherations about your house. Ever yours,

H. James

1. HJ included in *The Bostonians* (which dealt with reform movements in Boston) the character of an elderly former abolitionist whom he called Miss Birdseye. In Boston, his readers identified this fictional personage with the real-life Elizabeth Palmer Peabody (1804–1894), sister-in-law of Hawthorne, friend of Margaret Fuller, and a leading Transcendentalist and reformer. Miss Peabody, in 1860, had founded the first kindergarten in the United States.

2. Howard James (1866–1920), a cousin.

To William James
Ms Harvard

3 Bolton St. W.
Feb. 15*th* [1885]

Dear William.

Let me say as a p.s. to my letter of yesterday that I was wrong in telling you to take the $25 for Howard James from the Syracuse money you owe me, as I have assigned this as you know altogether to Alice, to whom of course you continue to pay it, and I want it to go to her intact. She appears scarcely to touch it, and her idea is to "save it up" for me, but I wish her to have it, all the same. The subtractions of the money to pay for my half of Father's book was an exceptional case, arranged between us. Therefore I will send you one of these very next days a postal order or a £5 note, for the $25. Today is a Sunday, and I can do nothing.—I have been thinking over the rest of my novel, in relation to Miss Birdseye, and it seems to me even if Miss Peabody *should* think I meant to portray her (which, however, heaven forfend!) she cannot on the whole feel that what I had in mind is not something very fine and is not tenderly and sympathetically expressed. The later apparition and death of Miss B. is the prettiest thing in the book, and even should it be resentfully insisted that the picture is a portrait (I am told, on all sides, here, that my *Author of Beltraffio* is a living and scandalous portrait of J. A. Symonds and his wife, whom I have never seen).[1] I believe the story will remain longer than poor Miss P.'s name or fame, and I don't hold that it will be an obloquy or ground of complaint for her, to be handed down as having suggested anything so touching and striking. In a word, after you have read the book I don't think it will seem to you any more wounding for her to be known as Miss Birdseye than to be known as Miss P. But probably later, if the episode *does* strike people as I think it will, they will deny *then* that I *did* have Miss P. in my mind or that they ever said so; they will never give me the credit of having wished to represent her gracefully!—As I told you yesterday I never wished or attempted to represent her *at all*, or dreamed of it, and to be accused of doing so is a poor reward for having labouriously bodied forth out of the vague of imagination, and with absolute independence of any model that my own wits did not afford me, a creature who is (as I think) interesting and picturesque. If you think it so bad a business now, perhaps you will think that the sequel does *not* better it—but I can do nothing more than I have done, at this last hour—except as I say, write a letter of absolute protest to Miss Peabody.—You don't tell me whether you had any rejoinder from Godkin to the letter you wrote about the review of your book.[2] When I had read the article it was absolutely impossible for me not to write to him on my own account, and as I told him that the notice was "contemptible," and, under the circumstances, "barbarous" he may see fit to terminate our acquaintance. Melancholy, after twenty years! Ever yours

H. James

1. HJ is guilty here of a certain amount of guile. Edmund Gosse had given him many details of Symonds's private life and they had discussed his homosexuality. Matthiessen and Murdock, eds., *The Notebooks of Henry James* (1947), pp. 57–58, show "The Author of Beltraffio" clearly derived from Gosse's account of the marriage. In *Letters* II, 99, HJ writes that he is about to meet Symonds. The meeting must have taken place, for HJ wrote to WJ that he found Symonds "a mild, cultured man, with the Oxford perfume, who invited me to visit him at Clifton."

2. The *Nation* published an unfavorable review of WJ's edition of *The Literary Remains of the Late Henry James* (1884). WJ wrote to E. L. Godkin, the journal's editor, not only complaining of the review but adding "Poor Harry seems always given out to critics with antipathy to his literary temperament; and now for this only and last review of my father—a writer exclusively religious—a personage seems to have been selected for whom the religious life is complete *terra incognita* . . . Make no reply to this! One must disgorge his bile" Henry James, ed., *The Letters of William James* (1920) I, 240.

To Edwin L. Godkin
Ms Harvard

3 Bolton St. Piccadilly
March 3*d* 1885

My dear Godkin.

Your delightful letter, in answer to my last, gives me more pleasure than I can say. I was morally sure that you had known nothing about the Review[1] in the *Nation*, and that it had found its way in by accident, but it soothes extremely, a certain wounded feeling which had taken possession of me to have your definite confirmation of this. I thank you moreover, most kindly, for the generous and affectionate way in which it is given. I have a tenderness for my poor Father's memory which is in direct proportion to the smallness of the recognition his work was destined to obtain here below and which (in spite of my own personal inability to enter into that work save here and there, or accept most of the premises on which it rests) fill[s] me with a kind of pious melancholy in presence of the fact that so ardent an activity of thought, such a living, original, expressive spirit may have passed into darkness and silence forever, the waves of time closing straight over it, without one or two signs being made on its behalf, to say, however little it might command general assent, how remarkable and rare it had been. I had a hope that one of such signs might come from the *Nation*, though I was well aware at the same time that it would be next to impossible, and had been in other cases, to obtain any proper hand for the work. The volume, with my brother's introduction, seemed to me to have a real literary importance, however, into which even a person outside of my father's religious ideas (as I am) might enter—and in short your critic (or Garrison's rather) inflicted on me a kind of *déception* which I mention only to explain my note, not to add to your regrets. *N'en parlons plus!*

—You say nothing about any chance of your crossing the seas this year, but I hope there is one, in spite of your silence. You will find England in a very interesting though a very lugubrious condition. Difficulties seem to be closing round her, and even at this moment the newsboys under my window are calling out the declaration of war with "Roosher" and the recall of the ambassador: which however is anticipating a little. The ministry is still in office, but hanging only by a hair, Gladstone is ill and bewildered, the mess in the Soudan unspeakable, London full of wailing widows and weeping mothers, the hostility of Bismarck extreme, the danger of complications with Russia imminent, the Irish in the House of Commons more disagreeable than ever, the dynamiters more active, the income tax threatening to rise to its maximum, the general muddle, in short, of the densest and darkest. I must confess that the ministry has none of my respect; anything more shiftless and uncourageous than their conduct as to foreign affairs it is impossible to conceive. The war in the Soudan makes every one simply sick, those who think it necessary as well as those who don't. Gladstone hates foreign relations and has tried to shirk them all, and is paying his penalty in the bitter censure of his own party as well as the execration of the other. It is a pitiful end of a great career. The people that abuse him most are the good old liberals.—I am expecting in a day or two to hear of poor Lowell being superseded—an event which will wring tears from my eyes. I don't know, or imagine, what will become of him; I don't see his future. The death of his wife would not in the least interfere with his remaining here if he were left. She had been much out of his life, lately, through her ill-health, and lived in her own manner. Moreover, as she had again been absolutely insane for a month before her death, this event only removes an anxiety.—My sister is at Bournemouth, wretchedly ill, I am sorry to say—not at all the better for a winter in England. I expect to join her about May 1st and to remain near her for the rest of the summer. London becomes impossible at that period for a literary person wishing to work and yet knowing 5000 people, and I already perceive the uncomfortable increase of the pace. I have had nine notes to write this morning, and have done no work as yet! If you come out I shall of course come up to town to see you and Mrs. Godkin, to whom I send the friendliest remembrances. I saw Mahlon Sands yesterday[2]—at F. de Rothschild's[3]—and he told me he was going home for a month; so he will take you a late—but exaggerated—impression of me. I wonder if you are at Washington today and what is Mrs. Adams's last. Farewell, my dear Godkin, with every friendly assurance and affectionate remembrance for both of you. Ever faithfully yours

Henry James

1. See preceding letter to William James.
2. Brother of Mrs. Godkin.
3. Ferdinand Anselm de Rothschild (1839–1898), descended from the Vienna branch of the Rothschild family, was a collector and a patron of the arts.

To Grace Norton

Ms Harvard

3 Bolton St. W.
March 4*th* [1885]

My dear Grace.

I am sorry to say that I am so pressed for time that I can write you only very briefly today. Your two—your three—last (including the note), about Mrs. Lowell, are before me, and I thank you tenderly. You *don't* do justice to George Eliot, and my article (in the *Atlantic*) won't help you, as it is thin, meagre and imperfect.[1] I had to stop work on my novel to write it, and hated the task; so hating it, I did it poorly. Nor do you do justice to Balzac, in the very clever and entertaining article on his costumes in the *Nation*. Excuse me for not propping up this impudent assertion by examples (I haven't time—I have written ten notes and letters today, my correspondence is *killing* me!) and taking refuge in the general statement that a woman *can't* speak properly of Balzac. The proof of this is that the only thing that it seemed open to you to call the *Contes Drolatiques* was "unmentionable." They are *not* unmentionable; they are magnificent, superb; and the feminine point of view here is inadequate! I think G. Eliot was really a very fine creature—and so do you, I believe; and so perhaps we don't differ. I will send you Lord Acton's article about her in the *Nineteenth Century*, which is the best thing about the *Life*. I have constantly been with poor Lowell for the last five weeks, and except that he seems really *aged* by his wife's illness and death, he is very quiet, and not harrowed up. She was horribly insane for a month, and the physical collapse, at the end, which was unexpected, was a great mercy, as her future would have been worth nothing. It was out of a clear sky, after the best winter she had had since her great illness. She had two thorough attendants, he never or almost never saw her, didn't even know how bad she was, and the whole thing took place with as little invasion (so to speak) of his own life as possible. His friends were devoted to him; *her* great friend the dowager Lady Lyttelton, Mrs. Smalley (*his* great friend), the Leslie Stephens, etc. I went to see him almost every day; the William Darwins have come to stay with him now, Mrs. Putnam and "Georgie" are to arrive later, etc. Meanwhile the nomination of his successor[2] hangs over him like a dark cloud (his wife's death, I think, makes him feel more than ever disposed to remain), and a few days more, I suppose, will settle the question. I don't know what will become of him then; he told me the other day he could never go back to live *alone* at Elmwood. That prospect was bad enough before; but now, I suspect, is impossible.—London is immersed in gloom, with the mess and muddle of public affairs. The government hangs by a hair only, and we live in suspense, anxiety and a kind of sickness. Sickening certainly is the tragic tangle in the

Soudan. *Do* like the *Bostonians,* dear Grace; it is something like Balzac!!! But the *Princess* will be even better.[3] I sent you *A Day of Days*[4] just now; I am digging up, refurbishing and reprinting some early tales and you shall have the rest also. Alice is still at Bournemouth, and I am sorry to say there is no good news of her. I don't know what it is all going to end in. The "Season" begins its vulgar throbs and my "quiet evenings" on which you congratulate me are wrenched from me by the world. But I leave town on May 1st for a long period of possession of my soul. *Then* I shall write you in a manner more worthy of your friendship and of yours ever

H. James

1. The review of J. W. Cross's biography of George Eliot. See letter to Miss Norton, 24 January 1885.
2. See letter to Miss Norton, 24 January 1885.
3. Serial publication of *The Bostonians* in the *Century* continued until February 1886. James was already at work on *The Princess Casamassima.*
4. "A Day of Days," *Galaxy,* I (15 June 1866), 298–312, which James revised for the first volume of *Stories Revived* (1885).

To Grace Norton
Ms Harvard

3 Bolton St. W.
March 21*st* [1885]

My dear Grace.

A word to thank you for yours of the 10th, and the notes on the *Day of Days.* It is very good of you to care for that product at all; I don't myself, *really.* I think you overestimate it; I hope that sounds neither vainglorious nor conceited! It was a very young thing, and it was, the other day, much rewritten and improved (verbally). I send you herewith another tale of the same early batch—prettily written but poorish and thinish in substance. Its merit is, I think, a certain picturesqueness. I sent you another lot (from "Stories Revived") by themselves, two or three weeks ago (*A Landscape Painter,* etc.) which I hope will have reached you. You shall have still one more: a thing (*A Most Extraordinary Case*) which I well remember Jane and you talking about to me one evening at Shady Hill, a thousand years ago, and our having an immense, interminable laugh over.[1] The heroine in it nibbled a cake, which you didn't like; and in this revision I have suppressed the cake and the nibbling, thinking of you, but with the feeling, throughout, that the lady must be hungry.—I wrote you the other day about Lowell, and if I was rather brief it is because there really isn't much to say. He is so simple and takes things so simply! A life less complicated I can't imagine. He is now perfectly natural, and if he is only kept here will do very well. I wonder if you will understand what I say when I tell you that he won't miss Mrs. Lowell much—*considering* that she *was* his wife and that he was very fond of her. They were so little together! He was at the Legation in the morning; in the afternoon they sat apart, he in his rooms, she in hers; and almost every night of his life he dined out, without her. William and Sara Darwin have been a week with him, and it was apparently a very successful episode. Mrs. Putnam and her daughter have come to London, but, I believe, are to stay with him only ten days. It would not be in their genius to "carry on" his home, which is a considerable affair. My whole sentiment with regard to him is summed up in the single solemn prayer—"Heavenly Providence, keep for him his post!" I absolutely don't see his future, without it.[2]—The East Wind blows, horribly, and the Season, even in the midst of wars, alarms, national pessimisms and private poverties, begins to palpitate. I am going tomorrow, Sunday A.M., with Mrs. Sands to the Comtist place of worship. I shall probably not remain in town later than May 1st. Ever, dear Grace, your very faithful

Henry James

1. Both these tales, included in vols. II and III of *Stories Revived,* had been published by HJ in the *Atlantic Monthly*—"A Landscape Painter" in XVII (February 1866), 182–202, and "A Most Extraordinary Case" in XXI (April 1868), 461–485.

2. HJ was wrong. Recalled by President Cleveland, Lowell rapidly adjusted to the change by making frequent visits to England.

To J. R. Osgood

Ms Yale

3 Bolton St. Piccadilly
April 18*th* [1885]

Dear Mr. Osgood.

I have sent to the *Century* all the copy for the *Bostonians* save a small fraction, which I am only waiting to receive from the type-writer who recopies it for me, and who, being the only operator of the sort in this whole big city, is over-burdened with work and delays interminably. At any rate, by the time you receive this the whole book will have gone to New York with the exception of 70 or 80 pages in the total ms. of 950. I shall not ask you for the complete sum we agreed upon as the price of the work till the last sheet is in Gilder's hands; and I shall be greatly obliged to you if you will send me at present the first *half* of it—i.e. $2000. I shall notify you a very short time hence of the despatch of the concluding pages (as I shall ask Gilder to do of its arrival); but meanwhile I am in pressing need of money. Please, therefore, at the earliest possible moment after the receipt of this, send me the sum above-mentioned. You will not, I trust, think this an unreasonable request. You will probably have already perceived that the *Bostonians,* like most of my things, transcends considerably the length to which I had originally intended to confine it. I consider that you have a wondrous bargain!

I wrote some three months ago (my letter was to Mr. Ticknor) to ask him that some half-yearly statement of account and cheque be sent me. But save a casual mention in a subsequent letter of his that he had spoken of the matter to you, I have not, though in a second letter I re-iterated my request, had to this moment any satisfaction on this point. The delay (though I don't know why it shouldn't have been explained meanwhile) has seemed to me to be perhaps owing to the fact that you were getting the *yearly* account ready, and that as so much of the year had elapsed (it has now elapsed completely), you did not think it worth while to anticipate it with a partial statement, by only a few weeks. It was on the 15th of this month, a year ago, that I last received a remittance, under this head, from you. In heaven's name, then, please send me the yearly statement, without further postponement. I have been much inconvenienced by this delay, and should have been glad if some notice—even merely explanatory—had been taken of my two requests.

Very truly yours
Henry James

To Frederick Macmillan

Ms British Library

St. Alban's Cliff
Bournemouth
May 5*th* [1885]

My dear Macmillan.

I am moved to write you a letter of somewhat bewildered inquiry by having culled from the *Times* this A.M. (in the American telegrams) the sweet flower of information that J. R. Osgood & Co., my dear Boston publishers, have failed. The news leaves me at sea in regard to one or two important facts, and it occurs to me that you, having many lights on such matters (I have none) may be able to answer two or three of my questions. If you can, I shall be greatly obliged. Osgood owes me about £1000, eight hundred of which constitute a sum that he was to give me for the *Bostonians* when the completed work was delivered. As the remaining £200 have not (for a long time) been forthcoming (the fact that two letters I had lately written him on the subject were not answered had led me to entertain suspicions that his solvency was not perfect) I see no reason to believe that, in the midst of his catastrophe, the larger amount will be paid me when the smaller is not. As the last instalment of the story (it has developed into a thing double the size I expected when I made my agreement with Osgood) has not yet been sent to America—it is in the hands of the interminable Mouchablon!—I have made no demand for the money; but it is obvious I shan't get it (from Osgood). He made terms of his own with the *Century* for it, serially, and what I want to know is whether, if the *Century* people haven't paid him that money, I can put forth a claim to it from *them*. If they have paid him, I suppose I must go unrewarded, as the money will have been swallowed up; but if they haven't, would it be a proper line, or mere verdancy, for me to expect they will give it to me, or respectfully to suggest the same? I fear the indebtedness of the *Century* to Osgood (only, and directly) is not altered by his having failed. If you have any idea or impression on the subject I should take it very kindly of you to let me have it, and to let me hear also this: Wouldn't the book become mine, as a book, to do what I please with, on the failure of J. R. O. & Co. to pay me $4000 on receipt of the whole? And can't I also do what I please with my other books (in their hands) for which I shall certainly receive no royalties—judging by all their recent dumbness when appealed to on the subject? I won't bother you with more interrogations (indeed I have no others), but leave the above to your convenience and discretion.

Bournemouth is very mild, in all senses, especially *not* climatic. In fact in that sense it isn't so particularly, though the quality of the air is of the finest. I have some pleasant rooms on the sea: in the day I work, walk a little and look after my sister, who is very feeble but tending to improve; and in the P.M. I go to see Robert Louis Stevenson, who lives here, consumptive and shut up to the house, but singularly delightful. The place itself is meagre and featureless; but the sea is a lovely colour and the Isle of Wight looks pretty on the horizon. I hope Mrs. Macmillan thrives. Ever faithfully yours

Henry James

To the Fellows of Pembroke College

Ms Pembroke

Mr. Henry James greatly regrets that engagements at a distance deprive him of the pleasure of accepting the invitation which the Master and Fellows of Pembroke College have done him the honour to send him for the 26*th* of May. He must content himself with being present in spirit and sympathy at the unveiling of the bust of Gray.[1]

St. Alban's Cliff
Bournemouth
May 6*th* 1885

1. Thomas Gray (1716–1771), the author of the "Elegy Written in a Country Churchyard," originally resided at Peterhouse in Cambridge but moved to Pembroke College in 1756.

To Frederick Macmillan

Ms British Library

St. Alban's Cliff
Bournemouth
May 7*th* [1885]

Dear Macmillan.

I am much obliged to you for your information in the matter of Osgood's failure—especially for the advice about not sending the last chapters of the *Bostonians*, which is much to the point. I shall keep them back for the present. I am strongly inclined to believe that the Century Co. has by this time paid Osgood the sum he agreed with them for the serial use of the novel; he is sure, by the time nearly nine-tenths of my copy had been sent, which was the case before his failure came out, to have extracted that money from them. He said something to me when he was in London in the summer (last) that suggested that he should get his cash as soon as they began to publish. Nevertheless, on the *chance* that he may have not been paid, I wrote to Gilder on Tuesday to inquire. The *Century* people, if they are very chivalrous, may give me something, but I don't see that they are bound to, as I chose to make the bargain (in an evil hour) with him and not with them; but I don't count upon it, and am resigning myself to going unrewarded for the work in its serial character—odious as that idea is. There will be some compensation if I recover the book; and I don't see how I can fail to, not having given it up, literally, nor where else the property can vest in. If this should appear plain, I shall probably offer it to you—that is if you are willing to give me a sum for the copyright. I shall be so out of pocket by the non-payment of the money due on the magazine use of it, that I shall want for funds, and have to make some such arrangement as that. Osgood's bankruptcy is a most beastly immediate inconvenience to me. My royalties (on five books) for the last year (three new ones), I don't expect to get at all, and limit my expectation to the books being rescued. I shall be very glad if your people over there will buy them (i.e. the plates), and you publish them in the U.S.[1] There is a sixth ("Tales of Two Cities")[2] of which Osgood owned the copyright (for five years), as well as the plates. I shall be glad to hear what your solicitor says about the effect of Osgood's insolvency on the *Bostonians* as that work stands. Yours ever

Henry James

1. Macmillan published a three-decker edition of *The Bostonians* in England in February 1886 and a one-volume edition in New York three months later.

2. HJ slips into the title of Dickens's novel *A Tale of Two Cities*, which he had imitated in his book published in 1884, *Tales of Three Cities*.

To Grace Norton
Ms Harvard

St. Alban's Cliff
Bournemouth
May 9*th* [1885]

My dear Grace.

My indebtedness to you (for letters) is so great that I can't begin to enumerate it in the items. Let me therefore confess to it, gratefully, and affectionately, in the lump, with the assurance that everything brought pleasure and profit with it, as in its due order, it arrived. And this applies to the things in the *Nation*, as well as to your private missives; I always read them with great interest and a sense that you write with extreme grace and point. I have tried to make up my mind whether the late articles [in the *Nation*] on G. Eliot were yours, and have decided not, on the whole, because they were (you will laugh at my reason) not written by a woman. But if they *were* written by a woman (you will laugh still more at my logic), they were written by you. Except that they are a little diffuse they are very good. But alas, no one seems capable of saying a word on G.E. on the side, or in the name, of *art!* My article on her in the *Atlantic*[1] is full of vile misprints.—I am down here looking after Alice, and have been for the last three weeks. I have very pleasant rooms, directly on the sea (which, here, is a splendid colour, with the Isle of Wight, like an immense marble toy, on the ultra-marine horizon), about three minutes' walk from hers. She has had a wretched winter, and is in a very weak and poor state now; though much better since I came. She has two people to look after her: I brought down with me a lady-nurse, or companion, who answers the purpose fairly well, and she has also a very good maid.

So I am not in great requisition, and see her but once or twice a day, for twenty minutes, when she is well enough. We want to move her to Malvern, but she is too weak for it now, and we are waiting from month to month. Katharine Loring, whose sister is wonderfully better, will probably soon come back to her, so that this episode will, for me, not last, probably, more than another month. It is a great luxury, however, for me to be out of London at this rampageous season, and it is probable that even if [I] should leave this place, it would not be to return to town. Bournemouth is not interesting, and only half pretty, with the universal British fault of being cocknified to death. But the air is splendid, the views have a certain colour, and I have so much to do, all day, that I am not thrown upon the place. I have a great resource, for the evening, in the presence here of Robert Louis Stevenson, who is an old acquaintance of mine, ripening now into a friend. I suppose you know his charming writings—and the adorable tale of "Treasure Island." He is deadly consumptive, and has not for two years been out of the house; is also married to a Californian divorcée older than himself, and wears on his emaciated person, ancient seal-skin garments of hers. But his face, his talk, his nature, his behaviour, are delightful, and I go to see him every night. He looks like, and reminds me a little of, Shelley—and Tasso!—I am hard pressed with my new novel (not the *Bostonians*) for the *Atlantic*, which is much behind; but am breathing a little easier, as I find this a very good place to work. I go up to London this coming week, for forty-eight hours, to transact some business and see the exhibitions. My friend Sargent has Lady Playfair at the Academy and Mrs. Mason at the Grosvenor; so that the American type will not be unrepresented.—The air, here, of course, is full of the Russian imbroglio,[2] of which you have an echo, doubtless even in Kirkland Street. England is distinctly breaking down, and her loss of room in the world will be proportionate. I have lost all patience with Gladstone, who is an incurable shirker and dodger. I don't want to see the war, but I don't want my dear old England to have her face too crudely slapped. The slap in the present case will resound all over India. The truth is the British Empire isn't what it was, and will be still less so. I take refuge in the idea of the *race*—yours and mine, as well. Lowell made a charming address on Coleridge in the Abbey a few days since, in which he said that he must ask (in some of his allusions) indulgence for a memory which was rapidly becoming "one of its own reminiscences." Think of calling away a man who can say such happy things as that. But he is to have a public banquet before he goes, and may reflect with complacency that he has certainly done *much* to draw together the two countries. He has done, simply by having filled his office, in a public way, so prettily, much really for the cause of civilization.—How do the days and weeks and months go with you, dear Grace, and what is the colour of your life? Don't think I don't think of you because I write so meagrely. I am silent only with my pen, and am constantly making inarticulate remarks to you. Don't imitate my long pauses, imitate only the affectionate friendship with which I am ever faithfully yours

Henry James

1. See letter to Miss Norton, 4 March 1885.

2. The "imbroglio" was a dispute between Britain and Russia over the northern borders of Afghanistan. Gladstone handled this with considerable firmness, and strife was avoided.

To Violet Paget (Vernon Lee)

Ms Colby

St. Alban's Cliff
Bournemouth
May 10*th* [1885]

My dear Miss Paget.

I take up my pen, as we used to say in our infancy; but who shall say what I can possibly do with it—in such a case? The difficulty is increased by the fact that I am on my knees, prostrate, humble, abject, in the dust. That is an awkward position for articulate and intelligible speech, and yet I can't hold up my head, or rise to manly stature again, till I have caught some glimpse of a hint of a hope—even from the mere tremor of one of your eyelids—that there lurks in your generous nature, some slight capacity to pardon my disgusting conduct, my odious, unmannerly and inconceivable delay in writing to you. It is more inconceivable to me than to you, I assure you, and I haven't the slightest hesitation in saying that it is the most discreditable act (if *act* it can be called!)

of an otherwise tolerably decent and virtuous life. Don't judge me by it, or if so, leave room for an appeal; for I hereby declare to you that the rest of my days shall be devoted to removing from your mind the vile implication my ignoble silence must have produced upon it. I am really not a bad person to be indebted to for compensation, and compensation you shall have, my dear Miss Paget, if I leave every other future duty and pleasure unregarded. There, I shall sit up again, and even with supplicating eyes, venture to look you in the face; not because I precipitately and fatuously assume that I have been forgiven, but because I do respectfully hope that you have listened. This has been for me a winter of infinite domestic worry, preoccupation and anxiety, and my correspondence and many other social duties have been woefully neglected in consequence. After I had allowed myself to be prevented a certain time from writing to you, the simple *shame* of my situation, I assure you, settled upon me like a spell and paralyzed me quite. Every week that —by a detestable fatality—I didn't write, the redemptory step became more difficult, till at last I began to feel that any interest you may have had in hearing from me had completely died out and that if I were at last to address you you would merely return my letter, as a document that had fallen below its opportunities and had no intelligible message for you. This of course is nonsense; you have tolerance for all aberrations that are not of purpose, but only of hapless and accidental form. I am down at this dull place looking after my poor sister, who is wretchedly ill, and who has been for me, these last six months, a great anxiety and occupation. She came from America just at the time *Miss B.*[1] came out, in very bad case, and I grieve to say, has steadily been getting worse. I am remaining with her for the present, and for I know not how much longer. My preoccupations on her account have had much to do with the *demoralized* state I sank into (there is no other word than that) on this subject of writing to you.

I read *Miss B.* with eagerness, of course, as soon as I received the volumes, and have lately read a large part of them over again. It is to me an imperfect, but a very interesting book. As regards the *idea* of it, the conception and presentation of the character of the heroine, I think it a very fine one. The girl is really a very noble and remarkable vision, and she is sustained with singular evenness, in the key in which you have pitched her—except, I think at the end, in regard to the last fact that you have to relate of her. Making every allowance for a kind of grand rigidity and mournful, dismal, heroism that you have attributed to her—her offering to marry Hamlin strikes me as false, really unimaginable. Besides, *he* wouldn't, I think: he must at last have been immensely afraid of her, and his fear would have been deeper than his vanity. But Anne lives in the mind (outside of that point) as a creature projected (from *your* intelligence) in all her strange, original, tragic substance and form, with real imaginative and moral superiority. The imperfection of the book seems to me to reside (apart from, occasionally, a kind of intellectualized rowdyism of style) in a certain ferocity. It will probably already have been repeated to you to satiety that you take the aesthetic business too seriously, too tragically, and above all with too great an implication of sexual motives. There is a certain want of perspective and proportion. You are really too savage with your painters and poets and dilettanti; *life* is less criminal, less obnoxious, less objectionable, less crude, more *bon enfant,* more mixed and casual, and even in its most offensive manifestations, more *pardonable,* than the unholy circle with which you have surrounded your heroine. And then you have impregnated all those people too much with the sexual, the basely erotic preoccupation: your hand has been violent, the touch of life is lighter. This however is a secondary fact, with regard to the book; the primary one (for me) is that it's after my own heart in this sense: that it is bravely and richly, and continuously psychological—that, for you, *life* seems to mean moral and intellectual and spiritual life, and not the everlasting vulgar chapters of accidents, the dead rattle and rumble, which rise from the mere surface of things. I find the *donnée* of *Miss Brown* exceedingly in the right direction—a real subject, in the full sense of the word; carrying with it the revelation of character which is the base of all things and finding its *perspective* in that; appealing too to the intelligence, the moral sense and experience of the reader. You have appealed—indeed, too much to that sense; and too little to two or three others—the plastic, visual, formal—perhaps. You have proposed to yourself too little to make a firm, compact work—and you have been too much in a moral passion! That has put certain exaggerations, overstatements, *grossissements,* insistences wanting in tact, into your head. Cool first—write afterwards. Morality is hot—but art is icy! Excuse my dogmatic and dictatorial tone, and believe it is only an extreme indication of interest and sympathy in what you do. I regard *Miss Brown* as a most interesting and (if the word didn't sound so patronizing I should say *promising*) experiment. It has, in this age of thinnest levity and claptrap, the signal merit of being serious. Write another novel; you owe it to yourself, and to me—to give me a chance to show how prompt I shall be on *that* occasion! Be, in it, more piously plastic, more devoted to *composition*—and less moral: for in that last way you will seem (if you care) to your probable readers less *im*moral than they appear to have found *Miss B.* Dear Miss Paget—I shall write you again—for my spirit is greatly friendly to you. I shall also soon send you a book. I hope you are well and are coming this summer to England. I don't venture to breathe a word of the hope of hearing from you: that would be much happiness for yours most faithfully

Henry James

1. For the question of Vernon Lee's novel *Miss Brown*, see letters to Grace Norton, 21 October 1884 and 24 January 1885. Her dedication read: "To Henry James I dedicate for good luck my first attempt at a novel."

To Theodore E. Child

Ms Barrett

St. Alban's Cliff
Bournemouth
May 13*th* [1885]

My dear Child.

I have two friendly letters to thank you for, or to be rapidly exact, a letter and a note, both of which were appreciated in their degree. I have been unprecedently taken up, both with domestic and literary cares, and that has prevented my writing to you before. When I am *pressed* with work, as I have been, and am still, my correspondence goes simply to the *devil*. I am down here looking after my sister, who is wretchedly ill, and I shall remain near her for some weeks to come. I like being out of London when once the rustle and crush of the Season has set in, as they have done now; for it is impossible in town to pursue one's work or possess one's soul. This is a decidedly dull south-coast "health resort," as you doubtless know—though I doubt whether you do know, or in the Rue de Constantinople can imagine, the depths of anti-literary British Philistinism which pile themselves up—or down—in such a place. However, I am not dead of it, yet. You see I have turned away from Paris, instead of toward it. I shan't get there this summer, I greatly fear. There are *entassements* of obstacles—culminating a week ago in the failure of J. R. Osgood and Co. my Boston publishers by whom I have lost a largeish sum of money. That puts a spoke in my wheel for the present. And in fact I shall be all summer a kind of *garde-malade*. That isn't gay, but it is necessary. Your account of poor dear old Huntington touches me greatly, and I can't say how sad I feel in thinking of him and in being able to do nothing for him. You do well to be so good a friend to him—that is the only cheer the image of the genial old sage and sufferer suggests to me. Please give him always my friendliest remembrance and the assurance of my constant sympathy.—Your Paris news has been duly appreciated and digested, but I can't say it makes me feel that a *souffle* of sweetness and sanity is blowing over the lovely city. I haven't yet seen Jules de Goncourt's letters, and the only thing I have read from *là-bas* is the wondrous, and I must say in ways admirable, *Germinal*. In Zola's work it comes directly after *L'Assommoir* for strength. I haven't seen a syllable of decent —or anything but the most ignoble—criticism of it here. I don't wonder that M. Zola *se fiche de l'angleterre*. There is nothing, written, or writing, here; literature scarcely exists. The exhibitions, in town, are all open—I saw them the other day, and crammed with infantine attempts at painting. Sargent has two portraits *de femme;* one a distinct hit and the other a failure. What do you mean to do this summer—to go *in villeggiature* in the banlieue? If you were in Paris in September I think I might find you there. But September is far ahead, though the time passes fast. When you next write try and give me some news of the little thing.[1] Heaven watch over him—with all his faults I love him still. I also languish for a new volume of Maupassant; there has [been] none since *Yvette*—full three months ago! I am greatly compromised here by the dedication of Bourget's novel—the story being so *malpropre*.[2] But I admire it much—not the story, but the ability of it. *Bien à vous,*

Henry James

1. An allusion to Alphonse Daudet, who had entitled a semi-autobiographical novel published in 1868 *Le Petit Chose.*

2. Like Vernon Lee, Bourget had dedicated his first important novel, *Cruelle Énigme,* to HJ, who squirmed at its fulsome nature. Bourget recalled "the time when I was beginning to write it and which was also the time when we became acquainted. In our conversations in England last summer, protracted sometimes at one of the tables in the hospitable Athenaeum Club, sometimes beneath the shade of the trees in some vast park, sometimes on the Dover Esplanade while it echoed to the tumult of the waves, we often discussed the art of novel writing, an art which is the most modern of all because it is the most flexible, and the most capable of adaption to the varied requirements of every temperament. We agreed that the laws imposed upon novelists by aesthetics resolve themselves into this: to give a personal impression of life." Bourget was feeding back to HJ "the lessons of the Master."

To Houghton Mifflin & Co.

Ms Harvard

Bournemouth
May 23*d* 1885

Messrs. Houghton Mifflin & Co.
Dear Sirs.

I beg to acknowledge with thanks your statement of sales of my books for the last half-year, and your draft on London for £14.15.1. —I am presently sending to Mr. Aldrich the opening chapters of *The Princess Casamassima,* my serial for the *Atlantic,* and in regard to these, I should like to make this inquiry. When, a year ago, the terms of this serial were agreed upon between us, Mr. Aldrich in writing to me, mentioned that those which you offered and which were settled upon ($350 for each number of the story) were such only as you could agree to for a novel in which your interest was to cease with the publication in the magazine. This appeared to convey an intimation that you would give a larger sum, if the subsequent publication of the story in a volume were also in your hands. I should therefore like to know whether I have rightly apprehended the matter and in case of your afterwards issuing the novel you would increase the above-mentioned $350 for the monthly instalments. In this event I shall be glad to make over the *Princess* to you as a book.[1]

Yours very truly,
Henry James

1. Macmillan contracted to publish the novel in the United States as well as in England.

To James Russell Lowell
Ts Lubbock

St. Alban's Cliff
Bournemouth
May 29*th* [1885]

My dear Lowell.

My hope of coming up to town again has been defeated, and it comes over me that your departure is terribly near. Therefore I write you a line of hearty and affectionate farewell[1]—mitigated by the sense that after all it is only for a few months that we are to lose you. I trust, serenely, to your own conviction of this fact, but for extra safety just remark that if you don't return to London next winter I shall hurl myself across the ocean at you like a lasso. As I look back upon the years of your mission my heart swells and almost breaks again (as it did when I heard you were superseded) at the thought that anything so perfect should be gratuitously destroyed. But there is a part of your function which can go on again, indefinitely, whenever you take it up—and that, I repeat, I hope you will do soon rather than late. I think with the tenderest pleasure of the many fire-side talks I have had with you, from the first—and with a pleasure dimmed with sadness of so many of our more recent ones. You are tied to London now by innumerable cords and fibres, and I should be glad to think that you ever felt me, ever so lightly, pulling at one of them. It is a great disappointment to me not to see you again, but I am kept here fast and shall not be in town till the end of June. I give you my blessing and every good wish for a happy voyage. I wish I could receive you over there—and assist at your arrival and impressions—little as I want you to go back. Don't forget that you have produced a relation between England and the U.S. which is really a gain to civilization and that you must come back to look after your work. You can't look after it there: that is the function of an Englishman—and if *you* do it there they will call you one. The only way you can be a good American is to return to our dear old stupid, satisfactory London, and to yours ever affectionately and faithfully,

Henry James

1. See letter to Grace Norton, 21 March 1885.

To Theodore E. Child
Ms Barrett

St. Alban's Cliff
Bournemouth
May 30*th* [1885]

Dear Child.

I ought already to have thanked you for your friendly thought and delicate attention in sending me Maupassant's ineffable novel,[1] which I fell upon and devoured, with the utmost relish and gratitude. It brightened me up, here, for a day or two, amazingly. It is as clever—as brilliant—as it is beastly, and though it has very weak points it shows that the gifted and lascivious Guy *can* write a novel. But what horrors it contains—e.g. the description of the love-making of poor Madame Walter! No one but a Frenchman can write such a page as that—but no one but a Frenchman *would*, either. *En somme, Bel Ami* strikes me as the history of a Cad, *by* a Cad—of genius! In fact, just now—à propos of the Panthéon, Victor Hugo, the red flags, etc., they strike me pretty well as *all* cads, in the holy city and sanctum sanctorum of the great and absurd Victor[2] himself. I like his leaving half a million sterling and wishing to be carried in the "corbillard des pauvres"! He proves that a great poet can be a humbug. Do write me a word about the situation—if you can. Ever yours,

H. James

1. Maupassant's *Bel-Ami* had just been published.
2. Victor Hugo had died the previous week. His body lay in state under the Arc de Triomphe, and he was interred in the Panthéon.

To Count Robert de Montesquiou[1]
Ms Unknown

[1 July 1885]

Cher monsieur, Je vous laisse ce mot à la hâte pour que vous ne fassiez pas d'engagement pour après-demain, vendredi, le soir, s'il est possible et que vous vouliez bien remettre à ce moment notre dîner. Je viens de voir Whistler[2] qui malheureusement est pris demain, mais qui s'engage solennellement pour vendredi. Je vous attendrai donc ce jour-là au même endroit, à la même heure, Reform Club, Pall Mall, huit heures, dans l'espoir que cela vous sera tout aussi commode. En attendant, à deux heures demain, nous irons voir tous les Burne-Jones et tous les Rossetti possibles. Tout à vous,

Henry James

3 Bolton St. Piccadilly

1. The text of this letter appears in Philippe Jullian, *Robert de Montesquiou, Un Prince* (1965), p. 128.

2. Count Robert de Montesquiou-Fezensac (1855–1921), descendant of an ancient French family related to European royalty, was a highly cultivated man of letters in France and a homosexual. Sargent gave him a letter of introduction to HJ, who promised to introduce him to Whistler. This he did at the dinner at the Reform Club scheduled in this letter. For an account of HJ's hospitality to Montesquiou see Edel, *The Middle Years,* the chapter entitled "The Peacock and the Butterfly." See also the following letter to Henrietta Reubell.

To Henrietta Reubell

Ms Harvard

St. Alban's Cliff
Bournemouth
[5 July 1885]

Dear Miss Reubell.[1]

I returned to this place last night, after a fortnight's absence, to find lying here, unforwarded, your letter of the 24th. As all my letters come to Bolton Street and are sent me thence I had not expected anything would come straight to me here, and therefore had left no directions about their being sent after me. My landlord therefore simply laid your letter on my table, and it is the only one I find. That I left London (to return thither) only yesterday—and therefore only missed you by a few hours. Woe is me! I *had* absolutely to come back, however, and apart from the wretched business of missing you I am glad, I confess, not to spend this roasting Sunday in town. I went up to London to take a house in the neighbourhood for my sister, and after a week's researches found one, for a couple of months, on Hampstead Heath. After that I was detained in town by two or three engagements, and finally was in the very act of leaving when there descended upon me from the skies—or rather from Paris—three Frenchmen bearing introductions from Sargent and yearning to see London aestheticism. They were Polignac, Montesquiou and the charming Dr. Pozzi,[2] and to do Sargent's introduction proper honour I put off my departure and devoted Thursday and Friday to entertaining them—which I did, I believe successfully. I escaped from town yesterday—only to learn on my arrival here, as I say, that you were just reaching it. I had wondered what had become of you, and as the days passed—apparently—without news, I was on the point of giving you up. But now, dear Miss Reubell I shall come back again and see you; as soon as I have made certain arrangements here for the transport of my sister to Hampstead. She is so ill that this is a very complicated business; she has to be carried on a litter, etc; and there are various winding-up matters to be attended to here. I have very good *hope* of being able to get up by *Thursday.* She will come to Hampstead, with nurses, a friend whom she has with her, etc., on the following Monday, and I shall then have to meet her and attend to her installation; but in the interval I shall have the pleasure of seeing you. Miss Strettell[3] has begged me to come to her picnic of the 10th, and sleep at King's Layley, and this for the sake of seeing you (though I love not picnics) I shall *in all probability* be able to do: (arriving in town the evening of the 9th). On the Sunday (today week) I will go with you to Hampton Court, or Windsor, or any other suburb you may be so good as to designate. I should have liked to see the exhibitions with you, but I can't flatter myself that you will wait for Saturday to go to them.—Very delightful sounds your plan of Trouville, the Boit's garden etc.; and still more delightful the Engadine and Venice. *Felicissima lei!* My Frenchmen, or two of them, are at your hotel. Montesquiou is curious, but slight.—I am delighted that you seem to assent to my idea that you will always be, for all of us, *la grande Mademoiselle.* That, at least, will always be *my* formula for you; since you won't marry *me!*[4] Till very soon, then: I shall probably communicate with you on Thursday evening. *Bien à vous, tout à vous,* very faithfully indeed, yours

H. James

1. HJ wrote more than one hundred letters to Henrietta Reubell, whom he had met in Paris in 1876. She was the original of Miss Barrace in *The Ambassadors.* An elegant American expatriate, with a distinguished French ancestor, Miss Reubell maintained a salon, mainly for painters and writers, at 42 Avenue Gabriel.

2. Dr. Samuel Pozzi, French society physician and Prince Edmond de Polignac, a composer of some distinction. For Montesquiou, see letter of 1 July 1885. All three belonged to Marcel Proust's world.

3. Alma Strettell (Mrs. L. A. Harrison) moved in London's society-bohemia, among painters and writers.

4. Compare this playful remark with HJ's earlier statement (*Letters* II, 42): "If I wanted to desire to marry an ugly Parisian-American, with money and *toutes les élégances*, and a very considerable capacity for development if transported into a favoring medium, Miss R. would be a very good objective. But I don't."

To William James
Ms Harvard

3 Bolton St. W.
July 24*th* [1885]

Dearest William.

Your letter has just come, with the news of your dear little boy's death.[1] I had begun to fear some such news, as you had been silent for some time, following the tidings of the first appearance of the whooping cough. You have my full sympathy, and above all Alice has it—in the loss of a little, tender innocent clinging belonging like that. Poor little mortal, with his small toddling promenade here below, one wonders whence he came and whither he is gone. But babies are soft memories and Alice will always throb to the vision of his little being. Give my very affectionate love to her, and tell her how much I hope she is rested and refreshed now—with recovered sleep and contact with her other children. I am very sorry to be able to have come no nearer to the little Herman than to see his small earthly mound nestling near father's. But that I shall some day see. *Requiescat!*—I wrote to Aunt Kate directly after Alice's[2] successful move on the 13th ult. It was effected much more easily than I feared, and for a day or two afterwards she seemed to have borne it very well. Then came a big collapse, which, however, was brief, and not at all excessive, and from which (save that her *legs* seem absolutely lifeless) she has already almost entirely emerged. The state of her legs varies, and they will probably soon be again at the point they were when she left Bournemouth—permitting her to walk about her room for several minutes at a time. They fluctuate and recuperate. The cottage at Hampstead is exceedingly diminutive—but she and Katharine fit into it and it is very salubrious and *gay*. You appear to underestimate the quality of the Hampstead air. The heath to which Alice is close, or on, is only forty feet lower than Malvern, and the atmosphere is exceedingly fresh and tonic. It is thought the most bracing air in this part of England and people come to it from a distance. What Alice needs is to *take* it, to breathe it, such as it is, and to get out of the close sickroom, with windows forever shut and fire, on the hottest days, forever burning, in which she has been immured for so many months. This she will probably do during the next month.—My transaction with Osgood's successor has dragged out long, partly through a delay, at the last, of my own; but before you get this he will to all appearance have paid over $4000 to Warner for me. I have instructed Warner immediately to take $1000 out of this and repay it to you: so that I trust the whole business will have been settled by August 1st.

I shall soon have straightened out completely as regards money, and am now in a position to promise to pay $1000 for the Syracuse building[3] before the bills are due, unless they are to be due unnaturally soon: that is I can easily pay the money by January 1st. *Therefore,* as this is a perfectly definite engagement, I would rather you did not keep back my share of the rents—but go on paying it to Alice. When I told you to do this I did not clearly understand that $1000 was the maximum I should have to contribute, even covering the advance to Bob. I thought the sum would be larger. This sum I now see I can pay out of current income from other sources; and, I repeat, hereby engage to do so if you will, when you next write, tell me the earliest moment at which you will have to settle for the repairs. I would do it *before* January 1st. In this case count upon me for the money and continue to pay my rents to Alice. I shall probably go on August 1st to Dover, for that month, to my rooms of last summer, and to such peace and control of one's time as one can simply *never* get in London.

I read in the papers here of long and intense heat in the U.S., and fear you have been much roasted. I hope at any rate you are now in some cool and calm country. I embrace you both, and Alice twice over, and am ever yours

Hy. James

1. This was William James's infant son, Herman. See letter to William James, 1 April 1884.

2. Readers will recognize from the context that it is a question of two Alices in these letters—Alice James, the sister, now in England, and Alice Howe Gibbens, the wife of William James.

3. HJ shared ownership with William of the James family's Syracuse real estate. They had decided to make extensive repairs in order to derive higher revenue from the buildings. The $1000 represented HJ's share of the outlay.

To Count Robert de Montesquiou
Ms Unknown

21 août 1885, 15 Esplanade Douvre

Cher monsieur de Montesquiou,[1] Je suis bien aise de savoir que vous avez gardé un aussi bon souvenir de votre trop court passage à Londres et vous envoie ce mot pour vous engager à y retourner sans crainte de voir se gâter vos belles impressions. Je crois que l'intérêt que vous avez trouvé à beaucoup de choses ne ferait que s'accroître avec une plus intime connaissance et que, pour vous comme pour tous ceux qui ont fini par s'attacher à la vie anglaise, le premier aspect et la surface un peu terne (de bien des éléments) se trouvent n'avoir été qu'un masque trompeur des jouissances qui vous attendent. Soyez certain dans tous les cas que chaque fois que vous reparaîtrez vous ferez bien plaisir à

Yours faithfully
Henry James

1. Text in Jullian, *Montesquiou*, pp. 128–129.

To Grace Norton
Ms Harvard

15 Esplanade, Dover
August 23*d* [1885]

My dear Grace.

It is absurd to pretend at this distance of time that this is an "answer" to your good letter of—I won't tell you when; but as an independent and irrelevant utterance it carries you my love, and every friendly wish that my heart can feel or my pen can form.

My imagination (perched close here on the edge of the sea) traverses that unprofitable element and figures you, though without enthusiasm, sitting in the bowery porch of your window and listening to the crickets shriek as they do in Cambridge on summer nights. I say without enthusiasm, because this is not the best position I could wish for you: I would rather believe you are in fresh fields, or even frivolous places, like Newport or Lenox, interposing a little absence, distance or even alienation, from the usual Kirkland Street. For me, I am spending a delightfully quiet month of August at this convenient though not intrinsically dazzling place, which I have at various times resorted to before, when I have wanted rest and retirement, and of which the principal merit is that it is salubrious and destitute of any possible social encounter. I returned from Bournemouth on July 10th, spent the rest of that month (worrying and panting through the hideous fag-end of the season) in London; escaped hither three weeks ago, and am meditating at the end of a fortnight a further escape, consisting of a visit to Paris, from September 10th to November 10th. Alice has been spending the summer at Hampstead Heath, with Katharine Loring to minister to her; and is very considerably better, though still an extreme invalid. K. P. L. stays with her till December (probably); and Alice spends the winter in London, not because it is an ideal place for an invalid, but because she has no strength for foreign journey. Such, dear Grace, is a rapid sketch of my domestic situation. Add to it that I am pegging away to finish the *Princess* (a long-winded novel which has just begun in the *Atlantic*), and that I have various other literary (ulterior) projects, and you will know almost all about me that is worth knowing. I went up to town the other day to attend the service for Grant[1] in the Abbey (hoping my name, as an eager assistant, would be in all the American papers: was it!). The service *per se* was fine and impressive and the number of English "illustrious" present creditable to international courtesy; but Archdeacon Farrar's address, or sermon (much praised) was, to my sense, so vulgar, so cheap and fifth rate, as to make the occasion rather a torture to me. I gave poor old Lord Houghton[2] my arm to come out, and that was the last I saw of him. I liked him (in spite of some of his little objectionableness), and he was always only kind to me. A great deal of the past disappears with him. I am *dying*, literally *dying*, to know something about Lowell: how he appears, gets on, comports himself, and how and where he intends to live—if he does so intend—in his native latitudes. Surely, he will come back: he ought to. Perhaps you will not think that; and if you don't perhaps you will tell me what you think he *"had"* ought to do? I can't make it out; but should be very thankful to you for news of him, or any personal impression. Mrs. Kemble[3] returns on September 1st from her annual Switzerland with her monumental punctuality: she has never failed of that day for forty years!—and I, as soon as possible afterwards, go up to town to embrace her—as one embraces a monument. (She lands at Folkestone—also for forty years!—or our embrace would take place on a plank of the vessel here.) I am spending the most *unsocial* summer—to my great delight—that has rolled over me since I came to England: having almost entirely succeeded in keeping out of engagements to pay "staying" visits—a process for which the small faculty I ever had is rapidly quite deserting me. They don't pay, compared with the inordinate amount of time they consume, and I, at the age I have reached, have purposes far too precious to put the rest of my few years to, to be able to devote long days to sitting about and twaddling in even the most luxurious country houses. I spent five days at Ferdinand de Rothschild's[4] the last thing before coming down here, and the gilded bondage of that gorgeous place will last me for a long time. Don't breathe it to a soul, but I am rather weary and sick of London. However, it is, on the whole, the best place for me to live, and the solution of the problem will be in learning to live there differently from what I have done hitherto. The London mind is now absorbed in the great "Dilke Scandal"[5]—no very edifying chapter of social history. It is, however, by no means without a certain rather low interest if one happens to know (and I have the sorry privilege) most of the people concerned, nearly and remotely, in it. Donald Crawford has applied for a divorce from his wife on account of her relations with Dilke, the lady being the sister of Mrs. Ashton Dilke, C.D.'s late brother's wife. Hearing of this, Mrs. Mark Pattison,[6] in India (staying at Madras with the Grant Duffs), heroically makes it known that she is engaged to be married to Dilke (by way of comfort to him), and the news is in all the papers. Meanwhile another London lady whom I won't name,[7] with whom for years his relations have been concomitant with his relations with Mrs. Pattison, and whose husband died (strangely enough) just at the moment as the Rector of Lincoln, has had every expectation that he was on the point of marrying *her!* This is a very brief sketch of the situation, which is queer and dramatic and disagreeable. Dilke's private life won't (I imagine) bear looking into, and the vengeful Crawford will do his best to lay it bare. He will probably not succeed, and Dilke's political reputation, with the "great middle class," will weather the storm.[8] But he will have been frightened almost to death. For a man who has had such a passion for keeping up appearances and appealing to the said middle class, he has, in reality, been strangely, incredibly reckless. His long, double liaison with Mrs. Pattison and the other lady, of a nature to make it a duty of honour to marry *both* (!!) when they should become free, and the death of each husband at the same time—with the public watching to see *which* he *would* marry—and he meanwhile "going on" with poor little Mrs. Crawford, who is a kind of infant—the whole thing is a theme for the novelist—or at least for *a* novelist. I, however, am not the one, though you might think it, from the length at which I have treated the topic! It will perhaps refresh you among New England bowers. Where are you, dear Grace, how are you, and what sort of life are you leading? Do give me some news of Shady Hill and what time brings forth there. I haven't seen Sara Darwin[9] since she came home, though she kindly asked me to Basset, at a moment when it was impossible to go. Your Montaigne, in the *Nation,* is delightful. Believe ever in the interest and friendship of yours most faithfully

Henry James

1. Ulysses S. Grant had died on 23 July 1885.

2. The literary Lord Houghton (Richard Monckton Milnes) had in earlier years been very hospitable to HJ. See Edel, *Henry James: The Conquest of London, 1870–1883* (1962) the chapter entitled "A Bird of Paradox," and *Letters* II, 114–115, 198–201.

3. Frances Anne Kemble. See *Letters* I, 319 and II, 240–241.

4. Ferdinand Anselm de Rothschild. See letter to Edwin L. Godkin, 3 March 1885. The patron of the arts had just completed Waddesdon Manor, his French chateau set into the English countryside, and HJ had visited it for the first time.

5. Sir Charles Dilke, described by HJ (*Letters* II, 218) as very skillful and very ambitious, had compromised his successful political career by his various liaisons.

6. Widow of the Rector of Lincoln. HJ had met her in 1869 (*Letters* I, 111) and described her then as "highly emancipated."

7. This lady was named soon enough during the court proceedings. She was Mrs. James (Christina) Rogerson, another friend of HJ's (*Letters* II, 101).

8. HJ was wrong. Dilke married Mrs. Pattison and retired from public life.

9. Mrs. Darwin, the former Sara Sedgwick, was a sister of Charles Eliot Norton's first wife. See *Letters* II, 143, 150.

To Robert Louis Stevenson
Ms Yale

Dover
September 10*th* [1885]

My dear Robert Louis.

When I hear, as I have done this A.M., from Sargent (of whom, till today, I had had no tidings since he paid his visit to you), that you have again been ill (and I fear seriously) I feel more than ever that I have been an incredible brute in not having written to you. But the motives of my silence have been pure. I knew that it was an effort and a fatigue to you to answer letters, and I didn't wish to seem to appeal to you for that sort of exertion. Had I known you had been laid up I would have made short work with these refined scruples! Even now I don't like to seem to ask questions of you, or to impose upon your misery the burden of having to produce unremunerated MS. about it. But perhaps your wife will at her perfect leisure (she will smile to hear me attribute to her that article) give me some brief information. All my arrangements are made for going over to Paris (for four or five weeks) tomorrow; and if this were not the case I should immediately come down and interrogate you with my eyes and ears, and with my heart. Sargent's mention of your case is of the briefest, as he evidently supposes I know all about you (naïf Sargent!) but it seems to point to your having had a much worse summer than there was reason to hope for when I quitted Bournemouth. Let me believe, at least, till I hear the contrary, that you are now on the rise again and encompassed with happy omens. At all events I give you, my dear Stevenson, my heartiest, friendliest sympathy, and to your wife as well, who, I fear, has been anxious and weary—no less than I know she has been brilliantly devoted. I have spent the last month at this place, trying to get ahead of the beastly serial in the *Atlantic,* which I hear panting at my heels. As soon as I come back from

Paris, I will come and see you: I have sworn it. I think, with all sorts of romantic embroidery and retrospective (though superfluous) glamour, of our sociabilities of the early summer, in which even Bogue[1] figures as an ingratiating personality. These fluctuations, my dear Stevenson, are mere *flamboiements* of genius, and your star is steady and I believe in it. Expect me at no distant date, and believe me always affectionately yours and your wife's—

Henry James

1. Stevenson's dog.

To William James

Ms Harvard

29 Rue Cambon
Oct. 9*th* 1885

Dear William.

This must be a very short effusion, mainly to enclose you another draft of $250, and to thank you for two letters, both received during the month that I have been spending in Paris. The first was from Cambridge and was about Bob's having made you his trustee etc.; the second from Keene Valley, acknowledging my former draft, the power of attorney etc., and containing several pages of advice and warning apropos of the "Bostonians." For these last I thank you heartily and think it very nice of you to have taken the trouble to write them. I concur absolutely in all you say, and am more conscious than any reader can be of the redundancy of the book in the way of descriptive psychology etc. There is far too much of the sort of thing you animadvert upon—though there is in the public mind at the same time a truly ignoble levity and puerility and aversion to any attempt on the part of a novelist to establish his people solidly. All the same I have overdone it—for reasons I won't take time to explain. It would have been much less the case if I had ever seen a proof of the *Bostonians;* but not a page have I had before me till the magazine was out. It is the same with the *Princess Casamassima;* though that story will be found probably less tedious, owing to my having made to myself all the reflections your letter contains, several months ago, and never ceased to make them since. The *Princess* will, I trust, appear more "popular." I fear the *Bostonians* will be, as a finished work, a fiasco, as not a word, echo or comment on the serial (save your remarks) have come to me (since the row about the first two numbers) from any quarter whatever. This deathly silence seems to indicate that it has fallen flat. I hoped much of it, and shall be disappointed—having got no money for it I hoped for a little glory. (What do you mean, by the way, by saying—"now that I am to lose nothing by Osgood!" I lose every penny—not a stiver shall I have had for the serial, for which he received a large sum from the *Century*.) But how can one murmur at one's success not being what one would like when one thinks of the pathetic, tragic ineffectualness of poor Father's lifelong effort, and the silence and oblivion that seems to have swallowed it up? Not a person to whom I sent a copy of your book, in London, has given me a sign or sound in consequence, and not a periodical appears to have taken the smallest notice of it. It is terribly touching and, when I think of the evolution of his production and ideas, fills me with tears. Edmund Gurney[1] spoke to me with extreme enthusiasm of your preface, but said he considered it dispensed him from reading the rest.—I have been all this month (from September 10th) in a perfectly empty and very dull and provincial Paris, which however I have enjoyed very much. I have had my time to myself, worked, gone to the theatre etc. I shall stay another two or three weeks, as some of my friends are coming back—including Bourget, who, to my great regret, has been wholly absent. The Bootts come next week. I can't give you any impressions of Paris—partly because they aren't much worth it and partly because I must catch the train to go and dine at Versailles with poor Charlotte King.[2] Alice is settled at 7 Bolton Row, and Katharine will probably be with her another month. I won't write about her now—I shall be sure to do it so much, later. Thank your wife for a sweet note, acknowledging my photographs. I am delighted that Keene Valley poured so much satisfaction into you. May it remain. I tremble to ask about Bob. Ever, in haste, your affectionate

Henry

1. Edmund Gurney (1847–1888), fellow of Trinity College in Cambridge, was one of the founders of the Society for Psychical Research. See *Letters* II, 73.

2. Charlotte King, a cosmopolitan cousin of HJ's, is described in chapters XX–XXI and XXVIII of HJ's autobiography, *A Small Boy and Others* (1913).

To Robert Louis Stevenson
Ms Yale

3 Bolton St. W.
Nov. *6th* [1885]

Dear Stevenson.

Five days ago, just as I was leaving Paris, came to me your delightful letter, which I promised myself to answer the moment I reached London. When, however, this conspicuous event did take place, I was in the throes of a savage neuralgic headache, which sent me to bed, kept me down for three days, and has but just permitted me to dedicate to you a few tremulous penstrokes. Tomorrow I shall be all right, but I won't wait even for tomorrow to tell you what a pleasure it has been to me to get news of you "over," as they say in the American land, your own signature. I have had anxieties and wonderments about you, and now, on the very first day I can manage it I shall come down and see with my eyes *à quoi m'en tenir*. I am afraid that, for many reasons, this will be unmanageable before the middle of the month, but I give you my solemn and affectionate vow that as nearly as possible at that moment my sedentary part shall press the dear old fire-side chair. There is a fundamental affinity between them, which yearns to be gratified. I shall not be able to stay for long—only a moment—but I shall very soon come again.—I haven't yet got hold of "Nine," but I shall find it presently, and shall, I am sure, enter largely into the joke. Poor Mr. Archer,[1] however, must have expressed only the conception that most of your readers catch from your pages when he sees you mainly in want of bloodletting and other emasculation; for the miracle of your achievement is that your extreme invalidism has coloured your literary production not at all, and you project upon the printed page a suggestion of a young Apollo unconscious of the doctor and unindebted to the chemist. I hope, very earnestly, that this indebtedness has not of late been going fast—that you have been in a good phase and have the prospect of an easy winter. I spent eight weeks in Paris, of which, however, I fear I shall have nothing proportionate to tell you. I find *Prince Otto*[2] here, the fruit of your munificence, and shall give you my impression of him from the vantage-ground of your grandfather's chair. I send you a corrected copy of the third *Princess*. Put me at the feet of your wife, till I can crouch there in the flesh. Courage, patience, my dear Robert Louis—though I know not why I should preach you virtues you possess far more richly than yours ever very faithfully

Henry James

1. William Archer (1856–1924) a critic and later a dramatist, had written an article on Stevenson in the November 1885 issue of the journal *Time*, emphasizing his robust qualities, without being aware of his chronic invalidism.
2. *Prince Otto*, a fairy-tale romance by Stevenson, had just been published.

To Grace Norton
Ms Harvard

3 Bolton St. Piccadilly
December 9*th* [1885]

My dear Grace.

If your last letters (all about James Lowell's return and prospects) seem to me, by this, ancient history, what will they—or this reminder of them—seem to you? The whirligig of time—all the while that I haven't written to you—has come round to the point that (in February) J. R. L[owell] is very confidently expected back here. So says Mrs. Procter, and Mrs. Smalley,[1] and various other Mrs.-es, and greater dames; but the outlook appears to me inscrutable—as inscrutable as the rumour, which reaches me, that he is spending the winter at Southborough, Mass., and greatly enjoying it! I know not whether it is a very kind or a very cruel world. Dear Grace, your last news came to me a little while before I went to Paris and contained a very natural implication that while I should be there I could give you some of mine. In the interval I have had time to spend a couple of months there and to have been back here some four weeks—and yet your friendly assumption I never justified. I won't undertake to describe to you why; each day brought some horrid little exasperating reason. September was very golden and hazy and pleasant on the banks of the Seine, but October was wet and muddy—rather prosaic. My Paris friends, however, for the most part, came back to town; but I saw little of any celebrities—nothing even of Daudet, who was mainly absent, and ill into the bargain. He is believed to be in a bad way, in health—"atteint de la moelle épinière." This, however, may be an exaggeration, and he is actively producing. I spent much of my time at the dying bed of poor Blanche Lee Childe,[2] who is gradually sinking through extreme suffering into the last stage of consumption. She has been confined to her bed for a year, has no voice, is fearfully emaciated, etc.; yet lingers on, with a strange, patient, irreducible vitality, and is—or was, a month ago—able to see visitors to a considerable extent, and to talk in a pathetic whisper, as well as to listen. She is a woman whom I never absolutely and completely liked while she was in health (though she never had much); but she appears to great advantage in illness, and her sweetness and serenity, her fortitude and patience in the midst of constant suffering and a kind of prostration particularly cruel to a woman who was always immensely occupied, made a great impression on me. She will be agreeable, graceful and intelligent to the last. Childe was more bored and *un*occupied and pessimistic and futile than ever; and I don't think I mistake in saying that his wife is partly dying of the *oppression* (for a woman who had begun by being proud and ambitious) of his complete failure in life and his curious, refined mediocrity—above all, of his idleness and his being always there. —Mrs. Strong, I saw a good deal of as usual, and went a good many times to the theatre with her. The theatre and the Madeleine, and the *couturière*, are the three props of her existence. She is bright and perceptive and very hospitable, but youth and happiness have left her. Paris was pleasant to me this year—very: and I was quite in the mood to have spent the winter there, if circumstances had favoured; which they didn't. But I was not inconsolable, for I am doing very well here.—England as you know has been in a state of the roughest electioneering topsyturviness, and the upshot of it is that the Liberals are apparently coming back; though they are not eager, I think, as they will have to face Parnell and the Irish question in a more colossal and insoluble shape than ever. It is a huge black monster, and civil war seems to me to be really in the air. I am not enchanted to see the Liberals back—with the help of the emancipated chawbacons; their wisdom doesn't seem to me superior. Gladstone is a dreary incubus, and "Dilke and Chamberlain" don't strike me as names and watchwords of magic. But *basta:* the air here is positively putrid with politics.—Alice lives five minutes off from me, and is better and every way more comfortable than she has been at any time since she came out. I have just taken a "residential flat," in Kensington, on a long lease; but it has to be finished and furnished, and I shan't get into it for at least three months. It is very good, with air, light, space, a lift (to the fourth floor, where it is "located"), and every other convenience—like a French *appartement.* I trust to a healthy and happy [life] there, for twenty-one years!—but will tell you more on the subject when I have got "fixed." There is positively nothing to read, in England or in France; the pen is fruitless and dumb. Party-politics, ferocious, dishonest and vulgar, are the only thing that exists. I hate 'em—that I do. Mrs. Kemble is wonderfully well this year, and (in conversation) full of action and passion. She sings, spouts, dances (almost), gives imitations and says fifty good things a minute. I have seen or heard nothing of Sara Darwin for many months; she was lately in town, but didn't come to see Alice. I am grieved dear little lonely Lily should have had to flee the too tranquil shores of Southampton water. But *si capisce.* I hope intensely and immensely that you are not reading, in their present form, my two long-winded serials. But do read 'em when they come out [in book form] and speak of them to me then. The *Princess* is not yet finished. When she is I am not going to write another long story for two or three years. The first next thing, I shall produce six or seven critical essays, not very long. Everyone here admires extremely the truth and power of "Silas Lapham," including myself. But what hideousness of life! They don't revile Howells when he does America, and such an America as that, and why do they revile me? The "Bostonians" is sugar-cake, compared with it. Dear Grace, I haven't asked you a question about yourself; but you don't need that to know the desire to hear everything, of your ever affectionate

Henry James

1. Mrs. Bryan Waller Procter, HJ's octogenarian friend (*Letters* II, 113, 199–201, 208), and Mrs. G. W. Smalley, wife of the European correspondent of the New York *Tribune.*

2. See *Letters* II, 61–62.

To Elizabeth Boott
Ms Harvard

3 Bolton St. Piccadilly W.
January 7*th* [1886]

My dear Lizzie.

My many thanks for your kind wish for the *bonne année,* which I give you back heartily, and to your dear father also, a hundred-fold. I hope the year announces itself well for you—as it so apparently does; it certainly will not be difficult for it to be a better one than 1885. It finds me struggling with the preliminaries of a new installation, a sort of thing I hate, having no genius for pots and pans, for estimating quantities of drugget or settling questions of gas and water. Alice, to whom I gave your letter and who thanks you tenderly for it, is doing very well, in all respects, and will probably do better as the rigour of the winter passes and she is able to trundle out. We are up to our necks in snow, and the hansom and the four-wheeler are alike as though they were not. The main artistic event is the exhibition of Millais's[1] pictures (ever so many), out of which he comes on the whole very well. He is a wondrous painter of children—it is on that his fame must rest. Sargent is still here, and evidently tends to remain. He is painting a pretty woman —Mrs. Robert Harrison—if he only won't stick his brush down her throat. In the long run he will thrive here, I am sure, and his social existence will be much larger and more prosperous than in Paris. Also there will be no Mrs. S.[2] to abuse him. I gather you are not *folle* of that lady; but be kind to her, because she is fond of me! I suppose you have heard the sad rumours (which appear founded) as to poor Clover Adams's[3] self-destruction. I am afraid the event had everything that could make it bitter to poor Henry. She succumbed to hereditary melancholy. What an end to that intensely lively Washington *salon.* I hope you fraternize with the tall Etta,[4] who has so much *cachet.* I am sure your father does, or if he doesn't it isn't Etta's own fault. I think there are more grounds for fearing he will marry her than there were for fearing he would marry (*dans le temps*) Miss Bartlett.[5] I embrace him whatever rash act he commits. Ever your affectionate

H. James

1. Sir John Everett Millais (1829–1896), one of the founders of the Pre-Raphaelite Brotherhood and a painter of great distinction.

2. Probably Mrs. Charles Strong. See preceding letter to Grace Norton.

3. Mrs. Henry Adams had committed suicide in Washington.

4. Henrietta Reubell. See *Letters* II, 41–42.

5. Alice Bartlett, now Mrs. Warren, had been one of HJ's friends in Rome during the early 1870s. See *Letters* I, 329.

To Edward Tyas Cook

Ms British Library

3 Bolton Street W.
January 21*st* [1886]

Dear Sir.

I must beg you to excuse me from sending you, as you do me the honour to propose, a list of the hundred best books.[1] I have but few convictions on this subject—and they may indeed be resolved into a single one, which however may not decently be reproduced in the columns of a newspaper and which for reasons apart from its intrinsic value (be that great or small) I do not desire to see made public. It is simply that the reading of the newspaper is *the* pernicious habit, and the father of all idleness and laxity. This is not, however, an opinion that I should have ventured to thrust upon you—without the pretext you have been so rash as to offer to

Yours very truly
Henry James

1. Swinburne supplied the list; Henry Irving gave only the Bible and Shakespeare. Matthew Arnold, like HJ, declined to participate.

To Edward Tyas Cook

Ms British Library

3 Bolton Street W.
January 23*d* [1886]

Dear Sir.

I must request you very earnestly and explicitly *not* to publish the note I was so reckless as to write you a couple of days since and which you have sent me, to my great alarm and surprise, in proof. It was a strictly private communication, intended simply to mitigate the dryness of my declining to comply with your invitation (to discourse upon the 100 books), and I have the best reasons in the world for wishing it not to appear in the columns of the *Pall Mall Gazette.* I depend upon your fine sense of honour not to let it figure there and remain truly yours

Henry James

To Edwin L. Godkin
Ms Harvard

13 De Vere Mansions West W.
Feb. *6th* [1886]

My dear Godkin.

You will perhaps have seen in the English papers some allusion to the sudden dismissal from the editorship of the *Daily News* of our friend Frank H. Hill[1]—an incident which has excited a good deal of sympathy and even a little indignation, among his friends. The manner in which he was turned off was abrupt and rough and he finds himself on the world, without, or almost without, an income, at a late hour of his life, and with very little eyesight. I have intended any time this fortnight past to write you a line of which the purport should be a suggestion that if it were possible for you to invite him specifically to do something for the *Post* or the *Nation,* the invitation would probably be extremely welcome to him. He must support himself in future by general writing—and as you no doubt know he writes with a great deal of force and knowledge. I am quite conscious that you *may* have done something of this kind—if you received from Hill the statement which he drew up and printed at the time of his leaving the *D.N.* It was not, I think, altogether well inspired; but he sent it about to most of his friends. Some of them have had a design of attempting, very privately, to raise a "testimonial" (of money) for him—but this idea will not be fruitful, owing to his want of personal popularity and some other causes. The *Daily News* was certainly doing badly, but it does not appear that it was by any means solely by reason of his shortcomings. At any rate if he *was* an unsuccessful editor he is an accomplished writer—and my regret at the presumption, though not yet proved, abandonment of the project to make up a purse for him (about which please say nothing) has prompted me to speak of him to you in this way—at the risk of your having already thought of him and my intimation appearing therefore importunate. I am very sorry both for him and his wife—for she has even less eyesight than he. They show great courage, and London is very sorry for them. But London is very busy, hurrying and indifferent.—I am delighted, my dear Godkin, to find myself writing to you—though this is but a partial realization of a plan I had at the New Year and have had repeatedly since, of writing to your wife. I wanted to wish you the *bonne année* and let you know how much the faith that I shall see you both here before many months is part of the force that sustains and cheers me amid the complications of existence. If you should be able to come out this summer I can promise you a social and political situation of thrilling interest. This you are doubtless theoretically aware of, but it has many features that can be appreciated only on the spot, amid the agitated saloons and more than British conversations, of Mayfair and South Kensington. I won't tell you what my own political opinions are, for my chief endeavour will be to conceal them from you while you are here. I doubt whether you will find the Liberals in office when you come; my prevision would be that the Tories will be back at the end of three months and streaking ahead of Gladstone (in the same sense) on the Irish business. A further inducement to you must be that in two or three weeks I am moving into more spacious quarters (should you kindly write me three lines, please address them to the Athenaeum Club, Pall Mall), and shall therefore be able to "receive" you in a manner more befitting your dignity and my own sentiments. I hear about you whenever I can from the Sands;—and they have been a long time absent, engaged in the winter diversions of their order. My sister is spending her winter in town, near me, and I am happy to say is much better than at any time since she came abroad. She is destined, I think, to get better still and be an ornament, yet, to society. She doesn't go out, and is confined to her sofa, but she sees people, and startles me by the breadth of her *aperçus* and her intimate knowledge of English public affairs. Please to give my heartiest greeting to Mrs. Godkin, and my most affectionate remembrance to Lawrence. I am sure he is having great success at the bar—but I hope he can lift his eyes long enough from his briefs to give a friendly glance at auld lang syne, as it already seems. I thought of you—and how you would be touched with the sad story, when poor Mrs. Adams found, the other day, the solution of the knottiness of existence. I am more sorry for poor Henry than I can say—too sorry, almost, to think of him. I have on my table your paper in the *Nineteenth Century*, and am to read it tomorrow during a three hours' railway journey. I hope you are not overworked—nor even overdined—and are well and happy and lucid, and that my hope of seeing you will prove to have had some solidity. It would give me much happiness to hear, especially if I might do so from herself, that your wife is having a comfortable winter, and I am, my dear Godkin, ever affectionately yours

Henry James

1. HJ had known Frank Harrison Hill (1830–1910) since 1877. Hill had been editor of the *News* for the past sixteen years, but was now turned out owing to his opposition to Gladstone's Home Rule policy. He is described as having "keen insight and a caustic pen." Soon after this letter was written he found employment on the *World*, where he was a leader writer until 1906.

To Elizabeth Boott
Ms Harvard

3 Bolton St.
Feb. 22 [1886]

My dear Lizzie.

I am heartily delighted and congratulate you with all the warmth and confidence of old friendship. Yes—today I am surprised, but I shouldn't have been three or four years ago. Better late than never—for me as well as for yourself, for I value greatly the prospect of renewing my relations with the gifted Frank,[1] whom I always liked and esteemed and whom I congratulate still more than I congratulate you. Give him, please, my friendliest regards, and tell him my interest in him, always great, will be redoubled. My interest in you, dear Lizzie, will be so much greater as may be possible in a sentiment in which there was so little margin for increase. I wish for you every happy and favouring consequence—and that it may all

At the Villa Castellani: left to right, Elizabeth Boott Duveneck, Francis Boott, Frank Duveneck, and Mrs. Duveneck's nanny, Ann Shenstone

take the form of you and Duveneck becoming the *Brownings* (more or less—in a sort of way) of pictorial art. Make *him* work—make him do himself justice, as he has never done. If your Father doesn't like it, he must come over and live with me—I have a room for him. But we shall all live together, surely: Europe *must* be your scene. Alice doesn't know it (unless she also heard from you this A.M.) but when she does she will enter into it as cordially as yours ever, dear Lizzie, most affectionately

Henry James

1. Miss Boott had become engaged to Frank Duveneck, the American painter, under whom she studied first in Munich and later in Florence.

To Francis Boott
Ms Harvard

3 Bolton St. W.
Feb. 22*d* [1886]

My dear Francis.

I was already on the point of writing to you that the Macmillans had been directed last week to send you the *Bostonians* and that I hoped it had by this time turned up (if it doesn't in a day or two kindly send me another post-card), when Lizzie's prodigious note dropped in! I hasten to express my sympathy in all you must feel on the subject of her engagement—the apprehensions (as to becoming No. 3) as well as the satisfaction that she is to take a step that has in it so little of precipitation and so much of experience, congeniality, maturity, community and other goods. Take care lest between two easels you fall to the ground, you can so easily trip over their legs. This is a caution very seasonable—after your long lameness. I trust you are better now and that the shock has cured you—brought you to your feet. Is it for that Lizzie has done it? You will be a delightful *beau père*—that is what strikes me most, and if you shouldn't be appreciated come and be that of yours ever affectionately

Henry James

À quand la noce?

To William James
Ms Harvard

13 De Vere Mansions West[1]
March 9*th* [1886]

My dear William.

Long before getting your most excellent letter of February 21st I had been pricked with shame and remorse at my long silence; you may imagine then how this pang sharpened when, three or four days ago, that letter arrived. There were all sorts of reasons for my silence which I won't take up time now with narrating—further than to say that they were not reasons of misfortune or discomfort—but only of other-engagement-and-occupation-pressure—connected with arrears of writing, consumption of time in furnishing and preparing my new habitation, and the constant old story of London interruptions and distractions. Thank God I am out of them far more now than I have ever been before—in my chaste and secluded Kensington *quatrième.* I moved in here definitively only three days ago, and am still rather upside down. The place is excellent in every respect, improves on acquaintance every hour and is, in particular, flooded with light like a photographer's studio. I commune with the unobstructed sky and have an immense bird's eye view of housetops and streets. My rooms are very pretty as well as very convenient, and will be more so when little by little I have got more things. When I have time I will make you a diagram, and later, when the drawing-room (or library: meantime I have a smaller sitting-room in order) is furnished (I have nothing for it yet). I shall have the place photographed. I shall do far better work here than I have ever done before.

Alice is going on the same very good way, and receiving visits almost daily. A great many people come to see her, she is highly appreciated and might easily, if she were to stay here, getting sufficiently better to exert herself more etc., become a great success and queen of society. Her vigour of mind, decision of character etc. wax daily, and her conversation is brilliant and *tressaillant.* She could easily, if she were to stay, beat the British female all round. She is also looking very well. I have given and lent her a good many things for her little sitting-room, so that her "setting" is "tasty" and becoming. The only draw-back in her situation is that her visitors are fatally apt to come several together—leaving her on some days with no one. This tires her too much, and then, after they are gone, she has slight—but only very slight—nervous fits. I found her in one yesterday, crying piteously, in consequence of an hour's visit from Edmund Gurney (whom she liked very much) superadded to two from two ladies before. But this in the long run will right itself; and I suppose it is moreover one of the essential inconveniences of people who "keep saloons." Sometimes, for several days, they are alone, and then every one comes at once. The great fact, with Alice, is that her ability to see people has sextupled since a year ago; and she takes the whole thing more and more easily. The weather continues bitterly cold and there will be no question of her going out for a long time to come.—The two great public matters here, have been the riots,[2] and the everlasting and most odious Dilke scandal. (I mean, of course, putting the all-overshadowing Irish question aside.) I was at Bournemouth (seeing R. L. Stevenson) the day of the émeute, and lost the spectacle, to my infinite chagrin. I should have seen it well from my balcony, as I should have been at home when it passed, and it smashed the windows in the houses (three doors from mine) on the corner of Bolton Street and Piccadilly. Alice was all unconscious of it till the morrow, and was not at all agitated. The wreck and ruin in Piccadilly, and some other places (I mean of windows), was, on my return from Bournemouth, sufficiently startling; as was also the manner in which the carriages of a number of ladies were stopped, and the occupants hustled, rifled, slapped or kissed, as the case might be, and turned out. The real unemployed, I believe, had very little share in all this: it was the work of the great army of roughs and thieves, who seized, owing to the very favourable nature of their opportunity, a day of license. It is difficult to know whether the real want of work is now, or not, so very much greater than usual—in face of positive affirmations and negations; there is, at any rate, immense destitution. Every one here is growing poorer—from causes which, I fear, will continue. All the same, what took place the other day is, I feel pretty sure, the worst that, for a long time to come, the British populace is likely to attempt. Dilke is decidedly, and most deservedly, ruined—as any man must be who sits and hears so foul a tale told of him as was told by Donald Crawford at the trial and is unable, and afraid (lest he should be cross-examined) to raise the least whisper to contradict it. He has behaved throughout with strange pusillanimity and want of judgment and taste; and the thing is too bad for him to get over. That is, if he does, the "moral tone" of London will show itself worse even than it has hitherto appeared, though I have never thought it very high. I am sorry to say that my old friend Mrs. Rogerson[3] has been much mixed up with the whole business, though rather by her misfortune than by her fault. Enough, however, to have been both made temporarily insane (she seems better now) and virtually ruined by it. A collection of episodes more hideous and abominable, in all their ramifications, it would be impossible to conceive, but I won't infect the pure air of Cambridge with them—though I have profited by them much as a novelist.—I can't talk about the Irish matter—partly because one is sick of it—and partly because I *know* too little about it, and one is still more sick of all the vain words on the subject, without knowledge or thought, that fill the air here. I don't believe much in the Irish, and I believe still less (consider with less complacency) the disruption of the British Empire; but I don't see how the management of their own affairs can be kept away from them—or why it should. I can't but think that, as they are a poor lot, with great intrinsic sources of weakness, their power to injure and annoy England (if they were to get their own parliament) would be considerably less than is assumed.

The "Bostonians" must be out, in America, by this time; I told them, of course, to send you a copy. It appears to be having a goodish success here. All your tidings about your own life, Bob,[4] etc. were of the deepest interest. I pity poor Alice[5] trying to "develop" for your use, qualities she may not have. I seldom see Edmund Gurney. His wife also has been (two or three times) to see Alice. I sent Bob the other day another box of apparel. I wish I could assist at your researches—and see the children—and commune with Alice—to whom I send much brotherly love. Ever your

Henry

1. HJ briefly used the name of the apartment he had moved into as his address, but soon began to use 34 De Vere Gardens, his street number.

2. These were the riots of unemployed laborers in the heart of London in February 1886.

3. See letter to Grace Norton, 23 August 1885, n.7.

4. Robertson James, HJ's youngest brother.

5. This allusion is to Mrs. William James.

To Henrietta Reubell
Ms Harvard

13 De Vere Mansions West W.
March 11*th* [1886]

Dear Miss Reubell.

It is always a delight to hear from you, and I lose as little time as possible in thanking you for your last letter, which I have just read over for the twentieth time, in the little skyblue and yellow boudoir *que je me suis ménagé* in my new apartment. (My grand salon, of the richest crimson, develops its noble proportions *à côté;* but it is yet a frugal and unfurnished void.) *Il faut que vous veniez voir tout cela.* I have thought of you constantly, in my legs. That sounds ambiguous, but you will understand. I am much interested, and very sympathetic, in *your* interest in Lizzie Boott's new departure. She is judging for herself, with a vengeance; but she is forty years old, and she has the right. Duveneck won't beat her, nor *la rudoyer,* nor perhaps even neglect her, and will be completely under her influence and control; but he is illiterate, ignorant, and not a gentleman (though an excellent fellow, kindly, simple etc.) and she gives away to him her independence and freedom. His talent is great, though without delicacy, but I fear his indolence is greater still. Lizzie, however, will urge him forward and be an immense help to him. For him it is all gain—for her it is very brave. You see I am far from enthusiastic, but I await results with a certain confidence, thinking they may be considerably better than some of the elements would promise. I have seen, for weeks and weeks, very little of Sargent—he being busy *de son côté* and I on mine. But I shall get hold of him more in future, having moved more into his quarter. I don't in the smallest degree agree with the idea that Sargent has done an unwise or an unfair thing to come to this place to live and work. He seems to me to have got from Paris all that Paris had to give him—viz. in perfect possession of his technical means. Paris taught him how to paint so well that she can't teach him better, and I don't see why he is not wise to apply all this acquired power here, where he can get such fine models and subjects. Besides I think an artist does his work better in the conditions in which the whole man is happier and finds a larger and more various life. I mean by this that Sargent seems to me to *like*

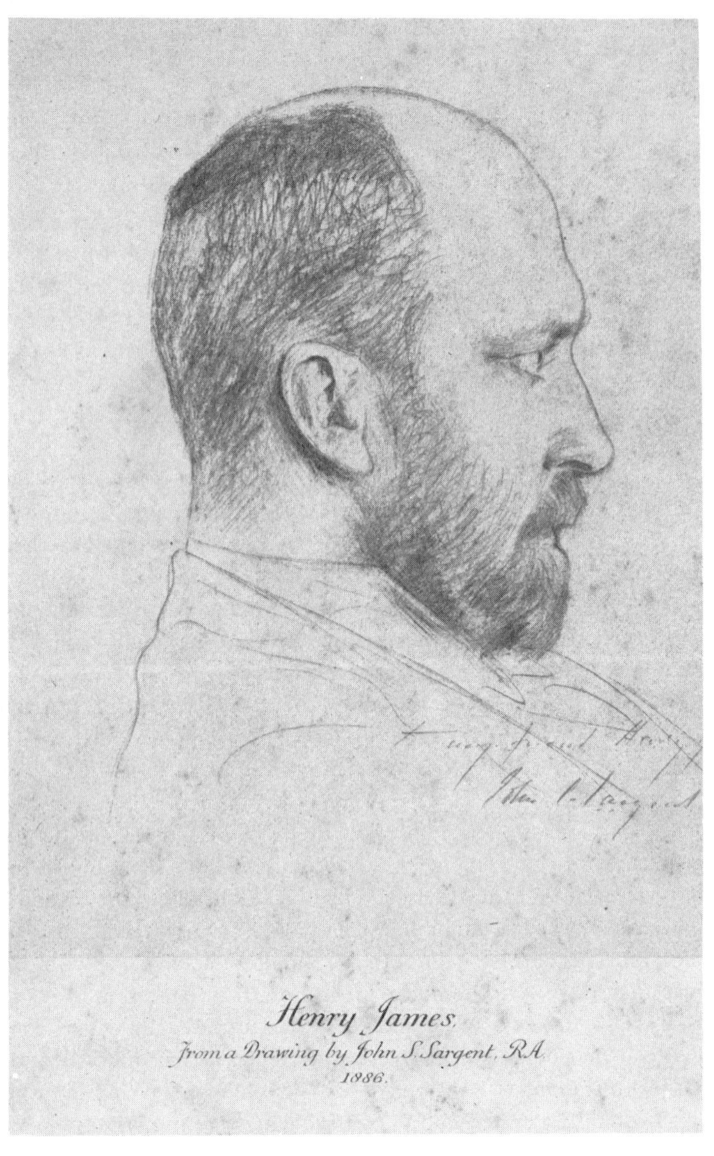

Henry James in 1886, from the pencil drawing by John Singer Sargent

London, its social opportunities and great variety, and that in itself is good for him, even as an artist. Why, therefore, should he be chained all his life to the school from which he has graduated? He appears to me today to be more qualified to teach than to learn, and his teaching is far more needed here than in Paris. And I don't speak selfishly, for up to this time I have scarcely seen him. Don't marry Edmond Fitzmaurice—he is a dry, political prig, and I suspect him of being stingy. However I would almost consent to it if it would bring you to live here, *auprès de votre très-dévoué.* I hope you will go to America even for three weeks, because it may make you *passer par ici* twice at short intervals. Also your impressions of the great, queer country might be distilled into the appreciative mind of yours, dear Miss Reubell, very affectionately

Henry James

P.S. Tell dear Mrs. Boit[1] with much love (to whom, you see, I am also affectionate) that I await her on the way to the U.S., and even have the fatuity to wonder a little whether I may not induce her to miss a steamer or two.

1. Mrs. Edward Boit. See letter to Elizabeth Boott, 14 October 1883.

To Francis Boott
Ms Harvard

13 De Vere Mansions West W.
May 25*th* [1886]

I wonder, my dear good Francis, whether you will do me rather a favour. My excellent and amiable friend Constance Fenimore Woolson[1] is in Florence, and I want to pay her your compliment and administer to her some social comfort. The finest satisfaction I can confer upon her will be to ask you to go and see her, at Casa Molin; the old pensione Barbensi, on the Lung'Arno, which you will know. She appears to know few people there (i.e. in Florence), and though she has not made any sort of request of me touching this proposal (by which I don't mean that I want you to "propose" to her, either for me or for yourself), I am sure the sight of you would give her joy. She is a deaf and *méticuleuse* old maid—but she is also an excellent and sympathetic being. If Lizzie could take a look at her and attract her to the villa I should be very glad—but I fear Lizzie's brush is so busy producing Boott-Duvenecks that she has little time for social felicities. (Miss W., by the way, is a good friend of Miss Greenough.) What a job the connoisseurs of the future will have—separating the Duvenecks, the Bootts, and the Boott-Duvenecks! I have no less than three Bootts on my wall, and am full of hope that I may be able to add specimens of the later manner: a not very modest hope, however, considering that the treasures in question were all acquired gratis. They *furnish* my apartment, simply—or rather richly. I send immense remembrances both to Lizzie and her spouse and should be delighted to hear from you something about them. When I think of what Bellosguardo must be at this superlative moment I grow quite limp and useless. Alice has just been joined by K. Loring for about three weeks and is just leaving for the provinces (Leamington to begin with) where she intends to spend the summer. She is really ever so much better, and has had a very good, and from her sofa, very considerable, social winter. Again I send my love to the queen of the Franks—Frédégonde[2] or Brunehaut I must begin to call her. You are doubtless Mayor of the palace. I bless you all, I think of you often, I shall write to you again as soon as I have another favour to ask, and I shall come and see you soon. Ever dear Francis very affectionately yours

Henry James

1. HJ's solicitude for Miss Woolson was inspired in part by her devotion to him. Four long letters from Miss Woolson to HJ of the early 1880s escaped the burning of his papers and are given in the Appendix to this volume.

2. HJ's ironic and humorous historical analogy does not bear close scrutiny. Lizzie Boott having married Frank Duveneck and having a father named Frank is now the "Queen of the Franks." And this was what Frédégonde became in Merovingian times when she married Chilpéric I. A passionate and murderous woman who achieved her ends by brutal killings, Frédégonde hardly resembles the meek and dutiful Lizzie Boott. HJ's tongue-in-cheek allusion may nevertheless contain some suggestion that he believed Miss Boott had shown a certain Frédégondian toughness in getting the easygoing bohemian Duveneck to marry her.

To William James
Ms Harvard

Osterley Park,
Southall, W.
June 13*th* 1886

Dear William.

As I have just written to Aunt Kate and asked her to forward you the letter it is bad economy, no doubt, to give you at the same moment, a letter for yourself. But on the other hand I have a moment of leisure and the sharp consciousness of having since I last gave you of my direct news heard copiously and liberally from you. So I will just seize this fleeting occasion to thank you for your letter received I think nearly a month ago, on the subject of *The Bostonians*. Everything you said in it gratified me extremely—and very superfluous was your retraction of what you wrote before (last autumn, while the thing was going on in the magazine and before you had more than dipped into it). I myself subscribe just as much to those strictures now as I did then—and find 'em very just. All the middle part is too diffuse and insistent—far too describing and explaining and expatiating. The whole thing is too long and dawdling. This came from the fact (partly) that I had the sense of knowing terribly little about the kind of life I had attempted to describe—and felt a constant pressure to make the picture substantial by thinking it out—pencilling and "shading." I was afraid of the reproach (having *seen* too little of the whole business treated of) of being superficial and cheap—and in short I should have been much more rapid, and had a lighter hand, with a subject concerned with people and things of a nature never near to my experience. Let me also say that if I have displeased people, as I hear, by calling the book *The Bostonians*—this was done wholly without invidious intention. I hadn't a dream of generalizing—and thought the title simple and handy, and meant only to designate Olive and Verena by it, as they appeared to the mind of Ransom, the southerner and outsider, looking at them from New York. I didn't even *mean* it to cover Miss Birdseye and the others; though it might very well. I shall write another: "The Other Bostonians." However, this only by the way; for after one of my productions is finished and cast upon the waters it has, for me, quite sunk beneath the surface—I cease to care for it and transfer my interest to the one I am next trying to float. If Aunt Kate sends you the letter I have just written to her you will receive it almost as soon as you do this one. It will tell you that Katharine L. came over about three weeks ago (she had left Louisa at Ems, with William Loring and his wife), and a few days later conveyed Alice to Leamington. Alice appears to have been greatly—too greatly, and somewhat disappointingly—fatigued by the journey; but she is now emerging from this bad sequel—and at any rate has suffered *less* than from any similar effort she has made since she came to England. K.L. will stay with her three weeks longer, and very possibly come back to her later in the summer. I have no doubt that during the next three months Alice will form *habits* of going out (in her chair) and that will be the beginning of a much better order of things. Katharine, who had not seen her for seven months, finds her, in spite of the knock-up of the journey, wonderfully better.—I am spending this Whitsunday down at this fine old place (close to London), of which Lord Jersey[1] is the happy proprietor. Lowell is in the house, and a few others, of no particular importance. Lowell, who has returned to England on a visit, as a private individual, is no less happy than when he was here as Minister; rather, indeed, I think, more so, as he has no cares nor responsibilities—and his "social position" is (bating precedence, as to which they let him off easily) quite as good. They are making, in London, an extraordinary lion of Dr. Holmes,[2] who strikes me as rather superannuated and extinct (though he flickers up at moments) and is moreover dazed and bewildered by the row. He is handicapped, unfortunately, by having with him his singularly, inexplicably, common daughter Amelia—who throws a kind of lurid light of consanguinity on some of *Wendell's* less felicitous idiosyncrasies.—Of course you are hearing all about Gladstone's defeat a week ago; which I don't deplore, for though it seems to me that Home Rule must come, his whole conduct in forcing it upon a House of Commons not in the least elected to pronounce for it—so that it might be done by *him* and him only—has been a piece of high political egotism. I don't know how the G[rand] O[ld] M[an] looks at the distance of across the seas, but seen on this spot he appears to me to have become rather baleful and demagogic. His talk about the "people's heart," the "classes" etc. is unworthy of a man having his responsibilities; and his influence, or rather his boundless authority, is demoralizing—his name is a kind of fetish with so many millions and the renunciation of personal judgment before him, so complete. But the whole drama is very interesting. There are to be new elections next month exclusively on the Home Rule issue, and it will be momentous to see what they bring forth. All the England one doesn't see may be for it—certainly the England one does is not. It seems highly probable that whatever happens here, there will be civil war in Ireland—they will stew, in a lively enough manner, in their own juice.—Edward Hooper, who is out here, lunched with me the other day and I pumped him vigorously for information about Cambridge and Boston. He would scarcely talk however of anything but poor Richardson—whose departure I much deplore. I hope the approach of the long vacation lifts you up. I am about to be called to lunch and can only squeeze in my love to Alice and many fraternal and avuncular assurances from yours ever affectionately

Henry James

P.S. You had better send this to Aunt Kate in exchange for hers.

1. Osterley was near London and impressed HJ sufficiently for him to use it as the country house in "The Lesson of the Master" and in his play *Summersoft*, later called "Covering End" (when it was converted into a short story). See Margaret, Countess of Jersey, *Fifty-One Years of Victorian Life* (1922).

2. Oliver Wendell Holmes (1809–1894), Boston's celebrated literary M.D. and "autocrat" of the breakfast table. Wendell, his son here alluded to, would be named to the Supreme Court by President Theodore Roosevelt.

To Grace Norton
Ms Harvard

13 De Vere Mansions West W.
July 16*th* [1886]

My dear Grace.

The reasons for this last long silence of mine are doubtless no better than usual—but they are also no worse. Your last good and generous letter has had time to become very familiar to me—and familiar to you, on the other hand, I fear, has become the idea that I am a dumb, ungrateful, animal, of the pre-human period, with whom it is of little profit to attempt intercourse. May this letter shake in some small degree that plausible conviction. The "Season" has come, and I was going to say gone—but that would be to speak too sweetly of it. It lingers and dawdles on in a most irritating manner—firing off last invitations after one had fondly hoped that the peace of God has descended upon this distracted city. The place has been supposed to be quieter than usual this year—on account of the interlude of the elections—but it is a quietness which annually almost costs me my life. However I have survived this year, and I shall again, I suppose—but the best way to do so is to quit the place altogether on the 1st of May. This I shall endeavour to do regularly in future, having only done it fitfully in the past; and having also now an apartment which I am told I can let—easily, for May, June and July, for a goodly sum—almost enough to pay my year's rent. You remark, by the way, in your last that I have never told you where the said apartment is, and I hasten, my dear Grace, to supply this lack of topographical tenderness. Behold a neat diagram. [HJ here draws a diagram of the surrounding streets and indicates in red the location of the apartment house.] From this it will appear to you that I am within three minutes of Kensington Gardens—the *far end,* away from Hyde Park—just out of the Kensington Road. My short but broad street (De Vere Gardens) is a sort of spacious cul de sac, and turns out of the said Kensington Road at a distance of five minutes' walk after you pass, coming from Piccadilly, the broad Queen's Gate, which you will remember, I suppose, as you lived there in 1868–69. My rooms are getting comfortable and even pretty—with being lived in, and I hope that, a year or two hence, when I shall have been able to supply some deficiencies, they will reach a certain modest perfection. They will always have a great deficiency, however, till you have seen them. That idea of letting them, of which I spoke just now, is loathsome to me—but I shall not scruple to do it if it will put money in my purse. I expect to spend the whole of this summer in town and to go abroad somewhere—that is to Venice and Florence—about September 1st. There is however, just now, a nastyish choleraic state of things in Italy which forbids one to form plans—and it is sufficient for me that London (if the temperature remains reasonable) really becomes pleasant after July 20th:—I mean pleasant for privacy and work. You will have heard before this of the defeat of the so-long-predominant Gladstone at the polls. I can't but feel that some sort of home-rule measure is destined to come sooner or later, by the irresistible march of things, but I cannot weep for the downfall of the G.O.M. whose ways seem to me to have become terribly personal and pernicious (he is really a furious demagogue) and the irresponsible subservience to whom of a party whose only idea and only programme is simply the eternal repetition of his name and his word, is a power that seems to me to "make," largely, as Matt. Arnold says, for evil. His errors and failures for a good while past have been so numerous that I don't think the voice of England in the future will pronounce him one of the most useful of her sons. In short I like him not—nor the cast of his mind, nor any of his ways and works: though of course that proves nothing against him—for I detest *all* the trickiness and brutality of the political spirit to which this unhappy country is now given over and which has converted it for the last year into a howling bear-garden. The oceans of talk that are required, more and more, for the smallest work of government make one long at moments for some fine dumb despot. Don't think I am turning into a heartless Tory, for I am not, in the least. The Tories, as such, are terribly stupid company, and I could never live long with them. All the same, I am curious to see what they will invent, on their impending return to power. The occasion demands an effort—but their inventive powers have never been great.—I feel as if I ought to give you some news of Lowell—as your last two letters contained such an interesting account of your own impressions of him during his months at home. But the truth is my dear Grace, that the first thing to say about him seems to me to be that he is such an extraordinary simple individual that there is *nothing* to be said! He is very nearly (though perhaps not *quite*) as "clever," to my mind, as he is thought here by most people (though by no means by all), but his whole relation to life and the world appears to me infantine—and infantine his judgment, his kind of observation. However, he is extremely pleasant (when he doesn't publicly correct people's grammar, pronunciation, pretensions to lineage—as compared with his own—and many other things!) and very contented and happy, apparently, as well as infinitely invited and caressed, as before. People in general take his rectifications and instructions with the sweetest docility (for though irritating, they are at the same time really genial, and almost always humourous, and are felt to be so), and he seems to me to have all the social advantages of his former position, with the simple difference that he has none of its annoying responsibilities. There is a persistent rumour that he is going to marry the dowager Lady Lyttelton; but I put no faith in it, if for no other reason than that it would break the heart of Mrs. Smalley, who loves him and whom he also (apparently) loves! She is a charming woman—with a husband that goes his way while she goes hers—and she devotes her life to J.R.L., who, I think, passes a portion of each day in her company. What is left over for Lady L. I know not—not much, I divine; and the rumour in question is of course nothing but an idiotic London invention—as the London mind sees matrimony in everything, when it doesn't see worse—which indeed is oftenest. (You had better by the way consign to the flames, this gossiping page, intended only for your diversion, and not for the reprobation of posterity.) I usually go out of town for Sunday at this season, and indeed am sometimes drawn into short excursions (of an afternoon) during the week. Yesterday I went to the annual garden party given at his pleasant old house out at Balham by my canny old publisher Alexander Macmillan—the Senior member of the firm, but not much my personal friend (if one's publisher can ever be such): that proud position being reserved for his nephew, the flourishing and convivial young Frederick, who has a pretty, dressy, worldly little American wife, and a very charming and hospitable house—also with a garden—in St. John's Wood. (Almost every one in London today has a pretty and dressy American wife.) Today I go (at six o'clock) down to a place called Limpsfield, in Surrey, to dine with Mrs. Jimmy Leigh (Mrs. Kemble's daughter—Mrs. K. is of course now among her beloved Alps); and come back at ten o'clock, in time to go to a kind of nocturnal garden-party at Lady Ardilaun's. Tomorrow I go out to Osterley, to Lady Jersey's—a beautiful old Georgian house, of which the internal decoration, remarkably homogeneous (urns, garlands, festoons, trophies etc.) is celebrated and makes it a kind of model of its class. The next week I go down to Highclere, Lord Carnarvon's, where I shall probably bore myself a good deal in very amiable and very respectable society. But I shall console myself by a ramble in an immense, divine park. In the interval I rush off to Bournemouth for thirty-six hours to see a poor sick friend—

and probably go also to spend a day with Alice at Leamington. All this while I am supposed to be looking after Mrs. Jack Gardner,[1] Mrs. Bronson,[2] the Dan'l Curtises,[3] and about thirty other Americans now in London, who are all holding by my coat-tails; to say nothing of polishing my periods for the purchase of my contemporaries and the admiration of posterity. So you see I am pretty well engaged. Alice went to Leamington, for the summer, some six weeks ago—but as I have not seen her since then, and she is up to very little writing, I have no very vivid realization of her present "form." I shall probably be separated from her till late next autumn, when we shall meet again, in London, for the winter, after my return from abroad. She has had a very fair year—much better than the preceding one—but is still a sad cripple. I have seen very little of Sara Darwin for a long time, and have not been to Basset for nearly—or quite—two years. But I am to go, for thirty-six hours, very soon. I feel as if I ought to respond, in some way, to your remarks about the *Bostonians,* in your last—but in sooth, I may say, without a grain of affectation, that my constant sense of the fragility of my own productions is such that at the first breath of criticism or first touch of censure they seem to me to crumble into dust. I can never defend them—I give them up without striking a blow; and indeed think that no work of art can ever be *justified.* If it doesn't strike you as happy it is so far a failure, and its greatest success is simply to escape! And then one *doesn't* fictionize for one's friends—but for the unknowing and the unknown!—Where are you, my dear Grace, and whither tending and what doing, and how feeling? Are you smelling the summer night in that lonelyfied Cambridge, or mingling your perspiration—so to speak—excuse my grossness!—with that of friends and relations? How are the Miss Arnolds—those nice girls you told me of? Tell me more—and deign, magnanimously, to respond, without too long and *vengeful* a delay, to yours ever affectionately

Henry James

1. Isabella Stewart Gardner of Boston. See *Letters* II, 266.

2. Katherine De Kay Bronson. See *Letters* I, 486–487, and II, 358–359.

3. Daniel and Ariana Curtis, of Boston, who lived in the Palazzo Barbaro in Venice.

To Robert Louis Stevenson
Ms Yale

34 De Vere Gardens W.
August 2*d* [1886]

My dear Louis.

I left you on Sunday P.M. without a farewell—but I thought it better to spare you that palaver, as there seems a probability of my seeing you so soon in town. I should have been very glad to stop over yesterday—but my time has been terribly ploughed into of late—and the hours become too sordidly precious to me here. In short I *had* to come back. This is to tell you *that,* in sorrow; and to relieve myself a little further on the subject of the unspeakable Haggard. Since I saw you I have finished Solomon and read half of "She."[1] Ah, *par exemple, c'est trop fort*—and the fortieth thousand on the title page of my *She* moves me to a holy indignation. It isn't nice that anything so vulgarly brutal should be the thing that succeeds most with the English of today. More even than with the contemptible inexpressiveness of the whole thing I am struck with the beastly *bloodiness* of it—or it comes back to the same thing—the cheapness of the hecatombs with which the genial narrative is bestrewn. Such perpetual killing and such perpetual ugliness! It is worth while to write a tale of fantastic adventure, with a funny man etc., and pitched all in the slangiest key, to kill *20,000* men, as in Solomon, in order to help your heroes on! In *She* the Narrator himself shoots through the back (I think) his faithful servant Mahommed, to prevent his being boiled alive, and describes how he "leaped into the air like a buck," on receiving the shot. He himself is addressed constantly by one of the personages of the tale as "my Baboon!" *Quel genre!* They seem to me works in which our race and our age make a very vile figure—and they have unexpectedly depressed, so that he looks to *you* for consolation, yours ever faithfully

Henry James

P.S. I mean consolation *printed*—don't think of answering this. I hope my visit didn't have a bad morrow.

1. Sir Henry Rider Haggard (1856–1925) wrote the popular romantic novels *King Solomon's Mines* and *She.*

To George du Maurier
Ms Harvard

34 De Vere Gardens W.
Thursday P.M. [5 August 1886]

My dear du Maurier.

Guy de Maupassant is coming to dine with me next *Thursday*, and I send you off this early line to express the hope that you will still be, then, *dans ces parages* and able to do the same. I will before that notify you of the time and place—I have thought of proposing Greenwich if that doesn't terrify you. In fact why shouldn't I take my chance of coming up to see you—that is, of finding you if I do so—tomorrow afternoon, Friday? I should come *late*, we might have a walk—and perhaps you would give me a crust of bread. I am assuming that you haven't yet left town and am ever with *bien des choses chez vous* yours ever faithfully

Henry James

To Francis Boott
Ms Harvard

34 De Vere Gardens W.
Aug. 15*th* [1886]

My dear excellent Francis the First.

I have a letter from you of some weeks old which has brought the blush of conscious shame to my cheek whenever I have come across it in the pile of unredeemed obligations which lies before me, eternally, on my table, any time the last month. (I say eternally because the number remains always the same—I subtract from the fatal heap on one side only to see it grow on the other.) Yesterday I heard from Alice that you are inquiring of *her* why I don't write to you, and I suppose she has replied to you with sisterly affection that it is because I am a low fellow. Your letter gave me great pleasure, and when I look over it now to renew that pleasure I see that it contains a request that I shall procure for you certain pens of which you give me the name. I had made a note of this at the time—but that didn't help me to remember the matter. I remember it now but today is Sunday—however I don't think I shall forget it tomorrow—I will send my servant out, your letter is in his hand, to scour the town until he finds them. If you had asked for a piano[1] I should have sent it to you the next day—but sixpenny orders get neglected. I am spending the summer in this capital summer place, whose only defect at present is that it is also a summer-resort. Americans crop up by the bushel, and the leisure to work that one had promised oneself in compensation for the wreck and ruin of the Season is very considerably compromised. I am taking breath a little—but Mrs. Lodge[2] arrives next week! I have but just escaped from the jaws of Blanche Roosevelt,[3] who used to sing in opera—didn't she?—and who is now here married to a Milanese, trying to be literary and assaulting me (with compliments) on my productions. Alice is at Leamington—in about the same form as usual. She likes the place, and will remain there a couple of months longer, after which she will come to town for next winter. I go to see her day after tomorrow. The D. Curtises (not the D—d) were here in the early part of the Summer, and I saw them two or three times. They were very nice and a little more and more Curtissy than ever. We talked much of you, that being a subject on which our common fastidiousness could relax itself. They have gone to the country somewhere—but I don't know where. Mrs. Bronson[4] is here *en permanence*—that is for the Summer. She has taken a house, brought Venetian servants etc. and as one sits in the smoke of her cigarettes one seems to hear the gondolier's cry and other sweet sounds of Venice wafted in from Hans Place. I heard lately from Lizzie who tells me you are in Switzerland, leading me thereby to infinite wonderments as to how you like it there as a lone orphan and how you face its terrible problems with only the inspiration of your OWN *bien être* (a stimulus never, in the past, sufficient for you) to hold you up. Perhaps you are not alone—I hope not; perhaps even you have met our friend Fenimore[5] somewhere. When I last heard of her she was at Geneva, in a balcony of the Hôtel National, hanging over the lake and thinking of—you! I have promised to go and see her after she is settled at Bellosguardo—but I am afraid (though I certainly shall get there sometime in the autumn) that I shan't get there so early as I originally hoped. Stern practical considerations will keep me here yet awhile; but if you have left Florence by the time I reach it I shall find you either in

Venice or in Paris. I wrote this much to Lizzie a few days ago, in a very meagre and inadequate letter, which expressed but a small portion of my continued close interest in her and her *sposo,* and which shall soon have a worthier successor. I was odiously pressed at the moment I despatched it. I expect to be in London through September. Why won't you come and pay me a visit here? The Americans I invidiously alluded to above were of the devouring sex—not like you, and me, of the devoured. How are the noonday walks, the Germans, the windows, and the smells? I must formally thank you for your great benevolence to Fenimore—though it is much of an injury to me, as it has given her a standard, which I fall so far below! Don't repay me by cold silence, but believe me, dear Francis, ever affectionately yours

Henry James

1. Boott was an amateur composer.
2. Mrs. Henry Cabot Lodge, the former Anna Cabot Mills Davis.
3. Blanche Roosevelt Tucker Macchetta, Marchese d'Alligri, an American opera singer who had made various international marriages and who pursued literary figures—from Longfellow to Victor Hugo, HJ and Maupassant.
4. Mrs. Bronson had come to London to avoid the cholera in Venice.
5. In his letters to the Bootts HJ always referred to Miss Woolson by her middle name, Fenimore.

To William James
Ms Harvard

34 De Vere Gardens W.
Sept. 10*th* 1886

My dear William.

Odious ages seem to elapse, nowadays, between the letters I succeed in writing to you; but the short letter of August 24th (written the day after your return from Mt. Desert) which I got from you a few days ago shall at least not go longer unanswered. I rather grieve to see that by August 24th you are already back in Cambridge—but perhaps you are to rejoin your family again at Jaffrey. However, I have agreeable recollections of the September quality of Cambridge. Sorrier still am I to hear that you apparently spent the greater part of your visit to Mt. Desert in bed—a business for which I altogether commiserate you. However, I trust that is wholly over. Mt. Desert is not a bad place to have *missed,* in that way—my recollection of it (from the three days I spent there with G. James the last thing before I came back last to England) is most unfriendly—or rather most horrible. I never saw a place of which I understood less that it should be raved about—or even endured. (I speak especially of Bar Harbour.) I have often desired to reproduce my brief impression of it in some tale—but that has grown now too dim. Mrs. F. Jones alleviated my stay and I remember her very gratefully, even to her Philadelphia accent. Mrs. Welman is affected, to a monstrous degree, and very "factitious"—but I think not quite so unprofitable as she seems. I spent three days lately, in the country, in the house with her useless husband; but to divorce him seems almost as unnatural a proceeding as if Carrie had divorced Wilky.—I am in London, as you see, and am making no further absence than an occasional short country visit. I have just come back from four days (my utmost limit of absence on a social basis) at Broadway, in Worcestershire, an extraordinarily fine and picturesque old village, where Frank Millet,[1] the American artist, has a house in which he spends six months of the year (he spends the others in New York); and which (beside his wife, who is charming, and his children) he shares with Abbey and Sargent, and various guests. There are other friends, and guests in the village, mainly Americans, though Edmund Gosse and Frederick Barnard (the man who makes the remarkable grotesque illustrations—to Dickens etc.) are there this year, and it is altogether a very pleasant and harmonious little artistic community, working in a manner very creditable to the good feeling of every one concerned, and "run" mainly by Millet who is a capital fellow and a prodigy of Yankee energy and practicality, combined with a very "nice" artistic feeling and a talent that is constantly bettering itself. The whole country is full of the stateliest, loveliest old stone villages, and the day before yesterday I took a drive of thirty miles in a dog-cart over the Cotswolds, and saw dozens of these picturesque hamlets. Sargent, who has left Paris, is domesticated there and has a studio in London in winter. He made (in three-quarters of an hour) a very pretty *small* pencil-drawing of me, which I shall present (probably) to Alice (here) when it is mounted.[2] I wrote to Aunt Kate not very long ago, just after having been to see Alice at Leamington. (I haven't been oftener because it's her wish: *it* tires her to have one there—"on her"—for several hours, and moreover she has had, most happily, Katharine there much of the time. Louisa Loring and Mrs. L. are in England, (North Devon), and K. goes to Alice again today, for a stay of two or three weeks. Alice's physical condition appears to be about the same—that is *much* better since the first knock-up of her journey to Leamington—or about as it was at the end of last winter in London. But her mental state is wonderfully bright and keen, and her spirit for the most part serene and sublime. Her fortitude is extraordinary, and my belief is that it will pull her through—as if she can hold out against time she will eventually get better. I am looking, or beginning to look, for rooms for the winter, for her; though she doesn't come back to town for some weeks she wants this question settled in advance. She will not return to her place of last year, and it is difficult to find what one wants, for a small price, or at least for a moderate one. But I shall end by doing so. She has had some thoughts of spending the winter in Leamington, seduced by its cheapness and by the desire to escape the strain of the journey back to town. But this would be desperate, and she would die of cold and loneliness. Katharine will probably be in England a couple of months more and will move her to London.—I am much obliged to you for wishing me the rustication which this year I shall not have got, save in an occasional visit of two or three days to friends. But I haven't wanted it and don't miss it. If I *had* wanted it I shouldn't have taken it, as I have had this year to put so much money into furnishing my apartment (for once in a lifetime) that I have had none left for taking other quarters elsewhere. Moreover my apartment itself, with its various pleasant idiosyncrasies, has given me, in the summer days, which this year have been very, very fine, plenty of "high air" and outlook into green gardens. About December 1st, if things are well with Alice, I hope to be able to go abroad for a few weeks—down to Florence to see the Bootts etc.—I have been taking the question of work very easily—in fact quite resting—since I finished the *Princess:* the production of the *Bostonians* and that work, one on top of the other and both so exceedingly long, especially the second, having quite exhausted me. This rest in town has really constituted an excellent holiday. But now I am tired, not of work, but of no work, and am again taking up my pen. I have plenty of engagements and am to do some short things—half a dozen little critical papers among others. The next novels I do are to be but half as long as these two last, and I never again mean to do anything nearly so long as the *Princess*.—I am to dine tonight with Lowell, who is in town for a day, prior to his near departure for America. He would like to remain here, I think, where his life is easy and his person much *choyé*—but he deems it necessary to spend the winter with his grim daughter, at that grim Southborough. His idea is to come back in the spring, but he seems to me old and rather vague now—so that one can't count very much on his prospective movements. Mrs. Lodge has been here and innumerable other Americans—a swarm of locusts. Mrs. L. was delightful—but the Howes, her sister and brother-in-law, with whom she was, have no discoverable *raison d'être*.—All this while I have never spoken to you of the horrible cataclysms in the South, which I suppose are the universal theme at present among you all. It is all very terrible—but I hope there is to be nothing worse. It all excites much commiseration here; subscriptions are opened—the Lord Mayor has started one of the great "Mansion House" funds, etc.—I have seen no particular friend of yours—nothing of Gurney for the last couple of months, etc. I shall write of course to Mrs. Gibbens, and do anything I can for her, or that she will let me. Tell Alice that I send her much love and wish infinitely I could commune with her better than in this way which is no way at all. I must go and wash—and am ever, dear William, your affectionate brother

H.J.

P.S. September 11th. I dined last night with Lowell, and Smalley was also there. The former goes back to make a speech at the Harvard 250th year, which I suppose will give you also plenty to do—or at any rate to see. I hope you won't be overdone with social burdens—but Lowell didn't seem to know at all what the function is to consist of. Smalley related a strange report of misbehaviour by Arthur Sedgwick[3] in Mexico: getting drunk and riotous etc. Is it true? I hope it's a fraud.

1. Francis D. Millet (1846–1912), the American painter and illustrator, had settled in the Cotswolds and gathered around him a friendly group of painters and writers, including Edwin A. Abbey, the illustrator from Philadelphia, and John Singer Sargent.

2. See the reproduction on p. XXX.

3. Arthur Sedgwick, formerly of the *Nation*. See *Letters* II, 56–57.

To Elizabeth Boott
Ms Harvard

34 De Vere Gardens W.
Oct. 18*th* [1886]

My dear Lizzie.

It is very kind and good of you to have written to me again; I myself really owed you another letter. It is a great pleasure to me to hear from you when your letters breathe such an air of matrimonial success and general well-being and well-doing. Delightful too is the glimpse you give of the golden autumn in your Florentine hills. Why am I not there to drivel with joy and what horrible despotism of circumstances is always fencing me off from the thing I want most to do. But my dear Lizzie, it shall not fence me much longer. I shall to a positive certainty (if nothing *monstrous* occurs to prevent) come down and see you this winter, as nearly as possible six weeks hence. My heart is set upon leaving England for a month or two about December 1st. I don't mean I shall spend *all* that time in Florence, because I want also to go to Venice and Rome; but I shall spend enough of it to have many a delightful and long-deferred talk with you. Our good Fenimore must also be worked in—but I shall be equal even to this. I am very glad you are nice to her, as she is a very good woman, with an immense power of devotion (to H.J.!). Tell your father I thank him for the kindness which she tells me he has shown her in profusion. (You mustn't apprehend from this that you will have occasion to look up some article for a teaset for *me!*) Tell your father also that I well, well know that I owe him a letter—and that he shall have it very presently. My correspondence is the struggle of my life!—Alice has lately come up to town and has taken rooms close to me for the winter—8 Gloucester Road; Palace Gate S.W. She is in very good form—in spite of her journey—and of an odious upset she had at Leamington in consequence of two clergymen getting "drunk and disorderly," in the house in which she was staying—and in which one of them had rooms also, and attempting to enter her apartments at one o'clock in the morning. (They pretended they had been "discussing theology" together below, and had become excited by so doing; but what they had been discussing was of course whiskey.) They were perfect strangers to her, and the whole thing, including the row and mess after it, made her very ill. But she is doing excellently now, and has a very good prospect for the winter. The incident was a vivid illustration of what horrible little cads and beasts there are in the church of England. Katharine Loring leaves England presently with her sister (who has been most of the summer at Torquay) to spend some months at San Remo. Louisa is supposed to be much better—but still requires great care. Frank Hall is painting a very fine portrait of Mrs. Loring—and is going to America, for a visit, thereafter, where he will probably find many sitters. Sargent is settled here at last (I mean in a permanent *installation*). It remains to be seen whether *he* will find many. Mrs. Bronson has returned to Venice—after a very sociable summer here; carrying with her a promise that I will come and stay a week or two with her in December or January. I am not sure how I shall enjoy that dear place (fond as I am of Mrs. B.) on that somewhat artificial footing. But I shall have to try it. Please, by the way, in Florence, *don't breathe a word of my advent in advance.* I don't intend to see *any one* there but you and Fenimore. Will you kindly ask *her* to observe an equal discretion? It must have been hard for you to see your husband go to Venice without you. I am much interested by what you tell me of his productivity, and can well believe in the gentle stimuli that you bring into play. Give him my friendliest greetings and tell him how anxious I am to see what he has been "up to." I send my particular love to your father; whom I beg to take on trust that I am very soon writing to him—till the poor retarded letter arrives. In you, dear Lizzie, I take more and more interest with the succeeding years and am ever very affectionately yours

Henry James

To Edmund Gosse
Ms Leeds

34 De Vere Gardens W.
October 26*th* [1886]

My dear Gosse.

I was afraid you wouldn't be able to dine with me—but I sent a word on the chance.

I am infinitely distressed that you should continue to be overturned by this whole beastly business[1]—and yet I understand it, for iteration will drive any man frantic. It is a matter of sensibility, and sensibility is much. All the same, sensibility apart, I really don't see what you have to consider except your own attitude—which I take to be simply that of continued and confirmed interest in your work, and ambition and purpose in regard to the literary life. Don't despair of that or of yourself—and the rest will be of course disagreeable, but still simple and superficial, like having been pushed without warning into a dirty pond, in which one splashes a moment and loses breath. The moment may seem long—especially if one is pushed again—but one scrambles out, as soon as one recovers one's surprise, without having left any vital part whatever behind. I repeat that the whole mass of the public *d'élite* feel the greatest sympathy for you as having been made to an almost unprecedented degree the subject of a peculiarly atrocious and vulgar form of modern torture—the assault of the newspaper—which all civilized and decent people are equally interested in resisting the blackguardism of. As for the *stupid* public, one must simply mind that at one time as little as at another. It is always there and is always a perfectly neglectable quantity, in regard to any question of letters or of art. Above all, however, what I wanted to say to you most especially is that I really don't see the smallest necessity for your *knowing* a word more about this odious matter, nor for your reading the newspapers. I can't too earnestly recommend you not to look at them—for an instant; I urge this upon you as one who has himself been tried. Under what earthly necessity are you, for instance, to know what idiotic rubbish on the subject may be shovelled out in America? Long ago I determined simply never to glance at such stuff and both as a man and an artist *je m'en porte à merveille.* Avert your eyes—and your nose—and the rest will take care of itself. I shall come in and see you, if you have time, on Thursday evening (night)—being engaged tonight and tomorrow. Take my advice, and your nerves will bloom again like roses in June. Ever, my dear Gosse, yours most faithfully

Henry James

1. Gosse had been fiercely attacked by a former friend, John Churton Collins (1848–1908). Writing in the October 1886 *Quarterly Review,* Collins

accused Gosse of slipshod scholarship in his book *From Shakespeare to Pope.* Some of the criticisms were justified, but they were crudely made and Gosse's reputation for accuracy was damaged.

To Francis Boott
Ms Harvard

34 De Vere Gardens W.
November 26*th* [1886]

My dear Boott

I am to see you so soon that it seems hardly worthwhile to write; nevertheless, I am in the receipt of such favours from you that I send this hasty precursive word, which gives me, besides, the pleasure of repeating once more than I am really coming. Your very pleasant letter of the other day and your genial cooperation with Fenimore in making the way smooth (though I can't say horizontal) for me at Bellosguardo are the benefits to which I particularly refer. I thank you for your kind deeds and your still kinder offers. Your fears that I shall "suffer" at the Villa[1] do credit to your sympathetic sensibility, but I think have no solider foundations. It is a question of comparison, and I shall be less incommoded there, and at a less cost, than if I am squeezed into some small tourist-hole in an insanitary Florentine hotel. I have lived at one time or another in all of them and detest them all. Besides, if one has been living for fourteen months without an absence (of more than a day or two at a time) in this unending Babel of a big city, one wants the *quietest* place, as the most of a change, and I go to Florence to hide myself. Please keep not only my approach, but my presence, a secret. It is very good of you to offer to put in *wood,* but I have an idea that Fenimore, whose devotion—like my appreciation of it—is *sans bornes,* has stacked me up a pile with her own hands. She is a gallant friend, but I am afraid she has bored you with me. Never mind, you will have your revenge; she will bore *me* with *you!* Next Wednesday is December 1st, but I have a fear that in spite of every effort I shall not be able to get off till the Thursday or Friday. I shall travel fast, however, and go straight through to Milan. There I shall stop a day—but whether I shall go to Pisa, in order to stop another and take my own hour for arriving (by a daylight train) in Florence, I don't yet know. Of course I shall keep my landlady punctually advised, that she may command a beefsteak *con patate* for me.—Just as I write, Lizzie's sweet letter comes in and stimulates terribly my impatience to depart. Please thank her for the affectionate welcome it conveys, and to which I respond as affectionately, and reassure her on the subject of my probable miseries at the house on the hill to which she apprehensively alludes. For what do you take me all—and for what do you take the divine Bellosguardo? I shall do very well, and shan't be blue, with cold or anything else, when I come to see you. You exaggerate the importance of that contemptible little notice in *Punch,* of the *Princess:* these things are not of my ken or my care. This sounds sublime—but really the idiocy and ill nature of the journals of my time have made me so. Don't speak of them. *À bientôt!* With much love to Lizzie and kindest *Grüssen* to Duveneck. Ever yours

H. James

1. This letter deals with HJ's arrangements for staying in Miss Woolson's Villa Brichieri during his visit to Florence. Miss Woolson had only just taken an apartment in this villa and had not yet moved into it. She offered HJ the apartment until she was ready to move from her own rooms in the Villa Castellani; it is for this reason that he speaks of her as his "landlady."

2
Italian Hours

1886–1887

2
Italian Hours

Henry James gave himself up to Italian romanticism for six months—from December 1886 to midsummer 1887. This was the most exhilarating of all his Italian journeys. He had shaken off the despondency of his break with "home," he had finally found a London anchorage in De Vere Gardens, he had written out his sadness and loneliness in his two long novels, and he felt himself free—free of deadline pressure, since he had made no commitments to write a serial for the American magazines and he was provided with ample funds for his holiday. Moreover, he found the expatriate world ready to receive him: his stay in Italy, save for a brief period in a Florentine hotel, was in splendid old villas, frescoed palaces, and in circumstances in which he could bask in the attention and homage of the surrounding world. One notices the satisfaction with which he describes how he is lionized by the polyglot hostesses of Florence; and then there is the greater satisfaction of his being at large in a beloved country—he likes the Italians, the art, the architecture, the constant spectacle of past and present, and not least the mildness and sweetness of the climate.

The result of this sense of freedom and well-being was seen soon enough in a series of brilliant tales, the most famous of which is "The Aspern Papers," written in a villa on Bellosguardo, in Florence. To this period we owe such stories as "Louisa Pallant" and such essays as "London" and his study of Robert Louis Stevenson. When his sister agreed to move into his flat during his absence, he was able to prolong his stay, and he paid a long visit to the Palazzo Barbaro of the Curtises in Venice; that palace he would later use as the scene for the latter half of *The Wings of the Dove.*

This is the period also of his deepest involvement with his compatriot Constance Fenimore Woolson. "Involvement" may be too strong a word for the friendship that developed between the demure and deaf spinster from the American provinces, who wrote novels, and the author of *The Portrait of a Lady.* The letters show that

James wanted to be kind to her because she was devoted to him. And he ended up staying in her Villa Brichieri on Bellosguardo, first as her tenant while she was still in the nearby Villa Castellani, but later as a visitor when he returned from Venice convalescent from a bad attack of jaundice. James and Miss Woolson burned their correspondence; but certain letters which escaped the flames, together with the image of Miss Woolson in the letters to the Bootts, tell us a story not unlike "The Aspern Papers." We do not know whether James ever realized that he had overplayed his gallantries to Miss Woolson; but we do know that she had to face her hopeless love for a man who had no thought of marriage. He continued to be loyal to her (she would later follow him back to England), but he always kept his distance and both were very discreet. During these crowded months, James led a much less lonely life than he did as the solitary bachelor of De Vere Gardens who leaned so much on his clubs and on "society" for his social recreation.

The climax of his Italian journey was his return to Venice to enjoy the ducal splendors of the Palazzo Barbaro, its frescoes and sculptured and painted ceilings, and the ease provided by the attendant gondoliers and servants. This was the grand style that James's innate aristocratic sense loved. The gilt and grandeur ministered to his feelings for past and present, the fruits of ripe civilization. He brought back to London a feeling of liberation and ease. And he was now more famous than ever—for during the succeeding months some eight or ten tales and essays appeared in the magazines, and his name was before the Anglo-American public with great consistency. Out of his Italian adventure came also one of his high-ironic short novels, *The Reverberator*, prophesying the course of American journalism in the succeeding decades.

To Charles Eliot Norton
Ms Harvard

Milan
December *6th* [1886]

My dear Charles.

I ought long ago to have thanked you for your very substantial present of Carlyle[1]—but I waited in the first place till I should have read the book (which business was considerably delayed), and then till I had wound up a variety of little matters—mainly matters of writing which pressed upon me in anticipation of my leaving England for two or three months. Now, when at last I seize the moment, I *have* left England—but you will be as glad of a letter from here as from out of the dense grey medium in which we had been living for a month before I quitted London. I came hither, straight from Dover, last night through the hideous but convenient hole in the dear old St. Gotthard, and I have been strolling about Milan all the morning, drinking in the delicious Italian sun, which fortunately shines, and giving myself up to the sweet sense of being once more—after an interval of several years—in the adorable country it illumines. It is Sunday and all the world is in the streets and squares, and the Italian type greets me in all its handsomeness and friendliness—and also I fear I must add not a little in its vulgarity. But its vulgarity is the exaggeration of a merit, and not as in England and the U.S., of a defect. Churches and galleries have such a fatal chill that being sorethroatish and neuralgic I have had to keep out of them—but the Duomo lifts all its pinnacles and statues into the far-away light, and looks across at the other white needles and spires of the Alps in the same bewildering cluster. I go to spend the remainder of this month in Florence and afterwards to—as I hope—take a month between Rome, Naples and Venice—but it will be as it will turn out. Once I am in Italy it is about the same to me to be in one place as in another. All this takes me away from Carlyle—and from the Annandale view of life. I read the two volumes with exceeding interest—for my admiration of Carlyle as a letter writer is boundless—and it is curious to watch the first steps and gradual amplification of his afterwards extraordinary style. Those addressed to his own family are most remarkable as dedicated to a household of peasants, by one of themselves, and in short for the *amateur* of Carlyle the book has a high value. But I doubt whether the general public will bite at it very eagerly. I don't know why I allude to this, though—for the general public has small sense and less taste, and its likes and dislikes, I think, must mostly make the judicious grieve. You seem to me a most perfect and ideal editor—and it is a great pleasure to me that so excellent and faultless a piece of editorial work should proceed from our rough and ready country—but at the same time your demolitions of the unspeakable Froude don't persuade me that Carlyle was *amiable.* It seems to me he remains the most disagreeable in character of men of genius of equal magnificence. In these youthful letters it appears to me even striking how his disagreeableness comes out more and more in proportion as his talent develops. This doesn't prevent him, however, from being in my opinion—and doubtless in yours—one of the very greatest—perhaps the very greatest of letter writers; only when one thinks of the other most distinguished masters of expression the image evoked has (though sometimes it may be sad enough) a serenity, a general *pleasantness.* When the vision of Carlyle comes to us there comes with it the idea of harshness and discord. The difference between the man and the genius seems to me, in other words, greater than in any other case—for if Voltaire was a rascal he was eminently a social one—and Rousseau (to think of a great intellectual swell who must have been odious) hadn't anything like Carlyle's "parts." All the same, I shall devour the volumes I am delighted to see you are still to publish.

I ought to have plenty of London news for you—but somehow I feel as if I had not brought it to Italy with me. Much of it, in these days, is such as there must be little profit in carrying about with one. The subject of the moment, as I came away, was the hideous Colin Campbell[2] divorce case, which will besmirch exceedingly the already very damaged prestige of the English upper class. The condition of that body seems to me to be in many ways very much the same rotten and *collapsible* one as that of the French aristocracy before the revolution—minus cleverness and conversation. Or perhaps it's more like the heavy, congested and depraved Roman world upon which the barbarians came down. In England the Huns and Vandals will have to come *up*—from the black depths of the (in the people) enormous misery, though I don't think the Attila is quite yet found—in the person of Mr. Hyndman.[3] At all events, much of English life is grossly materialistic and wants blood-letting.—I had not been absent from London for a year before this—save for two or three days at a time. I remained in town all summer and autumn—only paying an occasional, or indeed a rather frequent, country visit—a business, however, which I endeavour more and more to keep, if possible, within the compass of *hours.* The gilded bondage of the country-house becomes onerous as one grows older, and the waste of time in vain sitting and strolling about is a gruesome thought in the face of what one still wants to do with one's remnant of existence. I saw Matt. Arnold the other night, and he spoke very genially of you and of his visit to Ashfield—very *affectionately*, too, of George Curtis[4]—which I loudly echoed. M.A. said of Stockbridge and the summer-life thereabouts, etc. (with his chin in the air)—"Yes, yes—it's a proof that it's attaching, that one thinks of it again—one thinks of it again." This was amiably sublime—and amiably characteristic. I see Burne-Jones from time to time but not as often as I should like.—I am always so afraid of breaking in on his work. Whenever he is at home he is working—and when he isn't working he's not at home. When I *do* see him, it is one of the best human pleasures that London has for me. But I don't understand his life—that is the manner and tenor of his production—a complete *studio* existence—with doors and windows closed, and no search for impressions outside—no open air, no real daylight and no looking out for it. The things he does in these conditions have exceeding beauty—but they seem to me to grow colder and colder—pictured abstractions—less and less observed. Such as he is, however, he is certainly the most distinguished artistic figure among Englishmen today—the only one who has escaped vulgarization and on whom claptrap has no hold. Moreover he is, as you know, exquisite in mind and talk—and we fraternize greatly. Tell Sally that her friend Margaret is divinely fair—and, with her *detached* exterior, very humanly clever. Phil[5] painted last year a very beautiful little picture, of which he did me the honor to take the subject from a tale of mine—"The Madonna of the Future." I am happy to say that he sold it on the spot, to Agnew—and queerly enough, got an order to paint the same subject again with a different composition! I wept for Lowell, after Julian Hawthorne's[6] infamous trick—until I received his Harvard speech. Then indeed I continued weeping—but it was with pleasure and admiration. What a brilliant, felicitous thing! Every one expects him back here. J. Hawthorne has only kindled a blaze of indignation (against himself) which is a bonfire of sympathy for Lowell.

Dear Charles, I have written many pages, and not said a fifth of what I want. But my letters are many and my pen is bewildered and doesn't know where to turn. I should like to ask you questions innumerable—but I hope that some day—if the possible hour strikes for you—you will give me answers without that. Are you decently well—and not too indecently busy? But I am beginning when I ought to end. I send my love and blessing to all the house, and am ever dear Charles, very faithfully yours

Henry James

1. Norton's edition of *The Early Letters of Carlyle* (2 vols., 1886).

2. Four correspondents were named in this suit.

3. H. M. Hyndman (1842–1921), a wealthy Englishman of Evangelical zeal, who became one of the earliest Marxists in England and a founder of the Democratic Federation, which preceded the Fabians.

4. George William Curtis (1824–1892), the American travel writer and novelist, a close friend of the Nortons'.

5. Philip Burne-Jones, son of the painter, who also painted.

6. Julian Hawthorne, son of Nathaniel Hawthorne, had published an indiscreet newspaper interview with Lowell.

To William Dean Howells

Ms Harvard

Milan, Hotel de la Ville
December 7*th* [1886]

My dear Howells.

Though you *did* write to me some time ago, I can't despoil myself of a certain sense that in writing to you I drop my letter into an abyss too deep for echoes—nevertheless the impulse that drives my pen today is irresistible, and I write not for an answer—but just to write. The last thing I did before leaving London three days and a half ago was to purchase "Lemuel Barker"[1] (you never think of sending me your books—that is, I hope you don't, because you don't do it), and though I laid him down twenty-four hours ago I am still full of the sense of how he beguiled and delighted and illumined my way. The beauties of nature passed unheeded and the St. Gotthard tunnel, where I had a reading lamp, was over in a shriek. The book is so awfully good that my perusal of it was one uninterrupted Bravo. It is wholly perfect—better than anything yet—even than Bartley and Silas,[2] I think—in short quite your *capo d'opera.* And the best of it is that one sees you abundantly capable of doing better still, because you are so absolutely in the right track and the right sense. Where this comes from you will find no end more. Pause not, therefore, nor falter—but keep doing it every time! This whole thing is without fault or flaw—there isn't a false note, or a weak place. The girls are sublime, their speech and tone a revelation, and wonderful the way you have kept everyone and everything in exactly the very pitch and *nuance* of reality—without straying for an instant into the unobserved. You must be very happy to have done anything so good—and I am almost as happy for it as you can be. In short, I congratulate you from my heart—and I congratulate your wife and your children, and even the servants, and the furnace-man, and your butcher and baker. Manda Grier is so fine that I felt, as I went, as if I were writing her. Not everyone (great as the success of the book must be) will know how good she is—but that is but part of the general density and doesn't matter—it won't prevent you from doing "the like" of her again.—This is all I started to say—and I am waiting to be called for my train to Pisa. I am on my way to Florence to spend the rest of this month—after which I hope for two or three weeks of Rome and Naples, and a week of Venice. It is my summer vacation which I didn't take, by the almanac. When I left London the other day I had been there for thirteen months without an absence. It's joyous to be in Italy again—the sunshine is as yellow as of old and the colours of the shadows as pretty. I suppose you have heard from poor Gosse and know he has emerged—somewhat—from his *année terrible*. He has paid, fearfully, the penalty of a false position—for (between ourselves) I think he is in one in being at Trinity. But he stays there for the present—and he is right. Go on to glory, my dear Howells, and believe me ever your faithfully plausive

Henry James

1. "Lemuel Barker" is a character in *The Minister's Charge* (1887).
2. HJ is alluding to Bartley Hubbard in *A Modern Instance* (1882) and to *The Rise of Silas Lapham* (1885).

To William Archer
Ms British Library

Villa Bricchiere[1]
Bellosguardo, Florence
Dec. 19*th* 1886

Dear Mr. Archer.

I invoke the name of our dear and distinguished friend Louis Stevenson to protect me in this rough experiment; and have asked him to be so good as to forward you my note.—You published some months ago, in some periodical, a very ingenious and interesting essay on his literary character—which I have a particular desire to read over, as I have undertaken to express myself on the same inspiring subject. But I have idiotically forgotten the magazine, and as I'm, for the moment, in a foreign land, without consultative resources, I boldly take this short cut to arrive at my end. Would you very kindly inform me, at the above address, of the particular fact I mention?—that is, of the title and date of the periodical: (I have a vague idea it was *Time*—and I am in darkness as to the month.)[2] I shall then be able to send to London for the valuable document—and shall remain for this service (as I am already for the article itself) very gratefully yours

Henry James

1. HJ sometimes spelled Brichieri in this way.
2. The article, "R. L. Stevenson: His Style and Thought," appeared in the November 1885 issue of *Time*.

To Mr. and Mrs. William James
Ms Harvard

Villa Bricchière
Bellosguardo, Florence
December 23*d* [1886]

Dear William and Dear Alice.

I address you thus unitedly because I last heard from you both together—that is a week ago, when a letter from each of you, of December 2d, came in—William's containing a post office order for the books I sent him from London. I am very sorry you deemed it necessary to refund me for the same, as it has spoiled all my fun in sending them. You say (William) that your not doing so will establish the habit of my expecting to pay for the things you ask to be got for you. Precisely—it is just the habit I wish to establish; I grieve that you won't permit it. I intended the books for a Christmas present, with the simple—and very fortunate—irregularity of knowing in advance what you wanted. *Basta!* I sent both of your letters off to Alice—but though they are not before me they are pretty well graven on the tablets of my mind. It appeased my solicitude at last to learn from you (Alice) some of the facts about your mother's disembarkation—or rather about her unpacking. Woeful and sickening must this have been—and please assure her and Margaret again that I have mingled my tears with theirs—and with the salt horrors of their trunks. I am much touched by your mother's kind intention about the Afghan. I should have been delighted with it, and its bright American tints would have thrown a glamour over the already rather Londonish tone of my apartment—but I feel the loss of it to be the least of the disaster. I left London on the 3d of the month and have been here since the 8th. I have taken a three weeks' "let" of this furnished villa (that is of an apartment in it) from the proprietress (of the apartment), my old and excellent friend Miss Constance Fenimore Woolson—the gifted authoress. She has taken it for two years, and being in another villa is not ready to come into it till January 1st. I get it for the interval and meanwhile enjoy the space, the views, and the big wood fires. It is close to the Bootts' old villa (where Miss W. has a temporary apartment) but it has much finer views—and my perch on this hilltop lifted out of Florentine interruptions, has given me capital quiet hours for work. The Bootts are in Florence proper, and I suppose you will already have heard that Lizzie gave birth, six days ago, very quickly and quietly, to a robust male. She has been doing remarkably well ever since, and so has the child, and the whole affair has gone off much better than was feared. Her marriage, on a nearer view, doesn't seem any less "queer"—save that it seems always to have existed. Duveneck is a good frank fellow, without any small or nasty qualities—but it is impossible to converse with him for more than two minutes and he will be a weight for her to carry for the rest of her life—I mean socially, and in the world. He is only half civilized—though he is very "civil." Boott's acceptance of him, personally, *à toute heure de la journée,* is pathetic and heroic, and might have been made the subject of a little tale by Turgénieff. Duveneck's painting appears to have picked up since his marriage (it had languished much, before) but he has very few specimens in Florence. I go to Rome about a fortnight hence, for a week or two, and then proceed northward, with a stop in Venice and one in Paris. Alice was in excellent form when I left London—and her notes show that she continues so. My impression is that she more or less expects Katharine, for a month, about three weeks hence. If K. *should* come I may stay abroad longer. I congratulate you on Chocorua[1] (is that the name?) I hope it will bring you all rest and peace and joy; especially in the way of having it always awaiting you. I wish there were more of "that side" in my own existence. This is the ninth letter I have written this A.M. (though it is not A.M. but 4 in the afternoon and I have been at my table since 9.30). Therefore I will embrace you both and wipe my pen. I embrace the infants as well. I haven't seen the review of Edmund Gurney's book in the *Saturday*, but I can well believe it was "infamous." The latter is today a simply ignoble sheet—so ignoble for every kind of stupidity and malevolence as to be a discredit to the British mind. I bought Gurney's big volumes[2] just before leaving London—for Gurney's sake, but they were too big to bring along and I haven't read a word of them. Ever your affectionate Brother.

1. William James had purchased a large tract of land in New Hampshire and used the summer house there for the rest of his life.
2. Edmund Gurney's best-known work on psychical research, *Phantasms of the Living* (1886).

To John Hay
Ms Brown

Villa Brichieri
Bellosguardo, Florence
Christmas Eve [1886]

My Dear Hay.

Nearly three weeks ago I came to this place, to which your genial note of November 23*d* was the first gem of my London post-bag to follow me. Truly, you are an all-round man—you read my books, you loathe my critics—at least I hope you do—and you profess yourself, with a noble consistency, ready to undergo the friends of my friends. Do something, some day, to test me, my dear Hay, and you will see how I appreciate all this. I thank you most cordially for your gallantry in the face of the possible Ribot incident—"L'incident Ribot"—it sounds all right—and in fact very important and historic. I believe M. Ribot[1] is really a man of rare genius and virtue—but all the same I hope he won't have rung your bell. The permission extorted from me that he should do so was, after all, coldishly bestowed.—The Apennines are of the most delicate purple, and their summits are all crested with snow. Florence and all her towers lies in the valley at my feet, and a delightful yellow sunshine pours into my window from a terrace which, though it is not wonderful, is somehow a terrace of Italy. It has the effect of making me violate the injunction I once received from a "Boston lady" just before starting for Europe—"oh yes, write to me, do, but for heaven's sake don't describe the view from your windows!"[2] I could say more about it in this particular case—but I abstain. Besides they are not my windows—but those of our amiable and distinguished friend Miss Woolson, and I will leave her to deal with them. She has taken this roomy and rambling old villa, furnished, on a lease, and being still in possession of another and not able to enter it till the 1st day of January, has very obligingly sublet it to me for a month—with the services of a queer old melancholy male-cook, whom she had put in to take care of it. She dwells at five minutes' distance, and I see her every day or two—indeed often dine with her. She has done a brave thing in settling herself here (for two or three years) in a somewhat mouldy Tuscan mansion—but I think it clear that she will get much enjoyment and profit from it *à la longue*. She will get quiet, sunny, spacious hours for work (a prospect, on our part, in which I take an interest, in view of the great merit and progress of her last book)[3] and have Florence in the hollow of her hand.—And apropos of Florence, I wonder whether you would consider that I respond to a test—in the manner alluded to on the second page of this—if I say that I have not forgotten the singularly liberal and flattering request you made of me, three or four years ago, in regard to exposing my literary profile to the free assault of Larkin G. Mead.[4] I have not forgotten, either, that I blushingly assented to your suggestion, and yet now I hesitate, thinking it in the highest degree possible that the Cosimo de' Medici mood that dictated your rash invitation may have lived but an hour. Perhaps my going about the business now would only be a test of your own good nature. However, as there isn't time to hear from you, I shall assume that you are still willing gallantly to pay for your vagary, and one of these very next days shall knock at Larkin's doors. Meanwhile, heaven sustain you. I wish I might dine with you tonight—or rather tomorrow night; perhaps I should find Adams. But I shall find him in another manner yet. Let me add that it wasn't King who told me the tale of "Georgina's Reasons."[5] He has told me many—but for that ugly narrative I am not indebted to him. It was imparted to me by my dear old friend Fanny Kemble, to whom it had been told by her brother-in-law, Edward Sartoris, who had it from his queer little daughter-in-law Nelly Grant[6]—endowed for that occasion only, it would appear, with the favor of articulate speech. She gave it (as I understood the matter) as something that had befallen—or been transacted by—a girl she personally knew in some American—western—town. It struck me as a *theme,* and I pulled it about a little, put it in New York, Naples, etc. (*pour donner le change*) and made frankly, I think, a very bad and unsuccessful story of it. Is Nelly Grant's heroine and yours—and King's—one and the same person? Who I infer (I don't know her real habitat)—unless (which seems incredible) there are two—or even three—like the ducks of the lady in Tieck's picture, who mistook them for steamers. My dear Hay, I give you and your wife and your babes all sympathy of the Season and am ever faithfully yours

Henry James

1. HJ had given Charles Ribot a letter of introduction to Edwin L. Godkin and apparently to John Hay as a favor to Mlle Souvestre, headmistress of a French school in London, without having personally met Ribot.

2. The Boston lady was Mrs. Helen Olcott Bell (1830–1918), a daughter of Rufus Choate. She had a cultivated wit, and her sayings were much quoted in Boston.

3. Miss Woolson's most recent book was *East Angels* (1886).

4. Larkin G. Mead, Jr., the sculptor (1835–1910), brother of Elinor Howells, wife of W. D. Howells.

5. "Georgina's Reasons," published in the New York *Sun* in July and August 1884 and reprinted in *Stories Revived* (1885). See HJ's *Notebooks,* 59–60.

6. Nelly Grant, daughter of Ulysses S. Grant, had married Algernon Sartoris.

To Katherine De Kay Bronson
Ms Private

Hotel du Sud [Florence]
Saturday [15 January ? 1887]

Dear Mrs. Bronson.

I called yesterday on the McClellans,[1] which I have been meaning to do from day to day—since dining with them some time ago.

Mrs. McC., whom I found alone, broached the subject of the Venetian letter, and what she said about her daughter's distress and remorse, and about the general confusion and mortification of the family, was of a nature to suggest to me that I had better repeat it to you—as it may enable you to let them down more easily. They are evidently much ashamed of the matter—though she had nothing but this profession of regret and dismay (at the thing having come back to Venice) to say in exoneration. Evidently the thing was very thoughtlessly and above all *youthfully* done (though that last is no excuse for the mother), but it was done in perfect good faith as regards their utterly failing to realize that Venice would ever hear of it. As if everyone didn't hear of everything to-day! However, that was their naïveté—added of course to the daughter's flippancy. They have lived (as poor Mrs. M. herself said) as the great McClellan's family (though why so great I know not) in such an atmosphere of newspaper publicity and reporterism that they have lost all sense of perspective and proportion—though evidently they have not lost the sense of mortification when pulled up, and are very capable of learning a lesson. I am only very sorry they have learnt it at the expense of the poor little Montenegros.[2] I gave no sign whatever, of course, that you had written to me—and professed ignorance of the whole phenomenon. Mrs. M. thought your first letter "too impulsive"—but appeared to have derived satisfaction from the second. They despair of being able to go back to Venice—and want to be assured that they may *eventually* do so without finding every back turned to them. You will doubtless not be able to give them this assurance, but I took upon myself to say (for the mother's account of the girl's compunction rather touched me) that the breeze would blow over and that people would hold out the hand to her on feeling, after a while, that the thing had been a *péché de jeunesse* much repented of. All the same I think they ought to go back—they ought to take that penalty as their punishment. But I wanted to mention to you that the mother had *sfogatoed* to me and that humiliation reigns in their house—so that it will be rather humane of you to try and pour a little oil on the waters both here and in Venice if you have a chance. But good heavens, what a superfluous product is the smart, forward, over-encouraged, thinking-she-can-write-and-that-her-writing-has-any-business-to-exist American girl! *Basta!*—I am happy to say that I received this A.M. (sooner than I expected) a letter from my sister, telling me that she takes me at my word and that she will remain in my house as long as I see fit to stay abroad. That is all I want and it makes the difference that I can now look forward definitely to spending a good many weeks to come in this land of every charm. It also makes the difference, dearest lady, that I now *shall* decide to put in my three weeks in Rome. As I have settled, as I mentioned, to stay here till about February 5th, that will bring me to Venice only in the first days of March—a date which I fear will seem to you rudely distant. *Per contra,* when I do come it will be for a long time. If no odious inconvenient and unpleasant thing occurs in the meanwhile, I shall spend the *whole* of the spring there. For intrinsic reasons as well—I mean the sweetness of the place at that time, it will be much better for me to take those months—all the same, the more I think of your benevolence the more I wonder that I am anywhere but flat on my face before you. It is indeed almost in this attitude that I subscribe myself ever affectionately yours

Henry James

1. May Marcy McClellan, daughter of the Civil War general, had been introduced into Venetian society the previous winter and had written a gossipy letter to the New York *World* about Italian social life, ridiculing certain members of the nobility. Published on 14 November 1886, it created considerable scandal. See HJ's *Notebooks*, 82–85.

2. The Montenegro family were among the nobility lampooned by Miss McClellan.

To Robert Louis Stevenson
Ms Yale

Hotel du Sud
Florence, Italy
January 21*st* [1887]

My dear Louis.

I am much ashamed of myself for not having thanked you before this for your genial and charming note accompanying some of the sheets of your too deplorably delayed volume of tales.[1] I have been waiting for more and the arrival of another batch of proof (that word is batch—not botch) would have drawn eloquence from my lips. The fact of the new volume hanging back so much has depressed me altogether—for I have wanted to taste of it before invoking, on your behalf, the muse of appreciation. I have had to make up my mind at last that I appreciate you enough without it, and have just begun my genial tribute to your "exceptional powers."[2] I shall finish it by the end of next week—so for these impending days I shall really cohabit with you. Pray for me—that I don't offend you. If I do, it will only be by too thick a buttering—and yet I shall try to be not indecently greasy. I was charmed by your account of the concussion between your high spirits and your wife's moderate ones, and would have given much to assist at the debate, which I should have endeavoured to keep within parliamentary limits. Surely you have a right to a little spiritual cheer—you who minister so to that of others. (This is not a quotation from my article.) And on the other hand, by the same logic, your wife makes others so happy that she is entitled to make use herself of the misery that she saves them. That's the way I see it, my dear friends—who are yet dearer friends, I am sure, to each other.[3] I hear that you are having a bitter bad winter in your faraway North, and I am wondering much what sort of message it has had for you. I hope you haven't been be-frozen, after having been so be-fogged, and though not addicted to prayer I petition that at the present speaking you be in some tolerable pass. I shrink from the desperate course of pressing you to write, though it would agree with me wonderfully to have some clear ideas about you. I would fain know of the parents—and I would fain know of Sam. I hope the latter has by this time received his supplies—his pleasant conversation ought certainly to have supported him for awhile. My stay in these countries threatens to lengthen itself—and I am very willing. I have lent my rooms in London to my sister and if she keeps them awhile I shall continue abroad. (I mean it will be a matter of more weeks.) I find Italy peaceful for writing so long as it's not about its bescribbled self. I get good mornings and sunny withal. I salute you both, and am ever, my dear Louis, very faithfully yours, and your sterner consort's

Henry James

1. This was probably *The Merry Men* (1887).

2. The article on Stevenson that HJ had promised to the *Century*.

3. HJ's remarks are in response to Stevenson's having written him from Bournemouth a few days earlier in an undated letter: "My wife is peepy and

dowie: two Scotch expressions with which I will leave you to wrestle unaided, as a preparation for my poetical works. She is a woman (as you know) not without art: the art of extracting the gloom of the eclipse from sunshine; and she has recently laboured in this field not without success or (as we used to say) not without a blessing. It is strange: 'we fell out my wife and I' the other night; she tackled me savagely for being a canary-bird; I replied (bleatingly) protesting that there was no use in turning life into King Lear; presently it was discovered that there were two dead combatants upon the field, each slain by an arrow of the truth, and we tenderly carried off each other's corpses. Here is a little comedy for Henry James to write! the beauty was each thought the other quite unscathed at first. But we had dealt shrewd stabs." Sidney Colvin, ed., *Letters and Miscellanies of Robert Louis Stevenson* (1912), 224.

To Grace Norton
Ms Harvard

Florence, Hotel du Sud
January 25*th* [1887]

My dear Grace.

I have been "in," all the morning (it is now 2.30), but I swear that before I go out I will send you a greeting; and also (as soon as I can put my hand on it) a photograph. I have been in Florence ever since I wrote to you from Pisa—or was it from Milan? I dwell by the yellow Arno, and my sitting room is flooded with the splendid sunshine we have been having all this month. Florence is the same old Florence, and her sweet sad essence comes out into these first days that have a dim sense of spring in them. The first weeks I was here the cold and the wet and the "meanness" of so many of the circumstances turned up the prosaic side and made me feel very doleful—as if my love of Italy were quite an extinct volcano. But there has been an eruption since, and I find that I am capable—to my extreme satisfaction—of enjoying the dear old country as much—*almost*—!!! as I ever did. (I'm afraid there is no *repetition,* in life, that isn't qualified by an "almost.") I have the agreeable prospect of being able to remain here for a good many weeks—or even months—to come. I have lent Alice my rooms in London, on some which she had herself taken for the winter proving defective, and if I can persuade her to remain in them, and keep my servants from being demoralized by idleness, I shall hail the thing as a capital pretext for continuing abroad. The difficulty will be to persuade her that I am not doing so on purpose to give her the convenience of my apartment—but if I do so (and I probably shall)

I hope (D.V.) to remain in Italy till the summer—and go (sometime within a month hence) to Venice for the rest of my stay. It depresses me, rather, to find that committed as I am, morally and materially, to London, I don't leave it without finding that a weight is lifted from my physical and social, and even intellectual, life—that I can work better in other places (especially abroad) and have my time more my own and free from embarrassments and interruptions, and in short pursue existence on lighter and easier terms. This I feel each time I come to the continent—and yet I fain would not *live* anywhere but in the bothersome Babylon. The solution, of course, is to be in Italy when one can—not to live, in short, where one *does* live! I feel, my good Grace, as if I were rather flaunting these fine alternatives in your dear Cambridge face—but I would rather tell you my questions than let you think them perhaps worse than they are. I see a few people here—and am supposed to be "going out"—but it all amounts to very little. It is a very thin and flimsy society—with a few nice people. My poor clever, tactless and tasteless (intellectually) friend Vernon Lee lives here with a paralysed step-brother (from the legs down) formerly in diplomacy, and she and he are altogether the best people for talk—and indeed the only ones. There are lots of Russians—who have a *faux air* of being clever and are not. The Bootts are here, and Lizzie Duveneck (whose marriage is most interest-quenching) has an infant five weeks old. I have seen some rather entertaining women—the Marchesa Incontri, the Countess Gamba (niece of Byron's Guiccioli, by her husband) and various others whose names signify nothing. I go today to dine, near Fiesole, with a certain Baroness Zunch[1]—a kind of Anglo-Italian and a very kindly person. I dined last night with one compatriotic Mrs. Bronson (not her of Venice—but a cousin) to meet—or in company with—the "Bishop of New York" and a pleasant little Englishman, Sir Thomas Dick Lauder. I liked the Bishop (Potter) very much—better than those of his cloth in England. I don't speak of the pictures—I scarcely go to see them—they make me melancholy mad. I only visit Michelangelo, who being mad himself, pushes me back into sanity. I have been writing since nine this A.M.—and my head is heavyish. *La suite prochainement.* Ever yours faithfully

H. James

1. The identities of HJ's Florentine hostesses emerge in the ensuing letters written from Italy.

To Katherine De Kay Bronson
Ms Private

Hotel du Sud [Florence]
January 26*th* [1887]

Dear Mrs. Bronson.

Basta—basta! I shall take no more interest in the McClellan episode[1]—as the young lady strikes me as flippant and spoiled and deserving of any fate that may overtake her. I saw her this evening after I saw (as I wrote to you) her mother, and she spoke to me of the matter with less humility—with a certain resentment, as if she herself had been wronged. I doubt if they will return to Venice—and if I see them again I shall say nothing to them to encourage it—but on the contrary. The fact that they expected, and greatly desired, to return makes the girl's action—so extraordinary, at the best, for a young thing in good society—doubly inconceivable. But she is *Americanissima*—in the sense of being launched as a young person before the Lord, and no wonder the poor dear old Venetian mind can't understand such incongruities. I should like to write a story about the business, as a pendant to *Daisy Miller*, but I won't, to deepen the complication.[2] Don't jibe at me if I tell you that I am reconsidering my plans—and shall possibly drop Rome and get to Venice earlier than I told you last—i.e. sometime next month. You shall hear the first definite moment from yours ever faithfully

Henry James

1. See letter to Mrs. Bronson, 15 January 1887.
2. HJ changed his mind and wrote *The Reverberator* (1888), prophesying the modern American gossip column.

To Robert Underwood Johnson
Ms Harvard

Florence
January 27*th* 1887

Dear Mr. Johnson.

There goes to you today, in another packet from this, a type-copy of that article on *London* which I promised you last summer.[1]

I can only say of it that it proved damnably difficult to put so much into a little. The space of a magazine article is so small for so big a subject that I scarcely knew how to take hold or where to turn—but I have done the best I can. I hope I haven't made it too long—especially if there are to be illustrations (as I have assumed, by an allusion in the text); it was really impossible for me to turn round, or look about me, in a shorter space. If it is too long, won't you send it to Aldrich, telling him why, with my compliments—when I will write to him about it, on hearing that you have done so. As regards illustrations you will of course please yourself: I frankly confess that I hate them when attached to my own prose—and like them only as an incident of that of others. But no doubt, in your pages, this article will be held properly to require them. If I were in London at the present time I should take the liberty (assuming you would assent) of sounding Sargent, who is now settled there, on the subject of his making some drawings. But without knowing your idea I don't like to take the step of writing to him—especially as I am by no means sure it would produce fruit. The article itself is by no means so pictorial as I had at first intended—but perhaps it makes it up in other ways. At any rate, I trust it's not dull—. I am not in London, but on the banks of the yellow Arno, as you see. I came to Italy on December 1st to spend six weeks—and am staying and staying—as long as I can. I hope after this (I have been here all the time) to have a go at Venice. That dream of a couple of Sicilian papers[2] of which you spoke to me, I hesitate to say that I count upon realizing. I rather fear I shan't be able to get so far—and then I find, I confess, that everything is rather a loss to me which draws me off from writing fiction. That is the thing into which I can put most of what I want to do. I shall send you very soon a magnificent article on R. L. Stevenson[3] (I shall really do it with gusto), as I promised you last August—but when that is done I expect not for a long time to handle any but the fictive pen. To tell the truth I would much rather write you a story in a couple of parts than do two articles on Sicily—for I think that if I haven't the articles to do, and can enjoy the place platonically, I may venture to go there! But I fear that since the *Bostonians,* you are shy of my story-telling.—I hope you are still living happily on what you took home from Europe with you. Italy seems to me more charming than I believed I should ever again succeed in finding it. I happen to address this to you rather than to Gilder—but it is meant for both of you. I hope all prosperity is in your house—and houses—and I am ever faithfully yours

Henry James

34 De Vere Gardens
Kensington W.
London

1. Robert Underwood Johnson was an editor of the *Century*. HJ's article on London appeared in that journal, XXXVII (December 1888), 219–239, with illustrations by Joseph Pennell and was reprinted in *Essays in London and Elsewhere* (1893).

2. HJ never visited Sicily.

3. The article on Stevenson appeared in the *Century*, XXXV (April 1888), 868–879, and was reprinted in *Partial Portraits* (1888).

To Sir Frederick Pollock
Ms Rochester

Hotel du Sud
Florence
January 31*st* 1887

My dear Pollock[1]

I enclose you as to one of the Hon. Secs. of the Rabelais Club[2] a cheque for one guinea which I owe that institution—whose delightful meetings I am sorry to say I am for the present prevented from attending, by a longish absence from London. In this hungry and rather indecent country I am all the more with you in spirit—and am yours—individually—ever

Henry James

1. Third baronet (1845–1937), Corpus professor of jurisprudence at Oxford from 1883 to 1903. See *Letters* II, 94, 240.

2. The Rabelais Club, a literary dining club, was organized in 1879 by a dozen writers in a London tavern and dissolved ten years later. The members dined together half a dozen times a year. No speeches were countenanced. Toasts were reserved for Rabelais only. The members occasionally read literary trifles, some of which were privately published. HJ was a member from the start.

To Katherine De Kay Bronson
Ms Private

Hotel Du Sud [Florence]
February 5*th* [1887]

Dearest Mrs. Bronson.

I do seem, no doubt, to trifle with your friendly affection—by my interminable delays. But it is the old story, with me, that everywhere, and at every time, circumstances are too many for me—and I am not certainly indifferent nor frivolously insensible. It is now positive that I leave this place for Venice (I throw Rome to the winds!) on some day, yet to be designated, between the 10th and the 20th of this month. I shall make it as *nearly as possible* the 15th—and shall advise you, dearest lady, the first *instant* I am able to put my finger on the precise date. I pray for its speedy arrival. I am "going out" here a good deal—and am supposed to be "lionized"—heaven save the mark! I *do* dine daily, and mingle considerably in this thin polyglot world. I likewise leave a card on every woman on whose plain face (they are mainly deucedly ugly) my eyes happen involuntarily to have rested—in the most approved Florentine manner. Today I go (in half an hour) to have the day with Mrs. Ross[1] at Castagnola. Tomorrow I dine with the Marchesa Incontri. On Sunday at a villa with a literary friend. On Monday with a kinswoman of yours, the amiable Mrs. Bronson. On Tuesday with Vernon Lee to meet an Italian critic, Nencioni,[2] who has translated me. On the next day with Mme Matthews, etc. etc. Last night I dined with the good Mrs. Huntington. The night before with the more vicious Loftons—in extraordinary and overdone splendour. The night before that with the Cantagallis in company with that extraordinary and most amusing woman the Countess Gamba. The night still before with Edith Peruzzi[3]—to eat lark—Florentine homely dishes (about fifty of them) with her dear friends the whole Corsini brood—intermingled with Farinolas and Antinaris. I recite this list simply to show you that I am plunged in social embroilments that one can't be quit of from one day to another. But they shall stop absolutely—I tell you—on the first day possible after the 10th and before the 20th and then *vogue la galère*—or rather *la gondole!* When I reach Venice, I shall stay forever. I mean to stop twenty-four hours at Bologna—*vous me permettez bien cela?* Here it is almost already spring. I met the McClellans at their little Torregiani cousins where I went, by the latter's invitation, to see the pretended Raphael Madonna—which is no more a Raphael than Daisy Miller is a Shakespeare—and the young authoress served pimpante, in a Van Dyck hat. Dearest lady, have just a moment's more patience with me and je suis, à vous—but tout à vous

Henry James

1. Janet Ross (1842–1927), the former Janet Duff-Gordon, was a friend of George Meredith and John Addington Symonds. She had been painted by Watts and Leighton. She lived in a fine villa at Castagnolo and continued to entertain visiting Americans and Britons into the 1920s. See Virginia Woolf, *Letters* I (1975) 393.

2. Enrico Nencioni (1837–1896), an Italian critic, poet, and student of English literature.

3. Edith Peruzzi was the former Edith Marion Story, daughter of the American sculptor William Wetmore Story. She had married a descendant of the Medici, Simone Peruzzi di Medici, in 1876. See *Letters* I, 449.

To Grace Norton
Ms Harvard

Palazzino Alvisi
Venice
February 27*th* [1887]

My dear Grace.

Yesterday comes in your delightful letter of February 8th following (at a shorter interval than I deserved) a most benevolent one of November 23d, which reached me in Florence shortly after I had written to you at Pisa. Your letters always both gratify and sadden me; one ought to prevent the other, but somehow it doesn't. And neither prevents, my dear Grace, the stir of a thousand old-time associations, charged equally with the sad and glad elements that any *long* friendship must in the nature of things carry in its bosom, whenever I see your hand. You are, somehow, *austere*—but I suppose that that is good for me—living as I do in a world—or rather in twenty worlds, for that is a better description of my existence—of which such a quality can be but little predicated. I came to this place five days ago—after spending some ten weeks in Florence. I left England for six or eight—but it is now my hope that I may remain away till the summer. Alice has kindly taken my rooms and servants off my hands and this simplifies the problems connected with an empty habitation and "Mr. and Mrs. Smith" (my domestics!) demoralized by the master's long absence. As I dislike the Season, in London, "worse and worse," I felicitate myself on escaping it this year. The first month I was in Florence I had a villa at Bellosguardo, kindly sublet to me by a friend (Constance Fenimore Woolson the novelist—an excellent woman, of whom I am very fond, though she is almost impracticably deaf), who had taken it for three years and was not yet ready to go into it, having another on her hands. A cook went with it (a venerable—and veritable—chef) so that I was very comfortable—and blissfully lifted out of that little simmering social pot—a not very savoury human broth—into which Florence resolves itself today. It is a pity it is *personally* so tiresome, for (allowing for the comparative ugliness of its winter phase, with hard cold and dusty *tramontana*) it had never seemed to me, naturally and artistically, more delightful. And the views from the villas on the hills (I was at a good many) are as beautiful—really—as your memory must tell you. On January 1st my friend came into her villa and I descended into Florence —where (I am told) I went "out" a good deal. Why, I don't know— as it was very exactly what I had left London not to do. I am also told I was "lionized"—and the wherefore of this I know still less. On reflection, in fact, I greatly doubt it. But I did see a great many people; too many, for what they were. I won't tell you their names, or more than that they were members of the queer, promiscuous polyglot (most polyglot in the world) Florentine society. The Russians are the great factor there and the two pleasantest houses are supposed to be that of Mme de Tchiatchef and that of the Marchesa Incontri. The former is a remarkably nice and sympathetic Englishwoman married to a rich and retired Russian diplomat; the latter a singularly clever and easy Russian (with a beautiful villa outside of Porta S. Gallo) who, divorced from her first husband, Prince Galitzin, married a Florentine and became his widow. Mme de T. is very good (and yet not dull) and Mme Incontri I suspect of being *bad*—though not dull either. The latter receives both the serious and the "smart" people, is literary (writes poorish novels, under false names, in English, which she speaks in absolute perfection) and also, I think, rather dangerous. The most intelligent person in Florence is Violet Paget (Vernon Lee) who has lived there all her life, and receives every day, from 4 to 7, and as often in the evening as people will come to her. She is exceedingly ugly, not "well off," disputatious, contradictious and perverse; has a clever, paralysed half-brother, Edward Hamilton,[1] formerly in diplomacy—who is always in her salon, bedridden or rather sofa-ridden—and also a grotesque, deformed, invalidical, *posing* little old mother, and a father in the highest degree unpleasant, mysterious and sinister, who walks *all day,* all over Florence, hates his stepson, and hasn't sat down to table with his family for twenty years. Yet in spite of these drawbacks, Miss Paget's intellectual and social energy are so great, that she attracts all the world to her drawing room, discusses all things in *any* language, and understands some, drives her pen, glares through her spectacles and keeps up her courage. She has a *mind*—almost the only one in Florence. I saw also something of a very clever, natural, exuberant Countess Gamba,[2] who is one of the figures of the place—niece by her husband of Byron's Guiccioli (she has a lot of his letters to the G. which she declares shocking and unprintable—she took upon herself to burn one of them up!) a *putative* natural daughter of Giuseppe Giusti, the satiric Tuscan poet. (Her mother was some fine Florentine lady to whom G. was much devoted, and she—the "Euphrosyne"—is said much to resemble him.) She was the most of a "nature" of anyone I saw. I encountered no interesting man save [Adolf von] Hildebrand, the admirable, original German sculptor, who has the feeling of the Greeks and that of the early Tuscans too, by a strange combination, but is so little known, owing to his scorn of the usual claptrap and catchpenny arts. Willard Fiske our compatriot, a child of "Cornell," and supposed Icelandic scholar, who lives in Mr. Marsh's old villa, and has filled it with 5000 volumes of the Sagas and of Petrarch (!!) is, though friendly and hospitable, an absolutely colourless little personage. The other Americans there are *nil.*—I am staying here—provisionally—with my old friend Mrs. Bronson (who lived, a thousand years ago, at Newport and has lived here for ten). Her house directly faces the big doors of the Salute Church—and is next to the Pension Suisse, where I think you once stayed. But I am lodged in an old palazzo Giustinian-Recanati, which, in her rear, forms a kind of detached wing or appendage to her premises. It contains a very snug and comfortable little apartment of several rooms, including a private theatre, very well mounted, which she most benevolently puts at the service of her friends. Browning has often staid here—by the month at a time (he is a great friend of the padrona) and written crabbed verses at the table at which I sit. His son has been staying here for three months and departed just before I came in. They are looking for a palace—he and Robert—want to *buy* one—and thought they had, last year, till the vendor backed out. Mr. "Peabody Russell" of the U.S. has just bought two Contarini palaces, and is going to "knock them into one"! I tremble for what that one will be. This visit of mine (to Mrs. B.) has been promised again and again—but I shall make it short and soon look out for an independent lodging. Mrs. Bronson is a most benevolent, injudiciously (even) generous woman, adored by all the common people of Venice—and preyed upon by her servants. "Society" here presses more or less into her saloons—Layards, Hurtados, Mocenigos, Metternichs, Don Carlos (!!)[3] etc.—but I have kept out of them, mostly, save when she is alone (with her only daughter, a plain but pleasant girl, whose hand is sought here by penniless patricians who think her richer than she is, and whom she doesn't at all fancy. She doesn't like Venice—and would fain live in England). I am overdone with *people* and aspire to be quiet here, and do my work and possess my soul.—Yes, London is a *man's* city (not a woman's)—but even a man may sometimes be glad of something smaller. I am happy to say, however, that I always remain of the mind that if one can only have—or if *I* can only have—one domicile, London is the best place to have it. There it covers most ground. England is interesting at present—because it is heaving so, and cracking and fermenting. But the fissures are mainly political, and the exhalations often foul. Besides, I miss there the literary sense. *Il n'y en a plus!*—nor anywhere else, that I can see. I shall be delighted to see Lowell and Lily—so that I talk with her—and with him—about you. I envy you immensely your long *reads;* that is the curse of London—it is the worst place in the world for reading. Ever my dear Grace, your affectionate

Henry James

1. His name was Eugene (not Edward) Lee-Hamilton (1845–1907). He was Violet Paget's half brother, a writer of verse and a cultivated literary personality who ultimately recovered from his bedridden state. In one of their talks, he gave HJ the idea for "The Aspern Papers."

2. HJ in *Notebooks*, 72, alludes to the Countess and her letter-burning in his plan for "The Aspern Papers."

3. HJ's exclamations probably allude to the notoriety of the exiled Don Carlos (1848–1909), duque de Madrid, styled Charles VII by the Carlists (grandson of the first Carlist pretender to the Spanish throne), who had failed a few years earlier in his bid to become ruler. He was defeated by Alfonso XII and spent his remaining years in France and Italy.

To Sarah Butler Wister
Ms Congress

Venice, Palazzino Alvisi
Canal Grande
February 27*th* [1887]

Dear Mrs. Wister.

It would be a history to tell you why I have waited till this hour —and till I should be in this place—to answer your valued letter of so many weeks ago. To put that history in three words—I have been, from the moment it came—or from a certain time afterward —been expecting, from one week to the other, to go to *Rome,* and I wanted to give myself—and you!—the satisfaction (in the hour I should spend with you) of the Roman medium. Never, never have I forgotten how some of the most ineffaceable impressions of my life were gathered there fifteen years ago, in your society.[1] But month has followed month—and I haven't yet gone to Rome—and, strange as it may appear to you, it seems a little doubtful that I shall manage it. Therefore you must have your letter now and here. I came to Italy on December 1st; and have spent in Florence the whole time that has elapsed since then—until five days ago. My winter has taken a different turn from my first plan.—I am staying abroad twice as long, and dividing my time between Florence and Venice. I *was* to have gone to Rome on February 1st—but it proved just the thing, when the moment came, that I didn't want to do— owing to the shoals of *people* with whom my visit would have been associated. I came abroad to escape 'em (the human race— excuse my fastidiousness!) but I found myself much mixed up with them in Florence—so that it was more difficult than I had hoped to get time for reading (for which there is horribly little time in London—so that I depend on my foreign excursions to make it up) and generally possessing my soul. But behold, every one I had ever heard of, and didn't want to hear of again, was ascertained by me to be either in Rome or on the way there—so that I foresaw the shipwreck of all my hopes of concentration. I foresaw that inevitably my life would intertwine with a thousand irrelevancies. In a word, it was plain that I wouldn't be unknowing and unknown (excuse my fatuity!) so that I put it off. This was the easier to do as one's stomach is really turned here by the accounts of the hideous things that are being wrought upon the helpless seven hills. Destruction and vulgarization everywhere—and the Villa Ludovisi cut up into building lots. The Villa Ludovisi—*je ne vous dis que cela!* I staid in Florence till February 22d and then came here for an indefinite number of weeks. I find it delightfully quiet—though I am staying—for the moment—with the good Mrs. Bronson. She has a little apartment—a sort of detached wing or pavilion, in the rear of her house—which she kindly puts at the disposition of her friends.

I occupy it—in pursuance of a frequent promise—for the present, but shall seek an independent lodging as soon as I civilly may. Venice is wintry yet and so little *terne,* in consequence; also the *calles* and *campos* impress the sense with a kind of glutinous, malodorous damp. But it is Venice, none the less, and it is a ravishment to be here and to think that every week, at this season, will bring out a little more of the colour. I have a hope, if I stay in Italy late enough, of going down to Rome for ten days in May—when the damaging crowd shall have taken itself off. I dream then of also taking a little tour of old towns in Tuscany. If I am able to do this I shall certainly give you news of Rome. I passed my ten or eleven weeks rather well in Florence, in spite of more hard cold and dusty *tramontana* than one bargains for when one does so much as to go forth for a Southern winter; most of the essential aspects of the place seemed to me as lovely as ever (especially the divine hills—at the gates—and some of the old villas); but the queer polyglot promiscuous society—struck me as a vain agitation of insignificant particles. I saw many people—and am told I went out immensely—and even (tell it not in Philadelphia) that I was lionized. But if it was so I didn't perceive it, as the Princess Troubetzkoi, in Paris, is said to have remarked when it was stated to her that M. Thiers pretended to have made a particularly violent kind of love to her. I saw a good deal of Vernon Lee (Violet Paget), who has always lived there, and who though very ugly, disputatious and awkwardly situated *comme famille* (a paralysed sofa-ridden brother always in the parlour and grotesque, depressing, irrelevant parents) possesses the only mind I could discover in the place—unless the famous Mrs. Ross, whom I spent three days with at her picturesque old villa (or rather the Marchesa Stufa's) of Castagnola, may be said to have another. But I am not so sure of Mrs. Ross's mind as of her eyes, her guitar, and her desire to sell you bric-à-brac! She is awfully handsome, in a utilitarian kind of way—and an odd mixture of the British female and the dangerous woman—a Bohemian with rules and accounts.

—*February 28th*. I had to break off my letter yesterday, and since then we have been a good deal flurried by further *personal* accounts of the wretched contagious scare produced on the Riviera by the recent earthquake-shocks,[2] of which the full report will have come to you in the U.S.—that is, I saw last evening the Daniel Curtises of Boston (she, you may remember, a sister of that melancholy and strenuous, but estimable and superior, Miss Wormeley[3] of Newport, who has lately been so incongruously—as a New England old-maid, unacquainted with French—and other badnesses—mistranslating Balzac); which D. Curtises have just fled back from the frightened though not hurt Monte Carlo—to the splendid Palazzo Barbaro, of which they are the enviable owners (they have bought it) here. The Riviera has been full of people we know—and many, no doubt (lots of Bostonians) known to you; and the sudden violent, alarmed break-up and stampede of the luxurious colony (though unaccompanied by any real injury—except to the poor people who live by its presence there)—have been really melancholy and sickening. I hear of Mrs. Mason[4] and her Balfours, passing their nights in a *carriage* at Monte Carlo—where they have had a villa.

—*March 1st*. I was again interrupted—yesterday—but this time I vow I shall have my talk with you out. The day is lovely—and the golden glow of Venice streams into my room. On laying down my pen yesterday I went out and in the course of the afternoon paid a visit to a most remarkable woman—the Countess Pisani—a lady who vaguely suggests Caterina Cornaro[5] and makes one believe in the romantic heroines of D'Israeli and Bulwer. She has English blood in her veins—her father was the doctor who bled Byron to death at Missolonghi—and her mother a French odalisque out of the harem of the Grand Turk. The late Count Pisani married her thirty-five years ago for her beauty which must have been extraordinary and still is very striking (she is fifty-five and looks about forty); she has spent all her life in Italy; and today widowed, childless, palaced, villaed, pictured, jewelled, and modified by Venetian society in a kind of mysterious awe—she passes for a great personage and the biggest swell—on the whole—in the place. She is very little in Venice—living mainly at her villa on the mainland, where she farms a large property with un-Venetian energy. She made an impression—on me—as of one not formed of the usual social stuff of today—but the sort of woman one might have found—receiving on a balcony, here—at 2 o'clock on a June morning—in the early years of the century.—All this time I don't speak to you of your dear mother[6]—but it is three months since I have seen her. I did so often, as usual—regularly one night in the week—during the three months that elapsed between her return from the continent and my own departure—and she was in a very quiet, comfortable frame. With all abatements, her vitality is still great. I am so attached to her, and my periodical visits to her, of an evening, have become, after so many years, so much a part of my life—that the interruption of them really operates as a great drawback and loss to me, whenever I come abroad. I think of her constantly—I miss her—I worry about her—and I think she misses me. I almost hope she does!—and yet I have a bad conscience (that word is divided wrong),[7] when I consider that she may. That is much the case, for instance, this winter. If I remain abroad till toward the time she will be coming out, I shall certainly stretch it over long enough to go and pay her a visit in Switzerland. She has been most kind and attentive to my poor sister, who doesn't leave her sofa—and has sent her frequent flowers.—I hope things have gone well with you this winter; my absence from London has brought with it also that forfeiture—that I haven't had, as usual, from your mother, fresh and frequent news of you. I heard the other day in Florence from Mrs. Lockwood's incongruous friend, Miss Light (why are so many of her friends incongruous?—but it is perhaps not for us to decree the congruity), that she was perhaps coming to Italy for a few weeks—and to take the said Miss L. back with her. I heard also of the torment she had been traversing in the matter of her son's accident. Poor boy—and poor woman! I wouldn't be a mother! That's one of the reasons I have never married—because if I had

I should have been. And this unspeakable *sinister* horror of Jack Chapman[8]—which comes to me brokenly and roundaboutly—I fear even to ask what it means?—it suggests, so, madness and perversity. Let us close on a cheerfuller note—and say, dear Mrs. Wister, that I am ever your affectionate old friend

Henry James

1. HJ is alluding to their frequent sightseeing and horseback riding in the Campagna during 1872–1874.

2. The earthquake shocks felt largely along the French and Italian Riviera during the morning of 23 February 1887 extended as far as Genoa and were especially violent in the San Remo region, where a village above the town was destroyed.

3. Katherine Prescott Wormeley, older sister of Ariana Randolph Wormeley. Ariana married Daniel Curtis and lived in Venice. Katherine translated many volumes of Balzac.

4. Alice Mason, the former Mrs. Charles Sumner, a friend from HJ's and Mrs. Wister's stay in Rome in the early 1870s. Her daughter had married a Balfour.

5. Caterina Cornaro, a fifteenth-century Venetian lady of rank, married King James II of Cyprus, Jerusalem, and Armenia. On the death of her husband she was able to abdicate and convey her sovereign power, and that of her late husband, to the Venetian Republic.

6. Frances Anne Kemble.

7. In the holograph James had, at the end of the line, broken the word so as to read "cons-cience."

8. John Jay Chapman (1862–1933), the American writer, on an impulse, prompted by guilt after striking an acquaintance, had burned off the offending hand in his fireplace.

To James Russell Lowell

Ms Harvard

Palazzino Alvisi
Canal Grande
Venice
March 1*st* 1887

My dear Lowell.

Yes, of course I ought to have thanked you long ago for the beautiful letter you sent me after I had written to you in the autumn—especially as I had such a perfect added pretext in the pure delight I took in your noble Harvard address[1]—than which no piece of literature, in many a day, has made me more proud to belong, at however long an interval, to the same divine craft that taught you (or rather to which you have taught!) such an expression of such thoughts and such emotions—not to speak of the same country! This last is a bold speech for a man capable of perpetrating so long a sentence; but read it over, my dear Lowell, and you will see that there is a method in its madness—or at any rate a sentiment—a very tender one. I haven't written to you, because when I lay down the mercenary pen—my fingers ache too much to grasp the sentimental one. I write to you, really, whenever I turn a sentence that is less mediocre than usual—I know that if you happen to see it nothing of any merit it may have will be lost upon you. And now this isn't a letter—but only a little nod and beck—a writhed smile of friendship across the Grande Canal—and the grander one beyond. (I leave my absurd accidental "writhed" there—for wreathed—because it is so comical—it will make you laugh! The anguish of effort isn't in my smile!) I have been spending three months in Florence—and now have come here for as many weeks more as possible. I left London on December 1st for a short absence, but have been able to make it long through my sister, in London, having kindly taken my rooms and servants off my hands for the winter. This has left me without a preoccupation—or at least without that particular one. God knows I manage to have a sufficient number of others. You will probably get back to London before me, and it saddens me that I shall not be there to welcome you. Everyone else will, however, and your welcome will be great. I shall follow you at no very long interval. Venice—even at this crude season—is full of its old magic—but we are all over-shadowed, and morally *secoués* by the horrid earthquake on the Riviera, where desolation has descended in the course of a few moments. The Dan'l. Curtises have just arrived here from Monte Carlo, full of the most dismal stories—having been in the midst of it all. For those virtuous Bostonians an earthquake at Monte Carlo has been doubly Daniel in the lions' den. There has been nothing here—and I get quiet mornings for work. I hear very little from London—do give my love there. But only a little—keep the rest yourself. Ever, my dear Lowell, yours most faithfully

Henry James

1. At the celebration of the 250th year of Harvard. See letter to William James, 10 September 1886.

To George du Maurier
Ms Harvard

Palazzino Alvisi
Canal Grande
Venice: March 2*d* [1887]

My dear du Maurier.

I have got a tiresome headache and can't do my work this morning—but I think I *can* write to you. I fear, however, my letter will resolve itself into little more than an appeal to you to give me as much as possible of your own news. It is now just three months since I left England—and for that horrid period I have been—no doubt largely by [my] own fault—in the dark about you. I shall burst in ignorance—like Hamlet—if you don't relieve me. I have guessed from one or two stray copies of *Punch* that have fallen under my eye, that you have been at Brighton—but this imagination only torments me by what it leaves unexplained. I dwell among strange races and ways, in lands beyond seas, but I carry everywhere in my heart an interest, affectionate even perhaps to indiscretion, in your concerns and affairs. The last time I saw you, you were thinking of selling or letting your house—do tell me everything that has, or hasn't, happened. When I divine you at Brighton (*Punch* testifying—unless it was, frugally, a last year's memory), my fancy flies away with me and I wonder if the silver cord of Hampstead has really been loosed. If it has, *mon cher ami*, do tie yourselves together with it, labelled Venice, and come and spend the spring here. How it would furbish up this shabby old paradise for me *de vous y avoir!* I should think the Doge Partecipazio[1] (or all of them—I believe there were a dozen of the name) had returned. The weather glows—the lagoon twinkles and the old marble-fronted palaces look hungry for you. I came here a week ago from Florence, where I had been staying ever since I came abroad—and it is my hope to remain in this place as late as possible into the spring. My sister has taken my London rooms and servants off my hands for as many weeks more as I choose to lease them to her, and this liberates me for remaining abroad. I like London so much less during these proximate months than at any other time that I embrace the facility for being away. This place will go on improving up to the middle of June, when it will become too hot, and I have tested it, of old, at this season, for working-purposes. There is to be a senseless exhibition here a couple of months hence—but up to that time it will be blissfully quiet, delightfully entertaining and divinely beautiful. *Ça ne vous tente pas?* I wish I were like two or three friends of mine here, the possessor of some capacious old palace, whose marble arms I could throw open to you—but, alas, I myself am staying in a little apartment which an American friend has lent me—a humble appendage or *dépendance* to a *casa signorile.* Tell me some London news—and above all that Mrs. du Maurier enjoys such health as you could wish. There has been no *terremoto* here—but we are desolate at the other desolation. With a most affectionate greeting to your wife and children, believe me, *cher et excellent ami,* your *fedelissimo devotissimo*

Henry James

1. The first Doge Orso Partecipazio, in the ninth century, instituted reforms in the Venetian government that tended to broaden the ruling class. From the time of Giovanni Partecipazio's successor in 887, the office of the Doge became elective.

To Francis Boott
Ms Harvard

Palazzino Alvisi
Canal Grande
March 15*th* [1887]

My dear Francis.

I am much gratified by your letter, which renews the chain of intercourse. It comes to me on a dark dripping un-Venetian morning which is the third or fourth of a dismal series. Yesterday there were sinister carts in the Piazza and men who looked like Irishmen shovelling away snow. One was almost sorry to have left Boston. Can one indeed say one has, with Daniel Curtis, here, doing his best (though he abuses "over there" so much) to make the Grand Canal seem like Beacon Street. I see them pretty often and they are very friendly. But one calculates the time when one shall have worked through his anecdotes and come out the other side. Perhaps one never does—it is an unboreable—or unbearable—St. Gothard.

I have gone several times to see Laura [Wagnière-Huntington] and Mabel—and find the latter indeed, as you say, made of heroic stuff; to the impression of which her Medea-beauty greatly adds. Her situation is terribly touching—and you can form no idea, until you have heard it from their own lips and also those of the Curtises, of the *horrors* of that combined tragedy of the earthquake and Henry H[untington]'s unmanageable madness. The helplessness of the two women (after the Curtises left them) and the details of the whole thing were too miserable. Poor Mrs. Henry finds herself now, I fear, overwhelmed with demands for the payment of crazy debts contracted by her husband; and oddly enough the person in London who, in combination with the lawyers, is helping and advising her in the matter, is Lady Colin Campbell. The latter writes to her every day, and she commends immensely her kindness and sympathy. The quiet of this place is comfortable to me after the lively bustle of Florence. There are tea-parties here but one doesn't hear the clatter of the cups. I am accepting for the time the hospitality of this little palazzo Giustinian-Recanati in Mrs. Bronson's rear; but I have my own ménage, and reserve, pretty well, my freedom. Your Florentine Mr. B[rowning] is here—for a week, but is dimmed by a cold. I think I can never have written "very pleased" except dramatically—in the mouth of someone speaking —*è vero?* It is, however, very possible that I may have written very possible *in propria persona.* Tell Fenimore I forgive her—but only an angel would. She will understand. Much love to Lizzie and *tanti saluti* to the two gentlemen. Ever yours faithfully

Henry James

To Dr. W. W. Baldwin

Ms Morgan

Palazzino Alvisi
Canal Grande
Venice. March 23*d* [1887]

Dear Doctor:

I am much obliged to you for your long and lucid letter—especially as I judge you are sadly overworked and fatigued. I understand it perfectly and shall follow its directions religiously.[1] I return to Florence almost immediately (for the present at least), and shall therefore see you very soon. Since writing to you last I have been rather miserably unwell—and all these days in bed, which is rare for me. But I have not had the same sensations or symptoms as I wrote you of—only a horrid attack in my head, such as I am —or rather have been in the past—lamentably subject to—and which on this occasion has been distinguished for its long duration. But I am better now and shall leave Venice as soon as I can travel—for various reasons among others that the weather here is atrocious for one wishing to "get over" anything. If possible I shall get for a short time a perch at Bellosguardo—to be out of the turmoil of Florence. I wish *you* were less in it. I am very faithfully yours

Henry James

1. Dr. William Wilberforce Baldwin (1850–1910), an American M.D., had set up a practice in Florence some years before and had achieved international renown for his diagnostic skills. A friend of Princess May (later Queen Mary), he was consulted by British royalty and served as doctor to many itinerant writers passing through Florence—among them HJ, his brother William, Mark Twain, Miss Woolson, Edith Wharton, and W. D. Howells. During his stay in Venice, HJ had developed troublesome urinary symptoms and other discomforts and had written earlier to Baldwin, who understandably had difficulty diagnosing his illness from Florence. HJ finally consulted a Venetian doctor and discovered he had jaundice.

To William James
Ms Harvard

Venice, April 7*th* [1887]

My dear William.

I this moment hear, through your postcard to Alice, of the birth of your daughter.[1] I give you much joy, and to your Alice much love. I pray everything may have gone on well since the 24th and that the little *femminetta,* as they say here, has begun already to grow in grace and beauty. It is an excellent augury that she is the portrait of her mother—may the likeness constantly increase. I hope that by the time you get this Alice will be almost on her feet again. I had a letter from you more than ten days ago, dictated by her from the couch of pain, and which reached me, I am sorry to say, in a similar situation. I have been spending some seven rather unsuccessful weeks in this place, whence I depart two days hence to pass another month in Florence. I have taken some rooms at Bellosguardo[2] for that period—not wishing yet to return to London and oust Alice from my apartment. I began to be "poorly" shortly after I came here—had one of my odious violent headaches (lately so rare) of unparallelled magnitude (lasting day after day), and then wound up with a sharp attack of jaundice (a most loathsome malady), which kept me in my room, and mainly in bed, with a little fever, for sixteen days. This made it the *longest* illness I have had since I was laid up with typhoid fever, so many years ago, at Boulogne. But I had an excellent, tho' Venetian, doctor, and a very good gondolier-nurse, and am now completely well—but desiring much to get out of Venice for full recuperation. The air of Bellosguardo is most salubrious, and I shall spend a month there. But why do I tell you all this with your Alice perhaps filling all your thoughts. Tell her she is also constantly in mine. I come back to life, as it were, to meet a mountain of letters, and have lost a whole month of time. So I am brief—though I shall write soon again. I embrace the *fillette*. Alice seems now to flourish much in London. Ever your affectionate Brother

H. James

1. William James's youngest child was named Mary Margaret and usually called Peggy.

2. In Miss Woolson's Villa Brichieri. This time, however, HJ and Miss Woolson both resided in the villa, occupying separate apartments.

To Francis Boott

Ms Harvard

Venice, Wednesday
[13 April 1887]

My dear Francis.

Many thanks for your note and your kind offers of assistance. I am so revived and restored that I think that on Saturday P.M. I shall be well able to "fend for myself," with the assistance of the slave whom Fenimore has engaged for me and whom she will send to the station (with the mystic cab[1] of the Roman Gate) to meet me. Don't there *incomodarvi* to come out at that undue hour—with the tiresome accident of *waiting* so sure to happen. I am quite on my feet—and on my *feed*—the proof of both of which is that I go this noon to breakfast with the D—d Curtises. These days are lovely here—but I ween the *poderas* of Bellosguardo are lovelier; and I shall have been here, on Saturday, nearly seven weeks. I am glad to know that you are soon to tread the hilltop as a proprietor. We must take some walks together. I shall be delighted to see Duveneck's picture—as well as his smaller image. Much love to Lizzie. Yours ever faithfully

H. James

1. The "mystic cab" turned out to be the carriage of the vigilant Dr. Baldwin, who, in view of HJ's jaundice in Venice, came personally to escort his recovering patient to the hilltop villa occupied by Miss Woolson.

To Mrs. Emma (Wilkinson) Pertz
Ms Private

[April-May 1887]

Dear Madame Pertz[1]

Your invitation is most kind but I am sorry to say that I find myself in the impossibility, at present, of making engagements to lunch—except once in a while on Sunday. I have perched myself on my hilltop to lead a life of seclusion and finish some work, for which it is necessary to my salvation to make a *long* morning. I lunch at 12.30, get the best of my time afterwards, for a couple of hours, and don't go out till 3.30 or 4—or later. This makes it a kind of religion to me to deny myself the pleasure of a festive noon, but I am with many regrets, as well as many thanks, very truly yours

Henry James

Ville Bricchière
Bellosguardo
Saturday morning

1. HJ's ties with the Wilkinson family went back to his childhood. Emma Wilkinson was a daughter of Dr. J. J. Garth Wilkinson, the British Swedenborgian and intimate of HJ's father. See *Letters* II, 169, 339.

To Mrs. Daniel S. Curtis
Ms Dartmouth

Villa Bricchiere
Bellosguardo
April 23*d* [1887]

Dear Mrs. Curtis.

I send you this by the hand of my valued friend M. Paul Bourget, who will already have been very considerably introduced to you. He goes to Venice for a month; I take the greatest interest in him, and I can give him no better proof of it than to put it in his power to know Mr. Curtis and you. You will also not consider that I have been moved by anything less than extreme sympathy in making you acquainted with so agreeable and distinguished a person. Please let him see the flicker of the canal on your gilded roof—and take him over to the garden and show him the garden-house.[1] I envy him, at the mere thought! I hoped to have been in Venice during his stay—and then I should have brought him to you. But I shall assist in spirit at your *causeries* and shall bless your relations. Believe me, in advance, very gratefully yours, and Mr. Curtis's—

Henry James

1. The Curtises had one of Venice's rare gardens, a plot of land to which Curtis was rowed by his gondoliers and which he cultivated.

To Edmund Gosse
Ms Leeds

Villa Bricchiere
Bellosguardo, Florence
April 24*th* [1887]

My dear Gosse.

This won't be much of a letter—but let us make of it what we can. I made much of yours which came to me three days since. It was good of you to call back to me—across Alps and Channels—so promptly and cheerily. Apropos of cheerily how was it that you were "nearly drowned"! I palpitate for the items and heave a general *soupir* of relief.—*Il faut me raconter cela.* I have really nothing to relate to you save that I sit here making love to Italy. At this divine moment she is perfectly irresistible, and this delicious little Florence is not the least sovereign of her charms. I am fixed, till June 1st, in a villa which in England would be suburban, but here is supercelestial, whence the most beautiful view on earth hangs before me wherever I lift my head—which is one reason why I can only write short letters. The spring is in its flower and Florence is sweet *à faire pleurer*—but really, that is my only news. There is nothing personal or literary in the air. The only intelligent person in the place is Violet Paget—who is so, however, with a vengeance. She has one of the best minds I know—is almost worthy to be French—and makes one a little less ashamed of the stupid English race. She is disputatious and paradoxical, but a really superior talker. I suspect, however, that as a writer she has gone through all her paces—some of them very lively. She is trying to throw herself into fiction—for which she has not a distinct faculty. I will go and see Miss Marzials if I can—but she lives miles away from me—and *calls* are the scourge of Florence. I have a vivid recollection of her and her clever talk one evening, at supper at your house. I met in Venice that queer, uncanny person her brother, who made, in sooth, a disagreeable, painful impression on me.[1] Someone mentioned to me that you used to know him well—and you must tell me, some time, how he comes to be so.—I hear from Howells that he is coming this summer to Paris; but (once he has put his boy at the Beaux Arts) *que fera-t-il dans cette galère?* *Mont Oriol* has the supreme quality of *life*—but I don't think it is *du meilleur* Maupassant—any more than *André Cornélis*[2] is *du meilleur* Bourget. It has no idea—no *donnée*—except the smutty one of the water operating on the sterility of the young wife through the *robinet*—(I won't use a plainer English word though in connection with water it would be exact) of the young lover. And that has served many times. Your "crude" compliments to the *Princess* [*Casamassima*] are quite delicate enough to tickle. I am delighted the air of your life is clear again—I *did* foresee it would be.[3] One has only to hold fast, and it always is. I shall scarcely be in London before July 1st—but shall give you a sign as soon as I am. Ever faithfully yours

Henry James

1. In his earlier years, Gosse had been employed at the British Museum, where one of his fellow workers had been Theophilus Henry Marzials (1850–1920), a composer and song writer who had considerable vogue.

2. Bourget and Maupassant had both published these novels during 1887.

3. See letter to Gosse, 26 October 1886.

To William James
Ms Harvard

Villa Brichieri
Bellosguardo
May 3*d* [1887]

My dear William.

Have patience with me—I am bowed beneath my correspondence—as even at this distance London daily vomits forth notes and letters upon me. I shall be brief today but at least I will have speech with you. I have two letters from you, one long and delightful one of April 12th written just after you had been to the country to look after your place, and another of the 17th received but a few days since, condoling with me on my having been ill in Venice. I wrote to you from there just before I left, when I was already happily convalescent, and then again to Alice after my arrival here. So you will long since have known that I have left my troubles behind me. I am perfectly well again and only richer by the experience.—I had a good inspiration in taking this villa (or rather I mean, the corner of it that I occupy) till June 1st as it turns out a most timely refuge and a delightful habitation. Summer has begun here and the country is divinely fair. The most beautiful view in the world (literally I mean, as I believe) is there before one—all the livelong day—and there is all-sufficient quiet, space, and other suggestiveness, for work. I go down into Florence almost every day for my dinner and walk back again in the balmy night—a steep hillside, but up into light pure air—. I am working very well again—but my productions bury themselves—indefinitely, apparently, in the *Century* and *Harper*. I have just written for the former a longish article on R. L. Stevenson—but this, I think, I have already mentioned. I have written to Alice that she may stay in De Vere Gardens till the middle of July. If she does so, I shall remain as late as possible in Italy—and go awhile to Siena after leaving this.

Paul Bourget (who is in Venice, where he lately came expecting to find me) wishes me to spend a part of June with him somewhere, and I shall probably do so. There are great fêtes going forward here—or just beginning to—in celebration of the finished *façade* of the Cathedral—but they are down in the streets of Florence, and I give them a wideish berth. I have taken the greatest interest in the maiden—as I wrote to Alice the other day. She will variegate your house delightfully—and I am only sorry she is losing her resemblance to her mother. I hope the latter is now well on her feet. Also that Billy has come back to you *allégé*—poor dear little man. I divine that Alice (in De Vere Gardens) is now doing really very well. She will be glad to abbreviate her summer in the country at this end (having my quarters) and elongate it, if need be, at the other. This is a wretched answer, dear William, to all your brilliancies, but it is the eleventh letter (of letters and notes) I have written this morning. You shall have a better one as soon as I work out of some arrears fallen into during my illness. Much love to your Alice.

Ever yours
Henry

To Frances Anne Kemble
Ms Unknown

Bellosguardo
May 20*th* [1887]

Beloved Mrs. Kemble,

I wonder if you could very kindly give me a sort of notion of how you expect to proceed in Switzerland during the first half of your summer: I don't mean in the least in rigid detail—but in the main outline? I am staying in this sweet country so late that I should miss you if I were to go back to London now, and nothing would induce me to do that—I mean, to miss you. Neither do I find myself easily persuadable to return at present. I am waiting for the summer—and we don't have it yet. When it comes, I shall stop a little longer to enjoy it, and then I shall cross the Alps and jump down upon you. In other words, wherever you may be I will come to you and spend as many days as possible near you. I can't say now exactly when this will be—as I go back to Venice on the

25th of this month and the length of my stay there is uncertain. When the first *very* hot weather comes I shall probably take to my heels. Florence is lovely—and all the country about—to every sense but the sudorific; by which I mean that it isn't yet half warm enough. This remark will confirm your conviction that I am a salamander—but I ain't. I am only an American. We are just emerging from nearly three *weeks* (figgery-voo!) of fêtes à propos of the completion and unveiling of the famous front of the Duomo here—in the course of which I had the fatuity to assume a quattro-cento dress (of scarlet and black) and go to a very brilliant costumed ball that was given to the King and Queen in a wonderful tapestried hall of the Palazzo Vecchio here. I wish you could have seen me—I was lovely! We had also an historical procession in which the Florentine nobles of the present day (Strozzis, Guicciardinis, Gherardescas, etc.) represented, in accurate and splendid array, their medieval ancestors. This was really magnificent and interesting—the dresses, horses, trappings, etc. and the figures of the actors, etc. very noble and artistic. We have also had Rhoda Broughton[1] and Hamilton Aïdé—who, however, both departed before the best of the show began. You will have seen the latter and heard his adventures. Those of Miss Broughton, here, were, I think, happy—and liking her (in spite of her roughness) already, I liked her still more for liking Florence so much. She quite came up to my standard of appreciation. All this time I haven't thanked you for your last letter—of now nearly a month ago. But it is hard to thank you for telling me your gout was at that time so bad—though I should have appreciated still less your not letting me know it. I devoutly pray you may have been better since—though I gather that there has been small comfort in the season to make you so. I saw Mrs. Lockwood[2] two or three weeks ago—she had come out here for a month, from New York (not by way of England, but by a French or German steamer) to stay in Florence or elsewhere, with a certain queer English friend of hers, Miss Bianca Light; and she gave me very recent and very happy news of Mrs. Wister. She said she had *never* seen her so well, so active and so little knocked up by her activity. Write to me only at your leisure, dear Mrs. Kemble (always to 34 De Vere Gardens), and I will conduct myself accordingly. I haven't seen Thackeray's letters—but I *do* see Mrs. Procter's own, as she is so good as sometimes to write to me. What a capacity for *caring*—taking sides, resenting, etc. I don't see why, when one *minds* as much as that, one shouldn't live for ever. Your always affectionate

Henry James

1. Rhoda Broughton (1840–1920), the popular novelist, whom HJ had known from the middle 1870s and who spent an evening at this time on Bellosguardo with HJ and Miss Woolson.

2. Florence Bayard Lockwood, HJ's friend of his New York days in 1875. See *Letters* I, 470–471.

To Thomas Bailey Aldrich
Ms Harvard

Venice, June 12*th* '87

Dear Aldrich.

I send you herewith (in another parcel) the first half of the type-copy of a story—without having sounded you first on the subject. You may see in this a subtle desire to entrap you—to make you print it the more submissively from your having it on your hands. If you don't dislike it—and I don't see why you should, as it is brilliant, and of a thrilling interest—I should be very glad that you should print it early. If you do I will give you another of the same—or of a somewhat smaller length. This thing ("The Aspern Papers")[1] makes two parts of the maximum size—that of the longest instalments of the *Princess*. I think it would suffer grave injury from being cut otherwise. As you liked long instalments of the *Princess* I hope you won't object to them in this case. I should add that the tale is eminently proper. For the rest, *voyez plutôt*. The second half is in London, being type-copied, and I am expecting it *within a week*. The moment it comes it will follow its mate. It will thus reach you in about eight days after the latter. Will you please say to Messrs. Houghton and Mifflin that I shall be much obliged to them for sending me a cheque on your telling them that you print the story (and I hope you won't tell them that you don't). I blush to own it, but I am in want of money—and it would be a convenience to have it without waiting for publication. I leave them to fix the amount.—I have been spending the whole winter in Italy —and have pulled up here—in this effulgent steam bath—to say goodbye. I return to London in July—and my address is of course always *34 De Vere Gardens W*. When do *you* return?—A portion of the second part of my story has just come in from the copyist—and I send that too, in an envelope by itself. It makes about a third of the second part, which is a little longer than the first. So you will receive (with this) *two* oblong packets. I shall be very glad to hear they have reached you safely—and am ever, faithfully yours,

Henry James

1. Aldrich printed "The Aspern Papers" in the *Atlantic Monthly* in 1888 but in three instalments, not two. It appeared in book form the same year.

To Robert Underwood Johnson

Ms Harvard

Palazzo Barbaro
Venice
June 13*th* [1887]

Dear Mr. Johnson.

I am greatly obliged to you for the prompt cheque for my paper on Stevenson (for which I send a receipt) and for taking a part of your blessed, and I should suppose infinitely-needed Sunday of rest, to send me, with it, so pleasant a letter. I am very glad indeed the article seems about the right thing—and particularly rejoice at what you tell me of its seeing the light soon. The desire that it shall do so is confirmed, in my breast, by the fact that Stevenson lost his father a month ago—and this makes a considerable difference for the worse in his situation. The old man, while he could work, helped him to live, pecuniarily—but leaves an estate only sufficient for the maintenance of his widow. Therefore the sooner one can give his reputation a push, the better it will be for him. I haven't seen (he didn't show it to me last summer) Alexander's portrait—but I wish it well in the cutting. I am relieved that you don't like mine—and I didn't myself.[1] Somehow it didn't seem to go; and I pray that annihilation may overtake it.—I don't need your envying me Italy to make me feel that I love it about as much as ever. I am stretching out my stay and just now very happy in this effulgent steam bath. I shall probably spend three days in Florence again, before recrossing the Alps, and will carry your message to the Orcagna Madonna[2]—though I should never be bold enough to send her one myself. All his figures scare me. Bravo then—I shall send you a couple of short tales. Give my kind regards to Gilder and believe me ever faithfully yours

Henry James

P.S. You are right about the bells, the sunsets and every other beauty of Bellosguardo. I was lately there from April 8th[3] to May 25th—and grew to adore it as a habitation. You don't know what the view is till you live with it—and the bells of Florence talk to you, at a distance, all day long. The *feste* in Florence, for the unveiling of the new façade of the Duomo, were far more interesting than was to be supposed—especially a certain historical procession, of the mounted nobles and burghers, winding through the old palaced streets—very splendid and perfect.

1. The article on Stevenson appeared in the *Century*, XXXV (April 1888), 868–879, with an engraving by J. H. E. Whitney from a drawing by J. W. Alexander (1856–1915), an illustrator for magazines, notably Harper's for many years. The portrait of HJ, whether by Alexander or some other artist, has never turned up.

2. Andrea Orcagna (Andrea di Cione) (c. 1308–c. 1368), the most prominent Florentine painter, sculptor, and architect of the mid-fourteenth century. He is best known for his tabernacle in the guild oratory of Or San Michele, and HJ is apparently alluding to the figure of the Virgin in that tabernacle. Johnson reproduced a photograph of the Orcagna Madonna in the *Century*, May 1889.

3. HJ is mistaken in his dates. He was still in Venice on 13 April. See letter of that date to Francis Boott, in which he speaks of his journey to Florence the following Saturday, that is, 16 April.

To Catharine Walsh

Ms Harvard

Venice: June 16*th* [1887]
(Palazzo Barbaro)

Dearest Aunt.

As usual, when I am just on the point of writing to you comes in a good letter from you: with the date of May 30th. I have written to you but little this winter, not having had the opportunity of giving you news about Alice; and you have of course felt this to be the reason. It is now nearly seven months since I have seen her—and some five weeks will probably still elapse before we meet.

As soon as that happens I will give you a personal impression of her. I gather that in spite of a couple of bad episodes—one, however, much less serious than the other—she has had a half-year of substantial improvement. It is a proof of that, that she has been able to live—without distress—alone—with me in Italy and Katharine, for all but a few weeks, at a distance. I haven't heard from her, lately, for rather longer than usual—but this only indicates, I think, that her impediments have been a redundancy of visitors. More and more people appear to come to see her—and lately there have been many Americans in London. I have asked her to stay in De Vere Gardens till July 20th, and am much in hope that she will—as I don't expect to return to London before the 25th. About the 10th July there is a prospect of K. P. L[oring] coming over to her, after settling Louisa somewhere on the coast of Normandy. I believe she has settled to go to Leamington—somewhat to my regret—as I think a new place, and a more tonic, would have been better for her. But she dreads the unknown and the experimental—and her apartments at Leamington were cheap and good. I am very sorry that her house at Manchester hasn't let, as yet—but she has had an economical year, and I don't think she minds it much. I only hope it isn't a sign that the place isn't easily lettable—now that the Pratts have given it up.—I am in Venice as you see—for the second time since I have come abroad. My stay, which will have been of a month this time, draws to a close—I depart on the 25th. It is piping hot but as beautiful as ever. I have been paying a long visit—long for me, who like less and less as I grow older, to stay with people, to the Daniel Curtises, formerly of Boston but who have been living here for years and are the owners of this magnificent old palace—all marble and frescoes and portraits of Doges—a delightful habitation for hot weather. Mrs. Curtis is a sister of Miss Wormeley of Newport, whom she much resembles in face—and she and her husband are very intelligent, clever and hospitable people. I came for ten days, and they have simply kept me on. Dick Walsh came to see me a couple of days ago—and yesterday I took him over to the Lido. He seems a very good and gentlemanly little fellow—but without much "culture" or general information—though fond of art and artists. Mrs. Curtis has invited him to a party here, tonight. He is much with the McClellans, the General's widow, son and daughter—and very devoted to the latter, a rather flippant spoiled girl, who has got into a peck of trouble here by writing a strangely indiscreet and reprehensible letter to the New York *World* about Venetian "society," which received her very well last winter. The strange things of that sort that the American female does!—as witness the terrible Mrs. Sherwood, poor "Posy" Emmet's mother-in-law. She invited me (and some others) to dine with her in London last summer, and then wrote a fearful letter about it (I having gone, all unconscious) to the American journals, which she afterwards sent me as if I should be delighted to see it. I don't congratulate poor little Henrietta[1] (of whose bad condition I am really much pained to hear) on her relations by marriage—Mrs. Archie Pell having lately infested these parts, a terror of terrors. Alas, alas, I am grieved about the good little Henrietta. Life isn't gay. I am afraid you are making that reflection—shut up in New York for all these hot weeks. I am much distressed for you, knowing how little you like the bad days of summer. I hope you will get a chance to woo the breeze, somewhere, at some moment, as a holiday; and that in the meanwhile you will be sustained by the sense of alleviating Cousin Helen,[2] who must have much need of it. Please always give her my love. But a curse that she won't let Henry go off—his presence must be a wearisome oppression. But *pazienza!* as they say here. Will you send this to William?—though it is so stupid (it is really too hot for letters) that it will entertain him not at all. I will write again as soon as I get back to London, and am meanwhile ever your loving nevvy

Henry James

1. Henrietta, youngest of HJ's Temple cousins, had married Leslie Pell-Clarke of Newport in 1876.

2. Helen and her brother Henry Wyckoff, described in some detail in HJ's *A Small Boy and Others.* The Wyckoff great-aunt, who wore a green shade (like Juliana in "The Aspern Papers") was a sister of HJ's maternal grandmother. Helen's husband, described by HJ as "negligible," was named Perkins.

To Thomas Bailey Aldrich

Ms Harvard

Venice. June 21*st* [1887]

My dear Aldrich.

I send you today the remainder and end of "The Aspern Papers"—the Tale in two parts of which I sent you the First and a portion of the Second Part about ten days ago (on the 12th ult.). I wrote to you at some length about the story on that occasion—so that there is nothing now to add save the hope the accompanying may quickly and safely rejoin its predecessor. Ever yours

Henry James

3
A London Life

1887–1890

3
A London Life

After his return from Italy, Henry James settles back into the regular habits of his London life. For the next three years he works on his long novel, *The Tragic Muse,* about a young politician who wants to be a painter and a young actress who must make her way in the crowded world of the stage. He finds time to write short stories as well, and a brilliant series of essays on Flaubert's letters, the rise of Maupassant, the Goncourt journals. His correspondence, hitherto centered on his family, becomes increasingly diversified. But he is tired of the British social round, which attracted him when he was younger. He dines out less; he curtails country visits. He prefers to share the social and family life of his fellow writers and artists, and he enjoys long intimate tea-hours with worldly-wise London dowagers.

The glamour of England has worn off for him, but he is still a happy Londoner. He discerns laxities in British life and flaws in the British establishment; he likens the life of the British upper classes to the decay in the French aristocracy before the revolution. He follows, with some concern and an intense curiosity, the vagaries of political life—the endless Home Rule question and the scandals that cut short the political career of Sir Charles Dilke and brought about the fall of the Irish leader Parnell. As sex and politics are aired in the courts, James begins to feel freer to deal with sexual subjects in his work and with the London adulteries now opened up for public inspection. His tale "A London Life," written during this time, describes the hysteria of a puritanical American girl whose sister's adultery in her marriage with an Englishman will bring on a divorce.

These are the years of his sustained hours of work in his De Vere Gardens flat, a few doors away from his friendly neighbor Robert Browning. He would recall writing "by a wide west window that, high aloft, looked over near and far London sunsets, a half-grey, half-flushed expanse of London life." He remembered also the charm and intimacy of "the full projection, upon my very table, of the good fog-filtered Kensington mornings."

His letters reveal a deeper questioning of his role in the world of art. The sale of his books is declining, although he is still in many magazines. His correspondence with Macmillan about his royalties and his increasing dependence on his transatlantic friend William Dean Howells for advice show a certain anxiety about his future. He compensates for the decline of his earnings by strenuous overproduction. And in his novel, he returns to the questions he had tested in fiction years before: the artist's relation to an indifferent world, art and "public life," the creator who must make compromises to please a public little concerned with the act of creation. Behind his fictional masks we see him examining the meaning of his own considerable fame, his vocation, his literary role in British society. This will ultimately lead him to his experiments in the theatre.

Publishing conditions were in part responsible for James's dilemma. The use of illustration meant delay in the magazines while the sketchers did their work: and delay in payment. He also, at the beginning of the 1890s, has the unusual experience of having a short story rejected by the new editor of the *Atlantic*—the tale of "The Pupil," which posterity has judged among his finest. He absorbs the shock, but for the first time he consults a literary agent.

For the rest, his ever-widening correspondence testifies to his full participation in the life around him, his ability to feel and relate to private situations and to allow his mind to play over large areas of contemporary life. He attempts to bridge distance and mystery in imagining Stevenson in Polynesia; he is dogmatic in his criticisms of Bourget's failure to distinguish between sex and love. And as before, his letters of condolence are muted and exquisite prose elegies. The letters of these late middle years reflect the novelist's extraordinary energy, his humanity, and his professional problems. His goals are in full view; and he is, as always, very much the master of his personal situation.

To Grace Norton
Ms Harvard

34 De Vere Gardens W.
July 23*rd*, 1887

My dear Grace

I am ashamed to find myself back in England without having fulfilled the inward vow I took when I received your last good and generous letter—that of writing to you before my long stay on the continent was over. But I *almost* don't fail of that vow—inasmuch as I returned only day before yesterday. My eight months' escape into the happy immunities of foreign life is over and the stern realities of London surround me; in the shape of stuffy midsummer heat (that of this metropolis has a truly British ponderosity—it's as dull as an article in a Quarterly), smoke, circulars, invitations, *bills*, the one sauce that Talleyrand commemorated, and reverberations of the grotesque Jubilee. On the other hand my small home seems most pleasant and peculiar (in the sense of being my own), and my servants are as punctual as they are prim—which is saying much. But I enjoyed my absence, and I shall endeavour to repeat it every year, for the future, on a smaller scale: that is, to leave London, not at the beginning of the winter but at the end, by the mid-April, and take the period of the insufferable Season regularly in Italy. It was a great satisfaction to me to find that I am as fond of that dear country as I ever was—and that its infinite charm and interest are one of the things in life to be most relied upon. I was afraid that the dryness of age—which drains us of so many sentiments—had reduced my old *tendresse* to a mere memory. But no—it is really so much in my pocket, as it were, to feel that Italy is always there. It is rather rude, my dear Grace, to say all this to you—for whom it is there to so little purpose. But if I should observe this scruple about all the places that you don't go to, or are not in, when I write to you, my writing would go very much on one leg. I was back again in Venice—where I paid a second visit late in the season (from the middle of May to July 1st)—when I got your last letter. I was staying at the Palazzo Barbaro, with the Daniel Curtises—the happy owners, today, of that magnificent house—a place of which the full charm only sinks into your spirit as you go on living there, seeing it in all its hours and phases. I went for ten days, and, they clinging to me, I staid five weeks: the longest visit I ever paid a "private family." The Curtises are very private—and a most singular, original and entertaining couple. If I were lolling in one of your arm-chairs I could tell you more—but I can't describe them as I scribble here without the disloyalty of *incompleteness*—so it is better to reserve them for the great occasion of the future, whenever it may come, when I shall *talk* everything my pen hasn't been able to manage. They were most friendly and hospitable—but I don't *think* I shall stay with them again—if I can avoid it without rudeness. They can't keep their hands off their native land, which they loathe—and their perpetual digs at it fanned (if a dig can fan) my patriotism to a fever. In the interval between my two visits to Venice I took again some rooms at the Villa Brichieri at Bellosguardo—the one just below your old Ombrellino—where I had stayed for three December weeks on my arrival in Florence. The springtime there was enchanting, and you know what a thing that incomparable view is to live with. I really *did* live with it, and rejoiced in it every minute, holding it to be (to my sensibilities) positively the most beautiful and interesting in the world. Florence was given over to fêtes during most of those weeks—the fêtes of the completion of the façade of the Duomo—which by the way (the new façade) isn't "half bad." It is of a very splendiferous effect—there is doubtless too much of it. But it does great honour to the contemporary (as well as to the departed) Italian—and I don't believe such work could have been produced elsewhere than in that country of the delicate hand and the insinuating chisel. I stepped down into the fêtes from my hill top—and even put on a crimson *lucco* and a beautiful black velvet headgear and disported myself at the great *ballo storico* that was given at the Palazzo Vecchio to the King and Queen. This had the defect of its class—a profusion of magnificent costumes but a want of *entrain;* and the success of the whole episode was much more a certain really splendid procession of the old time, with all the Strozzis, Guicciardinis, Rucellais, etc., mounted on magnificent horses and wearing admirable dresses with the childlike gallantry and glee with which only Italians can wear them, riding through the brown old streets and followed by an immense train of citizens all in the carefullest quattro-cento garb. This was really a noble picture and testified to the latent love of splendour which is still in those dear people and which only asks for a favouring chance to shine out even at the cost of ruining them. Before leaving Italy I spent a week with Mrs. Kemble on Lago Maggiore—she having dipped over there, in spite of torrid heat. She is a very (or at least a partly) extinct volcano today, and very easy and delightful to dwell with, in her aged resignations and *adoucissements*. But she did suggest to me—on seeing her again after so long an interval, that it is rather a melancholy mistake, in this uncertain life of ours, to have founded oneself on so many rigidities and rules—so many siftings and sortings. Mrs. Kemble is *toute d'une pièce*, more than any one, probably, that ever lived; she moves in a mass, and if she does so little as to button her glove it is the whole of her "personality" that does it.—Let us be flexible, dear Grace; let us be flexible! and even if we don't reach the sun we shall at least have been up in a balloon.—I left Stresa on the 15th of this month, had a glorious day on the Simplon amid mountain streams and mountain flowers, and came quickly home. I found here a note from Eliot [Norton] and immediately sent to him to come and lunch with me—but as I have had no answer he evidently has left town. I depend on seeing him later. And I depend also on seeing Lily [Norton]—probably I shall spend a Sunday at Basset next month. To prepare myself, perfidiously, for that incident, let me echo your judgment of the mistress of "Ridgemount." She has indeed a plentiful inanimacy and a strange absence of predictable qualities. But she is very ill—and very nice! Verily also, I think, very "near."—Lowell is the only person I have seen since I came back—he very kindly knocked at my door the morning after my return. He continues to be the simplest person in London, as well as one of the cleverest—and seems well and "gay" (!!) and as much as ever of a diner-out. He has lapsed (most wisely) into more modest quarters than he has hitherto occupied in London, and is now separated by a comfortable interval from his ambassadorship. Mrs. Smalley watches over him tenderly and is a most useful and devoted friend; she is a woman of a very fine nature and a very gentle presence. I dined with him yesterday—and she was there—in red velvet—and not her husband. But it is all right and most excellent for both of them. Don't keep this page which looks (accidentally) like silly gossip—but is mere friendly history. I wrote a good many (short) things while I was abroad—but they are buried in the bosom of the *Century*, *Harper*,

Atlantic etc., who keep them, annoyingly, for what they suppose to be the mystic hour. *Pazienza* (that sounds conceited), and they will come. I am just beginning a novel about half as long (thank God!) as the *Princess*—and which will probably appear, at no very distant day, as a volume, without preliminary publication in a magazine. It will be called (próbably) *The Tragic Muse;* but don't tell of it. I haven't answered your letter in the least, as you see—in the sense of taking it up piece by piece and making appropriate remarks and responses. But you will know none the less that I have digested it all. If you get a chance to give the friendliest of possible messages from me to poor Frank Parkman, please do so. Tell him I hold him in the highest sympathy and honour.—I go tomorrow A.M. to spend a day with Alice at Leamington—not having seen her, to speak of, for a year. She was there all last summer, from May, and directly after she came to town, late in the autumn, I went abroad. I got her to occupy my rooms a part of the time that I was abroad, to keep my servants from suicide, but she departed a month ago. I shall be here for the rest of the summer—save for little blotches of absence —and I look forward to some quiet months of work. I am trying, not without success, to get out of society—as hard as some people try to get in. I want to be dropped and cut and consummately ignored. This only demands a little patience, and I hope eventually to elbow my way down to the bottom of the wave—to achieve an obscurity. This would sound fatuous if I didn't add that success is *easily* within my grasp. I know it all—all that one sees by "going out"—today, as if I had made it. But if I had, I would have made it better! I think of you on your porch—amid all your creepers and tendrils; and wherever you are, dear Grace, I am your very faithful and much remembering friend,

Henry James

To William James

Ms Harvard

34, De Vere Gardens W.
October 1*st* 1887

My dear Brother.

Your good and copious letter of September 20th, travelling swiftly, came in to me yesterday, and gave me great joy—our communications had so long been cut. I have written of late certain letters to Aunt Kate which I have always asked her to hand on to you (one only four days ago), but it's an age since I had any direct speech with you. I have an idea, however, that I wrote to you somewhile between the 25th July and the 1st August, just after my return from abroad. It was a great pleasure to me that your letter breathes a spirit of respectable well-being—though also alas, of "over-pressure" and tells of too many things perpetually to do. But that seems the universal law today, and if I feel it who have neither wife nor wean, I sometimes wonder that you don't faint by the wayside. But I suppose a wife simplifies as well as complicates—tell Alice I don't wish to seem to take too dark a view of *her!* I have always supposed that such a one (especially such a one as she) transacts for her husband some of the business of life and some of those relations with the world, that the lone bachelor has to transact for himself. My excellent but wooden-faced cook (who has exactly the same shy, frightened manner today that she had the first hour she was in my service) has just presented herself as usual (with a large, clean, white respectful apron) to ask for the "orders for the day." It is at these moments that I feel the want of assistance, especially as the lady in question is so reverent that she never presumes to suggest. On the other hand she and her spouse buy everything for me (I never have to go into a shop) and don't cheat me. They are on board-wages (i.e. have to provide their own food), and every bone that leaves my table comes back with a persistency that makes me say "Is your master a dog that you should treat him thus." But this is parenthetic. I take this morning to write to you because I am too much under the shadow of impending departure to concentrate on sterner work. My departure is only for the purpose of spending tomorrow (Sunday) and perhaps also Monday in the country. I am going down to the Frank Millets, who with the genial and gifted little Abbey form (there are usually two or three others, especially Sargent, but he has just gone to America to paint a portrait—I wrote about him, by the way, in the October *Harper*) a very friendly and entertaining small summer and autumn colony at the wonderfully picturesque old village of Broadway in Worcestershire.[1] Here they paint and walk and play lawn tennis and receive their friends, and the whole region is a delight to me—mainly on account of the interest of its magnificent monumental villages. I always get a couple of good walks while I am there—one of them usually over to Chipping Camden, which is a place of rapture especially when its wide long, wandering, grassy yet wonderfully architectural high-street is seen at the twilight hour. I have paid them a couple of days' visit for three years running, and I don't care to interrupt the tradition as it's American and fraternizing and does something to keep me "in touch," as they say here, with the land of my birth. Moreover, Millet is an excellent fellow who has ended by painting very well indeed (he didn't at all at first) as a consequence of mere hard Yankee "faculty"—and Abbey is a pure genius, with the biggest kind of Philadelphia twang and an inspired vision of all old time English aspects and figures. Apart from this I shouldn't care to go away again for many a week—it chaws up one's time so fatally. I have done a good deal of it since I returned—in brief but repeated dashes—which were more or less mistakes after a long absence from those friends with whom one keeps up some sort of visiting habits, and more or less irresistible from the influence of this splendid season. It has been the most glorious summer, not an hour that wasn't pleasant, and all the weather pure gold—one of the summers of one's childhood, as one remembers them, thinking they have left the world, come to life again. Even yet it doesn't break—all these last days have been magnificent. I went, the last of August, among other things, to spend three days with Lowell, at Whitby, on the Yorkshire coast, where he was spending a month. The place is delightful, and he is the same; wonderfully simple and genial, at the same time as "clever," and expressively kind to me. I get on with him well, though he belongs to a more primitive generation (essentially) and in spite of all his ambassadorial accretions, and the experience and fame that have come to him of late years, he is not a "man of the world." Du Maurier was also there, whom I like very much and who is a very charming and intelligent fellow and companion (one of the most so I know), into the bargain. We are excellent friends.[2] The other day I spent a week with the Roseberys (to make up for not having been near them for a year, thank heaven!) but Mentmore is always a peculiar experience, half pleasant and half insupportable, into which it would take too long to enter. Rosebery is a gifted being and has, in the opinion of all the world, a great future before him, and yet the conditions in which he has grown up and lives are such as to make it difficult for me to take him in some ways seriously—which no doubt is a proof of scoffing shallowness on my part. At any rate now that the autumn is closing in and one's fireside begins to glow I only long to settle down to work and gilded halls are a simple nuisance. They have been becoming so to me, more and more, for a long time past, and I begin to perceive, with delight, the fair fruit of a policy of letting them almost severely alone. I have tried for a good while now to get *out* of society, as hard as certain people are supposed to try to get into it: and I am happy to say I am perceptibly succeeding. I have very large accumulations (of "observation of the world" etc.) and I now simply want elbow-room for the exercise, as it were, of my art. I hope during the next ten years to do some things of a certain importance; if I don't, it won't be that I haven't tried hard or that I am wanting in an extreme ambition. I am able to work better, and more, than I have ever been in my life before; it isn't much, but it's enough, and at any rate it is so much more than has been the case in former years that I look back with wonder and pity to the wretchedly bad basis I have always been on. It makes me think rather well of myself to have done anything at all. Little by little I have grown less *sick*, especially as regards the relation of such sickness to the act of reading and writing.[3] Now I can do the essential—it's not too much to say that hitherto (I am particularly changed for the better within a year) I couldn't. I *ought* therefore to produce better stuff than ever before, especially as I have many more ideas and am not in the least tired of work—on the contrary. The damnation still is that I can't *read* a quarter as much as I should like. Indeed while my writing is going on I can read very little—the writing, unsubstantial as it may appear to some, so empties the measure of what I can do. So I can only read, to speak of, in *intervals*. But as I say, the whole case mends and may mend more. *Unberufen*, after all this swagger! I am glad you desire the sight of more of my prose, and very sorry that the mysterious ways of editors keep me apparently silent for so long. But I *am* productive, and in the course of this autumn shall have sent off the eighth or ninth fiction of about the length of "Daisy Miller" since I quitted England on the 1st December last.[4] These things will finally appear, I suppose, very much together, so that you will have a good deal of me at once. I haven't all this time said a word about Alice, but that is because I only the other day gave Aunt Kate a pretty full account of her, which you will receive. Her determination to remain at Leamington for the winter rests on all sorts of good reasons, and at any rate it is fixed. Her isolation there combined with her weakness seems rather pitiful but mainly to *us*—she doesn't think it so. She gave me, on Monday last, a very good account of herself, and her appearance bore it out. She misses Katharine but *elle en a pris son parti.* That she has been able to do it is a proof of strength. But of that sort of strength she has much. She is also very strong about [Irish] home-rule, and in various other ways. I miss her greatly here, as a communicant and talker. I *understand* her condition no better than I did two years ago; but I am more of the impression that eventually better years are in store for her. However, she lives from month to month—and in that sense I live with her. I should be very sorry to pretend to any views that she hasn't herself—her capacity for views is so large and excellent. Her patience is equally inexhaustible and admirable, and the coming months portend good to her much more than ill. I shall go to her, for a day at a time, with all possible frequency.—I mentioned Edith James in my recent letter to Aunt Kate, so as to let you know that I had given her (in one way or another—from three to four of them were for an ulster which I purchased and even fitted myself) £16—in order that you might feel easier as to donations. Poor girl, I didn't like her much, but I consoled her to the best of my ability when she mourned her father's removal as the loss of every good.[5]

October 5th. I had to stop the other day and keep over my letter. I paid my little visit at Broadway and came back yesterday. It shall be the last (I mean the last I shall pay there, tho' it was pleasant enough) as there is a limit, after all, to what one ought to do for people because they are Americans. I grudged the time so much that I didn't enjoy myself—but I won't add to the loss by talking about it. I'm afraid I must close my letter. Your plan is very interesting—the plan of your house in the country—and your existence there sounds very attractive from the loafing-out-of-doors point of view—an element of which my life is terribly destitute. It can't be got here save by "shooting"—and I don't shoot. Besides which if one shoots the loafing is the least part of it. Fishing costs £10 a bite. Switzerland is the only thing—and it is crammed with cockneys, and I never go there. But I mean to try and manage it next summer. I *did* spend one day there (on foot, on the Simplon) crossing from Italy the end of July, which was a rapture of wild flowers and mountain streams—but it was over in a flash. I am full of sorrow for the little girl's bad ear—but surely it will become a good one with time? And won't the other be all right? I just received a letter from Grace Norton, which I shall probably, though not certainly, answer this A.M. If I don't I'm afraid I shan't for a long time. Her letters breathe a kind of desolation—or rather a "thinness" of life, which I trust her sure existence doesn't so much express. This, however, is entirely unintentional on her part. Eliot (Norton) was here this summer and lunched with me twice. He struck me as the most portentous reproduction, in aspect, tone and manner, of his father (whom he however seemed to dislike very much) and as—moreover—appallingly aged. I have rarely been made to feel so much like a frivolous little boy. Other Americans I haven't seen: fewer this summer I think than ever before. Sometimes they have been too numerous—for what they were. I found Boott's card yesterday (on his way back from the U.S. where you perhaps saw him?) and I have written to him to return today. I saw him of course last winter frequently in Florence, and found him very shrunken and contracted, not that he was ever very capacious. But he is a mere pinch of his old smallness. In reading over the last two or three pages it strikes me that I will strike you as ill-natured. But I can't help it, and besides I don't think I am. At any rate it won't prevent me from saying that as to T. S. Perry, for instance (concerning whom you inquire), I have neither seen nor heard anything whatever of him, and don't want to.[6] He wrote me a most offensive and impertinent letter about a year ago—about what, I could scarcely make out, except that he disapproved of my living in London. It was too idiotic to notice and it was almost impertinent enough to return and it set the seal upon the conviction I have always privately had that he is a singularly poor creature. I had never failed, for years, for auld acquaintance sake, to pay him little occasional attentions—writing to him, sending him my books punctually, etc.—under the empire somehow of that superstition which he has to a certain extent managed to impose upon people in regard to his singularly helpless mediocrity—but it is really a relief to have nothing more to do with him. The letter, from him (it was but a short note), that I speak of, made me feel as if I had been "giving myself away" for thirty years, and as one has only one life—! I'm afraid you won't see Louis Stevenson, who is a most moribund but fascinating being, of whom I am very fond. If he were in health he would have too much "side," as they say here, but his existence hangs but by a thread and his almost squalid invalidism tones down the "*Erden* vein" in him, as well as any irritation that one may feel from it. He has a most gallant spirit and an exquisite literary talent; but don't read the verses to me in his new little volume of poems, as they happen, especially the first, to be the poorest things in the book. The second was occasioned by my giving his wife the little mirror he commemorates. Both were scribbled off at the moment—the first put on my plate one day I went to dine with him at Bournemouth—and I never dreamed that he had kept copies of them and would publish them.[7] Four or five other pieces in the thin volume are perfect and destined I think to live. He and Howells are the only English imaginative writers today whom I can look at. I hadn't seen the latter's "tribute" in the September *Harper*, but I have just looked it up. It gives me pleasure, but doesn't make me cease to deplore the figure that Howells makes every month in his critical department of *Harper*. He seems to me as little as possible of a critic and exposes himself so that I wish he would "quit," and content himself with writing the novel as he thinks it should be and not talking about it: he does the one so much better than the other. He talks from too small a point of view and his examples (barring the bore he makes of Tolstoi) are smaller still. There is, it seems to me, far too much talk around and about the novel in proportion to what is done. Any *genre* is good which has life—which of course is perfectly consistent with the fact that there are some that find it mighty hard to have it and others that one very much prefers to some. But I am sprawling into quires and reams. I hope indeed you may finish your *Psychology*[8] by the date you desire. It will be a tough morsel for me to chew, but I don't despair of nibbling it slowly up. What you tell me of poor Father's book would make me weep if it weren't somehow outside and beyond weeping. After that who shall be confident or believe that one's inner conviction is a voucher? I send no end of love to Alice and return (in another envelope) the queer, tragic Chicago letter. Ever your

Henry James

1. HJ's article on Sargent appeared in *Harper's New Monthly Magazine,* LXXV (October 1887), 683–691. HJ wrote an account of the Broadway group entitled "Our Artists in Europe," also published in *Harper's,* LXXIX (June 1889), 50–66. The two articles were reprinted in *Picture and Text* (1893).

2. HJ's recollections of his stay at Whitby were printed in his obituary article on George du Maurier in *Harper's,* XCV (September 1897), 594–609.

3. Compare HJ's reference here to his chronic invalidism (often quoted by critics) with his acknowledgment in his letter to his brother from Venice, 7 April 1887, that his attack of jaundice had been "the *longest* illness I have had since I was laid up with typhoid fever, so many years ago, at Boulogne." HJ was twelve when he had typhoid in 1857. In the light of this it is difficult to interpret what HJ meant by his "bad basis." We may speculate that this may have been his way of underestimating his capacity for vigorous literary action when he was writing to his elder brother.

4. HJ had written while in Italy, among other pieces, an article on Miss Woolson, his paper on London, his essay on Stevenson, and such tales as "Cousin Maria," "Louisa Pallant," "Two Countries," and "The Aspern Papers."

5. Edith James was the daughter of HJ's uncle Howard James, who had died two months earlier.

6. HJ had ceased writing to Perry, who had been his friend since their adolescent days in Newport in the 1850s. Their friendship was renewed in old age.

7. Stevenson's verses to HJ were published in *Underwoods* (1887) and are included in *Collected Poems,* ed. Janet Adam Smith (1971).

8. *Principles of Psychology* was not published until 1890.

To Robert Louis Stevenson
Ms Yale

34 De Vere Gardens W.
December 5*th* [1887]

My dear Louis.

I could almost hate poor Roderick H.[1] (in whom, at best, as in all my past and shuffled off emanations and efforts, my interest is of the slenderest), for making you write so much more about him than about a still more fascinating hero. If you had only given me a small instalment of that romantic serial, The Mundane Situation of R.L.S.! My dear fellow, you skip whole numbers at a time. Your correspondent wouldn't. I am really delighted you can find something at this late day in that work in which my diminutive muse first tried to elongate her little legs. It is a book of considerable good faith, but I think of limited skill. Besides, directly my productions are finished, or at least thrust out to earn their living, they seem to *me* dead. They dwindle when weaned—removed from the parental breast, and only flourish, a little, while imbibing the milk of my plastic care. None the less am I touched by your excellent and friendly words. Perhaps I am touched even more by those you dedicate to the less favoured *Portrait*.[2] My dear Louis, I don't think I follow you here—why does that work move you to such scorn—since you can put up with Roderick, or with any of the others? As they are, so it is, and as it is, so they are. Upon my word you are unfair to it—and I scratch my head bewildered. 'Tis surely a graceful, ingenious, elaborate work—with too many pages, but with (I think) an interesting subject, and a good deal of life and style. There! *All* my works may be damnable—but I don't perceive the particular damnability of that one. However I feel as if it were almost gross to defend myself—for even your censure pleases and your restrictions refresh. I have this very day received from Mr. Bain your *Memories and Portraits*, and I lick my chops in advance. It is very delectable, I can see, and it has the prettiest coat and face of any of your volumes.—London is settling to its winter pace, and the cool rich fogs curtain us in. I see Colvin once in a while *dans le monde*, which however I frequent less and less. My love to your wife and mother—I miss you too sensibly. My greeting to the brave Lloyd.[3]

Ever yours very faithfully,
H. James

P.S. I am unspeakably vexed at the *Century*'s long delay in printing my paper on you—it is quite sickening. But I am helpless—and they tell me it won't come out till *March*—d--n 'em all. I am also sorry—very—not to have any other prose specimens of my own genius to send you. I have really written a good deal lately—but the beastly periodicals hold them back: I can't make out why. But I trust the dance will begin before long, and that then you may glean some pleasure. I pray you, *do* write something yourself for one who *knows* and yet is famished: for there isn't a morsel here that will keep one alive. I won't question you—'twere vain—but I wish I knew more about you. I want to *see* you—where you live and *how*—and the complexion of your days. But I don't know even the name of your habitat nor the date of your letter: neither were on the page. I bless you all the same.

1. *Roderick Hudson* (1875).

2. Stevenson wrote to HJ in November or early December 1887: "I must break out with the news that I can't bear the *Portrait of a Lady*. I read it all, and I wept too; but I can't stand your having written it; and I beg you will write no more of the like. Infra, sir: Below you; I can't help it—it may be your favourite work, but in my eyes it's BELOW YOU to write and me to read." We may surmise that Stevenson did not appreciate HJ's art save in its ironic and satiric forms, as his poem on HJ's personages in *Underwoods* shows:

> . . . Lo, how these fair immaculate women walk
> Behind their jocund maker; and we see
> Slighted *De Mauves*, and that far different she,
> Gressie, the trivial sphynx; and to our feast
> Daisy and Barb and Chancellor (she not least!).

The stories alluded to are "Madame de Mauves," "Georgina's Reasons," "Daisy Miller," "Lady Barberina," and *The Bostonians*. It was the "jocund" HJ whom Stevenson appreciated rather than the serious meditative author of *The Portrait of a Lady*.

3. Lloyd Osbourne, Stevenson's stepson.

To Robert Louis Stevenson
Ms Yale

34 De Vere Gardens W.
December 18*th* [1887]

My dear Louis.

You are eminently accessible to any brilliant and accomplished young man, but I give this note of introduction to my young friend Owen Wister,[1] who answers closely to that description, just for the form and the lark. He will not be able to give you very late news of me, but I build hopes on his regaling me, after he has seen you, at your expense. I haven't the merit of sending him to you—he arrives on the wings of his own admiration—but I have that of giving him this push, with an eye to *détails intimes* about your health and circumstances, trifles which your adventurous muses (you have half a dozen—a shameless polygamy) refuse to a friend who cherishes the record of domestic manners. The bearer of this is the son and grandson of dear friends of mine, and combines the best parts of American and English descent. His mother's mother is my valued and distinguished neighbour Mrs. Fanny Kemble—his mother herself a beautiful and delightful lady, resident near Philadelphia, whom I hope you may some day know. But Owen Wister will speak for himself—and you ought to have no fault to find with that, for he intimates to me that such as he is you have had much to do with making him. *Vale et valeat!* Ever faithfully yours

Henry James

1. Owen Wister (1860–1938), grandson of Fanny Kemble and son of Sarah Butler Wister of Philadelphia, would gain fame as author of the archetypal "Western," *The Virginian* (1902), which helped to establish the cowboy as a mythic folk figure.

To William Dean Howells
Ms Harvard

34 De Vere Gardens W.
January 2*d* 1888

My dear Howells.

Your pretty read book (that is a misprint for *red* but it looks well, better than it deserves; and so I let it stand): the neat and attractive volume, with its coquettish inscription and its mystifying date, came in to me exactly as a New Year's gift. I was delighted to get it, for I had not perused it in the pages of *Harper,* for reasons that you will understand—knowing as you must how little the habit of writing in the serial form encourages one to read in that odious way, which so many simple folk, thank heaven, think the best. I was on the point of getting *April Hopes* to add to the brave array of its predecessors (mine by purchase, almost all of them), when your graceful act saved me the almost equally graceful sacrifice. I can make out why you are at Buffalo almost as little as I believe that you believe that I have "long forgotten" you. The intimation is worthy of the most tortuous feminine mind that you have represented—say this wondrous lady, with the daughter, in the very first pages of *April Hopes,* with whom I shall make immediate and marvelling acquaintance. Your literary prowess takes my breath away—you write so much and so well. I seem to myself a small brown snail crawling after a glossy antelope. Let me hope that you *enjoy* your work as much as you ought to—that the grind isn't greater than the inevitable (from the moment one really tries to *do* anything). Certainly one would never guess it, from your abounding page. How much I wish I could keep this lonely New Year by a long personal talk with you. I am troubled about many things, about many of which you could give me, I think (or rather I am sure), advice and direction. I have entered upon evil days—but this is for your most private ear. It sounds portentous, but it only means that I am still staggering a good deal under the mysterious and (to me) inexplicable injury wrought—apparently—upon my situation by my two last novels, the *Bostonians* and the *Princess*, from which I expected so much and derived so little. They have reduced the desire, and the demand, for my productions to zero —as I judge from the fact that though I have for a good while past been writing a number of good short things, I remain irremediably unpublished. Editors keep them back, for months and years, as if they were ashamed of them, and I am condemned apparently to eternal silence. You must be so widely versed in all the reasons of things (of this sort, today) in the U.S. that if I could discourse with you a while by the fireside I should endeavour to draw from you some secret to break the spell. However, I don't despair, for I think I am now really in better form for work than I have ever been in my life, and I propose yet to do many things. Very likely too some day all my buried prose will kick off its various tombstones at once.[1] Therefore don't betray me till I myself have given up. That won't be for a long time yet. If we could have that rich conversation I should speak to you too of your monthly polemics in *Harper* and tell you (I think I should go so far as that) of certain parts of the business in which I am less with you than in others. It seems to me that on occasions you mix things up that don't go together, sometimes make mistakes of proportion, and in general incline to insist more upon the restrictions and limitations, the *a priori* formulas and interdictions of our common art, than upon that priceless freedom which is to me *the* thing that makes it worth practising. But at this distance, my dear Howells, such things are too delicate and complicated—they won't stand so long a journey. Therefore I won't attempt them—but only say how much I am struck with your energy, ingenuity and courage and your delightful interest in the charming questions. I don't care how much you dispute about them if you will only remember that a grain of example is worth a ton of precept and that with the imbecility of babyish critics the serious writer need absolutely not concern himself. I am surprised sometimes, at the things you notice and seem to care about. One should move in a diviner air.—

Two or three nights ago Edmund Gosse came to share my solitude and my beefsteak, and we talked, *al volito,* of you. He has I think recovered from the immediate effects of his horrid imbroglio of a year and a half ago—out of which he came very well; but not from some of its remoter ones. Nor will he do this, I fear, so long as he continues to hold his Cambridge professorship.[2] I shall be glad when that is over, as I think he will then be in a much freer, sounder position. He is the only man of letters I ever see here—to speak of, or to speak to. I have many good friends here, but they are not in that class, which strikes me as mostly quite dense and puerile. I even confess that since the *Bostonians* I find myself holding the "critical world" at large in a singular contempt. I go so far as to think that the literary sense is a distinctly waning quality. I can speak of your wife and children only interrogatively—which will tell you little—and me, I fear, less. But let me at least be affirmative to the extent of wishing them all very affectionately, and to Mrs. H. in particular, the happiest New Year. Go on my dear Howells, and send me your books always, as I *think* I send you mine. Continue to write only as your admirable ability moves you, and believe me, ever affectionately yours

Henry James

1. Various critics have interpreted this statement as a prophecy of HJ's posthumous "revival." In reality, he is speaking here of the eight or nine essays and tales written during his Italian sojourn which the editors delayed in bringing out —some because the articles awaited illustration, others because they could not be scheduled earlier. In the ensuing months, these works did "kick off" their "various tombstones," so that Howells, reviewing some of them, spoke of "a massing of masterpieces."

2. HJ alludes here to Gosse's troubles with Churton Collins. See letter to Gosse, 26 October 1886.

To Edmund Gosse

Ms Leeds

34 De Vere Gardens W.
January 3*d* 1888

My dear Gosse.

I went yesterday to thank you for your excellent, friendly service, but found only your most amiable lady. I don't know why, indeed,

I should say "only," for I had so charming a chat with Mrs. Gosse that, after the first bitterness of disappointment, I was really quite consoled for your absence—especially as my fancy was led on to picture you at a bright convivial scene. I hope you have not returned from it in too cynical a mood to care for my very grateful sense of your quick, kind action in the matter of Mr. Watt.[1] It was immensely obliging of you to take the field with so little delay and I appreciate your benevolence. You are right in supposing that my talk with you the other night made me feel better. It quite set me up, as if I had received a cheque for £1000. I tremble on the verge of Mr. Watt—but shan't write to him till I can ask you, *viva voce,* two or three questions about him—as for instance whether I might interview him in a purely experimental or tentative manner without putting myself in his hands. I am beset with certain doubts and fears. I shall be delighted to come to you *any* evening next week that you may designate—I have very few engagements now. Let me beg Mrs. Gosse graciously to help you to choose one and believe me ever faithfully yours

Henry James

1. HJ's concern over delays in publication of his stories prompted him, on the advice of Howells, to seek a literary agent. He had hitherto handled his literary affairs himself. Gosse recommended the leading London agent, A. P. Watt, and HJ used him briefly before turning to J. B. Pinker.

To Grace Norton
Ms Harvard

34 De Vere Gardens W.
(This must have been begun on—
or about—Jan. 4*th*) [1888]

My dear Grace.

I had proposed to devote, today, the interval between breakfast and luncheon to writing to you; and now, behold, it wants already a quarter of an hour of the latter feast. The morning has been filled with attention to certain necessary, uncompromising letters which it has itself brought forth. But I can at least *begin,* and that will be a great point gained. As soon as I have swallowed my luncheon I must hurry off to keep a promise to Sir Frederick Leighton P.R.A.,[1] the urbane, the curly, the agreeably artificial, to the effect that I would join him at an afternoon performance of the Pantomime, at Drury Lane theatre, where he has taken a big box to entertain (it's his annual custom) certain children of whom I am also fond: the little granddaughters of Mrs. Sartoris, who was the love of his life (daughters of *her* daughter Mrs. Evans Gordon). Neither the mother, nor the grandmother, stand or stood, in that relation to *me;* and Leighton himself is not the person in England whom I most delight to consider: yet I shall desert you for him because I cannot, even after eleven years of London, tell a lie—how often it would be a blessing if I could!

10th. I broke off, my dear Grace, and not till this moment have I been able to go on. It is again within a measurable distance of lunch-time; and directly after that comes a fencing-master whom I have for an hour twice a week, to help me to combat not the possible enemies of the salon or the street, but a dreadful aggressor within myself: the symptoms of a portentous corpulence. It is a beautiful exercise: and I cultivate it in the teeth of Mrs. Kemble's classic and depressing dictum, that *with* that "hereditary tendency," "neither exercise, nor diet, nor *grief*" avails. I shall take grief in its order. Well, I went to my pantomime and enjoyed it—it was so highly and modernly artistic, a striking example of the elevation of taste that has been wrought in the British public in the last fifteen years. No such interesting and refined studies of colour, costume etc. would be possible today elsewhere in Europe. The box was full of rosy candid English children of whom I am very fond. I think they are the most completely satisfactory thing the country produces. The people are but the children magnified (not altered, not modified), and it is the children who are just of the right size. The elders strike one so often as too big for what they are. Leighton was genial and charming, and poor little Nelly Grant[2] was there (Mrs. Algernon Sartoris), with three very handsome but rather common youngsters. She is illiterate, lovely, painted, pathetic and separated from a drunken idiot of a husband. The Sartorises don't like her much, but they like her more, I suppose, than they do their disreputable "Algie." Whenever I see her there is something rather touching and tragic to me in this eminently chubby vision of the daughter of a man who in addition to being a great victorious warrior twice occupied what Hawthorne calls "the most august position in the world": in a strange land, quite without friends, ignorant, helpless, vulgar, untidy, unhappy, perfectly harmless and smeared over with fifteen colours. But I didn't mean to devote a page of this too brief epistle to her. Apropos of these people, you have, I think, asked me more than once for news of Mrs. Kemble—without, if I remember rightly, my finding the place to give it to you. I continue to see her about once every ten days: that is an immense intimacy for London, and a part of the habit and tradition of both of us. She is now of a robust eighty; and has lately been indulging in a recrudescence of literature—having produced within two or three months a tale, a comedy and being launched in what she herself calls a dull and disagreeable novel. The tale ("A Rose Lily"—and about Lenox etc.) appeared in the January *Temple Bar;* the comedy, a long farce founded on Daudet's *Tartarin sur les Alpes,* will not be acted; and Bentley will probably bring forth the novel if she finishes it. To write one's first novel at the age of eighty is a thing which could have happened only to a woman who has done everything, all her life, just exactly as others *don't.* Her peculiarities don't diminish as she grows older—but it is mainly the pleasant ones that have remained with her. Intensification and repetition are the laws of extreme old age—it's "siège est fait" and they dogmatise on dead premises. She has, of course, her share of all that, but if her perversities are old, so also is my affection for her. Her still older friend, Mrs. Procter (who hates her!) is declining, to the approach of ninety, and I am afraid dying. She is in her last illness. She has been as much of a "personality," in quantity, as Mrs. Kemble, but inferior I think in quality. She has taken her conventions ready-made, as Mrs. K. has made all hers.—One of the reasons I didn't get at my letter soon again was that four days ago I did the thing I most detest and yet that I don't succeed in shaking my skirts altogether clear of—though I am coming nearer to it: I paid a country visit of forty-eight hours. This led to my seeing (I was at Sir Trevor Lawrence's, a sweet little place near Dorking, with the perpendicular cliff of Boxhill rising straight out of its lawn, and, as everything is relative, looking quite Alpine), to my seeing again, I say, and possibly for the last time, a man of genius who always interests me—poor George Meredith,[3] the novelist, who, as a neighbour of the Lawrences, lives in a little green corner, all turf and old black yews, under the hill. He has a place quite apart here, grossly derided by the many and adored by the few. I don't adore him, but I scoff still less, for he is brilliantly intelligent and the wreck of a prodigious wit. He is much the wittiest Englishman, and the most framed for conversation, that I have ever known—for playing with intellectual fire. His main fault is that he thinks he is French, which he isn't. Today, he is alone, widowed, with a cold, comfortless hearthstone, and half consumed by an infirmity (he can scarcely walk straight) which he won't recognize. He has a little pretty, spoiled daughter who flirts up to London and neglects him. He, too, is sinking to his end—it is astonishing how one's wayside is strewn with *ends* after one has reached middle life! A very charming and clever man, a great friend of Meredith's, J. Cotter Morison,[4] is dying, I hear, and I go tomorrow to take leave of him. Though I have never seen much of him I have always liked him and feel much touched at his sending me a message to come. He has been a noted positivist in his day and written a very good life of St. Bernard.

February 5th! I take up my letter, my dear Grace, after a month, or almost, of interruption. Many occupations have come and gone—but the right moment for going on has not turned up till this grey, still, pleasant Sunday morning, full of mild English moisture, rainless but not dry, the kind of weather I am fondest of and of which we of course have plenty here. This winter is quite composed of it—a blessed absence of hard cold. The weather, in fact, is the softest thing in London. I scarcely know what I set out to tell you when I began my letter, just after the new year. I go to lunch an hour or two hence with Lady Playfair—it being my usual Sunday practise to lunch out. It is a pleasant London custom, and the only case here in which you may do anything intimate and informal, that in certain houses there are always, on Sunday, places at luncheon, for people to drop in—to offer themselves. There are four or five that I take, in this way in succession. Very often I lunch with Mrs. Pakenham—if you know who I mean; who used to be American, a hundred years ago, and flourish at Lenox (as "Miss Lizzie Clark," I think), and now is the wife of an amiable retired old General, with two sons in the Guards (one of whom is aide-de-camp to Lord Lansdowne, in Canada), great accumulations of "smartness" and a pretty friendly house, just out of Park Lane. She is full of tact and we have many common friends, but I don't know why I like her—and perhaps I don't, to distraction. Lady Playfair I don't see very often. She is a very natural and uncorrupted little American, who likes her life here greatly, and would like it still better, I imagine, if she had a little more health and a good deal more money—and also if poor little redfaced, but clever and canny, Sir Lyon, were not in the cold, officeless shade of opposition. *The* happy American here, beyond all others, is Mrs. Henry White, the wife of the First Secretary of the American legation—who is very handsome, young, rich, splendid, admired and successful, to a degree which leaves all competitors behind. A lady said to me the other day (a certain queer Lady Lothian), "She is very high up, isn't she?" "Very high up?" "I mean tremendously well-read; all the new books and that sort of thing." She has never read a book in her life; but she is "high up" all the same. So are the Phelpses, the minister and his wife, who are extremely popular: he a wrinkled old Democratic politician, but very capable, very well-dressed and well-mannered, and also humourous, making speeches without any of Lowell's *quality,* but which are thought by this perceptive public almost as good as Lowell's: and she a remarkably nice and graceful little woman of the pure American tradition—New Haven, Conn., and Burlington, Vt., who has been very pretty and still has a charming appearance, "receives" perfectly, and is thought delightful here. "Now there *is* a lady, if you like," old Lady Shrewsbury said to me of her, as I sat next her at dinner a while ago: a speech full of impertinence, as we had just been talking of American women in general, whom she evidently dislikes—poor painted and pencilled dowager. (Don't think I am imitating Major Pendennis, with my quotations from fine ladies: I am doing it, my dear Grace, cold-bloodedly, to amuse you!)—I see I spoke to you above of Cotter Morison whom I have been to see a number of times since then, and who is slowly and painfully, quite harrowingly, dying: he wants so to live—is so full of the love of the world and work and talk and curiosity. He is so weak now that I doubt whether I shall see him again—though I may speak of him once or twice more, before the end, with his two strangely insensible and inexpressive daughters, who illustrate the curious and striking laxity of the family tie in the country by having stodgy tea parties, at such a moment, in the melancholy house. Poor old Mrs. Procter is passing away inch by inch, in the deepest disapproval of her fate; and her only remaining daughter—an extraordinarily disagreeable person (save one, an idiot, who is a nun; they are all Catholics), hasn't even *seen* her, and won't! (Don't betray, for heaven's sake, *any* of these reckless confidences!)—I still can't remember what I started to tell you, originally. It wasn't that a remarkably intelligent and pleasant little Frenchman, Jusserand,[5] the *conseiller* of the French Embassy and author of three or four excellent studies of early English literature, has dined with me, and that I had Du Maurier and Claude Phillips[6] to meet him—for that was only two days ago. I have an idea that I meant to say something about a queerly, uncomfortable yet entertaining visit (of but two days, my limit), which I paid at Christmas to a wonderful old moated house, six miles from Sevenoaks, in Kent, Ightham Mote by name, which is celebrated far and wide for its picturesqueness and actually tenanted by some Colorado Americans, one General Palmer, a Mexican-railway-man, and his wife and children. I didn't know them much, but they nevertheless "secured" me, and the episode was the drollest amalgam of American and Western characteristics (there were also several English people there), in the rarest old English setting—which would have been rarer still, however, if the house, owned by an ancient race (the Selby-Biggs) which is so impoverished that they haven't a penny to spend on chair legs or window fastenings, were not in a state of almost perilous decrepitude. Its swift blue moat flows around it, its central court is an untouched piece of the fourteenth century, and its old garden and "pleasaunce" must be altogether adorable in summer. I slept in a room with a ghost and an oubliette; but fortunately the former remained in the latter. The good General Palmer arrived from Mexico, with the mud of his railway-making still on his boots, only two days before, to find his spontaneous, loquacious and really charming wife, installed in a moated grange and giving a Christmas feast to seventy rustics, tenants of the Selby-Biggs's, to whom she was under no obligation beyond what was suggested by her native and, I should suppose, characteristically Coloradoish, generosity. The landlords have so long been poor and parsimonious, that they (the lean tenants) hadn't, for generations, assisted *à pareille fête*, and the episode was very entertaining and successful. Seventy people were accommodated in the great high-roofed dining hall, and with our backs to the Yule log, we carved dozens of roast beefs, turkeys and plum puddings. There was a band in the court, a Christmas tree afterwards, and a dance, in costume, by the children of the house, and those of the guests (I mean of course those staying ones, who had brought their infants), and tea and speeches in the housekeeper's room. The affair was organized, perfectly, by the village inn-keeper, in that competent, immediate way in which you can get everything of that kind done in England—but the lady's butler was an Italian boatman from the Lake of Como and her major-domo a helpless German-American governess from the Rocky Mountains. It was all a curious little example of modern cosmopolitanism; but the bewildering heterogeneousness and incoherency of such *rapprochements* weary my conservative sense.

The winter wanes, and there will be, I think, no going-abroad for me this year. I lack not only the funds but also the keen desire—though I hate London in May, June and July as much as I like it at other times. Perhaps I shall be able to escape for the second and third of those three months; but meanwhile one's own little sitting room, and window and table and fireside are after all the safest (and cheapest) refuge, even in this bristling Babylon, for one who wishes to possess his soul and do his stint. Alice is spending the winter at Leamington, which she likes, and I pass several hours with her every month. She won't consent to more, having an almost morbid horror of taking my time. I am working well—you will see, little by little. But *don't* read anything of mine that you may perceive in periodicals till they come out, collected and revised, as books. I shall probably publish three or four volumes (I have put forth none for a long time) in the course of the coming year. Anything I should like you to read in a magazine I will send you.—I won't attempt to speak to you of "public affairs"—they are at once too stupid and too horrible. The violence of party division and party hatred is beyond any point it has ever reached before and it is beginning to ravage society in the manner in which it has long done so in France. People don't speak—don't see each other. The Home Rulers, socially, and judging by London, are nowhere. This doesn't alter my conviction that the gain of their cause is a certainty of the future. Otherwise—history is stupid, no doubt, but not so stupid as that. Meanwhile the flounderings, the phases, the embarrassments and transformations, the general ferment and fizzle, on the frying-pan of Clio (isn't she the right muse?) of this big, clumsy, fat and rich English race are full of entertainment to yours my dear Grace, ever affectionately

Henry James

1. P.R.A.—President of the Royal Academy.

2. See letter to John Hay, 24 December 1886.

3. HJ had known George Meredith since the late 1870s. See *Letters* II, 199.

4. J. Cotter Morison, whom HJ had met at the same time as Meredith. See *Letters* II, 199.

5. Jules Jusserand (1855–1932), diplomat and literary historian, would become a friend of HJ's. After the turn of the century (1902–1925) Jusserand served as French Ambassador to Washington.

6. Claude Phillips (1846–1924), son of a Court jeweller, was a writer on the arts and ultimately Keeper (1900–1911) of the Wallace Collection.

To Joseph Pennell
Ms Congress

34 De Vere Gardens W.
Jan. 6 [1888]

Dear Mr. Pennell.[1]

I am much obliged to you for your inquiry—for your interest in my article; though rather appalled that the *Century,* to whom I made it over just a year ago, is now only putting it into hand. I am afraid that at this rate it will be a long business.—As for the illustrations I have really nothing to suggest save that you follow your own fancy. If you too are fond of London let that fondness be your guide and you will fall in sufficiently with my text. The article from being so general is difficult to illustrate—and the thing, I should say, ought to be freely and fancifully done; *not* with neat, definite, photographic "views." Into that, however, you are not in danger of falling. Street vistas, characteristic corners (that of Hyde Park, say), something in the City, or on the way to it (say that church at the end of the Strand, where the road forks), etc. I should put in a plea for some view of (or in) the Green Park—with the dim and ugly pinnacles of Buckingham Palace. I lived close to it for nine years and was always crossing it. But do your own London, and it will be sufficiently mine.

Very truly yours
Henry James

1. Joseph Pennell (1857–1926), American illustrator, etcher, and lithographer, had been asked to provide illustrations for HJ's essay "London," written during his stay in Italy.

To Edmund Gosse
Ms Leeds

34 De Vere Gardens W.
Jan. 9*th* [1888]

My dear Gosse.

Alas, alas, I mourn for Morison—and am exceedingly touched by his caring to see me at such a time. Of course I will go with eagerness. It so happens that Thursday will be a good deal better day for me than Wednesday: I have promised on Wednesday to take Mrs. Kemble to the afternoon performance of a d---d, or rather damnable, play. On Thursday at four I shall be very, very glad to see the poor fellow. Will you kindly say so to him and thank him for the chance? Ever yours

Henry James

To Edmund Gosse
Ms Leeds

34 De Vere Gardens W.
January 19*th* [1888]

My dear Gosse.

I ought yesterday to have answered your good note about Morison—that is, to have thanked you for it. But when half my morning had gone in note writing I had to turn to mercenary composition—and I treated you as familiarily postponable. I went to see the *pauvre malade* on Tuesday—and found him visibly brighter and even seemingly stronger—moving about, making little exertions etc. It is only a vain lure, of course, but one feels as if it were a little gain—a little respite in the conscious process of dying. I shall probably go to him again tomorrow. I found Jusserand with him—and he talked to us both vigorously for three-quarters of an hour, and to me (as he had done to Jusserand before I came) for twenty minutes afterwards. I liked very much the bright little spark of France: just big enough to glow. What opposite poles they represent: the Frenchman three feet long, vivified and vitalized to his finger-tips, and the large Englishman, with a surface like a domain, whose central fire doesn't reach to it or to his extremities, his expressive parts. The Gaul is like one of those squeezed flowers that emit their odour. Excuse these flights of fancy—you will think I take you for a magazine. I have good hope of being able to come in about *five*, on Sunday. Ever yours

H. James

To Paul Bourget
Ms Private

le 23 février 1888
De Vere Gardens

Mon cher ami,

J'aurais répondu plus tôt à votre lettre de Milan, si éloquente et si subtile, si je m'étais senti de force à lutter avec vous sur les grandes questions qu'elle soulève. C'est aussi la faute à la vie forcément écrivassière que je mène ici, qui me condamne à tenir la plume toute la matinée mais me défend en même temps presque toute correspondance désintéressée. Sans cela je vous aurais déjà dit à quel point je trouve admirable et de premier ordre votre manière de *sentir* à propos des observations—restrictions que je me suis permises au sujet de *Mensonges.*[1] Votre façon d'accueillir ma rudesse vous fait le plus grand honneur et à moi presque honte. Elle a l'effet de me faire regretter encore davantage qu'une intelligence comme la vôtre ait cru devoir sacrifier à ce point à de fausses idoles! Car je les trouve toujours fausses, mon cher ami, en dépit de vos arguments et de votre générosité—je les trouve vains et erronés, le point de vue, le ton, le fond et la forme de *Mensonges.* Vos personnages, à mon sens, manquent tellement d'*importance* que je reste tout ébahi de vous voir apporter à leurs particularités ce raffinement d'attention. Ceci est surtout vrai pour Mme Moraines que vous grossissez (et dont vous grossissez les petites habitudes physiques et de toilette) de la manière la plus étrange, comme *illustration* (dans le sens anglais) de la vie. Cela touche à une véritable mystification au moment où vous passez de son côté, pour ainsi dire (sans avoir l'air de vous rendre compte) et où vous vous mettez à détailler les événements de son point de vue à elle, et en parlant comme avec *sa* conscience, en faisant le menu de ses raisonnements, de *ses* craintes, de ses angoisses et de ses espoirs. Nous n'en avons que faire et nous n'y croyons pas! Une Mme Moraines *subjective* devient une plaisanterie déplaisante; elle n'est subjective que parce que vous le voulez bien et vous le voulez, hélas, parce que —étant donné la vaste variété de la vie—vous lui consacrez, à elle et à son *underclothing*, une attention toute spéciale et toute malsaine—sans parler d'un talent d'interprétation, d'une puissance d'imagination sympathique, digne, comme nous disons, d'une meilleure cause. Quel "dedans" moral peut avoir une créature comme celle-là? Ça fait pitié de vous voir travailler à lui en bâtir un—comme s'il n'y avait que cela au monde. La vie se reflète si pauvrement dans une pareille nature que le lecteur se trouve tout outragé et tout trompé de la promenade que vous l'invitez d'y faire sous prétexte de psychologie de la souffrance! Croyez-moi, mon cher ami, laissez tout cela, c'est trop malpropre. Et vos jeunes écrivains, je ne peux pas les regarder comme plus substantiels. Ce garçon qui se rue en colère sur sa maîtresse et qui fait une maladie presque mortelle pour l'avoir supposée un ange de pureté—une femme sur le compte de laquelle toute sa donnée était qu'elle trompait son mari avec tous les signes de la facilité et qu'elle venait coucher avec lui en plein jour, porte à porte avec sa sœur, avant même qu'il ne l'y eût invitée! Il se peut que je n'entre pas entièrement dans vos intentions à l'égard de Vincy, car je dois vous dire, et vous avez dû vous en apercevoir, du reste, qu'il nous est profondément antipathique, cette figure si fréquente dans le roman français, du jeune homme sensible et distingué qui débute dans l'adultère, et que nous n'avons à son égard, nous autres Anglo-Saxons, presque pas d'autre sentiment que le désir de lui lancer un coup de pied dans le derrière. Il nous déplaît surtout lorsqu'il est poète ou qu'il nous est présenté comme d'essence supérieure, et je vous avoue que sa présence m'a bien gâté ma jouissance de vos autres [personnages].

Vous me dites que Paris est plein de Suzanne, de Desforges, de René et de Vincy; ce qui équivaut à dire que la vie est pleine de misères et de saletés. Ce n'est pas une raison pour nous nous en farcir la conscience. Plus elle est remplie d'autres choses, moins il y a de place pour celles autres [*sic*]. Vous me direz encore que cette épithète de "saleté" est un *begging of the question* et que cette saleté-là caractérise essentiellement la vie. Si l'amour est surtout une saleté, oui; mais il me semble que c'est trop prendre sur soi, dans le cas de chacun, que de l'affirmer, et surtout que de ne dépeindre la chose que par ses petits côtés. (J'appelle petits côtés le côté des détails précis qui ne regardent que ceux qui les pratiquent, tel que le nombre des étreintes, leur qualité, l'endroit où ça se passe, la manière dont ça se fait, et mille autres particularités plus intensément personnelles et moins *produisibles* au jour que tout autre chose au monde.) Qu'en savons-nous du reste et comment peut-on parler, dans toute cette matière, pour un autre que pour soi? C'est pourquoi il faut mieux en parler le moins possible puisqu'il y a de la fatuité, un manque de goût et de modestie, à en parler pour soi. Les procédés de l'amour me paraissent constituer une partie toute spéciale de notre être dont le caractère essentiel est de se prêter à *l'action,* et non pas à la réflexion. Cet élément de l'action est l'affaire de chacun mais aussitôt que la réflexion s'en mêle—aussitôt que l'on commence à patauger intellectuellement là-dedans, comme romancier, comme peintre, la chose devient malsaine et déplaisante. Voilà pourquoi il faut infiniment de tact et de goût pour ne pas y patauger—c'est une question d'application, question toute pratique. Je ne vous surprendrais pas en vous disant que vous me faites l'effet d'y avoir manqué à chaque page, à ce tact et à ce goût! Comment ça peut-il nous regarder, les détails des agaceries que Desforges, ou René et sa maîtresse [*sic*], se faisaient lorsqu'ils se couchaient ensemble et le plus ou moins de chemises ou de corsets qu'ils portaient? Jamais il ne me viendrait à l'esprit de vouloir savoir ce qui se passe dans leur chambre, dans leur lit, entre un monsieur et une femme; et je ne vois vraiment pas quel changement (surtout dans le sens de la publicité) le fait que ces personnes ne soient pas mariés fait à l'affaire.

Je sais que vous êtes à Paris, ayant appris par une excellente dame da ma connaissance ici que son beau-frère, Lord Lytton, avait causé avec vous et que vous lui aviez beaucoup plu. J'espère donc que les distractions de la capitale vous rendront insensible à ma dureté presque féminine. Je vois ici quelquefois Jusserand et je l'aime particulièrement. Il me fait espérer votre livre sur Balzac—c'est là que je voudrais vous retrouver. Urbain Mengin[2] m'écrit de douces et presque plaintives lettres (comme il écrit gentiment!), d'où je déduis qu'il ne mord pas à l'anglais. Je crois qu'il vous lit trop—ce n'est pas la manière d'apprendre la langue de votre féroce mais fidèle ami,

Henry James

1. Bourget's newest novel.

2. Urbain Mengin (1865–1955), befriended by Bourget when a young student seeking to learn English. When Mengin went to London as tutor to the future Duke of Sutherland, Bourget gave him a letter of introduction to HJ. In later life Mengin became an authority on the English romantics in Italy.

To Thomas Bailey Aldrich

Ms Harvard

34 De Vere Gardens W.
March 3*d* 1888

My dear Aldrich.

I succumb to your arguments and will undertake to manage a serial for the full twelvemonth of 1889. It shall be seventeen or eighteen pages—with the option of rising, *au besoin*, to twenty—and shall be paid for at the same rate as the *Princess*—i.e. $15 per page. And you shall have the opening chapters—numbers—by October.

1st.—To compass this end (I mean the end of giving you a longer rather than a shorter serial)—I shall probably run two stories (i.e. two subjects I have had in my head) together, interweaving their threads. But equally probably the thing will bear the name I gave you: "The Tragic Muse." She is an actress. But there will be much other richness, and the scene will be in London, like the *Princess*—though in a very different *monde;* considerably the "Aesthetic." There you are. It won't be improper; strange to say, considering the elements.

Yes, I have always thought Sargent a great painter. He would be greater still if he had one or two little things he hasn't—but he will do. Ever yours

Henry James

To Lady Constance Leslie[1]

Ts Lubbock

34 De Vere Gardens W.
March 10*th* [1888]

Dear Lady Constance.

I helped to consign our very remarkable old friend[2] to her last resting-place yesterday morning. It was fortunately mild and moist (yet without rain) and the whole long pilgrimage to Kensal Green was less lugubrious and dreary than I have sometimes seen it. I went in a carriage with Browning and there were a great many people there—almost all her old friends. It would have pleased her to know that she had a large following and that she passed away like a person of importance. She was buried in the Protestant Cemetery, but at a remote edge of it—where it touches the Catholic—to be near her daughter Edith. This settled the question of her faith—so far as she had any—for I had always vaguely supposed that she had quietly embraced the Catholic. But a person who knew told me that she had said almost on her deathbed that the adoration of the Virgin was, for her, an insurmountable stumbling-block and she had not that exalted idea of her sex! She was much harassed, I fear, by her infirmities and the nature of her malady, till within half an hour of the end, that is she struggled and suffered. It was a difficult physical extinction. Morally I am sure she had accepted it from the moment she saw it was really inevitable—but not before. Then when the end was definitely in view, she found out she really *was* weary (though she hadn't admitted it even to herself) and that the idea of rest was good to her. I saw her about three weeks before she died; she was very pathetic—it was such an image of defeat—almost of humiliation. I shall miss her greatly, for I saw her often and she was always fresh. I saw her often sad and bitter—but never dull, never common or commonplace. And then she was so historical. She was a kind of window in the past[3]—now it's closed there is so much less air.

I hope Ireland is sympathetic just now; London is wet and blowy, but there is a look of spring in the light and even a feeling of it in the March wind. But bring the reality with you when you come.

Believe me, dear Lady Leslie, ever faithfully yours

Henry James

1. Lady Constance Leslie, daughter of a Waterloo veteran and Minnie Seymour, the adopted daughter of Mrs. Fitzherbert (the wife of George IV) was a familiar figure in late nineteenth-century social and literary circles and had known Dickens and Thackeray.

2. Anne Benson Procter, widow of Bryan Waller Procter (Barry Cornwall) had died at an advanced age. See *Letters* II, 417–418.

3. Mrs. Procter had known all the great poets of England from Shelley to Browning.

To Laura Wagnière
Ms Unknown

[34 De Vere Gardens W.]
March 10*th* 1888

Dear Madame Wagnière.[1]

I don't think I know! Your curiosity is communicative and it makes me wish immensely I did.

But that isn't part of the story[2]—what Mrs. Pallant said to the young man. It was something pretty bad of course to make him give up, but the particular thing is a secondary affair whether it were true or whether it were false. The primary affair is that she told him something, no matter what—which *did* make him give up. The primary affair is also the nature and the behaviour of the lovely and inscrutable Linda. She thought Linda a monster of secret worldliness and in a fit of exaltation and penitence over her own former shabby conduct, wished to do something heroic and sacrificial to repair her reputation with her old lover. Therefore she abused the girl affectionately to his amorous nephew, but I have no light on what she said. She may have told him that she had been not as young ladies should be, but if she did I incline to think the statement was false. Linda was too careful of her future to have sacrificed to that extent to the present, and too little likely to have got into a mess that didn't pay—of course as you suggest (so sagaciously) it *might* have paid, and they were hard up etc.—But it wouldn't have paid in comparison with keeping straight and marrying—with patience—a lord or a millionaire. Yet I admit they were very hard up and that the thing *was* possible.

If it *had* happened, however, I think Mrs. P. would not, even in her exaltation, have mentioned it: whereas she might have done so if it were false. Do you understand? You see, I have in the story told you all I can for the money. I am as ignorant as you, and yet not as supposing!

It was charming to hear from you. I wish it were sight as well as sound. I shall pray for that and am ever faithfully yours

Henry James

I shall myself thank your mother for her delightful and generous letter.

1. Mme Wagnière, nèe Laura Huntington of Boston, a niece of Horatio Greenough, had married a Swiss-Italian banker "with affable manners and a talent for the violin" (HJ to Lizzie Boott, 24 July 1874).

2. James's "Louisa Pallant," which Mme Wagnière had just read and in which the mother of the young girl is so horrified by her daughter's calculating coldness that she warns a suitor against her. James, however, did not relate what the woman had said about her daughter; in his characteristic way he avoided "vain specifications."

To Frederick Macmillan

Ms British Library

34 De Vere Gardens W.
March 21*st* [1888]

Dear Macmillan.

I am just sending back the last proofs of my volume to Clark.[1] Therefore don't you think the enclosed title-page would perhaps do? I have thought of twenty things (Portraits Reduced, Figures Reduced, Faces and Figures, Smaller than Life, Essays in Portraiture, Likenesses, Appreciations etc. etc.—somehow they all sound—don't they?—like advertisements or *signs*); and this seems on the whole, the least objectionable.[2] It preserves the idea of the portrait, which is necessary, and conveys in a graceful and not obtrusive double meaning, both that the picture is *not* down to the feet, as it were, and that the appreciation is favourable—which in every case it happens to be. If however you should take a wild fancy to "Smaller than Life," I would give place to it. I think this improbable. If the title satisfies you will you please cause the note to Edinburgh to be posted. The sooner the book comes out the better, for I have an ardent wish that at as early a subsequent period as possible certain accumulated tales, which are panting to see the light in volumes, should be collected together. There will be by that time eight or nine of them—some of them rather long—and they will all have come out in periodicals by the time the last

Reverberator (July 1st) is published in *Macmillan*. Therefore one might be getting them ready. Yours ever

Henry James

P.S. I have left out six or seven of the original papers—and still the volume makes 408 pages!

1. R. & R. Clark, Edinburgh, the printers.
2. The title *Partial Portraits*.

To Theodore E. Child

Ms Barrett

34 De Vere Gardens W.
March 23*d* [1888]

My dear Child.

I thank you kindly for the two photographs which arrived very safely, beautifully "done up" this A.M. It is very good of you to have remembered the desire I had expressed for them. The mortuary sketch is gruesome and painful (to my sense), but the portrait is fine and interesting. It is, I think, quite admirable, and brings back the dear man to me and all that he had of most pleasing.[1] It is strong and charming painting. How strangely it is in the power of a good portrait to *revive*, recreate what is buried and finished. I shall hang the photograph in some familiar corner. I rub along with no great news. And I think of Paris without finding myself materially nearer to it. And indeed Paris has been here more or less—in the person of the Anglomane Dr. Henry Cazalis[2] (*le connaissez-vous?*) who has been more than once to see me, and that of the diplomatic (and delightful) Jusserand, who is a fixture—and not an Anglomane. And then Coquelin,[3] who can hardly be an Anglomane either, with the small houses that attend upon his seven weeks' season. I wish you would come over again and throw more light on the Parisian situation for me—though the effect of your impressions of London as contrasted with Paris, when you were here in the autumn, was to plunge me into deep gloom . . .[4]

The American picture-books pay far better—but they are such a damnable unliterary medium. I sympathise in your groanings over that terrible old Philistine of an Alden,[5] who has the literary and artistic ideal of Buffalo, N.Y., or Harrisburg, Pa. It must be dreary to work with him, or for him. Harris[6] has obtained from Bourget a dialogue on Science and Poetry, in thirty pages, which is to appear (I believe) in *French*, in the April *Fortnightly!*—an odd kind of *coup*. But I doubt whether *ces messieurs* will get £50 for their contributions. There will also be a great to-do here if they begin to invade the English periodicals—while the seedy Anglo Saxon crouches at the door. It is indeed not quite fair. Sargent has sent from America two big female portraits to the academy, admirable, almost incomparable (to my sense), for talent and life. One of them is a really noble picture of Mrs. Marquand. I find Maurice Barrès[7] *sick* with affection hiding real poverty, and I can't read his dreary little book. *Je connais le jeune homme*—he used to come and see me last winter in Florence. I have twenty letters to write, and am ever nostalgically yours,

H. James

1. This may have been the small portrait of Flaubert which HJ had in his study both in De Vere Gardens and later in Lamb House.

2. Dr. Henri Cazalis (1840–1909), a literary medical doctor, who was a minor Parnassian poet and a friend of Mallarmé. He adopted the pen name Jean Lahor.

3. Constant-Benoît Coquelin (1841–1909), a French actor, created the part of Cyrano de Bergerac in Rostrand's play. He was at this time touring with the Comédie-Française and had a season in London before going to the United States. HJ remembered him as a schoolmate from his days as a student in the *lycée* at Boulogne-sur-Mer in the 1850s.

4. The letter breaks off here, and the ensuing portion may be part of another letter.

5. Henry Mills Alden (1836–1919), associated at this time with *Harper's Magazine*.

6. Frank Harris (1856–1931), editor of the *Fortnightly Review*.

7. HJ did not revise his opinion of Barrès. The book alluded to consisted of imaginary conversations with Renan. In his diaries, Barrès says HJ described him as "*intelligent à faire peur.*" See Barrès, *Mes Cahiers* (1963), 17.

To Theodore E. Child
Ms Barrett

34 De Vere Gardens W.
March 27*th* [1888]

My dear Child.

Your charming letter deserves a quick response. We are both, apparently, gloomy, but the difference between your gloom and mine is that yours is relieved by the acquisition of charming works of art ("Kuehls" etc.—who is Kuehl?—excuse my British ignorance!) and that mine is quite unrelieved by anything. Perhaps if I could get Kuehls (or get cool) it would do me good; but I can't. Many thanks for your interesting little Parisian items—I wish I could *vous rendre la pareille.* I know Frank Harris not at all—to speak of. He is a queer brutal young adventurer who was once an hotel-waiter (*dit-on!*) in America and has lately married a very rich young woman, has a house in Park Lane, is spending the winter in Rome etc. The virtual and working editor of the *Fortnightly* is the Rev. John Verschoyle (19 Fitzroy Street W.) an odd but energetic young Irish parson (the ways of this country are droll), who pitchforks the magazine together *tant bien que mal* and without dangling before the eyes of the contributor *any* golden guerdon, to speak of. (Chapman and Hall are of a notorious stinginess.) I shall be very glad indeed to recall you to him as a former contributor and will do so, and abound in your praise, on the first opportunity. The pay for an article is pitiful as an equivalent of labour. I wrote a long *Maupassant* for the March number and received but £23 for it. I think they have only one price—and I have no art whatever of haggling for terms. It's beyond me—and I can't do it. So I am to do him a Pierre Loti for May, and then a Goncourt and a Flaubert (on the finish of F's correspondence), and a Daudet's Later Novels etc.[1] I sacrifice these things, because I want to do them and they appear in a conspicuous and legible form. I am afraid I can't call your attention to any literary or artistic news that will re-surround the British capital with a halo. There is to be a great New Gallery—a schism from the Grosvenor which I believe will be really a charming place. *Mais que diable* y *mettra-t-on?* Is there yet a III Journal des Goncourts? I ask with interest, as I have promised to write upon the book in the *Fortnightly.* And has Daudet terminated his novel—delightful day when he does? You needn't answer these idle questions, as the books will come to me duly from Hachette. The only—or the great literary event here—is Mrs. Humphry Ward's long religious novel.[2] It is quite remarkable—but *voyez la différence!* Ever yours with renewed thanks,

Henry James

1. The series of essays in the *Fortnightly Review* appeared as follows: Maupassant, XLIX (March), 364–386, reprinted in *Partial Portraits* (1888); Loti, XLIX (May), 647–664, reprinted in *Essays in London and Elsewhere* (1893); review of the Goncourt Journals, L (October), 501–520, also in *Essays in London and Elsewhere.* Flaubert's *Correspondance Générale* was reviewed in *Macmillan's Magazine,* LXVII (March 1893), 332–343 and reprinted in *Essays in London and Elsewhere.* The Daudet essay apparently was never written.

2. *Robert Elsmere* (1888), in which Mrs. Ward advocated the abandoning by Christianity of its miracles in favor of its social missions.

To Henrietta Reubell
Ms Harvard

Aston Clinton,
Tring
April 1*st* 1888

Dear Miss Reubell.

I wonder if you can give me any news of our poor desolate friend Boott—and of the helpless Duveneck as well? Have you seen them? —Have you heard from them or anything about them? I have heard from him of course but briefly and he is so simple and inexpressive that it is in [his] power to tell one very little about himself. I wonder much about him—in his hideously sad bereavement,[1] and if there were not great material obstacles and above all if one's *talk* with him would not be quite over at the end of the first three minutes—I would go over and see him. I wrote to him instantly that I would come if it would be a satisfaction or service to him, to see me, but he didn't take it up.

Lizzie's sudden death was an unspeakable shock to me—and I scarcely *see* it, scarcely believe in it yet. It was the last thing I ever thought of as possible—I mean before poor Boott's own surrender of his earthly burden. And the unnatural and most unhappy situation she has left behind her—those two poor uncongenial men tied together by that helpless baby—is something of which I don't see the solution. (I am writing in a room full of people talking—and they make me write erratically.) I have only wanted to ask you to send me three words when you *do* see Boott (whenever that is) and tell me what impression he makes on you—what he intends to do—what relation appears to exist between Duveneck and himself? Had you seen poor Lizzie long—or shortly?—before her death?

What a strange fate—to have lived long enough simply to tie those two men with nothing in common, together by that miserable infant and then vanish into space leaving them face to face! I shall miss her greatly. I had known her for twenty-three or four years—seen her for longish periods together—very familiarly, and I had a great affection for her. She was a dear little quiet, gentle, intelligent laborious lady. And the future looks dark for poor F.B.—one can only hope that it won't be long. The child is the complication—without it he and Duveneck could go their ways respectively—Duveneck to marry again in the fulness of time, and he to return to his Bostonian relationships and kindnesses, where he would be tenderly looked after to the end of his days. Have you seen any of D's work this winter—and especially the portrait of Lizzie? Is it good or interesting? I came down here yesterday (it is the house of the sweet and motherly little old Lady de Rothschild and her daughter and son-in-law, the Cyril Flowers)[2] to spend these two days of the Easter holidays. The house is full of people—Mr. and Mrs. Gladstone among others. So life goes on even when death, close beside one, punches black holes in it. This house is charming friendly and natural—by far the most cosy and homey of all the Rothschild houses.—I have seen the two great portraits which Sargent has sent over to go into the Academy—a month hence: Mrs. Marquand and Mrs. Boit. They are both full of talent life and style and as he only could have painted them, but very different from each other. Mrs. M. will do him great good with the public—they will want to be painted like that—respectfully honourably, dignement. It is a noble portrait of an old lady. Our dear Iza won't do him good—though she is wonderful and of a living! But she not only speaks—she *winks*—and the philistine will find her vulgar. Poor dear Iza![3] I hope you are in good form and am ever your *tout dévoué*

Henry James

1. Elizabeth Boott Duveneck had died of pneumonia in Paris on 22 March 1888.

2. Cyril Flower, later Lord Battersea, married Constance, granddaughter of Nathan Mayer Rothschild of London and daughter of Sir Anthony de Roy Rothschild.

3. Both portraits were a success; that of Mrs. Boit, the former Mary Louisa (Iza) Cushing, is in the Boston Museum of Fine Arts. See *Letters* I, 356.

To Francis Boott

Ms Harvard

34 De Vere Gardens W.
April *3rd* [1888]

My dear Francis.

Your letter which I find on my return from a country visit of two days gives me great comfort—because it puts the case of Lizzie's predicament (that really is the true name for it) exactly as I had inwardly *felt it*—and if you feel it in that way too, the solution (the moral situation) in which I see you enshrouded [is] by so much simplified and even illuminated. It is essentially true that she had undertaken an effort beyond her strength, that she staggered under it and was broken down by it. I was conscious of this as long ago as during those months in Florence when superficially she seemed so happy and hopeful. The infirmity was visible beneath the optimism—and the whole thing seemed to me without an issue. This particular issue is the most violent—but perhaps after all it is not the most cruel—the most painful to witness—for perpetual struggle and disappointment would have been her portion. I mean on account of the terrible *specific gravity* of the mass she had proposed to herself to float and carry.—It is no fault of *his*—but simply the stuff he is made of. There is something unspeakably pathetic to me in all the little heroisms of her plans, her faiths, her view of the future—quenched for ever—but quenched in a void—that is in a soundless rest—far sweeter than anything the hard ache of life has to give. I pity you, my dear Francis, almost more than anything else, for some of the canting consolations that must be offered you. I am more than glad that I can say that your vision of her situation happens to be the one which makes sorrow the least absolute. Don't answer this—I shall write soon again. Please say to Duveneck that he is very frequently in my thoughts. Ever faithfully yours

Henry James

To Francis Boott
Ms Harvard

34 De Vere Gardens W.
May 15*th* [1888]

My dear Francis.

Your kind letter only adds to my regret at not having been able to make act of presence in the last earthly offices paid to dear Lizzie. But my leaving England at any time during the last month has been the most rigid of impossibilities. At no period since I have lived here has it been so out of the question. I found your letter and the photograph last night on my return from a visit to Alice at Leamington. I go to see her every week or two—she continues, I am sorry to say, very weak and wretched. But the cessation of our interminable winter may bring her some assuagement.—It must have been very touching—to me indeed it would have been overwhelmingly sad—to stand with so many old friends and in the midst of so many years of close local recollections beside Lizzie's grave. Some day I shall stand there myself—and feel even then bewildered at the violence of the change. How glad I am that the dear old Florentine earth contains her[1]—it makes one love it more—adds to the tenderness of one's feeling about it. I am very glad too that you and Duveneck are able—or you at any rate—to remain for the present at Bellosguardo—in the midst of all that beauty and peace, out of the roughness of things elsewhere and with Lizzie's presence in every room and her voice in every air. Just a year ago now I saw her there—and wandered in the deep grass of the beautiful terrace with her and looked over the old parapet. I hope to go back to Bellosguardo often but I shall see *her* there, always, more than anything else. I needn't express the hope that Fenimore shows herself a good and friendly neighbour to you—she was too full of affection for Lizzie and is always so of every benevolent impulse not to hold out her hand to you in all sorts of soothing ways. It is a great satisfaction to me to think that you are within her bountiful sphere. I am sadly afraid I shall not, for the present, see the child—that is not before you bring him (as I suppose you will) to England to sail for Boston: I speak to Duveneck in all this—pray tell him so, with my love. I hope you will have some quiet and almost consoling weeks. Ever your affectionate old friend

Henry James

1. Lizzie Boott was buried in the Allori cemetery outside the Roman Gate, in Florence.

To Mrs. Humphry Ward

Ms Barrett

34 De Vere Gardens W.
July 3*d* 1888

Dear Mrs. Ward.

I am happy to say that I shall be able to dine with you on Friday 13th, as your husband was so good to propose to me yesterday (I told him I would say definitely). Meeting him at the Athenaeum brought vividly before me the circumstance that you had gone abroad and *returned* without my having despatched to you a certain letter which, written and rewritten again in my brain, had hopefully proposed to itself to overtake you in some foreign halt in a form as material (if legibility is the measure of that) as any letter of mine can ever be. But now it comes over me that everything has conspired to keep it unwritten till it is grotesquely late—every hindrance and hateful complication that belong in general to these depraved current weeks, multiplied, for my particular confusion, by damnable extras and bewildering accumulations. I have been sitting ever since the middle of April under a perfect smotheration of people, letters, notes, engagements, appointments and pressingly belated and overdue work. The fair, calm hour eluded me from day to day—whenever the clouds of letters cleared away a little *that* one (*this* one) was still unwritten. I feel now as if I were serving it up to you cold, coagulated and unappetizing, and you would simply "send it away"! It really glowed very brightly as jotted down in my brain as aforesaid. I thought you had achieved in your book[1] so many things—so much reality as well as so much beauty, done so much in effect as well as in intention. The hold you keep of your hero is I think very remarkable and especially in relation to the *kind* of hold you constantly attempt to make it; the intimate, lucid, completely perceiving and completely expository view. You never touch him but he lives—and much as you tell about him you never kill him with it: though perhaps one fears a little sometimes that he may suffer a sunstroke, damaging if not fatal, from the high, oblique light of your admiration for him. But fortunately you *see* him as much as you love him, and you feel him as much as you reason him—and your touch goes on animating and your intelligence goes on penetrating, and you do perpetual admirable things in the way of sounding chords, and playing tunes and crossing airs, on fine fibres that would break so easily. Of all that interesting moral realm—the vast dimness of character, of personal history intimate and difficult to write, you take, I think, really masterly possession and you fiddle there as brilliantly as Rose fiddled in her musical world. The interesting thing to me, in your book (and its great success) as I think I have hinted before, is that you have seen a personal history in the richest and most interesting way—the way that yields most fruit—seen the adventures of the real being, the intensely living inner nature and seen them (rendering them too) so vividly that they become exciting, thrilling, strongly attaching as a "story" and hold one's curiosity and suspense to the end. You have imagined for Elsmere matters of detail infinitely delicate and fine—both as regards his relations with his wife and as regards all his other fermentation and passion. This will tell you sufficiently what high successes I think both him and Catherine—for Catherine is admirably understood, and so temperately, so unvulgarly painted.—You are probably sick of hearing Langham praised—but he is a most interesting vivid study and seen more than any one else in the book, I think, as the pure *painter* sees his model. He is admirably *brown*—with his handsome pale head coming out of it—and he turns eventually to such a truthful dusky grey! The three people in the book whom I think, objectively, least completely achieved are the Squire, Rose, and Hugh Flaxman—but, alas, it would take me long to say all the whys and the wherefores! The Squire, one feels, is very elaborately and artistically composed—you have been full of composite intentions in regard to him, but he doesn't become, to my sense, simple and convincing—he has a symbolic part to play and that interferes—he is too much composed—and the pieces don't all hang together. I think the same may be said of Mrs. Darcy—all this strikes one as more invented than observed. One would have liked the agent of

Elsmere's disintegration to have been attended, somehow, with less machinery, less of the *picturesque* intention (à la "Amelia B. Edwards," or someone of that sort), though of course remaining the type most opposed to your hero. And so with Rose—here I am much in the dark—and I don't understand your full intention or quite see *où vous vouliez en venir.* Her general, and special, representative value—her opposition, her illustration of all the *other* side of life—*à la bonne heure*—I am with you altogether. But *why* —if she is only going *not* to act herself out—

July 5th. I was violently interrupted two days ago and since then have not had a moment to finish my letter. I almost forget what I was going to say about Rose,—but *voyons un peu*—it will come back in a moment. Yes, I was going to say that if she was only *not* to affirm the full artistic, aesthetic (I don't know what to call it—untheological?) view of life, I don't exactly see why you gave her so much importance. I think you have made too much of her coquetry, her flippancy, impertinence etc., as if that were a necessary part of her pursuit, her ambition. I can't help wishing that you had made her serious, deeply so, in her own line, as Catherine, for instance, is serious in hers. Then, if she had been strenuous and concentrated—the opposition would have been more real and complete. And I am afraid I don't like her rich, fashionable marriage and find it too conventionally third volume-y. You may say that though rich it isn't "fashionable" in any vulgar sense, and that Flaxman is a very interesting attempt to study conscience in a high place, or at least in a full pocket—to represent a fine, characteristic modern case of the sense of responsibilities of wealth, etc. He *is* such an attempt—and *per se* I think him (*per se* in his relation to Elsmere) an excellent figure. But somehow I resent him as the solution of Rose's problem, which a sort of desire for poetic justice in me would have craved to see fought out on lines more characteristic. And Catherine would have been in her own way a more effective figure—a more pathetic and tragic one—if to bewilderment on the score of her husband's strange, perverse life of the conscience, into which she couldn't enter, had been added bewilderment on the score of passions of another order on her sister's part, similarly intense and logical and equally closed to her. But I am magnifying perhaps—and I only wanted to express a sympathy. The whole book has inspired me with a very great awe, as a large, full picture of life, overflowing with experience, with atmosphere, with multitudinous touches and intentions of a kind I relish. The interest of any novel, in the last analysis, is as a view of the world, and your view is a great sweep on which I congratulate you. Don't answer this—but only tell me, on the 13th, that you have deciphered it. Ever faithfully yours

Henry James

1. *Robert Elsmere.*

To Frederick Macmillan

Ms British Library

34 De Vere Gardens W.
July 5*th* 1888

My dear Macmillan.

Will you please ask your people in America to have the enclosed title page copyrighted for me? It is the title of a tale[1] in two parts about to appear in the *Universal Review* here (July 15th and August 15th) which will of course be sure to reach the U.S. and be exposed to reproduction there.

And will you also direct that a copy of *The Reverberator*[2] be sent to:

Leslie Stephen esq.
Talland House
St. Ives.
Cornwall?

Making these little requests of you brings to the head a purpose I have entertained for several days past—and into which I will plunge without more delay. It is connected—I suppose I ought to be ashamed to confess it—with a certain need of money and a desire to learn if I may successfully *faire valoir*, as the French say, to the end of obtaining some from you, [for] various as yet unpublished but as I think eminently publishable productions. The case with me is that (stated as simply as possible) I have on the one hand a need for a considerable sum and on the other the sense that the material of three books of about the size of the *Reverberator* is about to burst (in so far as it has not already burst) from the periodical press. I think I have mentioned these things more or less definitely to you already, but I will enumerate them again for correctness' sake. Let me premise that each of the said books would make two volumes of rather fuller contents than the *Reverberator* —there is in each case, in other words, rather more copy.

First. There is: The Aspern Papers, which I sent you some time ago and which you sent on (I think you told me) to the printers. It consists of three tales.

Second. There is: A London Life (terminated in *Scribner* about August 20th). The Liar: (out of the *Century*).

Third. There is: The Lesson of the Master
The Patagonia
Mrs. Temperly.[3]

The first of these three last things appears in the July and August *Universal Review;* the second in the corresponding numbers (or rather the August and September numbers) of the *English Illustrated.* The third came out a year ago in *Harper's Weekly,* with big pictures by *Reinhart.*[4] Having them there I want to do something with them (in a pecuniary sense) and the question is What can I do? Are you able to answer this question, without inconvenience, in any accommodating sense? Of course I know that you don't wish to publish three books (or five, counting the two lately published) all in a heap: but nevertheless I can't forbear to sound you. Would there be any money owing me on the sale (already) of the two-shilling volumes lately put forth, and of which a parcel of copies—they are very pretty—came to me yesterday? Or on anything else? I am settling down to write a longish novel[5] (it begins in the *Atlantic* in January next and runs a year), so that for the next few months I shall be engaged on work without immediate returns—a strain I am sorry to say that I am not, just now, rich enough easily to stand. I may be asking something so unusual that it is impossible—but without asking I can't know. If it is consistent with your powers to make me such an advance as will ease off the said strain, I shall greatly appreciate the service to yours ever

Henry James

1. "The Lesson of the Master" appeared in the *Universal Review,* I (16 July and 15 August 1888), 342–365, 494–523

2. *The Reverberator* had been published on 5 June 1888.

3. Macmillan published *The Aspern Papers,* with "Louisa Pallant" and "The Modern Warning," in September 1888; and *A London Life,* with "The Patagonia," "The Liar," and "Mrs. Temperly," in April 1889. *The Lesson of the Master* did not come out until February 1892, in a volume with five other tales. "Mrs. Temperly" was serialized in *Harper's Weekly* under the title "Cousin Maria."

4. Charles S. Reinhart (1844–1896), the American illustrator.

5. HJ was writing *The Tragic Muse* for the *Atlantic Monthly.*

To Robert Louis Stevenson
Ms Yale

34 De Vere Gardens W.
July 31*st* [1888]

My dear Louis.

You are too far away—you are too absent—too invisible, inaudible, inconceivable.[1] Life is too short a business and friendship too delicate a matter for such tricks—for cutting great gory masses out of 'em by the year at a time. Therefore come back. Hang it all—sink it all and come back. A little more and I shall cease to believe in you: I don't mean (in the usual implied phrase) in your veracity, but literally and more fatally in your relevancy—your objective reality. You have become a beautiful myth—a kind of unnatural uncomfortable unburied *mort.* You put forth a beautiful monthly voice, with such happy notes in it—but it comes from too far away, from the other side of the globe, while I vaguely know that you are crawling like a fly on the nether surface of my chair. Your adventures, no doubt, are wonderful, but I don't successfully evoke them, understand them, believe in them. I do in those you write, heaven knows—but I don't in those you perform, though the latter, I know, are to lead to new revelations of the former and your capacity for them is certainly wonderful enough. This is a selfish personal cry: I wish you back; for literature is lonely and Bournemouth is barren without you. Your place in my affection has not been usurped by another—for there is not the least little scrap of another to usurp it. If there were I would perversely try to care for him. But there isn't—I repeat, and I literally care for nothing but your return. I haven't even your novel to stay my stomach withal. The wan wet months elapse and I see no sign of it. The beautiful portrait of your wife shimmers at me from my chimney-piece—brought some months ago by the natural McClure[2]—but seems to refer to one as dim and distant and delightful as a "toast" of the last century. I wish I could make you homesick—I wish I could spoil your fun. It is a very featureless time. The summer is rank with rheumatism—a dark, drowned, unprecedented season. The town is empty but I am not going away. I have no money, but I have a little work. I have lately written several short fictions—but you may not see them unless you come home. I have just begun a novel which is to run through the *Atlantic* from January 1st and which I aspire to finish by the end of this year. In reality I suppose I shall not be fully delivered of it before the middle of next.[3] After that, with God's help, I propose, for a longish period, to do nothing but short lengths. I want to leave a multitude of pictures of my time, projecting my small circular frame upon as many different spots as possible and going in for number as well as quality, so that the number may constitute a total having a certain value as observation and testimony. But there isn't so much as a creature here even to whisper such an intention to. Nothing lifts its hand in these islands save blackguard party politics. Criticism is of an object density and puerility—it doesn't exist—it writes the intellect of our race too low. Lang,[4] in the D[aily] N[ews], every morning, and I believe in a hundred other places, uses his beautiful thin facility to write everything down to the lowest level of Philistine twaddle—the view of the old lady round the corner or the clever person at the dinner party. The incorporated society of authors (I belong to it, and so do you, I think, but I don't know what it is) gave a dinner the other night to American literati to thank them for praying for international copyright. I carefully forbore to go, thinking the gratulation premature, and I see by this morning's *Times* that the banquetted boon is further off than ever. Edmund Gosse has sent me his clever little life of Congreve, just out, and I have read it—but it isn't so good as his Raleigh.[5] But no more of the insufferable subject I see—or have lately seen—Colvin[6] in the mazes of the town—defeated of his friends' hope for him of the headship of the museum—but bearing the scarcely-doubted-of loss with a gallantry which still marks him out for honourable preferment. I believe he has had domestic annoyances of a grave order—some embroilment in the City, of his feckless brother and consequent loss of income to his Mother etc.—Of all this however, I have only vague knowledge —only enough to be struck with the fine way he is not worsted by it. We always talk of you—but more and more as a fact not incontestable. "Some say he is going to such and such a place—there is a legend in another quarter that he was last heard of—or that it is generally supposed—" But it is weak, disheartened stuff. Come, my dear Louis, grow not too thin. I can't question you—because, as I say, I don't conjure you up. You have killed the imagination in me—that part of it which formed your element and in which you sat vivid and near. Your wife and Mother and Mr. Lloyd suffer also—I must confess it—by this failure of breath, of faith. Of course I have your letter—from Manasquan (is that the idiotic name?) of the—ingenuous me, to think there was a date! It was terribly impersonal—it did me little good. A little more and I shan't believe in you enough to bless you. Take this, therefore, as your last chance. I follow all with an aching wing, an inadequate geography and an ineradicable hope. Ever, my dear Louis, yours, to the last snub—

Henry James

1. Stevenson had gone to the South Seas, never to return.

2. S. S. McClure (1857–1949) had founded a literary syndicate in New York, purchasing short stories from writers and selling them at low prices to newspapers. Stevenson sold serial rights of *St. Ives* to McClure, and then a series of South Sea letters. McClure, while in England, had called on HJ with an introduction from Stevenson. In his memoirs, *My Autobiography* (1914), (written for him by Willa Cather) McClure says that James "questioned me minutely about everything pertaining to Stevenson. His interest was keen, sympathetic, personal."

3. *The Tragic Muse* ran from January 1889 to May 1890 in the *Atlantic Monthly*.

4. Andrew Lang (1844–1912) wrote much literary journalism, poetry, folklore, and anthropology, translated from the Greek; in addition to fiction, he produced a number of histories.

5. Gosse's *Congreve* had just been published; his *Raleigh* had appeared in 1886.

6. Sidney Colvin (1845–1927) had been Slade Professor of Fine Art at Cambridge and was now keeper of the prints and drawings at the British Museum. He was an intimate friend of Stevenson's.

To William James
Ms Harvard

Hôtel de l'Écu: Geneva
October 29*th* 1888

My dear William.

Your beautiful and delightful letter of the 14th, from your country home, descended upon me two days ago, and after penetrating myself with it for twenty-four hours I sent it back to England, to Alice, on whom it will confer equal beatitude: not only because so copious, but because so "cheerful in tone" and appearing to show that the essentials of health and happiness are with you. I wish to delay no hour longer to write to you, though I am at this moment rather exhausted with the effort of a long letter, completed five minutes since, to Louis Stevenson, in answer to one I lately received from his wife, from some undecipherable cannibal-island in the Pacific.[1] They are such far-away, fantastic, bewildering people—that there is a certain fatigue in the achievement of putting one's self in relation with them. I may mention in this connection that I have had in my hands the earlier sheets of the *Master of Ballantrae,* the new novel he is about to contribute to Scribner, and have been reading them with breathless admiration. They are wonderfully fine and perfect—he is a rare, delightful genius.—

I am sitting in our old family *salon*[2] in this place and have sat here much of the time for the last fortnight, in sociable converse with family ghosts—father and mother and Aunt Kate and our juvenile selves. I became conscious, suddenly, about October 10th, that I wanted very much to get away from the stale dingy London,[3] which I had not quitted, to speak of, for fifteen months, and notably not all summer—a detestable summer in England, of wet and cold. Alice, whom I went to see, on arriving at this conclusion assured me she could perfectly dispense for a few weeks with my presence on English soil; so I came straight here, where I have a sufficient, though not importunate sense of being in a foreign country, with a desired quietness for getting on with work. I have had sixteen days of extraordinarily beautiful weather, full of autumn colour as vivid as yours at Chocorua, and with the Mont Blanc range, perpetually visible, literally hanging, day after day, over the blue lake. I have treated myself, as I say, to the apartments, or a portion of them, in which we spent the winter of '59–'60, and in which nothing is changed save that the hotel seems to have gone down in the world a little, before the multiplication of rivals—a descent, however, which has the *agrément* of unimpaired cleanliness and applies apparently to the prices as well. It is very good and not at all dear. Geneva seems both duller and smarter—a good deal bigger, yet emptier too. The Academy is now the University—a large, winged building in the old public garden below the Treille. But all the old smells and tastes are here, and the sensation is pleasant. I expect, in three or four days, to go to Paris for about three weeks—and back to London after that. I shall be very busy for the next three or four months with the long thing I am doing for the *Atlantic* and which is to run no less than fifteen—though in shorter instalments than my previous fictions; so that I have no time for wanton travelling. But I enjoy the easier, lighter feeling of being out of England. I suppose if one lived in one of these countries one would take its problems to one's self also, and be oppressed and darkened by them—even as I am, more or less, by those which hang over me in London. But as it is, the Continent gives one a refreshing sense of getting *away*—away from Whitechapel and Parnell[4] and a hundred other constantly thickening heavinesses. Apropos of which I may say, in response to your speculation about Alice's homesickness (leaving her to answer the question directly for herself), that she doesn't strike me as made *unhappy*, nostalgically, so much as occupied and stimulated, healthily irritated. She *is* homesick, but not nearly so much so as if she had a definite, concrete nest to revert to—a home of her own; and as if she had *not* a habitation which, materially and economically, happens to suit her very well in England. I don't think she *likes* England or the English very much—the people, their mind, their tone, their "hypocrisy" etc. This is owing partly to the confined life she leads and the partial, passive, fragmentary, unreacting way in which she sees them. Also to her seeing so many more women than men; or rather *only* women, so far as she now sees anyone—and no men at all. Also to her being such a tremendously convinced Home Ruler. She *does* take a great interest in English affairs—and that is an occupation and a source of well-being (in the country) to her. It is always a great misfortune, I think, when one has reached a certain age, that if one's living in a country not one's own and one is of anything of an ironic or critical disposition, one mistakes the inevitable reflections and criticisms that one makes, more and more as one grows older, upon life and human nature etc., for a judgment of that particular country, its natives, peculiarities, etc., to which, really, one has grown exceedingly accustomed. For myself, at any rate, I am deadly weary of the whole "international" state of mind—so that I *ache*, at times, with fatigue at the way it is constantly forced upon one as a sort of virtue or obligation. I can't look at the English and American worlds, or feel about them, any more, save as a big Anglo-Saxon total, destined to such an amount of melting together that an insistence on their differences becomes more and more idle and pedantic and that that melting together will come the faster the more one takes it for granted and treats the life of the two countries as continuous or more or less convertible, or at any rate as simply different chapters of the same general subject. Literature, fiction in particular, affords a magnificent arm for such taking for granted, and one may so do an excellent work with it. I have not the least hesitation in saying that I aspire to write in such a way that it would be impossible to an outsider to say whether I am, at a given moment, an American writing about England or an Englishman writing about America (dealing as I do with both countries), and so far from being ashamed of such an ambiguity I should be exceedingly proud of it, for it would be highly civilized. You are right in surmising that it must often be a grief to me not to get more time for reading—though not in supposing that I am "hollowed out inside" by the limitations my existence has too obstinately attached to that exercise, combined with the fact that I produce a great deal. At times I do read almost as much as my wretched little *stomach* for it (literally) will allow, and on the whole I get much more time for it as the months and years go by. I touched bottom, in the way of missing time, during the first half of my long residence in London—and traversed then a sandy desert, in that respect—where however, I took on board such an amount of human and social information that if the same necessary alternatives were presented to me again I should make the same choice. One can read when one is middle-aged or old; but one can mingle in the world with fresh perceptions only when one is young. The great thing is to be *saturated*, with something—that is, in one way or another, with life; and I chose the form of my saturation. Moreover you exaggerate the degree to which my writing takes it out of my mind, for I try to spend only the interest of my capital.—I haven't told you how I found Alice when I last saw her. She is now in very good form—still going out, I hear from her, in the mild moments, and feeling very easy and even jolly about her Leamington winter. My being away is a sign of her really good symptoms. She was *wütend* after the London police, in connection with the Whitechapel murders, to a degree that almost constituted robust health. I have seen a great many (that is, more than usual) Frenchmen in London this year; they bring me notes of introduction—and the other day, the night before coming away, I entertained at dinner (at a club) the French Ambassador at Madrid (Paul Cambon), Xavier Charmes[5] of the French Foreign Office, G. du Maurier, and the wonderful little Jusserand, the *chargé d'affaires* in London, who is a great friend of mine, and to oblige and relieve whom it was that I invited the two other diplomatists, his friends, whom he had rather helplessly on his hands. THERE is the *real* difference—a gulf, from the English (or the American) to the Frenchman, and vice versa (still more); and not from the Englishman to the American. The Frenchmen I see all seem to me wonderful the first time—but not so much, at all, the second.—But I must finish this without having touched any of the sympathetic things I meant to say to you about your place, your work on it, Alice's prowesses as a country lady, the children's *vie champêtre,* etc. Aunt Kate, after her visit to you, praised all these things to us with profusion and evident sincerity. I wish I could see them—but the day seems far. I haven't lain on the ground for so many years that I feel as if I had spent them up in a balloon. Next summer I shall come here—I mean to Switzerland, for which my taste has revived. I am full of gratulation on your enlarged classes, chances of reading, etc., and on your prospect of keeping the invalid child this winter. Give my tender love to Alice. You are entering the period of keen suspense about Cleveland, and I share it even here. I have lately begun to receive and read the *Nation* after a long interval—and it seems to me very rough. Was it *ever* so? I wonder about Bole. Ever your affectionate

Henry James

1. This letter to Stevenson does not appear to be extant.

2. During the winter of 1859–1860 the James family had lived at the Hôtel de l'Écu, William James attending the Academy in Geneva and HJ the Institution Rochette, a preparatory school for engineers and architects. See *Letters* I, 7–21.

3. HJ had another reason for going to Geneva; he had promised to spend a few days near Miss Woolson, who was on holiday in Switzerland. See following letter to Francis Boott.

4. The sensational "Whitechapel murders" and the allegations in the *Times* that Charles Stewart Parnell, the Irish parliamentary leader, had condoned the Phoenix Park murders carried out in Dublin by Irish terrorists. The letters printed in the *Times* were later proved forgeries. See letter to Grace Norton, 25 March 1889, n. 3.

5. Pierre Paul Cambon (1843–1924) would later be French Ambassador in London and one of the makers of the Anglo-French alliance; François-Xavier Charmes (1848–1916) had served as an editor of the *Revue des Deux Mondes* before going to the Quai d'Orsay.

To Francis Boott
Ms Harvard

Hôtel de l'Écu: Geneva
Oct. 29*th* [1888]

My dear Francis.

I have a letter from you of too many weeks ago, for which I have inevitably delayed to thank you. I have been pressed with work and my correspondence has had absolutely to wait. Your letter was written just as you were alighting in the home of the free—the free-and-easy you doubtless quickly enough found it. Since then I have had news of you from Alice, of a sufficiently reassuring kind—and I have thought of you as bathed in the waters of kindness, kinship and hospitality. I hope that Duveneck and the dear little boy float at your side in the same warm moral gulf-stream. Please to give my love to both of them. If I were addicted to saying that, I should say now that your "ears must have burned" a good deal lately, for you have been a daily theme of conversation with me for the past ten days, with Fenimore. That excellent and obliging woman is plying her pen hard on the other side of this lake and I am doing the same on this one. Our hotels are a mile apart[1] but we meet in the evening, and when we meet she tells me, even at the risk of a repetition to which I am far from objecting, the story of your last months, weeks, days, hours etc. at Bellosguardo. We often talk of Lizzie and it is a great pleasure to me to do so with one who had entered so much into her life in so short a time. She had known you only a year or two—but the rate at which she went with you made it practically much longer. Fenimore goes back to

Florence in a day or two; and I then return to London via Paris, where I shall spend a fortnight. I expect to be at home all winter—but dream of Italy in the very late spring. How I shall miss you—how I shall miss Lizzie! I am literally *afraid* of Bellosguardo. I went to see Alice a fortnight ago, just before coming here, and found her in very good and cheerful form for her monotonous winter. I have enjoyed this familiar place, in extraordinarily beautiful autumn weather, with Mont Blanc, day after day, literally hanging over the blue lake, more than I almost believed I could ever again enjoy anything Swiss. I have sat in this little hotel, which is full of associations of my early years, pegging away at a long—a very long—novel I am doing for next year's *Atlantic*. I hope you have found some material harbour of refuge—hope rather sceptically when I remember how hard and how vainly *I* tried to do so the last time I was in America. But of course your friends and relations *le vous arrachent*. The boy, I know, has fallen upon flowers. I hope Duveneck *se tire d'affaire*, and repeat my friendly greetings to him. I trust you are both electing Cleveland. In this case he ought to send you Minister to England. Ever my dear Francis, affectionately yours

Henry James

1. Cf. HJ's tale "Louisa Pallant," *Complete Tales*, VI, 254. The narrator tells us: "I represented to him successfully that it would be in much better taste for us to alight at Stresa, which as everyone knows is a resort of tourists, also on the shore of the major lake, at about a mile's distance from Baveno. If we stayed at the latter place we should have to inhabit the same hotel as our friends, and this would be indiscreet, considering our peculiar relations with them. Nothing would be easier than to go and come between the two points, especially by the water . . ." It is quite likely that HJ was using the same strategy and the same discretion at Geneva.

To Rhoda Broughton
Ms Chester

Hôtel du Parc: Genoa
November 6*th* [1888]

Dear Miss Broughton.

I am, alas, in a foreign land and perversely unable to be the happier or the richer (this last figuratively speaking) for your visit to London. I am very sorry—and very cross—about it. I came abroad a month ago—but I would have staid at home—really, I think I would—had I known you were to descend, with your silken froufrou, on the metropolis. I am afraid I shall be away another month—about. Don't hate me too much when you see I'm in Italy. To appease you, I will quickly mention that the rain descends in torrents upon the dank autumn soil and lashes the windows of my frescoed apartment. I permit you to feel a savage glee about this and to remark grimly, to Mrs. Newcome, that it serves me right. This is partly because I wish to give *her* the opportunity of replying more tenderly that it doesn't. It is true that I am not certain that she ventures ever to contradict you. When you next dash up to town I pray I may be there. Wait, do wait, till I return—and don't spend all your money without me. Miss Woolson's address is Villa Brichiere, *Bellosguardo*, Florence. She is well and flourishing I know—but I have—this time—no hope of getting to Florence. I *may* go to Rome for a fortnight, straight from here along the coast. Bless you, there are no retributions in life: haven't you noticed that? The Flacks[1] always get off beautifully. Idiots have remarked to me that I have represented Francie as doing so, too much—but they are dense minds, which don't understand Francie. I am not a very particular enthusiast about the lady of the crimson tresses—but I do think *Robert Elsmere* touches her a little irritatingly in this, that the hero is avowedly a portrait of her late lamented husband. I will sing out to you, from De Vere Gardens to your quiet Oxford lane—proposing the latest thing out[2]—as soon as I escape from this "woman's land," as Browning calls it. Ever faithfully yours

Henry James

1. George Flack is the gossip-writer in *The Reverberator,* the short novel HJ had just published; Francie Dosson is the naive American chatterbox whose indiscretions Flack publishes.

2. Rhoda Broughton and HJ often went to the theatre together, Miss Broughton always militantly paying for her own ticket.

To Francis Boott
Ms Harvard

34 De Vere Gardens W.
Jan. 18*th* '89

My dear Francis.

I won't delay for a moment thanking you for the pleasure your genial and, thank God, fairly cheerful letter has just given me. You are terribly far away and the particular spot with which your farawayness is associated at present (for I never revelled in Cambridge) adds to the chill (if I were a *real* magazinist I should say the *pathos*) which the general fact has cast over your image. I hope it doesn't feel as "out of it" (as they say here) to *be* in Cambridge nowadays as it does to think of it! But of course not, for you are surrounded, thank heaven (you will think me become suddenly very religious) with all sorts of human warmth, some of which, I hope, abides in the company of William and *i suoi*. Besides you always really preferred Cambridge to "Tuscany." Therefore I won't pity you any more than I can help—though I shall continue to be as tender of you as if I did. Congratulate Mrs. Greenough very cordially for me on having "recovered" [from] her accident, as they say here. It is more to the point that she has recovered her leg. What is the use of being eighty, unless you can do independent and unconventional things? I came back from abroad on Christmas Eve, and spent a week at Leamington with Alice just afterwards. The revolving months bring her continuously a little more and a little more strength—I am always much struck with it in seeing her after an interval. On leaving Geneva I parted with Fenimore—she went back to Bellosguardo and I went (through the Mont Cenis) to Genoa and the Riviera. I spent two or three weeks at the delicious Monte-Carlo and the month of December in Paris. Fenimore's mind and talk are indeed full of her last year or two at Bellosguardo, and especially of the period of your return and your tragical departure. I questioned her so much on all this that that is partly why she dwelt upon it. But she cherishes the mystical survival there of dear Lizzie. She has her sister there now with the *pianterreno* all garnished and glorified for her—but she constantly speaks of giving up her villa. I can't imagine why unless to mortify the spirit and make Florida her ultimate Cambridge. I hope the

Boy is blooming. Please tell Duveneck to give me good notice of his advent *here*: I shall be very glad to see him. I wish you would come with him. Alice and I know about poor Aunt Kate and are very anxious for William's report. Ever my dear Francis, affectionately yours

Henry James

To William James
Ms Harvard

34 De Vere Gardens W.
March 22*d* '89

Dear William.

This is all I can afford today—a word to thank you for your letter from the hotel in New York after Aunt Kate's funeral, which Alice sent on to me today. By the same post, to me, came yesterday a singularly perfect and fine letter from Lila [Walsh][1] written at the same moment, which I straightway despatched to Alice. Both of these things make it *vivid* to me for almost the first time that the dear old Aunt's place on earth is vacant forever and that I looked upon her for the last time when before returning to London in the summer of 1883, six months after Father's death, I went down to bid her good-bye at the hotel at which she was staying with Aunt Margaret and Lila, at the Delaware Water-Gap. I seem to see her, familiar and characteristic, as one's eyes had known her for a lifetime—as you describe her in death. But I should have liked to speak to her in life once again. Her illness has entailed on me much writing—to Alice, to Lila, Helen Ripley etc.—and I have just written to Lily Walsh and Elly Morris (who had written to me), so I will be brief now, feeling rather exhausted. I am very glad your Alice could come on to New York with you, and I send her a message of affectionate gratitude for it. Sad must your visit to Newport, on your way home, have been,—I can't figure to myself the state of things there. Dismal must be the situation of poor old Tweedy[2]—if Aunt Mary be as far gone—and yet so much *not* gone—as I suppose. I mean very soon to write to him.—Henry's duration is rather a staggerer—when one had supposed him so near his end. If it's likely to be long I hope it's painless. I am very glad he has the familiar little 121 to protect his end. What a haunted little house by this time—how saturated with the history of a family. I shall soon write again. I haven't seen Alice for a month, but go to her in a day or two. Ever your

Henry

1. The Walshes, Ripleys, and other relatives mentioned here belonged to HJ's mother's side of the family.

2. Edmund Tweedy.

To Charles Eliot Norton
Ms Harvard

34 De Vere Gardens W.
March 25*th* [1889]

My dear Charles.

I have owed you a letter a prodigious time—but I haven't really thought it *fair* to pay my debt. I have been silent from delicacy and left you alone from kindness. I know what your correspondence is, and your work, and you know, a little, what mine are (and how much more limited are my powers), so that I have felt I could trust you to interpret my long failure to write, as a sign of greater interest rather than of less. But one must occasionally call attention even to one's finest sacrifice—especially when one has so pleasant an obligation to acknowledge as the gift of your two goodly new Carlyle volumes, which came in a fortnight ago. I thank you very cordially for them—they are an indispensable addition to my already copious Carlyle library. He remains to me, on the whole, the prince of letter writers, and the whole Carlyle domestic and personal history is a thing I have an insatiable appetite for, as for some inexhaustible interminable *roman des moeurs*, that one has got the habit of. Moreover it is a kind of patriotic pleasure to see such perfect editing proceed from our not too perfect country (whose lacunae, by the way, you would be less conscious of if you lived, at intervals rapid enough to make the comparison frequent, in this frumpy old England, where things are getting to be as slipshod from a want of freshness as they have long been with us from an excess of it). The things I am more particularly thinking of, those of the mind—and the higher parts of it—don't impress me here any longer so much with the ancient superiority that the imagination has always lent them. In a word the glamour, the prestige and the mystery have—subjectively, no doubt—been much rubbed away from the image of old England; she doesn't, no she doesn't strike me as so very "distinguished" and I am, I fear, glowingly conscious of the ugly and clumsy sides of what she has to show—the vast miseries and meannesses of London, e.g., which have been suffered to grow so myriad-headed, rather than of the rich and beautiful characteristics. But this sounds reckless and disputatious, and heaven forbid I should too crudely or too rashly generalize. Sometimes I feel still—*sentimentally*—quite the other way; one must always do that. I spent the autumn abroad but have been in town since the first days of January. I was a short time in Switzerland—then at Geneva for three weeks, then at Monte Carlo (charmingly, with only the exquisite beauty present and none of the base people yet arrived); and then for nearly a month in Paris—which struck me after a long intermission of habit there, as bright, charming, civilized, even interesting—in spite of Boulanger[1] and other vulgarities. London, in the empty (Christmas holidays etc.) midwinter phase, when I came back, looked like a big black inferno of fog, mud, drunkenness and pauperism. That impression, I hasten to add, has since then been balanced again by others—and I have enjoyed the home-feeling of the last three months, the best of the London year for one's occupations and one's fireside. Sometimes I see our friend Burne-Jones—though not so often as I like, so little is frequency of communication possible here. I am however to dine with him in a day or two—I wish you were to be of the party. He goes on working at (I believe) a great many large allegorical designs, in which his abundance and beauty of imagination are as striking as they have ever been, but which seem to me less and less in the direction in which painting becomes most interesting and most *itself*—more and more away from the open air of the world and the lovely study of the aspects and appearances of things, the real—or at any rate to me the fascinating—problems of the painter's art. He might paint exactly as he does if there were *no* open air, no light, nor atmosphere, nor aspects, nor appearances—nor moving, flushing, changing, *looking* ambient life. Phil follows him at a very long interval, but with, also, an apparent absence of suspicion of what painting really consists of which, as he has not his father's beatiful genius to give one something to *bite,* promises ill for his future career—or *would* promise ill in a society in which the sense of such matters was less hopelessly muddled than here. But Phil is such a delightful humourous amusing little social animal, with a *real* genius for talk and laughter, that he will flourish all his days even without help from the brush. He is a tremendous little Tory and—for sociability's sake—much launched in the Salisbury[2] world. Burne-Jones and I met a couple of times at the thrilling, throbbing Parnell trial,[3] during the infinitely interesting episode of the letters, when if one had been once and tasted blood, one was quite hungry to go again and wanted to give up everything and live there. Unfortunately, or rather, fortunately, getting in was supremely difficult. I don't know much how all this touched you in America—or whether you take any interest at all in the everlasting Irish question. My own has hitherto been largely confined to thinking some sort of State-government, over there, the least stupid solution of the mess—but as it all goes on and on, dreary as it is, it inevitably appeals to one as a drama with a deepening interest—a thickening plot—so that I find it impossible not to put a little passion into my general, very amateurish, conviction. If there were no other reason against the old state of things, there would always be this, that the English haven't the *tact* required for working the repressive attitude successfully. It seems to me impossible to have less. Arthur Balfour[4] is the darling of the government and their ideal of the perfect man—yet Arthur Balfour does things that make one almost understand Jacqueries[5] and French revolutions—and does them, I am convinced, from a high sense of duty and in perfectly good faith. Meanwhile the whole dispute converts English life (I say nothing of Irish) into a bear-garden of recriminations and spites. It is all very ugly, and I don't think home rule, putting it at the worst, could hurt *this* country so much.—I won't attempt to talk to you about your own affairs—I should be so distant and conjectural. I hear you are cutting up Shady Hill and I am vulgar enough to hope that it puts money in your purse. I was very sorry not to see Rupert when he passed through England in the autumn—it was just in the middle of my absence abroad. I hope his German experiment goes on well.—I wonder if I shall bother you unconscionably if I ask you for five words in relation to a matter which has been put upon me in the odd and unexpected way in which it sometimes befalls one here to be approached on business that one doesn't in the least consider one's own. If you receive, by this same post, a sort of circular on the subject of a portrait of Washington, the property of Lord Bury, you will understand a little, my predicament. The said Lord B.'s wife, an amiable woman,—whom I have known some time, but always, as *I* have considered, *very* slightly and superficially, asked me the other day to help her to dispose of the portrait (described in the circular) in America. I haven't seen it, but I have seen a photograph, and I judge the picture to be wholly without artistic, as distinguished from "historic," merit. I told Lady Bury I *could* do almost nothing—but that I would write a letter of inquiry for her. So, you see, I write! I only want to be importunate (and feel much ashamed even of that) to the extent of asking you whether there is any chance at all (in your opinion) that any public institution (Art Museum or historical society—) or any rich amateur, would buy such a picture? The amateur would have to be rich, as they have an idea they could get a big price—£10,000!! Their idea is absurd—isn't it?—but if I had a line from you, in the fulness of your benevolence, it would be a voucher that I *have* written. I send my love to the daughters, my dear Charles and am ever very faithfully yours

Henry James

1. General Georges Boulanger (1837–1891), the anti-Republican French military activist, was on the verge of being charged with treason for his royalist activities, and the French Chamber had been asked to lift his parliamentary immunity.

2. The third Marquess of Salisbury, Robert Arthur Talbot Gascoyne-Cecil (1830–1903), was Conservative prime minister at this time.

3. The *Times* had published a facsimile of a letter purportedly written by Parnell condoning the Phoenix Park murders in Dublin in 1882. Parnell called it a forgery, and it was demonstrated in court that the forger was one Richard Pigott.

4. Arthur James Balfour (1848–1930), Salisbury's nephew, held a key position in the British Conservative party for half a century. He had been appointed chief secretary for Ireland in the Salisbury government and was an unshakable opponent of Home Rule.

5. The French peasant revolt in 1358 was called a "Jacquerie" after the Jacques Bonhomme nickname given to peasants. HJ is referring to the rise of Fenianism in Ireland.

To Robert Louis Stevenson
Ms Yale

34 De Vere Gardens W.
April 29*th*, 1889

This is really dreadful news, my dear Louis, odious news to one who had neatly arranged that his coming August should be spent gobbling down your yarns—by some garden-window of Skerryvore—as the Neapolitan *lazzarone* puts away the lubricating filaments of the vermicelli. And yet, with my hideous capacity to understand it, I am strong enough, superior enough to say *Anything*, for conversation, later. It's in the light of unlimited conversation that I see the future years, and my honoured chair by the ingleside will require a succession of new cushions. I miss you shockingly—for, my dear fellow, there is no one—literally no one: and I don't in the least follow you—I can't go with you (I mean in conceptive faculty and the "realizing sense"), and you are for the time absolutely as if you were dead to me—I mean to my imagination of course—not to my affection or my prayers. And so I shall keep humble that you may pump into me—and make me stare and sigh and look simple and be quite out of it—forever and ever. It's the best thing that can happen to one to see it written in your very hand that you have been so uplifted in health and cheer, and if another year will screw you up so tight that you won't "come undone" again, I will try and hold on through the barren months. I will go to Mrs. Sitwell,[1] to hear what has made you blush—it must be something very radical. Your chieftains are dim to me—why shouldn't they be when you yourself are? *Va* for another year—but don't stay away longer, for we should really, for self-defence, have to outlive you. I saw poor Colvin three nights ago—dined with him, nearly alone, at the Museum, to welcome him back to London after a long regime of Charcot[2] and other severe remedies in Paris. He looks to me altered and spectral; but he maintained that he is better and I gathered that he really is. None the less I am very sorry for him—he looks like a man who has come back, if he *has* come back, from far. If you should communicate with him, however, take his condition wholly in the optimistic sense—he wants to be cheered about himself. I have seen no other near friend of yours—that I can think of—the pleasing Mrs. Sitwell excepted. Her brightness—her sympathetic quality—I always note. Edmund Gosse I occasionally see, and we never separate without having been very delicate over you. He writes in the reviews but he hasn't yet done the important thing that I hoped for as his answer to his assailant of three or four years ago. Rider Haggard is frequent, but has ceased to be importunate; his actuality has gone. He is doing, however, a *Cleopatra* in some illustrated sheet, and A. Lang lately told me that he, Andrew, had written a tale in collaboration with him—a kind of Helen of Troy. Poor Haggard, however, cannot be fairly made responsible for Lang's whims—he can't help it if Lang is so droll. I myself do little but sit at home and write little tales—and even long ones—you shall see them when you come back. Nothing would induce me, by sending them to you, to expose myself to damaging Polynesian comparisons. For the rest, there is nothing in this land but the eternal Irish strife—the place is all gashed and gory with it. I can't tell you of it—I am too sick of it—more than to say that two or three of the most interesting days I ever passed were lately in the crowded, throbbing, thrilling little court of the Special Commission, over the astounding drama of the forged *Times* letters. I have a hope, a dream, that your mother may be coming home and that one may go and drink deep of her narrations. But it's idle and improbable. A wonderful, beautiful letter from your wife to Colvin seemed, a few months ago, to make it clear that *she* has no quarrel with your wild and wayward life. I hope it agrees with her a little too—I mean that it renews her youth and strength. It is a woeful time to wait—for your prose as for your person—especially as the prose can't be better though the person may; and you must promise, and your mother and wife and Lloyd must promise, with you and for you that you will never again get into any floating or flying thing which will carry you out of sight of your very faithful

Henry James

1. Frances Sitwell (1839–1924), a friend of Stevenson's, later married Sidney Colvin.

2. Jean Martin Charcot (1825–1893), French neurologist and teacher. Freud, and later William James, studied with him.

To The Deerfield Summer School

Ms Unknown

Summer 1889

I am afraid I can do little more than thank you for your courteous invitation to be present at the sittings of your delightfully sounding school of romance,[1] which ought to inherit happiness and honour from such a name. I am so very far away from you that I am afraid I can't participate very intelligently in your discussions, but I can only give them the furtherance of a dimly discriminating sympathy. I am not sure that I apprehend very well your apparent premise, "the materialism of our present tendencies," and I suspect that this would require some clearing up before I should be able (if even then) to contribute any suggestive or helpful word. To tell the truth, I can't help thinking that we already talk too much about the novel, about and around it, in proportion to the quantity of it having any importance that we produce. What I should say to the nymphs and swains who propose to converse about it under the great trees at Deerfield is: "Oh, do something from your point of view; an ounce of example is worth a ton of generalities; do something with the great art and the great form; do something with life. Any point of view is interesting that is a direct impression of life. You each have an impression colored by your individual conditions; make that into a picture, a picture framed by your own personal wisdom, your glimpse of the American world. The field is vast for freedom, for study, for observation, for satire, for truth." I don't think I really do know what you mean by "materializing tendencies" any more than I should by "spiritualizing" or "etherealizing." There are no tendencies worth anything but to see the actual or the imaginative, which is just as visible, and to paint it. I have only two little words for the matter remotely approaching to rule or doctrine; one is life and the other freedom. Tell the ladies and gentlemen, the ingenious inquirers, to consider life directly and closely, and not to be put off with mean and puerile falsities, and be conscientious about it. It is infinitely large, various and comprehensive. Every sort of mind will find what it looks for in it, whereby the novel becomes truly multifarious and illustrative. That is what I mean by liberty; give it its head and let it range. If it is in a bad way, and the English novel is, I think, nothing but absolute freedom can refresh it and restore its self-respect. Excuse these raw brevities and please convey to your companions, my dear sir, the cordial good wishes of yours and theirs,

Henry James

1. During the summer of 1889 HJ was invited to attend the Summer School at Deerfield, Massachusetts, for a discussion of the art of the novel. He sent, instead, this letter, which was read during the proceedings and later published in the New York *Tribune* (4 August 1889).

To Edwin L. Godkin

Ms Harvard

Lord Warden Hotel
Dover: Sept. 20*th* [1889]

My dear Godkin.

I had already more than one welcome note, shot backward in your flight, to thank you for, when your very graceful letter of August 31st descended upon me the other day. I was delighted to get it and to gather from it that something of the genial spirit of De Vere Gardens still hangs about you. The weeks you spent there seem already tinted, to my vision, with history, poetry and romance, as I find everything does more and more, at the age I have reached, as soon as the gentle past rescues it from the perils of actuality. I keep thinking of all sorts of things which I might have done for you which I didn't—but even those things don't embitter my recollections, and some of them I cherish the hope of doing still. The summer seemed rather flat and tame after your departure: there was less to live for, somehow, and infinitely less to laugh about. Nevertheless I stuck fast to the feverish city all through the month of August, when I left it for a time of which the end is not yet. I went up and paid a short but very delightful visit to Lowell (who struck me as about twenty years old) at Whitby on the Yorkshire coast, and then I came down here (a place, with me, of old frequentation), with vague ideas of going to Paris. A week has passed and I haven't yet gone—and meanwhile I have accepted an invitation from Lord Coleridge to go down and spend three days with him in Devonshire, which relegates Paris to a later moment. He writes to me, by the way, that your valuable flask was found in your room *there* after your departure, and that they will give it to me when I come. I am delighted it has turned up, as its fate was much on my mind, and I can easily send it to you by Katharine Loring, my sister's great friend, who is spending a couple of months with her and who returns to the U.S. about November 1st. This I will make a point of doing—she will transmit the little object to you from Boston. Your account of your visit to Lord C. left me with so charming an impression that it bribed me to accept his invitation, though I have been sedulously avoiding the British country house almost ever since you left. I am less and less capable of it, though I managed, shortly after your flight, a glittering Saturday to Monday at Waddesdon, void of purpose or communion, save for some happy moments with Mrs. Mahlon [Sands]. I hope that gracious lady, whom I saw several times in London in August, is not far from you now. She was nervous about her voyage, but it must have been lovely, and I hope things have gone well with her since. I mean before long to write to her—but, *en attendant,* please give her my love and blessing. We are having the bravest September—the loveliest weather, and I walk here by the side of a Channel beautifully mild and blue, with the coast of France so distinct beyond it, that one can almost see the red legs of the little soldiers all ready for an invasion. On the days when the shores of the rival nation seem really hardly more than five miles away, the immensity of the moral and intellectual ocean between them becomes still more droll and extraordinary. Your slight but suggestive allusion[s] to some of your impressions of the U.S. since your return greatly excite my curiosity and challenge my powers of interpretation. The "horrible query" you propound as to "whether it's honest" and doing as much as may be done "for the best things of this life" to assume perpetually the great virtues of that civilization is one of which I feel even at this distance the full horror. I don't pretend to meet it or solve it and I confess I dodge it. But even dodging it—three thousand miles away—is a sufficiently difficult occupation. I have observed since I have been here at Dover, some "dreadful" compatriots, on their way to and from Paris: none, indeed, that were not dreadful—cheap, ugly, barbarous. But I am an incurable pessimist and have no comfort for any man. I would no more generalize than I would slide down the banisters. I have seen none of our particular friends—to speak of—all summer. I have corresponded with Mrs. Roundell[1] about her book—but I have evaded Mrs. Green,[2] who has taken, for the summer, a famous old tumbledown house (Hampden) with the Humphry Wards. Come back—come back and bring your wife. Give my love to her, please, meanwhile, and try and combine the maximum of remembrance with the minimum of impatience. *Vale*, my dear Godkin; and believe me always most faithfully yours

Henry James

P.S. I have mysteriously failed to write on this page—so I will add, postscriptively, what I was going to mention just now in speaking of the good Roundells, that I heard a while ago, in a roundabout way, that they considered that our visit at Darfold was altogether one of the most interesting and brilliant social occasion[s] of their lives—in all the records of their hospitality.

1. Mrs. Charles Roundell, the former Julia Elizabeth Anne Tollemache.

2. Irish historian Alice Sophia Amelia Green (1847–1929), better known as Mrs. Stopford Green, widow of the historian John Richard Green. She was an ardent advocate of Home Rule.

To Grace Norton
Ms Harvard

Lord Warden Hotel
Dover. Sept. 22*d* [1889]

My dear Grace.

I am spending a quiet fortnight by the murmuring sea—we are having a splendid September—and I have more leisure than I perhaps usually enjoy to think of many things. Those most present to me, I think, are my debilities and deficiencies as a correspondent. I reflect upon them with shame and penitence. But they are general, universal, not directed particularly at you; and they are aggravated in the present case, I may add, by my happening to have by me several atrociously bad pens and not being able, as the British Sabbath weighs upon the land, to procure any others. I look out on the blue straits and the white cliffs, and the picturesque old mass of the Castle clustered high above them—and at the gleaming, shining, shifting ships, and at the absurdly visible coast of France (absurdly visible considering what distant incommunicable things it represents here), where such momentous doings are taking place at this hour—I mean the big general election which is expected to settle more or less the "fate of the republic" or at least the Boulanger question. It all goes on today, but the placid mood of nature—the channel is as still as a glass—gives no hint of it. I came down here twelve days ago, with vague designs upon Paris (for two or three weeks only), which have not yet been enacted. I have lingered and walked and worked, enjoyed solitude and exercise and lovely weather, and the fit (of crossing the silver streak) has almost passed away. I shall probably go there two or three weeks later and in the interval return to attend to certain matters in London and to spend three days with Lord Coleridge (if you wish to know—or perhaps to wonder) in Devonshire. I am going in for a quiet autumn to make up for an anything but quiet summer. Up to August 1st, at least, there was far too much "on" for peace and comfort. You will have seen William, on his return, whose visit, all too soon over, was a delight to me, and he will have given you, I hope, a not too pessimistic interpretation of my existence. I remained in town to September 1st and then rushed up and paid a four days' visit, at Whitby, 'twixt the sea and the moors, to our dear old eternally juvenile Lowell, who appeared to particular advantage at that particular place, roughing in breezy lodgings, and striking one as younger than the youngest of the young Smalleys, who form his bodyguard. His powers of walking, talking, joking, smoking, drinking and playing host and guide—in the kindest gayest, most fifteen-year-old way seem literally to increase with each revolving twelve-month, and form the most amiable side of his nature. *He* doesn't, under these circumstances, wear an overcoat, either of cloth or of selfconsciousness, and that combined with his wondrous good fun and good temper renders him, at his age (and with the Yorkshire airs), miraculous to me. Bôcher[1] turned up, as he probably will have told you, and was so good as to come to lunch one Sunday when it was inevitable that I should not be without Mrs. Owen Wister, who talked in great floods and probably smothered the genial current of his soul. It came out however, after he went away, though he stayed too short a time, and he was very pleasant and "sensitive" and conversable. I liked him much both as your friend and as a mind and nature evidently charming—but wondered at him as (apparently) the least French Frenchman I have ever encountered. He is different from all the others I have ever seen—but that is natural enough, doubtless, transplanted years ago to a different *ambiente*. The odd part was that he struck me as having acquired the peculiar American quality, far from characteristic of the Frenchman, or of any European, indeed, in general, of seeming to belong to no particular *ambiente* at all. It was a pleasure to me to meet and talk with anyone [who] cares apparently for the sweet Italy as much as I do (little as I succeed in going there), and that is peculiarly unFrench—*they* have the sentiment of Italy less I think, than any other European people save, doubtless, the Spaniards. Then—or before that—I had a visit from the big deep-voiced Rupert [Norton], and two or three hours with the gentle ironic Lily. I dined with the latter at the little Margaret Burne-Joneses who are both very pretty—the female one lovely—and do their best apparently to help one to circumvent their slightly undue hightonedness. I was very glad to see Rupert so strong and pleasant and good-looking and baritonish and apparently at home in the world. I envied him his youth, his Germany, his Egypt and Greece and everything that was his except his rather puckered and melancholy companion, poor little George Ashburner,[2] so "clever" and refined and yet such a prematurely aged little failure. It seems in the dim past—the beginning of the summer that your young Ballard nephew came one day to lunch with me (looking more extraordinarily like you surely than nephew ever looked before like aunt); but I vividly remember that I reviled myself vigorously, just afterwards, for not having written to tell you how superfluous your warnings about him seemed to me and how exempt from embarrassments—for me—our meeting was. He seemed to me much more brilliant than you described him—very intelligent, indeed, and amiable. Living so much as you do with the great wits of the past you probably have grown to think the present—outside Cambridge etc.—more remarkable by analogy, than it is! Perhaps you even think *me* more brilliant than I am, or more requiring of brilliancy in those introduced to me! When I have told you that I was never less so in my life than I find myself at the end of thirteen years of London (not through satiety, but through simple solid *rust*), I shall have mentioned everything about myself that I can scrape together for your entertainment just now. I shall return to London to a quiet, dusky, fire-lighted and lamplighted winter, and early-closing autumn such as I like. I have plenty of work, thank heaven, in view—I say thank heaven because I don't on the whole tire of it, but find it the indispensable movement that keeps up vital heat. I dream of going to Italy next spring—but I dream so much more of that than do it that it isn't worth mentioning. If I go to Paris in the course of next month it will be to look at some pictures in the exhibition before a general *acquit de conscience* (though I hate the whole *genre* of the big world shows and the deluge of number and quantity); and not to see any particular people or persons. I shan't see any *literati*—one's relations with the few I have known inevitably die out through want of reciprocity and curiosity on their part, and their ignorance of all one's Anglosaxon background, combined with a fine contempt, largely justified, for it. Yet I *am* going to translate for pure and copious lucre (for the Harpers) a new *inédit* novel of Daudet's,[3] warranted innocuous, and I *may* see him about that. Don't, please, mention this. I found, by the way, at Whitby your little *ci-devant* friends and protégées the "Josie Swifts" of New York—one of them, the younger sister, who used to live in Paris with Mme de Stoeckel, married to a young Englisher by name St. Johnston the author of books and apparently a kind and clever and honourable youth—with the fat, common and good-natured "Josie" and the more or less ditto mama (isn't there something mysterious the matter with her?) domesticated familiarily with them. They were all much intertwined with the young Smalleys, and St. Johnston was the *boute-en-train* of the circle. Let me not take leave of you, my dear Grace, without telling you that I should like to cover this sheet with sympathetic inquiries about yourself, your own life, health, spirits and occupations. But you won't like that—so I forbear: a virtue the more commendable as I have no hope that you will be quick to write to me after my dull, ungraceful silences and insufficiencies. I have heard you have been as usual all summer at home (how I understand that!) and I have also heard you have been at Nahant—which I equally comprehend. I am so vulgar as to hope your land goes off, or goes on—and that you don't mind William and his big shingles. Let me not burst in ignorance and believe me ever my dear Grace affectionately yours

Henry James

1. Ferdinand Bôcher, a friend of the Nortons.
2. The Ashburners were neighbors of the Jameses in Cambridge.
3. HJ's translation of *Port Tarascon* was published on 30 October 1890. HJ received £350.

To William James
Ms Harvard

Hotel de Hollande
r. de la Paix
Paris: Nov. 28*th* [1889]

My dear William.

Don't curse me for sending you the young Leonard Huxley,[1] who has written me the enclosed appeal; and to whom I have, after anxious searchings, ventured to give a note to you. I don't think you *will* objurgate me; in the first place because his plan in the U.S. seems respectable, useful and interesting, and in the second because he is such a charming fresh, manly, cleanly type of young English master at a great school. He is a son, of course, of the great Thomas—and is highly esteemed at Charterhouse. He is married, *of course,* to a "niece of Matt. Arnold"—sister of Mrs. Humphry Ward! I have the pleasantest recollection of him—of his face, type and speech.—I pray he be not an utterly inacceptable burden—and am pretty sure he won't.—I send you this from Paris, where I have been for the last five weeks. Toward the end I relented in regard to the exhibition[2] and came over in time for the last fortnight of it. It was despoiled of its freshness and invaded by hordes of furious Franks and fiery Huns—but it was a great impression and I'm glad I sacrificed to it. So I've remained on—I go back December 1st. It happens that I have been working very hard all this month—almost harder than ever in my life before—having on top of other pressing and unfinished tasks undertaken, for the bribe of large lucre, to translate Daudet's new *Tartarin* novel for the Harpers—whereby the proof sheets (the thing is the delightful work of a slowly dying man[3]—he has motorataxia), hot from his pen of genius have been pouring in upon me and have had to be attended to even in the midst of matters still more urgent. I had a talk of an hour and a half with him the other day—about "our work"(!!) and his own queer, deplorable condition, which he intensely converts into *art,* profession, success, copy, etc.—taking perpetual notes about his constant suffering (terrible in degree), which are to make a book called *La Douleur,* the most detailed and pessimistic notation of pain *qui fût jamais.* He is doing, in the midst of this, his new, gay, lovely, "Tartarin" for the Harpers *en premier lieu;* that is, they are to publish it serially with wonderfully "processed" drawings before it comes out as a book in France—and I am to represent him, in English (a difficult, but with ingenuity a pleasant and amusing task) while this serial period lasts. I have seen a good deal of Bourget, and as I have breakfasted with Coppée[4] and twice dined in company with Meilhac, Sarcey, Albert Wolff, Goncourt, Ganderax, Blowitz,[5] etc., you will judge that I am pretty well saturated and ought to have the last word about *ces gens-ci.* That last word hasn't a grain of subjection, or of mystery, left in it: it is simply, "Chinese, Chinese, Chinese!" They are finished, besotted mandarins, and their Paris is their celestial Empire. With that, such a Paris as it sometimes seems! Nevertheless I've enjoyed it, and though I am very tired, too tired to write to you properly, I shall have been much refreshed by my stay here, and have taken aboard some light and heat for the black London winter. I shall see Alice on December 4th or 5th—I haven't seen her (through the sufficiency of Katharine's long visit) since the day I stopped with you on your way to Liverpool. I suppose the house has been the great cinder in your eye, though not, I trust, to producing tears all the autumn. I hope you are all sifting down and that your life seems larger for it. I am afraid, however, Alice can't be anything but very tired—and I send her much love. Did Millet ever write to you? I wrote to him urgently, but had no answer. I hope that above house and college and life and everything, you still hold up an undemented head, and are not in a seedy way. Ever your affectionate

Henry

1. Leonard Huxley (1860–1933), son of the scientist Thomas Henry Huxley and future father of Aldous Huxley.

2. The Paris Exhibition of 1889.

3. Daudet did not die until 1897.

4. François Coppée (1842–1908), poet and dramatist, whose stories of drab existences and humble people had considerable appeal.

5. Henri Meilhac (1831–1897) was librettist for Offenbach and a well-known playwright, collaborator with Ludovic Halévy in drawing-room comedies; Francisque Sarcey (1827–1899) was drama critic of *Le Temps.* Henri de Blowitz (1825–1903) was the special Paris correspondent of the *Times.*

To Thomas Wemyss Reid
Ms Barrett

34 De Vere Gardens W.
December 30*th* [1889]

My dear Wemyss Reid.[1]

Here is my misbegotten article, in which I have taken the license of *2000* words that you gave me as your maximum. I hope it will pass muster—I have done my best for it—and so far as it falls short please remember that

First: It was really very difficult.

Second: I didn't want to do it—oh, I didn't!

and

Third: I have, I fear worked quite away, in general, from the easy journalistic form—and don't faintly *pretend* to be master of it. Let me add nevertheless that my proofs will receive my instantaneous attention.

Ever yours
Henry James

P.S. Kindly remember that I go in for inscrutable anonymity!

1. Sir Thomas Wemyss Reid (1842–1905) founded *The Speaker* in 1890 and edited it until 1897. It was a weekly liberal organ.

2. HJ's anonymous article in the newly founded *Speaker*, on the burial of Browning in Westminster Abbey, was reprinted in *Essays in London* (1893).

To Francis Boott
Ms Harvard

34 De Vere Gardens W.
Jan. 11*th* 1890

My dear Francis.

As usual I have infinitely procrastinated. But it may help you to think less ill of me for not having answered your last letter to know that that negative has a reverse of many positives—if I have been speechless it is really because I have lived with my pen in my hand. I spent several hours yesterday with Alice, and we talked inevitably about you and smacked our lips together over your last fine letter to her, and she showed me the various photographs she had lately received from you: notably the group of four on the old terrace at Bellosguardo, in which dear Lizzie stands there beside you with such a vivid actuality that for the moment, it startles one into wondering why one hadn't heard from her for so long. At any rate it made me ask myself again how in the world you can make anything of life today. You will tell me, of course, that you don't, save in so far as the dear little boy helps you—one of the two portraits of whom (with his father holding him up from behind) I extorted from Alice and brought away with me. Of the other picture, the group of four on the terrace, with you in a chair and Anne in the background, you doubtless have too few *exemplaires* to be able to spare me one—and you have given me too many photographs in the past. But if you did have one at your disposal I should value it exceedingly—it is, somehow, so full of Bellosguardo and the past. I forget when I last wrote to you—but it is since then, at any rate, that the rupture of our last tie with that consecrated spot has really taken place—in the unmitigated secession of our (apparently) so deeply-rooted Fenimore.[1] She has gone, with her sister, to Corfu and the East, and she will probably have written you that at the last she left Florence with (seemingly) a kind of loathing: loathing, I mean, for the crowd, the interruptions and invasions, the final rapacity and trickery of the unmasked Brichieris, and the conditions consequent upon her extravagant propensities for "packing" —the most envious virtue that ever a woman was cursed with, and the blight of her whole existence. It appears to have taken her upwards of two months of incessant personal labour, night and day, to get out of a Brichieri bed or two. But she is out now, evidently never to return—and is on her way to Athens and Cairo—a capital sort of change of life for her. She spent a month of the autumn here—that is at Richmond, and *raffolēd* of the English country.—I lately came back from six weeks in Paris—no Italy for me now—unless I manage a few weeks in May and June, when London becomes a burden. I saw Miss Reubell often and your name was tenderly mentioned. I go on liking Paris exceedingly and yet being glad I don't live there. I came in for the last three weeks of the monstrous yet agreeable exhibition—to the American department of which I was full of regret that Duveneck hadn't even contributed. Does he like his western work?—I hope so, and that you will give him my love. We have buried Browning, whom I believe you don't like. Would you have left him unburied? An alacrity to inter is indeed rather a sign of hostility I suppose. The great abbey, at any rate, grandly entombs him. I hope you continue to acknowledge no influence in resisting the queer epidemic. It is too strange for me to figure you at Cambridge in the horse-car-world. Yet I would fain do it more vividly for it—that world—is the better for you. I'm afraid, however, I don't like it enough to be glad of that. Ever dear Francis—and kiss the sweet little boy for me—most faithfully yours

Henry James

1. After her Mediterranean journey, Miss Woolson settled in England. Boott had returned with his grandson to live in Cambridge, Massachusetts.

To Katherine De Kay Bronson

Ms Private

34 De Vere Gardens W.
January 12*th* 1890

Dear Mrs. Bronson.

You will probably think me a sad brute never to have written you a word of sympathy or condolence since the death of our illustrious old friend, by whose grave in the great Abbey I the other day respectfully stood. The simplest thing is for me to admit frankly that I *am*—only pleading that I have, every moment, been a very busy brute as well, and at no moment an unthinking or unrepentant one. *Your* loss was really the first reflection I made after I heard we should never see Browning again. I thought immediately what it meant for you, before I thought what it meant for any one else. And then, wrongfully, no doubt, even that sympathy was submerged in my sense of its being a supremely happy and enviable death—such as one would wish with all one's heart to any great man for whom one cared—so at the right moment and in the right condition—in the fulness of years and honours, immediately, without taking the visible turn for the worse (inevitably close at hand but for the quick rescue); without pain or delay, too, and in the congruous, romantic, poetic place. This is all very well, you will say—but it makes an immense difference in your life. I am conscious of that too—for he was very much in our life here—that of all of us who knew him and met him often and liked him, as I did, as I always had. Even this big brutal, vulgar, indifferent London will miss him—and that says everything. But his funeral was charming, if I may call it so—crowded and cordial and genuine, and full of the beauty and grandeur of the magnificent old cathedral—which looked really exquisite for the occasion—in its dim, sublime vastness, with the boy-voices of the choir soaring and descending angelic under the high roof. They were really national obsequies[1] . . . [con]ditions possible—I mean after long illness and pain and with a valid usual right to a much greater number of years.[2] She was a delightful woman and I was much attached to her. I shall miss her—for I was always looking for her again. But *basta*—let me wish *you* all comfort and tranquillity—*poveri noi!* I hope you and Edith haven't been bothered with the ridiculous little pestilence. *State bene! tutte due.* I give you both the most affectionate assurance of yours, dear Mrs. Bronson, most faithfully

Henry James

1. A page is missing in the holograph.
2. Apparently HJ discussed the death of Lizzie Boott after his account of the Browning funeral.

To W. Morton Fullerton
Ms Harvard

34 De Vere Gardens W.
March 11*th* [1890]

My dear Fullerton[1]

Do come on *Thursday* at 2, as the nearer day. And don't, oh don't, my dear boy, insert the hard wedge of the "Mr."—as if for splitting friendship in twain—into your communications with one so very amicably yours as

Henry James

1. This letter marked the beginning of a long friendship with William Morton Fullerton (1865–1952). Born in Norwich, Connecticut, Fullerton was twenty-five when he arrived in London and found employment with the London *Times*. HJ was charmed by him and always wrote to him with great affection. Very early he was sent to Paris to assist Blowitz (see letter to William James, 28 November 1889), and he remained in the French capital. Shortly after the turn of the century he was Edith Wharton's lover. In his later years he was political writer on American affairs for *Le Figaro*. The London *Times* said Fullerton's copy was so influenced by HJ "as to often involve a very drastic process of sub-editing before it was suitable for publication in a daily newspaper."

To Grace Norton
Ms Harvard

34 De Vere Gardens W.
March 12*th* 1890

My dear Grace.

I am full of desire to know something definite about Lowell and yet if I write to you I shall probably only add to the number of importunate information-seekers you have probably had to meet. On the other hand I can't write to Elmwood without any present expectation of an answer, and, after all I have as good a right to write to you as anyone, and better than most. Last night, I met Sybella Lady Lyttelton and she told me she had just had a distinctly encouraging telegram from Dr. Wyman. But we live in considerable anxiety—and I haven't yet even ventured to go and see Mrs. Smalley. This will give you a pathetic—perhaps more—even an ironical—sense of the importance to us of our dear annual and alternative *grand homme.* I am not at all clear as to what his malady has been—nor does that particularly matter; if only you should find yourself magnanimously able, within any measureable time after the receipt of this, to send me a kind and candid word as to his actual condition and to any possibility you may discern in it of his pulling himself together sufficiently to be able to come out here this summer. That possibility has seemed to me of late years so much of his life that I can't help thinking that (if it, of course, isn't taken too rashly for granted) it may again do something to minister to that life. Yet I should be sorry to see him come alone, and who is to come with him? These questions may bother you and seem to you insufficiently to concern you, or your imagination or your interests—and they are really only a way of saying that if you can write me a word about him of any sort I shall be very glad.— It's so long since I either wrote to you or heard from you that I have lost all count of it. I continue to become a worse and worse correspondent; but perhaps you will say there can be no intensification of the superlative bad. A mild and poisonous winter, with us, is ushering in a still milder but apparently somewhat purified spring. It has been pestilential, but also delightfully "quiet," and the consequence has made me forgive the cause; inasmuch as I "had it" only in a bland and benevolent form and could sit up and read and yet do nothing else, which in London is a supreme blessing. I have had a very good working winter, and by its fruits, in due time, you shall know it. I hope to leave London after the 25th April for some more sequestered scene, but I can't say as yet whither I shall seek that scene; in the British islands or on further shores. (I make this plan, for the season, every year, and only carry it out in the minority of cases. But I think this year will be one of the minority.) Did I tell you much about the couple of months that I spent in Paris, in the autumn—just as the exhibition was closing? They have however already become rather dim, and there was, moreover, at the time, not much to say about them, inasmuch as for a long time I haven't had so peaceful and personal a time there. (By which I mean *im*personal—personal to myself.) I saw Daudet who is slowly dying and making a book about it, and Coppée who is slowly living and doing the same, and a good deal of Bourget, who has given his measure, I think, and two or three others. But none of these are *really* very interesting people. Here it's another affair, since Mrs. Humphry Ward is founding an outward and visible church, somewhere in Bloomsbury with a Lord (not a God) to lead off the list of the faithful (poor Geo. Howard, now Carlisle); and giving us thereby out of hand, and in her own person, a finer "case" of serene, sublime and imperturbable self-complacency than any analytic foreigner can do who is only *looking* for cases.—Your faithful "nieces" and nephew the good little St. Johnston and Swift house (what kinship by the way, does the relation to you confer on Mrs. Swift?) hold out hopes to me that you are coming out here to take a house? Heaven speed the day! I saw those pleasant young people the other day and "Aunt Grace" was much to the fore. Do take the house in advance, through me.—I hope, dear Grace, your winter has been worryless and that pestilence and famine have kept away from your door. I hope you have been able to study and to scatter the flowers thereof with a free mind and a free hand. *My* hand isn't free—it is rheumatic (in the wrist, alas), which helps to account for my rudely-formed cuneiform characters. But whatever you fail to decipher let it be distinct to you that I am ever faithfully yours

Henry James

To Mr. and Mrs. Robert Louis Stevenson

Ms Yale

34 De Vere Gardens W.
March 21*st* 1890

My dear Louis and my dear Mrs. Louis

It comes over me with horror and shame that, within the next very few months, your return to England may become such a reality that I shall before long stand face to face with you branded with the almost blood-guilt of my long silence. Let me break that silence then, before the bliss of meeting you again (heaven speed the day) is qualified, in prospect, by the apprehension of your disdain. I despatch these incoherent words to Sydney, in the hope they may catch you before you embark for our palpitating England. My despicable dumbness has been a vile accident—I needn't assure you that it doesn't pretend to the smallest backbone of system or sense. I have simply had the busiest year of my life and have been so drained of the fluid of expression—so tapped into the public pitcher —that my whole correspondence has dried up and died of thirst. Then, somehow, you had become inaccessible to the mind as well as to the body, and I had the feeling that, in the midst of such desperate larks, any news of mine would be mere irrelevant drivel to you. Now, however, you *must* take it, such as it is. It won't, of course, be news to you at all that the idea of your return has become altogether the question of the day. The other two questions (the eternal Irish and Rudyard Kipling) aren't in it. (We'll tell you all about Rudyard Kipling—your nascent rival—he has killed one immortal—Rider Haggard—the star of the hour, aged twenty-four and author of remarkable Anglo-Indian and extraordinarily observed barrack life—Tommy Atkins—tales.) What I am pledged to do at the present moment (pledged to Colvin) is to plead with you passionately on the question of Samoa and expatriation. But somehow, when it comes to the point, I can't do it—partly because I can't really believe in anything so dreadful (a long howl of horror has gone up from all your friends), and partly because before any step so fatal is irretrievably taken we are to have a chance to see you and bind you with flowery chains. When you tell me with your own melodious lips that you're committed, I'll see what's to be done; but I won't take a single plank of the house or a single hour of the flight for granted. Colvin has given me instantly all your recent unspeakable news—I mean the voyage to Samoa and everything preceding, and your Mother has kindly communicated to me her own wonderful documents. Therefore my silence has been filled with sound—sound infinitely fearful sometimes. But the joy of your health, my dear Louis, has been to me as an imparted sensation—making me far more glad than anything that I could originate with myself. I shall never be as well as I am glad that you are well. We are poor tame, terrified products of the tailor and the parlour-maid; but we *have* a fine sentiment or two, all the same. Your return will probably do dear old Colvin more good than any other remedy—especially as, after some very dark days, or months, he has lately seemed really to have turned his face quite in the right direction. Don't disappoint him—don't fail him. He's sadly thin, but you'll make him stout. (See how cunning I am when I wish to seem disinterested.) Seriously, it will be a cure to him to behold you—as it will be the opposite to lose you again. I, thank God, am in better form than when you first took ship. I have lately finished the longest and most careful novel I have ever written (it has gone sixteen months in a periodical!) and the last, in that form, I shall ever do—it will come out as a book in May. Also other things too flat to be bawled through an Australasian tube. But the intensest throb of my literary life, as of that of many others, has been the *Master of Ballantrae*—a pure hard crystal, my boy, a work of ineffable and exquisite art. It makes us all as proud of you as you can possibly be of *it*. Lead him on blushing, lead him back blooming, by the hand, dear Mrs. Louis, and we will talk over everything, as we used to lang syne at Skerryvore. When we *have* talked over everything and when all your tales are told, then you may paddle back to Samoa. But we shall call time. My heartiest greeting to the young Lloyd—grizzled, I fear, before his day. I have been very sorry to hear of your son-in-law's bad case. May all that tension be over now. *Do* receive this before you sail—*don't* sail till you get it. But then bound straight across. I send a volume of the Rising Star[1] to goad you all hither with jealousy. He has quite done for your neglected even though neglectful friend,

Henry James

1. Kipling.

To Frederick Macmillan

Ms British Library

34 De Vere Gardens W.
March 24*th* 1890

Dear Macmillan

I find your note of today on coming in—having posted you a letter on the subject of it[1] three hours ago.

I will send you the revised copy therein alluded to, by hand tomorrow A.M.—you can then estimate its length. It is complete save for 17 pp. (*Atlantic* pages), which I haven't yet had the sheets of from Boston—but am daily expecting. I should considerably doubt whether the book will come in Boston so *early* as the end of April; that is, the date of their receipt of revised copy over there would make this a hurry greater than I should suppose Houghton, Mifflin & Co. likely to take. I imagine some time in May more probable. You will judge how long the matter represented by the 332 *Atlantic* pages will take yourselves to produce as a book.

Oh yes, I translated three months ago an unpublished Tartarin novel of Daudet's, the last, killing the hero off, for the Harpers, who are to produce it as a six-months serial (and then as a book) in their magazine in advance of its issue in France. It begins in the U.S. I think in June—and appears in France only for Christmas. I was bribed with gold—more gold than the translator (as I suppose) is accustomed to receive. The book is charming. Yours ever

Henry James

1. The subject in question was book publication by Macmillan of *The Tragic Muse*, whose serialization in the *Atlantic Monthly* had just been completed.

To Frederick Macmillan

Ms British Library

34 De Vere Gardens W.
March 26*th* 1890

My dear Macmillan

I am afraid I can't meet you on the ground of your offer in regard to the publication of "The Tragic Muse" in this country—two thirds profits in the future. That future is practically remote and I am much concerned with the present. What I desire is to obtain a sum of money "down"—and I am loth to perish without a struggle—that is without trying to obtain one. I gather that the terms you mention are an ultimatum excluding, for yourselves, the idea of anything down—which is why I make this declaration of my alternative. But I should be sorry to pursue that alternative without hearing from you again—though I don't flatter myself that I hold the knife at your throat. Yours ever

Henry James

To Frederick Macmillan

Ms British Library

34 De Vere Gardens W.
March 28*th* 1890

My dear Macmillan.

I thank you for your note and the offer of £70.0.0.[1] Don't, however, think my pretensions monstrous if I say that, in spite of what you tell me of the poor success of my recent books, I still do desire to get a larger sum, and have determined to take what steps I can in this direction. These steps I know will carry me away from you, but it comes over me that that is after all better, even with a due and grateful recognition of the readiness you express to go on with me, unprofitable as I am. I say it is "better" because I had far rather that in those circumstances you should *not* go on with me. I would rather not be published at all than be published and not pay—other people at least. The latter alternative makes me uncomfortable and the former makes me, of the two, feel least like a failure; the failure that, at this time of day, it is too humiliating to consent to be without trying, at least, as they say in America, to "know more about it." Unless I can put the matter on a more remunerative footing all round I shall give up my English "market"—heaven save the market! and confine myself to my American. But I must experiment a bit first—and to experiment is of course to say farewell to you. Farewell then, my dear Macmillan, with great regret—but with the sustaining cheer of all the links in the chain that remain still unbroken.

Yours ever
Henry James

P.S. I am not unaware or oblivious that I am actually in your debt to the extent of whatever fraction of £200 on account (which you paid me July 9th 1888) is represented by the third of the books then covenanted for here and in the U.S.—the *Aspern Papers* and *A London Life* being the two others. I will engage that this last member of the batch (about five short tales) shall appear in the autumn—if that will suit you.—H.J.

1. Macmillan bought a five-year lease of *The Tragic Muse* and gave HJ an advance of £250. Sales of the book were poor, and at the end of the five years HJ still owed Macmillan £170.

To Violet Paget (Vernon Lee)

Ms Colby

34 De Vere Gardens W.
April 27*th* 1890

Dear Miss Paget.

Your gruesome, graceful, *genialisch* "Hauntings"[1] came to me a good bit since; but, pleasure-stirring as was the gift, I have, to thank you for it, been able to control what George Eliot would have called my "emotive" utterance until I should have had the right hour to reassimilate the very special savour of the work. This I have done within a day or two and the ingenious tales, full of imagination and of Italy are *there*—diffused through my intellectual being and within reach of my introspective—or introactive—hand. (My organism will strike you as mixed, as well as my metaphor—and what I mainly mean is that I *possess* the eminently psychical stories as well as the material volume.) I have enjoyed again, greatly, the bold, aggressive speculative fancy of them—and, in addition to this, what I always taste, deeply, in all your work, the redolence of the unspeakable Italy, to whose infinite atmosphere you perform the valuable function of conductor and condenser. You are a sort of reservicer of the air of Italian things, and those of us who can't swig at the centuries can at least sip of your accumulations. Italy seems to have been made on purpose to have a past, whereas other countries are as if they had one by accident and didn't quite like to confess it—as if they were maidservants with an illegitimate brat! Italy doesn't blush for *her* prodigal son, and you are one of the most accomplished interpreters of the parable. The short tale is a divine form—I have the face to say it, I who should already have sent you the longest three-volume novel ever written, if it hadn't failed, as yet, to come out. (It comes three or four weeks hence—when it will trundle to you over the Alps like a *banal* tricycle. Ride it but a few minutes at a time—unless—or until—you learn how: which perhaps you won't.) The supernatural story, the subject wrought in fantasy, is not the *class* of fiction I myself most cherish (prejudiced as you may have perceived me in favour of a close connotation, or close observation, of the real—or whatever one may call it—the familiar, the inevitable). But that only makes my enjoyment of your artistry more of a subjection. As for the land unspeakable, I hope to say something to it, if not of it, one of these very next few weeks. I start for Italy *ces jours-ci*—by the 10th, I hope, at latest. The business is to consist mainly of Venice—I have promised Palazzo Barbaro a visit—but I shall be very unhappy—more unhappy than I can afford to, in a world spiritually so expansive, if I don't get down to Florence for a few days. But I shall not know *when* I shall take these few days (whether before or after Venice—or as an interlude) till I get to Milan (Hôtel de la Ville). Probably before—but I want to do so many things—Urbinos and Volterras and Urbanias: for which I lack the golden hours and the golden coin. I have seen lately a few of your friends: Mme Darmesteter[2] at Easter, very much alive, very fresh and happy, apparently—*quand même;* Miss Marie MacKenzie, thoroughly and securely agreeable; and Lady Wolseley, at last (just these days) facing the music and sounding the charge (*her* social Tell el-Kebir)[3] to bring her daughter a second time into the world; to which end she has taken a flat in London for the Season. I believe it's over (Frances's first ball a couple of nights ago), and both of them doing very well. Will you give my very friendly remembrances and assurances to your brother? As to how he is and how you are I hope to have ocular, or auricular, confession some day in May. Sargent is, I believe, adding up dollars (still) in America as fast as is possible to one *qui se fiche* to such an extent of arithmetic! Believe me, dear Miss Paget, your most truly,

Henry James

1. A volume containing four of Vernon Lee's ghost stories, published in 1890.

2. The former Mary A. F. Robinson. See letter to Violet Paget, 21 October 1884.

3. Lady Wolseley, the former Louisa Erskine, whose daughter was "coming out" that Season. James is referring to the celebrated battle fought by Sir Garnet (later Viscount) Wolseley near Cairo in 1882—the last in which British soldiers wore red coats.

To Robert Louis Stevenson

Ms Yale

34 De Vere Gardens W.
April 28*th* '90

My dear Louis.

I didn't, for two reasons, answer your delightful letter, or rather exquisite note, from the Sydney Club, but I must thank you for it now, before the gulfs have washed you down, or at least have washed away from you all aftertastes of brineless things—the stay-at-home works of lubberly friends. One of the reasons just mentioned was that I had written to you at Sydney (c/o the mystic Townes) only a few days before your note arrived; the other is that until a few days ago I hugged the soft illusion that by the time anything else would reach you, you would already have started for England. This fondest of the hopes of all of us has been shattered in a manner to which history furnishes a parallel only in the behaviour of its most famous coquettes and çourtesans. You are indeed the male Cleopatra or buccaneering Pompadour of the Deep—the wandering Wanton of the Pacific. You swim into our ken with every provocation and prospect—and we have only time to open our arms to receive you when your immortal back is turned to us in the act of still more provoking flight. The moral is that we have to be virtuous whether we like it or no. Seriously, it was a real heartbreak to have September substituted for June; but I have a general faith in the fascinated providence who watches over you, to the neglect of all other human affairs—I believe that even *He* has an idea that you know what you are about, and even what *He* is, though He by this time doesn't in the least know himself. Moreover I have selfish grounds of resignation in the fact that I shall be in England in September, whereas, to my almost intolerable torment, I should probably not have been in June. Therefore when you come, if you ever do, which in my heart of hearts I doubt, I shall see you in all your strange exotic bloom, in all your paint and beads and feathers. May you grow a magnificent extra crop of all such things (as they will bring you a fortune here) in this much-grudged extra summer. Charming and delightful it was to me to see you with a palate for *my* plain domestic pudding, after all the wild cannibal smacks that you have learned to know. I think the better of the poor little study in the painfully-familiar, since hearing that it could bear such voyages and resist such tests. You have fed a presumption that vaguely stirs within me—that of trying to get at you in June or July with a fearfully long-winded but very highly-finished novel which I am putting forth in (probably) the last days of May. If I were sure it would overtake you on some coral strand I shouldn't hesitate; for, seriously and selfishly speaking, I can't (spiritually) afford *not* to put the book under the eye of the sole and single Anglo-Saxon capable of perceiving—though he may care for little else in it—how well it is written. So I shall probably cast it upon the waters and pray for it: as I suppose you are coming back to Sydney, it may meet you there, and you can read it on the voyage home. In that box you'll *have* to.—I don't say it to bribe you in advance to unnatural tolerance—but I have an impression that I didn't make copious or clear to you in my last what a grand literary life your Master of B. has been leading here. Somehow, a miracle has been wrought for you (for you they are), and the fine old feather-bed of English taste *has* thrilled with preternatural recognitions. The most unlikely number of people *have* discerned that the Master is "well written." It has had the highest success of honour that the English-reading public can now confer—where it has failed (the success, save that it hasn't failed at all!) it has done so through the constitutional incapacity of the umpire—infected, by vulgar intercourses, as with some unnameable disease. We have lost our status—*nous n'avons plus qualité*—to confer degrees. Nevertheless, last year you woke us up at night, for an hour—and we scrambled down in our shirt and climbed a garden-wall and stole a laurel, which we have been brandishing ever since over your absent head. I tell you this because I think Colvin (at least it was probably he—he is visibly better—or else Mrs. Sitwell) mentioned to me the other day that you had asked in touching virginal ignorance for news of the fate of the book.

Its "fate," my dear fellow, has been glittering glory—simply: and I ween—that is I hope—you will find the glitter has chinked as well. I sent you a new Zola the other day—at a venture: but I have no confidence that I gratified a curiosity. I haven't read The Human Beast[1]—one knows him without that—and I am told Zola's account of him is dull and imperfect. I would read anything new about him—but this is old, old, old. I hope your pen, this summer, will cleave the deeps of art even as your prow, or your keel, or whatever's the knowing name for it, furrows the Pacific flood. Into what strange and wondrous dyes you must now be qualified to dip it! Roast yourself, I beseech you, on the sharp spit of perfection, that you may give out your aromas and essences! Tell your wife, please, to read between the lines of this, and between the words and the letters, all that I miss the occasion to write directly to *her*. I hope she has continued to distil, to your mother, the honey of those impressions of which a few months ago the latter lent me for a day or two a taste—on its long yellow foolscap combs. They would make, they *will* make, of course, a deliciously sweet book. I hope Lloyd, whom I greet and bless, is living up to the height of his young privilege—and secreting honey too, according to the mild discipline of the hive. There are lots of things more to tell you, no doubt, but if I go on they will all take the shape of questions, and that won't be fair. The supreme thing to say is Don't, oh *don't*, simply ruin our nerves and our tempers for the rest of life by *not* throwing the rope in September, to him who will, for once in his life, not muff his catch:

H.J.

1. Zola's novel *La Bête Humaine* had just appeared in France.

To William Dean Howells
Ms Harvard

Hôtel de la Ville, Milan
May 17*th* [1890]

My dear Howells.

I have not been writing to you at a tremendous, an infamous rate, for a long time past; but I should indeed be sunk in baseness if I were to keep this pace after what has just happened. For what has just happened is that I have been reading the *Hazard of New Fortunes*[1] (I confess I should have liked to change the name for you), and that it has filled me with communicable rapture. I remember that the last time I came to Italy (or almost) I brought your Lemuel Barker,[2] which had just come out, to read in the train, and let it divert an intensely professional eye from the most clamourous beauties of the way—writing to you afterwards from this very place I think, all the good and all the wonder I thought of it. So I have a decent precedent for insisting to you, now, under circumstances exactly similar (save that the present book is a much bigger feat), that, to my charmed and gratified sense, the *Hazard* is simply prodigious. I read the first volume just before I left London—and the second, which I began the instant I got into the train at Victoria, made me wish immensely that both it and the journey to Bâle and thence were formed to last longer. I congratulate you, my dear Howells unrestrictedly, and give you my assurance—whatever the vain thing is worth—that, for me, you have never yet done anything so roundly and totally good. For, (after the flat-hunting business is disposed of) the whole thing is almost equally good—or would be, that is, if the Dryfooses[3] were not so much better than even the best of S. Lapham, and the best of what has been your best heretofore. I don't know whether you can bear to see the offspring of your former (literary) marriages sacrificed so to the last batch—but it is the sort of thing you must expect if you *will* practise so prolific a polygamy. The life, the truth, the light, the heat, the breadth and depth and thickness of the *Hazard*, are absolutely admirable. It seems to me altogether, in abundance, ease and variety, a fresh start for you at what I would call "your age" didn't I fear to resemble a Dryfoos—so that I'd say instead that to *read* the thing is a fresh start for me at mine. I should think it would make you as happy as poor happiness will let us be, to turn off from one year to the other, and from a reservoir in daily domestic use, such a free, full, rich flood. In fact your reservoir deluges me, altogether, with surprise as well as other sorts of effusion; by which I mean that though you do much to empty it you keep it remarkably full. I seem to myself, in comparison, to fill mine with a teaspoon and obtain but a trickle. However, I don't mean to compare myself with you or to compare you, in the particular case, with anything but life. When I do that—with the life you see and represent—your faculty for rendering it seems to me extraordinary and to shave the truth—the general truth you aim at—several degrees closer than anyone else begins to do. You are less *big* than Zola, but you are ever so much less clumsy and more really various, and moreover you and he don't see the same things—you have a wholly different consciousness—*you* see a totally different side of a different race. Man isn't at all *one* after all—it takes so much of him to be American, to be French, etc. I won't even compare you with something I have a sort of dim stupid sense you might be and are not—for I don't in the least know that you might be it, after all, or whether, if you were, you wouldn't cease to be that something you are which makes me write to you thus. We don't know what people might give us that they don't—the only thing is to take them on what they do and to allow them absolutely and utterly their conditions. This alone, for the taster, secures freedom of enjoyment. I apply the rule to you, and it represents a perfect triumph of appreciation; because it makes me accept, largely, all your material from you—an absolute gain when I consider that I should never take it from myself. I note certain things which make me wonder at your form and your fortune (e.g.—as I have told you before—the fatal colours in which they let *you*, because you live at home—is it?—paint American life; and the fact that there's a whole quarter of the heaven upon which, in the matter of composition, you seem consciously—*is* it consciously?—to have turned your back); but these things have no relevancy whatever as grounds of dislike—simply because you communicate so completely *what* you undertake to communicate. The novelist is a particular *window*, absolutely—and of worth in so far as he is one; and it's because you open so well and are hung so close over the street that *I* could hang out of it all day long. Your very value is that you choose your own street—heaven forbid I should have to choose it for you. If I should say I mortally dislike the people who pass in it, I should seem to be taking on myself that intolerable responsibility of selection which it is exactly such a luxury to be relieved of. Indeed I'm convinced that no reader above the rank of an idiot—this number is moderate I admit—can really fail to take any view that is really *shown* them—any gift (of subject) that's really given. The usual imbecility of the novel is that the showing and giving simply don't come off—the reader never touches the subject and the subject never touches the reader; the window is no window at all—but only childishly *finta*, like the ornaments of our beloved Italy. This is why, as a triumph of *communication*, I hold the *Hazard* so rare and strong. You communicate in touches so close, so fine, so true, so droll, so frequent. I am writing too much (you will think me demented with chatter); so that I can't go into specifications of success. It is *all* absolutely successful, and if a part or two are better than the others it isn't that the others are not so good as they ought to be. These last have the deuce of an effort in making it appear that nothing ought *ever* to be less good than they. That is, you set a measure and example of the prehensile perception—and so many things in future will seem less good than they ever *could* be, for not coming up to such a standard. The Dryfooses are portraiture of the very first magnitude, the old man magnificent without flaw or faintness anywhere, and the whole thing, in short, so observed, so caught, so felt, so conceived and created—so damningly and inexplicably American. How can they stand each other? (so many of them!) I asked as I read, reflecting that they, poor things, hadn't *you*, as I had, to make me stand them all. Or rather they *had* you, really—and that's the word of the enigma. You pervade and permeate them all, my dear Howells, just enough to save them from each other and from the unlimited extension of the movement of irresistible relief by which Christine D. scratches Beaton's face and even old Dryfoos smites his blank son (an admirable, *admirable* business, the whole of that). Go on, go on, even if *I* can't—and since New York has brought you such *bonheur* give it back to her with still larger liberality. Don't tell me you can't do anything now, or that life isn't luxurious to you, with such a power of creation. You live in a luxury (of that kind) which Lindau would reprehend, or at any rate have nothing to meet, and that I am not sure even poor March would be altogether easy about. Poor March, my dear Howells—what tricks you play him—even worse than those you play Mrs. March! Just let me add that Conrad D. is a *first class* idea, as the son of his father and a figure in the Dryfoos picture. But *all* the picture, I expect, is of the highest worth. How the devil did you do it? You'll found a school—that of your "third manner" and I shall come to it.—I left London four days ago, with the cunning purpose of staying away from it for June and July and returning to it for August and September. I hope to spend June in Venice—July perhaps in some blue Giorgionesque background. I continue to scribble, though with relaxed continuity while abroad; but I can't talk to you about it. One thing only is clear: that henceforth I must do, or half do, England in fiction—as the place I see most today, and, in a sort of way, know best. I have at last more acquired notions of it, on the whole, than of any other world, and it will serve as well as any other. It has been growing distincter that America fades from me, and as she never trusted me at best, I can trust *her,* for effect, no longer. Besides I can't be doing *de chic,* from here, when you, on the spot, are doing so brilliantly the *vécu.*—The *vécu* indeed reached me in a very terrible form, in London, just before I came away, in the shape of the news of the rejection at Washington of the International Copyright Bill.[4] That was the great news there, and it has made a very bad state of things—so that I was glad to come away, for a time at least, from the shame and discomfort of it. It seems as if this time we had said, loudly, that whereas we had freely admitted before that we in fact steal, we now seize the opportunity to decide that we *like* to steal. This surely isn't what we really *mean,* as a whole people—and yet apparently we do mean it enough not to care to make it clear that we mean anything else. It is a new sort of national profession, under the sun, and I am sorry the originality of it should belong to us. Of course however there will be another big fight before the civilization of the country accepts such a last word. I have lately seen much the admirably acute and intelligent young Balestier,[5] who has been of much business use to me, and a great comfort thereby—besides my liking him so. I think that practically he will soon "do everything" for me. Also your (also acute) young friend H. Harland,[6] whom I had to fish out of a heaped-up social basket *as* your friend. I shall be glad to make him mine if he'll be so—he seems a very clever fellow. But why won't you ever project these young stars into my milky way? If it's to "spare" me you don't, because I always—at last—discover them and then have to try to lavish myself on them the more to make up to them for the unnatural rigour with which you've treated them. Please give my love to Mrs. March and tell her I could "stand" *her* if she'd only give me a chance. Do come out again, with Tom and Bella, whom I press to my heart and will take you to a better hatter, in London, than Dryfoos did. Ever my dear Basil,[7] enthusiastically yours

Henry James

1. *A Hazard of New Fortunes* had just been published.

2. Lemuel Barker is a principal character in *The Minister's Charge* (1887). See letter to Howells, 7 December 1886.

3. The Marches (including Tom, Bella, and Basil), the Dryfooses (including Christine and Conrad), Lindau (the old man), and Beaton are characters in *A Hazard of New Fortunes*.

4. This was the defeat of the Chace bill, the twelfth international copyright bill to be defeated in the United States since 1843. Under the leadership of prominent writers and editors including James Russell Lowell, E. C. Stedman, and Robert Underwood Johnson, the same measure obtained a favorable vote in 1891. Before this there was much pirating of British works in America and cheap reprinting of American works in England.

5. Wolcott Balestier (1861–1891), a young publisher's representative, had come to England to make contractual arrangements with British authors so that their American rights might be protected.

6. Henry Harland (1861–1905) had published, under the pseudonym of Sidney Luska, a series of novels dealing with the lives of immigrant Jews in America. He had now come abroad to write under his own name and would shortly be named editor of the *Yellow Book*.

7. Basil March in Howells's novel is partly autobiographical.

To Alice James
Ms Harvard

Palazzo Barbaro, [Venice]
June *6th* [1890]

Dearest Sister,

I am ravished by your letter after reading the play[1] (keep it locked up, safe and secret, though there are three or four copies in existence) which makes me feel as if there had been a triumphant première and I had received overtures from every managerial quarter and had only to count my gold. At any rate I am delighted that you have been struck with it exactly as I have *tried* to strike and that the pure *practical* character of the effort has worked its calculated spell upon you. For what encourages me in the whole business is that, as the piece stands, there is not, in its felicitous form, the ghost of a "fluke" or a mere chance: it is all "art" and an absolute address of means to the end—the end, viz., of meeting *exactly* the immediate, actual, intense British conditions, both subjective and objective, and of acting in (to a minute, including entr'actes) two hours and three-quarters. Ergo, I can do a dozen more infinitely better; and I am excited to think how much, since the writing of this one piece has been an education to me, a little further experience will do for me. Also I am sustained by the sense, on the whole, that though really superior acting would help it immensely, yet mediocrity of handling (which is all, at the best, I am pretty sure, that it will get) won't and can't *kill* it, and that there may be even something sufficiently general and human about it, to make it (given its eminent actability) "keep the stage," even after any first vogue it may have has passed away. *That* fate—in the poverty-stricken condition of the English repertory—would mean profit indeed, and an income to my descendants. But one mustn't talk of this kind of thing yet. However, since you have been already so deeply initiated, I think I will enclose (keep it sacredly for me) an admirable letter I have just received from the precious *Balestier* in whose hands, as I wrote you, I placed the settlement of the money-question, the terms of the written agreement with Compton. Compton saw him on Monday last—and I send the letter mainly to illustrate the capital intelligence and competence and benevolence of Balestier and show you in what good hands I am. He will probably strike you, as he strikes me, as the perfection of an "agent"—especially when you consider that he has undertaken this particular job out of pure friendship. Everything, evidently, will be well settled—on the basis, of course, which can't be helped, of production in *London* only about the middle of next year. But by that time I hope to have done a good bit more work—and I shall be beguiled by beginning to follow, in the autumn, the rehearsals for the country production. Keep Balestier's letter till I come back—I shall get another one from him in a day or two with the agreement to sign. You will see how much he confirms my good personal impression of Compton. If Compton's maximum in the country is £100 (gross-receipts) a night it ought to be taken (always assuming, of course, the play to be successful) as his *average* in a London theatre, where prices are higher—twice as high—and seats, above all, stalls, more numerous. Therefore with weekly matinées my ten per cent would certainly bring me upwards of £80 a week—and this, going on steadily for some time, would make up a sum very well worth while. But, further, a nightly "take" in London of only £100 for a *successful* play, is moderate—and I might probably look for £350 a month: which, as a steady thing, would seem to me a fortune. But the *real* fact is that any play, in *London,* which should bring me £350 a month, would so soon get into swing in America that the larger (simultaneous) profits would come from there—to say nothing (vide Balestier letter) of the simultaneous country company and of Australia! These castles in Spain are at least exhilarating. In a certain sense I should like you very much to communicate to William your good impression of the drama—but on the whole I think you had better not, for the simple reason that it is very important it shouldn't be talked about (especially so long) in advance—and it wouldn't be *safe,* inasmuch as every whisper gets into the papers—and in some fearfully vulgarized and perverted form. You *might* hint to William that you have read the piece under seal of secrecy to me and think so-and-so of it—but are so bound (to me) not to give a sign that *he* must bury what you tell him in tenfold mystery. But I doubt if even *this* would be secure—it would be in the *Transcript* the next week.—Venice continues adorable and the Curtises the soul of benevolence. Their upstairs apartment (empty and still unoffered—at forty pounds a year—to any one but me) beckons me so, as a foot-in-the-water here, that if my dramatic ship had begun to come in, I should probably be tempted to take it at a venture—for all it would matter. But for the present I resist perfectly—especially as Venice isn't *all* advantageous. The great charm of such an idea is the having in Italy, a little cheap and private refuge independent of hotels etc., which every year grow more disagreeable and German and tiresome to face—not to say dearer too. But it won't be for this year—and the Curtises won't let it. What Pen Browning[2] has done here, through his American wife's dollars, with the splendid Palazzo Rezzonico, transcends description for the beauty, and, as Ruskin would say, "wisdom and rightness" of it. It is altogether royal and imperial—but "Pen" isn't kingly and the *train de vie* remains to be seen. Gondoliers ushering in friends from pensions won't fill it out. The Rodgerses[3] have turned up but are not oppressive—seeming mainly to be occupied with being constantly ill. That is Katie appears everywhere to collapse badly and expensively, and I judge she has something gravely the matter with her. She has "doctors" at every place they go—is in bed for days etc.—and yet they go every-

Angle of the drawing room in the Palazzo Barbaro

where. I don't encourage them (I have indeed seen them but once—when I took them on the water by moonlight) to talk about "the will"—as it's disagreeable and they really know nothing about it. I am thinking, after all, of joining the Curtises in the evidently most beautiful *drive* (of upwards of a week, with rests) they are starting upon on the 14th, from a place called Vittorio, in the Venetian Alps, two hours' rail from here, through Cadore, Titian's country, the Dolomites etc., toward Oberammergau. They offer me, pressingly, the fourth seat in the carriage that awaits them when they leave the train—and also an extra ticket they have taken for the play at Oberammergau if I choose to go so far. This I shall scarcely do, but I *shall* probably leave with them, drive four or five days and come *back*, via Verona, by rail—leaving my luggage here. Continue to address here—unless, before that, I give you one other address while I am gone. I shall find all letters here, on my return, if I do go, in the keeping of the excellent *maestro di casa*—the Venetian Smith. I should be back, at the *latest*, by the 25th—probably by the 20th. In this case I shall presumably go back to Florence to spend four or five days with Baldwin (going to Siena or Perugia); after which I have a dream of going up to Vallombrosa (nearly 4000 feet above the sea—but of a softness!) for two or three weeks—till I have to leave Italy on my way home. I am writing to Edith Peruzzi, who has got a summer-lodge there, and is already there, for information about the inn. If I don't go there I shall perhaps try Camaldoli or San Marcello—all high in the violet Apennines, within three or four hours, and mainly by a little carriage, of Florence. But I *want* to compass Vallombrosa, which I have never seen and have always dreamed of and which I am assured is divine—infinitely salubrious and softly cool. The idea of lingering in Italy a few weeks longer on these terms is very delightful to me—it does me, as yet, nothing but good. But I shall see. I put B.'s letter in another envelope. I rejoice in your eight gallops—they may be the dozen now.

Ever your
Henry

1. The dramatized version of HJ's novel *The American.*
2. Son of Robert and Elizabeth Barrett Browning.
3. Maternal relatives traveling abroad.

To Francis Boott
Ms Harvard

Palazzo Barbaro. Venice
June 12*th* [1890]

My dear Francis.

I am extremely sorry to be so far away and to miss you so completely for the present. May this catch you at Liverpool with as little delay as possible. I hope to be away from London till August 10*th* as it is to keep out of the outermost eddy of the Season that I have come abroad; and it won't be safe to venture back before the first days of that month. Besides I want to complete my three months on the Continent. I shall not go to Switzerland—I want to stick to Italy to the bitter end. All this muddle is of the sweetest. The Curtises leave this place on Saturday, *via* Cadori, Tyrol, Oberammergau, Davos (to see Symonds) etc. for England, and bid me tell you that they will be *about* July 1st at *5. A. Cork St. Bond St. W.* till July 15th and greatly hope to see you there. I go with them through Titian's country and then come back hitherward and pay Mrs. Bronson a little visit at Asolo. After that I may stay on in Venice, *may* go to Vallombrosa—*may* do other things. But I mean at least to try to cling to Italy. I haven't the faintest thought of "Lucerne." I came to Italy a month ago, and to Venice eleven days. I lately spent a week with Baldwin in Florence. I am delighted at your coming out—may it do you lots of good. It's a capital inspiration. I am sure Alice will rejoice to see you if she possibly can. She will tell you how and when. *Go to see Fenimore—without fail*—at *4 Promenade Terrace, Cheltenham.* It's a three or four hour journey—and a very pretty one—from London. After the first week in August—and possibly before—I shall be continuously in London—having had my cake. Come and stay with me then—I can easily put you up, and shall be delighted to do so—though it will be a moment when London won't be very interesting to you. Your last letter I have been on the very edge of answering—and should have done so from Florence had I not spent all my time there at the Dentist's. If Alice should be ill I would come back *before* August 10th. Otherwise not. *Si diverta!* Can't you pass the Alps? Probably you hate the idea. The Curtises send you much love, and so does yours ever faithfully

Henry James

To Lady Gregory

Ms Berg

Palazzo Barbaro: Venice
June 13*th* [1890]

Dear Lady Gregory.

Even at this distance and borne over the smooth lagoon, which softens all sounds, the elephant's footfall has a very friendly music. But I wish I were at home to hear it more distinctly. When I do get back, however, I shall become intimate with its other charms and uses and feel still more grateful for your benevolent thought of taking so much trouble to supply me with a picturesque luxury.[1] It is very charming of you, and please be sure you are as cordially thanked as the exotic convenience will be deeply appreciated. You shall have more news of its complete domestication.—Like you I am spending the London Season in quieter waters—I have been these several weeks in Italy. The peace and leisure of it, the exemption from "pressure" are not to be said—they are blessings only to be devoutly inhaled. I hope you have something like them. Oddly enough (in a sense), I was relating only late last night how kind you have been to P[aul] H[arvey][2] (relating it to my good hosts—old friends here), and the first thing this A.M. your letter comes. I hope P.H. continues to deserve well of you and that Sir William returned in due course and due condition. Kindly give him, and take unto yourself, the very friendly remembrances of yours most truly

Henry James

1. Lady Gregory had apparently sent HJ from India a small carved elephant souvenir.

2. Paul Harvey, private secretary to the Marquess of Lansdowne and later a diplomat and man of letters, was related to Blanche Lee Childe, a friend of HJ's Paris days. See letter to Grace Norton, 23 February 1884. HJ had met Harvey, then a small boy, on the estate of the Childe relatives near Varenne in 1876. Both James and Lady Gregory took a particular interest in Harvey's career.

To Dr. W. W. Baldwin
Ms Morgan

Innsbruck
Austria
[20 June 1890]

My dear Doctor:

It was only yesterday that your cordial and charming note overtook me—and I snatch a moment to answer it before I step (apparently in a pouring rain) into the carriage which is to convey me —forty miles—to Oberammergau—for even to that have I come, dragged along by an irresistible current. The friends with whom I stayed in Venice and who have brought me thus far are determined to put me through the mill. But thus far the mill has ground merrily enough—our three days' drive through the Venetian Alps, the Ampezzo, etc. has been enchantingly beautiful. The performance at Oberammergau takes place on Sunday 22d—and lasts (in the open air and in the rain, *if* it rains) from 8 A.M. to 5.30 P.M.! It would give you many patients, I think, if you were here. However, I hope to survive it, and drive back here, alone (my companions go elsewhere), on Monday 23d. On Tuesday 24th I jog back over the Brenner, in five hours, to Botzen, whence on Wednesday, if all goes well, I take an Einspänner and drive (for two days) back into blessed Italy, to *Asolo,* where I spend a couple of days with Mrs. Bronson, who, as perhaps you know, has a little house there. (Asolo is in the sweet Venetian hills, near Bassano, and Pen Browning, the other day in Venice, recommended me highly to take the drive in question—from Botzen to Bassano, by Primiero and San Martino, other beautiful Dolomites.) I mention these details simply to let you see that I have a certain amount of work still cut out before going back to Florence. But I won't fail you! I hope to leave Venice (to which I return, from Asolo, simply to pick up my luggage) by the end of next week. I will write you again before that. I deplore your defunct patients and don't envy you your groggy apostle. You must tell me all about him. I have the charmingest recollection of my week in your delicate Villino and of the hospitality you and Mrs. Baldwin lavished on me. Kindest regards to her. Ever dear Doctor your *devotissimo*

Henry James

To Isabella Stewart Gardner

Ms Gardner

Garmisch
Bavaria
June 24*th* 1890

Dear Mrs. Gardner,

There are many things I must ask you to excuse. One of them is this paper from the village grocer of an unsophisticated Bavarian valley. The others I will tell you when we next meet. Not that they matter much; for you *won't* excuse them—you never do. But I have your commands to write and tell you "all about" something or other—I think it was Venice—and at any rate Venice will do. Venice always does. Therefore I won't give you further grounds for rigour by failing to obey your behest on this point. I have just been (three days ago) to see the Passion Play at Oberammergau, and with my good friends and hosts the Curtises, with whom, twelve days ago, I left Venice to drive hither delightfully through the Venetian Alps, the Dolomites, Cadore, Cortina, and Ampezzo etc., I am resting, after that exploit, in this sweet recess among the mountains—which has been (it is but two hours away by carriage) our *point de départ* for the pilgrimage. Tomorrow we drive back to Innsbruck and separate—they to go to England and I back to Italy, for two or three weeks more. The Passion play is curious, tedious, touching, intensely respectable and intensely German. I wouldn't have come if I hadn't been brought (by Mrs. Curtis and Miss Wormeley); and I shall never go again even if I *am* brought by syren hands. But all these Tyrolean countries are beyond praise—and the several days' drive was magnificent. Venice was cool, empty, melancholy and delicious. They "sprang" upon me (the Curtises) the revelation that you are to have the Barbaro for August, torturing me thus with a vision of alternatives and preferences—the question of whether I would give up the happy actual (the secure fact of really *being* there in June) for the idea of a perhaps even happier possible or impossible, the romance of being there in August. I took what I had—I *was* there a fortnight. Now I am going back, to stay but a day or two, and then do some other things —go again for ten days to Florence and to two or three Tuscan excursions. Why are you so perverse?—Why do you come to London when I am away, and away from it just when I come back? Even your bright presence there does not make me repent having fled this year from the Savage Season. You wouldn't have made it tame—so what good should I have got? I hope you have found it as wild as you like things. The Palazzo Barbaro is divine, and divinely still: don't make it spin round. If I am in Italy still when you arrive *je viendrai vous y voir.* But I take it you have arranged your court. My clothes are there still (I only brought a necktie here). But I shall get them out of your way—you would perhaps pitch them into the Adriatic. I shall write to you again and am ever, dear Mrs. Gardner, most faithfully yours

Henry James

To Grace Norton
Ms Harvard

Palazzo Barbaro
Venice
June 30*th* [1890]

My dear Grace.

I begin this grateful letter to you with vague ideas as to when I shall finish it—being at the present moment on a branch that sways beneath me: i.e. in Venice only for twenty-four hours, *di passaggio,* on my way to other parts. But the great thing *is* to begin—for after all I should never properly and justifiably end—telling you how I glow with genial appreciation of the two magnanimous letters I have received from you since I came to Italy, and more particularly with gratitude for the second one, on the subject of my latest "work" (date of June 12th), which I found here last evening on my return from an excursion (mainly driving), of fifteen days through the Dolomites and to the Oberammergau Passion Play. I came hither originally June 1st, to spend a fortnight with my old friends and entertainers the D. (*you* will say the d--d) Curtises, according to a promise made and renewed any time these three years. This promise I redeemed, very agreeably (to myself), and then unexpectedly started off with my hosts, who had made their plans—and *mine* (which *I* hadn't) to proceed by carriage through the Venetian Alps, Cadore, Cortina, the Ampezzo, etc., to (by the aid of five further hours of rail) Innsbruck, and thence by carriage (forty miles) through the Bavarian Highlands and the pastoral valley of Garmisch, to the before-mentioned inevitable Ammergau—which is the "boom" this summer and every tenth year. To make a long story short, I started with them, to see Cadore etc., and then was wooed on by adorable scenery, genial society and lovely weather to do, from day to day, the whole thing—which I have gratefully survived but not allowed to cheat me out of a return to Italy, where I hope to remain till August 1st. I posted back to Innsbruck with my friends (after the curious, tedious, touching Ammergau episode—very honourable on the part of the earnest and practical peasants and artisans who act the play, but well nigh threatened with extinction by vulgarity and cocknification from Cook, Gaze, etc.—the entrepreneurs of British and American travel); and there we separated, the kind Curtises to betake themselves to England to see their younger son who dwells there in country-gentlemanliness (at least attempted) and matrimony, and I to come back and pick up my luggage and clothing—represented during our drive only by an exiguous wallet. I go with them tomorrow to Florence—and meanwhile I am spending this splendid summer day in this beautiful empty house, under the care of the suavest and most obsequious of old Venetian butlers. Such is a succinct account of my recent doings—to which let me add, that I go to Florence, first to stay four or five days with a good friend I have there—a dear little American physician of genius, W. W. Baldwin by name; who makes the rain and the fine weather there now; and then to go up (if I can find a perch at the inn) and spend the rest of July on the divine hilltop of Vallombrosa—which is high enough to be cool and lovely enough to be warm. After that, my holiday finished, I shall post back to London, where work awaits me and where I shall not scruple to spend, most contentedly and unfashionably, the rest of the summer.

July 3d (three days later): *1 Via Palestro, Firenze.* I take up my little story again here—having been interrupted just after those last words and transferred myself day before yesterday from Venice to this place. This is a delightful moment to be in Italy, and really nowadays, the only right one—for the herd of tourists has departed, the scramble at the stations is no more, and one seems alone with the dear old land, who at the same time, seems alone with herself. I am happy to say that I am as fond as ever of this tender little

Florence, where it doesn't seem a false note even to be staying with an "American doctor." My friend Baldwin is a charming and glowing little man, who, coming here eight or ten years ago, has made himself a first place, and who seems to consider it a blessing to him that I should abide a few days in his house. I accept the oddity of the view, and perhaps even regard it as another oddity, all round, that on leaving him, I shall probably go up and spend a week with the Edith Peruzzis, *née* Story,[1] at Vallombrosa. As to this I am temporizing—but I am distinctly *pressed;* or should say I was if my modesty permitted me to. I should have liked to tell you how fascinating I found the Italian Alps and the Tyrol—what a "revelation" they really struck me as being—revelation, I mean, of the sympathetic, and loveable in great mountain scenery. I never "sympathised" much with Switzerland—but I can with the Dolomites. When, three mornings ago, I rose early, to take the train for Florence, and in the cool, fresh 7 o'clock light, was rowed through the delicious half-stirred place and the imbroglio of little silent plashing waterways to the station, it was really heartbreaking to come away—to come out into the dust and *banalité* of the rest of the world. (Venice clings closer to one by its dustlessness than perhaps by any other one charm.) But already the sweetness of Florence *tastes.* I am, however, seriously thinking, or rather *dreaming,* of putting my hand on some little cheap permanent refuge in Venice—some little perch over the water, with a bed, and a table in it, to call one's own and come away to, without the interposition of luggage and hotels, whenever the weight of London, at certain times, is no longer to be borne. For the moment, however, I am just solicited back there by a local (or would be) Lorelei in the shape of Mrs. Jack Gardner, whom the absent Curtises have lent Palazzo Barbaro to for the month of August and who requests the favour of my company (she seems to think I am "thrown in") after the second or third. I have left to the end, my dear Grace, thanking you properly for the very "handsome" way in which you speak of the massive [*Tragic*] *Muse.* I am delighted that it strikes you as a success, for I tried so hard to make it one that if it hadn't been it would have been a failure indeed. That's all I can say about it—as I never have begun to understand how one can "justify" a work of art or imagination or *take up* anything said on the subject. One's own saying is what one has tried to say *in* it. This is there or it's absent, and when the thing is done nothing will make it better or worse. Thank you for reading. Good-bye: I wish you had a little change as they say in London. May this bring you a moment of such. Ever faithfully yours

Henry James

1. See letter to Mrs. Bronson, 5 February 1887.

To Theodore E. Child

Ms Barrett

Villino Rubio, 1, Via Palestro
Florence. July 4*th* 1890

My dear Child.

I have been moved by my indignation at the gross mutilation practised in this month's *Harper*, on the combined integrity of Daudet and myself, to write a few glowing words of disavowal to the author of *Port Tarascon*—lest he should think I had a hand in the *inqualifiable* trick;[1] as to which I am also addressing Messrs Harper a few *vertes* remarks. But I have utterly forgotten Daudet's number and as I wish to be very sure my note reaches him am constrained to ask you kindly to close, address, stamp and post it. I shall be *infinitely* obliged. I am where you see—for as much of the summer as possible. I hope you have happily returned—I take for granted you have—from the dim (to me) Antipodes. I have hopes of Paris in the autumn if I don't take too much Italy now. But I can't take enough! Ever yours,

Henry James

1. HJ's protest was over the omission in the serial form in *Harper's Magazine* of his translation of the fifth chapter of Daudet's work, the so-called anti-Christ episode. Daudet, himself a Catholic, had indulged in a certain kind of humor generally acceptable to French Catholics; but Henry Mills Alden, the editor of *Harper's*, wrote to HJ: "There are many readers to whom the whole chapter would seem blasphemous. The more thoughtful reader would comprehend the true meaning of the episode. I found by actual test that there was a chance of its being misunderstood. We followed our usual rule in such a case, and left it out." See J. Henry Harper, *The House of Harper* (1912), 620–621. The chapter was restored in the book publication.

To Henrietta Reubell
Ms Harvard

Villino Rubio, 1 Via Palestro
Florence
July 7*th* [1890]

My dear Miss Reubell.

You really ought to have met me or joined me somewhere—your genial note only reminds me how pleasant that would have been. You see, as I am still in Italy, what a long, social southern time of it we might have had together. This summer aspect of the land of lands is exceedingly sweet and sympathetic; for the barbarian hordes have departed and one has the whole place to one's self and is quite en famille with it. I don't know what, or how, to tell you about all I have been doing, as I have been up and down the place considerably and have had a succession of episodes which might bewilder you. Yesterday I spent 3000 feet in the air, at the divine, the delicious Vallombrosa. Today—an hour or two hence—I go to Sienna for four or five days. On the 12th I start on a little tour of the most romantic and untrodden corners of Tuscany[1] with my excellent hospitable friend Baldwin (the wonderful little American doctor—a man of genius—did you ever hear of him? with whom I am spending a few days here). We are to take with us a very pleasant and wily Italian friend of Baldwin's, who is connected with the Ferrovie and very *pratico* of the out of the way places, and he engages to give us impressions which the herd of tourists never have. See how you might have made a fourth in our little party and what wonderful episodes and adventures you might have shared. You should trust more—risk more. Take care lest the rising tide of your Parisian skepticism submerge you. I have just come back here from two or three weeks of Venice (I originally spent a week here when I first came to Italy) and a wonderful unexpected hors d'oeuvre or excrescence in the shape of a fifteen days' excursion through the Dolomites etc. over into the Tyrol, the Bavarian Highlands and the Oberammergau Passion Play. See again what you might have tasted. I went with the Daniel Curtises (with whom *auparavant,* I spent, most appreciatively, the first fifteen days of June at their delicious Barbaro). They, it is true, might not have been your affair; but if *you* had crossed the Alps they would also have been less mine—I would have gone with you. The Oberammergau play is a good deal like the Français—if you imagine the Maison de Molière more or less unroofed and set in a sweet little circle of mountains. Also the *crowds* much better done—quite wonderful and the Crucifixion to the life, a perfect illusion—only that neither Worms nor even Febvre nor Le Bargy[2] could have begun to represent it or look it. The Tyrol, the Dolomites etc., which I didn't know, are divine and knock the poor dear old Swiss "fine scenery" to pieces. This is a crude way of speaking—I mean I found all that region more sympathetic and friendly, a Dolomite somehow more personal and sociable than an Alp. I stay about here till August 1st and then, my holiday over and the London crowd dispersed, I return to my humble home. As you probably know, Mrs. J. L. Gardner has borrowed the Palazzo Barbaro for the month of August, and has kindly asked me to come back there and pay *her* a visit: but I fear I am already nearly at the end of my tether. When I whiz through France you will have left Paris—therefore I shall probably, in the dog days, not stop there. But I dream of a month of it in the autumn. I have read *Notre Coeur* but haven't looked at Bourget in the *Figaro*. I am waiting for the volume. Is his "coeur" of the same sort? What a droll name for the organ in question! What a droll subject, that of Maupassant, every way—the drollest I think, when one considers what it really is—ever treated in fiction, and showing to what lapses, or intermissions (the *treatment* shows) the great French perception of the ridiculous is liable. I don't think it, *Notre Coeur*, very good. The woman's a character, if you like—*and encore;* but the man surely isn't. But the work is too unedifying to write to a lady about. I hope you will enjoy the Canton de Genève and I look forward, with eagerness, to some early opportunity of exposing you to the assiduities of yours, dear Miss Reubell most faithfully

Henry James

1. HJ and Baldwin hiked to several Tuscan towns with Baldwin's friend, a stout Italian named Taccini, and on one occasion slept in a farmhouse where HJ insisted on having his morning bath. No bathtub being available, the huge dough-tub used for kneading bread was conscripted into service. The suffocating summer heat made the adventurers give up the trip after four days. But the name Taccini was carried by HJ into *The Wings of the Dove*—he is the doctor

who takes charge of Milly Theale when Sir Luke Strett is in London; and this suggests that in some of his characteristics Sir Luke himself derives from Dr. Baldwin.

2. Gustave Hyppolyte Worms (1837–1910), Alexandre Frédéric Febvre (1835–1916), and Charles Gustave Auguste Le Bargy (1858–1936) were among the most celebrated actors of the Théâtre Français in the late nineteenth century.

To William James

Ms Harvard

Paradisino, Vallombrosa, Tuscany
July 23*rd*, 1890

My dear Brother:

I had from you some ten days ago a most delightful letter written just after the heroic perusal of my interminable novel[1]—which, according to your request, I sent off almost too precipitately to Alice, so that I haven't it here to refer to. But I don't need to "refer" to it, inasmuch as it has plunged me into a glow of satisfaction which is far, as yet, from having faded. I can only thank you tenderly for seeing so much good in the clumsy thing—as I thanked your Alice, who wrote me a most lovely letter, a week or two ago. I have no illusions of any kind about the book, and least of all about its circulation and "popularity." From these things I am quite divorced and never was happier than since the dissolution has been consecrated by (what seems to me) the highest authorities. One must go one's way and know what one's about and have a general plan and a private religion—in short have made up one's mind as to *ce qui en est* with a public the draggling after which simply leads one in the gutter. One has always a "public" enough if one has an audible vibration—even if it should only come from one's self. I shall never make my fortune—nor anything like it; but—I know what I shall do, and it won't be bad.—I am lingering on late in Italy, as you see, so as to keep away from London till August 1st or thereabouts. (I stay in this exquisite spot till that date.) I shall then, returning to my normal occupations, have had the best and clearest and pleasantest holiday of three months, that I have had for many a day. I have been accompanied on this occasion by a literary irresponsibility which has caused me to enjoy Italy perhaps more than ever before: let alone that I have never before been perched (more than three thousand feet in the air) in so perfect a paradise as this unspeakable Vallombrosa. It is Milton's Vallombrosa, the original of his famous line, the site of the old mountain monastery which he visited and which stands still a few hundred feet below me as I write, "suppressed" and appropriated some time ago by the Italian Government, who have converted it into a State school of "Forestry."[2] This little inn—the Paradisino, as it is called, on a pedestal of rock overhanging the violet abysses like the prow of a ship, is the Hermitage (a very comfortable one) of the old convent. The place is extraordinarily beautiful and "sympathetic" and the most romantic mountains and most admirable woods—chestnut and beech and magnificent pine-forests, the densest, coolest shade, the freshest, sweetest air and the most enchanting views. It is full twenty years since I have done anything like so much wandering through dusky woods and lying with a book on warm, breezy hillsides. It has given me a sense of summer which I had lost in so many London Julys; given me almost the summer of one's childhood back again. I shall certainly come back here for other Julys and other Augusts—and I hate to go away now. May you, and all of you, these weeks, have as sweet, or half as sweet, an impression of the natural universe as yours affectionately,

Henry James

1. *The Tragic Muse.*

2. The Benedictine Abbey and mother house of an Italian order founded by Gualbert in 1015. The later edifice was built in 1637 and appropriated by the Italian government in 1866. The School of Forestry was housed there in 1870. Milton's allusion in *Paradise Lost* was in the celebrated lines (Book I, 302–303) "Thick as autumal leaves that strew the brooks / In Vallombrosa . . ."

To Horace E. Scudder

Ms Harvard

34 De Vere Gardens
October 5*th* 1890

Dear Mr. Scudder.[1]

I send you, in a heavy registered packet, by this post, a tale called *The Pupil,* which I have tried to make as short as possible. Do what I would (and I boiled it down repeatedly), it insists on being of dimensions that represent, as I measure them, about twenty-three and a half pages of the *Atlantic*. This, obviously, you will regard as long for a "short" story—though it isn't very long for *me;* at least until, after much disuse of the practice, I succeed, with more trials, as I fully mean to do, in working myself back to an intenser brevity. At any rate I greatly hope you will, on looking on this performance, fancy it justifies itself sufficiently to go in as one thing—not as two. I can't but think it would suffer greatly by partition. I have given it much care, and it hangs all together—it has *one* long rhythm. If you will print it as one I promise you, for the next time, a thing that will take only ten pages. I hope *The Pupil* comes in time for me to see a proof of it. Yours very truly

Henry James

1. Horace Elisha Scudder (1838–1902), Boston novelist and biographer, edited the *Atlantic Monthly* from 1890 to 1898.

To Frederic W. H. Myers
Ts Lubbock

Reform Club
Oct. 7*th* [1890]

My dear Myers.[1]

I have waited a day just to think a little whether my complete detachment from my brother's labour and pursuits, my *outsideness,* as it were, to the S.P.R., my total ignorance of Mrs. Piper[2] and my general aversion to her species ought not (to myself, who have the full and inner measure of these limitations) to appear to disqualify me from even such a share in your proceedings as would be represented by, and restricted to, the lending of my (barely audible) voice to his paper. But even after so much reflection I *can't* make up my mind! Therefore I don't pretend to make it up—but give *sentiment* the benefit of the doubt. If it will do the paper the least good—or do *you* either—I will read it, as pluckily as possible, on the day you designate. Might you very kindly let me have a look at it before that? Ever yours

Henry James

1. Frederic William Henry Myers (1843–1901) was one of the founders of the Society for Psychical Research (S.P.R.).

2. Mrs. William J. Piper, a Boston medium, had interested William James for some years, and he had written a paper on her for the "Proceedings of the S.P.R." in London. It was entitled "Certain Phenomena of Trance." HJ read the paper for his brother in Westminster Town Hall on 31 October 1890. See letter to WJ, 7 November 1890.

To Urbain Mengin

Ms Harvard

34 De Vere Gardens W.
October 19*th* 1890

My dear Mengin.

Hasn't the best way to "forgive" you (for nothing) been to give you an occasion to forgive me—and make us more than equal—by delaying (more days than I meant) to thank you for your last most graceful letter? We must, however, cherish an easy rule in all these matters; for the correspondences of this world are well-nigh too heavy to be borne. But I like to hear from you and to know that you remember me and that you don't forget, and don't detest, this poor dear old London, against which you have—tous vous autres—si beau jeu. Don't be discouraged and don't let go your tangled English thread. Keep hold of it, fasten it to some thing on your person, and some day the other end (perhaps when you least expect it) will give a responsive twitch and you will be drawn into the heart of the mystery, the centre of the labyrinth, the seat where you can sit down. Happy you, at any rate, to have a French home-background to your life—I mean a well of sentiment and piety into which you can dip; a nest in your sweet, bright, human, national *midi* to which you can sometimes flutter back. At this moment I am afraid your vacation is over and the greyness of active pedagogy closes you in. All the same I shall send this letter to Pau, to be forwarded to you—as I am not sure of your other address. I had myself this year a very pleasant holiday-time, and I took it, with a particularly successful perversity, at the moment when London is most recommended. I went to Italy the 1st May and stayed there till the middle of August. I loved it better than ever—at that moment the barbarians who overrun it in winter and spring have returned to their northern caves, and one is en famille with the dear old indigènes and their lovely land. But neither going nor coming did I stop in Paris; so that it is nearly a year since I have seen

Bourget. I heard, the other day, of his being at Genoa—so he has been spending his honeymoon in Italy.[1] He has not written to me for ages, and save by the formal faire-part, ne me touche pas un mot de son mariage. Ce mariage s'est fait, paraît-il, d'un jour à l'autre—dans les conditions les plus singulières. La jeune fille, qui n'a pas le sou, était très jolie et tout à fait folle de lui. Elle écrivit l'autre jour à une dame de mes amies, amie aussi de Bourget, et qui se trouvait alors à Venise: "Venez donc trouver mon poète à Gênes, Madame—il a si besoin de consolations!"—Après un mois de mariage, diable! Enfin j'espère les voir à Paris, où je compte passer trois semaines en novembre ou décembre. Que vous semble-t-il de *Coeur de Femme?*[2] Je l'y vois prendre de plus en plus un pli que je déplorais déjà dans ses commencements mais que je mettais alors sur le compte du manque de sûreté de goût propre à la jeunesse: je veux dire l'étalage trop complaisant of the knowledge of "high life"—detestable expression. Et puis, bien que ce livre contienne des pages d'analyse magistrale, c'est de l'analyse appliquée tellement à tort, l'analyse de M. Casal, et d'une, en somme, si pauvre créature! Et puis, il y a autre chose encore. Bourget est tragique—mais est-il sérieux? C'est bien plus difficile.—I hope you don't find the insidious melancholy of these autumn days too much for you; and that so far as your professional duties don't make your joy, you have some "consolations," as Mme P.B. says, in your life—some agreeable friendship or other, some human compensation. You have, my dear Mengin, the compensation of youth: that is everything. Believe your desperately mature friend

Henry James

1. Bourget had just married Minnie David.
2. Bourget's most recent novel.

To William James
Ms Harvard

34 De Vere Gardens W.
November 7*th* 1890

My dear William.

Both Alice and I have fresh bounties—recent letters—to thank you for. Katharine, I know, will already have written you that it has been definitely settled that Alice is for the present—that is, for the winter—to remain just where she is, instead of embarking on the somewhat bleak and precarious experiment of Tunbridge Wells. She is not fit for *any* experiments, or any journey; especially now that the winter (or what is winter to her) has definitely begun. Fortunately she is in excellent quarters—better rooms than she has ever had, since she has been in England—an excellent quiet modern hotel, close to me. The "improvement" that took place in her first coming up to town has, unfortunately, been much interrupted—she has relapsed and collapsed a good deal. Still, she has sometimes better days. At any rate K.P.L. will not leave her while she is in the present condition. She told me the other day that she should consider it "inhuman"—and this is a vast relief to me. Alice is, really, too ill to be left; and the difficult question of doctors (owing to A's extreme dread of them, and her absolute inability, which they can't understand, to take tonic doses, drugs etc.—this put her into a fearful nervous state) may loom up again. On the other hand, she may re-"improve": though her extreme, her really intense weakness is against that. At all events, and in any case, she is at present in the least bad place to encounter either contingency. Her little "improvements"—where she emerges out of a bad period—discourage her really more than her relapses: she wants so to have done with it all—to sink *continuously*. But her great vitality prevents her doing that. Don't, however, worry about her: she is "fixed," and on a good extrinsic basis, for the winter. Her not being away is a great simplification to me.—It was a week ago today that I read you at the S.P.R., with great éclat—enhanced by my being introduced by Pearsall Smith as "a Bostonian of Bostonians." You were very easy and interesting to read, and were altogether the "feature" of the entertainment.[1] It was a full house—and Myers was rayonnant. I will be thus brief today because I am in a very busy phase, which however will not prevent me from writing soon again. That is I have to keep dashing off into the country (I came only last night from two days at Portsmouth) for the hard *énervant* work of rehearsing[2]—something that as yet, for a few weeks longer, I absolutely don't speak of—*so please don't you*. It consumes much time and infinite "nerve power"; especially if taken as seriously (all and *only* for the dream of gold—*much* gold) as I take it, immersing myself in it practically up to the eyes, and really *doing* it myself, to the smallest detail. It is all for preliminary "country production" —to be followed later by the London. I spent upwards of five hours yesterday on the deadly cold stage of the Portsmouth theatre (the "ladies" had *such* red-noses!) going at them tooth and nail, without pause; and then two more with my *grand premier rôle* at his lodgings, coaching him with truly psychical intensity, *acting,* intonating[3] everything *for* him and showing him simply *how!* The authorship (in any sense worthy of the name) of a play only *begins* when it is written, and I see that one's creation of it doesn't terminate till one has gone with it every inch of the way to the rise of the curtain on the first night. (I will tell you *when* to pray for me then.) I go to Brighton next week for another bout, and the next to Northampton etc.; for my company is "on tour" with the rest of its repertory. It is fatiguing, largely owing to the terrible want of plasticity of one's British material; but if I have, from the experiment, and from other ventures of the same kind that are closing round me, the results that are perfectly *possible,* I shall be superabundantly rewarded. The conditions (of the Anglosaxon stage) are really so base that one would be unpardonable for going to meet them if one's inspiration were *not* exclusively mercenary. But to provide for one's old age one is *capable de tout*—and it is a revelation to me to find how "capable" I am, in the whole matter.—Meanwhile, to compare great things with small, your *Psychology*[4] has never turned up—though you told me you had ordered an early copy sent. Has there been some error or non-compliance? Will you kindly see? I yearn for the book—to lift me out of histrionics. Love all round—Ever your

Henry

1. William James wrote to HJ on 20 October 1890: "I think your reading my Piper letter . . . is the most comical thing I ever heard of. It shows how first-rate a business man Myers is: he wants to bring variety and *éclat* into the meeting . . 'T is the most beautiful and devoted brotherly act I ever knew, and I hope it may be the beginning of a new career on your part, of psychic apostolicism. Heaven bless you for it!"

2. Rehearsals had begun for Edward Compton's production of HJ's dramatization of his novel *The American,* while the Compton Comedy Company was on tour.

3. HJ was coaching Compton in the American accent for the part of Christopher Newman.

4. William James's *Principles of Psychology,* recently published.

To Horace E. Scudder
Ms Harvard

34 De Vere Gardens W.
November 10*th* [1890]

Dear Mr. Scudder.

I am very sorry to learn we have made such a bad start, and to this regret is added the shock of a perfectly honest surprise.[1] I sent off *The Pupil* with a quite serene conviction that I had done a distinctly happy thing, and when I asked for indulgence for its length on the score of its probable value, I expressed a confidence which was deeply genuine, though the event now makes me smile at it. The tale, in truth, was the fruit of much labour—and I regarded it as a little masterpiece of compression (I so boiled and re-boiled it down), of the effort to give a large picture in a small compass. It was precisely this tender treatment of it that made me long in getting it off. But I have, thank heaven, no pretension at all to never making a mistake—no such uncomfortable glory, and I am very glad you have been perfectly frank in pointing out the occasion on which it seems to you that I *have* done so. For me, artistically, the sense of a mistake is a still more fertilizing excitement than that of a success; and I shall be perfectly ready to admit that I have gone astray with the *Pupil* if doubts of it are born to me, as is perfectly possible, on a reperusal of it in the light of *your* impression. But the thing I most regret is that your impression makes me feel nervous and insecure about the things I have had it in mind still to send you. I mean that if I was mistaken about *The Pupil*—and badly mistaken, given my really exceptional confidence—I may be deluded about things produced with, after all, similar hopes. However, I shall face this risk about a shorter story (it is called *The Servant*),[2] which I am just sending off to be typecopied and which when it comes back, I shall despatch you—*if* in reading it over with the test of the vivider surface, I am *not* panic-stricken in regard to its possible fate. But even in this case I shall try again—though deploring such delays. Please keep *The Pupil* in your desk for me till I can consider what I had best ask you to do with it.[3] Perhaps I should like it sent to an address in the U.S.—I shall have the MS. recopied and study it afresh—and then perhaps ask you to destroy your copy. Your[s] very truly

Henry James

1. Scudder had rejected "The Pupil." We may infer he did not want to print in the *Atlantic* a tale about a mendacious, itinerant, and drifting American family.

2. Later renamed "Brooksmith."

3. "The Pupil" was sold to *Longman's Magazine* in England and appeared in XVII (March–April 1891), 512–531, 611–632. It was reprinted the following year in the collection of tales entitled *The Lesson of the Master.*

To Rhoda Broughton
Ms Chester

34 De Vere Gardens W.
December 5*th* [1890]

Dear Miss Broughton.

Rudyard and I *have* met and foregathered; nevertheless I shall be glad to see him again (we met at dinner last Saturday), if *he* can stand it: which I think problematical.[1] I am afraid the distant Saturday—13th—of next week is what would suit *me* best: at 5 o'clock[2]—and if, under the circumstances, and having had his dose, Rudyard doesn't, like Oliver, ask for more, I will at any rate come on the said Saturday (unless you warn me off) and read you Acts II and III of my melodrama.—I may remark that III (in particular) isn't particularly adapted to the ears of guileless young things—in the short perspective of a drawing room.[3] I might have to omit my *grand coup.*—Perhaps this latter programme would be better. But determine yourself. I liked Rudyard: and I hope you—with your nobler initiations now—*didn't* like *Called Back.*

Most truly yours
Henry James

1. HJ and Rudyard Kipling became very good friends, although HJ grew increasingly critical of Kipling's work.

2. HJ wrote on the envelope in which he sent this letter: "4.30 would suit better than 5. And Friday as well as Saturday."

3. To selected theatre-going friends (with constant reminders that they should maintain secrecy) HJ was reading various acts of *The American.*

To William Archer

Ms British Library

34 De Vere Gardens W.
Dec. 27*th* 1890

Dear Sir.

I am much obliged to you for your interest in an obscure and tremulous venture.[1] It *is* true that a play of mine is to be produced at a mysterious place called Southport, which I have never seen, a week from tonight, and it is further true that the production is one to which I myself, and every one concerned, have, and has, contributed as seriously as the particular conditions would allow. The performance is *not* a "scratch" one, to establish copyright, but a carefully prepared one to which I have lent a zealous hand and in which the performers, wholly deficient in celebrity, but inflamed, I think, with something of the same zeal, will do their individual best. I won't deny that I should be glad to know that the piece was seen by a serious critic, and by yourself in particular, but I shrink from *every* responsibility in the way of recommending such a critic to attempt so heroic a feat. The place is far, the season inclement, the interpretation, *extremely* limited, different enough, as you may suppose, from what I should count on for representation in London. The circumstances *may* be definitely uncomfortable. I have carefully followed rehearsals, but the whole thing is a leap in the dark, and my hope is greater than my confidence. On the other hand it is apparently to be months before the play comes to town—as I accepted at the outset the essence of the proposal made me (and of which the general attempt was the direct result): the proviso, namely, that the piece should be produced (and only *occasionally!*) in the provinces for upwards of a year before being brought out in London. England, Scotland and Ireland therefore will behold it before the starved metropolis. But it will come—I believe—before long, considerably nearer town than Southport, and probably in more seductive weather. At any rate I have hopes that I may be represented otherwise in London before the drama in question is revealed here; for if I have made up my mind to make a resolute theatrical attempt, I am far from considering that one makes it with a single play. I mean to go at it again and again—and shall do so none the worse for knowing that you may give some heed to the undiscourageable flounderings of yours very truly

Henry James

1. William Archer, by this time an authoritative drama critic, had been urging men of letters to write for the stage. The first night of the out-of-town run of *The American* took place in Southport, near Liverpool on 3 January 1891.

To Mrs. Hugh Bell
Ms Private

34 De Vere Gardens W.
Dec. 29*th* [1890]

Dear Mrs. Bell.[1]

How kind and friendly and undeserved by my own bald silence, your sympathetic note! I *do* "proceed" into the wilds of Lancashire (what an inexplicably droll place for my artistic *tâtonnements*) on Thursday next, in time for a "dress rehearsal." I wish indeed, selfishly, you might be there, to support a wholly unsupported (and as the public *may* judge, unsupportable!) one. But, on every other ground, may furs and fires protect you from all such magnanimous exposure. It's a leap in the dark, and it's much more seemly that I should take it alone. My heroine and my hero are both, at the present speaking, ill in bed—and the curtain may never rise. But if it does you shall hear on what it falls—on my suicide in the *Times* (or perhaps even in the *Era*—I must subscribe!) if on nothing better. What I have for ten days owed you a letter for is the rich cluster of comedies—unacknowledged, uncommemorated only because they have been, through jealous and emulous efforts of my own, unread. I have, to tell the truth, been giving every moment to a third *chef d'oeuvre*—a comedy in three acts, of which I wished to finish the first *immediately*, for a particular purpose. I did so brilliantly, of course, yesterday—and now I can breathe, and turn your ingenious pages and you shall hear from me.—Mrs. Vibert,[2] all this while, reposes in the silent bosom of John Hare, which as yet emits no sound. I am a little disappointed in our friend G's[3] apparent command of the situation—which is seemingly less complete than my belief in it represented when I made such haste with my play for her. It is not only that

Hare doesn't appear to "rise," for her sweet sake, but that she shows no glimpse of any other string to her bows for mine! All the more reason for deeper absorptions! And Hare *may* rise, of course, even with G. as a plummet—and it is of course inconsistent with the dignity of his species to rise quickly.—Your suggestion about returning by Redcar has an hospitable glow—but I fear it's unmanageable. I have already promised to return by Cheltenham,[4] and they are not side by side. I shall watch for you more than ever *here,* and I am with the heartiest New Year's wishes to yours and husband's and all your house, most truly yours

Henry James

1. Florence Bell, writer of closet dramas—one of which had been produced by the Comédie Française—was a strong supporter and confidante of HJ in his pursuit of success in the theatre. She was married to a wealthy Yorkshire colliery owner, and was the mother of Gertrude Bell (1868–1926), the celebrated traveler and British administrator in Arabia.

2. "Mrs. Vibert" was the tentative title of a play HJ later called *Tenants.* He was hoping the actor-manager John Hare would produce it.

3. The allusion is to the singer-actress Geneviève Ward. HJ hoped she would play the feminine lead in *Tenants.*

4. To visit Miss Woolson.

4
The Dramatic Years

1891–1895

4
The Dramatic Years

During the five years Henry James devoted to writing plays, from 1890 to 1895, he ceased to be master of his personal situation. Accustomed for more than a quarter of a century to dictating terms to editors and publishers, he found himself unable to dictate to producers and actor-managers—although he tried. He pretended he was meeting the "theatric conditions," but with all the independence of his craft, he in reality had contempt for the stage, for the simplifications of on-stage presentation, for the self-exhibition of the actors. Players were "mountebanks" to him; managers were shifty and untrustworthy people, who expressed enthusiasm one day and became apathetic the next. James tended to develop a paranoid view as managers held back his scenarios only finally to reject them. Actors found James's plays hard to act—for he provided more verbal play than dramatic action. Verbal play could work in the hands of a wit like Oscar Wilde; but James, whose wit was more refined, lacked Oscar's common touch. The result was a succession of rejected comedies. One play was produced by a country touring company, but it eked out only seventy performances when brought to London. The second play, at the end of James's period of play-writing, was a disaster. James was booed out of the theatre.

This is the story we can read in the ensuing letters. And as we read we become conscious of the way in which the years he devoted to the drama were "dramatic" in life as in art: the sudden death of his friend the young publisher Wolcott Balestier, the lingering death of his sister Alice, the death on the other side of the world of Robert Louis Stevenson, whom James deeply mourned, and the suicide in Venice of his friend Constance Fenimore Woolson. James had a sense of a disintegrating world, and his long unremunerative period of writing plays made him feel more of a financial failure than ever. The booing of *Guy Domville* was the ultimate rejection. Harboring guilt feelings in connection with Fenimore's death, carrying a burden of grief for his sister and his friends, James found himself, at the end of his "dramatic years," in a deep state of depression. The years had seemed treacherous; he had come to the theatrical "abyss" with a sense of defeat. In these letters he plays his epistolary game and hides his anger and his aggressions behind a thick veil of exaggerated politeness. We find him at his most paranoid—or could we call it megalomaniac?—in the long letter he writes to Augustin Daly, a busy manager, who had ordered scenery and costumes for James's play but found the vehicle lacking in action and force at its first rehearsal. James accuses the manager of "staging" the rehearsal in order to get him to withdraw the play. One doubts whether a tough theatre-man like Daly needed such a subterfuge. And then we have James's castles in the air, his high hopes for huge royalties at the box office, his belief that he had mastered the drama, his discovery of Ibsen, and his final cry that he may have been made for the Drama but "I certainly wasn't meant for the Theatre!" It is a rude awakening. And it will take several years for James to recover from the shock.

To Edmund Gosse

Ms Leeds

Prince of Wales Hotel
Southport
Jan. *3d* [1891]

My dear Gosse.

I am touched by your *petit mot. De gros mots* seem to me to be so much more applicable to my fallen state. The only thing that can be said for it is that it is not so low as it may perhaps be tomorrow—after the vulgar ordeal of tonight. Let me therefore profit by the few remaining hours of a recognizable *status* to pretend to an affectionate reciprocity. I am yours and your wife's while yet I *may* be. After 11 o'clock to-night I *may* be the world's—you know —and I may be the undertaker's. I count upon you both to spend this evening in fasting, silence and supplication. I will send you a word in the morning—wire you if I can—if there is anything at all to boast of. My hopes rest solely on intrinsic charms—the adventitious graces of art are not "in it." I am so nervous that I miswrite and misspell. Pity your infatuated but not presumptuous friend,

Henry James

P.S. It would have been delightful—and terrible—if you had been able to come. I believe Archer is to loom.[1]

P.P.S. I don't return straight to London—don't get there till Tuesday or Wednesday. I shall have to wait and telegraph you which evening I can come in.

1. See letter to Archer, 27 December 1890.

To William James
Ms Harvard

Prince of Wales Hotel
Southport
Saturday, Jan. 3*d* [1891]

My dear William.

Yesterday came to me here your note (with photograph of your charming house) announcing the birth of your third son.[1] I am delighted that he has come easily and smoothly into the world and that dear Alice was, as they say here, at the moment you wrote, in good form. I ardently pray that she may have remained so, and that the little boy, as yet pretty indefinite I judge, may find a spare corner in the crowded world. We shall be now very anxious for later and more "evolved" news. The anecdote of Margaret Mary and her babe [is] most delightful. It seems trivial at such a time to trouble you with *my* deliveries, but by the time this reaches you, you and Alice will have got a little used to yours. However, you are to receive news of the coming into the world of *my* dramatic first-born (which takes place here tonight) some time tomorrow, through Alice from London, as I am to wire her early in the morning the upshot of the dread episode (tomorrow unfortunately is Sunday), and she expressed to me before I left town day before yesterday the ardent wish that *she* might be allowed to cable you, as from herself, my report of the verdict that I am so oddly (till my complicated but valid material reasons are explained) seeking of this Philistine provincial public. The omens and auspices are good—the theatre is bad but big and every seat in it has been taken for a week. The principal London critic William Archer, of the Weekly *World* (I will send you his pronouncement) is coming down and can scarcely get one. The play will owe nothing whatever to brilliancy of interpretation, and the mounting is of the meagrest—it will all, if the thing isn't damned, be a success of intrinsic vitality. We are resting and quaking today—but we had yesterday a supreme, complete, exhaustive rehearsal, during which I sat in the stalls watching and listening as to the work of another: the result of which (I boldly say it—on the untried eve) was a kind of mystic confidence in the ultimate life of the piece—and even in the immediate. God grant that tonight—between 8 and 11 (spend *you* the terrible hours in fasting, silence and supplication!) I don't get the lie in my teeth. Still, I *am,* at present, in a state of abject, lonely fear—sufficient to make me say in retort to my purpose of trying again, again and yet again,—"What, a repetition of *this* horrid and quite peculiar preliminary?" I am *too* nervous to write more —and yet it's only 3 o'clock and I've got to wait till eight.—But I shall finish, either with triumph or resignation, tomorrow.—

Thursday, January 8*th:* 34 De Vere Gardens. I haven't had a moment to add a word since I wrote the foregoing last Saturday. But meanwhile I knew Alice had cabled you, and I asked her to send you off immediately the letter I wrote her the A.M. after my première. I paid a country visit[2] after leaving Southport and my leisure has undergone complete extinction till this moment. At present I shall only scribble a few lines to catch the steamer and say that my ordeal *did* blossom into a complete and delightful success—limited only by the intrinsic limitations of a place like Southport in the matter of conferring success. But that circumstance works in two ways: I mean that if the *cachet* of a biggish provincial town isn't authoritative on the other hand the play had to suffer from the want of adventitious aid conferred by provincial production—ill-mounted, meagrely interpreted etc.—and yet quite overcame that drawback. I *think* it has a strong life and will surmount the more formidable tests in store for it. At any rate there was no drawback to our felicity on Saturday and the Comptons are delighted. He will, I surmise, make a "big" creation (with more time to live into it) of the principal character—I mean for the

English public. Only an American can do it for the Americans. Only these raw words today—I want to write you properly by the next mail—or the next. Ever your affectionate

Henry

P.S. Quantities of love to Alice and the Babe.

1. Alexander Robertson James, William James's youngest son.
2. HJ had gone to Cheltenham to visit Miss Woolson.

To Urbain Mengin
Ms Harvard

Prince of Wales Hotel
Southport
Ce 3 janvier [1891]

Mon cher ami.

Je ne suis point à Paris—je suis dans un coin perdu de l'Angleterre occupé de la chose du monde la moins vraisemblable: la "première" d'une pièce en quatre actes, qui se trame ici ce soir. "Je fais du Théâtre"—je suis tombé bien bas—priez pour moi. Pour des raisons particulières, trop longues à expliquer, mon drame voit le jour, ou plutôt la nuit, en province avant d'être joué à Londres, et son sort là-bas dépendre de l'acceuil qui lui aura été fait ici. Comme vous pensez bien, c'est la soif de l'or qui me pousse dans cette voie déshonorante. Si cette soif est apaisée je m'en irai la faire repousser à Paris vers la fin de janvier. Tous mes projets ont été bouleversés par cette existence cabotine. Je vous ferai savoir ce qui en sera dès que j'y verrai clair. En attendant, aussitôt que je rentrerai à Londres la semaine prochaine je compte vous envoyer pour vos étrennes les deux gros volumes de mon frère.[1] The happiest possible New Year. Ever yours

Henry James

1. The two-volume *Principles of Psychology,* recently published.

To Alice James
Telegram
Ms Harvard

[Southport, 4 January 1891]

Unqualified triumphant magnificent success universal congratulations great ovation for author great future for play Comptons radiant and his acting admirable writing Henry

To Alice James and Katharine P. Loring
Ms Harvard

Prince of Wales Hotel
Southport
[4 January 1891]

My dear Children.

I wired you an half hour ago a most veracious and historical account of yesterday's beautiful evening. It was really *beautiful*—the splendid success of the whole thing, reflected as large as the surface presented by a Southport audience (and the audience was very big indeed) could permit. The attention, the interest, the outbursts of applause and appreciation hushed quickly for fear of losing (especially with the very bad acoustic properties of the house) what was to follow, the final plaudits, and recalls (I mean after each act) and the big universal outbreak at the end for "author, *author*, AUTHOR!" in duly *delayed* response to which, with the whole company grinning delight and sympathy (behind the curtain) I was led before by Compton to receive the first "ovation," but I trust not the last, of my life—all this would have cured you (both) right up if you could only have witnessed it. The great feature of the evening was the surprising way Compton "came out," beyond anything he had done, or shown, at rehearsal,—acting really exceedingly well and putting more force, ability and above all art and charm and *character* into his part than I had at all ventured to expect of him. He will improve it greatly, ripen and *tone* it, as he plays it more, and end, I am sure, by making it a *celebrated* modern creation. He *may* even become right enough in it to do it in America—though as to that one must see. The Comptons of course are intensely happy, and their supper with me here, with Balestier[1] for a fourth, was wildly joyous, as you may infer when I tell you it lasted from 11 to 1.45 A.M. Mrs. Compton was "cured right up" by our success—she acted, in her own Mrs. Comptonish way, *very* neatly and gracefully, for a lady who had been ill in bed for a week. She was exceedingly well-dressed—all Liberty, but very good Liberty. Every one, in fact, worked his and her hardest and did his and her best; and though some of them, notably Valentin, who made himself very handsome, were much impaired by extreme nervousness, there was no real flaw on the extreme smoothness of the performance, which "went" as if it were a fiftieth. On the other hand, of course, I felt freshly the importance of a change of Mme de B[ellegarde] and Mrs. Bread, of Lord Deepmere and perhaps, or probably, even of Valentin and the Marquis for the London production. As for Newman, Compton simply *adores* the part and will, I feel sure, make it universally beloved. Well, he *may* like it, for though I say it who shouldn't, I was freshly struck, in my little "cubby" beside the curtain in the right wing (where I stuck all the evening, save to dash out and embrace every one in the entractes), I was more than ever impressed, I say, with its being *magnificent*—all the keyboard, the potential fortune of an actor. The wondrous Balestier dashed out between the third and fourth acts and cabled to the *New York Times* fifty vivid words which will *already* have been laid on every breakfast table (as it were) in that city. I strongly suspect they will bring in prompt applications for the "American rights." I will tell you a droll anecdote of William Archer's behaviour and attitude.[2] I go part of the way to Cheltenham[3] tonight, sleep at Birmingham and spend tomorrow at C. Expect to see you Tuesday evening. If Katharine could send me a word—telegraphic—about how you are —to 4 Promenade Terrace C.—I should be glad. I am writing to William, but you might send him on this letter just as it stands. Ever yours

Henry James

P.S. *Sunday noon.* Compton has just come in to tell me that he has already seen a number of people present last night who were *unanimous* about the success of the piece, the great hit he has made it—and ergo—the large fortune that opens to it. His own high spirits indeed tell everything.

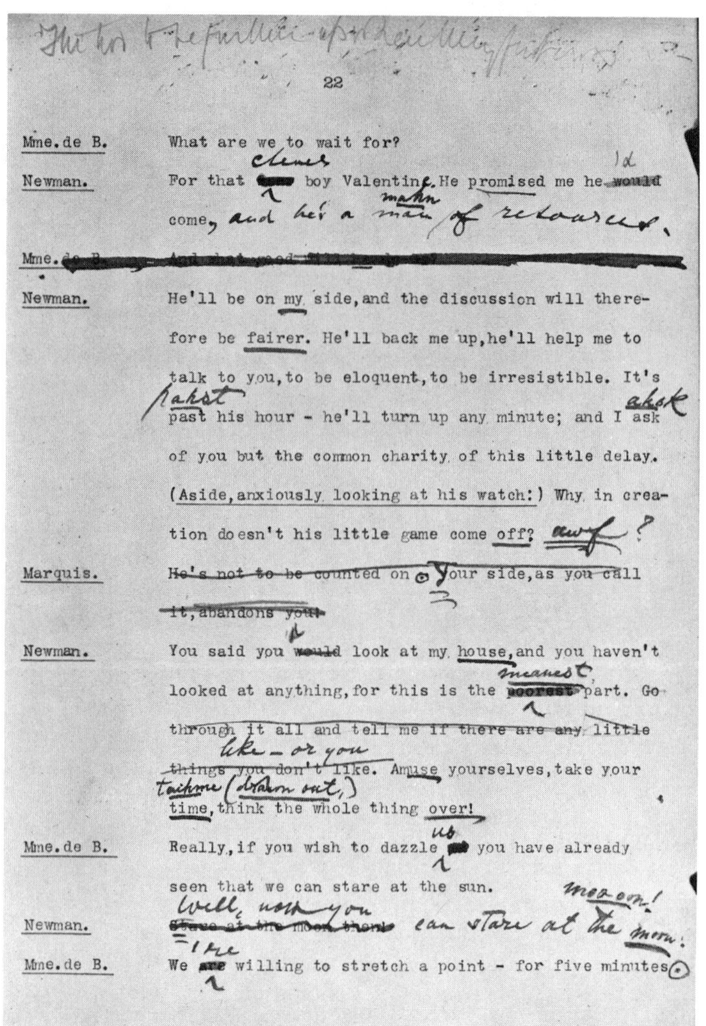

22

Mme. de B. What are we to wait for?

Newman. For that [illegible] boy Valentine. He promised me he would come, and he's a man of resources.

Mme. de B. [illegible]

Newman. He'll be on my side, and the discussion will therefore be fairer. He'll back me up, he'll help me to talk to you, to be eloquent, to be irresistible. It's past his hour – he'll turn up any minute; and I ask of you but the common charity of this little delay. (Aside, anxiously looking at his watch:) Why in creation doesn't his little game come off?

Marquis. He's not to be counted on. Your side, as you call it, abandons you!

Newman. You said you would look at my house, and you haven't looked at anything, for this is the poorest part. Go through it all and tell me if there are any little things you don't like. Amuse yourselves, take your time, think the whole thing over!

Mme. de B. Really, if you wish to dazzle [illegible] you have already seen that we can stare at the sun.

Newman. Stare at the moon then!

Mme. de B. We are willing to stretch a point – for five minutes.

Page 22 of Henry James's dramatization of *The American,* showing the American accent prescribed by James for Edward Compton

1. HJ had invited Balestier as his guest at the first night.

2. Alice James recorded in her diary on 7 January 1891 that Archer told HJ on the first night, "I think it's a play that would be much more likely to have success in the Provinces than in London." She added that "these uncalled for and depressing amenities from an entire stranger seemed highly grotesque." *The Diary of Alice James*, ed. Edel (1964).

3. His visit to Miss Woolson.

To Mr. and Mrs. Hugh Bell
Ms Texas

34 De Vere Gardens W.
Jan. 8*th* [1891]

Dear Mrs. Bell
and Dear Hugh Bell.

Your most kind congratulatory note deserved an answer more gracefully prompt than this. But I extended my absence from town to a short visit at Cheltenham, and the whole thing was virtually, till yesterday, a complete extinction of leisure. Delightful of you to want "details." I think if I were to inflict them on you, they would all be illustrative of the cheering and rewarding side of our feverish profession. The passage from knock-kneed nervousness (the night of the première as one clings, in the wing, to the curtain-rod, as to the *pied des autels*) to a simmering serenity is especially life-saving in its effect. I flung myself upon Compton after the first act: "In heaven's name, is it *going?*" "Going?—*Rather!* You can't [can] hear a pin drop!" Then, after that, one felt it—one *heard* it—one blessed it—and, at the end of all, one (after a decent and discreet delay) simpered and gave one's self up to *courbettes* before the curtain, while the applausive house emitted agreeable sounds from a kind of gas-flaring indistinguishable dimness and the gratified Compton publicly pressed one's hand and one felt that, really, as far as Southport could testify to the circumstances, the stake was won. Of course it's only Southport—but I have larger hopes, inasmuch as it was just the meagre provincial conditions and the limited provincial interpretation that deprived the performance of all adventitious aid. And when my hero and heroine and another friend supped with me at the inn after the battle, I felt that they were really as radiant as if we were carousing among the slain. They *seem* indeed wondrous content. The great feature of the evening was the way Compton "came out" beyond what he had done or promised at rehearsal and acted really most interestingly and admirably—if not a "revelation" at any rate a very jolly surprise. His part is one in which I surmise he really counts upon making a large success—and though I say it who shouldn't—it is one of incontestable opportunities. However, all this is to come—and we stumble in judgment. Amen. *Voilà mes chers amis.* You have been through all this, and more, and will tolerate my ingenuities.—I am still afloat in the crepuscular vague with Geneviève,[1] and the oracle is dumb. I shall soon go to see her—I mean not the oracle, but the priestess, to pull her sleeve. All merriment to *your* "full house." Yours most truly

Henry James

1. See letter to Mrs. Bell, 29 December 1890.

To Robert Louis Stevenson
Ms Yale

34 De Vere Gardens W.
January 12*th* 1891

My dear Louis.

I have owed you a letter too shamefully long—and now that I have taken my pen in hand, as we used to say, I feel how much I burn to communicate with you. As your magnanimity will probably have forgotten how long ago it was that you addressed me, from Sydney, the tragic statement of your permanent secession, I won't remind you of so detested a date. That statement, indeed, smote me to the silence I have so long preserved: I couldn't—I didn't—protest; I even mechanically and grimly assented; but I couldn't *talk* about it—even to you and your wife. Missing you always is a perpetual ache—and aches are disqualifying for gymnastic feats. In short we forgive you (the Muses and the soft Passions forgive *us!*) but we can't quite *treat* you as if we did. However, all this while I have many things to thank you for. In the first place for Lloyd.[1] He was delightful, we loved him—*nous nous l'arrachâmes.* He is a most sympathetic youth, and we revelled in his rich conversation and exclaimed on his courtly manners. How vulgar you'll think us all when you come back (there is malice in that "when"). Then for the beautiful strange things you sent me and which make for ever in my sky-parlour a sort of dim rumble as of the Pacific surf. My heart beats over them—my imagination throbs—my eyes fill. I have covered a blank wall of my bedroom with an acre of painted cloth and feel as if I lived in a Samoan tent—and I have placed the sad sepia-drawing just where, fifty times a day, it most transports and reminds me. To-day what I am grateful for is your new ballad-book,[2] which has just reached me by your command. I have had time only to read the first few things—but I shall absorb the rest and give you my impression of them before I close this. As I turn the pages I seem to see that they are full of charm and of your "Protean" imaginative life—but above all of your terrible far-off-ness. My state of mind about that is the strangest—a sort of delight at having you poised there in the inconceivable; and a miserable feeling, at the same time, that I am in too wretched a back seat to assist properly at the performance. I don't want to lose *any* of your vibrations; and, as it is, I feel that I only catch a few of them—and that is a constant woe. I read with unrestrictive relish the first chapters of your prose volume[3] (kindly vouchsafed me in the little copyright-catching red volume), and I loved 'em and blessed them quite. But I *did* make one restriction—I missed the *visible* in them—I mean as regards people, things, objects, faces, bodies, costumes, features, gestures, manners, the introductory, the *personal* painter-touch. It struck me that you either didn't feel—through some accident—your responsibility on this article quite enough; or, on some theory of your own, had declined it. No theory is kind to us that cheats us of *seeing*. However, no doubt we shall rub our eyes for satiety before we have done. Of course the pictures—Lloyd's blessed photographs—*y sont pour beaucoup;* but I wanted more the note of portraiture. Doubtless I am greedy—but one *is* when one dines at the Maison d'or. I have an idea you take but a qualified interest in "Beau Austin"[4]—or I should tell you how religiously I was present at that memorable première. Lloyd and your wonderful and delightful mother will have given you the agreeable facts of the occasion. I found it—not the occasion, so much, but the work—full of *quality,* and stamped with a charm; but on the other hand seeming to shrug its shoulders a little too much at scenic precautions. I have an idea, however, you don't care about the matter, and I won't bore you with it further than to say that the piece has been repeatedly played, that it has been the only honourable theatrical affair transacted *dans notre sale tripot* for many a day—and that Wm. Archer *en raffole* periodically in the "World." Don't despise me too much if I confess that *anch' io son pittore. Je fais aussi du théâtre, moi;* and am doing it, to begin with, for reasons too numerous to burden you with, but all excellent and practical. In the provinces I had the other night, at Southport, Lancashire, with the dramatization of an early novel—*The American*—a success *dont je rougis encore.* This thing is to be played in London only after several months—and to make the tour of the British Islands first. Don't be hard on me—simplifying and chastening necessity has laid its brutal hand on me and I have had to try to make somehow or other the money I don't make by literature. My books don't sell, and it looks as if my plays might. Therefore I am going with a brazen front to write half a dozen. I have, in fact, already written two others than the one just performed—and the success of the latter pronounced—really *pronounced*—will probably precipitate them. I am glad for all this that you are not here. Literature is out of it. I miss no occasion of talking of you. Colvin I tolerably often see: I expect to do so for instance to-night, at a decidedly too starched dining-club to which we both belong, of which Lord Coleridge is president and too many persons of the type of Sir Theodore Martin[5] are members. Happy islanders—with no Sir Theodore Martin. On Mrs. Sitwell I called the other day, in a charming new habitat; all clean paint and fresh chintz. We always go on at a great rate about you—celebrate rites as faithful as the early Christians in the catacombs. Gosse has just published a singularly clever, skilful, vivid, well-done biography of his father—the fanatic and naturalist—very happy in proportion, tact and talent. Filial pity *lui a porté bonheur*—it is one of the good biographies. He is altogether prosperous and productive—concerning himself, however, I think, too much with the "odd jobs" of literature and too little with the finer opportunities. But I find him one of the very few intelligent and, on such matters, conversible creatures here.

January 13*th*.—I met Colvin last night, after writing the above—in the company of Sir James Stephen, Sir Theo. Martin, Sir Douglas

Galton, Sir James Paget, Sir Alfred Lyall, Canon Ainger, and George du Maurier. How this will make you lick your chops over Ori and Rahiro and Tamatia and Taheia—or whatever *ces messieurs et ces dames,* your present visiting list, are called. He told me of a copious diary-letter he has just got from you, bless you, and we are discussing a day on which I shall soon come to meat or drink with him and listen to the same. Since yesterday I have also read the ballad book—with the admiration that I always feel as a helplessly verseless creature (it's a sentiment worth nothing as a testimony) for all performances in rhyme and metre—especially on the part of producers of fine prose.

January 19*th.*—I stopped this more than a week ago, and since then I have lacked time to go on with it—having been out of town for several days on a base theatrical errand[6]—to see my tribute to the vulgarest of the muses a little further on its way over the provincial circuit and re-rehearse two or three portions of it that want more effective playing. Thank heaven I shall have now no more direct contact with it till it is produced in London next October.—I broke off in the act of speaking to you about your ballad-book. The production of ringing and lilting verse (by a superior proser) always does *bribe* me a little—and I envy you in that degree yours; but apart from this I grudge your writing the like of these ballads. They show your "cleverness," but they don't show your genius. I should say more if it were not odious to a man of my refinement to write to you—so expectantly far away—in remonstrance. I don't find, either, that the canibalism, the savagery *se prête,* as it were—one wants either less of it, on the ground of suggestion—or more, on the ground of statement; and one wants more of the high impeccable (as distinguished from the awfully jolly), on the ground of poetry. Behold I *am* launching across the black seas a page that may turn nasty—but my dear Louis, it's only because I love so your divine prose and want the comfort of it. Things are various because we do 'em. We mustn't do 'em because they're various. The only news in literature here—such is the virtuous vacancy of our consciousness—continues to be the infant monster of a Kipling. I enclose, in this, for your entertainment a few pages I have lately written about him, to serve as the preface to an (of course authorized) American *recueil* of some of his tales.[7] I may add that he has just put forth his longest story yet—a thing in Lippincott which I also send you herewith—which cuts the ground somewhat from under my feet, inasmuch as I find it the most youthfully infirm of his productions (in spite of great "life"), much wanting in composition and in narrative and explicative, or even implicative, art.[8]

Please tell your wife, with my love, that all this is constantly addressed also to her. I try to see you all, in what I fear is your absence of habits, as you live, grouped around what I also fear is in no sense the domestic hearth. Where do you go when you want to be "cosy"?—or what at least do you *do?* You think a little, I hope, of the faithful forsaken on whose powers of evocation, as well as of attachment, you impose such a strain. I wish I could send a man from Fortnum and Mason's out to you with a chunk of *mortadella.* I am trying to do a series of "short things" and will send you the least bad. I mean to write to Lloyd. Please congratulate your heroic mother for me very cordially when she leaps upon your strand, and believe that I hold you all in the tenderest remembrance of yours ever, my dear Louis,

Henry James

1. Lloyd Osbourne, Stevenson's stepson.
2. *Ballads* (1891).
3. Fifteen of the thirty-five letters Stevenson had written from the South Seas were gathered into the privately printed volume *The South Seas* (1890) and were published serially during 1891 in the New York *Sun.*
4. A play Stevenson had written in collaboration with W. E. Henley.
5. Sir Theodore Martin (1816–1909), Scottish man of letters who wrote for the theatre and prepared for Queen Victoria a five-volume life of the Prince Consort.
6. HJ continued to attend performances of *The American* in country towns.
7. A preface to the American edition of *Mine Own People* (1891).
8. The *Lippincott* issue of January 1891 contained an installment of Kipling's *The Light That Failed.*

To William James
Ms Harvard

34 De Vere Gardens W.
Feb. 6*th* [1891]

My dear William.

Bear with me that I haven't written to you, since my last, in which I promised you a better immediate sequel, till the receipt of your note of the 21st, this A.M., recalls me to decency. Bear with me, indeed, in this and other ways, so long as I am in the fever of dramatic production with which I am, very sanely and practically, trying to make up for my late start and all the years during which I have *not* dramatically produced, and, further, to get well ahead with the "demand" which I—and others *for* me—judge (still very sanely and sensibly) to be *certain* to be made upon me from the moment I have a *London*, as distinguished from a provincial, success. (You can form no idea—outside—of how a provincial success is *confined* to the provinces.) Now that I have tasted blood, *c'est une rage* (of determination to *do*, and triumph, on my part), for I feel at last as if I had found my *real* form, which I am capable of carrying far, and for which the pale little art of fiction, as I have practised it, has been, for me, but a limited and restricted substitute. The strange thing is that I always, innermostly, knew *this* was my more characteristic form—but was kept away from it by a half-modest half-exaggerated sense of the difficulty (that is, I mean the practical odiousness) of the conditions. But now that I have accepted them and met them, I see that one isn't at all, needfully, their victim, but is, from the moment one *is* anything, one's self, worth speaking of, their *master;* and may use them, command them, squeeze them, lift them up and better them. As for the form *itself,* its honour and inspiration are (*à défaut d'autres*) in its difficulty. If it were *easy* to write a good play I couldn't and wouldn't think of it; but it is in fact damnably hard (to this truth the paucity of the article—in the English-speaking world—testifies), and that constitutes a solid respectability—guarantees one's *intellectual* self-respect. At any rate I am working hard and constantly—and am just attacking my fourth!

No. 2 is in the hands of a high London manager,[1] in conditions as to which I prefer at present to maintain absolute silence—suffice it that he tells me (I quote a letter) that it is "a masterpiece of dramatic construction": a good phrase for a "high London manager" to apply to the first production he has read of a beginner.

No. 3[2] is committed to Compton, in pursuance of a promise I made him as soon as *The American* was finished, to give him another piece to follow it up with—to "have up his sleeve," as they say, for the London theatre which he has taken on a several years' lease and to which he intends to transfer his career.

No. 4[3] has a destination which it would be premature to disclose; and, in general, please breathe no word of these confidences, as publicity blows on such matters in an injurious and deflowering way, and interests too great to be hurt are at stake. I make them, the confidences, because it isn't fair to myself not to let you know that I may be absorbed for some months to come—as long as my present fit of the "rage" lasts—to a degree which may be apparent in my correspondence—I mean in its intermittence and in my apparent lapse of attention to, or appreciation of, other things. For instance, I blush to say that I haven't had freedom of mind or cerebral freshness (I find the drama much more *obsédant* than the novel) to tackle—more than dipping in just here and there—your mighty and magnificent book,[4] which requires a stretch of leisure and an absence of "crisis" in one's own egotistical little existence. As this is essentially a year of crisis, or of epoch-making, for me, I shall probably save up the great volumes till I can recline upon roses, the fruits of my production fever, and imbibe them like sips of sherbet, giving meanwhile all my cerebration to the condensation of masterpieces.—The winter is less brutally cold—and much less densely black than it has been; but Alice's state doesn't change, save in its perpetual variation from one manifestation of extreme weakness to another. Her weakness is utter and complete—such an effort as taking her breakfast, in bed, with every aid, prop and service, quite overcomes her. Katharine sticks to her post and will stick *late*—indeed I have no clear vision of *any* state of Alice's that will now make her *leavable*. However, the day must come when Katharine *must* go—and it will be sufficient to deal with it when it comes. I have seen a good deal of Elly Emmet[5] these last weeks with great enjoyment of her charm—though she doesn't strike me as "interesting." (Her daughter presents—to my sense—*no* source of interest—save the "pathos" of her bad relations with her mother and her mother's with *her*. I am very sorry for Minnie.) At present (this is *utterly* private and confidential—don't betray that you know anything of it *from* me!) my sentiments on the subject of Elly are all merged in an acute apprehension and indeed almost painful nervousness as to the possibility of her marching to the altar with a Scotchman whom she met, knew, and was apparently "addressed" by in America, with whom she is evidently fearfully in love—and he with her—but about whom no one here knows anything at all (no one has *seen* him) save that he has lately lost money (with a great vagueness as to how much he has had or kept)—in the Argentine smash. It is unknown, as I say, what he *is*—but it is tolerably clear what he *isn't*—and I am rather alarmed at Elly's apparently crude and irresponsible disposition in the matter—considering, I mean, her age, her children, his admitted deficiencies and the complications of her fitting a new and foreign husband—whose means are *dim*—and a new foreign home, into an existence already encumbered with her four girls. Nothing may come of the danger—but she has gone to stay in Scotland with his three or four maiden sisters—in a small country town—where *he* is staying. She speaks of sailing for America on the 22d—but that may change; I may not see her again, as I am thinking of going to Paris for two or three weeks the middle of next week. Meanwhile Minnie, who is to remain in London (while her mother is in Scotland), doesn't suspect the situation—and please breathe it not to any—least of all to the other children. All Elly's Rose cousins here are delighted with her; and she has had a "lovely" time.

Farewell, dear William—and bear with my sawdust and orange-peel phase till the returns begin to flow in. The only hitch in the prospect is that it takes so *long* to "realise." *The American,* in the country, played only on Friday nights, with the very low country prices, gives me nothing as yet to speak of—my royalty making only about £5–0–0 for each performance. Later all this may be thoroughly counted upon to be totally different.

Ever your
Henry

1. John Hare. See letter to Mrs. Bell, 29 December 1890.

2. A play entitled *The Album,* which HJ published in *Theatricals: Second Series* (1895).

3. Play no. 4 was probably *Disengaged,* the comedy HJ wrote for Ada Rehan. It was published in *Theatricals: First Series* (1894).

4. William James's *Principles of Psychology.*

5. Ellen James Temple (1850–1920), a younger sister of Minny Temple, had married Christopher Temple Emmet in 1869. Now widowed, she married the Scot of whom HJ speaks and became Mrs. George Hunter. The Minnie alluded to in this letter is her eldest daughter, Mary Temple Emmet.

To William James
Ms Harvard

34 De Vere Gardens W.
February 12*th* [1891]

My dear William.

I wrote to you at some length the other day—but your letter to Katharine, from Newport, which she has just showed me, makes me want to add a belated postscript. You make a hopeful enquiry about the great question of one's theatrical profits—and though I think—but am not sure—I touched on the matter to you the other day, I have *à coeur* to dot, briefly, the *i*'s of the question, lest you shouldn't be living, as it were, in a fool's paradise in relation [to] my *actual* unearned increment. It is only from the moment a play is produced in *London* and thereby played nightly, and during a *long run,* that profits begin to figure up to great heights, whether for manager or author. I fear I didn't make it clear to you that *The American* isn't played by the Comptons *every* night of their provincial tour—or anything like it. No play *can* be, in the smaller towns—the company stays a week and *must* give (the public is too small else) a nightly change of bill. My play is therefore acted only on Fridays—the "fashionable" night. It will thus be given only about some twenty-five times at the most between now and the late summer vacation; and as country prices are very low—the stalls usually only four shillings—my royalty is proportionately scant. Moreover I have already had it, in a lump—£250 paid down as soon as my contract was signed. I never expected to make money in the country—it's impossible; but London is the reverse of the medal, as later the U.S. (*and* the country there), and would make the story totally different. If my play succeeds here I can't get *less* than £100 a week from it, and I may easily get more. (There is now a great success here, at the Haymarket, called *The Dancing Girl,* by one Henry Arthur Jones—the clumsiest trash, alas, of a play—and the said Henry Arthur, with a largeish theatre and full houses derives £180 a week—and will evidently go on doing it for months: which will make him, by the end of six months, £5,000, and, at the end of a year, during which the play may perfectly run, £10,000—not counting his American or Australian profits, or the eventual country-tours of his play *by itself,* played every night (not as one of a repertory, which is the only thing that can be done, as is being done with mine, *before* London production). It is the American proceeds of a play that are much the biggest now; so that Henry Arthur, if the *Dancing Girl* is a success in the U.S., may easily with that help, at the end of a year, double his £10,000. You see all this is worth waiting for; and it was inevitable that beginning late, I should be a longish while getting *en train;* especially with the peculiar complication that I agreed at the outset to wait for Compton, as he so took me by the hand, to finish his ten years (ghastly thought) of "Touring" and settle down deliberately and preparedly with a London Theatre of his own. I think I told you that he has taken one on a long lease—a very good one, in spite of its awkward name, the Opéra Comique: it is where all Gilbert and Sullivan's earlier productions were performed. There is every present appearance that as soon as the London run, whatever it may prove to be, of *The American* is over, he will produce there an admirable three-act comedy by the same author. I go into these vulgarities (which *please* keep utterly to yourself—there was a phrase in your letter to Katharine about the "Irving St. and Kirkland St. circle" which makes me shiver!—with a sense as of extreme ventilation of one's privatest affairs), I say I bore you with these details simply that you may not for the present look to me to ship over nuggets for investment under your eye. Later I do expect to give your eye plenty to do.—I am afraid that in writing last week I seemed to overstate a little Alice's weakness inasmuch as she has "stayed up" to her dinner (I mean got out of bed at about six, for perhaps the second time, and had it, with much assistance, on the sofa) several times lately—though these very last days have been bad with her. However, all the same, her feebleness is extreme, and if a somewhat extreme description of it is not true one day, it is another; so that the above rectification is more for "form" than anything else.—I take the greatest interest in your new Babe's name;[1] but frankly, I am rather unhappy about the one you mention as virtually settled upon—so much so as to feel strongly moved—even to tears—to supplicate you to *un*settle it. I have thought over your combination, wondering much at your reasons for it—and reflecting, at any rate, on the whole thing deeply. *Francis* is very good, and I suppose it a friendship—certainly most just and grateful to F. J. Child.[2] Besides I like the name in itself. *Tweedy* I hate in itself—I think it woefully ugly—but accept willingly enough for its associations—though, as to this, they are essentially yours, not the child's, who will carry the name through life wondering, rather, why he was *affublé* with it. It is for *Temple* that I reserve all the horrors that an uncle and a brother may be judged by you to have a right to express; I don't understand it—I don't like it—I can't away [*sic*] with it anyhow. That it may be a sign, on your part, of attachment to Aunt Mary's maiden name, to the far-off dead Minny, or to the very near (me) living Elly (whom as I wrote you, I *suspect* of an intention to *change* hers—for the second time—to Hunter!)—these things seem to me to count for nothing in favour of it, as compared with the *odiousness* of the false air it has of *our*—I mean of any of us—trying to connect ourselves so with the T. family—hook ourselves on to the name or make use of it because it is "aristocratic." It doesn't matter that you are so sublimely incapable of any such motive—and that it will dawn upon you in these words for the first time. It is enough that there is a *fatal* air of elastic snobbishness about it—from the moment we have cousins of the name—cousins too who have always made so much of it, under circumstances which would, had they been wiser, made them keep silent or even drop it. They come by it through illegitimacy and through an individual who was horribly dishonoured. Aunt Mary's father was a *bastard* son of Sir John Temple, the "founder" of the family in America, and he housed himself, after burning the public office of which he was in charge, to cover the tracks of his peculations. This doesn't prevent the Roses, here, from taking a great stand on the name (so that Sir William, the late Sir John's eldest son, has bought Moor Park, Sir William Temple's old place); and one hates to be connected even by implication, and in spite of all the good faith possible on one's own part, with all the general American and Canadian swagger about it. Nothing would induce me to let it appear to a "Temple" that I wished to make my child seem to be connected with them by *that* strain in his blood; which is what any Temple would inevitably assume! If the word is a tribute to Aunt Mary T. isn't this surely, for one child covered by the *Tweedy*? Why give the boy so much of it? I, moreover, hate all surnames given to children when they are not own *family*-names. The boy grows up to find himself nominally and thereby hollowly and uncomfortably connected with people who are nothing to him, or he to them, ten to one, and yet whom he seems to hook himself on to. For instance I am more glad than I can say today that it was not *me* whom Father named "Garth Wilkinson"—dangling onto Wilkinsons here who are no Wilkinsons of mine. The Wilkinson who was *his,* father's, would have been long departed, when I should be still in that false position with his children. If I were the father of children I should say: "Go to, let us use what we *have,* when to simplify an always difficult problem, we *can*"; and I would give one of my boys the name or one of the names of mother's maternal grandfather,* the worthy Alexander Robertson, who came from Scotland to the U.S. in the middle of the last century and was a good and solid burgess of New York. That's an association worth perpetuating—it means something, preserves the continuity one likes to preserve, connects itself with something which is *of* us—and not of other people. Our Bob, as having the Robertson, needn't be a stumbling block, with a proper Christian name [before] it. I, for my part, think Alexander Robertson James a very good name—though I should think Francis R. J. almost equally good—and can't help wishing your New Boy, who I hope won't be a Newsboy, had either of them. At any rate think better of the "Temple"—do, *do,* DO! Alice feels as intensely on the subject as I do[3] . . . the warmth of them, dear William, and dearest Alice—*c'est plus fort que moi.* I am sure, moreover, that *you,* dearest Alice, are not eager to contend for the luckless idea. But I have deluged you.—I take Minnie Emmet, who dines with me tonight, to the theatre. Elly is still in Scotland[4] . . . Paris . . . 17th I shan't see her, I fear, before she returns to the U.S. (the end of this month), unless Scotland does for her on the spot. Ever both of your affectionate

Henry James

* Or even "Hugh Walsh (James)" her Newburgh *pa*ternal grandfather.

1. HJ made repeated pleas to his brother to be careful in naming his children. William named his youngest son Francis Tweedy—the Tweedy after the old Newport family friend—but the child, on reaching maturity, changed his name to Alexander Robertson, the name HJ suggests in this letter.
2. Francis James Child (1825–1896), the Harvard professor and eminent authority on English ballads.
3. A portion of this letter shows burned edges, and there is a gap in the text.

Three words are discernible—"feelings . . . my own . . ."—suggesting that HJ, after his earlier vehemence on the question of names, reminds his brother that these feelings are his own.

4. There is a further gap here, and the condition of the holograph suggests that a lighted cigar or cigarette was laid on the last page

To Robert Louis Stevenson
Ms Yale

34 De Vere Gardens W.
Feb. 18*th* 1891

My dear Louis.

Your letter of December 29th is a most touching appeal; and I am glad my own last had been posted to you two or three weeks before it reached me. Whether mine has—or will have been—guided to your coral strand is a matter as to which your disclosures touching the state of the Samoan post inspire me with the worst apprehensions. At any rate I did despatch you—supposedly via San Francisco—a really pretty long screed about a month ago. I ought to write to you all the while; but though I seem to myself to live with my pen in my hand I achieve nothing capable of connecting me so with glory. I am going to Paris tomorrow morning for a month, but I have vowed that I will miss my train sooner than depart without scrawling you and your wife a few words tonight. I shall probably see little or nothing there that will interest you much (or even interest myself hugely)—but having neither a yacht, an island, an heroic nature, a gallant wife, mother and son, nor a sea-stomach, I have to seek adventure in the humblest forms. In writing the other day I told you more or less what I was doing—*am* doing—in these elderly days; and the same general description will serve. I am doing what I can to launch myself in the dramatic direction—and the strange part of the matter is that I am doing it more or less seriously, as if we *had* the Scène Anglaise which we haven't. And I secretly dream of supplying the vile want? *Pas même*—and my zeal in the affair is only matched by my indifference. What is serious in it is that having begun to work in this sense some months ago, to give my little ones bread—I find the *form* opens out before me as if there were a kingdom to conquer—a kingdom forsooth of ignorant brutes of managers and dense *cabotins* of actors. All the same, I feel as if I had at last *found* my form—my real one—that for which pale fiction is an ineffectual substitute. God grant this unholy truth may not abide with me more than two or three years—time to dig out eight or ten rounded masterpieces and make withal enough money to enable me to retire in peace and plenty for the unmolested business of a *little* supreme writing, as distinguished from gouging—which is the Form abovementioned. Your loneliness and your foodlessness, my dear Louis, bring tears to my eyes. If there were only a parcels' post to Samoa I would set Fortnum and Mason to work at you at this end of the line. But if they intercept the hieroglyphics at Sydney, what would they do to the sausage? Surely there is some cure for your emptiness; if nothing else why not coming away? Don't eat up Mrs. Louis, whatever you do. You are precious to literature—but she is precious to the affections, which are larger, yet in a still worse way. It's passing strange to me that the coral strand is trodden by John LaFarge and Henry Adams.[1] The former is one of the two or three men now living whom (outside of my brotherhood), I have known longest since before the age of puberty. He was very remarkable then—but of late years I've seen less of him and I don't know what he has become. However, he never can have become commonplace—he is a strange and complicated product. Henry Adams is as conversible as an Adams is permitted by the scheme of nature to be; but what is wonderful to me is that they have both taken to the buccaneering life when already "on the return"—LaFarge many times a *père de famille.* Who knows what may be the pranks of my own *cinquantaine?* I shall certainly do my utmost to get to Egypt to see you, if, as is hinted to me by dear Colvin, you turn up there after the fitful fever of Samoa. Your being there would give me wings—especially if plays should give me gold. This is an exquisitely blissful dream. Don't fail to do your part of it. I almost joy in your lack of the *Tragic Muse;* as proving to me, I mean, that you are curious enough to have missed it. Nevertheless I have just posted to you, registered, the first copy I have received of the one-volume edition; but this moment out. I wanted to send you the three volumes by Lloyd, but he seemed clear you would have received it, and I didn't insist, as I knew he was charged with innumerable parcels and bales. I will presently send another *Muse,* and one, at least, must reach you. Our public news is small—unless you count in the "Card Scandal"; the imputed cheating at Baccarat of Sir William Gordon Cumming, of the Scots Guards, while playing with the Prince of Wales.[2] I posted you today two numbers of the *World,* with two articles thereanent which constitute the most interesting discussion of the matter that I have seen. Gordon C. is to bring an action for libel against five gentlemen and ladies—yet he *did* sign an abjuration (from play), which implied his guilt. It is a curious, complicated, ugly *fin de siècle* drama of the "great" world—with the extraordinary stamp of vulgarity on it that is on everything the Prince of Wales has to do with. The Irish chasm yawns wider than ever—you can *taste* a general election in the air. Poor Gosse has just passed through one of his periodical episodes—a ferocious attack from William Archer, in the P[all] M[all] G[azette] on the subject of his translation of Ibsen's last (and queerest) play *Hedda Gabler.* Again he has been almost saved by the extravagant malevolence (as it seems to me) of his critic. But he *has* a genius for inaccuracy which makes it difficult to dress his wounds. Colvin is really better, I think—if any one can be better who is so absolutely good. I hope to God my last long letter will have reached you. I promise to write soon again. I enfold you all in my sympathy and am ever your faithfullest

Henry James

1. John LaFarge (1835–1910), the painter, an old friend from HJ's Newport days, had accompanied the widowed Henry Adams on his long journey into the South Pacific. For an account of their visit to Stevenson see Edel, *Henry James: The Treacherous Years, 1895–1901* (1969), the chapter entitled "A Romantic Fable."

2. The Prince of Wales, later Edward VII, was forced to testify in court in the Baccarat case (called the Tranby Croft Case) after one of his companions was accused of cheating.

To Horace E. Scudder

Ms Harvard

Paris, Hotel Westminster
Rue de la Paix
March 4*th* 1891

Dear Mr. Scudder.

Your letter demands a frank answer. My "deathly silence" has been the result of the fact that when after last writing to you I read over *The Pupil* in the light of your remarks about it, I quite failed to see that you had treated me fairly: I could *not* see that it was a performance that the *Atlantic* ought to have declined—nor banish from my mind the reflection that the responsibility, in any case, as regards the readers of the magazine, the public, should, when it's a question of an old and honourable reputation, be left with the author himself. The editor, under such circumstances, may fairly leave it to him—and I should not have shrunk from any account the readers might have held me to. These impressions were distinctly chilling as regards the production of further work. I had in my hands a little story which I had meant to send to you—but there was nothing in it to assure me that it would seem to you to have a different quality from its predecessor, and I couldn't bring myself to despatch it. The pen fell out of my hand and I took refuge in other work, which has proved fruitful and [in] which I am now immersed. I fear I shall remain so—certainly all this month—which I am spending in this place. But on my return to London on April 1st I will do my best to get back to some tales. I feel uncertain as to how I shall do them—and as if the spell, for today, were rather broken. But you shall have a couple of specimens and I will do my best to keep them really short. Please destroy the copy of *The Pupil* you have—if you still have it—in your hands. I sent the story to *Longman,* to which I had long promised a tale, and it presently appears.[1] The other little thing comes out in the new Illustrated weekly London periodical *Black and White.*[2]

Yours very truly
Henry James

1. See letter to Scudder, 10 December 1890.
2. "Brooksmith" appeared in *Black and White* (2 May 1891), 417–420, 422, and in *Harper's Weekly* (2 May 1891), 321–323.

To Edmund Gosse
Ms Leeds

34 De Vere Gardens W.
Apr. 28*th* [1891]

My dear Gosse.[1]

I return the Ibsenite volume[2] with many thanks—especially for the opportunity to read your charming preface which is really *en somme* and between ourselves (I wouldn't say it to Lang) more interesting than Ibsen himself. That is I think you make him out a richer phenomenon than he is. The perusal of the dreary *Rosmersholm* and even the reperusal of *Ghosts* has been rather a shock to me—they have let me down, down. Surely the former isn't *good?*—any more than the tedious *Lady from the Sea* is? *Must* I think these things works of skill? If I must I will—save to you alone: to whom I confide that they seem to be of a grey mediocrity —in the case of "Rosmersholm" *jusqu'à en être bête.* They don't seem to me dramatic, or dramas at all—but (I am speaking of those two particularly) moral tales in dialogue—without the objectivity, the visibility of the drama. They suggest curious reflections as to the Scandinavian stage and audience. Of course they have a serious —a terribly serious, "feeling for life," and always an idea—but they come off so little, in general, as plays; and I can't think that a man who is at odds with his form is ever a first-rate man. But I may be grossly blind, and at any rate don't *tell* it of yours tremulously

Henry James

1. On the flap of the envelope of this letter HJ wrote: "Your preface perfect, granting premises."

2. Gosse, a specialist in Scandinavian languages and a translator at the Board of Trade, had long championed Ibsen. The preface to which James refers appeared in Volume I of the Lovell's Series of Foreign Literature edition of Ibsen's works (1890).

To Elizabeth Robins

Ms Texas

34 De Vere Gardens W.
May 29*th* [1891]

Dear Miss Robins.[1]

I am greatly hoping that you will kindly agree to see my friend Edward Compton, who was with me last night at the Vaudeville, on the subject of such possibilities as may exist of your doing Mme de Cintré in my *American* on its production here in September next. He was exceedingly interested, of course, in your Hedda, and I have undertaken to ask him, on your behalf, if you can give him half an hour either on *Sunday, Tuesday,* or *Wednesday*— preferably in the afternoon: no matter how early. He would be delighted to come and see you, or if you are away from home at those hours I should be delighted, that he should meet you *here*—when you can have the place to yourselves. Will you kindly address a word directly to *him*—

Edward Compton Esq.
54 Avonmore Road,
Kensington, W.?

mentioning such time as will suit you and to which he will conform?—I have been hoping for some news of you ever since the day I last saw you—when you expected to clear up the prospect of Henry Arthur [Jones]. I am *now* hoping that it is sufficiently clearer for you to take some little interest in *us*—even if on the basis of simply *starting* us in the *early* autumn, if H.A. is to come on (as would seem probable) in the later. You can desert us for him on the day he wants you. Yours most truly

Henry James

1. Elizabeth Robins (1863–1952), a Kentucky-born actress, created major Ibsen roles on the London stage with considerable success. On retiring from the stage she became a popular novelist and a champion of women's rights.

To Isabella Stewart Gardner

Ms Gardner

34 De Vere Gardens W.
June 7*th* [1891]

My dear Mrs. Gardner.

You always do graceful and generous things promptly and swiftly, and I always thank you for them a hundred years too late. Don't deny it—your magnanimity is capable even of that—for the present is a crowning proof. Your sympathetic word about my poor little play[1] went to my heart when it came—and it has lain locked up there ever since. I pull it out, with a violent effort, to turn it over and handle it a little again—but the frowning portals of that organ gape wide for me to put it quickly back among the slumbering echoes and dried roseleaves. There it goes—don't you hear the click of the lock? I wish indeed I were going to America to "produce" my dramatic production—for heaven knows how that ticklish business will go off when the time comes. The time will not come till it has been a *London* success—if success it is to be. I have refused the most glittering American offers in order to elicit still more glittering ones on the basis of the triumph in *this* place. The thing has only been acted as yet in the provinces—but I am happy to say its success in the big cities (the bigger the place the better it goes) constitutes a basis for home. Meanwhile London doesn't see it till the 26th September next—when one *does* hope that it will run all winter. These are rash words to utter—so please kindly scratch them out yourself—to make sure. The piece is really very well cast, as things go on the *scène anglaise* for town, and I am to have really quite adorable scenery—which it has been very amusing to go into the gorgeous details of. A young American actress[2] who never made a mark I believe, *chez vous,* has lately revealed herself, strikingly, here as Ibsen's *Hedda Gabler,* and has quite leaped into fame. She is slightly uncanny, but distinguished and individual, and she is to do my heroine; a short part, but a very pretty one.—It's a bad business that you don't come out this summer, for I shouldn't miss you by going to Italy. If it didn't sound vain-glorious I should add that neither would you, by going there—miss me. However, perhaps you would go all the same—I only meant that I fear there are, this year, no loose palaces knocking about. The Curtises go to India—or believe they do—in the autumn; so I suppose they summerize at the Barbaro. Happy thought—you come out in the autumn and occupy the Barbaro during their absence. Give me then a lease of their top-floor. They won't—so this will be my only way to get it. This is a pale, dim, cold, sceptical season—a season that doesn't believe in itself. It's a thousand pities you are not here to stimulate its credulity. My sister has a very nice house to be very ill in—and it isn't a waste. Katharine Loring is, still, the very foundation of our Universe. I hope *yours,* dear Mrs. Gardner, keeps in tolerable repair—your Universe I mean. But everything of yours is always in lovely order—except indeed a thing so very peculiarly and intensely yours, as

Henry James

1. This is an allusion to HJ's dramatization of *Daisy Miller* in the early 1880s. He had given Mrs. Gardner a copy of the privately printed version of this play and had read it to her on two successive evenings. See *Letters* II, 384.

2. Elizabeth Robins.

To John Hay
Ms Brown

34 De Vere Gardens W.
Sunday [June ? 1891]

My dear Hay.

H.A.'s[1] letters are most interesting, but I always want more account of the look of things—places—people. No one ever renders that—R.L.S. doesn't touch it, in some things he is now publishing.[2] But many thanks for these. What a power of baring one's self—hitherto unsuspected in H.A.—I hope you are alive for the moment.

Ever yours
Henry James

The poor old dirty MS. will have gone to you by hand today.

1. Hay had apparently sent HJ a typescript of Henry Adams's letters from the South Seas.

2. Stevenson's letters about his life in the South Seas. See letter to Stevenson, 12 January 1891

To William Archer
Ms British Library

34 De Vere Gardens W.
June [July] 5*th* [1891]

Dear Mr. Archer.

I owe you much acknowledgment of your very interesting and gratifying letter,[1] and should be able this morning to make it more complete if it were not that I am almost bent double with a vile attack of lumbago which I was threatened with when I saw you yesterday and which at the present moment makes it anguish for me to sit up and write. I am very glad you found my article in any degree remunerative. As regards your own various remarks—on Ibsen's style, his poetic element etc., I take them with the full sense of your infinitely more complete initiation and without having meant to put forth my own as the last word about him. Only on *our* data—those of the mere English reader—they are (my own) almost *inevitable* strictures. Remember how very imperfect our means of approach to him are, while you practically inhabit the citadel. I should indeed like to hear as much as possible of *Peer Gynt* and *Brand,* and hope the occasion—the opportunity—may come to me, of doing so with your aid. Aren't those productions translatable—on the system of Hayward's *Faust* or some prose Dante? However, you will tell me this some day. But no, decidedly, I do *not* find the general atmosphere of imagination, the transporting tone, in *Rosmersholm,* interesting as that work is; though no doubt in the portions you allude to one misses it least. *Yes,* on the other hand, many times yes, *Hedda* as against *Francillon*—for a big sense of life.[2] Dumas *fils* is no great god of mine—*phraseur,* intensely prosaic I find him—with all his hundred clevernesses. Ibsen is much deeper and more various—the *Wild Duck* is altogether beyond the contemporary neat everlastingly and exclusively adulterous Frenchmen, who are never *strange.* In short I like Ibsen, I think quite as much as you ought to ask one who deals with him on our restricted basis to do. And more than this, I *respect* him peculiarly, an odd, unwonted sentiment to be prompted to—and which one enjoys much for its rarity. I shall be very glad to find opportunity to have a talk about him with you some day—about him and others. Believe me meanwhile very truly, and lamely, yours

Henry James

1. HJ had begun by disliking Ibsen and finding him limited (see letter to Gosse, 28 April 1891). Then, on seeing some of his plays, and in particular Miss Robins's *Hedda,* he had begun to find him interesting. In the midst of the general attacks on Ibsen from other critics, HJ wrote for the *New Review,* IV (June 1891), 519–530, "On the Occasion of Hedda Gabler," in which he praised Ibsen's "angular irony" and described his realism as providing "a charmless fascination" in "his perfect practice of a difficult and delicate art, combined with such aesthetic density." He also praised Ibsen's "admirable talent for producing an intensity of interest by means incorruptibly quiet." William Archer, the drama critic, wrote a long letter to HJ calling this piece "one of the very few really sane and luminous things that have been said on the subject in English." As one of the principal translators of Ibsen, Archer challenged James, however, to see that Ibsen was to be admired not so much as a realist "but rather (I might almost say) as a symbolist." James, in his preoccupation with Balzacian realism, had not yet grasped the full impact of the symbolist movement, and it may be judged that Archer's timely remonstrance had a profound influence on him. It modified his judgments of Ibsen and marked the beginning of an influence that would extend from *The Spoils of Poynton* to *The Golden Bowl.* Archer wrote: "I feel that the real secret of Ibsen's power is a very simple one—to wit, that he is incomparably the greatest *poet* who has as yet enslaved himself to the condi-

tions of realistic, or perhaps I should say, everyday drama. What we feel—at any rate what *I* feel—behind *Ghosts, The Wild Duck, Rosmersholm* and *Hedda Gabler* is a gigantic imagination, seizing upon a few fragmentary episodes of life with unexampled rotundity and marvellous vitalization of the smallest detail . . . *Rosmersholm,* for example, delights me simply because it has what I should call style in the largest sense—because it takes a piece of real life and impregnates it with poetry and with meaning, while presenting it in an atmosphere of the poet's own creation, a 'light that never was on land and sea' " (Archer to HJ, 3 July 1891, Ms Harvard).

2. Archer had compared Ibsen with Dumas *fils* in his letter: "take *Hedda Gabler,* and compare it with such a play as Dumas's *Francillon*—to my mind a masterpiece in its way: does not one feel that the sheer mental energy of *Hedda,* the intellectual horse-power as it were, is far and away greater than that of *Francillon*—there is greater pressure of thought to the square inch?" *Francillon* was produced in 1887.

To Grace Norton
Ms Harvard

Marine Hotel
Kingstown
Thursday [19 July 1891]

My dear Grace.

Though I haven't been able to write and thank you for a couple of days, I have been full of the impression of Lily's saddening note. My soul is grieved indeed for dear old J.R.L.[1] and for the painful, darkened, unhelpable *end*—from which, always, he seemed to me—as I knew him and saw him—personally far. I echo Lily's hope—and yours probably and that of those who are on the spot, that the great release may descend upon him soon. I shall miss him much and think of him with all kinds of warm and bright and distinguished (I mean eminent and happy) association. There will be a deluge of mediocrity of criticism of him in the London papers. But we will talk of him. I start homeward toward the end of next week. The weather here is of an extraordinary perfection; and doubtless still better than Irish with you. How hateful you leave your cottage on September 1st. But I will come down every day or two before that: as often as you will give me dinner. Ever yours

Henry James

1. Miss Norton was in England and had just learned from Lily Norton that James Russell Lowell was dying.

To James Russell Lowell
Ms Harvard

Royal Marine Hotel
Kingstown, Ireland
July 20 [1891]

My very dear Lowell.

Too seldom have I written to you, considering how often I think. I have fled from the brutal London July and sought this alien strand, where I find comparative leisure and obscurity—that sounds as if I were celebrated!—so that I ought to bombard you with *ma prose*—the more easily that from here, as it were, Cambridge is only across the way. We are very American in Ireland. But alas I have also brought with me a thousand unanswered letters—which I have taken an expensive sittingroom at the inn on purpose to work off. Therefore when I stop please know it isn't from failing interest (on my own part), but only to begin again and from economy, get back the price of my salon. My departure from London was quickened by the desire to lighten the burden that an attack of influenza had left me to carry—I was "ordered" as they say so humbly in London (it's their own humility!) to the sea, and I chose a *plage* as distant as possible. This isn't exactly a plage, but a kind of watery suburb of Dublin—representing apparently the only water in the connection. It is a very charming coast, in this lovely weather, with great blueness of sea and greenness of shore, and all kinds of graceful Wicklow mountains and hills of Howth and Killiny. The very waves have a brogue as they break—and they broke Bray Head, the fine southernmost limit of the bay, long ago. But let me not have the air of inflicting upon you that deadliest of all things, a scenery-letter, when my foremost wish is to throw myself into *your* environment. I have, somehow a vision of you which makes my heart ache a good deal—and makes me brush from my eye the tear in which old London pictures—other pictures —are reflected. Your non-arrival—this spring—made me for the first time in my life willing to say that I "realised" a situation. I seemed to see that you were tied down by pain and weakness, that you were suffering often and suffering much. I don't like to ask for fear of a yes, and I don't like not to ask for fear of your noticing my silence. In point of fact I *have* asked—every time I have seen

Mrs. Leslie Stephen. When I read in the *Times* that the heat in America is exorbitant, I try to think it's only perfidious Albion, so as not to figure you unable to move from the torrid Cambridge —if it be true that you *may* not do this. A letter from my brother some weeks ago mentioned that, on his seeing you just before writing it, you had spoken to him of your having for the first time that day—the first for many weeks—been able to eat a mutton chop without nausea.[1] This gave me the note of the condition that I haven't liked to think of, and which I *have* yet thought of, with infinite sympathy and infinite sense of how little we can interfere with the doom of our friends to *endure*. But, my dear Lowell, I don't write to rehearse to you your own incommodities. I have walked across the Park alone this summer and when I have had to go to Paddington I have slackened my step—oh, so vainly—in Radnor Place, in the hope that from the little afternoon sittingroom you would call me in. These melancholies haven't prevented the London Season from roaring and elbowing along, in a manner less and less to my taste. When the German emperor arrived the other day I fled before the exhibition of such abysmal platitude—if your renowned literary sense admits that collocation. I went to see Mrs. Smalley the day before that—she and Eleanor and Evelyn were very kind to me while I was Influenzed. They were all influenzed themselves too, and I think their sky is a little duskier. Smalley's invulnerability strikes me as having failed him—since the serious illness he had in the winter. He looks altered and humiliated—older and softer; but this remark is for your private ear alone. I trust it bodes them all nothing but a more domestic life. They kindly wish me to promise for Whitby in August—but, as I told you last summer, I have no heart for Whitby on any but *your* terms —the little house in the lane with the view of the Abbey through the loophole in the barn—or whatever it was—and the religious rite of your coffee-making to usher in the summer's day. I believe the du Mauriers go again, but poor Alfred St. Johnston seemed a part of it to me—and there is something discordant in his senseless young death. The Leslie Stephens had already, when I left town, repaired to St. Ives, with a poor little *stabbed* Toby[2]—stabbed at school, by a little brute of a mate, to form him an English character. I believe he will get better of it—I mean of the stabbing, I'm afraid not of the character. Leslie seems vaguely better, and can work so long as he *doesn't,* in these things, make his wife shine with a more and more beautiful light.[3] Grace Norton has a cottage —very spacious and shabby and pleasant, with all Crofton Croker's reviewed books[4] in it, at Hampton Court, on the Mole, if you please, which is a tributary of the Thames and holds a boat with a one-legged boatman, who is in her service. If he were a biped I fear it would run aground. The Lord Chief Justice invites me again to Ottery, but I'm afraid he wants to marry me to his sister-in-law —he can't any one else. The Miss Lawrences are more unanimous than ever, especially when they ask after you. And I too, my dear Lowell, have only one mind—but I won't bore you more with its sameness. I wish I had twenty, that they might be all filled with participation in your lot and with the ever affectionate sentiments of yours devotedly

Henry James

1. Lowell had cancer of the stomach.
2. Thoby Stephen (1880–1906), the elder brother of Virginia Stephen, later Virginia Woolf.
3. Julia Jackson Stephen. HJ seems to be referring to the Stephens' marriage in the same light in which Virginia Woolf depicted it in *To the Lighthouse.*
4. Thomas Crofton Croker (1798–1854), the Irish folklorist.

To William James
Ms Harvard

Marine Hotel
Kingstown, Ireland
July 31 [1891]

My dear William.

I wrote you a letter of many pages one of the first days of this month—mainly about our poor Alice; but when you despatched to her the long one which was lately sent me to read, from Argyle Road, and of which I forget the date, mine hadn't reached you, and you only remarked that you hadn't heard from me for three months. I trust, however, that, just afterwards, my twenty earnest pages turned up. I left London for an absence of four or five weeks, now nearly spent, on July 7th. I came hither not especially to come to Ireland; only to get far, far from the burdensome London of July. I have plentifully succeeded and have been blissfully "out of it." When I get back—about the 12th—not to move again, to speak of—peace will have descended on the metropolis. I have unadventurously subsided, here, on the spot where I landed, and where I have found a very good quiet hotel, a charming summer sea and air, a very pretty coast, though too suburban (to Dublin), and a command of my time which has enabled me to do a London month's work in a fortnight. I have also purged myself of the lingering blight of influenza. At the same time I have not seen Alice for nearly four weeks, and have only Katharine L.'s brief but frequent communications to go by. They have been soothing, reassuring, or I shouldn't have staid away; reassuring, I mean, in the sense that Alice's condition presents no essentially new feature—only a pretty steady and I fear pretty painful development of the old. The great circumstance is that, as you probably will already know, she has seen W. W. Baldwin, the American doctor of Florence (detested, I don't know why, of Boott), who, passing through London, on a flying visit to the U.S., was sent for, at my telegraphed solicitation, by Katharine, and made Alice four very beneficial visits. He is very "live"—clever, intelligent and ingenious and remarkable in his way; and, as a good friend of mine, has taken an added interest in her, besides having evidently been most careful and attentive. He appears to have been almost the only doctor that she has ever *liked* to see; she at any rate saw him, each time, without nervousness or exhaustion. Of course I have *not* seen him—as all this has taken place within the last ten days; but (he sailed on the 29th) I shall do so, as well as Alice and Katharine again, of course, on his return in September. He will probably stay a few days with me then. K.P.L. will presumably already have let you know that he pronounced that poor Alice's tumour *is* cancer—"not immediately fatal," and probably in the last stage painless. Before he came I fear she was having a great deal of pain—and he was mainly occupied with her, I judge, in going, happily, into the question of how to most successfully combat this misery with morphia. It is clear he has been very suggestive and help-giving, and he has already, evidently, done poor Alice much good. K's report of his *effect* has been joyous. I will write you more as soon as I return to town. Alice must have greatly appreciated your beautiful and interesting long letter—as *I* did. You do not exaggerate her *force d'âme*—which is extraordinary; and cannot, without seeing it, appreciate the serenity of her present attitude, which strikes me, strange as it may appear to you, as a condition of greater *comfort* than she has known for years, or probably *ever* known. The "nervousness" engendered by (or engendering) her intense horror of life and contempt for it is practically falling away from her in view of her future becoming thus a definite and not long—a rapidly *shrinking*, term. She is easier about it—ever so much—than before, and her state is simplified by this new and possibly great, but (comparatively) *maniable* suffering. Her easy intercourse with Baldwin is a striking sign of this. Don't, therefore, be too much *haunted* with her: I am less so now than I have been for years. Her outside material environment, taking all morphia can do for granted, will be (D.V.) perfect for her, in all probability, so long as an environment matters. Her thoroughly sanitary little house, her nurse, her cook, and her housemaid are everything that could possibly be wished. As for Katharine,—abysses of gratitude only can respond to her name. Her brother (*Me!*) also works in very well. I have been supposing that K. would absolutely have to go home, for a couple of months, late this summer—though unable even to fancy how nurse and I alone could meet the stress of Alice's formidable state. But I now am pretty sure that she will abide with her uninterruptedly to the end—whenever that may be. Her father and sister seem to me almost as much one of the "Lord's mercies" to us as she herself. Fortunately she gets much out of her London life—has a hundred independent activities and dozens of friends and a much more free and uncompromising life than in her narrow home.—But enough of this tolerably tragic chapter: I will report freshly after again seeing Alice.—Your letter, to *her*, gave me a very sympathetic but very unhelping sense, of all *your* responsibilities and complications—not that I am ever without it! Your summer sounds serious, with all these things, and so big a task on your hands as distilling so big a book thrown in. I respond joyously to the idea of seeing you all here a year hence—please tell Alice that my welcome is already waiting at her door, to come over with her and minister to her on the way. But my own wifeless, childless, houseless, classless, mother- and sister-in-lawless, horseless, cowless, and useless existence seems too spare indeed and lean and unheroic, in the lurid light of your fireside, and probably strikes you in the same way. Yet strangely, this attenuated being is, practically, about all I can manage, which shows how little nature constructed me for fringes and frills and ramifications. May the manual you will squeeze out of your two big volumes be worth real income to you as a textbook. Apropos of which the main thing, counting out Baldwin, that has lately happened to Alice, appears to have been the disgust and indignation experienced by her over the idiotic review of your Psychology in the *Nation.* I don't know what to make of the way the *Nation* treats, and has mainly always treated *us*—and it alienates me from Godkin. It never notices anything of mine at all till six months after publication and then pitchforked in with a lot of baser matter. It is some vicious, pig-headed *parti pris* of Garrison's.[1]—I expect to be in London, after the middle of this month, straight on end indefinitely. I have *entirely* given up country-visiting, thank God: I haven't paid one for a year. The last days of August begin the rehearsals for the London production of *The American*—on September 26th, at the Opéra Comique. I went into all the scenery with Compton before leaving town, and it will be very well done. The cast remains the same as in the provinces as regards most of the men, but the women are all changed. Miss Elizabeth Robins, a very intelligent young American "artiste," who has lately scored here heavily in Ibsen, does the heroine. Mrs. Crowe, the "Miss Bateman" ("Leah" etc.) of our youth, who is Mrs. Compton's eldest sister, returns to the stage on this occasion, after retirement, widowhood, loss of fortune etc., to play "mothers" for the rest of her days, and is to do Mme de Bellegarde. Miss Louise Moodie, who is supposed to be one of the two or three first "old women" in London, does Mrs. Bread, and Noémie is [in] the hands of a young French actress who has embarked (in English of course) on the London stage, Adrienne Dairolles. I give you these copious items to diversify the voices of Chocoruan nature. I embrace you all, dear William and dear Alice, and long unspeakably to press to my bosom the little heroine of anecdote, Margaret Mary. She must come and stay with me in De Vere Gardens and let me "take her out." Ever your

Henry

1. Wendell Phillips Garrison, book editor of the *Nation.* See *Letters* II, 68.

To Julia Jackson Stephen
Ms Berg

August 13*th* [1891]
34 De Vere Gardens W.1

Dear Mrs. Stephen.

I found your letter here on Tuesday night, on my return from four or five weeks in Ireland—and the next morning I sent your very kind enclosure to Mrs. Smalley, with a letter of my own. But yesterday afternoon brought us the news that you will by this time know, transforming all our suppositions and sadnesses to the absolute loss. Now that the beloved man[1] has gone, how swift and violent seems the event—and how difficult to believe—and how miserably much to come home to us hereafter. If it was hard to believe that his abounding life was really stricken—and that he was *marked,* how little, as yet, can I take in the eternal silence! But we can talk *of* him and resist it a little. It seems as if we measured only now how much we loved him. I shall miss him singularly and be long getting rid of the fancy that I shall meet him some day walking across the park. The papers will chatter profusely—but that will do us no good. You know all the depth of his attachment to yourself and Stephen, but you can't know how often I heard him tenderly express it—and to your children. Poor Mrs. Burnett—she will "hear of it" now! I shall write again to Mrs. Smalley.—London is apparently destined to be my portion at present—and I have no particular plans of absence, but only certain particular reasons for not going far. I am afraid I *shan't* achieve such a flight as to Cornwall, and yet I don't banish hope and shall certainly come straight to St. Ives if I get within a county or two of it. Many thanks for your kind invitation. The loss of one of his oldest friends will probably not conduce to Stephen's present well-being, but I hope some other things have done so. I found, and left, lovely weather in Ireland. Believe me, dear Mrs. Stephen, in great sympathy yours

Henry James

1. James Russell Lowell had died on 12 August 1891. He had been a close friend of the Stephens and was godfather to their daughter Virginia.

To Charles Eliot Norton
Ms Harvard

34 De Vere Gardens W.
August 28*th* 1891

My dear Charles.

It is only the conspiracy of hindrances so perpetually characteristic of life in this place, even when it is theoretically *not* alive, as in the mid-August, that has stayed my hand, for days past, when it has most longed to write to you. Dear Lowell's death—the words are almost as difficult as they are odious to write—has made me think almost as much of you as of him. I imagine that you are the person in the world to whom it makes the most complete and constant difference that he is no longer here; just as you must have been the one most closely associated with the too vain watching of his last struggle with the monster. It is a dim satisfaction to me, therefore, to say to you how fond I was of him and how I shall miss him and miss him and miss him. During these last strange English years of his life (it would take me long to tell you why I call them strange), I had seen a great deal of him and all with the effect of confirming my affection for him. London is bestrewn, to my sense, with reminders of his happy career here, and his company and his talk. He was kind and delightful and gratifying to me, and all sorts of occasions in which he will ever be vivid swarm before me as I think of him. The "press" has been copious and extremely worshipful about him—but all with that colourless perfunctory note, that absence of the personal tone and of individual talent, which makes English journalism almost unreadable to me nowadays and has kept me from sending you, or any one else, the articles I have seen. But they have been full of the most commemorative intention—reminding me afresh that the dear man had become indeed a very high and honourable personage here. Strange was his double existence—the American and the English sides of his medal, which had yet so much in common. That is, I don't know how English he was at home, but he was conspicuously American here. However, I am not trying to characterize him, to you least of all who had known him well so much longer and seen all, or most, of the chapters of his history; but only letting you see how much I wish we might talk of him together. Some day we will, though it's a date that seems unfixable now. I am taking for granted, and Grace confirms my impression, that you inherit the greatest of literary responsibilities to his memory.[1] I think of this as a very high interest, but also a very arduous labour. It's a blessing, however, to feel that such an office is in such hands as yours. The posthumous vulgarities of our day add another grimness to death. Here again is another matter as to which I really miss not having the opportunity to talk with you. This is a brief communication, my dear Charles, for I am literally catching a train. I go down to the Isle of Wight half an hour hence. I saw Grace last night—on her way from Hampton Court to the lakes. I think she has had a summer with great elements of pleasure tantalizingly nipped and clipped by weather and people—the two curses of this island. Her existence strikes me as having been breathless and damp—and she came to lie on the grass! I have seen Lily less than I like, but it isn't over yet. I rejoice in Sally's promised advent—as much as gnawing envy permits. I think I shall write you again, my dear Charles; indeed I am very sure I shall do so if you risk the rash encouragement of a few lines (tho' I feel like a beast, as they say here, to suggest them to a man of your burdens) to yours ever affectionately

Henry James

1. Norton was to edit Lowell's letters.

To William James
Ms Harvard

34 De Vere Gardens W.
September 1*st* [1891]

My dear William.

Coming home last night from three days in the Isle of Wight I find your good letter from Asheville, N.C. It is delightful to hear of you from such a place—after the execution of your big job, with such a sense of holiday earned. I was in very truth on the point of writing to you, and as you see, I don't lose an hour. I have wished to tell you how I found Alice on my return from five weeks in Ireland—but I came back to occupations immediately pressing. She is of course *more* ill, weaker, and her state more precarious; but she is also, thank heaven—and Baldwin—easier. She has less pain, with constant morphia. It acts quite as it's desired to, and makes all the difference. I haven't seen her for several days (she was too ill for two days before I left town, and since last evening I have had no time to go 'round), and in general she is able to see me much less and for shorter moments: only between 5 and 7, and many days not at all. This shows a great increase of feebleness. I am not going out of town, however, even for a day, for some weeks to come. My rehearsals begin in a few days—the scenery has had the very last touches; the furniture (or portions of it) is just (as it is all French) arriving from Paris, and the dresses have had my personal superintendence. These things will all be of prime perfection; and oh, if the success can only be to match! I haven't spoken of my *other* theatrical preoccupations, because they are anxious and bothering and somewhat confused—and I would rather not do so till after the *American* has been played in London. *That,* if it is the success I hope, will have a direct and immediate action on everything else; and consecrate and fix my theatrical position—the terms on which I may deal with the barbarous, the ignorant, the sickening race of managers, etc. The great stumbling block in the whole business is the question of *time*—the slowness, the waiting, the delays which are a large part of the very essence of managerial production. They talk of years as we talk of months. I am handicapped by having begun too late—being too old: I ought to have done it ten years ago. But I shall vanquish, all the same. The only thing I *do* care to speak of now (and *only* to you) is the drama in three acts, *Mrs. Vibert,* which John Hare is to produce at the Garrick some time this season. But here there are irrepressible delays—indeed almost wholly—produced largely by the intense difficulty of casting. One tries to write as simple and feasible a thing as possible, and still—with the ignoble poverty of the English-speaking stage—the people capable of *beginning* to attempt to do it are not findable. *There's* a career for talent—to act my plays! *Mrs. Vibert* is blocked, largely by the difficulty of putting one's hand on a young man who can *touch* an important little part of a boy of twenty—who must be a *character,* a touching one. But, as I say, if the *American* prospers it will clear up many things.—Very interesting, very touching is your description of dear old Lowell—your last impressions of him. Yes he was an extraordinary *boy*—I was as much struck with it the year before his fatal illness as I ever was. All my relations with him were of the most affectionate character, and I shall infinitely miss him.—Grace Norton has just given up her pretty cottage and gone to Windermere till she sails, October 1. I have seen her when I could and so far as the drawback of her strange domestication of the boresome and incongruous Bôchers has permitted. They seem practically to live with her. We have had the vilest, coldest, wettest summer of all the vile, cold, wet ones I have known here—they disagree with me more and more as I grow older—far more than the winters. A tempest rages as I write. Your *warm* rusticity is a balmy image. Ever your faithful

Henry

To James McNeill Whistler

Ms Glasgow

34 De Vere Gardens W.
Sept. 29*th* [1891]

My dear Whistler.[1]

Heinemann[2] tells me that you and Mrs. Whistler are aimiably[3] disposed to go and see "The American."[4] (*8.20*) Kindly accept the enclosed—for Thursday night—on presentation of which at the box-office you will be instantly and obsequiously conducted to the two best stalls in the house. Ever yours and Mrs. Whistler's

Henry James

1. HJ had known the American painter since the 1870s. See *Letters* II, 167.
2. William Heinemann (1863–1920) had set up business as publisher during the previous year.
3. An example of HJ's occasionally resorting to an older Anglo-French form of the word.
4. *The American* had opened its London run at the Opéra Comique on 26 September.

To Edmund Gosse

Ms Leeds

34 De Vere Gardens W.
October 2*d* [1891]

My dear Gosse.

Your good and charming letter should have been answered on the spot—but my days are abnormal and perspective and relation are blurred. I shall come and see you the moment you return, and then I shall be able to tell you more in five minutes than in fifteen of such hurried scrawls as this. Meanwhile many thanks for your sympathy and curiosity and suspense—*all* thanks, indeed—and, in return, all eagerness for your *rentrée* here. My own suspense has been and still is great—though the voices of the air, rightly heard, seem to whisper *prosperity*. The papers have been on the whole quite awful—but the audiences are altogether different. The only thing is that these first three or four weeks *must* be up-hill: London is still empty, the whole enterprise is wholly new—the elements must assemble. The strain, the anxiety, the peculiar form and colour of such an ordeal (not to be divined in the least in advance) have sickened me *to death*—but I am getting better. I forecast nothing, however—I only wait. Come back and wait with me—it will be easier. Your picture of your existence and circumstance is like the flicker of the open door of heaven to those recumbent in the purgatory of yours not *yet* damned—ah no!—

Henry James

To Mrs. Mahlon Sands
Ms Private

34 De Vere Gardens W.
Sunday [October 10? 1891]

Dear Mrs. Sands.[1]

I find these days bring me many notes, or I should have sooner answered yours of Friday. Many thanks for it and for your honourable "candour." The latter charms me—I accept it in the friendliest spirit. But the *Becauses* that swarm up in answer to your "Why shouldn'ts!" etc., are too numerous for me to attempt to express here. They are, to my sense, very final and ultimate ones—the result of infinite ponderation and threshing out. My play suffers from being a novel dramatized—the original rigid story rides it through a country not otherwise, doubtless, to be traversed. I shall never dramatize a book again—but let my subject and my form be born together. Meanwhile I am glad you were held, as it were, even when you weren't pleased. I note with an expression of face so angelically tender that it's a pity you don't see it, the arrangement you suggest instead of Valentine's death scene—and feel that, after all, it would be charming to perish *with* you! However, we shan't perish, but live to tread a firmer and flowerier soil. I *am* unhappy about Miss Robins's hair—but *que voulez-vous?—I* can't dress it! You've seen *her*—but I wish she could see *you!*[2] I shall do so (happier than Miss R.) very soon, and I am yours most faithfully

Henry James

1. Mary Morton (Hartpence) Sands (1853–1896) was a great American beauty who moved in high English circles and was a friend of the Prince of Wales. See *Letters* II, 408.

2. In his tale "Nona Vincent," *English Illustrated Magazine*, IX (February–March 1892), 365–376, 491–502, which embodies his experience during the production of his play *The American*, HJ incorporates this idea—the beautiful woman providing an actress with the proper image of the character she must portray.

To William James
Ms Harvard

34 De Vere Gardens W.
Oct. 10*th* [1891]

My dear William.

It was an unspeakable relief for me to hear, from the office,[1] of your safe restoration to *les vôtres*—so conscious was I of the heavy price you so heroically paid for your visit to us. I thought it a tremendous tribute while you were here—but now I think [it] a still greater one; and I feel as if worried and worrying, preoccupied and detached as I was during those days, I had given you a very meagre and unamiable hospitality. I should think you would have a shuddering recollection of your visit—and I heartily forgive you if you have. I hope your homeward course was comfortable—as comfortable as any such misery can be. But I won't waste conjecture and curiosity, but simply wait to hear from you. Alice has undergone no particular change since you were here—though the last couple of days she has been too ill to see me. Yesterday she had a bad condition of the heart—great distress, with, however, too much weakness to allow of the violent agitations of it that in such moments she used to have. The remedy that Baldwin sent her as a substitute for morphia appears very beneficent and operative—I forget its name. The other invalid—the ill-starred play—is having a difficult infancy—a very difficult one—owing to the still extreme emptiness of the town (as to its stall-taking population) and to the injury done to it first by the newspapers and second by the four bad actors—which is too terrible a number for any play to carry. We shall probably fight it through this month and then the fates must decide. Unfortunately their decision appears already only too clear. Don't, however, *say* this in America—and say simply that it's too soon to determine *how* it's going. The strain is great and was at first intolerable; but I am getting a little used to it. Meanwhile, every night, the thing *appears* to succeed admirably, afresh—it is listened to with an absolute *tension* of stillness and interest—it plays closer and shorter—judicious excisions have improved it—Claire is better and Compton continues excellent. But my friends—mostly—shun the subject like a dishonour. The thing has been a revelation to me of how queerly and ungracefully friends can behave. I shall only live, henceforth, for my *revanche.* This is all today—save to express the tenderest sentiments to Alice. I hope the house is sound and still. Ever your

Henry

1. HJ had called the office of the shipping line to learn of the safe arrival of his brother's ship in the United States. William had come over for a few days at the end of September, mainly to see Alice, whose death was approaching. He had also attended the first night of *The American.*

To Robert Louis Stevenson

Ms Yale

34 De Vere Gardens W.
Oct. 30*th* 1891

My dear Louis.

My silences are hideous, but somehow I feel as if you were inaccessible to sound. Moreover it appears that my last letter, despatched many months ago, I admit, never reached you. But Colvin tells me that a post leaves tomorrow via San Francisco, and the effect of diminished remoteness from you is increased by the fact that I dined last night with Henry Adams, who told me of his visits to you months and months ago. He re-created you, and your wife, for me a little, as living persons, and fanned thereby the flame of my desire not to be forgotten of you and not to appear to forget you. He lately arrived—in Paris—via New Zealand and Marseilles and has just come to London to learn that he can't go to China, as he had planned, through the closure, newly enacted and inexorable, of all but its outermost parts. He now talks of Central Asia, but can't find anyone to go with him—least of all, alas, me. He is about to ship [John] La Farge home—now in Brittany with his French relations (and whom I have not seen). I feel as if I ought to make my letter a smoking porridge of news; but it's a bewilderment where to begin. Nothing, however, seems more foremost than that Colvin is really in a state of substantially recovered health. I dined with him a few days since at the Athenaeum and he gave me a better impression than he had done for years. He has passed through black darkness—and much prolonged; but I think he sees daylight and hears the birds sing. That little black demon of a Kipling will have perhaps leaped upon your silver strand by the time this reaches you—he publicly left England to embrace you many weeks ago—carrying literary genius out of the country with him in his pocket. As you will quarrel with him at an early day, for yourself, it is therefore not needful I should say more of him than that nature languishes since his departure and art grunts and turns in her sleep. I am told you and Lloyd are waking them both up in *The Wrecker,*[1] but I have had the fortitude not to begin the Wrecker yet. I *can't* read you in snippets and between the vulgar covers of magazines; but I am only biding my time and smacking my lips. I am a baser cockney even than you left me, inasmuch as now I don't even go to Bournemouth. I have made, in a whole year, but two absences from London—one of six weeks, last spring, in Paris, and another of the same duration, in the summer, in Ireland, which has a shabby foreign charm that touches me. Yet I'm afraid I have little to show for such an adhesion to my chair—unless it be holes in the seat of my trousers. I have written and am still to write a goodish many short tales—but you are not to be troubled with them till they prop each other up in volumes. I mean never to write another novel; I mean I have solemnly dedicated myself to a masterly brevity. I have come back to it as to an early love. "La première politesse de l'écrivain" says lately the exquisite Anatole France, "n'est-ce point d'être bref? La nouvelle suffit à tous. [That word is nouvelle.][2] On peut y renfermer beaucoup de sens en peu de mots. Une nouvelle bien faite est le régal des connoisseurs et le contentement des difficiles. C'est l'élixir et la quintessence. C'est l'onguent précieux." I quote him because il dit si bien. But you can ask Kipling. Excuse me for seeming to imply that one who has distilled the ointment as you have needs to ask anyone. I am too sceptical even to mention that I sent you ages ago the *Tragic Muse*—so presumable is it that she never reached you. I lately produced here a play—a dramatization of my old novel *The American* (the thing was played last spring in various places in the country), with circumstances of public humiliation which make it mainly count as an heroic beginning. The papers slated it without mercy, and it was—by several of its interpreters—wretchedly ill-played; also it betrays doubtless the inexperience of its author and suffers damnably from the straight-jacket of the unscenic book. But if I hadn't done, on solicitation, this particular thing I shouldn't have begun ever at all; and if I hadn't begun I shouldn't have the set purpose to show, henceforth, what flower of perfection I presume to think I can pick from the dusty brambles—ah meagre vegetation!—of the dramatic form. The play is in its fifth week—and will probably traverse a goodish many others; but it has been a time (the first, God knows!) when I have been on the whole glad you are not in England. Adams has made me see you a little—both, and I look to John LaFarge to do so a little more. (He comes in a few days.) Colvin has read me your letters when he discreetly could, and my life has been a burden from fearing to unfold the *Times* every morning to a perusal of Samoan convulsions. But apparently you survive, little good as I get of it. We are all under water here—it has rained hard for five months—and the British land is a waste of waters, as in the first pages of geologies. I am consumed with catarrh and rheumatism and lumbago—and when Adams talked to me last night of the tropics I could have howled with baffled desire. My poor sister—slowly and serenely dying—is too ill for me to leave England at present: she has a house in London now. I don't know whom to tell you about more than you would care to hear of. Edmund Gosse has written a novel—as yet unpublished—which I wot little of. Hall Caine[3] has put forth *A Scapegoat* to the enrichment, I believe, of all concerned—but I am not concerned. I will send you the work as soon as it is reduced in bulk. The Frenchmen are passing away—Maupassant dying of locomotor paralysis, the fruit of fabulous habits, I am told. *Je n'en sais rien;* but I shall miss him. Bourget is married and will do good things yet—I send you by this post his (to me very exquisite, as perception and as expression—that is as literature) *Sensations d'Italie.* I saw Daudet last winter, more or less in Paris, who is also *atteint de la moelle épinière* and writing about it in the shape of a novel called *La Douleur,* which will console him by its sale. I greet your wife, my dear Louis, most affectionately—I speak to you too, dear Mrs. Louis, in every word I write. I desire to express the very friendliest remembrance of your heroic mother—who accounts for her son, and still more wonderfully for her daughter-in-law and grand young stepson. My love to the gallant Lloyd. Vouchsafe me a page of prose and believe in the joy that a statement that you bloom with a tropic luxuriance, will, if made in your own hand, convey to your flaccid old friend

Henry James

1. *The Wrecker,* which Stevenson wrote in collaboration with his stepson, Lloyd Osbourne, was published in 1892.

2. HJ's brackets. He had probably been reading Anatole France's *Causeries* in *Le Temps,* published as *La Vie littéraire* (1888–1892). Anatole France was the pseudonym of Jacques-Anatole-François Thibault (1844–1924).

3. Henry Hall Caine (1853–1931), author of romantic-sentimental novels, had just published *The Scapegoat.*

To William James
Ms Harvard

34 De Vere Gardens W.
Nov. 18*th* [1891]

My dear William.

I have immediately seen Katharine on the subject of your further letter—of the 4th—about Carrie's property: with the result of learning that I had unconsciously misinformed you in one or two particulars about Alice's will.[1] She *had,* in making the will, thought it right to take account of the probabilities of Carrie's prospects—so she made it in a way in which it may well now stand. She left Alice, the child, as her *namesake* a legacy of about $4000—Cary (I *think*) another of $1000, and Carrie $1000. This it will be well not to alter—it doesn't matter sufficiently—especially in her present state. She also thought it right—and I agree with her—to take some slight account of the apparently *very* substantial wealth of Bob's children's grandfather—whose meanness during life—constitutes —by what almost inveterately happens—a strong presumption that he won't leave his money *away* from his daughters—it being the during-life generous men who mostly do that. She has left Bob $10,000 and Mary and her children legacies amounting to *about* $5000 more—besides having, a few days since, sent Mary a present of $1000 as a contribution to Ned's college expenses. She has left you and me and Katharine about $20,000 apiece. If she were to break this $60,000 into *four* shares, to include Bob equally, it would make $16,000 apiece—giving Bob but about a thousand or two more than what he and his wife and children already have—in prospect—from her. I think this slight discrimination a very fair allowance for the fact that Holton has a fortune which enabled him the other day to leave $75,000 to a college. *Such* a man wouldn't have done this unless there had been much more behind. He and his wife are very fond of little Mary—their granddaughter. I write in haste and thus briefly. I wrote two days since—but my letter will probably reach you only with this.—Alice seems to be distinctly *soothable* by hypnotism.[2] Fifty-third night of *American*. Ever your

Henry

A *P.S.* to say that I find on seeing K.P.L. again for a minute, that what Bob and Mary will have from Alice will be about *$13,000;* but that I feel very strongly that the discrimination is extremely just in the face of the fact that whereas you and I have not (*except* Alice) a relation in the world from whom we can inherit a penny, and you have four children—and I have given A. all my (possible) care and the use of my little (fixed) income for these last years—Mary and her children have a father and grandfather likely *at the meanest computation* to benefit them more than Carrie and her offspring have been benefitted. The difference would be about *$3,000* more for Bob, therefore, if the four of us (including Katharine, who has most justly been placed on the footing of a brother) got $16,000 a piece.

1. Alice James divided her estate among HJ, William, and Miss Loring and left gifts for nieces and nephews. Carrie James was the widow of HJ's younger brother, Garth Wilkinson; her children were Alice and Joseph Cary. Robertson

James, the youngest brother, and his wife, Mary, were the parents of Edward (Ned) and Mary Walsh James. Miss Loring was treated in the will as if she were a member of the family.

2. William James suggested that hypnosis might ease Alice James's sufferings. This therapy was tried by a hypnosis specialist, Dr. Charles Lloyd Tuckey, a graduate of Aberdeen.

To Edmund Gosse

Ms Congress

Europaeischer Hof
Dresden. Thursday
[10 December 1891]

My dear Gosse.

I delay as little as possible to tell you *où nous en sommes*. We arrived at 9 last (Wednesday) night after a deadly, dreary journey and a miserable delay on Monday night at Dover. The funeral,[1] most happily—if I may use so strange a word—had been successfully delayed till this A.M.; when it took place most conveniently and even picturesquely according to arrangements already made by the excellent Heinemann ladies and the American consul Mr. Knoop. The English chaplain read the service with sufficient yet not offensive sonority and the arrangements were of an admirable, decorously grave German kind which gives one, really, a higher idea of German civilization. The three ladies came, insistently, to the grave—the others were Heinemann, his mother and I, and the excellent Mr. Knoop. The little cemetery is suburbanly dreary, but I have seen worse. The mother and sister are altogether wonderful, and so absolutely composed—that is Mrs. B. and Josephine—that there is scarcely any *visible* tragedy in it. By far the most interesting is poor little concentrated, passionate Carrie,[2] with whom I came back from the cemetery alone in one of the big black and silver coaches, with its black and silver footmen perched behind (she wanted to talk to me), and who is remarkable in her force, acuteness, capacity and courage—and in the intense—almost manly—nature of her emotion. She is a worthy sister of poor dear big-spirited, only-by-death-quenchable Wolcott, and if we judged her—in speaking of a certain matter lately—"unattractive," her little vivid, clear-talking, clear-*seeing* black robed image today (and last evening) considerably—in a certain way—to my vision—modifies that judgment. What is clear, at any rate, is that she can do and face and more than face and do, for all three of them, anything and everything that they will have to meet now. They are going home (to the U.S.) as soon as they can—and they are going to London first: I suppose about a week hence. One thing, I believe, the poor girl would *not* meet—but God grant (and the complexity of "genius" grant) that she may not have to meet it—as there is no reason to suppose that she will. What this tribulation is—or would be, rather, I can indicate better when I see you. Please tell your wife that gladly and piously I carried her pot of English flowers to the poor women—and Josephine had them in her hand during all the service this morning. When the clergyman had said his last words at the grave—they were the first flowers dropped into the horrid abyss—poor Josephine tottered to the edge and let them fall. Strange enough it seemed to stand there and perform these monstrous rites for the poor yesterday-so-much-living boy—in this far-away, alien city. Even after them, and at this hour—it all seems like some deadly clever game or invention—to beat Tauchnitz[3] of his own. I stay three or four days and rest—see the Museum, etc.—and then I go back, the same way—by Cologne, Brussels, etc.—but not so fatiguingly fast. There seems little appearance that I shall travel with them—or wait for them—the three women: they are now perfectly capable themselves. They will probably write your wife their plans. They have plenty of present money. I am very tired—*auf Wiedersehen* to both of you. Yours always—

Henry James

1. HJ's young friend Wolcott Balestier had suddenly died in Dresden.
2. Balestier's sister, Caroline Starr Balestier (1865–1939), who married Rudyard Kipling in 1892.
3. Balestier, in partnership with Heinemann, had organized a new soft-cover publishing house to compete with the continental Tauchnitz editions.

To Mrs. Mahlon Sands

Ms Private

Hôtel de l'Europe
Dresden
Dec. 12*th* [1891]

Dear Mrs. Sands.

Just a word—in answer to your note of sympathy—to say that I am working through my dreary errand and service here as smoothly as three stricken women—a mother and two sisters—permit. They are however very temperate and discreet—and one of the sisters a little person of extraordinary capacity—who will float them all successfully home. Wolcott Balestier, the young American friend beside whose grave I stood with but three or four others here on Thursday, was a very remarkable creature who had been living in London for some three years—he had an intimate *business*-relation with literature and was on the way to have a really artistic and creative one. He had made himself a peculiar international place—which it would take long to describe, and was full of capacities, possibilities and really big inventions and ideas. He had rendered me admirable services, become in a manner a part of my life, and I was exceedingly attached to him. And now, at thirty, he dies—in a week—in a far-away German hospital—his mother and sisters were in Paris—of a damnable vicious typhoid, contracted in his London office, the "picturesqueness" of which he loved, as it was in Dean's Yard, Westminster, just under the Abbey towers, and in a corner like that of a peaceful Cathedral close. Many things, many enterprises, interests, visions, originalities perish with him. Oh, the "ironies of fate," the ugly tricks, the hideous practical jokes of life! I start for London some time next week and shall very soon come and see you. I hope all is well with you. Yours always

Henry James

To Sir John Clark

Ms Barrett

Hôtel de l'Europe
Dresden: Dec. 13*th* [1891]

My dear Laird.[1]

I am ashamed of my long and odious silence—for your second kind letter, the other day (after Henry Adams had been with you), only heaped coals upon my head and served to remind me of favours already received. I live alas in a press of penmanship—and struggle vainly at moments with unremunerated "copy," and mainly depend, for making up arrears, for chance hours like this, in foreign lands, when I have left my work at home. I was called to Germany a week ago, suddenly, by necessities arising from the sudden death, from typhoid here (very virulent and rapid), of an American friend, whose helpless and desolate mother and sisters there was nothing for me but to make some movement to befriend. But when I have followed the poor dear fellow to his ugly and alien German grave I have done all I can and I presently return to the irresponsible (comparatively) peace and obscurity of De Vere Gardens. I have been delighted to hear, dear Laird, that you are decidedly victor over your ills. I hope I don't state the case with frivolous optimism. Adams, God knows, is not an optimist, and he assured me you seemed to be virtually mending, mended. For pity's sake don't, dear Laird, do yourself any more of these gallant harms. You can bear them, it would seem, but *we* can't—we are made of stuff less heroic. I wish the dear Lady had better chroniclers—for, alas, though they all tell me that she is as delightful as ever, they intimate that she suffers even more. I wish I might have come to your Hieland home—since I was in for a pious pilgrimage—rather than to this grey rococo capital of the bull-necked military. Everything human is shabby here except Raphael's Divine Madonna *and* the bull-necked military. I can't do much with the Germans—they are somehow not in my line. One must either really know them or leave them alone. They are ugly and mighty—they have (I think) lots of future, but a most intolerable present. I am going to the opera tonight at 6.30—and coming home at 10 to cold Kalbfleisch and Moselblümchen. Many thanks for your sympathetic words about Adams. I like him, but suffer from his monotonous disappointed pessimism. Besides, he is what I should have liked to be—a man of wealth and leisure, able to satisfy all his curiosities, while I am a penniless toiler—so what can *I* do for him? However, when the poor dear is in London I don't fail to do what I can. I don't know where he is now. He kindly forsakes the fleshpots of the Bristol for the very dry *casseroles* of my lofty-lowly garret. I wish you could have had at Tillypronie his and my very old friend (and his late travelling companion) John La Farge, one of the most extraordinary and agreeable of men, a remarkable combination of France and America, who spent the other day with me in London on his way back to New York, causing me to wonder afresh at his combination of social and artistic endowments and yet how Adams and he could either of them have failed to murder the other in Polynesia. Fortunately each lives to prove the other's self-control.—My sister's condition draws out its long and painful, its slightly intermittent but perfectly inexorable decline. Everything declines but Katharine Loring. She accepts, endures and performs. I bless the old house on the mountain and its genial and bountiful tenants. Are they coming to London never, never, never again? Look out, or at such a rate you'd have me up there at your very door! Always, dear laird and lady, your friendliest

Henry James

1. Sir John Clark Bt., a diplomat, the son of one of Queen Victoria's doctors. He lived with Lady Clark in Tillypronie, Aberdeen, where HJ first visited them in the late 1870s. See *Letters* II, 184, 242.

To Ada Rehan
Ms Penn

34 De Vere Gardens W.
Jan. *6th* 1892

My dear Miss Rehan.[1]

The New Year has brought me, with many other things less agreeable, a most interesting note from our so sympathetic friend Mrs. Eric Barrington in which she is so good as to communicate to me some friendly expression of yours toward my own imperfect work which I almost venture, gratefully, to interpret as a message. Nothing could give me greater pleasure than to hear that you see in it any possibilities on which you may rest an even very contingent hope. I am addressing myself very seriously to the theatre, and such ambition would be wonderfully confirmed if I should find myself able to offer you a part which should directly appeal to you. Already the vision of making, for this purpose, a very discreet and tentative approach to you begins to take form in my overweening spirit. I hammered away, some months ago, at a three-act comedy[2] in which as I wrote it, I saw you at every turn and in every phrase which seemed to me to be, indeed, intensely and exclusively *you.* I took tremendous pains with it, but still it doesn't satisfy me. I fondly believe there is too much in it *not* to send [it to] you to look at some day, and yet I as lucidly see that I haven't got it as yet irreproachably *right.* If you were here I should ask leave to read you a letter that John Hare wrote me about it. I intend at my earliest opportunity to sit down to it and have the question out. I want to send it to you as nearly as possible impeccable only; plated with steel and stuffed with flowers. Unfortunately I have another piece of dramatic work and perhaps even yet another, to struggle with in the meanwhile. But all the time I shall be lifting the curtain from the picture already on the easel. I greatly deplore the accident of your non-arrival here this particular summer. But if 1892 is not to give you London I heartily hope it will give you all other good things to make up for it. Believe me, dear Miss Rehan, most cordially and responsively yours

Henry James

1. Miss Rehan, born Crehan in 1860 in Limerick, Ireland, was taken to the United States at five. She played first with John Drew and from 1879 became the leading lady in Augustin Daly's company, acting both modern and classical comedy roles and Shakespeare. She was very popular with English audiences, and Daly built his London theatre for her.

2. A comedy that HJ first called *Mrs. Jasper* and later *Disengaged.*

To Mrs. Hugh Bell

Ms Private

34 De Vere Gardens W.
Jan. 7*th* '92

Dear Mrs. Bell.

It was—last night—what you might suppose—a very, very simple affair, reminding me of the pathetic and virtuous little Domestic Drama of fifty years ago, in the tradition of Dickens and the old goody-goody actors. Only the infatuated Mrs. B.[1] had still further diluted and simplified her Dickens—so that her little picture has become much too primitive and provincial, I fear, to take this preoccupied town. It is like something intended for purely country consumption—in very outlying parts, and I fear even Redcar would be cynical about it and Coatham[2] profane. It was listened to by a very friendly pit and gallery—and a very decorously-clapping group of stalls—and the evening passed very smoothly and with quite the air of a little "popular" success. The curtain at the end rose upon the rotund little Muse in person alone on the stage—pale and curtseying—and then a second time with the said Muse surrounded by her choir! I spoke to her afterwards—

very tenderly—and she was under the impression, I judge, that she has achieved something. But I am sadly afraid she hasn't—in relation to her formidable predicament—of a theatre on her hands—taken, however, I suppose (or hope), by the week. The stalls won't go near her—and the shilling and 2/ places—even if they groan beneath the popular weight,—as they *may*—can't, unaided, keep the house open long. The Dyly Pipers—as you see—let her down gently, but with a fatal brevity—and she has too much to compete with. She is a fatally deluded little woman, and I'm afraid cunning hands are plucking her of her downy plumage. I wish she would gather up her few remaining feathers while yet there is time and flutter them westward, where she has, after all, a husband and a child. I hope yours is really mending as my possessive pronoun applies only to your little Scarlatino not to your other belongings—your husband or *your* pinions, my singular verb is strictly grammatical. Peace be with you. Yours

Henry James

1. Mrs. B. was HJ's compatriot Frances Hodgson Burnett (1849–1924), the author of *Little Lord Fauntleroy*. HJ had attended, the previous evening, the opening of Mrs. Burnett's play *The Showman's Daughter* at the Royalty Theatre. The play's run was curtailed the following week by the death of the Duke of Clarence and the closing of the theatres during public mourning.

2. The village in Yorkshire where Red Barns, the country house of the Bells, was located

To W. Morton Fullerton
Ms Harvard

34 De Vere Gardens W.
Jan. 18*th* 1892

It is always charming, *mon cher enfant*, to see a scrap of your predestined publicity perverted toward me and to consume in private what was meant for mankind. I echo almost hysterically your sage animadversions about the bards of the breakfast. Vulgarer crudities never usurped a vulgarer chance. The floods of verbiage of your personal organ and of all the others bow me down with unassuagable melancholy. We have—over here—the genius of frumpy hypocrisy and clumsy cant. The *Times* would be worse without you—that is all I can say. *I* am worse without you (than I was with you), so that the induction is justified. London is pestilential and I am seedy. You asked me some time ago sometimes to send you something I write—so I risk the January *Atlantic* with a paper on Lowell[1] which you perhaps won't have seen. I *have* a sick sorethroat or I would pour forth a profuse strain. *Soignez-vous,* my dear child, and *soignez bien* any sympathy that you may continue to entertain for yours always

Henry James

P.S. I today, at All Souls', Langham Place, "gave away" Carolyn [Caroline] Balestier to Rudyard Kipling[2]—a queer office for *me* to perform—but it's done—and an odd little marriage.

1. "James Russell Lowell," *Atlantic Monthly,* LXIX (January 1892), 35–50, reprinted in *Essays in London and Elsewhere* (1893).
2. See letter to Gosse, 10 December 1891.

To Mrs. J. T. Fields
Ms Huntington

34 De Vere Gardens W.
Jan. 26*th* 1892

My dear Mrs. Fields.[1]

Please accept my heartiest thanks for your most kind and sympathetic note about my somewhat embarrassed and stammering but essentially affectionate paper on J.R.L.[2]—the only echo of any kind that I can perceive it to have evoked. I said what I could and laid my meagre little garland on the cold new slab—feeling mainly how impossible it was—once one had the opportunity—not in some manner to testify. But one feels, in this terrible hurrying age and roaring place, as if one were testifying in the desert. In London, at least, the waves sweep dreadfully over the dead—they drop out and their names are unuttered.[3] This makes me all the happier to have heard from you and to know that Miss Jewett[4] was associated with your kind thought of me. Please again believe I thank you both. I hear nothing of Mrs. Burnett[5]—and fear—from my impression of her last summer (it was a very tragic little sequel to her father's happy living presence here), that there is no good to hear. Are not you and Miss Jewett coming once more to England? I should be delighted to see you, and I am, dear Mrs. Fields, yours and hers most faithfully,

Henry James

1. HJ had known Mrs. Fields, widow of the *Atlantic* editor, since his youth.

2. See letter to Fullerton, 18 January 1892.

3. HJ here adumbrates an idea that will develop into his tale "The Altar of the Dead."

4. Sarah Orne Jewett (1849–1909), the American writer of short stories, and Mrs. Fields were close friends.

5. Lowell's daughter Mabel was married to Edward Burnett, who served briefly in Congress as a Democrat.

To Mrs. Hugh Bell

Ms Private

34 De Vere Gardens W.
Tuesday
[23 February 1892]

Dear Mrs. Bell.

I am very sorry you are *not* here to mingle with these things—it would make them so much more interesting. In your absence they are, honestly, scarcely enough so to kindle in me the flame of the valued reporter. Still, I have seen them as through a glass darkly and you are welcome to the faint repercussion. Oscar's play (I was there on Saturday)[1] strikes me as a mixture that will run (I feel as if I were talking as a laundress), though infantine to my sense, both in subject and in form. As a drama it is of a candid and primitive simplicity, with a perfectly reminiscential air about it—as of things *qui ont traîné,* that one has always seen in plays. In short it doesn't, from that point of view, bear analysis or discussion. But there is so much drollery—that is, "cheeky" paradoxical wit of dialogue, and the pit and gallery are so pleased at finding themselves clever enough to "catch on" to four or five of the ingenious—too ingenious—*mots* in the dozen, that it makes them feel quite *"décadent"* and *raffiné* and they enjoy the sensation as a change from the stodgy. Moreover they think they are hearing the talk of the *grand monde* (poor old *grand monde*), and altogether feel privileged and modern. There is a perpetual attempt at *mots* and many of them *râter:* but those that hit are very good indeed. This will make, I think, a success—possibly a really long run (I mean through the Season) for the play. There is of course absolutely no characterization and all the people talk equally strained Oscar—but there is a "situation" (at the end of Act III) that one has seen from the cradle, and the thing is conveniently acted. The "impudent" speech[2] at the end was simply inevitable mechanical Oscar—I mean the usual trick of saying the unusual—complimenting himself and his play. It was what he was there for and I can't conceive the density of those who seriously reprobate it. The tone of the virtuous journals makes me despair of our stupid humanity. Everything Oscar does is a deliberate trap for the literalist, and to see the literalist walk straight up to it, look straight at it and step straight into it, makes one freshly avert a discouraged gaze from this unspeakable animal. The Mitchell-Lea affair[3] was naturally, yesterday afternoon before a fatally female and but languidly *empoignée* house, a very different pair of sleeves. It is a perfectly respectable and creditable effort, with no gross awkwardness or absurdity in it, nothing in the least calculated to make the producers redden in the watches of the night. But it is too long, too talky, too thin and too colourless, rather flat and rather grey. I should think that it was capable of compressibility into a quite practicable three-act drama (there are *five,* just heaven) which would produce an effect. Marian Lea was clever and pretty.—But come up to town and stir up the pot yourself. Miss Robins spoke a prologue, very well save that one couldn't hear her. I'm delighted the gallant boy is disrubescent. May he soon release you to your natural duties. Thanks for your kind attention to *Nona V.*[4]—a very small and simple *fantaisie* of which the end is soon. I greet all your house and am yours, dear Mrs. Bell, most truly

Henry James

1. HJ attended the opening of Oscar Wilde's *Lady Windermere's Fan* at the St. James's Theatre on 20 February 1892. The cast included George Alexander as Lord Windermere and Marion Terry as Mrs. Erlynne.

2. Wilde appeared before the audience wearing a metallic carnation in his buttonhole and holding a lighted cigarette in his hand.

3. Marion Lea and Langdon Mitchell were a producing team in London and friends of Elizabeth Robins, very much involved in Ibsen.

4. The first of two installments of HJ's short story "Nona Vincent" in the *English Illustrated Magazine,* in which Mrs. Bell may have recognized herself as the gifted "theatrical" woman whom HJ called Mrs. Alsager.

To William James
Ms Harvard

34 De Vere Gardens W.
March 5*th* 1892

My dear William.

I wrote to you on the 2d and this morning I dispatched you dear Alice's touching cable-message[1]—her last word, as it will probably be, of farewell. It will probably startle you a good deal, as our last (previous) news will not have prepared you for so sudden a fall. In a few days, however, you will receive my letter which is now on its way and one from Katharine written on the same 2d. Nothing particular has happened (since I wrote) save an accelerated increase of weakness. Katharine, and I think the doctor too, judge that she cannot live more than three or four days—yet she *may* linger (I can't help believing) some little time at the very last—I mean, however, only counting by days. Yet when I saw her this A.M. (K. had sent round for me quickly,—and I hadn't seen her—she couldn't—yesterday) I was struck with the great change—a supreme deathlike emaciation—that had come over her in forty-eight hours. Her lungs, her heart, her breast are all a great distress, and she has constant fever, which rises and falls. She has a most distressing, choking retching cough, which tries her strength terribly —*but* since last evening, thank heaven, there are symptoms that she has become too weak to be actively nervous. She slept not a moment all night—yet she remained *quiet,* with it, Katharine tells me: which is a very new phenomenon. Therefore we greatly hope *that* condition will be every day less and less a feature of this last period. It will greatly simplify—though hypnotism does hold the nervousness in arrest. Only the heroic, the colossal Katharine has to go at it every twenty minutes—when it is bad. We *haven't* said much, as you remind me, of the local tumour because there has not been much to say—it has only been one feature among several, and though it has greatly increased in size and hardness its painfulness does not seem to have *proportionately* increased. Morphia has always checked the feeling of it—and though the distress of it has been constant it has seemed as if she felt it more by reason of her great weakness than by that of its own increased intensity. But it has been a constant element in all her recent suffer-

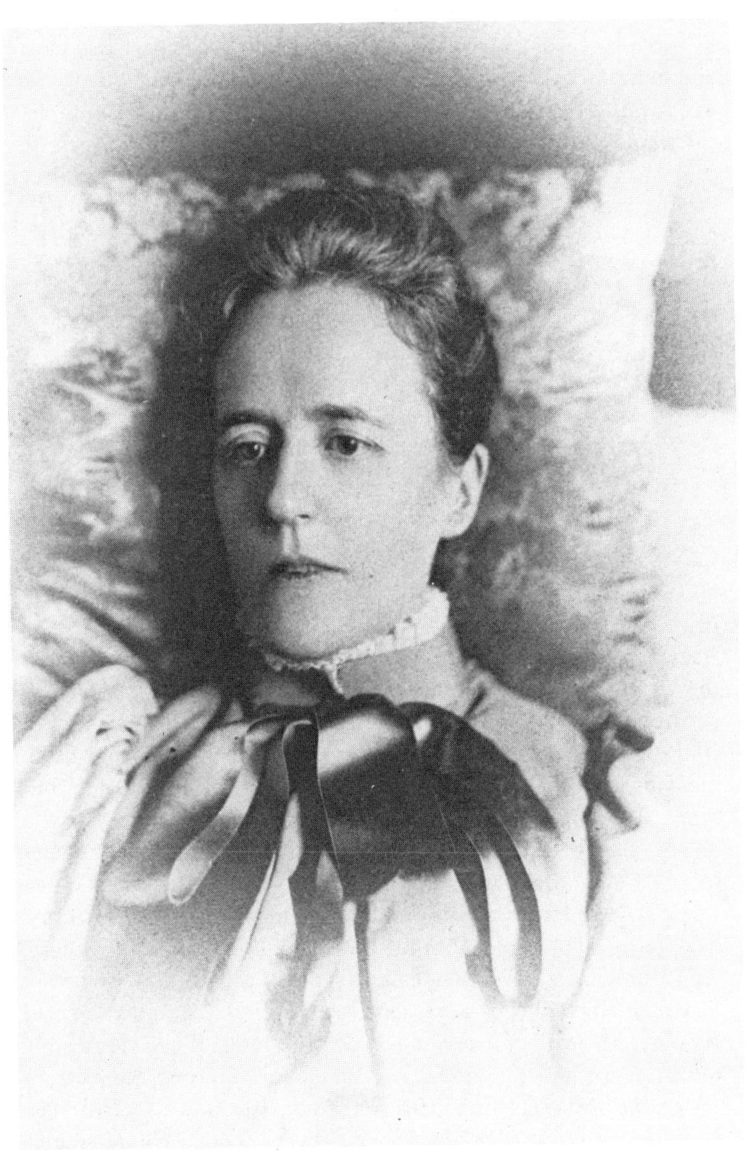

Alice James in 1891, a short time before her death

ing. She fainted away, quite painlessly, last night and felt as if she were dying—and hopes that that is the way she *will* pass away. K. was just sending for me when she came to. She is perfectly clear and humourous and would talk if doing so didn't bring on spasms of coughing. But she does speak in a whisper—and gave me, in my ear, very distinctly, three words to cable to you. I will of course cable instantly whenever the end comes, and write you meanwhile by next post. Thanks for your last letter and all your Syracuse[2] trouble. I bless you for this. Ever your

Henry

1. Alice had cabled to William: "Tenderest love to all. Farewell. Am going soon."

2. A reference to the property HJ and William owned in Syracuse, New York.

To William James
Ms Harvard

34 De Vere Gardens
March 8*th* 1892

My dear William.[1]

Alice died at exactly four o'clock on Sunday afternoon (about the same hour of the same day as mother), and it is now Tuesday morning. But, even now the earliest moment my letter can go, or could have gone, to you is tomorrow P.M.—and there were innumerable things yesterday to do. Yesterday afternoon came your cable. You wouldn't have thought your warning necessary if you had been with us, or were with us now. Of course the event comes to you out of the comparative vague and unexplained, for you won't get our letters of Wednesday last and of Saturday for some days yet, alas. I wrote you as fully as I could on both of these days. On Saturday the end seemed near—yet also as if her strange power to *last* might still, for a few days, assert itself. The great sign of change on Saturday A.M. and, as I wrote you, the inexpressibly touching one, was the sudden cessation of all suffering and distress, which, up to Friday night, had been constant and dreadful. The pleuritic pain, the cough, the fever, all the sudden complications of the previous few days which came, so unmistakably, as *the* determining accident at the mercy of which we had felt her to be (and without which she might still have lived on for some weeks—even possibly,—though this I greatly doubt—some months): all these things which, added to the suffering they already found, were pitiful to see, passed from her in the course of a few hours, fell away blissfully and left her consciously and oh, longingly, close to the end. As I wrote you on Saturday, the deathly look in her poor face, added to this simplification, and which, in its new intensity, had come on all together in the night, made me feel that the end *might* come at any moment. I came away on Saturday afternoon, not to break the intense stillness which Katharine wished to create near in order that she might sleep—for though she was quiet she didn't sleep. Lloyd Tuckey saw her, that evening, for the second time that day, and I was back there for the hours before 10. I wanted to stay the night—but Katharine thought I had better not—and it turned out better. For I couldn't have been in the room or done anything. She became restless again—but without pain—said a few barely audible things—(one of which was that she *couldn't,* oh, she COULDN'T and begged it mightn't be exacted of her, live *another* day), had two or three mouthfuls of nourishment at 1 or 2 and then, towards 6, sank into a perfectly gentle sleep. From that sleep she never woke—but after an hour or two it changed its character and became a loud, deep, breathing—almost stertorous, and this was her condition when I got to the house at 9. From that hour till 4 P.M. Katharine and Nurse and I sat by her bed. The doctor (who had doubted of the need of his returning, and judged that she would *not* live till morning) came at 11.30—but on Katharine's going down to him and describing exactly Alice's then condition, asked leave *not* to come into the room, as he preferred not to, in the last hour before death, when there was nothing to do or to suggest, unless it was insisted on. For about seven hours this deep difficult and almost automatic breathing continued—with *no* look of pain in the face—only more and more utterly the look of death. They were infinitely pathetic and, to me, most unspeakable hours. They would have been intolerable if it had not been so evident that all the hideous burden of suffering consciousness was utterly gone. As it is, they were the most appealing and pitiful thing I ever saw. But I have seen, happily, but little death immediately. Toward the end, for about an hour, the breathing became a constant sort of smothered whistle in the lung. The pulse flickered, came and went, ceased and revived a little again, and then with all perceptible action of the heart, altogether ceased to be sensible for some time before the breathing ceased. At three o'clock a blessed change took place—she seemed to sleep—I mean to breathe—without effort, gently, peacefully and naturally, like a child. This lasted an hour, till the respirations, still distinct, paused, intermitted and became rarer—at the last, for seven or eight minutes, only one a minute, by the watch. Her face then seemed in a strange, dim, touching way, to become clearer. I went to the window to let in a little more of the afternoon light upon it (it was a bright, kind, soundless Sunday), and when I came back to the bed she had drawn the breath[2] that was not succeeded by another.

I went out and cabled you about half an hour later—I knew you would be in great suspense every hour after her cable of the day before. Since then I have sat many hours in the still little room in which so many months of her final suffering were compressed, and in which she lies as the very perfection of the image of what she had longed for years, and at the last with pathetic intensity, to be. She looks most beautiful and noble—with *all* of the august expression that you can imagine—and with less, than before, of the almost ghastly emaciation of those last days. Only last night (I have not yet been at the house today) had a little look of change begun. We have made all the arangements—they have been on the whole simple and easy—with the Cremation Society, for a service tomorrow afternoon (early) at Woking. Of course you know her absolute decision on this point—and she had gone into all the details. For myself I rejoice, as you doubtless will, and Katharine does, that we are not to lay her, far off from the others, in this damp, black alien English earth. Her ashes shall go home and be placed beside Father's and Mother's. She wished we should be simply four—Katharine and I, her Nurse, and Annie Richards, who, though almost never seeing her, has shown devoted friendship to her ever since she (Annie) has been in England. I will try and send you a line tomorrow after it is over. Katharine is the *un*broken reed, in all this, that you can imagine, and I rejoice, unspeakably in the rest and liberation that have come to her. The tension—the strain and wear—of these last months has been more serious than any before—and I hope she won't go back immediately to new claims and responsibilities. She has, practically, a large margin of convenience here, as Alice's lease of that pleasant little house runs on till May 1st. She will probably stay yet a month. She considers that there were almost unmistakable signs, in the last weeks of Alice's life, of the existence of the *internal* tumour (the second one), which Baldwin last summer pronounced probable. The final "accident"—brought on (though at a moment when her strength was at the last ebb and her distress from the tumour in the breast and all her nervous condition and her perpetual gout and rheumatism was absolutely unbearable from day to day, and she was simply living from day to day, and night to night, on the last desperate resources of morphia and hypnotism)—this strange complication which simply *made* a sudden collapse of everything was ostensibly a mysterious cold, communicated by nurse (who had a bad one) and producing all the appearance of pleurisy—with a sharp pain in the side (she lived only in perpetual poultices the last three or four days—up to Saturday night when she wished everything off) and a dreadful cough which shook her to pieces and made impossible the quiet which was the only escape from the ever-present addition of "nervousness." But Katharine thinks that an internal tumour close to the lung, where Baldwin placed it, was accountable for much of this last disorganization. However, she will tell you, later, of all these things—perhaps you will think I try to tell too much. I shall write by this post briefly to Bob, but won't you please immediately send him this. I hope he got a prompt echo of my cable.—Katharine will probably also tell you immediately that Alice very wisely under the circumstances, I think, in an alteration made *lately* in her will, after your plan of coming abroad this summer for a year came home to her, named her (K.P.L.) and J. B. Warner[3] her executors. She had first named you and me—but she came later to think it probable that she would die this summer—live *till* then—during the months you would probably be in Europe—which would be for the execution of the will on your part a burdensome delay. Besides, with all the load upon you, she wished to spare you all trouble. But I *must* close this endlessness—even if I send you more of it by the same post. Ever yours, and your Alice's, and Bob's affectionate

Henry James

1. This letter, and those of the next few weeks, are written on heavy mourning stationery, with a half-inch black border.

2. At this point HJ wrote the words "last breath" then crossed out the word "last" and added "that was not succeeded by another."

3. Alice's lawyer.

To William James
Ms Harvard

34 De Vere Gardens W.
March 8*th* (Tuesday night) [1892]

My dear William.

I posted a very long letter to you this afternoon—but I add this word (as no other letter will go, after tomorrow, until Saturday) by way of postscript on a matter that will interest you. Katharine read me this evening Alice's will—I have been for several hours in Argyll Road—and the men have been to bring the "shell" or light, but perfectly substantial and decorous receptacle, in which her remains are, tomorrow, to be transported to the Woking Crematorium. She lies there still as inaccessibly serene as before—and will be undisturbed till 10.30 in the morning. Her will seems to me a very enlightened and admirable document and I hope it will strike you in the same way. She leaves $2500 to each of her nieces—Wilky's, Bob's and your daughters. A $1000 to Lila Walsh, a $1000 to Henrietta Child (F.J.C.'s daughter) and a $1000 to Miss Alice Gray (Asa G.'s[1] niece) the history of whose struggles with poverty in the pursuit of such art-culture as would enable her to obtain a post in the Boston Art Museum had inspired her with much sympathy. She leaves Bob $10,000 and all (I think) her silver. The remainder of her property she divides (save some trifling legacies, the biggest one $100) equally between you, Katharine and me. As the total of her estate is upwards of $80,000 this will make, Katharine says, *about* $20,000 (rather less, presumably) to each of us. She leaves you all her furniture that you have had in use; and me the objects of hers that I have had here—the "Venice," Grandmother Walsh's portrait, etc. She distributes definitely all her little personal possessions. The discrimination as regards Bob on the ground of the expectations of his wife and children and the no-expectations of yours or of myself, seems to me very just. She sent Ned $1000 a short time ago. His house will thus have had $13,500 from her. I hope all this will strike you as well as it strikes me. Katharine speaks tonight of returning *about* April 1st. She wishes to join her father and sister in California. Alice expended a month ago £270 in an annuity for her nurse. I think those are the principal facts in the matter. I will write no more—I am weary. Ever your

Henry

1. Asa Gray (1810–1888), the botanist, an old friend of Henry James, Sr.

To Francis Boott
Ms Harvard

34 De Vere Gardens W.
March 9*th* [1892]

My dear old friend.

You will, long before this reaches you, have heard of the great sorrow that has come to us all in dear Alice's death. I call it a great sorrow in spite of all the complicated suffering from which she is liberated, perhaps more particularly from my own personal point of view—because, even with everything that made life an unspeakable weariness to her, she contributed constantly, infinitely to the interest, the consolation, as it were, in disappointment and depression, of my own existence. But it's all over, and the peace, for her, had been intensely and pathetically desired. One of the very last things that she had cognizance of was the arrival of your letter of February 26th. Nothing gave her more pleasure than the reminders of your faithful friendship. I needn't remind you that she was tenderly attached to you. She had had a winter of miserable suffering, but at the end the burden was lifted more swiftly than she had hoped. Her death was in a manner sudden—her weakness was so great that any accident could determine it. And it was painless and unconscious—except that, a dozen hours before, she knew and rejoiced in the knowledge that it was at hand. We take her remains today out to Woking, to surrender them to the process of cremation that she particularly desired.

10*th:* It is all over—yesterday, sleety, snowy with blustering March intervals, was the final day. We were a little company of only four—K.P.L., Annie Richards, Alice's devoted Nurse and myself. It was all, somehow, less dreadful than I had feared; and at night it was even a positive joy to me that we hadn't left her alone, and far off, in the wintry earth. To me her death makes a great and sad personal difference—her talk, her company, her association and admirable acute mind and large spirit were so much the best thing I have, of late years, known here. But for her it is only blessed and bountiful. She had lived in it, as it were, for months and months before. K.P.L. is to tell you, I think, of a strange and striking dream that she told her of a night or two before she died—a vision of Lizzie with Annie Dixwell in a boat, standing up, putting out into a tumbled sea (as they seemed to pass from under the shadow of a cloud) and looking back at *her*. It impressed and agitated her much, and it is curious. Katharine returns to the U.S. about April 1st and she will tell you everything. I think she hopes to be able to join her father and sister in California. I hope your winter has been clement and your personal case what you would like it. It was delightful to learn by your letter of the expanding powers of the Boy. Greatly, greatly shall I like to see him again—he is consecrated for me by innumerable memories. Poetic justice should make him tend steadily toward "Tuscany," as poor Anne used to say, to its most renowned villa. Our poor Fenimore, at Oxford, which she likes, has had a very painful illness—an affection of the head, brought on by trying *false drums* (a new invention) in her ears. But she is better, though her hearing isn't. I go to see her next week. I sent you, through Macmillan of New York, my last book of tales;[1] and I am, my dear Francis, always affectionately yours

Henry James

1. This book of tales was probably *The Lesson of the Master*, published in February in New York.

To William James
Ms Harvard

The Reform Club
March 9*th* [1892]

My dear William.

It is all over—the painful business at the Crematorium achieved. I have just returned, and I stop here on my way from Waterloo home to scribble a word which will catch tonight's post. We went there by the 11.45 from Waterloo this A.M. The people came to Argyll Road with a hearse and a carriage, and the hearse and horses were put on the train—separate of course. At Woking we had a couple of miles' drive. The arrangements are all excellent—and have made me a convert to cremation—if I needed to be. Katharine, A. Richards and Nurse were only present but myself. There was a short and simple service, read by an inoffensive, sweet-voiced young clergyman (I remember Alice's saying a month ago, that this would be the only "form" of which, in her life, she would have been made the subject); after which the incineration (while we waited in a very warm and comfortable waitingroom *attenant* to the chapel) was proceeded with and took but an hour and a quarter. It is the last, the last forever. I shall feel very lonely in England at first. But enough. Ever yours

Henry James

To Robert Louis Stevenson
Ms Yale

34 De Vere Gardens W.
April 15*th* [1892]

My dear Louis.

I send you by this post the magnificent Mémoires de Marbot,[1] which should have gone to you sooner by my hand if I had sooner read them and sooner, thereby, grasped the idea of how much they would probably beguile for you the shimmering tropical noon. The three volumes go to you in three separate registered book-post parcels and all my prayers for an escape from the queer perils of the way attend and hover about them. Some people, I believe, consider this fascinating warrior a *bien-conditionné* Munchausen—but perish the injurious thought. Me he not only charms but convinces. I can't manage a letter, my dear Louis, to-day—I wrote you a longish one, via San Francisco (like this), just about (it was the last post) a month ago. But I mustn't fail to tell you that I have just read the last page of the sweet collection of some of your happiest lucubrations put forth by the care of dear Colvin.[2] They make a most desirable, and moreover a very honourable, volume. It was indispensable to bring them together and they altogether justify it. The first one, and the Lantern-Bearers and two last, are of course the best—these last are all made up of high and admirable pages and do you the greatest credit. You have never felt, thought, said, more finely and happily than in many a passage here, and are in them altogether at your best. I don't see reviews or meet newspapers now (beside which the work is scarcely in the market), so I don't know what fortune the book encounters—but it is enough for me—I admit it can hardly be enough for you—that I love it. I pant for the completion of *The Wrecker*—of which Colvin unwove the other night, to my rapturous ear, the weird and wondrous tangle. I hope I don't give him away if I tell you he even read me a very interesting letter from you—though studded with critical stardust in which I a little lost my way—telling of a project of a dashing *roman de mœurs* all about a wicked woman. For this you may imagine how I yearn—though not to the point of wanting it before the sequel of *Kidnapped.* For God's sake let me have them both. I marvel at the liberality of your production and rejoice in this high meridian of your genius. I leave London presently for three or four months—I wish it were with everything required for leaping on your strand. Sometimes I think I have got through the worst of missing you and then I find I haven't. I pine for you as I pen these words, for I am more and more companionless in my old age—more and more shut up to the solitude inevitably the portion, in these islands, of him who would really try, even in so small a way as mine, to *do* it. I'm often on the point of taking the train down to Skerryvore, to serenade your ghosts, get them to throw a fellow a word. Consider this, at any rate, a plaintive invocation. Again, again I greet your wife, that lady of the closed lips, and I am yours, my dear Louis, and Lloyd's and your mother's undiscourageably

Henry James

1. The three volumes of General Marcelin Marbot's memoirs, written for his children, were published in 1891 and revived interest in the Napoleonic era. Marbot (1782–1854) was with Napoleon in Spain, Portugal, and Russia and became a general on the eve of Waterloo. HJ's copy, elaborately bound, has many penciled markings.

2. *Across the Plains.*

To Ariana Curtis

Ms Dartmouth

Hôtel de Sienne
Siena
June 11*th* [1892]

Dear Mrs. Curtis.

Only a word to thank you for your so good ones and to send my blessing with you as you go. I feel really infamous at being absent from London at the very (so exceptional) hour that you embark for it (by "exceptional" I don't mean unnatural—but rare); and am filled with the desire to do something to contribute to your comfort while there. Hampered persons, like myself, have to do things (i.e. come to Italy) when they just happen to be able—under penalty of not doing them at all. *All* the good conditions never meet. Won't you go and stay in my rooms, which are absolutely and heartily at your disposal—and where you will not be worse even than in Cork Street? They are pretty dirty, but otherwise comfortable, filled with books and armchairs and writing-tables—and with two pious servants who *à défaut* of the Angels and the Titanic Grace, have a fine British regularity, and are wasting and pining in idleness. If you won't live in them won't you *use* them? especially go and take from them any and every *book* you may like? There they are—and I should be delighted.—Mrs. Jack, in London the other day, gave me (not altogether unexpectedly) to understand that she would pass this way (*ces jours-ci*)—en route (?) for Venice. I think she knows that Bourget is here and her *coeur de Femme* reaches out to him. But Bourget won't see her. His intense desire is to avoid people—but from no more complex or mystical motive than an intense chronic pressure of work. He is writing intensely hard and making money—as they make it now in France—and he wishes to keep that up uninterruptedly. He dreads the "relations" that lead to things. I don't think he is jealous or exclusive about his wife—but she is his devoted shadow. She is charming altogether—but a frail, nervous, sensitive, intensely intelligent and really quite beautiful *child*. I find in her a strange and touching little charm—and don't see her future at all. I don't see her life as long. He, on the *contraire*, is stout, red and robust—much less *névrosé* than in former days and more solid and concentrated. His marriage has evidently been an excellent thing for him, for although his wife is infinitely susceptible and *souffrante* she ministers to him like a little quivering pathetic priestess on a bas-relief. They are infinitely kind and friendly to me here—and the beauty and charm of this place this season—in this fresh, cool splendid youth of the summer—is not to be said. Oh, land of Italy—oh, eternal resource and inexhaustible *spell!*—How sad and superfluous seems to be what you tell me about the poor little Pens.[1] Oh "New England conscience," oh American spine, oh ineradicable mistake.—I don't know the Coolidges—but shall doubtless find them during the next year or two a part of the Comédie Humaine. They follow people who were in Paris, against all expectation, a very remarkable and very opulent success.—I conceive what you mean by calling *Sensations d'Italie*[2] dull—but I found a great beauty and interest in them—they seem to me indeed very exquisite, and on the whole *ce qu'il a fait de mieux.* I prefer so that side of his talent to that of the *romancier.* Please don't dream of answering this in your last hurry-worry. If you have time to give me of your news from London I shall be delighted—especially if you can make it come from De Vere Gardens. Yours and Curtis's most faithfully

Henry James

1. An allusion to Robert Wiedeman Barrett Browning (nicknamed "Pen"), the maritally troubled son of Elizabeth Barrett and Robert Browning.
2. Paul Bourget's Italian travel writings, published in 1891.

To Charles Eliot Norton
Ms Harvard

Hôtel de Sienne, Siena
July 4*th* [1892]

My dear Charles.

Too long have I owed you a letter and too many times have your generosities made me blush for my silence. I have received beautiful books from you and they have given me almost more pleasure as signs of your remembrance than as symbols of your wisdom and worth. The Purgatorio[1] reached me just before I came abroad—or a short time—and I was delighted to know that you continue to find time and strength for labours so various and so arduous. Great glory is yours—for making something else come out of America than railway-smashes and young ladies for lords. During a singularly charming month that I have been spending in this most lovable old city I have often thought of you and wished I had a small fraction of your power to put the soul of history into Italian things. But I believe I shouldn't love Siena any better even if I knew it better. I am very happy indeed to feel that—as I grow older—many things come and go, but Italy remains. I have been here many times—regularly every year or almost, for many years now, but the spell, the charm, the magic is still in the air. I always try, between May and August, to give London a wide berth, and I find these parts far and away most pleasant when the summer has begun and the barbarians have fled. As one stays and stays on here—I mean on *this* spot—one feels how untouched Siena really is by the modern hand. Yesterday was the Palio of the ten contrade, and though I believe it is not so intense a festival as the second one—of August 15th (you have probably—or certainly—seen them both)—it was a most curious and characteristic (of an uninterrupted tradition) spectacle. The Marchese Chigi asked me and a couple of friends—or rather asked *them,* and me with them—to see it from the balcony of his extraordinarily fine old palace, where by the way he has a large collection of Etruscan and Tarentine treasures—a collection to break the heart of envy. My friends were Paul Bourget, the French essayist and novelist (some of whose work you probably know), and his very remarkably charming, cultivated and interesting young wife. They have been living in Italy these two years—ever since their marriage, and I have been living much *with* them here. Bourget is a very interesting mind—and figure altogether—and the first—easily, to my sense—of all the talkers I have ever encountered. But it would take me much too far to *begin* to give you a portrait of such a complicated cosmopolitan Frenchman as he! But they departed, alas, this morning, for the Piedmontese Alps, and I take my way, in a couple of hours, to Venice, where I spend but a few days—with perhaps a few more at Asolo—before joining my brother William and his wife for a month in Switzerland. After that I expect to return to London for the last of the summer and the early autumn—the season I prefer there above all others. But before I do this I wish I could talk to you more about this sweet old Siena. I have been talking for a month about it with Bourget—but how much better it would have been for both of us if you could have broken in and taken up the tale! But you did, sometimes, very happily—for Mme Paul knows you by heart (she is the Madonna of cosmopolitan culture) and cites you with great effect. Have you read P.B.'s *Sensations d'Italie*? If you haven't, *do*—it is one of the most exquisite of books. Have you read any of his novels? If you haven't, *don't*, though they have remarkable parts. Make an exception, however, for *Terre Promise*,[2] which is to appear a few months hence, and which I have been reading in proof, here—if on trial, indeed, you find you can stand so suffocating an analysis. It is perhaps "psychology" gone mad—but it is an extraordinary production. A fortnight ago, on a singularly lovely Sunday, we drove to San Gimignano and back. I had never been there before, and the whole day was a delight. There are of course four Americans living at San G.—one of whom proved afterwards to have been an American "lady-newspaper-correspondent" furious at having missed two such birds as Bourget and me—whom a single stone from that rugged old quarry would have brought down. But she didn't know us until we had departed and we fortunately didn't suspect her till a suppliant card reached us two days later at Siena. We were in the hands of the good old Canonico—the *proposito*, as they call him—and he put us gently through. You remember well enough of course—though to such a far-away world your Siena summer must seem to belong—the rich loveliness, at this moment, of this exquisite old Tuscany. One can't say enough about it, and the way the great sea of growing things—the corn and the vines and the olives—breaks in green surges at the very foot of the old golden-brown ramparts, is one of the most enchanting features of Siena. There is still never a suburb to speak of save in the quarter of the railway-station, and everywhere you look out of back-windows and back-doors and off terraces and over parapets straight down into the golden grain and the tangled *poderi*. Every evening we have gone to walk in the Lizza and hang over the bastions of the Castello; where the near views and the far, and the late afternoons and the sunsets and the mountains have made us say again and again that we could never, never go away. But we are coming back, and I greatly wish *you* were. We went the other day to the archivio—which I had never seen before, and where I was amazed and fascinated. (It is a great luxury to be in Italy with a *French* celebrity—he is so tremendously known and well treated, as the "likes" of *us* can never be, and one comes in for some of his privileges.) You of course probably know, however, what the fullness, detail, continuity and curiosity of the records of this place are—filling with their visible, palpable medievalism the great upper chamber of Pal. Piccolomini.

Basta—I have my trunk to pack and my reckoning to pay. I am very glad to have shaken hands with you before I go. I saw dear Burne-Jones tolerably often this spring—often unwell, but almost always stippling away. He is the most loveable of men and the most disinterested of artists, but sometimes I wish that he set himself a different order of tasks. *Painting*—as I feel it most—it is true I have ceased to feel it very much—is, with him, more and more "out of it." There remains, however, a beautiful poetry. I'm sorry to say I missed Lily by a day or two—but I shall see her on my return. I want to ask you twenty questions about J.R.L.'s papers—but I feel it isn't fair—and I must wait and see. I hope this work—and your masses of other work don't take all your holiday. I gladly take for granted that Sally still glows with all sorts of acquired orientalisms. I shall send this to Ashfield, and if you are there will you give, for me, a very cordial greeting to that mythical man George Curtis? I embrace all your house and am, my dear Charles, very affectionately yours,

Henry James

1. Norton's translation of Dante, a work of many years, was issued in three volumes during 1891 and 1892.
2. *La Terre promise* was published in 1892.

To Ariana Curtis
Ms Dartmouth

Palazzo Barbaro
Venezia
July 10*th* [1892]

Dear Mrs. Curtis.

J'y suis—would that I could add *j'y reste!*—till you return. Many thanks for your kind London note. I rejoice in everything that may be comfortable in your situation or interesting in your adventures. I came hither two days ago and Mrs. J.L.G.[1] has kindly put a bed for me in this divine old library—where I am fain to pass the livelong day. Have you ever *lived* here?—if you haven't, if you haven't gazed upward from your couch, in the rosy dawn, or during the postprandial (that is after-luncheon) siesta, at the medallions and arabesques of the ceiling, permit me to tell you that you don't *know* the Barbaro. Let me add that I am not here in wantonness or disorder—but simply because the little lady's other boarders are located elsewhere. I am so far from complaining that I wish I could stay here forever. I don't—I go out with the little lady, and even with the boarders. It is scorching scirocco, but I don't much care; it is the essence of midsummer, but I buy five-franc alpaca jackets and feel so Venetian that you might almost own me. I believe I am to go to Asolo for a day or two next week—and I confess that I have a dread of exchanging this marble hall for the top of a stable. But there is a big lady as well as a little one in the case—and I must execute myself. They went (Mrs. Jack and her three friends and Mr. Jack) last night to a première at the Malibran—an opera with libretto by Viel, who had sent boxes and other blandishments. They roasted, I believe, all the more that they frantically applauded*—while I met the wandering airs on the lagoon. Mrs. Bronson is at Asolo and I've not seen her; Edith is with the Edens and I have, thank heaven, no cousins at the pensions. So it is a rather simplified Venice—save always for the boarders. I believe we are going—or they are going—to Fusina (by steamboat) this evening: the little lady is of an energy! She showed me yesterday, at Carrer's, her seven glorious chairs (the loveliest I ever saw); but they are not a symbol of her attitude—she never sits down. I hope you have seen Dorchester House—it is, however, but a public imitation of this. Yet the pictures are wondrous and Mrs. Holford herself almost the best.—No, I haven't—thank heaven—a single political opinion, unless it be one to be glad I'm out of it—out of the sweetness and light of the elections, I mean. I stay here, alas, but from day to day; when I haven't a cousin in Venice I have a brother in Switzerland. But oh, how I dream of coming back! Please tell the Paron' how I pity him for not being here, and remind him that pity is akin to love. Ever yours, dear Mrs. Curtis, with the same pity

Henry James

* Que faire in a sent box à moins que l'on n'applaud?

1. Mrs. Gardner had rented the Palazzo Barbaro from the Curtises.

To Isabella Stewart Gardner

Ms Gardner

Hôtel Richemont
Lausanne
Friday July 29*th* [1892]

Dear Donna Isabella—

I have waited to draw breath here before writing to you—and I arrived here only yesterday. Italy is already a dream and Venice a superstition. The Barbaro is a phantom and Donna Isabella herself but an exquisite legend. You all melt away in this hard Swiss light. But I have just bought a tinted (I believe they call it a "smoked") pince nez, and I am attempting to focus you again. I carried my bleeding heart, last Sunday, all the way to Turin, where I literally spent two days (the Hôtel de l'Europe there is excellent) and finished the abominable article.[1] With that atrocity on my conscience I deserved nothing better, doubtless, than the melancholy Mont Cenis, which dragged me last Wednesday, through torrid heats, straight out of Paradise, fighting every inch of the way. Switzerland is much hotter than Italy, and, for beauty, not to be mentioned in the same cycle of time. It's a pleasantry to say it has charm. I have been here (in this particular desolation) since yesterday noon, intently occupied in realizing that I am an uncle. It is very serious—but I am fully taking it in. I don't see as yet, how long I shall remain one—but sufficient unto the day are the nephews thereof. Mine, here, are domiciled with *pastore* in the neighboring valleys, but were let loose in honour of my arrival. They are charming and the little girl a *bellezza.* My brother and his wife send you the friendliest greetings and thank you for all you have done—and are doing—for me. My windows, from this high hillside, hang over the big lake and sweep it from one end to the other, but the view isn't comparable to that of the little canal end from the divine library of the Barbaro. I am utterly homesick for Venice. *Il n'y a que ça.*—Our smash on the way to the station is almost an agreeable recollection to me—simply for being so Venetian. Gardner will have told you all about it, but I hope there have been no tiresome sequels. I don't know, but I *think* it arose from a want of competence on the part of the fallible Domenico, who had the prow-oars. I shall be eager to hear from you some day *ce qui en suivit.* I am hungry for Venetian and Asolan gossip. I want to know everything you have *bought* these last days—even for yourself. Or has *everything* been for me? I pray this may catch you before you start for this cruel country. I enclose the introducing word for Lady Brooke, to whom I am also writing. My station here is precarious, as my brother, I believe, thinks of going somewhere else[2]—so I won't venture to ask you to write anywhere but to De Vere Gardens (34)—if you are so charitable as to write—or if you ever *can* write again after the handkissing extraordinary that I ween the Barbaro will witness on Monday. Please give my friendliest remembrance to Gardner, whom I thank afresh for his company and protection last Sunday A.M.—how long ago and far away it seems! If he hadn't been there to steady the boat Domenico would probably have sent me to the bottom. I am more and more determined, however, in spite of such perils, to secure a Venetian home. I largely depend upon you for it and I am, dear, generous lady,

Your *Devotissimo*
Henry James

1. The article was an essay on the Grand Canal which appeared in *Scribner's Magazine,* XII (November 1892), 531–550. See ensuing letter to Edward L. Burlingame.

2. William James was abroad on a sabbatical and for the first time had brought his children to Europe. HJ went to Lausanne hoping to spend a little time with his brother and family, but William left almost at once on a walking tour. HJ remained briefly, then returned to London.

To Edward L. Burlingame
Ms Arents

Hôtel Richemont
Lausanne
Aug. 5*th* 1892

Dear Mr. Burlingame—[1]

"The Grand Canal,"[2] delayed a little alas, but I hope not infamously late, goes to you today, apart from this, as a registered letter. I am hoping that it will catch the next steamer at Queenstown, that the steamer will be a quick one and that my copy will therefore reach you by, or on, the 15th: in time to save my reputation. It was written a week ago in Venice, where I had however trusted myself to private hospitality, which meant, alas, postponement and interruption; and since then I have been waiting for the return of the typecopy from London. I didn't write to thank you for the little pictures you sent me so many weeks ago, and I am afraid you will think my paper doesn't much conform to them.[3] I didn't write because I was expecting to let you know much sooner that my paper was starting—but in the event I had to wait to go to Venice. *There* it was not on the cards for me to obtain much inspiration from the little pictures—it came if it came at all, from the bigger ones. In truth I can't write for illustration, I am too greedily jealous for my own prose. I hope there is neither too much nor too little of this. You said "about ten" pages, and I make it out that my copy is about eleven (without the illustrations), that is, upwards of eight thousand words. May it reach you safely and swiftly and answer your purpose. Yours very truly

Henry James

1. Edward Livermore Burlingame (1848–1922) editor of *Scribner's Magazine* from its first number in January 1887 until his retirement in 1914.

2. See previous letter to Mrs. Gardner.

3. Sketches by the illustrator Alexander Zezzos of people and places along the canal, for which HJ had been asked to provide a text.

To Grace Norton
Ms Harvard

34 De Vere Gardens
Aug. 23*d* [1892]

My dear Grace.

I have two delightful letters to thank you for. I lately (a week ago) returned from Italy and Switzerland and I had hoped to write to you from some sympathetic spot in the former country; but the spots were too sympathetic as it proved, for anything but wholesale postponements. I spent June in Siena and most of July in Venice, with "Mrs. Jack" (most strange to say!) and then ten days with William and his little group at Lausanne. Now I am back from all this romance in the prosaic London of the fag-end of August. I enjoyed my Italy, as I always do—rather more, perhaps, than sometimes; and if I had been able to write you at the moment I was there I might have wafted you a whiff of the old delightful charm.

But now it has gone where the old moons go—it is like an echo that has trembled away. While one is there it is still a blessing to find that Italy remains firm while other things come and go—remains, on the whole, I mean, the sweetest impression of life. I would have staid all summer if I had not had to recross the Alps to meet William and to do some necessary business at home. My month of Siena was admirable and it often made me think of you and Jane, in days and conditions which must seem to you at present to have belonged, in their far-awayness, to some strange dim antenatal state. I tried to go to Villa Spanocchi, but when I drove my coachman seemed vague and mystified about it—as about a place where only Pia Tolomei might have mediaevally lived. Paul Bourget and his charming young wife were there—very harmonious companions for enjoyments for which "cleverness and culture" are required! Mrs. Jack in Venice, with the Barbaro full of her guests, may strike you as less in the right key; but you would be mistaken if you fancy she is not, as people go, a super-subtle Venetian. It was delightful there (as delightful as it can ever be to me to "stay" with any one!). And I cursed my fate more than ever that I haven't a little asylum of my own to flee to, in a place where, during many months of the year, it would suit me so well to have one. The difficulty is that though asylums in Venice are cheap, they are terribly few—if one wants one in a position. I was near William and his family in Switzerland rather than with them, as they were much dispersed—William himself in the Engadine, the two boys planted with Vaudois pastors, the mother and babies in a rural *pension*. They have plans as numerous as the leaves of the forest, and much more various: but will probably spend next winter in Florence—a resolution I greatly applaud. It is more possible than Paris and less impossible than Stuttgart. London is a desert peopled for the day by Boott, who has just sailed, by J. B. Warner, of Cambridge, by the Godkins and by Lily and Dick (last not least), who lunched with me a day or two ago and are to do something or other as yet undefined, delightful, slightly vulgar and nocturnal, with me on Thursday next. Lily is so charming—she has so much personal grace and so true a "social gift" that it is a pleasure to be with her. Also it's a great pleasure to see Dick such a fine, fresh courteous young man. He is a very taking youth, and they are bohemianizing together at an hotel in Sackville Street, which I think exactly the right thing for them to be doing. On Thursday we shall try and help each other in this direction. I hope Dick's winter at Athens will represent more reality than you seem to see in it. It seems to me at any rate quite a *pretty* thing to have done with him.—Your letter from Lenox gives me a sad account of poor George Curtis, confirmed by a letter from Sally to Godkin. Little as I have ever seen or known him I feel a real pang of sorrow in the knowledge that he suffers. I think of him with an affectionate sympathy out of proportion to any relations we have ever been able to have. And what you tell me, and the newspapers tell of the infernal heat in the U.S. makes a really dreadful picture of the dear man lying in such a temperature at Staten Island—though perhaps, after all, that is a cooler corner. I only remember its sordid ugliness. I am finishing this month in London, but going away, if I can, for September. I shall probably go abroad for a part of the winter—if William *does* go to Florence—or wherever he goes. I have two other sisters-in-law with their two children apiece (pretty well grown up) touring on the continent now. All this makes me feel "many-sided." Gladstone's government is weak and its reign will be short. But Sir Lyon Playfair is a peer! "Lord Playfair" seems to me a reduction to the absurd. I greet you, dear Grace, very affectionately and am always yours

Henry James

To Augustin Daly
Ms Harvard

Hotel Metropole, Brighton
September 1*st* 1892

My dear Mr. Daly.

I am much obliged to you for reading my play[1]—as to which I think I may say that I haven't any illusions—any that prevent my understanding that you shouldn't be "satisfied" with it. I am far from satisfied myself, but as the thing cost me, originally, a good deal of labour and ingenuity, I was unable to resist the desire to subject it to some sort of supreme probation. If it had a fault of which I was very conscious, I thought it perhaps had other qualities which would make it a pity that I shouldn't give it a chance—since a chance so happily presented itself. To tell the truth now that I have given it this chance my conscience is more at rest and I feel as if my responsibility to it were over. Its fault is probably fundamental and consists in the slenderness of the main motive—which I have tried to prop up with details that don't really support it; so that—as I freely recognise—there is a lack of action vainly dissimulated by a superabundance (especially in the last act) of movement. This movement cost me such pains—and I may add such pleasure!—to elaborate that I have probably exaggerated its dramatic effect—exaggerated it to myself, I mean. The thing has been my first attempt at a *comedy*, pure and simple, and as first attempts are, in general, mainly useful as lessons, I am willing to let it go for that. At any rate I am far from regarding it as my necessary last word. You will wonder perhaps that as I defend *Mrs. Jasper* so feebly I could still care to talk with you about her. But this will give me pleasure, all the same, and I shall avail myself of your leave to do so. I am spending a few days at this place, but I shall be in London tomorrow, Friday, and if I hear nothing from you, here, to the contrary, will call on you at (say) *three* o'clock. I can't forgo any opportunity of seeing a manager! Believe me,

Yours very truly,
Henry James

1. See letter to Ada Rehan, 6 January, 1892.

To William James
Ms Harvard

34 De Vere Gardens W.
Nov. 15*th* '92

My dear William.

Your pale-green postcard follows your letter in pencil from Venice. I have taken the greatest satisfaction in your week at Padua and Venice—and especially in the words (contained in one of your notes to Alice from Padua, which she enclosed to me) "I surrender to Italy." I rejoice to hear it—for it is what I did twenty-three years ago—once and for all—when it was revealed to me in

September 1869. And with all the lapse of life, the changes of sensibility and even exhaustion of the same, the place is still to me one of the greatest of comforts. I will try and clear up the question of the *Daily News* responsibility—but don't worry about it, for what I paid (for only three months) was the merest of trifles. I have no personal news for you at all—unless it be that I came back yesterday from a day at Bath, whither I went to carry Compton a completely rewritten and reconstructed (in a comedy-sense—heaven forgive me!) fourth act of *The American*. The actual fourth act (the old) militated markedly by its grimness against the *remaining* of the play in his repertory. He has now played it every Friday for several months and had time to feel country audiences, *very* friendly indeed up to the end of 3d, *regimber* and droop over the fourth. So the fourth is now *another* fourth which will basely gratify their artless instincts and British thick-wittedness, and thanks to it the poor old play will completely save one's *honour* (which is all I care for) as a *permanent* and regular thing. It will be much for it to "keep the stage." The Comptons are delighted with the new act (a feat of unspeakable difficulty), and it is played for the first time at Bristol next week (without, of course, the smallest reference to any change. Please never *make* any). I am expecting to hear this week from Daly exactly *when* he is to produce my comedy in New York. There are various indications that it will be very soon—perhaps immediately. I shall at any rate know definitely in a few days.—We are living in horrors of foul black fog—an atmospheric misery (lamplight from early morn every day for a week) that makes me almost frantic when I think there are Florences and Romes. I cherish more and more the dream of getting away in January. If I *can* manage it I will go down, then, through France. The Bourgets are to be at San Remo and have appealed to me strongly to spend another month near them. I shall not spend so much—but I shall see them, unless the whole thing fails. Mrs. Cuyler, Mary's sister, writes to ask me to come and see her—where she has come to see her daughter's prospective mother-in-law. I hate to be even so much mixed up with their affairs. A very contented (save with her niece's marriage!) letter from Mary herself at Dresden. Yours and Alice's always

Henry

To Edmund Gosse
Ms Leeds

34 De Vere Gardens W.
Jan. 7*th* [1893]

My dear Gosse.

It was very kind of you yesterday, to supply—or rather to remedy—the injury of fate by bringing me those marvellous outpourings.[1] I had at the B[oard] of T[rade] a lurking suspicion that you *were* within, but my natural modesty—though strangely impaired since yesterday P.M.!—made me shy of too grossly insisting. I was evidently avenged upon the erring janitor—but don't give him the sack (as I believe you fellows say), for then *I* shall have to support him!—J[ohn] A[ddington] S[ymonds] is truly, I gather, a candid and consistent creature, and the exhibition is infinitely remarkable. It's, on the whole, I think, a queer place to plant the standard of duty, but he does it with extraordinary gallantry. If he has, or gathers, a band of the emulous, we may look for some capital sport. But I don't wonder that some of his friends and relations are haunted with a vague malaise. I think one ought to wish him more *humour*—it is really *the* saving salt. But the great reformers never have it—and he is the Gladstone of the affair. That perhaps is a reason the more for conveying him back to you one of these next days. I will drop in with him and defy the *consigne.* I am very very melancholy with the first attack of gout—in my left leg toe-joint—that I have ever had in my life. I feel it's the beginning of the end. But I shall hobble to Whitehall. Yours—if I may safely say so!—ever

H.J.

1. Gosse had loaned HJ Symonds's "A Problem in Modern Ethics," his privately printed pamphlet on homosexuality. Symonds's friends had difficulty in keeping him from an outspoken advocacy of his active homoeroticism at a time when it would have proved ruinous to his career and reputation. HJ in this letter, as we can see, is being coy about the entire subject.

To W. Morton Fullerton
Ms Harvard

34 De Vere Gardens W.
January 16*th* [1893]

I don't think I *apprehend,* my dear boy, the charming conundrum you propound—but we will talk it over and thresh it out, for I am coming to Paris as soon as possible after this week. I *was* to have gone today, but I have been laid up with gout—anguish intense—and can't walk straight or wear the Christian shoe. Some days hence therefore you will guide me through the summer twilight of your brave young thought—*not* holding on, however, please, yourself, any tighter than you need, to the hem of the somewhat scanty robe of the irrepressible Vernon Lee. Excuse me if I don't enter into your bright allusion—but you have more than once found me, I know, of a strangely gelid wit. I think there is an initiation that I lack—but please don't give it to me. I believe (as I have been told) the said Vernon has done something to me ("Lady Tal?")[1] but I don't know what it is and if I should know I should have to take upon myself the burden of "caring" in some way or other established of men, or of women—and oh, I don't *care* to care, for I am preoccupied and weary and fastidious, and only care, my dear Fullerton, to care for sympathy and affection, and for such words of magnanimous gentleness as you address to yours always

Henry James

1. Vernon Lee had just published a volume of short stories entitled *Vanitas.* One of the stories, "Lady Tal," satirized HJ.

To Sarah Butler Wister
Ms Congress

34 De Vere Gardens W.
January 20*th* 1893

Dear Mrs. Wister.

I have just written to Mrs. Leigh, and she may send you my letter—but I must speak to you a direct, and very old friend's, word. I stood by your mother's grave[1] this morning—a soft, kind, balmy day, with your brother-in-law and tall pale handsome Alice, and a few of those of her friends who have survived her, and were in town—and were not ill—as all the world lately has been. The number is inevitably small—for of her generation she is the last, and she had made no new friends, naturally, for these last years. She was laid in the same earth as her father—and buried under a mountain of flowers—which *I* don't like—but which many people, most people do. It was all bright, somehow, and public and slightly pompous. I thought of you and Mrs. Leigh "far away on the billow," as it were—and hoped you felt, with us here, the great beneficence and good fortune of your mother's instantaneous and painless extinction. Everything of the condition at the last, that she had longed for was there—and nothing that she had dreaded was. And the devotion of her old restored maid, Mrs. Brianzoni, appears to have been absolute—of every moment and of every hour. She stood there this morning with a very white face and her hands full of flowers. Your mother looked, after death, extraordinarily like her sister. Indeed the resemblance to Leighton's last drawing of Mrs. Sartoris[2] was *complete.* I mention these things—to bring everything a little nearer to you. I am conscious of a strange bareness and a kind of evening chill, as it were, in the air, as if some great object that had filled it for long had left an emptiness—from displacement —to all the senses. It seemed—this morning—her laying to rest— not but that I think, I must frankly say, the act of *burial* anything but inacceptably horrible, a hideous old imposition of the church— it seemed quite like the end of some reign or the fall of some empire. But she wanted to go—and she went when she could, at last, without a pang. She was very touching in her infirmity all these last months—and yet with her wonderful air of smouldering embers under ashes. She leaves a great image—a great memory.—I have greatly regretted to hear lately that you have not been well. Please receive, dear Mrs. Wister, all my sympathy—all my participation, which though far is not faint, in everything which touches you closely—and believe me when I say that I hope you will look upon me ever as your very constant old friend

Henry James

1. Mrs. Kemble had died on 15 January at eighty-three. Mrs. Leigh, like Mrs. Wister, was a daughter of Mrs. Kemble.

2. The former Adelaide Kemble, Mrs. Kemble's sister.

To William James
Ms Harvard

34 De Vere Gardens W.
Jan. 20*th* [1893]

My dear William.

I wrote you a few days since a letter which you will have got by this time—but meanwhile comes in your own of the 17th (inclosing Katie Rodgers's[1]—poor, poor Katie?) and picturing the sad [state] of things *in casa tua*—with which this is designed as a hasty word of sympathy. May the acuteness, or at any rate the simultaneity of those *disgrazie* already have waned. Keep up a good heart. You will soon have had the last kick of winter and the divine Italian spring, breaking out intermittently but early, will have begun to throb and *gazonner* around you.[2] Then you will be in for a long stretch of clear joy of life; part of which I shall share with you. My letter will have told you of my interrupting attack of gout. It is a fortnight yesterday since it began; but I have only, for a second time, today put on a shoe—and a shoe gashed, excised, alas, to allow me to go to Mrs. Kemble's funeral. You will have seen her death in the *Daily News*. She died—at the last, happily—in a *second,* with only time to give a faint little "oh!" (She was letting her maid quietly put her to bed.) But she had failed and changed so for two or three years that it was as if she had gone a good while ago. Don't be disgusted with my procrastination when I tell you that as Bentley (her publisher for twenty years past and a great personal friend) has asked me to write twenty-five pages on her memory for the earliest number possible of *Temple Bar,*[3] I shall probably hang on here long enough to do it —to get it off my hands before starting abroad. Wait in other words to about February 7th. It will all be a gain for the time that I shall be abroad, I mean giving me the lengthening days and the milder weeks. I have first to finish an article on G. Flaubert's lately completed *Correspondance* for *Macmillan*[4]—otherwise I could do the paper on Mrs. K. more immediately. And I shall be able to stay away till *May*—as Daly's advent is delayed by the impossibility of finishing his theatre so soon as he first announced.—

Afternoon. I am back from Mrs. Kemble's funeral at Dreary Kensal Green—a small knot of old friends by her grave in the centre of a rabble of pushing, staring indelicate populace, with the British female of the lower orders as insufferable as on such occasions she always is.—Poor great and extraordinary woman!—Receive from me (apropos of extraordinary women) a word of warning about Vernon Lee. I hope you won't throw yourselves into her arms—and I am sorry you offered to go and see her (after she wrote to you) *first.* My reasons are several, and too complicated, some of them, to go into; but one of them is that she has lately, as I am told (in a volume of tales called *Vanitas,* which I haven't read), directed a kind of satire of a flagrant and markedly "saucy" kind at me (!!)—exactly the sort of thing she has repeatedly done to others (her books—fiction—are a tissue of personalities of the hideous roman-à-clef kind), and particularly impudent and blackguardly sort of thing to do to a friend and one who has treated her with such particular consideration as I have. For God's sake don't betray that I have *spoken* to you of the matter or betrayed the faintest knowledge of it: I haven't read these tales and never mean to. They are moreover, the others, excessively, to my sense, brutal and bad. But *don't* caress her—not only on this ground but because she is as dangerous and uncanny as she is intelligent—which is saying a great deal. Her vigour and sweep of intellect are most rare and her talk superior altogether; but I don't agree with you at all about her "style," which I find insupportable, and I find also that she breaks down in her books. There is a great second-rate element in her first-rateness. At any rate draw it mild with her on the question of friendship. She's a tiger-cat!—You will of course no doubt, all the same, as I'm your brother, find the bad taste of her putting me *en scène* (and the whole treachery to private relations of the *procédé*) a thing to be judged as on her part *deserving*—and at any rate with a hundred attenuations. *But,* at any rate, show *her* no glimpse of knowing anything about it—I know only by hearsay—and I should be glad if (though I am quite conscious of the loss of good talk entailed on you by it—as she is far-away the most able mind in Florence) you could oblige yourself not to respond to her any further than mere civility requires. Ask Mme Villari[5] some day about her!—What a terribly sad image of poor Katie Rodgers—and what courage and cheerfulness—to be dragging herself about Europe in such a state and living in the contraction of cheap hotels and pensions! I shall of course go to see her in Paris—but what can one do for her? But I must draw breath. I hope Alice gets some leisure—that it isn't all baby, and all Peggy—and cook! Much love to her—and many assurances in the course of next month she will begin to be glad to live—in Florence. Yours always

Henry

1. A maternal relative.

2. William James and his family were spending the winter in Florence.

3. HJ's memorial to Fanny Kemble appeared in *Temple Bar,* XCVII (April 1893), 503–525, and was reprinted in *Essays in London and Elsewhere* (1893).

4. HJ's review of the Flaubert letters appeared in *Macmillan's Magazine,* LXVII (March 1893), 332–343.

5. Wife of the Italian historian, Pasquale Villari.

To Mrs. William James
Ms Harvard

34 De Vere Gardens W.
Jan. 30*th* [1893]

My dear Alice.

I am grateful to you for your gentle response to my perhaps rather too earnestly uplifted fingers on the subject of poor Miss Paget. After I had uttered my word of warning I had expressed the total of my interest in the situation—and only feel now genially indifferent about it. Her *procédé* was, under the particular circumstances, unqualifiable,—and that's all I wished to mention. Should I meet her (or when I do go to Florence), I should myself be perfectly civil to her. *Basta.* I'm sorry William was exposed to the rigour of a repast under her roof[1]—for she is as innutritive in that respect as she is hospitable, and the big, bland, harmless humbug of a Miss Anstruther-Thompson is always there.[2] Poor death-in-life Hamilton![3] It is a bliss to gather from your letter that you do in a manner rise superior to the Florentine winter—at least that it hasn't vanquished your spirit. I'm afraid these last have been weeks of tribulation to Peggy and the baby. I hope heartily to hear that William *has* gone to Rome and Naples. This is the right moment. At Naples he will meet the spring. Don't be shocked to find that I haven't yet got into motion. The usual thing is happening—which inevitably happens before I start for the continent—the desire to finish last bits of *work* before quitting my quiet little winter-room here—and so be able to start with my hands free. My present delay is a longish article on Mrs. Kemble (an excellent subject) to do *quickly* for Bentley—I can do it so much better here than in Paris. But I am getting on with it—and in ten days more shall be ready.—William speaks of my bringing him certain things from here, which looks as if you were *not* coming to London in the early summer. Surely you *are?*—you are not giving that up? But I will bring him everything possible that he asks of me. Tell him, however, that I have *all* Vernon Lee's books here and that he can take his choice when he comes. I will however, bring him—or rather send him, two—*Belcaro* and *Baldwin.*—I am glad you like Mme Villari—she is excellent—and safe! You never speak of Baldwin (W.W.) but I hope you have seen something of him and that he is something of a resource. I have had a rather unhappy (I mean disappointed) letter from Carrie from Dresden—but telling me *nothing* of any intended later movements—so that I am bothered as to how, when, or where I must see her. I am glad Mary is getting back to Italy. I hope there are already vernal odours in the Cascine. How I should like to play with Peggy and the little brother there. Tell them I am expecting some great excursions with them. Ever, dear Alice, affectionately yours

Henry James

P.S. Oh yes, I was very happy over the boys' two sweet letters.

1. William James, having already dined with Vernon Lee, nevertheless wrote her a letter saying: "The portrait of my brother in the first story is clever enough, and I cannot call it exactly malicious. But the using of a friend as so much raw material for 'copy' implies on your part such a strangely *objective* way of taking human beings, and such a detachment from the sympathetic considerations which usually govern human intercourse, that you will not be surprised to learn that seeing the book has quite quenched my desire to pay you another visit." (11 March 1893, Ms Colby.) Vernon Lee wrote a penitent reply, and William answered, "A woman in tears is something that I can never stand out against! Your note wipes away the affront as far as I am concerned, only you must never, *never*, NEVER, do such a thing again in any future book! It is too serious a matter," (18 March 1893, Ms Colby.) HJ told William he was "partly amused and partly disconcerted" by this exchange; he would have preferred silence. See letter to William, 21 March 1893.

2. Clementine (Kit) Anstruther-Thompson became an intimate of Vernon Lee after her earlier friend, Mary A. F. Robinson, married the eminent scholar James Darmesteter.

3. Miss Paget's bedridden half-brother, Eugene Lee-Hamilton. See letter to Grace Norton, 27 February 1887.

To W. Morton Fullerton
Ms Harvard

The Reform Club
Feb. 4*th* [1893]

My dear Fullerton

You must have immense merits to make a fellow forgive you for being so ingeniously tormenting. You write me in mystic mazes of wit and grace which tell me nothing whatever about yourself, your life, your occupations or impressions. And you won't say these things are none of my business (even tho' they may not be), simply because—you won't. On re-reading your last letter, for the 10th time (five of them directly after it came), I recognised a collocation of words in it as one of my own peerless felicities.[1] I confess I hadn't done so till then—I am the father—obviously—of so many more children of glory than I keep the list of. But I'm none the less sorry to have given you a *banal* moment by a vulgar recurrence. What traps life lays for us!—I have written no article on Mrs. Humphry Ward[2]—only a civil perfunctory *payé* (with *worlds* between the lines) to escape the gracelessness of refusing when asked. No, I haven't been false to the Divine—I am imaginative but consistent—even in the sentiments with which I am yours, my dear Fullerton, ever

Henry James

P.S. Santyana's sonnets[3] are very delicate indeed and verge upon the exquisite—or *would,* if one didn't feel they were not *naïfs*—not somewhat painfully distilled. Who may he be? I haven't read the *Apologist*—but I will. Nor have I read or seen *Le* [illegible] *Présent* —only Jules Lemaître *on* it. The "moral aspirations" of the French —their reciprocal *agaceries* to virtue—seem to me to have all the naïveté that Santyana lacks—prodigious for an ironic people—droll as monkeys trying to smoke or poodles on their hind legs!—

1. Fullerton imitated HJ's style to such an extent that he even wrote to HJ himself in it, as this letter reveals.

2. HJ's brief article on Mrs. Ward, signed only "H.J.," appeared in the *English Illustrated Magazine,* IX (February 1892), 399–401, and like certain other such articles confined itself to graceful generalities. From this remark we may judge that HJ regarded such an article as the equivalent of a bread-and-butter social note.

3. George Santayana (1863–1952), then thirty, had just published his first book, *Sonnets and Other Verses.* He was an instructor at Harvard under William James, but HJ had apparently never heard of him and misspelled his name.

To Robert Louis Stevenson
Ms Yale

34 De Vere Gardens W.
Feb. 17*th* 1893

My dear distant Louis.

The charmingest thing that had happened to me for a year was the advent of your reassuring note of December 5th (not *1891*—my dear time-deluded islander: it is enviable to see you so luxuriously "out." When you indulge in the eccentricity of a date you make it eccentric indeed). I call your good letter reassuring simply on the general ground of its making you credible for an hour. You are otherwise wholly of the stuff that dreams are made of. I think this is why I don't keep writing to you, don't talk to you, as it were, in my sleep. Please don't think I forget you or am indifferent to anything that concerns you. The mere thought of you is better company than almost any that is tangible to me here, and London is more peopled to me by your living in Samoa than by the residence of almost anybody else in Kensington or Chelsea. I fix my curiosity on you all the while and try to understand your politics and your perils and your public life. If in these efforts I make a poor figure it is only because you are so wantonly away. Then I think I envy you too much—your climate, your thrill of life, your magnificent facility. You judge well that I have far too little of this last—though you *can't* judge how much more and more difficult I find it every day to write. None the less I am presently putting forth, almost with exact simultaneity, three little (distinct) books—two volumes of penny fiction and one of little essays,[1] all material gathered, no doubt, from sources in which you may already have encountered some of it. However this may be the matter shall again be (D.V.) deposited on your coral strand. Most refreshing, even while not wholly convincing, was the cool trade-wind (is the trade-wind cool?) of your criticism of some of *ces messieurs*. I grant you Hardy with all my heart and even with a certain quantity of my boot-toe. I am meek and ashamed where the public clatter is deafening—so I bowed my head and let "Tess of the D.'s" pass.[2] But oh yes, dear Louis, she is vile. The pretence of "sexuality" is only equalled by the absence of it, and the abomination of the language by the author's reputation for style. There are indeed some pretty smells and sights and sounds. But you have better ones in Polynesia. On the other hand I can't go with you three yards in your toleration either of Rider Haggard or of Marion Crawford. Let me add that I can't read them, so I don't know anything about them. All the same I make no bones to pronounce them shameless *industriels* and their works only glories of Birmingham. You will have gathered that I delight in your year of literary prowess. None the less I haven't read a word of you since the brave and beautiful *Wrecker.* I won't *touch* you till I can feel that I embrace you in the embracing cover. So it is that I languish till the things now announced appear. Colvin makes me impatient for *David Balfour*[3]—but doesn't yet stay my stomach with the *Beach of Falesá.*[4] He is very well—interruptedly but recoveringly. I mean of course relatively to his sad bad years. Mrs. Sitwell, who has wonderful theoretic irons on strange imaginary fires, *me fait part* of every savoury scrap she gets from you. I know what you all magnificently eat, and what dear Mrs. Louis splendidly (but not somewhat transparently—no?) wears. Please assure that intensely-remembered lady of my dumb fidelity. I am told your mother nears our shores and I promise myself joy in seeing her and pumping her. I don't know, however, alas, how long this ceremony may be delayed, as I go to Italy, for all the blessed spring, next week. I have been in London without an hour's absence since the middle of August last. I hear you utter some island objurgation, and go splashing, to banish the stuffy image, into the sapphire sea. Is it all a fable that you will come some month to the Mediterranean? I would go to the Pillars of Hercules to greet you. Give my love to the lusty and literary Lloyd. I am very glad to observe him spreading his wings. There is absolutely nothing to send you. The Muses are dumb, and in France as well. Of Bourget's big seven-franc *Cosmopolis*[5] I have, alas, purchased three copies—and given 'em away; but even if I were to send you one you would find it too round and round the subject—which heaven knows it is—for your taste. I will try and despatch you the charming little "Etui de nacre" of Anatole France[6]—a real master. *Vale—age.*[7] Yours, my dear Louis, in a kind of hopeful despair and a clinging alienation

Henry James

1. *The Real Thing and Other Tales, The Private Life,* and *Essays in London and Elsewhere,* all published in 1893.

2. Hardy's *Tess of the D'Urbervilles* had appeared in 1891.

3. Serialized as *David Balfour* and published as *Catriona* in 1893.

4. In the volume *Island Nights' Entertainments*, published in 1893.

5. Bourget's *Cosmopolis* had just been published.

6. Anatole France published *L'Étui de nacre* in 1892. It contained two well-known tales, "Le Jongleur de Notre-Dame" and "Le Procurateur de Judée."

7. HJ's exclamation *Vale—age!* ("Farewell, then!") is explained in the next sentence—his mixed feelings about Stevenson's remoteness from him. He is using the imperative second person singular of the Latin verb *ago*.

To Mr. and Mrs. William James

Ms Harvard

Hôtel Westminster
rue de la Paix
March 21 [1893]

Dear William and dear Alice.

Your two letters—of the 16th and 17th gratify me *outre mesure*. I am delighted that you recognise the essential propriety of your coming to England; so much the simplest, yet richest, solution of the question of your remainder. I would have *wailed* at the thought of Alice's departing from Europe without a substantial British impression. It would have been at once a crime and a *bêtise*. It seems to me that the question of *where* is one that may be sufficiently left for future discussion. So that as I am to see you *here*—an idea with which I am also delighted—there is no need of our going into it yet. I congratulate both of you on your *sagesse*. I needn't add that my house, my person, my experience and everything I *have* (reserving only a certain quantity of my *time*) will be at your service. I am very sorry you react so against the lax and lovely Italy. But I can understand it—and your circumstances. So much the better that there is a stodgy Albion to strike such a different variety of notes. I see every reason to believe, then, that I shall hang on here till you come. Paris is at present wonderfully mild and bright—blond and fair. The air is full of *"décadence"* (to my sense), but the light is vernal and the spectacle beguiling.—I am partly amused and partly disconcerted by the William-Paget correspondence: though much gratified indeed at his having felt the throb of resentment on my behalf and acted upon it—for which I thank him. I desired however that the thing (as to which I am utterly in the dark save in my very vivid sense—and other experience—of Violet's possibilities enlightens me) should not have been "noticed," directly, at all. However 'tis doubtless well as it is. I don't find her note at all convincing;—she is doubtless sorry to be disapproved of in high quarters; but her *procédé* was absolutely deliberate, and her humility, which is easy and inexpensive, after the fact, doesn't alter her absolutely impertinent nature. *Basta—basta!*—I am very happy about William's design for the tomb[1]—and I don't *hold* to my shorter inscription: all I hold to is the "Kensington." I rejoice that it is in artistic hands. I hope everything will go well with you till you again get into movement. I have this A.M. a perfect mountain of forwarded letters and proofs—from London—so I break off. Please notify me, as you see your way—about what sort of *dates* you tend to. It will be useful to have a general sense of them in advance. Many caresses to the infants. Yours, dear Alice, dear William, always

Henry James

1. Alice James's ashes had been buried in Cambridge cemetery, in the James family plot. While in Italy, William James arranged for a marble urn to be carved with an inscription from Dante, *Paradiso* X, 128–129: *ed essa da martiro e da essilio venne a questa pace* ("and from martyrdom and exile, he came to this peace").

To Edmund Gosse
Ms Leeds

Hotel Westminster
Friday [21 April 1893]

My dear Gosse.

I am very glad of the emotion that led you write to me immediately about the sudden—the so brutal and tragic extinction, as it comes to one, of poor forevermore silent J.A.S.[1] I had never even (clearly) seen him—but somehow I too can't help feeling the news as a pang—and with a personal emotion. It always seemed as if I *might* know him—and of few men whom I didn't know has the image so much come home to me. Poor much-living, much-doing, passionately out-giving man! Various things, however, seem to me to have made—to have contributed to make—his death—in the conditions—fortunate and noble. The superabundant achieved work—I mean, the achieved maturity—with age and possibly aberration (repetition and feverish overproduction) what was mainly still to come; and now, *instead,* the full life stopped and rounded, as it were, by a kind of heroic maximum—and under the adored Roman sky. I hope he will be buried there—in the angle of the wondrous wall where the Englishmen lie—and not in his terrible Davos. He must have been very interesting—and you must read me some of his letters. We shall talk of him. *Requiescat!* I hope it isn't to the same "roundedness"—heaven save the mark! —that R.L.S. is coming home, if his return be not again merely one of the lies in the dense cloud of mendacity in which *on se débat*—in these days. I wrote to you yesterday. The *heat* here is simply fierce! Do let me know of any *circumstance* about Symonds —or about his death—that may be interesting. Yours always

Henry James

1. John Addington Symonds had died in Rome on 19 April.

To Edward Compton
Ms Texas

Hotel Westminster
rue de la Paix
Tuesday [2 May 1893]

My dear Compton.

I answer your note immediately, as it contains some words about a point, in the play,[1] which should be cleared up without loss of time. Of course I never dreamed of looking to you for any "criticisms"—and to tell the truth wouldn't have *wanted* any, this time, as they mainly disturb and disconcert while the work is under way and one's nerves are in tension. I only expected—what you have *given* me—a voice, on the question of whether or no you *liked* the act—as a spectator, an irresponsible outsider in your stall —thought it interesting as a *beginning,* the first chapter of a story etc. This hope you have answered very agreeably and I have been delighted that you and your wife have been able to say so emphatically that, sitting there in your box, you *are* interested. It was all that was to be expected or desired that you *should* say. But— Oh, monstrous *but!*—it behoves me to let you know without even a day's delay that the "ending" that you express a dread of *is* the only ending I have ever dreamed of giving the play. I oughtn't to talk of "giving" it to the play—it *is* the play, the very essence and meaning of the subject—which is what I meant by telling you (as I recall that I did) that the subject was a case of "magnanimity." The idea of it is that Domville throwing up the priesthood to take possession of his place in the world etc. finds, in fact, that he comes into the world only to make himself happy at the *expense* of others—a woman in one case (act 2), a man in the other (act 3); and in the face of this reality—ugly and cruel—turns back again to his old ideal, renounces his personal worldly chance, sacrifices himself and makes the others happy. *That* subject seemed to me simple, charming, touching—very pretty. To make him come out (of his old ideal) simply to *marry* Mrs. Peverel is, for me, not only no subject at all, but a very ugly and displeasing (as well as flat and undramatic) substitute for one. To make a Catholic priest, or a youth who is next door to one (the interest of the play is that he is just all *but* one) *marry*, really, when it comes to the point, *at all*, is to do, to spectators—a disagreeable and uncomfortable thing: the utmost length one may go to is represent him as thinking, as dreaming, for an hour, that he innocently and blissfully *may*. The subject, as I have entertained it, appears to me *charming*—picturesque, tender, human, dramatic, and with the pathos of it not too grave to injure the pretty comedy atmosphere. But of course if your public is such a public that it can't see any of that charm, and wants such a *bêtise* instead, we are engaged in a blind-alley—and the sooner we recognise it the better. My *dénouement* is my very *starting-point*—and my subject is my subject, to take or to leave. If your conviction is that the piece won't *go* unless Guy marries Mrs. Peverel (for he *doesn't* of course marry the other female), then it is a blessing (though mingled with bitterness) that the words of your letter have revealed it to me without a further prolongation of our illusion. They have caused the pen to drop from my hand this morning and my work is suspended till I hear from you again. I can't work of course straight *into* the thing (with my eyes open) that is going to prove an objection. What I want to hear from you is that—or *whether*—you, *after reflection*, are still strongly convinced that Domville's return (after his misleading erratic episode) to the holy place he had forsaken, will be fatal for an audience.

You *seem* to feel it very strongly—you allude to it as an impossibility. But I ask you to look at it as a *possibility*—and *then* to tell we what you think. If you are still then of the same mind we must simply drop Guy Domville. (I shall in that case probably go on with him *myself*—I am so fond of him; addressing him to other conditions.) What happens in II and III is in three words that he finds (discovers) on the very eve of marriage, that Mary Brasier is being *sacrificed* to him, and then, in dismay and remorse, throws up, on the spot, all the advantages and prospects, her fortune, her young beauty, the pleasures of the life he has been introduced to [through] her, and *ensures*—brings about—her union to the man she really loves. Yearning still, after this, for the fuller taste of life that has been dashed from him, he swings back to Porches—only to realise that his happiness there will, if realised, be on the ruins of that of his old friend—and he determines to bring about the union of Humber and Mrs. Peverel—and then to steal beneficently back to the cloister. He *does* this and ends in beauty and glory, as it were. This is a bald account of the matter and I only write the meagre words because as I just definitely *sound* you on the subject of the dénouement I thought it not fair not to add a few sentences that will show you a little more what I mean by it. *Do* I mean something that your audience won't understand? It is a *complete* surprise to me to suppose so, for I have been going on with a great sense of security. Your note of alarm is a blight that comes now far better than later, but such as it is it has cast such a shade over the future that I shall not be able to recover myself before I hear from you again—and time, alas, is precious. Be absolutely frank, on this point, and as clear as you can *see*. I feel that I must, moreover, add this: that my plan, such as it is, is an absolutely *final* one. I can make another (which will be another play), but I can't touch *this* one. Above all don't if you *are* distinctly sceptical try to persuade yourself that you *do* believe. I'll take hold—as soon as I can *get* hold—of another subject—but this effort is wasted. Yours ever

Henry James

1. HJ had sent Edward Compton the first act and a scenario for the remaining two acts of a play titled *Guy Domville*. He considered it suitable for the Compton Comedy Company, which specialized in romantic plays. The Comptons liked the first act and the scenario, but (as with their production of *The*

American) asked for a "happy ending." To give the earlier play that kind of ending, HJ had written a new fourth act. This letter, one of a series of long letters to Compton, expresses HJ's bewilderment—as he said in an earlier letter written three days before this one: "I have a general strong impression of my constitutional inability to (even in spite of intense and really abject effort) *realise* the sort of simplicity that the promiscuous British public finds its interest in—much more, after this indispensable realisation, to *achieve* it. Even when I think I am dropping most diplomatically to the very rudiments and stooping, with a vengeance, to conquer, I am as much 'out of it' as ever, and far above their unimaginable heads." (29 April 1893, Ms Texas.)

To Robert Louis Stevenson

Ms Yale-Harvard[1]

34 De Vere Gardens W.
June 8*th* 1893

My dear Louis.

I send you by this post (June 10th via San Francisco, registered) two little volumes of tales[2] that I have lately put forth—all oldish things that have had their small dim hour in magazines where, like faint glowworms in an obscure lane of literature, one or two of them may have chanced to glimmer up at you. I fear their glimmer will quite go out, however, in your tropical light. I can't tell you with what regret and sympathy I learned—two days ago—from Colvin—that that light had lately been darkened to you by anxiety on the subject of your wife's health. I returned only a week since from three months on the continent (mainly in Paris), and this was the first news I had had of such a tribulation. Please believe, and ask Mrs. Stevenson to believe, in my very friendliest participation in it. Sad enough to me it sounds—that off there in your lone immensities—you should have such poignant aches to bear. But you are such a hero that you have taught the gods to treat you as one and to play on your pulses to the top of their unspeakable bent. By this time I trust they have learned that in such a game the last word is always yours and have turned their attention to victims more gratifying.

I seem to be making phrases, my dear Stevenson, when in reality I am thinking of you with the simple longing of my helplessness to aid. It may well be, however, I take it, that the conditions are by this time better and the future brighter—and for such a consummation I heartily pray.—Thanks to my absence from England

I wholly missed your mother—a few weeks ago—when she was in London.[3] The nearest I came to seeing her was corresponding earnestly and elegantly with a kinswoman of yours with whom she was staying. It was a disappointment of magnitude, so pressingly am I disposed to question her. But the chance will come, as I learn with joy that she is to be here many months. It was only when I came back the other day that I could put my hand on the *Island Nights,* which by your generosity (please be tenderly thanked) I found awaiting me on my table. They have for me all the same old charm, and I read them as fondly as an infant sucks a stick of candy. Fortunately, unlike the candy they are still there after sucking—to be freshly reabsorbed into the system. The art of *The Beach of Falesá* seems to me an art brought to a perfection and I delight in the observed truth, the modesty of nature, of the narrator. Primitive man doesn't interest me, I confess, as much as civilized—and yet he *does,* when you write about him. However, a part of my impatience for *David Balfour*[4] to become a book held in the hand and caressed by the eyes, springs from the apprehension that it deals with more complicated folk. I have seen lately so few of your friends that my news of them is very *éventé.* Colvin looks and appears quite like himself of the untroubled years. I hear —you have heard perhaps—there is a question of his coming in for the ideal post (on the superannuation of Sir Frederick Burton) of director of the National Gallery.[5] It would be to his friends as a personal happiness of their own were he to be appointed to it; but they can only hold their breath and hope, remembering uneasily that he has one or two formidable competitors. One, I believe, is Edward Poynter, R.A.[6] Literature is thin and Kipling is silent. That is he *has* been—at Brattleboro', Vermont (the strangest of all wife-beatings—I mean beatings *by* the wife), but I believe a book (of tales) comes out today. Bourget I haven't seen for a year; he has wintered in Greece and in Syria, (where he still is—at the French consulate at Beyrout), but he returns to Europe presently to embark in July for the United States of Chicago. I hope he now feels that he has achieved the cosmopolitan. In Paris was nothing nutritive save the sonnets of Hérédia,[7] which decidedly I must send you: they are to me of a beauty so noble and a perfection so rare. They make the English muse (of the hour) seem (strange combination) both illiterate and dumb. (The book goes also by this post). I saw Daudet

—who appears to be returning from the jaws of slow death—getting *over* creeping paralysis. Meredith I saw three months ago—with his charming *accueil,* his impenetrable shining scales, and the (to me) general mystery of his perversity. That perversity is flowering, I believe, into two soon-to-be-published serials—one in *Scribner.*[8] He is wonderfully gallant and brilliant. For myself I am doing work and following a homely plan which it will scarcely be decent to speak of even if they are successful.[9] To do so at present would therefore be quite shameful. There is nothing for me but to pass for a while for a finished (in both senses of the term) vulgarian. But I will send you a third little book by the next post.[10] Vale. My kindest, heartiest, faithfullest remembrances to your wife and to Lloyd. You make me *feel* more than ever that a man's mind—his talent—is his experience. Ergo, I want yours (ah, *some* of it—and not the pain!)—and yet I want to keep my own as well—as *with* the pain! Who shall choose? But experience settles it. For yourself, my dear Louis, I grasp your hand and am yours always

Henry James

1. This letter has been pieced together out of holograph double-sheet pages [1]–3, 8–[12], which are at Yale, and pages 4–7, which are in the Houghton Library at Harvard.

2. *The Real Thing and Other Tales,* published in March 1893, and *The Private Life,* which appeared the week this letter was written.

3. Mrs. Thomas Stevenson had returned from a stay with her son in Samoa.

4. See letter to Stevenson, 17 February 1893.

5. Colvin did not receive the appointment and remained keeper of prints at the British Museum.

6. Edward Poynter (1836–1919), the painter, was named director of the National Gallery in 1894.

7. José María de Heredia (1842–1905), born in Cuba of a Spanish father and a French mother. The sonnets in his *Les Trophées,* published in 1893, are considered to be among the most beautiful in French literature.

8. Meredith was completing *Lord Ormont and his Aminta.*

9. The "they" in this sentence apparently is a reference to HJ's plays rather than to any tales he was writing.

10. *The Wheel of Time,* a third collection of tales, was published in September 1893.

To George Alexander
Ms Unknown

2 Wellington Crescent,
Ramsgate
Sunday [2 July 1893]

Dear Mr. Alexander.

I counted fully when I last saw you on sending a *part* of what I spoke of to you, the other day, before so many days had elapsed. But I counted without a good many complications—in fact an unprecedented number of domestic hindrances—from which, finally, however, I have fled, and shall not return—remaining out of town—"in spite of all temptations"—for the present. At the same time I wanted to wait to send you *with* the finished first act (of one of the subjects I alluded to) the scenario, as detailed as possible, of the other two acts. But, not to delay longer, I have determined to dispatch by the same post as this note, in another cover, a fresh type-copy of the said first act, which has just come in and which I have been waiting for. A detailed Scenario of Act Second goes this evening to the copyist—who will quickly return it, so that you shall have it in three or four days. A statement of Act III will come to you two or three days later. In the meanwhile you will perhaps find time to read the complete first act. These things will constitute "exhibit" No. I.[1]—In the group of three subjects I spoke to you of.

"Exhibit" No. II is the scenario of a three-act comedy pure and simple, on an intensely contemporary subject,[2] which you shall receive in the course of a small number of days after getting the statement of Act III of this first thing. The Scenario in question was drawn up two months ago—but I want to recopy it and send it to be type-copied. This will take but little time.

Exhibit No. III is a three-act contemporary play, less purely a comedy,[3] but on a subject very beautiful to my sense—of which the complete Scenario is yet to write. Now that I have quiet conditions, however, I can promise you that you shall not have to wait for it very long. These three subjects have of course in common that they are essentially subjects with a hero—dealing with a *man's* situation. In the second the man is scarcely ever off the stage.—It occurs to me that I may perhaps have some difficulty this Sunday afternoon in getting my big first-act book into a Ramsgate letter-box. Please understand therefore that if it doesn't reach you with this tomorrow morning it will in the evening.

Yours very truly,
Henry James

1. This was *Guy Domville,* in three acts, which HJ wrote at Ramsgate.

2. It is difficult to say which scenario this was; it might have been the one based on his short story "The Chaperon." See *Complete Plays,* ed. Edel (1949), 457–462.

3. From HJ's description this would probably have been his scenario for *The Reprobate,* published in *Theatricals: Second Series* (1895).

To Francis Boott
Ms Harvard

2 Wellington Crescent
Ramsgate
July 14*th* [1893]

My dear Francis.

Your last charming letter lies (or to avoid all misconception I should say *stands*) too long unanswered. I have waited, to write you, to thank you for it, to enter upon the comparative calm of this refined retreat. I surrendered my London habitation a short time since to William and his wife and am far from the madding crowd. There is a crowd here but they're only madding when one knows them, *è vero?* It is composed altogether of 'Arry and 'Arriet, and they at least don't know *me,* or pretend they don't—which is a delicacy I don't find in Mayfair. A few days ago, spending a few hours in town, I found there, by the kind care of Duveneck—*via di* Rolshoven[1]—two admirable photographs of the magnificent monument.[2] They gave me more pleasure than I can say—a pleasure almost as great, I think, as the honour the work does to its author. Please thank Duveneck very heartily for the photographs and tell him how noble and beautiful, and simply serene and unique I think his inspiration has been. Forever (practically) will that exquisite image lie there to enshrine it. One sees, in its place, and its *ambiente,* what a meaning and eloquence the whole thing has—and one is touched to tears by this particular example which comes home to one so—of the jolly great truth that it is *art* alone that triumphs over fate. Poor long-silent Lizzie speaks and lives there again and will be present to generations and generations and have a continuity and a beauty superior to ours. It is a great thing to have done—please ask him to accept from me directly, my small proportionate share of the general gratitude. And for *him*—what a happiness to have achieved it—to have made such a present! I want intensely to stand there before it in fact—though there is something terrible in such an evocation, at first. I am sorry there should have to be a question of waiting another whole year, to send the marble comrade to the Salon. But it ought to be most eminently and universally seen. The Boy, I suppose, is of an age, now, to enter into it. What a happiness for him—at least when you shall take him to Florence. When will that be, however? I fear *I* shan't see him till you *do*. We must make an appointment there; all the more that there has been no Italy for me, alas, this year. I spent three months abroad but squandered two of them in Paris. Then I had another—divinely beautiful—at the exquisite Lucerne of early summer, meeting William and his little group on their egress from Italy. You will have heard of the *ingress* thither of our excellent friend C. F. W. [Miss Woolson]; of her at last actual domestication (for which a permanent "flat" is indeed still needed) at Venice. She is looking at palaces. I hope to see her there in the autumn—and shall of course go to Florence *apposto*. The Williamses go back to you the last of August. Their children are in Switzerland, and they return thither (though I wouldn't in their place!) to pick them up. Will this find you all doubled up with the great American summer question? Surely it must be easily solved this year by *not* going to Chicago. If that simple device fails, try Ramsgate, the real headquarters of your favourite *cibo* of muffins and shrimps. *Tornate subito,* dear Francis. Please give my kindest remembrance, apart from the monument, to Duveneck and believe me affectionately yours

Henry James

1. Julius Rolshoven (1858–1930), an American painter, had been a pupil of Duveneck's in Munich and received high honors for his work in Europe and later in America.

2. Duveneck executed a life-size monument in bronze of his wife, showing her recumbent like a knight's lady in flowing robes. This was placed on her grave in the Allori Cemetery outside Florence's Roman Gate.

To W. Morton Fullerton
Ms Harvard

2 Wellington Crescent
Ramsgate, July 14*th* [1893]

My dear Fullerton.

No, I'm not a brute for having failed so long to thank you for the good offices, proffered at least, of your last letter, and for the touching two words you had the friendly thought of sending me when the indignity that life had heaped upon poor Maupassant found itself stayed.[1] I wanted moreover to applaud your energy and vivacity during the *journées de juin* and the art with which you brought internecine warfare home to us.[2] But not till this hour, as ever is, have I been sufficiently my master to thank you for these luxuries. The detail of my servitude would not interest you; but knowing my feeble powers of resistance you will believe in the fact. I don't know what prevented my wiring you a crystalline tear to drop on Maupassant's grave. Or rather, I do. Everything prevented it, including the fact that my tears had been already wept; even though the image of that history had been too *hard* for such droppings. I have taken refuge from the abominations and over-populations of London in this refined retreat, where there is no one I know—no one but 'Arry and his female, who don't know me—or at least pretend they don't, a delicacy of which Mayfair is incapable. *J'y suis, j'y reste.* It was very good of you to offer to send me the last distillation of Bourget and the last chunk of Zola.[3] They lie at present on my intellectual board. What *won't* the French write about next? Strange are the loves of a sick sexagenarian and his niece. Yet I love my Zola. Also my Fullerton and am his ever

Henry James

1. Guy de Maupassant had died on 6 July 1893 in an insane asylum in Paris, his insanity a consequence of syphilis.

2. Fullerton had written a series of dispatches for the *Times* on France's political situation.

3. The Bourget novel was *Un Scrupule;* Zola's novel was *Le Docteur Pascal* in the Rougon-Macquart series.

To Ariana Curtis
Ms Dartmouth

2 Wellington Crescent
Ramsgate, July 14*th* [1893]

Dear Mrs. Curtis.

I rejoiced to hear from you the other day, even though it was to gather that you have been under a misconception as regards what must have seemed to you an attitude (on my part) of really criminal levity on the subject of the beloved Venice. No such levity was intended; I haven't been heartlessly toying with its affections; and the case is less hopeless, thank heaven, than you perhaps suppose. I expressed myself clumsily to Miss Woolson in appearing to intimate that I was coming there to "live." I can only, for all sorts of practical reasons, *live* in London, and must always keep a habitation "mounted" there. But whenever I have been in Venice (especially the last two or three times), I have felt the all but irresistible desire to put my hand on some modest pied-à-terre there—modest enough to be compatible with the retention of my London place, which is rather expensive; and such as I might leave standing empty for months together—without scruple—in my absence, and deposit superfluous luggage in, when I wished to "visit" Italy. This humble dream I still cherish—but it is most vivid when I'm on the spot—i.e. in Venice; it fades a little when I'm not there. The next time I am there I shall probably act in harmony with it—and then find myself unable (such are the tricks of fate) to occupy the place for a long time afterwards. But *pazienza;* and above all more thanks than I express to you for having taken an interest in the sordid little inquiry. I think it will be a part of the fun to pursue it myself on the spot; and as it would be a question of a lowly rental (£50 a year, I fear, is my limit—one can get a palatial country bower—with a garden—for that here), there will not be the same narrowness of choice as in the case of something smart. *Basta*—and again all thanks. I have the fondest hope of going to Italy next winter—but I am learning by stern experience not to make hard and fast plans. It is only the unexpected that happens—nevertheless I fear I shall never go to India. That is only the *délassement* of leisure and fortune. The most I can hope to do is to be there to send you off—with mingled reluctance and benedictions. But these things are vague. I am very sorry indeed Miss Woolson has trouble in finding a house, or a piano. But I had an idea she wanted—I think she does want—to abide for a winter experimentally, first, in a *quartiere mobiliato.* I am far from the madding crowd, beside these sordid sands. There *is* a crowd, but it's vulgar and comfortable, and the air is as destitute of an edge as the language of an *h.* How charming your young lovers, and what a pleasure to have such frames to offer to such tableaux! Yours dear Mrs. Curtis and the Paron's[1] always devotedly

Henry James

P.S. I must take another sheet to say Yes—I hear that the young Kipling is serenely content at Brattleboro, and takes the greatest interest in the "frame" structure, as I suppose it is, that he has built there to live in for aye. He is *en puissance de femme—che vuole?* And moreover I take it that the wonder is really very much less than it appears under the first glamour of his work; that is that he has very few needs that the Brattlesboros of the world can't satisfy; almost *none* of the civilized order—London, English life, "culture" etc., were for instance altogether a superfluity for him. He charged himself with all he could take of India when he was very young, and gave it out with great effect; but I doubt if he has anything more of anything to give. All sorts of things—i.e. symptoms and indications—seem to me to point to that. But what he *did*—in two or three years—remains wonderful.—The poor dear Ranee[2] is lately back from her winter in the South of France, Florence, Rome etc., with her boy better but endlessly ill. It is very miserable. Poor Mrs. Bronson. What a life!

1. *Paron* is Venetian dialect for *padrone,* HJ's pet name for Daniel Curtis at the Palazzo Barbaro.

2. Margaret Brooke, the Ranee of Sarawak.

To Isaac Austen Henderson

Ms Private

[Ramsgate]
July 18*th* [1893]

My dear Henderson.[1]

You will see from the enclosed that I am at least rapidly *qualifying* for Scarborough. I wish greatly you were here, that I might, on the question, ask you, pressingly, for a word of valuable advice. As a substitute for that I venture to entreat you to very kindly transmit to me by pen such an impression as the perusal of the little document may if it awakens *any*—arouse in you. I rise—tottering—from thirty-six hours of influenza to throw myself on your charity. (I came back from the refined Ramsgate on Saturday—and return to it tomorrow. Excuse my tremulous incoherence—I got out of bed but an hour ago. My little go was of course very slight—but it's absurd how even a few hours of it weakens one.) The facts are, very briefly, these: George Alexander has just accepted from me with instantaneous *rapture* a three-act play for *near* production. He has indeed in his hands only the first act completely finished; but *elaborately full* and detailed Scenarios of II and III. The rest he is to have in a month or two. Modesty forbids me to relate to you even at this distance the expressions, the enthusiasms, the promptitude with which this transaction has been accomplished—the *instantaneity,* above all, of his surrender. "The most beautiful 'poetical play' produced in this country *since*" (hold your breath and wait—) "since *Olivia*!" (Not a word about any *Criterion*[2] productions!) Furthermore my impression is that he *wants* to make it —really—follow Mrs. Tanqueray[3] *directly*—and hopes that our dear Henry Arthur [Jones] will not have finished a promised masterpiece in time to hold him to a contingent understanding already existing: he has intimated to me that there are symptoms that he (H.A.) will *not.* Lastly I find that he has *already* written to Alfred Parsons—did in fact the moment he had read scenario of third act—about the scene for Act First—an old Somersetshire garden a hundred years ago! I mention these things as indications of zeal. Now these things being so, does his offer of terms—frankly—strike you as adequate? Will you take the trouble to say to me—if possible—what you think one *ought* to have? What sticks in my crop is the surrender of the piece to him personally after £2000. For what that amounts to—is it not?—is that I dispose to him of the play for ten years, for his own performance, for that rather moderate sum gradually paid. The other element—the share in other performances, the half share with him—strikes me as very indefinite and possibly very small as a compensation. And yet I don't know what to propose instead—and am in the dark—helpless. A word from you would be a word of light. Forgive my laying this burden on you—but I know you throw off this sort of wisdom with the puffs of your cigar. Would you very amiably address your precious missive to *Ramsgate?* I shall probably have to write to Alexander tomorrow—but shall only say I *don't* like his terms. So that I shall have heard from you perhaps before I say what I do like. I hope your paradise of the successfully produced is full of refreshment and inspiration. Ramsgate is good enough for me *yet.* But who knows, how long that will last? Will you kindly treat this communication as intensely private and confidential—and forgive my ricketty scrawl?

Yours always
Henry James

P.S. Many greetings please to Mrs. Henderson and the menagerie.

1. Isaac Austen Henderson was the former assistant publisher of E. L. Godkin's *New York Evening Post.* He retired in 1881 and settled in England. HJ probably met him through Godkin. Faced with the offer of a contract for his play *Guy Domville,* HJ now consulted Henderson. HJ had ceased to use a literary agent some time before, and carried on his theatrical negotiations himself.

2. *Olivia,* a play in four acts by W. G. Wills founded on incidents in Goldsmith's *Vicar of Wakefield,* was produced at the Court Theatre on 22 March 1878 with Ellen Terry as Olivia and Hermann Vezin as Dr. Primrose. Henry Irving revived it at the Lyceum on 22 April 1891, playing the part of the Vicar himself. In his review of the 1878 production HJ had written that "the idea of making an effective play . . . of Goldsmith's delicate and humorous masterpiece, whose charm is almost wholly the exquisite narrative style, could have originated only with a playwright desperately at a loss for a subject." The Criterion Theatre in Piccadilly Circus, opened in 1874, was for a long time associated with the production of farce and light comedy.

3. Arthur Pinero's *The Second Mrs. Tanqueray,* with George Alexander and Mrs. Patrick Campbell, was at this moment one of the most successful plays in London.

To George Alexander
Ms Unknown

Ramsgate
[19 July 1893]

Dear Mr. Alexander:

I have considered the terms that you offer me in your note of Monday—with the result of being moved to say that they *don't* strike me as all I could desire. It seems to me that in the arrangement you propose you would become very easily and quickly possessor, owner—for your personal use—of the play for the rest of the ten years. I can't help considering the enjoyment of the half share with you in the profit arising from the use of the piece by others as too indefinite and undetermined a compensation for this. I am perfectly willing to make an arrangement with you by which you shall have control of the play *everywhere* for ten years. But I don't like my share in your performances stopping at £2000. Does not this limit very unduly my profit if the play is successful? If it isn't, my profit will stop of itself; but if it is, I think my gains ought to run further—from *your* performance, I mean, which will be *the* performance. Also is £5.0.0 a night as much as I ought to receive? If this is your definite conviction—and I have no other source of information on the subject—I should probably be willing to let it stand so; but in this case I should like the enjoyment of the £5.0.0 to run a good deal longer. I should be very glad if you would let me have an alternative proposal. Is there none you can make me that should be more attractive to me than this, based on a royalty? I spoke to you myself of a fixed sum, but I am not wedded to it. At any rate I should be obliged to you if you can put the case to me more dazzlingly another way.

I came back here yesterday and am already launched very promisingly in my second act. I think I shall be able to send it to you in a really very moderate space of time—a quite near date. It *goes* so. Yours very truly,

Henry James

To Isaac Austen Henderson
Ms Private

2 Wellington Crescent, Ramsgate
Saturday [22 July 1893]

My dear Henderson.

I must thank you more fully for your luxurious advice. It was most kind of you to rise so benignantly to my appeal. You shall certainly have a couple of good stalls to reward you (at the first); or better still a private performance (a first *before* the first) all for you and Mrs. Henderson, if she will come, at the Boltons—or even in De Vere Gardens! "Fancy that!" Your advice, however, is braver than I. I am too modest or perhaps only too timorous to ask Ten—and the case is apparently being settled on the basis of Seven for London and America—and Five for everywhere else—and for the whole ten years; (to which also I have said Yea). I am informed (by G[eorge] A[lexander]) that Irving gives the Tennysons Ten (on account of their name—no pun!) for *Becket*—and I don't dream of approaching *Becket*.[1] It is the moral support of your communication that has assured me the Seven.—I have desired to write to you disinterestedly ever since I had your charming letter on the eve of your great exodus. I hope your caravan is encamped in a pleasant place. What with saints and vicars Cromer ought to be blessed to you. I stick fast here some days more. It keeps me in touch with the pit and gallery. Daly opens on September 13th with the *Foresters*; and tells me that I come next.[2] It ought to be a near next; but I am even *yet* a child of disappointment and doubt. His company, alas, is woeful. But of these things we will discourse after the East Coast has worked its will on you. I hope that will takes kindly shapes. Be reassured. Yours on no sliding scale

Henry James

1. Tennyson's posthumous play, produced by Sir Henry Irving on 6 February 1893.

2. *The Foresters* was Tennyson's play about Robin Hood, which Augustin Daly produced originally in 1891. Daly had begun preparations to produce HJ's comedy *Disengaged*.

To Richard Watson Gilder
Ms NYPL

2 Wellington Crescent
Ramsgate
July 24*th* [1893]

My dear Gilder.

Again, with a burning blush, I am obliged to decline an invitation of yours. I *can't* write about Mme Duse. She is exquisite—a revelation of the art that sails supremely unprecedently close to nature and relegates vulgarity—and in particular *all* the old vulgarities of the footlights—to a far-away limbo; but mountains of hindrance interpose. I have laid down the critical pen forever, and am very intensely and pressingly occupied in driving another. These are the big obstacles. I couldn't do it *now*—I am too hurried with something else to break off even for a day; and by the time I *could*, it would be too late. Moreover I have seen her in too few parts—only five; and she plays fifty! Excuse the verbosity of my Nay; which however is brought to a close by the temporary work-weariness of yours (and Mrs. Gilder's) ever

Henry James

To Robert Louis Stevenson
Ms Yale

34 De Vere Gardens W.
August 5*th* 1893

My dear Louis.

I have a most charming and interesting letter, and a photographic representation of your fine head which I cannot so unrestrictedly commend, to thank you for. The portrait has its points as a memento, but they are not fine points as a likeness. I remember you, I think of you, I evoke you, much more plastically. But it was none the less liberal, and faithful of you to include me in the list of fond recipients. Your letter contained all sorts of good things, but best of all the happy news of your wife's better condition. I rejoice in that almost obstreperously and beg you to tell her so with my love. The Sydney photograph that you kindly announce (of her) hasn't yet come, but I impatiently desire it. Meanwhile its place is gracefully occupied by your delightful anecdote of your mother's retrospective Scotch friend—the pale, penetratin' and interestin' one. Perhaps you will permit me to say that it is exquisitely Scotch; at any rate it moves altogether in the highest walks of anecdote.—I get, habitually, the sympathetic infection, from Colvin, of so much general uneasiness and even alarm about you, that it is reassuring to find you apparently incommoded by nothing worse than the privation of liquor and tobacco.—"Nothing worse?" I hear you echo, while you ask to what more refined savagery of torture I can imagine you subjected. You would rather perhaps—and small blame to you—perish by the sword than by famine. But you won't perish, my dear Louis, and I am here to tell you so. *I* should have perished—long ago—if it were mortal. No liquor—to speak of—passes my wasted lips, and yet they are capable of the hypocrisy of the sigh of resignation. I am very, very sorry for you—for I remember the genial tray which, in the far-off, fabulous time, used to be placed, as the evening waxed, under the social lamp at Skerryvore. The evenings wax at Vailima, but the tray, I gather, has waned. May this heavy trial be lightened, and, as you missionaries say, be even blessed to you. It wounds, I repeat, but it doesn't kill—more's the pity. The tobacco's another question. I have smoked a cigarette—at Skerryvore; and I shall probably smoke one again. But I don't look forward to it. However, you will think me objectionably destitute of temperament. What depresses me much more is the sad sense that you receive scarcely anything I send you. This, however, doesn't deter me from posting to you today, registered, via San Francisco (it is post-day), a volume of thin trifles lately put forth by me and entitled *Essays in London and Elsewhere.* It contains some pretty writing—not addressed to the fishes. My last letter to you to which yours of June 17th [was a reply]—the only dated one, dear Louis, I ever got from you!—was intended to accompany two other volumes of mine, which were despatched to you, registered, via San F., at the same moment (*The Real Thing,* and *The Private Life*). Yet neither of these works, evidently, had reached you when you wrote—and you asked me not to send you the former (though my letter mentioned that it had started), as you had ordered it. It is all a mystery which the fishes only will have sounded. I also post to you herewith Paul Bourget's last little tale (*Un Scrupule*), as to which nothing will induce me to utter the faintest rudiments of an opinion. It is full of talent (I don't call *that* a rudiment), but the French are passing strange. I am very glad to be able to send you herewith enclosed a *petit mot* from the said Paul Bourget, in response to your sense of outrage at his too-continuous silence. He has been in London these three days with his exquisite young wife, on his way to the United States (he sails today), where he intends apparently to spend the winter and write a volume of observations—on the model of Taine's *Notes sur l'Angleterre.* He will never know how little he knows or can understand our great and glorious Anglo-Saxon civilization—as to which, however, he is full of almost anomalously flattering (given some of his other dispositions) judgments and sympathies. He was fuller still of compunction and shame (when I spoke to him) at not having written to you. His intentions, I can answer for it, had been the best; but he leads so migratory a life that I don't see how *any* intention can ever well fructify. He has spent the winter in the Holy Land and jumps thence in three weeks (from Beyrouth) to this queer American expedition. A year ago—more—he earnestly asked me (at Siena) for your address. I as eagerly gave it to him—*par écrit*—but the acknowledgment that he was then full of the desire to make to you succumbed to complex frustrations. Now that, at last, here it is, I wish you to be able to *read* it! But you won't. My hand is the hand of Apollo to it.—I have been at the sea-side for six weeks, and am back in the empty town mainly because it *is* empty. *My* sea-side is the sordid sands of Ramsgate—I see your coral-reefs blush pink at the vulgarity of the name. The place has for me an unutterable advantage (in the press of working-weeks) which the beach of Falesà would, fortunately, *not* have—that of being full of every one I don't know. The beach of Falesà would enthrall but sterilize me—I mean the social muse would disjoint the classic nose of the other. You will certainly think me barren enough as I am. I am really less desiccated than I seem, however, for I am working with patient subterraneity at a trade which it is dishonour enough to practise, without talking about it: a trade supremely dangerous and heroically difficult—*that* credit at least belongs to it. The case is simplified for me by the direst necessity: the *book,* as my limitations compel me to produce it, doesn't bring me in a penny. Tell it not in Samoa—or at least not in Tahiti; but I *don't* sell ten copies! and neither editors nor publishers will have anything whatever to say to me. But I never mention it—nearer home. "Politics," dear politician—I rejoice that you're getting over them. When you say that you always "believed" them beastly I am tempted to become superior and say that I always knew them so. At least I don't see how one can have glanced, however cursorily, at the contemporary newspapers (I mean the journal of one's whole time) and had any doubt of it. The morals, the manners, the materials of all those gentlemen are writ there more large than any record is elsewhere writ, and the impudence of their airs and pretensions in the presence of it revolts even the meekness of a spirit as resigned to everything as mine. The sordid fight in the House of Commons the other night seemed to me only a momentary intermission of hypocrisy. The hypocrisy comes back with the pretended confusion over it. The Lives of the Stevensons (with every respect to them) isn't what I want you most to write, but I would rather you should publish ten volumes of them than another letter to the *Times*. Meanwhile I am languishing for *Catriona*—and the weeks follow and I must live without you. It isn't life. But I am still amicably yours and your wife's and the insidious Lloyd's,

Henry James

To Grace Norton
Ms Harvard

Marine Hotel, Ventnor: I[sle] of W[ight]
Aug. 20*th* [1893]

My dear Grace.

I have been outrageously silent; but I also have been outrageously taken up. I know you know—you have often so generously said—that when I interpose these big black intervals, like the viewless tunnels of a railway-journey, there is something in the formation of the country one is passing through to require them. My country for a long time past has been rather mountainous—but I have kept blushing in the tunnels—over my misfortune. News of me of a sort—of a good sort I hope—will go to you presently with William and his wife, who sail for Boston on the 24th and whom I go up to town tomorrow to meet on their arrival from Switzerland and help to beguile the brief interval for. I came down here three days ago to breathe, for England, this summer, has known how to be as hot as Africa—and the heat *solid*, and in big stodgy chunks, like some other English things, a bun or an editorial. I have been much out at the seaside—for, before this I was capable of five or six weeks at Ramsgate—the favourite hunting ground of my classic namesake 'Arry; and altogether have succeeded this year *almost* as much as I wanted in keeping out of London during the months of "squash." I spent March and April in Paris, May on the lake of Lucerne with the Williams, and then escaped again as soon as I returned from abroad, in spite of the said Williams having come over to pay me a charming visit. I left them in possession of my little home and went off to scribble by the sea—and, strange to say, everyone was pleased! I won't tell you of them—you will see them so soon; they will perhaps rather (if you are patient to the infliction and no better subject *always* supervenes) tell you a little of *me*. I confess, however, I wonder a good deal what they *can* tell you—so little, as I think of it, there appears for me [to] tell you of myself. The tenor of my life is more and more quiet, and I have almost wholly cut loose from "society." In a country in which "society" is as terrifically numerous as in this, that means a very great gain of time for the cultivation of any little private ambitions, however lame, one may have. The result comes about almost of its self if one ceases to accept invitations to "stay" with people—even for a day—as I have been doing these two or three years; and if in addition one discovers that in London the only way not to dine out too much is not to dine out at all. This sounds eremitic—but it isn't: the chapter of accidents, here, is so great. Long after I have ceased to dine with people, moreover, I trust they will sometimes dine with me. If *you* only would, dear Grace! You are the one person with whom *I* would! You always think I have a much more wonderful time in Paris than I do: therefore I feel humiliated at not being able to glitter with anecdote on the subject of the two months I spent there during the unprecedentedly early, long, hot, beautiful and above all fabulously rainless spring with which, this year, all Europe was visited. (No drop of rain fell *anywhere* from February to nearly July.) But save that Paris was, in these conditions, singularly beautiful to behold, I gathered very few intense impressions there. My little circle there is, through all the changes the revolving years bring, much smaller than it used to be; and (I suppose I may say it in Cambridge) not particularly interesting. Almost the only man of letters I saw was Daudet—several times—dining with him twice. I don't count some babyish little Decadents. I was spared the sight of Goncourt. Daudet is pathetic, through incurable illness, for which Brown-Séguard is treating him (he is crippled and shrunken and almost wholly shut up): but in spite of his coloured little Provençal *faconde*—like the waving of some spotted bright handkerchief—even he is not "interesting" through his ignorance of everything but his little professional Paris horizon. He is too simple—and I am afraid has nothing more to write; though I beseech you not to say *I* said it!—Bourget and his wife were all the spring in the Holy Land—and, as you will know, are by this time in the Unholy. It's the strangest, to my sense, of all jumps, moves and errands. None the less, while they were in London four days, a fortnight ago, I gave them a letter to Charles and ventured also to give them a note to you. I don't even know whether they will eventually turn up in Cambridge—so impossible do I find it to predicate anything but disaster of their American tour: they seem to me (confidentially—oh *so* confidentially speaking!) so ill equipped for it. Bourget has some big engagement to "write a book" about America, and yet his preliminary equipment of acquaintance with his subject is absolutely *nil.* He understands scarcely any English and no American—and speaks neither (to speak of), and will never do so. But his ability is immense—especially, I think, as shown in talk—he is a talker altogether superior—though needing to be inspired to the effort, and by the *ambiente;* and some strange product or monstrous birth will ensue. His little melancholy, complicated, exquisite wife is, besides being very young and very pretty, intensely accomplished and polyglot. They are great Catholics and "reactionaries," and have a hundred letters from priests and the Comte de Paris; but *que diable vont-ils faire dans cette galère?* I don't expect to hear from them—but I should be glad to know of anything you hear or see. I mean to write to Charles to tell *him* also of the liberty I have taken. Your charming antedeluvian last letter lies open before me; but I am almost afraid to refer to anything *it* refers to, lest this should betray to you how long I have had it. I miss not having had Lily in England this year to talk about you to—but perhaps she is here by this time. Heaven send I presently see her—I would go almost anywhere (but to Basset!) to do so. I hope that by this time all your painful preoccupations on the question of Rupert's condition have passed away. Has he not had time to become again reconciled to life and reconstituted in health? This I should be so glad to hear. I am hoping Dick may turn up with the finest Attic tone; but fearing at the same time that the probability of my being away from London much of September may make me miss him. I am in this place but for a few days—to escape some particularly intolerable London heat—unequalled for many years and sickening in its ponderosity. But I shall shun the metropolis again after I have guided the Williams to Euston—on Thursday next. I am vaguely looking for a humble permanent cot beside the sea (preferably), which may serve as a refuge from De Vere Gardens at such bad London moments as make a refuge necessary. Your Hampton Court habitat is grander and much too dear—but I want just such a garden. As yet however, I don't find it; and shall probably end with something sordid at Brighton or Ramsgate; and then repent and chafe at having cut off my little margin for going "abroad." As I read over your letter I find you speak of Maurice Barrès. I met him at Daudet's—but he was an old acquaintance, as five or six years ago, during a stay I was making in Florence, he brought me a note of introduction there. He was then very young, uncelebrated and undecipherable. His books are still utterly the latter to me—I find them a pure galimatias—but he has since then fought duels, married a rich wife and become a deputy and a personage. He strikes me (though I may do him injustice) as a *poseur* and a mystificator of the first water—an adventurer whom it isn't really (in spite of his cleverness) important to keep the run of. The other people you speak of (I mean the young talents, "Vandermenen" in the Revue [des Deux Mondes] and the Hollandais à Paris) I must plead a shameful ignorance of. I have read nothing in the Revue for ages save Augustin Filon's[1] remarkably interesting and able papers on Mérimée. (Augustin, by the way, who has married an English wife and has undergone terrible surgical mutilation of the head (what would he be if he had it *all?*) lives at Ramsgate.) The young men in France seem to me dying of nothing to say; and of such a vain agitation about "how" to say it. It is all an intense *rabâchage*. The French publication that has given me most pleasure for an age is Heredia's[2] volume of sonnets—*Les Trophées*. That is awfully honourable. Jules Lemaître[3] is going down and down, and perishing, somehow, of the monstrosity of his agility. He has taken to the novel and the play; but *Les Rois* was incredibly feeble for so clever a man—and his plays (I saw two of them in Paris—both failures) were worse, really much worse, than that one of mine that you saw in London. They quite restored my self-respect—all the more that he himself wrote about them in the newspapers.—Where are you, my dear Grace, if you are not in your overcreepered window-porch, that delightful summer-*recoin*, of which I have so pretty a photograph? I have an impression the Misses Ashburner are on your mind and that the warm circle of Cambridge is traced about your steps. You live in the Land of Mutual Offices—therefore you will miss Mrs. Cleveland (haven't I heard of her death?) the more sensibly. I won't ask you about Charles and the others, for I try to be in communication with him. I have commanded the Harpers to send you two new books of mine of which they have the American publication; but they have such bad manners that there is no counting on them. Please let me know if the books *don't* come—one a volume of very thin "essays," another a collection of thinner tales. Do you ever see Howells?—I fear not, as he is so of New York. I met Miss Hogarth[4] last Sunday close to Palace Gate, faring through the dead hot afternoon from the Gloucester Road station to read a book to some old invalid friend. She looked bright, though historic, and reminded me of the cottage on the Mole: such a strange bewildering *flash* that cottage seems to me to be as I look back upon it: a kind of *wit* flash, like *Turner's* railway-train in the rain. She spoke to me very tenderly of you; and I spoke of you to her in a manner quite to match it. After this will you despair, or *never* despair? of hearing again from yours so intermittently but so eventually and affectionately—always—

Henry James

1. Pierre Marie Augustin Filon (1841–1916), French man of letters, who was tutor to the Prince Imperial in England and wrote a history of English literature (1883) under the pen name of Pierre Sandrié. His book on Mérimée was published in 1894.

2. See letter to Stevenson, 8 June 1893.

3. Jules Lemaître (1853–1914), for many years drama critic of the *Journal des Débats*. The two plays HJ saw were *Le Député Leveau*, a political satire, and *Mariage blanc*—both produced in 1891.

4. Georgina Hogarth, niece of Dickens's wife, who lived with the Dickens family from her early years until the novelist's death.

To Edwin Austin Abbey

(Telegram) *Ms Unknown*

[1893]

Will alight precipitately at 5.38 from the deliberate 1.50.

Henry James

Robert Louis Stevenson, from the engraving by J. H. E. Whitney (based on a drawing by J. W. Alexander) that appeared in the *Century*, April 1888

Jonathan Sturges, from the portrait by Albert Sterner

To Jonathan Sturges
Ts Lubbock

34 De Vere Gardens W.
Oct. 19*th* 1893

My dear Sturges.[1]

Suffer me to mention an intense recent preoccupation as a reason for my delay to acknowledge your letter. Also the inevitable dejection consequent on finding you fled—after the elaborate (intellectual) provision you had invited me to make for your (decorous) hibernation. These things chilled me for the hour. But you've doubtless been hugging the Russian bear and having better fun than any you would have enjoyed in this passionless town. How much more amusing is France than any country of the earth whatsoever, and how dreary would the human family be if it were not for that distinguished—the only distinguished—member! Be diverted then, on the spot. You would not, I think, have been diverted at Whitby, which I found arduous, cold and *décousu,* and quitted before my time—to look at cathedrals and things. When you get tired of "distinguishing shades of difference"—"curious" or other—between the quartier latin and the quartier Montmartre, come back here where there are no shades to be distinguished—*pas de nuances, pas de nuances!* Come back all the same and revel in chunks and lumps. You will always find a few such for luncheon in this house at 1.45. Meanwhile go and see Miss Reubell by all means, and give her, when you do, my love. She keeps a saloon for gifted infants—but apart from it is a most delightful person and a friend of mine from very long ago. I will write to her and tell her I told you to go. Loeser has been to see me and so has Dauphin-Meunier, but I scarcely know to what use to put them. If you were here you would advise me. Keep up the tradition of Whistler as long as you can—but don't *lancer* the "big Titianesque red-haired model"—I mean into literature.[2] Literature feels the weight of her already. Keep her for Life. Keep also for life, if you can, yours ever, my dear Sturges,

Henry James

1. Jonathan Sturges (1864–1909), a Princeton graduate, was crippled early by polio but led an active expatriate life in London, where he lived at Long's Hotel and had a circle of friends that included Whistler and Henry James. In

later years, he often visited HJ in Lamb House for weeks at a time. It was Sturges whom Howells advised to "live all you can," a remark, made in Whistler's Paris garden, that led James to write *The Ambassadors.* After Sturges's death HJ's letters to Sturges were returned to the novelist and he destroyed them. This one survives thanks to a copy taken by Percy Lubbock.

2. Perhaps an allusion to George du Maurier's forthcoming *Trilby,* in which Whistler is a character.

To Francis Boott
Ms Harvard

34 De Vere Gardens W.
Oct. 21*st* 1893

My dear Francis.

I have one of your gentle gossamer screeds again to thank you for. I enjoy the Tuscan tradition of letter-paper a shade less painfully as a reader than as a writer. Does Ann stuff it into the pockets of her little Bersaglieri? I am delighted the dear little boy has assumed his national costume. The wasted exiles on the Waltham roads (those whom their situation *piace poco*) must snatch him up and embrace him. You wrote from the legendary Lenox, which (though I have seen Naples and survived) I am evidently destined to descend into the tomb without having beheld. I feel all the same as if I had been brought up on the glory of it by Mrs. Tappan. *Io so che sia morte, poveretta!*[1] I lately came home from a summer of British sea-sides, which are all right if one can only choose them vulgar enough, for then they are delightfully full of people one doesn't know (unless one is vulgar oneself, which of course *may* be). I am glad the sight of you in Cambridge has gilded again the Williams's American fetters. They were here long enough for me to miss them now in their *éloignement.* But the London autumn is always convenient to me, and I shall support existence here until—some time in the spring, I may be free to peregrinate to "Tuscany." I shall take Venetia by the way and pay a visit to our excellent friend Fenimore. She has taken, for the winter, Gen. de Horsey's Casa Semitecolo, near the Pal[azzo] Dario, and I believe is materially comfortable; especially as she loves Venice, for which small blame to her! But I figure her as extremely exhausted (as she always is at such times), with her writing and re-writing of her last novel—a great success, I believe, in relation to the particular public (a very wide American one) that she addresses. She is to have, I trust, a winter of bookless peace. The Curtises, you probably know, are just leaving for India (what ever-greenness!) and their withdrawal (as they have been most kind to her) will make the Venice winter rather bare, I fear. Apropos of which things I hear that the bloated Rezzonico is offered for sale, with all Pen Browning's hideous luxuries—except, I believe, the "Tuscan" model whom he has taken to his side in place of his truly unfortunate wife. For a poet's double child (or a double poets') he is singularly prosy. I rejoice in the good you tell me of Lizzie's boy, and long for the day when I may take him by the hand. Shan't you bring him over soon for indispensable initiations and pilgrimages? Give him, please, the love of one who loved his mother. I hope Duveneck's admirable work is now adequately *known*. Does not a train of solicitation follow on this? I hope he is in some stable equilibrium; and send him cordial greetings. What will become of my books when *you* stop reading them? They will droop; but on the other hand the American home will bloom again. Spurn it—sacrifice *me* first. You wouldn't scruple to if you knew how I hate everything I've ever written. *Stià bene.* Yours, dear Francis, evermore

Henry James

1. "I know she is dead, poor thing!" Caroline Sturgis Tappan (Mrs. William A.) was an old friend of the Jameses, the father having known her in Emersonian circles and actively corresponded with her. See *Notes of a Son and Brother,* chapter VII. Mrs. Tappan was an aunt of Mrs. Henry Adams.

To Robert Louis Stevenson
Ms Yale

34 De Vere Gardens W.
October 21*st* [1893]

My dear Louis.

The postal guide tells me, disobligingly, that there is no mail to you via San Francisco this month and that I must confide my few lines to the precarious and perfidious Hamburg. I do so, then, for the plain reason that I can no longer repress the enthusiasm that has surged within me ever since I read *Catriona*. I missed, just after doing so, last month's post, and I was infinitely vexed that it should not have conveyed to you the freshness of my rapture. For the said *Catriona* so reeks and hums with genius that there is no refuge for the desperate reader but in straightforward prostration. I'm not sure that it's magnanimous of you to succeed so inconsiderately—there is a modesty in easy triumph which your flushed muse perhaps a little neglects.—But forgive that lumbering image—I won't attempt to carry it out. Let me only say that I don't despatch these ineffectual words on their too watery way to do anything but thank you for an exquisite pleasure. I hold that when a book has the high beauty of that one there's a poor indelicacy in what simple folk call criticism. The work lives by so absolute a law that it's grotesque to prattle about what *might* have been! I shall express to you the one point in which my sense was conscious of an unsatisfied desire, but only after saying first how rare an achievement I think the whole personality and tone of David and with how supremely happy a hand you have coloured the palpable women. They are quite too lovely and everyone is running after them. In David not an error, not a false note ever; he is all of an exasperating truth and rightness. The one thing I miss in the book is the note of *visibility*—it subjects my visual sense, my *seeing* imagination, to an almost painful underfeeding. The *hearing* imagination, as it were, is nourished like an alderman, and the loud audibility seems a slight the more on the baffled lust of the eyes—so that I seem to myself (I am speaking of course only from the point of view of the way, as I read, *my* impression longs to complete itself) in the presence of voices in the darkness—voices the more distinct and vivid, the more brave and sonorous, as voices always are (but also the more tormenting and confounding) by reason of these bandaged eyes. I utter a pleading moan when you, e.g., transport your characters, toward the end, in a line or two from Leyden to Dunkirk without the glint of a hint of all the ambient picture of the eighteenth-century road. However, stick to your own system of evocation so long as what you positively achieve is so big. Life and letters and art all take joy in you.—I am rejoiced to hear that your wife is less disturbed in health and that your anxieties are somewhat appeased. I don't know how sufficiently to renew, to both of you, the assurance of all my friendliest sympathy. You live in conditions so unimaginable and to the tune of experiences so great and so strange that you must forgive me if I am altogether out of step with your events. I know you're surrounded with the din of battle, and yet the beauty you produce has the Goethean calm, even like the beauty distilled at Weimar when the smoke was over Jena. Let me touch you at least on your bookish side and the others may bristle with heroics. I pray you be made accessible some day in a talkative armchair by the fire. If it hadn't been for *Catriona* we couldn't, this year, have held up our head. It had been long, before that, since any decent sentence was turned in English. We grow systematically vulgarer and baser. The only blur of light is that your books are tasted. I shall try to see Colvin before I post this —otherwise I haven't seen him for three months. I've had a summer of the British seaside, the bathing machine and the German band. I met Zola at luncheon the day before he left London and found him very sane and common and inexperienced. Nothing, literally nothing has ever happened to him but to write the Rougon-Macquart. It makes that series, I admit, still more curious. Your tour de force is of the opposite kind. Renew the miracle, my dear Louis, and believe me yours already gaping,

Henry James

P.S. I have had to keep my poor note several days—finding that after all there *is*, thank heaven, a near post by San Francisco. Meanwhile I have seen Colvin and made discreetly, though so eagerly, free of some of your projects—and gyrations! Trapezist in the Pacific void! Colvin is lucid and firm, and we are all praying he be made head of the National Gallery *vice* Sir Frederick Burton. But I am too "out of it" to *measure* his chances—and desire the thing too amicably to appreciate them coolly. *Ora pro nobis.* I saw Gosse last night—going to lecture at Sunderland and gratified at a charming article (on his genius) in the *Débats*—by Augustin Filon (not *filou*): both circumstances, I take it, irrealisable in your white ether. "Catriona" is more and more BEAUTIFUL. There's the rub!

H.J.

To Charles Eliot Norton

Ms Harvard

34 De Vere Gardens W.
Nov. 15*th* 1893

My dear Charles.

The two beautiful volumes of dear J[ames] R[ussell] L[owell][1] constitute a gift for the substantial grace of which I lose as little time as possible in affectionately thanking you. I think it most kind of you to have sent me the work, when I think also of all the people to whom, as his correspondents, you owed (exactly) a more literal duty. I have read the whole thing with absorption and with a delightful illusion. It has been the dear man's *company* again—irresistibly, audibly, visibly; and I have felt precisely as if I were face to face with him and could see him fill his pipe in the intervals of the letters. I expected a great deal from them—it was impossible to have known Lowell and not do so; but I think they have given quite all I imagined. They have less of other people in them than I should on the whole have thought—I mean are less peopled and figured, as it were; but all they have of himself—and it is so much—is of a sort to do the greatest honour to his memory. They form a singularly beautiful monument—everyone must agree—to his nature equally with his gifts. The sweet humanity of them and the robust manhood are as unmistakeable as the admirable literary genius. It seems to me that the best of them must rank with the best letters in the language—and they are so unlike most of the chatter of the day and so untainted with its cheapness, that they strike one indeed already as full of pages that time and criticism have consecrated. The total impression has remarkable beauty. If I allude, however, to criticism, it is not that I have any impression worth mentioning of any your volumes may have elicited in this place. It is long since I looked at an English review—I was "choked off," in past years, by their strange mediocrity and commonness. Therefore I have no notion at all of what "the papers" (to which it seems to me, by the way, Lowell himself gave more attention than he might) say about them. I can't help wishing, however, frankly, that I might have had a chance of putting in a very deferential voice, once or twice, on the editorial question—perfectly as you seem to me, for the far greater part, to have viewed it. I mean that there are passages (which since you *were* selecting and omitting) I should have liked to talk with you on the propriety —the advisability—of *not* printing (I don't mean allusions to persons,—I wish there were more of these, but of the cumulative effect of the frequent repetition—in the absence of certain other elements to dilute and balance it—of a certain kind of allusion to his own work). All this will sound to you mighty vague, so long as I don't give you examples of what I have in mind. But I *could* have done so had I been with you! It is one more reason for me to regret, my dear Charles, that I am *not* with you. You will doubtless reply that there was never any editor since editing began who didn't render himself liable to this particular observation—and who could have escaped from it otherwise than by plumping straight up against another. None the less I will persist to the point of saying that I can't help wishing the second volume might have contained more letters illustrative of his London life—in its extreme variety and extension, I mean of his English life at large. It was the richest period of his existence, surely, in the particular way in which letters are an expression of "richness"—and would have given a picture very delightful to possess of the play of his mind in a far greater multitude of contacts than he had ever had before. I may be invidious—but I care comparatively so little for the play of his mind in contact, say, with R. W. Gilder and T. B. Aldrich! For me—who was more or less nearly present at the whole evolution of his relations and humours in this country—the book gives almost a sense of (in this particular) complete *omission*. There are people who were in the very forefront of his life (not the Miss Lawrences, blessed virgins, who weren't) who are too vividly absent. And there was a whole *kind* of distinction public and private which it—the book—seems to me too dimly to reflect. You may easily reply—very easily indeed —that what you had to deal with was the material you *had,* and that you used to the best of your judgment simply the letters that reached you. This I can perfectly conceive—and what my remark amounts to is therefore only a hope that you may still be able to put forth a second crop. I may be mistaken about the *existence* of the material for it (or the accessibility); but I can't help thinking (till the contrary is proved) that there must be enough for a very interesting appendix—if you should be able or disposed to make a second appeal. He wrote to so many people—and *always* wrote so characteristically; and I should suppose he never did either more than while he was here—never did the former indeed so much.—Forgive this long parenthesis—which has left me scarce space to say once more how grateful I am for the book as it stands and how above all I find the total effect of it strangely *touching.* I don't know how much it will interest or amuse or please you to know that sitting the other night beside Grant Duff[2] at dinner (the dinner of a somewhat drearily-distinguished club that meets for the purpose once a month) I spoke of Lowell's letters (which he hadn't yet seen) and of how good they are. "Are they as good as Charles Norton's own?" "They are too different to compare." "Charles Norton's own are the very best I know." "They are admirable indeed." "They are perfect *models.*" This warmed my heart so that I instantly accepted an invitation to spend next Sunday at York House—an experience of which, with my heart in its normal slightly tepid state (toward G.D.—not toward *you*) I am apt to be conspicuously incapable.—And apropos of your letters I have just got one from Richard[3]—in Berlin—which is marvellous in its reproduction of your hand. I am sorry for some of the lonesome experiences to which his work dedicates him. But it is such a beautiful work to be dedicated to that I think it is not too much to ask of him, for that sake, to see them through. I saw a little of him here in October with such relish that I had written to him to say how sorry I was not to have seen more. Ten days hence is unveiled in a dark passage out of the Abbey cloisters the memorial[4] which the energy of the Leslie Stephens—hers in especial—has succeeded in placing there in default of a place that was impossible from the first. I *don't* wish you were to be there; and yet I am, my dear Charles, ever affectionately yours

Henry James

1. Norton had sent HJ advance copies of his *Letters of James Russell Lowell,* published by Harper & Brothers in New York early in 1894.

2. Sir Mountstuart Elphinstone Grant Duff (1829–1906), statesman and author, undersecretary of state for India 1868–1874 and governor of Madras 1881–1886.

3. Norton's younger son, Richard, an archaeologist, later was director of the School of Classical Studies in Rome.

4. See ensuing letter to Sir Leslie Stephen.

To Leslie Stephen
Ms Berg

34 De Vere Gardens W.
November *29th* '93

My dear Stephen.

I was forced to leave the Abbey with little delay yesterday—through having made an engagement to lunch; and I did so with regret, because I wanted to see you for a moment—long enough to congratulate you on your achieved work. It is well done—and I shared, strongly, the emotion with which you so perfectly, in your address, acquitted yourself. I thought you did this admirably—both with eloquence and temperance—and combining happily the spokesman and the friend. It was all thoroughly right and clear and sincere—and was felt by everyone to be so. Now it's over, and the storied window will stand for all the time we need calculate. The window is beautiful—I take great and superior comfort in it—and it seems to me not only a memorial of Lowell's distinction, but a record of your and Mrs. Stephen's fine friendship—which I infinitely esteem. I renew to both of you the assurance of my sympathy, and am yours, my dear Stephen always

Henry James

To Elizabeth Robins
Ms Texas

The Athenaeum,
Wednesday 2 P.M.
[6 December 1893]

Dear Miss Robins.

Only a word to say that the result (for your very sympathetic ear) of the ghastly—yes, it's the word!—two hours I have just brought to a close at Daly's is that I write to him to-night to withdraw my piece.[1] The "rehearsal" left me in such a state of nervous exasperation that I judged it best—or rather I could only control myself and trust myself enough—to say, simply, to him, after the last word was spoken: "I shall take some hours to become perfectly clear to myself as to the reflections which this occasion—taken in connection with your note of Saturday, causes me to make. And then I will write to you—" and then to walk out of the theatre. To Ada Rehan (white, haggard, ill-looking almost in *anguish*) I couldn't bring myself to *speak*. I know Bourchier[2] and said good-bye to him—but I was not given a single *second's* opportunity of having the least contact or word with any other member of the company; who began and stammeringly *read* their parts the instant I came in, and vanished the instant the third act ended. Don't pity me too much—rather rejoice with

Yours always
Henry James

1. HJ's three-act comedy *Mrs. Jasper*, later renamed *Disengaged*.
2. Arthur Bourchier (1863–1927), actor-manager and a founder of the Oxford University Dramatic Society.

To Augustin Daly
Ms Harvard

34 De Vere Gardens W.
Dec. 7*th* 1893

Dear Mr. Daly.

My play may *not* contain the elements of success, and at my stage of relationship to the theatre I am much too nervous a subject not to accept as *determining*, in regard to my own action, any sound of alarm, or of essential scepticism, however abrupt, on the part of a manager. That makes my nervousness operative and simplifies the case. I should none the less have been very glad to be informed at an earlier moment (of the year it has been in your hands) of your discovery that the piece is fundamentally unsuited to your purpose—an earlier moment, I mean, than the eve of what I had been looking forward to as a serious preparation. Your few words of Saturday so definitely express, in spite of their brevity, or perhaps indeed by reason of the same, the sudden collapse of your own interest in it, that I withdraw it from your theatre without delay and beg you to send me back the MS. For myself—I cannot for a moment profess that the scene I witnessed on your stage yesterday[1] threw any light on the character of the play that might not have been thrown by *any* repetition on re-reading of the lines.

The only slightly fresh or somewhat intenser impression I derived from it was that of the quick brevity of the three acts and their closeness and crispness of texture. I could recognise it in no degree as a test constituted by even an approach to the tentative or experimental *representation* of a delicate and highly-finished piece, each of whose steps and stages was to have been essentially dependent on expression. I was, in other words, unable to see in it, any measure or any intimation of what *acting* could do for my intentions. Nor can I meet you on the ground—which if I mistake not there was a moment when you invited me to do—of taking account of the actor's "conception" (and least of all of its finality) either of the parts or of the total—in a piece that I am surprised the author was deprived of the indispensable preliminary of communicating to them or giving them a hint about, and as to which not one of them had had the interest or curiosity to approach him for a suggestion; or, in illustration of the said conception, and even while uninterruptedly reading from the book, to seek to exhibit an acquaintance with the text.

Truly yours
Henry James

1. HJ seemed to think he had been denied the privilege of explaining *Mrs. Jasper* (*Disengaged*) to the actors, who read their parts in a manner that seemed to him an attempt to get him to withdraw the comedy. Daly replied on the following day that there had been "no pretence on my part, or that of the actors to give you anything approaching a performance. The players merely gave you a reading of their lines and an indication of their movements and positions on the scene—from a view of which I had hoped you might have gathered, as I had already, that something was needed (beside accentuation or expression) to make a success of the work: a success for which you could not hope or labor more than myself." Daly said that his having ordered scenery and costumes in Paris that summer showed that he had acted in good faith. He added: "I am sure that calmer reflection will lead you to a more just and generous appreciation of the efforts of Miss Rehan and her fellow artists, to give you their conception of your characters upon your written lines: which conception you were entirely free and welcome to correct at subsequent rehearsals; but I believe it was distinctly understood between us that on the rehearsal you attended everything was to be allowed to pass without interruption." Daly concluded, "it was you who offered me the play in the first instance and it is you who now request its return. I am satisfied to accept your word as compliment to my judgment now as then." (Daly to HJ, 8 December 1893, Ms Harvard.)

To Augustin Daly
Ms Harvard

34 De Vere Gardens W.
December 11*th* 1893

Dear Mr. Daly.

I cannot let your letter accompanying the return of my play pass without a rejoinder; which you should have had sooner had I not gone on Saturday morning to a distant country visit—during which none of my time was my own and from which I have but just returned. In my letter of Thursday I contested in no degree whatever your right to change your mind about my play; and my observations bore—and still bear—exclusively on your very imperfect achievement of that courtesy of the *demonstration of grounds* which every dramatist in such a situation has a right to expect. I cannot admit that the dozen words on the subject in your note of December 2d, and the reading of Wednesday, which constituted the sole occasion of my having, up to that time, been admitted to any sort of contact with our experiment, amount to such a courtesy or to such a demonstration. Therefore please believe that I should have appreciated more the disappointment to which you allude, and which I greatly regret that you should have suffered, if I had not been so taken up with appreciating the want of ceremony, under the circumstances, with which you addressed yourself to the business of getting rid of me.

I say "under the circumstances" because I hold that it is quite to fail of justice to them to say that I in the first instance *offered* you my play. My own recollection of the matter is that you *invited* me to offer you something—invited me, very distinctly, by a message which Miss Rehan kindly conveyed to me on an occasion of my meeting her (at Mr. and Mrs. Barrington's) in the autumn of '91, some months, many months indeed, before the piece eventually came into your hands. I then intimated to you (through Miss Rehan) that I had every hope of being able on your next return to England to communicate to her, as representing you, a finished and discussable play. I parted with Miss Rehan on that occasion with the very definite sense that you would, as a sequel to it, as definitely *expect* such a communication. In August '92 I read to her, at Mr. and Mrs. Barrington's (the date had been fixed long in advance) the first form of "Mrs. Jasper," and she kindly took the MS. up to London and handed it to you. You wrote to me, within two or three days, that the play "pleased but did not satisfy you"; but also that, should I feel disposed to talk with you about it, you would be at home to see me. I answered you, from Brighton, in a manner than which nothing could have been more candid and less pressing, fully accepting your restriction and quite "giving away" my piece, as it then stood, by my frankness; but also saying that I should like to call on you.

I called accordingly—not in the least to plead for "Mrs. Jasper," but with the idea—and, I confess, the hope—that our conversation would possibly lead to your inviting me to attempt to submit to you some *other* play, some play which might satisfy as well as please you. What I learned, however, in talking with you was that "Mrs. Jasper" didn't *need* any other plea than an undertaking to alter and amend, to reconstruct and rewrite it, to the best of my ability. I remember, in my positive desire *not* to appear importunate, saying that I was willing to accept this, or anything else, on the *chance*—without asking of you a pledge, and your replying that as regards an altered "Mrs. Jasper" that should *content* you, you were perfectly willing then and there to take a responsibility. I left you with the promise to consider the practicability of rewriting my play, and a few days later, just as you were leaving England, I let you know that I thought I had found a way ("seen the light") and that I would take the job in hand. I *took* it in hand with extreme punctuality and zeal, as a definite commission for your theatre, and devoted many weeks of patience and ingenuity to bringing it to success. I addressed the principal part as elaborately as I could to Miss Rehan (you had intimated to me that this was the line you should desire taken) and endeavoured to produce a result which should be closely associated with her artistic personality. This was essentially the basis of my labour. When I sent you the play—finished and highly finished on this basis—you immediately, in however few words, accepted it. I surrendered it to you hereupon without a single condition of any sort. I neither discussed the terms you offered me nor asked for any information even (much less any promise) in respect to time, place, or circumstances of production. You would have been free to run the play, at the end of five years, for a single night if it had suited you. From that moment till the moment I got your note of December 2d, I never approached you in any degree or manner on the subject, asking no question and bringing during the year that elapsed, not the hint of an impatience to bear on you. I recite these circumstances to remind you that I have not exposed myself to an exceptional and in the code of relations between manager and author, very irregular want of consideration, and to suggest to you that it is not I who exhibit it. In regard to the zeal of your performers, on which you insist, I can only again express my regret that it should not have been exercised in a way to convince me that the question (of the practicability of my piece) was being seriously dealt with. I should have been very willing not to introduce Miss Rehan's name into our correspondence, but since you have done so I must express myself in consequence. My play, in its ultimate form, was, as I say, essentially addressed to her, conceived, at your suggestion, wholly in the light of the hypothesis that she would show me what she thought could—or could not—be done with the leading part. I am therefore, naturally, only the *more* sorry not to have been more enlightened by her as to the process by which she so rapidly ascertained that nothing could be done with it at all. I met Miss Rehan on Sunday November 25th—definitely before the rehearsals (of which I was so surprised to learn only after the fact) had begun. She then casually mentioned to me that—a couple of days later—my play was to "be read." She didn't mention by *whom*—in my absence, and as I thought it in better taste (presuming her quite irresponsible in the matter) not to ask her, she left me only bewildered and uneasily wondering and confidently expecting to be informed on the morrow. Not a word dropped from her on this occasion, as it had never dropped before (of course I don't refer to allusions to the circumstance that a play of mine with a part in it for her was in your hands), to indicate that she had taken any cognizance of the new piece or the new character. I waited for some such word—on the eve of rehearsal—but not a syllable reached me; and "Mrs. Jasper" will have performed its long and complete revolution without my having had the advantage of exchanging a word with Miss Rehan on a single one of the points which I had looked to her to subject to the test of her great talent. That makes one more regret to add to the rest—the regret that the actress who has been willing to act the parts I have, for the most part, seen her act this winter, should not have been moved even to *study* that of the heroine of my comedy.

Truly yours,
Henry James

To Mr. and Mrs. William James
Ms Harvard

34 De Vere Gardens W.
Dec. 29*th* 1893

My dear brother and my dear sister:

The most gratifying incident that has befallen me this quiet Christmastide has been the arrival of your two deeply interesting letters, each of December 18th. They have crowned with felicity the exceptionally quiet and comfortable manner in which the dread Season has passed away. London has been very still; very empty and of an air extraordinarily soft and clear. I have passed no more selfishly complacent Christmas in the cheerful void left by the almost universal social flight to the country. The autumn has been wholly fogless, and even the mists which have now at last gathered, are harmless and silvery—though I *am* writing to you with the aid of a not absolutely indispensable lamp. Very interesting and thrilling to me is your vivid combined chapter about the Bourgets; and, frankly speaking, confirmatory, altogether, of impressions more or less forced upon me by all my late observations of them, and especially by that of the five days which they spent near me here last August on their way to embark for the U.S. (Confirmatory, that is, of everything but the idea of "Minnie's" bad temper. That is something of a surprise to me; though I saw enough at Siena, of her terrible nerves and constant *crises*.) About Bourget himself I never had *any* delusions. He has, I think, a distinctly charming and affectionate side, but it loses itself in an abyss of *corruption* and in a sort of personal avidity, a habit of inconsiderate manners, over which his unmistakeable absence of "early training" (as Aunt Kate used to say), never established a control. Hélas, with all his brilliancy, all his literary *mondanité* etc., he isn't a gentleman. They both "took for granted" when they were here in August to a degree that startled me and which it was that determined me (so fruitlessly alas!) not to give them a letter to you. (My systematic withholding of letters never avails, it appears, to save you, after all, from victimization.) I gave them introductions only to three or four whom I thought it would *please,*—Mrs. Jack, Mrs. Whitman and the two Nortons: (the pleasing of the Bourgets themselves, in the matter, I had already renounced, or was in the act of renouncing as a motive; for I have done, in proportion, enough of that). Oh yes, you are right in saying that in a manner he has got much more out of me than I out of him—and yet you are wrong. I have got out of him that I know him as if I had made him —his nature, his culture, his race, his type, his *moeurs,* his mixture —whereas he knows (as a consequence of his own attitude) next to nothing about me. An individual so capable as I am of the uncanniest self-effacement in the active exercise of the passion of observation, always exposes himself a little to *looking* like a dupe —and he doesn't care a hang! And yet I *like* Bourget and have an affection for him; he has a great deal of individual charm, sensibility, generosity; and the sides by which he *dis*pleases are those of his race and the in so many ways abominable *milieu* in which his life has mainly been passed. Your remarks (William's) about the putrefactions of the French character are admirable—and oh, how Bourget lights them up! He can *talk* of them better than anyone! His wife is a strange little mystery to me—and the end of her revelation is not yet. It strikes me indeed that they have complicated possibilities ahead of them. Their *matrimones* has hitherto gone on the basis of the most complete and cautious absence from Paris; but he has had (the comparative failure of *Cosmopolis* admonishes him, and Zola spoke of the matter to me very strongly in September) to recognize that his literary security now demands his again taking up his life there and re-entering into "touch"; so that when they are steeped together into that absolutely seething caldron, the latent elements of lively times will, I fear, rise to the surface. They both have a strange terror of it in advance—a terror which, when I have heard him speak of it, has seemed to me to *en dire long* on the subject of their whole view of life and fate and character and conduct—their whole innermost "tone," as it were. To me, let me add (and I have three letters from him—three weeks ago quite a long one, almost fatally illegible) he has not dwelt on the "horribleness" of the U.S.; but spoken of the interest and imposingness of *ce colossal abri de vu*, etc. On the other hand he has spoken with no detail of his impressions. I am intensely grateful to you for what you did for them—I *dreaded* their invasion of you. And as for the wasted and unacknowledged courtesy of it all, don't regard that as squandered, for the luminosity of your remarks about him show[s] a valued accession of experience. Please bury in secrecy my own foregoing candid observations!—I rejoice greatly in Alice's announcement (which you, William, coyly don't mention) of the presidency of the [Society for Psychical Research]. I hope it's all honour and kudos and pleasantness, without a tax of botherations. I wish I could give you some correspondingly good tidings of my own ascensory movement; but I had a fall—or rather took a jump—the other day (a month ago) of which the direction was not vulgarly—I mean theatrically and financially—upward. You are so sympathetic about the whole sordid development that *I* make a point of mentioning the incident. It consisted simply of the abrupt and disgusted termination of my really quite unnatural connection with that hopeless cad of a Daly. I *withdrew* my play from him after a single (absolutely, humbugging) rehearsal, and in consequence of an attitude on his part of unmistakeable provocation to do so. The whole manoeuvre and whole situation were as plain as day. He has so blundered and muddled away his whole season here that he has lost money appallingly—has not had a *single* success—pursuing with a third rate company an utterly third rate policy, which has landed him on the verge of ruin. Under these circumstances I became for him simply an author to whom he had the dreadful prospect of having "royalties" to pay—and he addressed himself crudely and odiously to getting rid of. Pledged to me these fourteen months and wholly by his own initiative he could only do so circuitously—that is could only make *me* stop the production. This he did—I won't go into details—by reading and pretendedly rehearsing the play in secret once or twice (in defiance of the rigid[1] and only decent usage in such cases between author and manager), and then admitting me to one ghastly make-believe, to the end that I might be disgusted. I *was*, at his bad faith, and at Miss Rehan's singular artistic (and social!) baseness, and I walked straight out of the theatre with the play as it were in my pocket. On the other hand my whole sense of his discredited and compromised situation, of his theatre, of his company, of his *procédés* and of the "mean" person to deal with that he is—to say nothing of my vision "close-to," of Ada Rehan's unmistakeable unintelligence: all this gave me a sense of relief and escape—escape as from a sinking ship. It was none the less for a while a lively disgust and disappointment—a waste of patient and ingenious labour and a sacrifice of coin much counted on. But *à la guerre comme à la guerre.* I mean to wage this war ferociously for one year more—1894—and then (unless the victory and the spoils have by that become more proportionate than hitherto to the humiliations and vulgarities and disgusts, all the dishonour and chronic insult incurred) to "chuck" the whole intolerable experiment and return to more elevated and more independent courses. The whole odiousness of the thing lies in the connection between the drama and the theatre. The one is admirable in its interest and difficulty, the other loathsome in its conditions. If the drama could only be theoretically or hypothetically acted, the fascination resident in its all but unconquerable (*circumspice!*) form would be unimpaired, and one would be able to have the exquisite exercise without the horrid sacrifice. However, Alexander's preparations of my play are going on sedulously, as to which situation and circumstances are all essentially different. He will produce me at no distant date, infallibly (his joy in his own part is a guarantee of that), but the managerial policy at a given moment is an abyss, and he *may* put into rehearsal first something that he is also simultaneously preparing. As this something is, I believe, a play of the celebrated [Henry Arthur] Jones, nothing is more possible than that it may be a failure. In that case I am pretty sure I should come on with a rush—and after a delay not substantially greater than if I follow *Mrs. Tanqueray* straight. If it's a success, of course I shall have to wait longer. But meanwhile I am working heroically, though it every month becomes more difficult to give time to things of which the pecuniary fruit is remote. Excuse these vulgar confidences. I *have* come to *hate* the whole theatrical subject. Only let me add that the rehearsal at Daly's was a mere mumbled *reading* of their parts, book in hand, by actors whom I beheld at that moment (in private, as it were) for the first time, to whom I hadn't been allowed, and wasn't then allowed, an instant's access, and whose proceedings constituted no more a tentative or experimental *expression* of my play than a closed piano constitutes a sonata. Ada Rehan, white, haggard, ill, really with the effort of her bad faith, was too ashamed of what she was doing—of the farce to which she had lent herself—to come near me or to look me in the face. It was a horrid experience—and an interesting illustration of what may happen, in the vulgar theatrical world, to one who is not yet cased in the only success there recognized—the success *not* of the Book. When once one is cased in that success, however, one's position wholly changes, and I think the *revanche* must be great and sweet.—There, I have written you twenty pages about these *misères* and have left myself no more time and space. I am giving up this little remnant of the year's end to terrific arrears of letters, and still day follows day without my having worked through my list. Therefore I will only express very briefly my sympathies with your better and your worst. I am horrified at that loss of money that you speak of—through the sacrificed sale of bonds etc. while you were away. Such things are very dreadful—and your year in Europe was a devouring maw. However, you have got much and you feel much, to show for it. But be hospitable and be adventurous no more! They are the saddest but the clearest lessons, and I have learnt them, in general, for myself. Solitude is more and more my portion but nothing fine was ever done without a large measure of it. You have my tenderest compassion for your late horrible friction with Bob. I lately had a letter from him which I couldn't accept as *sane;* and in consequence of my rejoinder to it—though I didn't say so to him—I am quite prepared that he will cast me off.[2] When the drama becomes successful Harry must come out and pay me a visit. Poor little Miss Grace Ashburner's disparition must leave Miss Anne standing there more and more like a gnarled and blasted tree. Katharine P. L[oring] wrote to me the other day that your arrived sepulchral stone for Alice seemed to her very beautiful —by which I judge that it is in place. How much I wish I might have a photograph of it! Embrace me for your two Vaudoises, and each other, and all the young. Don't write to condole with me about the Daly business. I don't in the least "require" it. May the new year not have too many twists and turns for you, but lie straight and smooth before you.

Evermore your
Henry

1. HJ is referring here to an old tradition of the French stage—the reading of the play by the dramatist to the players. It did not necessarily apply to the British or American stage.

2. HJ alludes to the continued alcoholism and irresponsibility of their younger brother Robertson.

To Grace Norton
Ms Harvard

34 De Vere Gardens W.
December 31*st* 1893

My dear Grace.

Long, long have I been the happy possessor of your last beautiful letter—the one from Arlington Heights (that name gives me away!) and I am now trying to save my credit for a decent responsiveness by catching at the very last hours of the old year to keep myself in some sort of temporal relation to you. My credit, however, was long ago gone—it is only your charming indulgence that remains. Be greeted, anyhow, my dear Grace, on this threshold of another age; be wished everything that I can suppose you to agree with me in wishing you, and be assured that the amount of thinking of you that I luxuriously achieve is out of all proportion to the amount of epistolizing. May the coming time be easy to your feet—by which I don't mean to say may it be all downhill! A gentle incline, however, is I think better than a dead level, and may yours and mine be turned the right way! I have thought of you apropos of many things—J.R.L.'s letters, Frank Parkman's death,[1] and very intensely, let me say in your ear, apropos of the Bourget's visit. I have received from William and his wife a very interesting, very convincing, and very you-know-what-I-would-say-so-I-wouldn't-say-it account of the last named phenomenon. (I mean by that preceding ambiguous qualification that I am as certain of every impression every one of you got from every moment of his presence—and hers —among you, as if I were writing it all in a little tale. Indeed it strikes me exactly as one of my own stories. But now I wish you would translate it into one of *yours!*) I wanted much to write to you when that heroic Frank Parkman passed away—and I wanted equally to write to his sister. But I did neither, and now, as regards Miss Parkman, I shall never repair the omission. Circumstances imposed it on me—and now it's late. Do you ever see her?—And if you do, will you tell her I asked you to give her my very friendliest remembrance and participation? Words and vain motions seem uncalled for when a man has lived his life so well and cut his mark so deep. I shall always think of him as one of the manliest spirits and finest Americans it has been given me to know. His books have a peculiar and abiding nobleness, and he painted great things with a great capacity for them. I think that with all trials and struggles he was happy in his fate. So too, in so far a different way, has dear Lowell been. The beauty of his Letters has been a benediction, a consecration to his memory. Such is felt to be the case even here, where such perceptions are not, I think, of the finest. They do him great honour—only there ought to have been more of them—there ought, I think, still to be; especially illustrative of those years during which he most lived, succeeded and transformed himself—I mean the years in this country. (By "transformed himself" of course I only mean went through an initiation and an adjustment (if one may say he really did!—he *didn't,* too!) unusual for a man of his years and his former *moeurs.*) However, the letters are all to the good for his name and fame—and we are greatly and gratefully indebted to Charles. Has Miss Grace Ashburner's extinction made any particular personal or social difference to you? Miss Anne must stand there alone like an only doorpost. I have been passing through a deliciously mild and quiet Christmas-tide —one of only three or four who have not gone out of town. It has been soft and unsocial and leisurely, and this is my sixth day of letter-writing. I've been making up the arrears of six months. Forgive me therefore if the pen drops from my hand. Do write to me, dear Grace. Tell me about everything, and especially about William and his house. I have been hearing twice from Richard—poor unenjoying boy! But who *does* enjoy Berlin? Yours, my dear Grace always and altogether

Henry James

1. Francis Parkman, the historian. See letter to Parkman, 24 August 1884 .

To Mrs. Mahlon Sands

Ts Lubbock

34 De Vere Gardens W.
[1894]

Dear Mrs. Sands.

I meant to delay less to answer your two interesting notes; but even now that I *am* scrawling a few lines to you I feel that my *matter* so overflows my space and time, that abstention is almost the line most practicable. I want to give you a bushel of good advice, in short—advice about the supreme wisdom, in a situation like yours, of the policy of self-surrender to the artist—that of giving him his head and letting him utterly alone. Trust him completely and ask no questions. "So love me not at all or all in all."[1] From the moment one trusts him enough to ask for a portrait at all—trust him enough to leave him his ways, his variations, his mysteries and circumgyrations and idiosyncrasies. You can't keep step with him and you can't assist at the process. You can't collaborate or co-operate, except by sitting still and looking beautiful, in your own portrait. You are outside of it altogether and you will—you always *must*—consult the highest interest of the result by preserving this perfectly helpless and detached attitude!! Cultivate indifference, cultivate not looking at it nor thinking about it. Don't challenge him by the way and give him a tremendous margin. It's *his* affair—yours is only to be as difficult for him as possible; and the more difficult you are the more the artist (worthy of the name), will be condemned to worry over you, repainting, revolutionizing, till he, in a rage of ambition and admiration, arrives at the thing that satisfies him and that enshrines and perpetuates you. There are as good eyes on his palette as ever were caught and yours, on Sargent's canvas, will still be the mystification of posterity, just as they often are that of yours most didactically

Henry James

1. HJ seems to be thinking of "And trust me not at all or all in all" from Tennyson's "Merlin and Vivien" in *Idylls of the King.*

To Dr. W. W. Baldwin

Ms Morgan

34 De Vere Gardens W.
January 26*th* [1894]

My dear Baldwin.

I write you in much embarrassment and perplexity. Mrs. Benedict's cable was the first news I have had of poor Miss Woolson's being—having been—even ill,[1] and it was accompanied with the expression of the wish that I should go to Venice. In my horror and distress I began to make preparations to get off as soon as possible—but a second cable from her a few hours later, mentioning, or implying, that Miss [Grace] Carter had come, combined with your own two most kind telegrams—these things have made me delay and ask myself if what can be done is not being done so effectually by Miss C. and the American consul (whose immediate and adequate action I have taken for granted,) that, reaching there on Tuesday or Wednesday (the earliest moment I *can*,) I should probably find myself confronted with mere accomplished facts. Her (Miss Carter's) wiring you not to come even from Florence seems to me to suggest all this. But I wired her yesterday afternoon asking her to tell me if she *desired* me—and getting no answer, I have again repeated the inquiry. I know you are deadly busy, and infinitely worried, but if you can find time to tell me *something* of what has so strangely and sadly happened I shall be very very grateful. To me it is all ghastly amazement and distress. I hadn't even heard Miss Woolson was ill. Hadn't she sent for *you?* I have a dismal, dreadful image of her being alone and unfriended at the last. But what sudden disaster overtook her—pneumonia supervening on influenza? That her funeral is to be in Rome—where she would have wished—is in some degree a comfort. But poor isolated and fundamentally tragic being! She was intrinsically one of the saddest and least happy natures I have ever met; and when I ask myself what I *feel* about her death the only answer that comes to me is from what I felt about the melancholy, the limitations and the touching loneliness of her life. I was greatly attached to her and valued exceedingly her friendship. She had no dread of death and no aversion to it—rather a desire and even a passion for it; and infinite courage and a certain kind of fortitude. Eternal peace be her portion! *Can* you write to me—no matter how briefly? This won't reach you for two or three days—but even then if I can do any good by coming I will do so. I expect at any rate to come about April first—at least I fondly hope it. I have written to Miss Carter and told her what I tell you. I take it, however, the funeral can be delayed a very small number of days, and that I should now, with whatever speed it would be at all possible to make, miss it. Do tell me about it—it must have been difficult to arrange. Your last letter to me is still unacknowledged. You have my tenderest compassion in your hideous, your cruel loss of money. What burdens you carry and what blows you get! Very sad indeed, and very characteristic of a dreadful American type of life and character, your brother's dreadfully painful story. I can well believe how it has overdarkened you. But I hope it is all growing less bad. Meanwhile I rejoice that you have struck a vein of such terrible interest in your poor infinitely to be helped and pitied *contadini*.[2] The Sicilians have profoundly one's sympathy. Poor Italy—but how I want to see it! *Poveri noi!* Excuse my haste and incoherency. Yours, my dear Baldwin, evermore

Henry James

1. HJ at this moment had no details of the death of Miss Woolson in Venice on 24 January under circumstances that suggested suicide. Mrs. Clara Benedict, Fenimore's sister, first informed HJ of her death; and Grace Carter, a cousin, who happened to be in Munich, went to Italy to make the funeral arrangements.
2. Dr. Baldwin devoted much time to the health of the Tuscan peasants in the Abruzzi.

To Rhoda Broughton
Ms Chester

34 De Vere Gardens W.
Sunday [28 January 1894]

Dear Miss Rhoda.

I have been terribly overwhelmed by some shocking news, the death of my old and dear friend Miss Woolson in Venice—with deplorable attendant circumstances, and was this morning to have started for Rome to be present at her funeral. This proves to be impossible and I shall probably *not* go to Italy. But you will easily see how miserably upset I have been—(the whole event is unspeakably tragic); which is why I haven't written to you. Shall you be at

Mrs. Hudson's—whom I *have* met—till *Wednesday?* If so I will come in with pleasure at 5. I am afraid it is impossible tomorrow or Tuesday.

Yours always
Henry James

P.S. If you are leaving town again immediately I will come and see you—some afternoon soon—*not* Wednesday—at Richmond. In fact I should like that *better*—a walk and a talk with you (now the afternoons are longer), without others.

To John Hay
Ms Brown

34 De Vere Gardens W.
January 28*th* 1894

My dear Hay.

Your telegram, and Nevin's[1] share in it, last night, lifted a terrible weight off my spirit, and I can scarcely express to you the comfort I take in the knowledge that you are in Rome and that poor Miss Carter, with her burden of dreadful exertion and responsibility, has been able to look to your sympathy and cooperation. Up to five o'clock yesterday afternoon I expected to start this morning for Rome, arriving, if I should make my connections, at 6 on Tuesday morning—in order, simply, to stand, that day, by that most unhappy woman's grave. But coming in—from Cook's office—with my preparations made—I found on my table a note from Miss Fletcher[2] (of Venice—who is now in London), enclosing a cutting from a Venetian newspaper which gave me the first shocking knowledge of *what* it was that had happened. Before the horror and pity of it I have utterly collapsed—I have let everything go, and last night I wired to Miss Carter that my dismal journey was impossible to me.[3] I have, this morning, looked it more in the face, but I can't attempt it. I shall wire you tomorrow morning—one can do nothing here to-day; but meanwhile I must repeat to you that with the dreadful *image* before me I feel a real personal indebtedness to you in the assurance I have of your beneficent action and tenderness—in regard to offices that you will scarcely know how to make soothing and pitying enough. Will you very kindly express to Nevin my appreciation (as an old friend of his as well as of hers) of every consoling honour that he may pay? Miss Woolson was so valued and close a friend of mine and had been so for so many years that I feel an intense nearness of participation in every circumstance of her tragic end and in every detail of the sequel. But it is just this nearness of emotion that has made—since yesterday—the immediate horrified rush to personally *meet* these things impossible to me. I can't *think* of Venice for the present—nor of any other inevitable vain contacts in Rome (apart from the immense satisfaction of seeing you and your wife); from the moment there is nothing of value for me to *do*. She had always been, to my sense (and I think must have been to that of almost all her friends—those who were not too stupid), a woman so little formed for positive happiness that half one's affection for her was, in its essence, a kind of anxiety; but the worst sensibility to suffering or exposure to disaster that I ever apprehended for her was far enough from this brutal summarized tragedy. I have, as yet, no understanding of it or of its monstrous suddenness—and can only, till I know something, take refuge in a dim supposition of the ill (spoken in this hideous Venetian paragraph) that always haunted her—some misery of insomnia pushed to nervous momentary frenzy. But what a picture of lonely unassisted suffering! It is too horrible for thought! The only image I can evoke that interposes at all is that of the blest Roman cemetery that she positively *desired*—I mean in her extreme love of it—and of her intensely consenting and more than reconciled rest under the Roman sky. *Requiescat.* I shall wire you tomorrow asking you to kindly see that some flowers with my name attached are laid beside her there. Will there not be, for kindness' sake, and that of her so extremely honourable literary position, a few Americans (having known her or not) to stand with you there? I should be grateful to you if you would express to Miss Carter for me (though I have already done it myself and shall do it again) my sense of what all Miss Woolson's friends owe to her devotion in surmounting the added difficulties of burial in Rome.—I didn't know, my dear Hay, till last night, that you were in Rome, or at all where you were; beyond the general supposition that you were still in Europe. When you were in London last summer I was abroad, and I have had no chance—until this so somber one—to find myself in relation with you since. But there was an occasion—almost equally somber—a couple of months ago when only the constant over-pressure that one's life seems never to cease to bring with it prevented me from writing to you. Indeed the intention to write has remained all the while at the back of my head. Miss Woolson, in a letter from Venice, briefly mentioned to me the startling fact of Clarence King's mental illness—without any details.[4] I was infinitely shocked; you were the first person I thought of and I had the most cordial impulse to write to you. But I didn't know in the least where you were; other occupations and pre-occupations overbore it, and I daresay you were conscious of my silence. But please believe that there was a sympathy for you in it. The fact itself is tragic enough—but I don't know what the real truth may be—for better or worse. What a history—what a denouement! Won't you, my dear Hay, write to me now—(with something of yourselves too, and of your movements and whereabouts these next weeks and months?) You have my heartiest wish for your own exemption from ills. It has been a real balm to talk with you this morning, and I am yours more than ever

Henry James

1. John Hay, an old friend of Miss Woolson's (later to be named American ambassador to London), was in Rome and helped with the funeral arrangements. Robert Jenkins Nevin was for many years rector of St. Paul's American Church in Rome.

2. Constance Fletcher (1858–1938), who wrote under the name of George Fleming, was an old friend of HJ's and a long-time resident of Venice. Among her popular works was *Kismet.*

3. Miss Woolson's death was reported as a suicide by newspapers in Venice, London, and New York. Her family claimed that she had fallen from a small window into the little Venetian street behind the palace in which she had her apartment. HJ seems from the first to have accepted the idea of suicide. Miss Woolson was buried 31 January in the non-Catholic (commonly called the Protestant) cemetery in Rome near the graves of Keats and Shelley, and next to the graves of Richard Henry Dana, Jr., and George P. Marsh. Hay wrote to Henry Adams: "We buried poor C.W. last Wednesday . . . laying her down in her first and last resting place—a thoroughly good, and most unhappy woman, with a great talent, bedeviled by disordered nerves. She did much good, and no harm in her life, and had not as much happiness as a convict." William Roscoe Thayer, *The Life of John Hay* (1915), II, 107.

4. Clarence King (1842–1901), first head of the U.S. Geological Survey and a close friend of John Hay and Henry Adams. See *Letters* II, 387–389.

To Rhoda Broughton
Ms Chester

34 De Vere Gardens W.
January 29*th* [1894]

Dear Miss Rhoda.

Many, many thanks for your letter.

Frankly speaking, *instead* of coming to you on Wednesday afternoon I would rather see you at Richmond, in your own house. I should like much to talk to you; and if the day is good we will take a stroll in the park. I will propose to you, soon, something for next week; and will come early.

The tragedy of Miss Woolson's death remains—till I have more light (I have none as yet), terribly obscure—as obscure as it is shocking. It is explicable only on the hypothesis of some sudden explosion of latent brain-disease. But it is unspeakably sad and pitiful. I remember well our lovely May night at Bellosguardo.

Yours always
Henry James

To Francis Boott
Ms Harvard

34 De Vere Gardens W.
Jan. 31*st* [1894]

My dear Francis.

I had a letter from you a fortnight ago which about this time I should be answering—thanking you for. It is not for that I write you now, however, but because I feel how, like myself, you must be sitting horror stricken at the last tragic act of poor C.F.W. I can't *explain* it to you—it is with my present knowledge, too dreadfully obscure—and I am tired with the writing and telegraphing to which I have had to give myself up in consequence—especially with the exhaustion of a second long letter to poor Mrs. Benedict (258 Fourth Avenue, New York). Besides, I am still too sickened with the news—too haunted with the image of the act—and too much, generally, in darkness. For three days I only knew (by a cable from Mrs. Benedict) that she was dead—and I was almost in the very act of starting for Rome—to be present at her funeral (she is buried *there* today—Mrs. B. had asked me to go to Venice, and I hadn't been able to get off), when the evening papers here told the rest of the dreadful story. (She had had influenza and I simply supposed at first that it had quickly taken some fatal form.) The event seems to me absolutely to demand the hypothesis of sudden *dementia* and to admit of none other. Pitiful victim of chronic melancholy as she was (so that half one's friendship for her was always anxiety), nothing is more possible than that, in illness, this obsession should abruptly have deepened into suicidal mania. There was nothing *whatever*, that I know of, in her immediate circumstances, to explain it—save indeed the sadness of her lonely Venetian winter. *After* such a dire event, it is true, one sees symptoms, indications in the past; and some of these portents seem to me now not to be wanting. But it's all unspeakably wretched and obscure. She was not, she was never, wholly sane—I mean her liability to suffering was like the *doom* of mental disease. On the other hand she was the gentlest and kindest of women—and to me an admirable friend. She wished to be buried in Rome. Her cousin Miss Carter came instantly from Munich and did everything. I will write you more of it all when I know more. You will be immensely touched and compassionate. What a world!—and life what a "treat"! Yours, dear Francis, always

Henry James

To Dr. W. W. Baldwin

Ms Morgan

34 De Vere Gardens W.
Feb. 2*d* 1894

My dear Baldwin.

I am most grateful for your two letters—they are the only written words, or rays of faint knowledge, that I have received during these horror-haunted days. Miss Carter will doubtless have written to me (I have entreated her to), but probably not till after the ceremony of Wednesday. I grieve more than I can say to hear you have been *ill* in the shock of all this tragedy—and you have my closest sympathy. Have courage and have patience—they see everything through. Meanwhile, for myself, though completely without *information* (from Venice) I can't help seeing and reading that unspeakable event in the light of some of my general impressions and anxieties. I don't know how much your own (after all tolerably close) knowledge and observation will confirm what I say—but I had two or three years ago very gloomily and dolorously made up my mind that she was not positively and wholly *sane*. My reasons are too many and too private to give you here; but when I see you we will talk about them. To my own vision the horror of last week throws an ineffably sad but very distinct light far away back on symptoms and idiosyncrasies. She was exquisitely morbid and tragically sensitive; in other words she was the victim of chronic melancholia and of the tendency to suffer and to *insist* on suffering, more than [any] human being I have met. A beneficent providence seemed to have constructed her—pitilessly—for the express purpose of suffering, with an ingenuity worthy of a better cause. Half of my friendship for her was a deep solicitude, a deep compassion, a vigilant precaution, so far as was possible, about all this. The world didn't see it—she didn't show it socially—but I think you will agree with me that it was impossible to know her well without being conscious of it. I at any rate knew her well enough to be painfully so—though the event has far surpassed my worst apprehensions of tragedy. If it had not been, however, for certain scattered and definite symptoms to the contrary (suggestions of a bad, a very morbid phase), I should have thought that the *general* tendency of her circumstances was to make for an easier, a brighter prospect.—*Basta*. I can't write more about the dark business—we must keep it till we meet; and the haunting obsession of the fact, the act, is a thing to try with all one's might to get rid of.—A letter from Miss Carter just comes in. It tells me, I take it, just what she told you. Miss Woolson's evident determination not to send for you seems to me insane—just as her silence to me does: in spite of letters which in a *normal* state she would infallibly have answered. She kept us both ignorant—with a perversity that was diseased. But infinite pity is the only word one can have for her and the joy that, horrible as was the gate through which she passed, she is eternally and inaccessibly at rest. Go on my dear Baldwin, with your numberless good works and in as few weeks as possible I will come stand beside you. Yours evermore

Henry James

To Katherine De Kay Bronson
Ms Private

34 De Vere Gardens W.
February 2*d* 1894

Dear Katrina Bronson.

I have thought of you often ever since the horror of last week—and in writing to Edith [Bronson], which I have repeatedly done, have felt almost as if the words reached *you* as well. I came within an ace of seeing you, for I was twice on the very verge of rushing off to Italy. My first knowledge of Miss Woolson's death was by a cable from her sister in New York telling me only that fact and *asking* me to go. I made instant preparation, but a few hours later heard, afresh—from New York—that Miss Carter was already on the spot—and then, before night, both from Miss Carter herself and from Baldwin, dissuasively in regard to coming. Later, I prepared to start for Rome—to her funeral—but at the very moment heard, for the first time, of the unimagined and terrible manner of her death—which sickened and overwhelmed me so, on the spot, that I had no heart for the breathless, sleepless rush that I had before me to reach Rome in time. So I have been kept away from you—and I can't, while the freshness of such a misery as it all must have been is in the air, feel anything but that Venice is not a place I want *immediately* to see. I had known Miss Woolson for many years and was extremely attached to her—she was the gentlest and tenderest of women, and full of intelligence and sympathy. But she was a victim to morbid melancholia, and one's friendship for her was always half anxiety. The worst mine had ever made me fear, however, was far enough from the event of which you must still be feeling the inexpressible shock. It was an act, I am convinced, of definite, irresponsible, delirious insanity, determined by illness, fever as to its form, but springing, indirectly, out [of] a general depression which, though not visible to people who saw her socially, casually, had essentially detached her from the wish to live. But it is all too pitiful and too miserable to dwell on—too tragic and too obscure. You were so close to it that it must have filled all the air of your life for several days—and this publicity of misery, this outward horror and *chiasso* round her death, was the thing in the world most alien to her and most inconceivable of her—and therefore, to my mind, most conclusive as to her having undergone

Constance Fenimore Woolson, from a photograph taken in Venice

Henry James at the time of *Guy Domville*

some violent cerebral derangement. Nothing could be more incongruous with the general patience, reserve and dainty dignity, as it were, of her life. Save her deafness, she had absolutely no definite or unusual thing (that I know of) to minister to her habitual depression; she was free, independent, successful—very successful indeed as a writer—and *liked*, peculiarly, by people who knew her. She had near relations who adored her and who were in a position to do much for her—especially as she was fond of them. But it was all reduced to ashes by the fact that a beneficent providence had elaborately constructed her to suffer. I can't be sufficiently grateful that Edith had the blessed inspiration of placing with her that competent and excellent Miss Holas. I have just had, from Rome, a long letter from Miss Carter—for whose nearness and prompt arrival I am also devoutly thankful. What she tells me is very interesting and touching, but it doesn't penetrate the strange obscurity of so much of the matter. But that has indeed the im . . .[1] distant date. Believe me meanwhile always affectionately yours

Henry James

1. A page is missing in the holograph.

To Katherine De Kay Bronson

Ms Private

Grand Hôtel de Gênes: Genoa
Tuesday [20 March 1894]

My dear Katrina B.

Will you render an old friend a very gentle service—such a service as may accelerate the hour at which he shall find himself at your feet? A combination of circumstances, some of which I would have wished other, but which I must accept (I am speaking of course quite apart from the question of *inclination*, and intense desire to see you),[1] make it absolutely necessary I should be in Venice from the 1st April. This being the case, as I have work in hand, I must get into some quiet and comfortable material conditions—and I peculiarly detest the Venetian hotels: loathe in fact to be in an hotel, in Venice, even for a day. It occurs to me that the apartment occupied by Miss Woolson last summer before she went to Casa Semitecolo and which I believe she found very comfortable, may be free and obtainable—or if not the other set of rooms in the same house. But I have forgotten the address and don't know the woman's name. I only seem to remember vaguely that the house was *Casa Biondetti* and that it's quite near where Paul Tilton used to live. The Hohenlohes, or some such people, had occupied the rooms before Miss Woolson. You will probably easily identify the place, and what I service to ask of your great kindness is to go and see if one of the apartments *is* free. If so I think I should like to take it from Sunday or Monday next—for a month, with liberty to renew; that is if the woman will give it to me on the same terms on which she gave it to Miss Woolson and will *cook* for me as she did for her. (I have ceased, in my old age, to be able to prowl about for my food.) I don't at all know what Miss W. paid—but I remember her mentioning in a letter that the *padrona* "did" for her very well. Should you be able to cause this inquiry to be made the day you receive this—and should you then be able to address me here a few lines of information? If dear Edith had got back I would appeal directly to *her* kindness in the matter —and her more violent activity. But I shall thank you with all my heart. It is delicious to me to think I shall see you, dear Katrina B., so very soon. I arrived here but a couple of days ago and shall be here till I go to Venice; where I trust I shall find you in all respects at your ease—or as much so as we worried mortals ever can be. I suppose Edith is well on her way home by this. I saw less of her in London than I desired, but I shall make it up in Casa Alvisi. I shall make *everything* up in Casa Alvisi. Casa Curtis, I suppose, is empty for another two or three weeks?—If Casa Biondetti (if that be its name) is all occupied, I will come on, at the same date, and simply go to the Britannia till I can find something—unless by chance you beneficently know and are able graciously to suggest, something *like* the place I speak of—and as good. A word from you at any rate will rejoice my heart and add wings to my approach. This place is charming and the sense of recovered Italy inexpressibly dear to me. There is nothing like it. *Stià bene—sempre bene.* I can't tell you how happy I am to be able to try to say to you "à bientôt!" Yours, my dear old friend, very tenderly

Henry James

P.S. If by a miracle *both* the apartments should be free I should like, I think, the *better* one—if there is a difference, even if it be not the one Miss Woolson had.

1. This parenthesis was inserted in the letter as an afterthought.

To William James
Ms Harvard

Hôtel de Gênes: Genoa
March 24*th* [1894]

My dear William.

Your good letter of the end of February reached me some days before I left London; but I kept putting off my acknowledgment of it from the eve to the morrow of my intended departure. There was much to do and to finish before I left home—and I knew that on the blessed soil of Italy I should immediately have a greater sense of margin. It has come, that happy sense, with my first real stop. (Quitting London nearly a week ago I spent two days in Paris and one in Turin.) It is as delicious as ever to find one's self again in a climate and to meet the Ligurian spring. I sit here with the sun pouring in through my open window and the friendly clatter and chatter of the market-place making the light a part of the sound. I have come abroad for three or four months—for as long as London is not quiet again. I started rather earlier than I originally meant—by reason, mainly, of a sort of smothered attack of influenza, which left me seedy and sore, interminably coughing and lumbago-ing—till I began to yearn for balmier air. So I pulled myself together and fled—and I find the balmier air in perfection and an instant restoration in it. I am glad I like Italy as well as I do—it is a great convenience. If I didn't I don't know what I should like enough instead. Another consideration that made me start sooner is the arrival here on the 29th, from New York, of poor Mrs. Benedict and her daughter, Miss Woolson's sister and niece. I had from her a month ago a letter telling me of her intended sailing for Genoa, and breathing such helpless misery and implied appeal, that I instantly wrote to her I would meet her here on her landing. She comes, apparently, to stand, primarily, by her sister's grave in Rome—and then, if she can face it, to go to Venice, where the house Miss W. had taken, the servants, and all the possessions and affairs, tolerably numerous and accumulated, have to be responsibly discharged and wound up. I have told her I will go there, later, and help her in every way I can (she speaks no word of Italian), and there will be inevitably a very painful side to it—though probably simple enough and rapid, as her means etc. are large. But it won't be altogether a gloom—strange as it may sound to say so; so joyously, almost, does one assent to the liberation from life of a person for whom life primarily meant almost unqualified suffering. Your impression of Miss Woolson's "gaiety" was natural and inevitable enough—as it was, in general, for everyone who knew her but little. But it was a purely superficial and social, and purely exterior manifestation. She was, in general, so shut up to solitude by her extreme deafness and her absence of pleasure in ordinary intercourse, that all contacts, meetings, conversations, new people etc. were *special,* isolated occasions, for her, constituting momentary liberations, reactions and excitements. This combined with her admirable constitution—her tragically conscientious *politeness*—to give her, for the hour, the air of a cheerfulness which was really intensely mechanical and which left her whole general feeling about life, her intimate melancholy, utterly unexpressed—any more than the flowerpots in the window of a room express the figure lying on the bed. My own belief is (I say this of course in intense confidence) that she had been on the very verge of suicide years ago and that it had only been stood off by the practical interposition of two or three friendships and affections, which operated (to their own sense) with a constant vague anxiety. All *intelligent* interest in her was an *inevitable* anxiety.[1] Of course the manner of her death (with a violence, publicity, etc. utterly foreign to her) was determined by the irresponsible delirium of fever; but this delirium worked upon a predisposition unmistakeable—a predisposition which sprang in its turn from a constitutional, an essentially, tragic and latently insane *difficulty in living*—; an element rendered unspeakably touching by her extraordinary consideration for others—those to whom she was attached; a dire multiplication only of her own difficulty—and an ingenious, elaborate, passionate effort to minimise theirs. To me she had the spirit of beneficence and friendship in their most disinterested form; which is why I inflict on you this long digression on a person whom you after all scarcely at all knew. The few words in your letter called it forth. Will you read or show the foregoing remarks, by the way, to Boott—telling him I asked you to? I have a letter from him which I shall presently answer—but to a phrase or two of his own (about her joy in life!!—he mistook for it her joy in *him!*)—they constitute a provisional answer. He *amused* her so delightfully and attachingly that she put for him *all* the flowerpots in the window. But very few people amused her—which was all the greater service he rendered her. Please give my love to him if you have a chance and tell him I shall write him an Italian letter.—It is such a blessing to be in a place (after London—for so many months) in which one knows no one, that I shall probably be here for some days—till indeed I go to Venice; having plenty of work in hand. The Curtises, just back from India, beseech me to stay with them there—but I am hanging fire: even the kindest hospitality interferes so with the freedom of one's occupations. Baldwin, from Florence, puts forth the same insistence—he has a *pianterreno* which he has arranged on purpose for me—and his wife writes me in the same terms. It is all rather difficult—but there are obviously worse troubles. It gives me great joy that you speak on the whole well of yourself, your endurance, your work, your exchequer and your *cuisine.* My heart goes out to Alice on it as well as to yourself. May all continue practicable with you till summer and alleviations (if such they be) come. Your allusion to a possible union between C.E.N. and T.S.[2] fills me with horror—that *she* should be supposed capable of putting herself in such an intolerable relation to his daughters. Let us hope she will sacrifice the bliss—and go on as she is. I saw lately in London Arthur S.,[3] whom I hadn't seen for an eternity—and whose big-barrelled unloadedness made me wonder at one's having, in the dim past, thought him promising—if one did. Also I tried to pass (to myself) for talking with Lawrence Godkin, Edward Hooper and Sturgis Bigelow. The latter is interestingly shy—but is he interestingly anything else? I embrace you individually and collectively. My time with Alexander draws so much nearer as that the last nights of *Mrs. Tanqueray* approach—sooner than I supposed, and the probabilities are all in favour of the interposing and idiotic Jones being a failure—in which case my hour will sound. But even if a very moderate success, Jones *must* be worked till the end of the season; and it leaves me at best over till the autumn—which is what the whole thing is reducible to. Indeed I should be very sorry to be called back from Italy this summer, to dingy rehearsals. Ever, dear William, yours

Henry

1. This sentence was inserted as an afterthought, and the word "intelligent" inserted after that.

2. Apparently an allusion to gossip that Charles Eliot Norton might marry Theodora Sedgwick (*Letters* II, 150, 158), the younger sister of his dead wife. Miss Sedgwick remained a spinster, and Norton never remarried.

3. Arthur Sedgwick. See *Letters* II, 56–57.

To Grace Norton
Ms Harvard

Hôtel de Gênes, Genoa
March 29*th* 1894

My dear Grace.

I sit here waiting for the steamer from New York which is to bring out some friends whom I have promised to meet (it threatens indeed, by what I can learn, to be laden with half one's American circle); and while I do so I can invent no better pastime than to read over your last generous letter. As usual in such cases I studiously conceal from you—hoping you will have forgotten it—the remote date at which you wrote. I have just been writing to Bourget moreover (whose last communication to me was from Thomasville, Georgia!) and the association of ideas is irresistible. I thank you tenderly, dear Grace, for your "action in the matter" of my letter of introduction—that is for your lavish and *soignée* hospitality and still more for your charming and interesting account of it. Oh yes, you told me as much—and much more—than I could possibly have explained to you that I desired to know. In fact you explained to me myself *what* I wanted to know—and just why I wanted to know it. Somehow the occasion represents to me, myself, a great missing of opportunity—of new lights and new reliefs; but I have by this time sufficiently tamed my chagrin to be affectionately grateful. I knock at my forehead in vain for some divination of what Bourget's book will be—the only thing that comes out to me is the conviction that there'll be a page about that dinner. I left London ten days ago, and am on my way to Venice, where I hope to spend some weeks—keeping at any rate away from home during April, May and June. Italy is almost as convenient as she is beautiful, and I don't know what I should do without her. She has wholly ceased to be exciting to me—which is a part of the convenience; for I always come nowadays with work in hand and looking for passive and plastic conditions. Familiarity has toned down everything but the loveableness—and Venice has come to seem to me (granting that one keeps at bay the social and tourist side) the perfection of a place to write in. I have been in this brave coloured, sonorous Genoa a week—and a long stretch of preliminary London has made it exactly the right thing. I have two or three good friends along the divine coast (beyond Nervi), and one of them particular, the delightful Lady Brooke, Ranee of Sarawak, I go out in the afternoon to drive and dine with. The whole shore is a paradise of liberal beauty.—

Rome, June 4th. Instead of destroying the foregoing wretched scrap I accept the omen that fate, or chance, has kept it safe in my portfolio these absurdly many weeks. I take it up and go on with it without stopping to puzzle out the knotty question of whether you will [be] less outraged at perceiving that I did begin a letter to you at a date considerably distant—or more outraged at perceiving that I didn't finish it. My general sense that you are blessedly safe and kind and tender and wise floats me serenely over all problems of the sort. I have been these two months in Venice and I can't begin to tell you all the successful conspiracies that worked together from hour to hour to prevent my resuming my talk with you. At last, you see, I have had to come away to do it. I have been in Rome these eight days, after an absence of many years. Delightfully empty and still, at this moment, and by good fortune delightfully cool, it pleases me almost as much, and speaks to me almost as much with its old *most-loved* voice, as if the thousand vulgarities perpetrated during the last fifteen years had never been. There are a few "people"—the curse of Italy now (and nine-tenths American, so that the voice and tone of our compatriots and all their allusions and "atmosphere," are practically an ingredient, and an incorrigible one, in all the *most* Italian impressions one has peregrinated to revel in!) but they have pressed lightly, permitting me to cull *this* precious hour! I lunched however, yesterday, with a certain youngish Count Primoli[1] (an old acquaintance—and an offshoot of the Bonapartes, whom he resembles), where I learned from the astonishing Matilde Serao,[2] whom I sat next to, that Paul Bourget has just got his exaltation to the Academy—got it, so well everything succeeds with him, just in time to be so much wind in the sails (and in the sale—excuse my vulgarity!) of his so-soon-to-appear American book. I mention this as we talked together a little of him at Genoa two months ago!—Did you ever hear of the Serao—the she-Zola of Italy?—or read any of her really "talented" fictions? She is a wonderful little burly Balzac in petticoats—full of Neapolitan life and sound and familiarity. There were other strange Roman types, male and female, in a picturesque old palace in Via Tor di Nona—overhanging all the ruinations of the modern bedevilment (embankments etc.—all unfinished and half-relinquished) of the Tiber—which have made it too unsightly even to approach. I smile as I read over a passage in the first page or two of this in which I stated that Venice is a sweet place to work! It is so little so that I honestly think I shall never go there again. That won't sound to you a fearful or a difficult threat, however; and I must ask you to forgive my talking so much as one pursued—Apollo fleeing from the furies. I think you will easily do so when you remember your little history at Hampton Court—how it *bristled* with the impossibility of quiet. Very well, it's the little history everywhere. *C'est le mal moderne*—and every year augments it. But when I go back to England I shall discover a burrow somewhere,—a nameless rock of ocean that figures in no chart; or else give up everything that I still want to do with the rest of my life. When I return to Venice I shall go to Asolo with Mrs. Bronson! and when I go to Florence a week hence I shall stay (five days) with a dear inevitable friend there! I go to Naples tomorrow, for four days, to stay, thank heaven, with no one; no one but the delightful human old bronzes of the museum, which I haven't seen for years. I hear from Lily that she and Miss Felton are "due" in Venice!—and I shall try and get some solitude *with* her. (I mean of course with Lily.)—

I had again to break off my letter, but only for a few hours. My aforesaid friend Primoli came to take me and drive to the Villa Pamfili, which we had all to ourselves and which, in this splendour of summer, is of a beauty quite divine. The views of the Campagna, and the way the whole place hangs over and commands St. Peter's, as it were, make it a "fairy scene." I go back to England by August 1st, and shall try and spend July on some mountain. I haven't your last letter here—I left it in Venice; and feel as if there must be things in it to "answer." If there are, they are, for you, probably too old. I hope your summer will be a thing of peace. I somehow think of you happily in July, August and September in your bowery house in the deep quietness of Cambridge. I saw Arthur Sedgwick in England—for the [first] time for years and years—and am reminded of him by the sense that some old elements of neighbourly sadness are now absent from you. But I believe you miss them! Write me about William and his house only what cheers—if there *is* anything. Everything else breaks my heart! Yours, my dear Grace, evermore

Henry James

1. Count Joseph-Napoléon Primoli (1851–1927), son of Pietro Primoli and Charlotte Bonaparte. Charlotte was the daughter of Charles-Lucien, who had been Prince of Canino, and of his consort Zenaïda, daughter of Joseph Bonaparte. An intimate of the Princess Matilde, Count Primoli was Franco-Italian in his literary associations. See Marcello Spaziani, *Pages Inédites de Joseph-Napoléon Primoli* (1959).

2. Matilda Serao (1856–1927), Neapolitan novelist, regarded as one of the best of the southern Italian realists. HJ published a long essay on her in the *North American Review*, CLXXII (March 1901), 367–380, reprinted in *Notes on Novelists* (1914).

To Dr. W. W. Baldwin

Ms Morgan

Casa Biondetti
San Vio, 715. Venice
Tuesday [17 April 1894]

My dear Baldwin.

I am overwhelmed by the hospitality of your ever-kind attitude. It finds me, I grieve to say, considerably distracted with this terrible people-question which ravages one's existence, when one comes abroad—to these lovely centres of gravitation—flying, in desperation, from other forms of the same scourge in London. It leaves me scarcely time to write you these words. My present situation is, at any rate, that I can't leave Venice while the poor clinging helpless Benedicts are here. I find myself of great use and comfort to them—they arrived here utterly prostrated and seemed to have been fearfully knocked up by their interview with you in Florence. They are taking their duties here (to all Miss Woolson's accumulated and complicated *effects*) in a very serious manner, which will carry them on two or three weeks longer. Then they will go: *about,* I think, the fifth May. They have no one here to look to but me—and to remain near them is an act of common humanity—though not of exhilarating enjoyment. Next month, my dear Baldwin, I will come with great pleasure and spend a few days with you. Meanwhile I shall also try to get on with some pressing work. Venice is full, the hotels overflow, and I meet every hour (that I am out) somebody I know or who knows me. Today at last, the long-delayed rain has come. Your account—your good and bright account—of your own actual relative peace and plenty delights me. I rejoice in every word of it—and am impatient to come and behold it. Yes indeed, I will go to the Seaside with you for a Sunday and grub and wade with Mrs. Baldwin and the bambini if they are still there. That you are personally better makes *me* feel so. Keep at it. Evermore yours, my dear Baldwin

Henry James

To Mr. and Mrs. William James

Ms Harvard

Ravenna, May 25*th* [1894]

Dearest brother and sister.

This letter is but a stopgap till I can (in two or three days) write you both properly. A fine letter from each of you since last I wrote makes me feel how strangely long my silence will have seemed to you—especially in face of my receipt of Alice's magnificent diary.[1] It has been caused by insurmountable hindrances—mainly a pressure of work in Venice to make up for the dreadful interruptions and adversities in general of that place and in particular for the great hole bored in my time and my nerves by the copious aid and comfort I couldn't help giving to poor Mrs. Benedict—Miss Woolson's sister, who, staying there five weeks, made daily demands of me to help her in the winding-up of Miss W.'s so complicated affairs, all left, so far as Venice was concerned, at sixes and sevens. This proved a most devouring, an almost fatal job, and as at the same time I had just promised a splendid work of art, in London, for the second number of the *Yellow Book*[2] I had to *fight* for every hour to finish it by the promised date. Three quarters of an hour ago I posted, in this place, the last of the covenanted 25,000 words to London, and though I am exhausted with the effort and the heavy heat I scrawl you these feverish lines to keep you in patience —till I can get a quieter hour. I leave in an hour for five days in Rome and seven in Florence (with Baldwin); after which I return to Venice till July 1st. Another reason I didn't instantly *sfogare* to you on the subject of Alice's wonderful Diary was that in addition to my immense *impressedness* by it, and during the first days superseding even that, I was terribly scared and disconcerted—I mean alarmed—by the sight of so many private names and allusions in print. I am still terrified by this—as I partly feel responsible as it were—being myself the source of so many of the things told, commented on etc. This kept me from being, at first, able to express anything but my anxiety—and my regret that K. P. Loring hadn't sunk a few names, put initials—I mean in view of the danger of accidents, some catastrophe of publicity. The book is rare—wondrous; and I will express *everything* from Rome—including all my sympathy with your melancholy illness—which I now feel that I must have looked "heartless" not to have poured forth about. But my horrid predicament in Venice made me simply ferocious till my promise—in London—should be redeemed. God send you have been long ere this wholly well. I really wept for you. *À bientôt.* Ever your

Henry

1. Katharine P. Loring, who had the manuscript of the diary kept by Alice James during the last three years of her life, printed four copies intended for herself and Alice's three brothers. The title page reads: "The Diary of Alice James. Four Copies Printed. Cambridge: John Wilson and Son. University Press. 1894." William's copy is in the Houghton Library at Harvard; Miss Loring's copy is in the Barrett Collection, University of Virginia, and Robertson's copy is in the Bancroft Library at Berkeley. It has been assumed that HJ destroyed his copy. Miss Loring left the manuscript to the family of Robertson James. A truncated version, edited by Anna R. Burr, was published in 1934. The entire diary, edited by Leon Edel, was published in 1964.

2. "The Coxon Fund," HJ's story about a Coleridge character, appeared in the *Yellow Book*, II (July 1894), 290–360.

To Mr. and Mrs. William James

Ms Harvard

Grand Hotel, Rome
May 28*th* 1894

My dear William—my dear Alice—I wrote you a scrappy note from Ravenna a few days since—but I must follow it up, without delay, with something better. I came on here an hour afterwards, and shall remain till June 1st or 2d. I find Rome deliciously cool and empty and still very pleasing in spite of the "ruining" which has been going on so long and of which one has heard so much—i.e., the redemption and cocknefication of the ruins. It is "changed" immensely—as everyone says; but I find myself, I am afraid, so much *more* changed—since I first knew and rhapsodised over it, that I am bound in justice to hold Rome the less criminal of the two. I am thinking a little about going down—if the coolness lasts—for three or four days to Naples; but I haven't decided. I feel rather hard and heartless to be prattling about these touristries to you, with the sad picture I have had these last weeks of your—William's—state of suffering. But it is only a way of saying that that state makes me feel it to be the greater duty for me to be as well as I can. *Absit omen!* Your so interesting letter of the 6th, dictated to Alice, speaks of the possibility of your abscess continuing not to heal—but I trust the event has long ere this reassured, comforted and liberated you. Meanwhile may Alice have smoothed your pillow as even she has never smoothed it before. I turn quite sick when I hear from you that on top of this tribulation you have had to undergo another of Bob's fits of madness. This time it seems to me really a little too strong—too strong and too cruel—and I don't know what to say or to do to help you. Is the state produced in him by a difficulty in re-investing his capital? What else had he before him, for months, but this question of the *suites* of his withdrawal? Alas, alas, I bleed. Apropos of these things I have just received from Warner (from London) the legal paper to have executed in regard to my participation in the Wyckoff[1] compromise—he asking me to do this before a U.S. consul. But the paper is all drawn explicitly up to be put through before the consul in *London*—so that I am afraid I must wait till I get back there to have the thing done. Warner's note makes no allusion to this point—from which I judge he takes for granted I will do it simply on my return. I will go to see the consul here or in Florence and ask him if *he* can be substituted for the London one; but I am afraid he will say no—so that, as I have been desiring not to get back to De Vere Gardens before August 1st, I fear I may entail on you and Bob the wait of these intervening weeks—unless I go home sooner. Such delay as I may inflict upon you (making you *tarder* to come into your share of the $3000), I beg you both to forgive me. You speak of the question of the sending of the fourth copy of Alice's Diary to Bob (in his present profane state), as if it were a matter still under discussion—whereas I have been assuming that action was taken by Katharine in the sense in which I immediately wrote you that I had written her (in the 1st days of April), on hearing from you that the book had *not* been sent, and on hearing from Katharine that you judged it ought to be. I had instantly judged likewise, and as Katharine had written to me that she was only waiting for my voice in the matter, I immediately expressed to her that I begged her without delay to transmit the copy to Bob. This seemed to me the only safe, and normal course, the only one putting us *à l'abri* from some violent resentment on his part. But it shows what "safety" is in dealing with a madman—that *now* the danger, the resentment, may be in his *having* it. At any rate is not his having it a *fait accompli?* I don't know for sure—for I haven't heard from Katharine since then. When I wrote to her (to send the book), I hadn't yet received my copy—delayed in London; and it only came a few days later—on which I wrote her again a letter which (discreet—on the subject of her editing—as it was) she may not have liked—perhaps; though this idea may be groundless on my part. At any rate I haven't as yet heard from her again—and am therefore in the dark as to Bob's possession or non-possession. As soon as I had *seen* the Diary the question began greatly to worry me—though I still hold that—given the fact that it *exists,* in the (to me!) regrettable form it does—the only thing that didn't put us (practically) too much in the wrong was to make him an equal inheritor of it with us. In other words—as I mentioned to you in my note from Ravenna—the printedness-*en-toutes-lettres* of so many names, personalities, hearsays (usually, on Alice's part, through *me!*) about people etc. has, through making me intensely nervous and almost sick with terror about possible publicity, possible accidents, reverberation etc., poisoned as yet a good deal of my *enjoyment* of the wonderful character of the thing—though it has not in the least dimmed my perception of that character. This has been above all really why (in addition to a peculiar pressure of occupation) I haven't written to you sooner on the subject. I was too depressed to face it! The other day, in Venice, Miss Wormeley,[2] who is with the Curtises, said to me, as if she knew all about it, "I hear your sister's *letters* have just been published, and are so delightful": which made me almost jump out of my skin. It will probably seem to you that I exaggerate; in fact I am sure it will, as neither of your letters makes any allusion to this disturbing feature—which to me was almost all (as it were) that I could *first* see. At any rate what I am *now* full of, as regards Bob's possession of the book, is the possible angry, irresponsible *communication* of it in his hands—or the equally irresponsible well-meaning but very dreadful-to-me-to-think-of adventures it may have in those of the two Marys.[3] I seem to see them showing it about Concord—and talking about it —with the fearful American newspaper lying in wait for every whisper, every echo. I take this side of the matter hard, as you see—but I bow my head to fate, and am prepared for the worst. *All* my sense of danger would have been averted if Katharine had only had a little more—had in about *twenty places* put blanks or initials for names. When I see that *I* say that Augustine Birrell[4] has a self-satisfied smirk after he speaks—and see that Katharine felt no prompting to exercise a discretion about the name—I feel very unhappy, and wonder at the strangeness of destiny. I used to say everything to Alice (on system) that could *égayer* her bedside and many things in utter confidence. I didn't dream she wrote them down—but this wouldn't have mattered—the idea of her doing so would only have interested me. It is the printing of these privacies *telles quelles* that distresses me, when a very few merely superficial discriminations (leaving her *text*, sacredly, really untouched) would have made all the difference! It is a "surprise" that is too much of a surprise, though meant so well. My observations about Birrell ("coloured" a little too to divert Alice!) were for instance made at a dining-club of which we both are members and about which I gossiped to the sister—on my principle of always bringing in the world to her and telling her in her sick solitude everything I could scrape together. As regards the life, the power, the temper, the humour and beauty and expressiveness of the Diary in itself—these things were partly "discounted" to me in advance by so much of Alice's talk during her last years—and my constant association with her—which led me often to reflect about her extraordinary force of mind and character, her whole way of taking life—and death—in very much the manner in which the book does. I find in its pages, for instance, many things I heard her say. None the less I have been immensely impressed with the thing as a revelation of a moral and personal picture. It is heroic in its individuality, its independence—its face-to-face with the universe for-and-by herself—and the beauty and eloquence with which she often expresses this, let alone the rich irony and humour, constitute (I wholly agree with you) a new claim for the family renown. This last element—her style, her power to write—are indeed to me a delight—for I never had many letters from her. Also it brings back to me all sorts of things I am glad to keep—I mean things that happened, hours, occasions, conversations—brings them back with a strange, living richness. But it also puts before me what I was tremendously conscious of in her lifetime—that the extraordinary intensity of her will and personality really would have made the equal, the reciprocal life of a "well" person—in the usual world—almost impossible to her—so that her disastrous, her tragic health was in a manner the only solution for her of the practical problem of life—as it suppressed the element of equality, reciprocity, etc. The violence of her reaction against her British *ambiente,* against everything English, engenders some of her most admirable and delightful passages—but I feel in reading them, as I always felt in talking with her, that inevitably she simplified too much, shut up in her sick room, exercised her wondrous vigour of judgment on too small a scrap of what really surrounded her. It would have been modified in many ways if she had *lived* with them (the English) more—seen more of the men, etc. But doubtless it is fortunate for the fun and humour of the thing that it wasn't modified—as surely the critical emotion (about them), the essence of much of their nature, was never more beautifully expressed. As for her allusions to H.—they fill me with tears and cover me with blushes. What I should *like* to do *en temps et lieu* would be, should no catastrophe meanwhile occur—or even if it should!—to *edit* the volume with a few eliminations of text and dissimulations of names, give it to the world and then carefully burn with fire our own four copies. I find an immense eloquence in her passionate "radicalism"—her most distinguishing feature almost—which, in her, was absolutely direct and original (like everything that was in her); unreflected, uncaught from entourage or example. It would really have made her, had she lived in the world, a feminine "political force." But had she lived in the world and seen things nearer she would have had disgusts and disillusions. However, what comes out in the book—as it came out to me in fact—is that she was really an Irishwoman!—transplanted, transfigured—but none the less fundamentally national—in spite of her so much larger and finer than Irish intelligence. She felt the Home Rule question absolutely as only an Irishwoman (not anglicised) could. It was a tremendous emotion with her—inexplicable in any other way—and perfectly explicable by "atavism." What a pity she wasn't born there—and had her health for it. She would have been (if, always, she had not fallen a victim to disgust—a large "if") a national glory!—But I am writing too much—and my late hindrances have left me with tremendous arrears of correspondence. I thank you, dear Alice, *caramente,* for your sweet letter received two or three weeks before William's. I crudely hope you won't let your house—so as to have it to go [to] in the summer. Otherwise what will become of you? I dig my nose into the fleshiest parts of the young Francis. Tell Peggy I cling to her—and Harry too, and Billy not less.—Thanks for the allusion to the Jones-Alexander situation. I judge, in fact, however, it is *not* a fiasco (*The Masqueraders*) but a success with a certain quantity of run in it—that will take it through the summer. The question of the rehearsals of my piece will probably loom before me early in the autumn. However I know nothing till I get back—and the unspeakable Jones, even for one of his minor achievements, may have months and months *dans le ventre.*—I haven't sent you "The Yellow Book"—on purpose; and indeed I have been weeks and weeks receiving a copy of it myself. I say on purpose because although my little tale which ushers it in ("The Death of the Lion") appears to have had, for a thing of mine, an unusual success, I hate too much the horrid aspect and company of the whole publication.[5] And yet I am again to be intimately—conspicuously—associated with the second number. It is for gold and to oblige the worshipful Harland[6] (the editor).

Wait and read the two tales in a volume—with two or three others. Above all be *debout,* and forgive the long reticence of your affectionate

Henry

1. In the settlement of the estate of HJ's Wykoff cousin.
2. The literary sister of Ariana Curtis.
3. Robertson James had settled with his family in Concord, Massachusetts. The two Marys were Mary Holton James, Robertson's wife, and their daughter, later Mary James Vaux, who did indeed publish portions of the diary in 1934.
4. Augustine Birrell (1850–1933) would later be president of the Board of Education and also chief secretary for Ireland. He was an essayist whose "Obiter Dicta" were widely read.
5. "The Death of the Lion" appeared in the *Yellow Book,* I (April 1894), 7–52, and was reprinted in *Terminations* (1895).
6. Henry Harland (1861–1905), expatriate American novelist and first editor of the *Yellow Book.*

To Edmund Gosse
Ms Leeds

34 De Vere Gardens W.
Friday [10 August 1894]

My dear Gosse.

You were very happily inspired in writing me about Pater's interment—and, in particular, in writing so charmingly. Your letter makes me much regret that, having, as I had, fifty minds to go to his funeral, I didn't have the fifty-first which might have carried me there. If I had known you would go I would have joined you—very possibly. But I was deterred by considerations—that of my very limited acquaintance with Pater, my non-communication with him for so long, and above all by (what I supposed would be) the compact Oxfordism of it all; in which I seem to feel myself to have no place. And now I feel, still more, that I should have liked to *faire acte de présence.* Meanwhile you are very vivid and interesting about it. It was not to be dreamed of, however, I think, that the event should have been more "noticed." What is more delicate than the extinction of delicacy—and what note more in place than that of "discretion"—in respect to the treatment of anything that might have happened to Pater—even the last thing that *could* happen? It presents itself to me—so far as I know it—as one of the successful, felicitous lives and the time and manner of the death a part of the success.[1] But you must tell me more. I don't cease to regret that being last February (I think) at Oxford, and Herbert Warren taking me on the Sunday afternoon to see him, took me to the spare little house where Miss Pater only was drearily visible, instead of to Brasenose, where I learned with a pang, that coming from the curious Bussell, W.H.P. had been "disappointed" at my non-arrival. Yes, the President of Magdalen is incurably young: I forgive him the youth only on account of the incurableness. I have been dividing my time between Rudyard Kipling and Hugues Le Roux:[2] and if I stay in town all through next week (I leave it tomorrow till Tuesday) I will come and see you of a night. Thanks, thanks again for your letter. Yours always

Henry James

1. Walter Horatio Pater (1839–1894) fellow of Brasenose College, had died on 30 July, five days short of his fifty-fifth birthday. HJ is probably alluding to the success of his books—his *Plato and Platonism* of the previous year having confirmed the already large reputation of the author of *Marius the Epicurean.*

2. Hugues Le Roux (1860–1925), a French journalist and a friend of Paul Bourget's. See HJ *Notebooks*, 212.

To Edmund Gosse
Ms Barrett

Tregenna C[astle] Hotel
St. Ives
August 22*nd* [1894]

My dear Gosse.

I should have been very glad to hear from you yesterday if only for the sweet opportunity it gives me of crying out that I told you so! It gives me more than this—and I *didn't* tell you so; but I wanted to awfully—and I only smothered my wisdom under my waistcoat. Tell Arthur Benson[1] that I wanted to tell *him* so too—that guileless morning at Victoria: I knew so well, both then and at Delamere Terrace, with my half century of experience, straight into what a purgatory you were *all* rushing. The high Swiss mountain inn, the crowd, the cold, the heat, the rain, the Germans, the scramble, the impossible rooms and still more impossible anything else—the hope deferred, the money misspent, the weather accurst: these things I saw written on your azure brows even while I perfidiously prattled with your prattle. The only thing was to let you do it—for one can no more come between a lady and her Swiss hotel than between a gentleman and his wife. Meanwhile I sit here looking out at *my* nice, domestic, inexpensive English rain, in *my* nice bad stuffy insular inn, and thanking God that I am not as Gosses and Bensons are. I am pretty bad, I recognise—but I am not so bad as you. I am so bad that I am fleeing in a day or two—as I hope you will have been doing if your ineluctable fate doesn't spare you. I stopped on my way down here to spend three days with W. E. Norris,[2] which were rendered charming by the urbanity of my host and the peerless beauty of Torquay, with which I fell quite in love. Here I go out for long walks on wet moors with the silent Stephen, the almost speechless Leslie.[3] In the morning I improve the alas not shining hour, in a little black sitting-room which looks out into the strange area—like unto that of the London milkman—with which this *ci-devant* castle is encompassed and which sends up strange scullery odours into my nose. I am very sorry to hear of any friends of yours suffering by the *Saturday Review*,[4] but I know nothing whatever of the cataclysm. It's a journal which (in spite of the lustre you add to it) I haven't so much as seen for fifteen years, and no echoes of its fortunes ever reach me.

23rd. I broke off yesterday to take a long walk over bogs and brambles, and this morning my windows are lashed by a wet hurricane. It makes me wish I could settle down to a luxurious irresponsible day with the *Lourdes*[5] of your approbation, which lies there on my table still uncut. But my "holiday" is no holiday and I must drive the mechanic pen. Moreover I have vowed not to open *Lourdes* till I shall have closed with a final furious bang the unspeakable *Lord Ormont*,[6] which I have been reading at the maximum rate of ten pages—ten insufferable and unprofitable pages, a day. It fills me with a critical rage, an artistic fury, utterly blighting in me the indispensable principle of *respect*. I have finished, at this rate, but the first volume—whereof I am moved to declare that I doubt if any equal quantity of extravagant verbiage, of airs and graces, of phrases and attitudes, of obscurities and alembications, ever *started* less their subject, ever contributed less of a statement—told the reader less of what the reader needs to know. All elaborate predicates of exposition without the ghost of a nominative to hook themselves to; and not a difficulty met, not a figure presented, not a scene constituted—not a dim shadow condensing once either into audible or into visible reality—making you hear for an instant the tap of its feet on the earth. Of course there are pretty things, but for what they are they come so much too dear, and so many of the profundities and tortuosities prove when threshed out to be only pretentious statements of the very simplest propositions. Enough, and forgive me. Above all don't send this to the P[all] M[all] G[azette]. There is another side, of course, which one will utter another day. I have a dictated letter from R.L.S., sent me through Colvin, who is at Schwalbach with the horsey Duchess of Montrose, a disappointing letter in which the too apt pupil of Meredith tells me nothing that I want to know—nothing save that his spirits are low (which I would fain ignore) and that he has been [on] an excursion on an English man-of-war. The devilish letter is wholly about the man-of-war, not a word else; and at the end he says "I *decline* to tell you any more about it!" as if I had prescribed the usurping subject.[7] You shall see the rather melancholy pages when you return—I must keep them to answer them. Bourget and his wife are in England again—at Oxford: with Prévost[8] at Buxton, H. Le Roux at Wimbledon etc., it is the Norman conquest beginning afresh. What will be the end, or the effect, of it? P.B. has sent me some of the sheets (100 pp.) of his *Outremer*,[9] which are singularly agreeable and lively. It will be much the prettiest (and I should judge kindest) socio-psychological book written about the U.S. That is saying little. It is very living and interesting. Prévost's fetid *étude* (on the little girls) represents a perfect bound, from his earlier things, in the way of hard, firm, knowing ability. So clever—and so common; no ability to imagine his "queenly" girl, made to dominate the world, do anything finally by way of illustrating her superiority but become a professional cocotte, like a *fille de portier*.

Pity's akin to love—so I send that to Mrs. Nellie and Tessa and to A. Benson.

Yours ever
Henry James

1. Gosse and his family had gone to Switzerland for a holiday with Arthur Christopher Benson (1862–1925), then a Master at Eton. The Gosses lived at Delamere Terrace, in London.

2. James's friendship with William Edward Norris (1847–1925), a minor

Victorian novelist who lived at Torquay with his daughter, dates from this time.

3. HJ had gone to Cornwall to be near Leslie Stephen and his family, visiting the house and scenes later described by Stephen's daughter, Virginia Woolf, in her novel *To the Lighthouse.*

4. *The Saturday Review,* the weekly periodical founded in the Liberal interest in 1855, was being reorganized by the American literary entrepreneur Frank Harris, who had been editing the *Fortnightly Review.* Gosse wrote to a friend that the *Saturday Review,* to which he was a contributor, "has been bought by a wild kind of Sioux or Apache called Frank Harris, who has driven all the old staff out into the street with cuffs and kicks, and is trying to run it with young braves and scalp-hunters of his own." Evan Charteris, *The Life and Letters of Sir Edmund Gosse* (1931), 241.

5. Zola's novel, published in 1894, the first of his trilogy *Les Trois Villes.*

6. Meredith's *Lord Ormont and His Aminta* had just been published.

7. HJ, in his insistence that Stevenson was not giving him sufficient visual testimony of his life in the South Seas, misquoted this letter. What Stevenson wrote from Vailima was "I decline any longer to give you examples of how not to write." Sidney Colvin, ed., *The Letters of Robert Louis Stevenson* (1901), II, 339.

8. Marcel Prévost (1862–1940) had just published a sensational novel entitled *Les Demi-Vierges.*

9. Bourget's travel book describing his trip to the United States.

To T. H. Huxley
Ms Imperial College

34 De Vere Gardens W.
Oct. 27*th* 1894

Dear and illustrious Professor.

I am overwhelmed with emotion at the arrival from Messrs. Macmillan & Co., of the goodliest offering which, in the course of a long connection, they have ever approached me with—the complete set of your beautiful little red volumes—with a label attached which makes me almost as red as themselves. It is the flush of pride and gratitude, for the label literally declares that the bounty is your own, and I have ended at last by believing it. I am really, dear Professor, more gratified and touched than I can tell you—and I am asking myself when I can make the moment for rushing down to Eastbourne to try and help myself out more practically. How I wish I had already found the little habitation which I spoke to you at Tunbridge Wells of desiring there! Then I should really have a basis for active acknowledgment. But at least your generosity shall add zeal to that quest! When I come down to look for the fivepenny cottage it will be first to look for you and Mrs. Huxley. I very greatly hope that she is more completely better of her illness than at Tunbridge. Please believe how much more valued a recollection to me our meeting there now becomes; and try to hear, in the wind that must be roaring today round your ears, the very sincere accents of yours most devotedly

Henry James

To Frederic W. H. Myers

Ms Private

34 De Vere Gardens W.
Nov. 13*th* 1894

My dear Myers.

To such a reader as you, such a delightful observer, rememberer, liker, who would not concede anything? It costs me no struggle of pride whatever to say that you must be absolutely right: there is a clear luxury of gratitude in it. Of *Georgina's Reasons*[1] I mainly remember that I thought them pretty bad at the time—I mean thought the tale a feeble one, and that impression has remained with me. I daresay it is one of the worst I was ever guilty of. I have been looking for it this A.M.—to appreciate your remarks better, but I find that I seem to be without the volume that contains it. The thing is dim to me; what they did, and what they should have done; there only sticks to me rather definitely the memory of the limited anecdote (told me by a friend, a lady, as something told to *her*—and having happened in some American western town) in which I originally saw the adumbration of a story. In general, moreover, I think that after one has done, *tant bien que mal,* a thing of that sort, one becomes intensely irresponsible about it—getting away from it as from a kind of relinquished execution or terminated connection. That, at least, is the feeble way *I* feel. One saw it, one did it, with all the vividness that was in one at the time; but the act accomplished, and the spasm over, one can't *relive* that experience, one can only thirst for another with different material. So it is that I, at least, can never lift my finger to defend or to explain. There they are, poor things, and *why* they were I did once seem to know; but I have always consentingly forgotten. So moreover it is that when the ingenuous ask which of one's "things" one likes best, I am filled [with] a secret horror at being supposed to "like" any of them. I loathe them all! What I "like" is the art—more than I can say; and the works have only a temporary tolerance—reflected from that. None the less I am inconsequent enough to like immensely those who also tolerate. You are admirably generous. I remember Miss [? Van W.] as an affliction—a distinct distress—and I am glad she continues to be eluded. I don't know Lord C. or his veritable bride. You make me want awfully to be more flagrantly "productive": to really go it well. I (somewhat subterraneously) *am* going it.

Yours *always*
Henry James

P.S. Let me add that I regretted more than I could express at the time the mutilation of that meeting of ours at Torquay. I should have been exceedingly glad of another day or two and more talk beneath the hawthorn shade. And . . .[2] H.J.

1. "Georgina's Reasons" had originally been published by HJ in the New York *Sun*, 20 and 27 July and 3 August 1884. It was reprinted in *The Author of Beltraffio* (1885) and again in *Stories Revived*, II, 1885. In the story Georgina, a New York girl, commits bigamy and disposes of the child of her first marriage to an Italian family. The reasons for her strange conduct are never given.

2. Here eight lines—about forty words—have been erased, clearly not by HJ and probably by the recipient.

To William Heinemann
Ms Unknown

34 De Vere Gardens W.
November 22*nd* 1894

My dear Heinemann.

All thanks for your prompt and adequate relief—the last "go" at Act II.[1] It is a very great little affair. If Act III doesn't drop, it will be Ibsen's crown of glory—I mean the whole thing will. It is a little masterpiece. It seems to me that he doesn't make quite enough —(in form, in the pause to take it in, and the indication of the amazement and emotion of Allmers)—of the revelation of the non-relationship; but that is a detail, and the stroke itself—coming where it does—immense. The thing must and *can* be represented.

This Act II is such a crescendo on I that if III is an equal crescendo on II, the fortune of the thing will be made, and it will be a big fortune. I hope III is already on the stocks of translation. It's a fine case for the British manager's fine old demand for a "happy ending"! What I seem dimly to divine is that the she-Eyolf goes the same way as the He! i.e. the way of the fiord.

I don't see what *complete* tragedy there is for it *but* that. But the Devil knows what queer card the old Roué has up his sleeve!—perhaps Rita "has" the roadmaster publicly on the stage, while Asta throws herself into the fiord. Yes, Eyolf No. 2 does by design what Eyolf No. 1 did by accident—and does it conjointly *with* Alfred (at the risk of repeating Rosmersholm and Hedda and the Wild Duck), while Rita falls upon Borgheim and the Rat wife returns leading in a wild dance of rodents! That, at least, is the way it *should* be. But come to my aid! I was so full of it yesterday that, being near you, I popped in—tho' I had already written, but only missed you.

Yours ever,
H.J.

1. William Heinemann, the publisher, who had fallen in love with the actress Elizabeth Robins, joined in her Ibsen enthusiasms, in which HJ also participated, and sent HJ the acts of *Little Eyolf* as quickly as the manuscript of the English version reached him.

To Urbain Mengin
Ms Harvard

34 De Vere Gardens W.
November 27*th* 1894

Mon cher ami.

Please believe that I am touched by the really angelic generosity of your beautiful letter. I have neglected you brutally, though only by the cruelly perverse force of things—of things independent of my will; and yet your charity still has kind thoughts of me and your admirable pen beautiful accents as well as perfections more formal, even though microscopic. I have been so long silent simply because I had arrived at a crisis bringing it home to me that either I or my correspondence must perish—so I let it go to save my own life. But this same silence left me leisure to think of you, to wonder what your fortune had been and to hope it was proving in some degree congruous with your ambition. Now you tell me, and though I am sorry to hear of your philosophic discouragements I rejoice in your return to our poor dear patient old language, because it brings you nearer to me again and seems to furnish me with a presumption that we shall meet once more. This time you must keep well hold of your English[1]—you must not give it up. You will find much to do with it—only you must *live* with it if you expect it to live with you. One's own language is one's mother, but the language one adopts, as a career, as a study, is one's wife, and it is with one's wife that *on se met en ménage.* English is a very faithful and well-conducted person, but she will expect you too not to commit infidelities. On these terms she will keep your house well. I am afraid you have had some dark hours and many dismal thoughts—have been, in short, through rather a cruel experience. But renouncement is the larger half of success and one's mistakes the best part of one's certitude. Read, read, read, and speak to your pupils from a full and easy mind. Know more than they want to know—for if you only knew as much you would know nothing. Work for the day when you can come back to London. It will be a much better and more fruitful visit than your last. I am glad Bourget advises and assists you. A man so intelligent and so sagacious can't *touch* you without giving you something. I can't talk to you of myself save in a very superficial sense. I am utterly unable, always, to speak of what I am "doing"—for when I speak of it I seem to expose it to some hard profaning light; even when I speak to an ear as receptive as yours. If it were of importance you would hear of it—and you must believe in me on general grounds. To give up Greek and Greece—that must indeed have been a sorrow; but it is something—a great deal—to have loved such things enough to weep for them. Weep no more—but work and live and love, rejoice in your charming mind and your delicate soul and believe in the pleasure with which I see them reflected in what you write to me. Whenever London again becomes possible to you write a word in advance to yours, my dear Mengin, very faithfully

Henry James

1. Mengin, who had been a French tutor in England, had now returned to France and was teaching English at the Lycée d'Albi.

To Edmund Gosse

Ms Congress

34 De Vere Gardens W.
Thursday [13 December 1894]

My dear Gosse.

I return with much appreciation the vivid pages on Pater.[1] They fill up substantially the void of one's ignorance of his personal history, and they are of a manner graceful and luminous; though I should perhaps have relished a little more insistence on—a little more of an inside view of—the nature of his mind itself. Much as they tell, however, how curiously negative and faintly-grey he, after all telling, remains! I think he has had—will have had—the most exquisite literary fortune: i.e. to have taken it out all, wholly, exclusively, with the pen (the style, the genius) and absolutely not at all with the person. He is the mask without the face, and there isn't in his total superficies a tiny point of vantage for the newspaper to flap its wings on. You have been lively about him—but about whom *wouldn't* you be lively? I think you'd be lively about *me!*—Well, faint, pale, embarrassed, exquisite Pater! He reminds me, in the disturbed midnight of our actual literature, of one of those lucent matchboxes which you place, on going to bed, near the candle, to show you, in the darkness, where you can strike a light: he shines in the uneasy gloom—vaguely, and has a phosphorescence, not a flame. But I quite agree with you that he is not of the little day—but of the longer time.

Will you kindly ask Tessa if I may *still* come, on Saturday? My visit to the country has been put off by a death—and if there is a little corner for me I'll appear. If there isn't—so late—no matter. I dare say I ought to write to Miss Wetton. Or will Tessa amiably inquire?

Yours always,
Henry James

1. Gosse's paper on Pater was included in his volume *Critical Kit-kats* (1896).

To Francis Boott

Ms Harvard

34 De Vere Gardens W.
December 15*th* 1894

My dear Francis.

Let me not suffer the year to close, as it is so nigh doing, without carrying you some sign of my ancient but not faded affection and my too often inarticulate but not unconscious remembrance. You are just made vividly present to me by a word or two in a letter I have just had from Fanny Morse[1]—faithful and loyal maid: in which she says that she had lately seen you come into some concert, "looking so handsome, young and fresh"—and (she intimates) the cynosure of every eye. I seem to see you before me when I thus authentically hear that you preserve your beauty and your "taste for music." I hope the former represents health and ease and the latter many quiet private joys as well as brilliant public appearances. It is incredible, the time I *haven't* written to you—though the last words that passed between proceeded so liberally from your pen. What makes it peculiarly abnormal is the fact that all last spring which (from mid-March to mid-July) I spent in the countries adjacent to "Tuscany," as Anne would say, there was scarcely an hour at which I hadn't the theory—the actual *afflatus,* of a letter to you on the end of my pen. In truth, however, Italy is more and more a snare and a trap to one's freedom and one's quiet—it was last year, if I may be allowed the expression, the mere *vomitorium* of Boston. Half America was gathered there—*all* of Marlborough Street and the Back Bay—and leisure and repose fled howling at the sight—or rather at the sound! Therefore, though I had immense opportunities for talking about you, I had none for directer intercourse. I went to Chioggia to see Duveneck and spent several hot and rather smelly hours with him—unrewarded, I grieve to say, with the sight of a single stroke of his brush. He would "show" us nothing—save the beauties of Chioggia and his robust and pleasant self. He seemed wondrous well, and made me most welcome, and I felt sorry for his lonely and uncompanioned life. In Florence, where I spent a few days on my way to Rome, I made an intensely pious pilgrimage to the spot where Lizzie lies in majestic and perennial bronze.[2] Strange, strange it seemed, still, to see her only so—but so she will be seen for ages to come. I climbed to Bellosguardo and dined at Villa Castellani with the impoverished but still social Wagnières; but the whole place is now such a perfect cemetery of ghosts that there is little joy in it left for me—or rather there *would* be little if I had not deep-seated dispositions to find myself secretly, even whenever so sadly, fond of the company of the relics of the dead. Villa Brichieri seemed to stare down at one with unspeakably mournful eyes of windows. Apropos of which all my first weeks in Venice were populated with the dolorous *detail* of the two poor Benedicts, who occupied Miss Woolson's sad death-house and took elaborate possession of her immensely accumulated effects. However, *"non ragionam di lor!"*—I mean of the Benedicts. It was a sufficiently tragic fact that all the knowledge poor Mrs. B. collected (and it was much) of her sister's last weeks tended directly to confirm the conviction she had already formed that an unmistakable lapse from sanity had occurred some time before her death—that some cerebral accident had been determined the previous summer. The sight of the *scene* of her horrible act is, for that matter, sufficient to establish her utter madness at the time. A place more mad for *her* couldn't be imagined. But I don't know why I remind you of these things, which only deepen the darkness of the tragedy. The Curtises I of course often saw, *retour des Indes,* and Daniel for the first time out of sorts and showing his years. But they came to England in the autumn and he revived so much that *mots* and puns and other witticisms began freely to flow. E.g., they (Mrs. C.) has struck up a great friendship with a very charming Irish "distressed landlady," Lady Kenmare. He had seen here Lady Kenmare's daughter and I asked him if she thought her like her mother. "No; I think she must take less after Kenmère than after Kenpère!" The *mot* has had great—immense—success here: the combined British and Irish minds had never thought of it before! I am what they call here "doing a little play" (at the St. James's theatre) and doing it for lucre and nought else; and if it brings lucre I shall do others for the same unblushing end. But it comes on in less than three weeks and exceedingly thorough and patient rehearsals make a great hole in the middle of each day. Therefore I have scant time, my dear old friend, to do more than assure you that I am always affectionately yours

Henry James

1. Frances Rollins Morse (1850–1928), a Boston friend of the James family.
2. The Allori Cemetery.

To Edmund Gosse

Ms British Library

34 De Vere Gardens W.
Dec. 17*th* 1894

My dear Gosse.

I meant to write you tonight on another matter—but of what can one think, or utter or dream, save of this ghastly extinction of the beloved R.L.S.?[1] It is too miserable for cold words—it's an absolute desolation. It makes me cold and sick—and with the absolute, almost alarmed sense, of the visible material quenching of an indispensable light. That he's silent forever will be a fact hard, for a long time, to live with. Today, at any rate, it's a cruel, wringing emotion. One feels how one cared for him—what a place he took; and as if suddenly *into* that place there had descended a great avalanche of ice. I'm not sure that it's not for *him* a great and happy fate; but for us the loss of charm, of suspense, of "fun" is unutterable. And how confusedly and pityingly one's thought turns to those far-away stricken women, with their whole principle of existence suddenly quenched and yet all the monstrosity of the rest of their situation left on their hands! I saw poor Colvin today—he is overwhelmed, he is touching: But I can't write of this—we must talk of it. Yet these words have been a relief.—And I can't write, either, of the matter I had intended to—viz. that you are to rest secure about the question of [January] 5th[2]—I will do everything for you. *That* business becomes for the hour tawdry and heartless to me. Yours always,

Henry James

1. Stevenson had died of a cerebral hemorrhage at Vailima, his home in Samoa, on 3 December 1894 in his forty-fifth year, but the news had only now reached the outside world.
2. HJ wrote June 5th instead of January 5th—the date of the first night of *Guy Domville*, which Gosse was to attend.

To Elizabeth Lewis

Ms Private

34 DeVere Gardens W.
Saturday [15? December 1894]

Dear Lady Lewis.

I throw myself upon your charity with the tremulous confidence of an old friend. I have been looking forward fondly to the great pleasure of dining with you on Monday—but all my happiness is undermined by the nervousness and the exhaustion (to speak frankly) consequent upon the rehearsals of my play at the St. James's. In these rehearsals I am steeped up to my eyes—and I take everything hard and agitatingly. There is to be one on Monday *night* (as well as on Tuesday and Wednesday), at which it is of extreme importance I should be present—and which I am too uncomfortably preoccupied to miss. In short, dear Lady Lewis, I am *too* preoccupied, too terrified, too fundamentally distracted, to be fit for human intercourse. At the theatre it passes a little—but everywhere else it squeezes me till I turn sick. Therefore I won't inflict my misery upon your glorious revels. I should be a death's head at the feast. Forgive me and pity me. I *may* be meant for the Drama—God knows!—but I certainly wasn't meant for the Theatre. I repeat, forgive, forgive, dear Lady Lewis, your demoralized but faithful old friend

Henry James

To Mr. and Mrs. Frank Millet

Ms Private

34 De Vere Gardens W.
Christmas [1894]

Beloved Millets.

How kind your friendly thought of me, whom you have already loaded with your bounty—so loaded that this added touch causes the cup verily to overflow. Occupied and preoccupied as I know you to be, my dear Millet, I take your Christmas greeting for one of the very gracefullest things that ever happened to me. Broadway brings forth nothing that isn't good—and more things that *are* than any other place. (Hasn't it also brought forth a manifestation from "Edgar T." and from "Elsie"?) You were already in my thoughts, and I had already expressed it haltingly by sending Jack[1] a little reminder of our October acquaintance. I hope the modest—very modest—offering reached the dear boy safely. It took with it my most tender remembrance. I have felt moreover lately much under the blessing of Broadway through being shoulder to shoulder with Alfred P[arsons][2] in shifting the scenery of the St. James's—for which he has produced some admirable, some lovely pictures. It has been a luxury to clutch at him in the desert sands of the British stage. I hope you are both enjoying to the full the peace, the plenty, the reunion of your quiet old-world corner. You must feel like rescued swimmers—gently palpitating on terra firma. I hope the pictures palpitate too. I thank you both, I embrace you both, and I am yours and Jack's (oh, how I hug *him!*) forever

Henry James

1. The Millet son, named after John Singer Sargent and Alfred Parsons, John A. P. Millet, later a distinguished psychiatrist in New York.
2. Parsons had designed the sets for *Guy Domville.*

To Mrs. Robert Louis Stevenson
Ms Yale

34 De Vere Gardens W.
December 26*th* [1894]

My dear Fanny Stevenson.

What can I say to you that will not seem cruelly irrelevant and vain? We have been sitting in darkness for nearly a fortnight, but what is *our* darkness to the extinction of your magnificent light? You will probably know in some degree what has happened to us —how the hideous news first came to us via Auckland, etc., and then how, in the newspapers, a doubt was raised about its authenticity—just enough to give one a flicker of hope; until your telegram to me via San Francisco—repeated also from other sources—converted my pessimistic convictions into the wretched knowledge. All this time my thoughts have hovered round you all, around *you* in particular, with a tenderness of which I could have wished you might have, afar-off, the divination. You are such a visible picture of desolation that I need to remind myself that courage and patience and fortitude are also abundantly with you. You are all much to each other, I am sure, and the devotion that Louis inspired—and of which all the air about you is surely full—must also be much to you. Yet as I write the word, indeed, I am almost ashamed of it—as if anything *could* be "much" in the presence of such an abysmal void. To have lived in the light of that splendid life, that beautiful, bountiful being—only to see it, from one moment to the other, converted into a fable as strange and romantic as one of his own, a thing that *has* been and has ended, is an anguish into which no one can enter with you fully and of which no one can drain the cup *for* you. You are nearest to the pain, because you were nearest to the joy and the pride. But if it is anything to you to know that no woman was ever more felt *with,* and that your personal grief is the intensely personal grief of innumerable hearts and devotions—know it well, my dear Fanny Stevenson, for during all these days there has been friendship for you in the very air. For myself, how shall I tell you how much poorer and shabbier the whole world seems and how one of the closest and strongest reasons for going on, for trying and doing, for planning and dreaming of the future, has dropped in an instant out of life. I was haunted indeed with a sense that I should never again see him—but it was one of the best things in life that he was *there,* or that one had him, at any rate, one heard him and felt him and awaited him and counted him into everything one most loved and lived for. He lighted up a whole side of the globe and was in himself a whole province of one's imagination. We are smaller fry and meaner people without him. I feel as if there were a certain indelicacy in saying it to you, save that I know there is nothing narrow or selfish in your sense of loss—for *himself,* however, for his happy name and his great visible good fortune, it strikes one as another matter. I mean that I feel him to have been as happy in his death (struck down that way, as by the gods, in a clear, glorious hour) as he had been in his fame, and, with all the sad allowances, in his rich, full life. He had the *best* of it—the thick of the fray, the loudest of the music, the freshest and finest of himself. It isn't as if there had been no full achievement and no supreme thing. It was all intense, all gallant, all exquisite from the first, and the recognition, the experience, the fruition had something dramatically complete in them. He has gone in time not to be old—early enough to be so generously young and late enough to have drunk deep of the cup. There have been—I think—for men of letters few deaths more romantically right. Forgive me, I beg you, what may sound cold-blooded in such words—and as if I imagined there could be anything for *you*, "right" in the rupture of such an affection and the loss of such a presence. I have in my mind, in that view, only the rounded career and the consecrated work. When I think of your own situation I fall into a mere confusion of pity and wonder—with the sole sense of your being as brave a spirit as *he* was (all of whose bravery you endlessly shared) to hold on by. Of what solutions and decisions you see before you we shall hear in time—meanwhile please believe that I am most affectionately with you. You will question this last declaration indeed, perhaps, after all—at *first*—when you hear that I have (in infinite distress of spirit) seen no way but to ask to be excused from acting as one of the executors to Louis's will—the office to which I learned from Mr. Mitchell of Edinburgh a few days ago that that will conjointly with C. Baxter appointed me. My dear Fanny Stevenson, let me ask you to believe that I have taken in this matter the sole course—absolutely—that the peculiar circumstances have left open to me, the course which if you were only here and I might speak to you, in my infinite regret and sorrow—my deep tribulation—face to face, I should be able in three minutes to make you not only composedly but most eagerly accept. The peculiar circumstances are that, though beloved Louis had, in his great imagination, no conception of it, I am utterly and absolutely the creature in the world most abjectly and most humiliatedly unfit for the discharge of any such duties or any duties remotely approaching or dimly resembling them. I am more touched than I can say by such a sign of confidence and affection, and it makes me blush to my depths and my ears tingle with pain—so abnormally *not* am I a man of business or acquainted with the rudiments of any business transaction whatever. I have always had a constitutional incapacity for everything of the sort and an insurmountable aversion to it, and circumstances have happened, from the first, to confirm me in my habits of ignorance and helplessness. I am utterly unacquainted with my *own* little affairs, which are entirely in the hands of my brother and my lawyer, of whom I have literally never asked a question concerning them (save, vaguely: "*When* shall I get a remittance?")—and indeed shouldn't be able intelligently to ask one. When my sister died three years ago my being "out of it" was so comfortably recognised between us that although I was her only relative in this country and the person nearest to her in intimacy and affection, there was not even a question of her naming me *her* executor—and another person had to be found. I mention this, though it doesn't redound to my glory, to show you how fearfully broken a reed I am and how I am—or was, till I had answered Mr. Mitchell's letter of announcement—paralysed with terror at the idea of being expected to administer, or aid in administering Louis's estate in the interest of his heirs. It would be a dreadful disaster to these heirs that I should *touch* the business in any way —but indeed I should be wholly unable even to blunder into the most preliminary formality. I have never in my life had anything to do with accounts, never kept one since I was born, can't do the simplest sum in arithmetic, and have only the sketchiest and dimmest idea of how my own small means are invested. I tell you all this—excuse the almost brutal candour of it—only to make vivid to you that if I have had to ask to be exonerated from the danger of doing you dreadful damage, it is for reasons which, monstrous as they sound, I have not even faintly exaggerated (it would be impossible), and which it costs me no small pain to state to you, but which when they *are* stated you will fully feel the force and perhaps slightly be sensible to the pity of. If it had only been something in my *line,* in the line of my aptitude and possibility, in the line of his papers, his relics, his genius, his renown, that Louis had dreamed of asking of me! Then I would have performed the job with joy to the last extremity! But enough of all this, I feel after all that you won't have needed so feverish an explanation to be sure that if so old a friend has failed in a particular case he has failed only because it was right for him to fail. I could have wished that Mr. Baxter hadn't happened already to have started—but he will probably have reached you about the time you get this. I hope Mr. Mitchell will have sent him the letter. I have written you a long letter, but I haven't said half that I wanted to. You shall hear from me again as soon as we have had more news of you. I write by this post to Mrs. Stevenson—however briefly. I send my love to Lloyd and the assurance that no man can understand better than I the difference that has fallen on his life. Poor Lloyd indeed—with the rupture of such a tie! How much he will have to be, how much he already is to you! I haven't the pleasure of knowing your daughter, but I thank her as if I did for all her devotion and service, of these last years, to him. What a happiness ended for her! I won't pretend to speak for Colvin—he will speak for himself to you. He is infinitely stricken. You will know that there has been but one universal dolorous acclaiming voice. You would have felt what the place is he occupied had you been here. The press all full of his honour—and of a peculiar tone of peculiar affection that quite humanised it—and not one dissentient or anything but spontaneous note. More than I can say, I hope your first prostration and bewilderment are over, and that you are seeing your way and feeling all sorts of encompassing and supporting arms—all sorts of outstretched hands of friendship. Don't, my dear Fanny Stevenson, be unconscious of *mine*, and believe me more than ever faithfully yours

Henry James

To John A. P. Millet

Ms Private

34 De Vere Gardens W.
Dec. 27*th* 1894

My dear little Jack.

Your old friend was delighted with your lively—in fact lovely—little letter, and really excited by it. I liked everything in it, but I liked the Signature most of all. I don't mean because the signature was the end, but because it somehow *looks* like the brave little writer—out for a walk to school—with his little cap and muffler. Oh, and the handkerchief too—I just *loved* that! I thank you, dear Jack, with all my heart for such a useful little present. I shall keep it always and it will remind me of you and of the good fairy who so beautifully worked my name on it. I am greatly wondering which of the good fairies it is—there are so many, you know, and a few—a very few—bad ones. I think you are a very happy little boy to be such chums with the good sort. Be always kind and loving to them and you will be able then always to count on their help in all your little doings. I suppose you are up to your bright little eyes in holidays and things. Well, enjoy them hard and sleep sound at the day's end. Good-bye, dear little happy, hearty, healthy Jack. Don't forget me and I will come again one of these days to see you. Till then and always I am your faithful old friend

Henry James

P.S. It usually isn't thought good manners to speak of the spelling, but yours is so beautiful I hope you don't mind my mentioning *it.*

To Edmund Gosse

Ms Leeds

34 De Vere Gardens W.
Dec. 27*th* '94

My dear Gosse.

It will be all right—and I will take care. None of the seats can have been sent out yet: they will go in a day or two. Those you will receive are not to be paid for—they are direct from the author. I shall be delighted if Norris can go with you—though appalled at his making that midwinter journey to such an end. The responsibility of it!—Yes, I should like much to talk with you. The ghost of poor R.L.S. waves its great dusky wings between me and all occupations—and I am haunted for another reason that I will tell you. I am unable to say whether Friday or Saturday will be free evenings for me—the damnable theatre is now given over to nocturnal as well as diurnal rehearsals. But I shall probably know tonight. I have been reading with the liveliest—and almost painful—interest the two volumes[1] on the extraordinary Symonds. They give me an extraordinary impression of his "gifts"—yet I don't know what keeps them from being tragic. Yours ever

Henry James

1. A memoir by Symonds's close friend, Horatio Brown (1854–1926), a British historian whom HJ had met in Venice.

To Elizabeth Robins
Ms Texas

34 De Vere Gardens W.
Monday [31 December 1894]

My Dear Elizabeth Robins.

Something deep and strange within me tells me that your letter is a really good omen; and for a moment it stills the quite ridiculous frenzy of my nervous pulses. All thanks then for it—from a heart which devoutly echoes your invocation. No one—not even Mrs. Bell (please tell her) can wish for me more than I wish for myself! The portents, on the whole, I think, are as good as they can be—or as I can *read* them—in the case of a thing as to which I now mainly feel that it *has* been abbreviated and simplified out of all *close* resemblance to my intention. I have worked and participated with unremitting zeal and intensity—and my afflicted consciousness has been divided between desolation at the immensity of my sacrifices (of things—touches, passages, details—indispensable to real interest and coherence) and exultation over the very absence of things not left in the piece for them *not* to do! The bare minimum (excuse my awful writing) is at once so much the worse and so much the better for my play! Not that they are not, poor dears, doing their zealous best. There is *one* actor in the affair, little Esmond,[1] and a remarkably clever and capable, an (on usual and obvious but most sensible lines) quite *masterly* stage-manager—I mean of course G[eorge] A[lexander]. They have all been most comfortable and decorous, and the rehearsals very human and tranquil—I mean without "incidents." As for the poor little play itself, aching in every fibre from its wounds—*valeat quantum:* which means "I shall do the next time so much better." It will be a very creditable performance, and a very finished production. Only I feel more and more that I *may* be made for the Drama (God only knows!) but am not made for the Theatre! I rejoice more than I can say in the plain ivory Satin Duchess "pikestaff." I hope Mrs. Bell will be equally ascetic. I am told [that] I shall receive the tickets for your stall and Mrs. Bell's *to-day*—to send them to you myself—so they will come to you to-morrow or Wednesday—and Mrs. Clifford[2] is, I believe, to be alongside of you.—I am sorry to say there is a bad (theatrical) *wind* rising—which is always a worry:

that is, Grundy's[3] play at the Garrick is described to me on several sides as a hopeless failure—and the wretched papers this A.M. seem to really say as much. I have a superstitious sense that such influences are contagious. Still, contagion means contact, and I can't say I do think there are many points of contact between *Slaves of the Ring* as I hear (and see) it confoundingly described and *my* little clutch at lucidity. Poor Miss Calhoun[4]—I am told her part is impossible, but her art excellent. Bless the Barns![5] Yours in all gratitude

Henry James

1. H. V. Esmond, a gifted actor who also wrote plays. He had a key role in *Guy Domville.*

2. Mrs. W. K. Clifford, HJ's friend for many years, wrote popular novels and plays.

3. Sydney Grundy's *Slaves of the Ring* had just opened.

4. Eleanor Calhoun (1865–1957), a native of Visalia, California, had been playing in both French and English plays in Paris and London but was considered by HJ to have limited talents as an actress. She later became the Princess Lazarovich-Hrebelianovich, marrying a Serbian who claimed descent from royalty.

5. An allusion to Red Barns, the Yorkshire house of the Hugh Bells.

To Edmund Gosse
Ms Private

34 De Vere Gardens W.
Thursday. [3 January 1895]

My dear Gosse.

Don't, after all, trouble to come to seek me on Saturday evening at the little nestling pub;[1] for I have changed my policy. I recognize that the only way for me to arrive at 10 o'clock with any patience is to *do* something active or at least positive; so I have had the luminous idea of going to see some other play. I shall go and sit at the Garrick or the Haymarket till about 10.45—or 11—and then I will come into the theatre; at which moment you will be, I trust, in your enraptured stall. All thanks for the charitable intention I frustrate. The 2d act isn't over till 10.15, or 10.30, even, and it is to get *to* that period (at the pub, or at home) that would be the devil. My remedy covers the ground; and I am more or less, already under chloroform. I shall be at home all day—Sunday—won't you come in in the afternoon—to tea—or earlier—if you have people at home? Come to lunch at 2—I have asked Norris. Yours ever,

Henry James

1. Gosse had planned to report to HJ in a nearby pub during the intermissions of *Guy Domville* on the opening night.

To Marion Terry

Ms Colby

Reform Club, Pall Mall, S.W.
Saturday noon [5 January, 1895]

Dear Miss Terry.[1]

I don't want to worry you—on the contrary; so this is only a mere word on the chance I didn't say a couple of nights ago *distinctly* enough that your business of the end of Act I—your going and leaning your face against the pillar of the porch—couldn't possibly be improved. Please believe from me that it is perfectly beautiful and *right*—like, indeed, your whole performance, which will do you great honour. Rest quiet, this weary day, at least about *that*. Yours most truly

Henry James

1. Marion Terry, sister of Ellen Terry and an accomplished actress, played the leading role of Mrs. Peverel opposite George Alexander's Guy Domville.

To Minnie Bourget

Ms Private

34 De Vere Gardens W.
January 5*th* 1895

I am greatly touched by your memento, dear Madame Paul, and you should long ago have had a little of my news had I not been for the last six or seven weeks quite exceptionally occupied. I exceedingly regret to hear that your rheumatism has returned, but I hope that if you have fled from it to Cannes it will at least not overtake you in that stronghold, stronghold, I mean, of the painless elements and of all sweet airs. I write to you at a very nervous moment, and you must forgive me if I don't hold my pen very straight; but it is a moment when I particularly like to be in contact with Bourget and you—a moment when one almost *begs,* superstitiously, for every good wish of every really good friend. It is 5 o'clock in the afternoon and at 8.30 this evening *le sort en est jeté*—my poor little play will be thrown into the arena—like a little white Christian Virgin to the lions and tigers. Since you have already heard of it (I offer Mrs. Wharton[1] all thanks for her sympathy), I venture to send you the enclosed florid *horreur,*[2] which will bring my situation home to you. I hoped *you wouldn't* hear of the little adventure save in the event of its being a success; but now I make haste to get this note off to you before my possible dishonor becomes actual. —*Domine, in manus tuas*—! At any rate, I have been rehearsing all these weeks so continuously and uninterruptedly that I have achieved nothing else besides—not even the translation into a few written lines of all my curiosities and imaginations *sur votre compte.* And I don't ask either of you for a letter now—because you must have something better from myself than these words of incoherent trepidation before that charity becomes a debt. *Vous voilà de nouveau sur les chemins.* I hope it isn't because that lovely chimney-piece smokes. The history of your installation, of your re-initiation, of your endurance, rebellion and escape—all this would be, for me, matter for palpitation—if there is any palpitation left in me after the next few hours are over. Give at any rate my fond love to Bourget—whose "plane" of performance makes me feel like a monster of vulgarity. I do it—because I simply *have* to; *mais je ne m'en vante pas.* All the *midi,* the distinguished, almost Wagnerian Midi, is in your word "Cannes." More than ever, this evening, I wish I could be distinguished! But I cling to *you,* both, with the agitated clutch of this instant; and please say to Mrs. Wharton that I cling a little, if she will permit it, even to *her.* May the remaining 360 days of 1895 not seem to you too many. *Stià bene,* dear Madame Paul, and believe me yours and Paul's very affectionate

Henry James

1. Edith Wharton was a friend of the Bourgets, but several years would elapse before she and HJ would formally meet. She had not yet published any fiction.
2. The *Guy Domville* poster.

To Mr. and Mrs. William James
Ms Harvard

34 De Vere Gardens W.
[5 January 1895]

Dear William and Alice.

I stick this florid "poster" into an envelope this tremulous afternoon, to help to beguile the hours until 8.30—and to bring my trepidation home to you. I am counting on some Psychical intervention from you—this is really the time to show your stuff. I shall possibly cable tomorrow A.M. The omens, thank God, are decently good. But what are omens? *Domine in manus tuas*—! This is a time when a man wants a religion. But Alexander told me yesterday that "the Libraries" had taken in advance £1600 worth of seats! But my hand shakes and I can only write that I am your plucky, but, all the same, lonely and terrified

Henry
Saturday January 5*th*
5.45. P.M.

To William James
Ms Harvard

34 De Vere Gardens W.
Jan. 9*th* 1895

My dear William.

I never cabled to you on Sunday 6th (about the first night of my play) because, as I daresay you will have gathered from some despatches to newspapers (if there have been any, and you have seen them), the case was too complicated. Even now it's a sore trial to me to have to write about it—weary, bruised, sickened, disgusted as one is left by the intense, the cruel ordeal of a first night that—after the immense labour of preparation and the unspeakable tension of suspense—has, in a few brutal moments, not gone well. In three words the delicate, picturesque, extremely human and extremely artistic little play, was taken profanely by a brutal and ill-disposed gallery which had shown signs of malice prepense from the first and which, held in hand till the end, kicked up an infernal row at the fall of the curtain. There followed an abominable quarter of an hour during which all the forces of civilization in the house waged a battle of the most gallant, prolonged and sustained applause with the hoots and jeers and catcalls of the roughs, whose *roars* (like those of a cage of beasts at some infernal "zoo") were only exacerbated (as it were!) by the conflict. It was a cheering scene, as you may imagine, for a nervous, sensitive, exhausted author to face—and you must spare my going over again the horrid hour, or those of disappointment and depression that have followed it; from which last, however, I am rapidly and resolutely, thank God, emerging. The "papers" have into the bargain, been mainly ill-natured and densely stupid and vulgar; but the only two dramatic critics* who count have done one mere justice. Meanwhile all *private* opinion is apparently one of extreme admiration—I have been flooded with letters of the warmest protest and assurance. The horridest thing about the odious scene was that Alexander lost his head and made a speech of a dozen words in which (in his nervous bewilderment) he had the air of deferring to the rumpus as to the "opinion of the public," an accident that excited, outside of the obstreperous gallery, universal reprobation and of which he has since been, I think, signally ashamed. It is what Archer alludes to in the provisional few words in the *World,* which, with Clement Scott's article in the *Telegraph,* I sent you by this post. I add two or three letters that will show you the "key" of the aforesaid "private" opinion. Every one who was there has either written to me or come to see me—I mean every one I know and many people I don't. Obviously the little play, which I strove to make as broad, as gross, as simple, as clear, as British, in a word, as possible, is over the heads of the *usual* vulgar theatre-going London public—and the chance of its going for a while (which it is too early to measure) will depend wholly on its holding on long enough to attract the *unusual.* I was there the second night (Monday, 7th) when, before a full house—a remarkably good "money" house Alexander told me—it went singularly well. But it's soon to see or to say, and I'm prepared for the worst. The thing fills me with horror for the abysmal vulgarity and brutality of the theatre and its regular public**—which God knows I have had intensely even when working (from motives as "pure" as pecuniary motives *can* be) against it; and I feel as if the simple freedom of mind thus begotten to return to one's legitimate form would be simply by itself a divine solace for everything. Don't worry about me: I'm a Rock. If the play has no life on the stage I shall publish it; it's altogether the best thing I've done. You would understand better the elements of the case if you had seen the thing it followed (*The Masqueraders*) and the thing that is now succeeding at the Haymarket—the thing of Oscar Wilde's.[1] On the basis of *their* being plays, or successes, my thing is necessarily neither. Doubtless, moreover, the want of a roaring actuality, simplified to a few big *familiar* effects, in my subject—an episode in the history of an old English Catholic family in the last century—militates against it, with all *usual* theatrical people, who don't want plays (from variety and nimbleness of fancy) of different *kinds,* like books and stories, but only of *one* kind, which their stiff, rudimentary, clumsily-working vision recognizes as the kind they've had before. And yet I had tried so to meet them! But you can't make a sow's ear out of a silk purse.—I can't write more—and don't ask for details. This week will probably determine the fate of the piece. If there is increased advance-booking it will go on. If there isn't, it will be withdrawn, and with it all my little hope of profit. The time one has given to such an affair from the very first to the very last represents in all—so inconceivably great, to the uninitiated, is the amount—a pitiful, tragic bankruptcy of hours that might have been rendered retroactively golden. But I am not plangent—one must take the thick with the thin—and I have such possibilities of another and better sort before me. I am only sorry for your and Alice's having to be so sorry for yours forever,

Henry

P.S. I can't find the letter I wanted most to send you—it was so singularly eloquent and strong from (on the part of her husband too) Mrs. Frank Hill, wife of the ex-editor of the *Daily News*—both very old friends of mine. I have stupidly lost it somehow. But I stick in a little one from the dramatic critic of the *St. James's Gazette.* Clement Scott's article in the *Telegraph*—is the work of a man crudely awfully vulgar and Philistine—but I only mention it to show how he has been "drawn." But their standard of "subtlety"! —God help us! With one's i's all dotted as with pumpkins!—

* W. Archer and Clement Scott. I will send you Archer's next week notice.

** I mean as represented by most of the Newspaper people—a really squalid crew.

1. HJ had attended, on the first night of his own play, Oscar Wilde's new play at the Haymarket, *An Ideal Husband.*

To W. Morton Fullerton

Ms Harvard

34 De Vere Gardens W.
January 9*th* 1895

My dear Fullerton.

Your sympathy enters into the soul of a man singularly accessible to affection and with whom sensibility to certain manifestations of it is a pleasure akin in its quality—almost to pain.—The vulgar, the altogether brutish rumpus the other night over my harmless and ingenious little play was the abomination of an hour—and an hour only. Deep and dark is the abyss of the theatre. Even in the full consciousness of the purity and lucidity of one's motives (mine are worthy of Benjamin Franklin) one asks one's self what one is doing in that *galère.* However, nothing matters but one's honour and one's sanity. The little play in question presents to the uncivilized the unpardonable anomaly of not belonging to the kind which is the only kind they know—a roaring actuality of intention united to a "bloody" crudity of execution. In the presence of that howling mob I felt once for all what an utter non-conductor such an atmosphere, even when comparatively cleared, must ever be to even the most simplified ingenuity and the most studied Britishness of which I am capable. You *can't,* after all make a sow's ear out of a silk purse—which is what I have been too heroically trying. The future is exquisitely rosy to me with the invitation to purge myself of that heroism and return to the exercise of diviner functions. I am purged—the other night purged me. Anderson's[1] part of the work was exquisite. I have innumerable notes to answer. I *have* been deluged with reassurance and admiration. But the play is wounded, probably to death. Fortunately it is not a vital member of yours, my dear Fullerton, very exhaustedly, preoccupiedly and responsively,

Henry James

P.S. If the thing comes off I shall probably publish it, and then you shall have a copy.

1. Percy Anderson, the stage designer.

To William Dean Howells

Ms Harvard

34 De Vere Gardens W.
January 22*d* 1895

My dear Howells.

I have two good things—and have had them for some time—to thank you for. One is John's charming paper about the Beaux Arts which I was delighted you should have sent me—so lovely it is and young and fresh and vivid and in every way calculated to minister to the "fondness of a father" and the frenzy of a mother—to say nothing of the pride of an affectionate old friend. The dear boy seems to have been born to invent new ways of being filially gratifying—generally delectable. Happy you—happy, even if you had *only* him! Surely, surely you *must* all come out this summer to visit him with your condign tenderness. Any other course will be utterly shabby of you. I regard this as quite settled.—Secondly (or firstly it should have been), I am indebted to you for your most benignant letter of December last. It lies open before me and I read it again and am soothed and cheered and comforted again. You put your finger sympathetically on the place and spoke of what I wanted you to speak of. I *have* felt, for a long time past, that I have fallen upon evil days—every sign or symbol of one's being in the least *wanted,* anywhere or by any one, have so utterly failed. A new generation, that I know not, and mainly prize not, had taken universal possession. The sense of being utterly out of it weighed me down, and I asked myself what the future would be. All these melancholies were qualified indeed by one redeeming reflection—the sense of how little, for a good while past (for reasons very logical, but accidental and temporary), I had been producing. I *did* say to myself "Produce again—produce; produce better than ever, and all will yet be well"; and there was sustenance in that so far as it went. But it has meant much more to me since *you* have said it—for it *is,* practically, what you admirably say. It is exactly, moreover, what I mean to admirably do—and have meant, all along, about this time to get into the motion of. The whole thing, however, represents a great change in my life, inasmuch as what is clear is that periodical publication is practically closed to me—I'm the last hand that the magazines, in this country or in the U.S., seem to want. I won't afflict you with the now accumulated (during all these past years) evidence on which this induction rests—and I have spoken of it to no creature till, at this late day, I speak of it to you. But, until, the other month (two months ago), Henry Harper, here, made a friendly overture to me on the part of his magazine, no sign, no symbol of any sort, has come to me from any periodical whatever—and many visible demonstrations of their having, on the contrary, no use for me. I can't go into details—and they would make you turn pale! I'm utterly out of it *here*—and *Scribner,* the *Century,* the *Cosmopolitan,* will have nothing to say to me—above all for fiction. The *Atlantic,* and Houghton and Mifflin, treat me like the dust beneath their feet; and the Macmillans, here, have cold-shouldered me out of all relation with them. All this, I needn't say, is for your *segretissimo* ear. What it means is that "production" for me, as aforesaid, means production of the little *book* pure and simple—independent of any antecedent appearance; and, truth to tell, now that I wholly *see* that, and have at last accepted it, I am, incongruously, not at all sorry. I am indeed very serene. I have always hated the magazine form, magazine conditions and manners, and much of the magazine company. I hate the horrid little subordinate part that one plays in the catchpenny picture book—and the negation of all literature that the insolence of the picture-book imposes. The money-difference will be great—but not so great after a bit as at first; and the other differences will be so all to the good that even from the economic point of view they will tend to make up for that and perhaps finally even completely do so. It is about the distinctness of one's *book-position* that you have so substantially reassured me; and I mean to do far better work than ever I have done before. I have, potentially, improved immensely

—and am bursting with ideas and subjects: though the act of composition is, with me, more and more slow, painful and difficult. I shall never again write a *long* novel; but I hope to write six immortal short ones—and some tales of the same quality. Forgive, my dear Howells, the cynical egotism of these remarks—the fault of which is in your own sympathy. Don't fail me this summer. I shall probably not, as usual, absent myself from these islands—not be beyond the Alps as I was when you were here last. That way Boston lies, which is the deadliest form of madness. I sent you only last night messages of affection by dear little "Ned" Abbey, who presently sails for N.Y. laden with the beautiful work he has been doing for the new Boston public library.[1] I hope you will see him—he will speak of me competently and kindly. I wish all power to your elbow. Let me hear as soon as there is a sound of packing. Tell Mildred I rejoice in the memory of her. Give my love to your wife, and believe me my dear Howells yours in all constancy,

Henry James

1. Edwin A. Abbey's mural of "The Quest for the Holy Grail," in which HJ had taken a particular interest.

To Mr. and Mrs. William James
Ms Harvard

34 De Vere Gardens W.
February 2*d* 1895

Dearest William and Alice.

You will think that I haven't been very communicative for a month—but I have had to do from day to day, what seemed possible and seemed best; and I wanted, moreover, to wait till I should have received your response to my letter of January 8th, as to answer *that* (what you would write after you had heard from me) would be more to the point than to reply to your earlier words—which however have most liberally and soothingly come to me. The first of these signs was a good and generous letter from you, dear Alice, from Philadelphia—of January 5th, enclosing a couple of the notes you had received from William in your absence. Two days ago came William's letter of January 19th, telling of the arrival of mine of the 8th, which appears to have been long in reaching you, but which went by the very first post that departed after the 5th. The poor little play seems already, thank God, ancient history, though I have lived through, in its company, the horridest four weeks of my life. Produce a play and you will know, better than I can tell you, how such an ordeal—odious in its essence!—is only made tolerable and palatable by great success; and in how many ways accordingly non-success may be tormenting and tragic, a bitterness of every hour, ramifying into every throb of one's consciousness. Tonight the thing will have lived the whole of its troubled little life of thirty-one performances and will be "taken off," to be followed on February 5th by a piece by Oscar Wilde that will have probably a very different fate. On the night of the 5th, too nervous to do anything else, I had the ingenious thought of going to some other theatre and seeing some other play as a means of being coerced into quietness from 8 till 10.45. I went accordingly to the Haymarket, to a new piece by the said O.W. that had just been produced—"An Ideal Husband." I sat through it and saw it played with every appearance (so far as the crowded house was an appearance) of complete success, and *that* gave me the most fearful apprehension. The thing seemed to me so helpless, so crude, so bad, so clumsy, feeble and vulgar, that as I walked away across St. James's Square to learn my own fate, the prosperity of what I had seen seemed to me to constitute a dreadful presumption of the shipwreck of *Guy Domville;* and I stopped in the middle of the Square, paralysed by the terror of this probability—afraid to go on and learn more. "How *can* my piece do anything with a public with whom *that* is a success?" It couldn't—but even then the full truth was, "mercifully," not revealed to me; the truth that in a short month my piece would be whisked away to make room for the triumphant Oscar.[1] If, as I say, this episode has, by this time, become ancient history to me, it is, thank heaven, because when a thing, for me (a piece of work), is done, it's done: I get quickly detached and away from it, and am wholly given up to the better and fresher life of the next thing to come. This is particularly the case now, with my literary way blocked so long and my production smothered by these theatrical lures: I have such arrears on hand and so many things seem to wait for me—that I want far more and that it will be nobler to do—that I am looking in a very different direction than in that of the sacrificed little play.

Partly for this reason, this receiving from you all the retarded echo of my reverse and having to live over it and go over it with you (you must excuse me if I don't do so much) is the thing, in the whole business, that has been most of an anguish and that I dreaded most in advance. As for the play, in three words, it has been, I think I may say, a rare and distinguished private success and scarcely anything at all of a public one. By a private success, I mean with the even moderately cultivated, civilized and intelligent *individual,* with "people of taste" in short, of almost any kind, as distinguished from the vast English Philistine mob—the regular "theatrical public" of London, which, of all the vulgar publics London contains, is the most brutishly and densely vulgar. This congregation, the things they do like sufficiently judge; and while the successful "Masqueraders" was going on, before my play, at the St. James's, heaven knows how anxiously I asked myself what would become of me, even with every precaution taken, in the very atmosphere in which such a thing as that could live. The stupid public is the big public, and the perceptive one the small, and the small doesn't suffice to keep a thing afloat. What appears largely to have enabled *G.D.* to go on even a month is the fact that almost every one who has been to see it at all appears to have been two or three times. I have been deluged with letters of admiration and interest, and, as I think I wrote to K. P. Loring the other day in a note which I hope she will have sent you, this little drama has brought me in two or three weeks twenty-five times more letters than a career of refined literary virtue has brought (about my books) in twenty-five years. These things have mainly (most of all when they were, as they largely were, from strangers) [been] such as I felt I must answer; and that has consumed a formidable amount of time, and been a considerable part of the reason I haven't written to you more. These letters I haven't kept—they were mementoes of too horrid an experience; some two or three of the latest to come, which I enclose, as they may strike you. Please burn them up. The papers I have simply, in a single case, not read —and it was *impossible* for me to traffic in them—to gather them up and send them to you. I am told that many were very rude indeed—but that those that weren't were very genial. It hasn't mattered to me—for I have too long and too carefully watched their pronouncements, their standards, and know too much what they are, in the light of the things that draw them out. The London theatre-man *can't* be anything but a gross vulgarian. You will *ricaner* perhaps, at *my* pretending, in my own case to speak: but I very quickly consider that I am *absolutely* clear-sighted about my piece, and know the rights and the wrongs of it far better than all the rest of them (I mean of those who have publicly spoken) put together. The play has failed because it has been *unfamiliar.* It is an exceedingly skilful, considered and expert piece of construction—with a neatness of art, in this particular, that their measurement, their utterly uninitiated sense, is too coarse and too stupid for. It has shipwrecked not in the least in the treatment (save, I hasten to add, in those fatal particulars in which the treatment was the acting); but definitely, measurably, fatally, on the subject. I knew the subject had this danger of unfamiliarity—but what I hoped was that (especially as it was intrinsically beautiful—as seemed to me, at least—and human and warm and touching) I should be artfully able to draw it near and make it (especially with the aid of the best representation, as I hope, and the most perfect picture, to the eye and aesthetic sense, that London could give) intimate, vivid and convincing. What I believed—or almost!—was that it would be so objective, so picturesque, so neat as a little coloured drama, so interesting as a little old-time story, far enough off to have a certain "Henry Esmond" quality and yet near enough for all reality—that it would have enough of all these things to justify itself and form, by itself, as it were, a little class of one happy specimen. This was plainly what Alexander thought, who absolutely jumped at the play. But I no sooner found myself in the presence of those yelling barbarians of the first night and learned what could be the savagery of their disappointment that one wasn't perfectly the *same* as everything else they had ever seen, than the dream and delusion of my having made a successful appeal to the cosy, childlike, naïf, domestic British imagination (which was what I had calculated) dropped from me in the twinkling of an eye. I saw they couldn't care one straw for a damned young last-century English Catholic, who lived in an old-time Catholic world and acted, with every one else in the play, from remote and romantic Catholic motives. The whole thing was for them, remote, and all the intensity of one's ingenuity couldn't make it anything else. It has made it something else for the *few*—but that is all. Such is the bare history of poor G.D.—which, I beg you to believe, throws no light on my "technical skill" which isn't a light that that mystery ought to rejoice to have thrown. The newspaper people muddle things up with the most foredoomed crudity; and I am capable of analysing the whole thing far more scientifically and drawing from it lessons far more pertinent and practical than all of them put together. It is perfectly true that the novelist has a fearful long row to hoe to get into any practical relation to the grovelling stage, and his difficulty is precisely double: it bears, on one side, upon the question of method and on the other upon the question of subject. If he is really in earnest, as I have been, he surmounts the former difficulty before he surmounts the latter. I have worked like a horse—far harder than any one will ever know—over the whole stiff mystery of "technique"—I have run it to earth, and I don't in the last hesitate to say that, for the comparatively poor and meagre, the piteously simplified, purposes of the English stage, I have made it absolutely my own, put it into my pocket. The question of realising how different is the attitude of the theatre-goer toward the quality of thing which might be a story in a book from his attitude toward the quality of thing that is given to him as a story in a play is another matter altogether. *That* difficulty is portentous, for any writer who doesn't approach it naively, as only a very limited and simple-minded writer can. One has to *make* one's self so limited and simple to conceive a subject, see a subject, simply enough, and that, in a nutshell, is where I have stumbled. And yet if you were to have seen my play!—I haven't been near the theatre since the second night, but I shall go down there late this evening to see it buried and bid good-bye to the actors. There will have been a matinee this afternoon as well—and there was an afternoon performance at Brighton two days ago as successful as the one of a fortnight since. And there was a Wednesday matinee last week as well as a Saturday, and every *raffiné* in London (I mean of course only the people who *don't* go to the usual things) has been to see it, and yet it doesn't "go!" I am very sorry for Marion Terry, who has delighted in her part and made the great hit of her career, I should suppose, in it, and who has to give it up thus untimely. Her charming acting has done much for the little run. Of Alexander I can't bear to speak.—The money disappointment is of course keen—as it was wholly for money I adventured. But the poor four weeks have brought me $1,100—which shows what a tidy sum many times four weeks would have brought; without my lifting, as they say, after the first performance, a finger.—I have written you so long-windedly on this matter that I have left myself neither time nor space for anything else. I must catch the post and will write more sociably something by the next one. I wish very much you would let Katharine see this—and the enclosures, as letters have begun to flow in to me from America too, and I must economize. One's time, in the whole history, has gone like water—and still it pours out. *Please* don't send me anything out of newspapers. Always your

Henry

1. Oscar Wilde's *The Importance of Being Earnest* succeeded *Guy Domville* at the St. James's.

To William James
Ms Harvard

34 De Vere Gardens W.
Feb. 4*th* [1895]

My dear William.

Since I posted my letter to you on Saturday all the enclosed have come in (this is Monday A.M.), and as they are in the same line as the two or three notes I sent you, I add them thereto as a relevant postscript. I would send some of the earlier ones if I had only *kept* them. I went down to the theatre on Saturday night, to find that the play goes on into *this* week—its *fifth* week; so that instead of the $1,100 I spoke of (which was under the mark) I shall have made upwards of $1,300. That is a vulgar detail; a much greater consolation is the sense—brought to me by all the things *said* to me, and all the things in the air—that my "position" is much more "distinguished" in consequence of *Guy Domville,* than before—is in fact very distinguished. Read the notes—if they care for them—to Boott and to Grace N. As regards the phrase in Miss Robins's about Alexander, it is a relief to have the dreadful truth fairly and frankly out—he *is* atrocious. *But burn this letter and don't say I say so, for the world.* His whole treatment of, and attitude to, the *material* of the part was, from the first, fatal—portentous to me in its gross want of perception of the intentions delicacies and atmosphere, of the character generally. He wanted everything "out" that an actor with any fine sense of his material, his opportunities, wouldn't have sacrificed for the world. Oh, the mutilated brutally simplified, massacred little play!—I speak of course solely from the point of view of what complete interpretation (something of the Thé[âtre] Français order) would have done with it. To do a thing "out" of which all the best things have to come, because the actors can't *do* them, can't touch them! and I speak of things absolutely theatrical, that ought to be the air they breathe. I can't help idly wishing the Season were later—the period of the American advent. I have an idea the compatriots would come in their hundreds and keep the thing on a couple of months longer—or some weeks at least; and not merely *as* compatriots, but as feeling the play better. Miss Bessie Minturn "raves" about it—she is here now. See the Abbeys, who have been staying with her here, if you can—when he arrives in Boston with his beautiful work for the new Public Library. You can see them though Warner. Ever yours

Henry

To Alphonse Daudet

Ms Harvard

34 De Vere Gardens W.
ce 12 février [1895] Londres

Cher ami et confrère.

Je n'ai pas voulu, avant de l'avoir longuement savouré, vous remercier de votre nouveau livre, que vous m'avez envoyé l'autre jour si amicalement. Je suis très touché et tout réchauffé (au temps où nous sommes), de ce signe de votre bon souvenir. J'ai lu *Petite Paroisse* comme je vous lis toujours—dans un doux recueillement traversé de frissons pénétrants. Il n'y a pas de manière de faire qui me contente aussi pleinement que la vôtre; je l'avais constaté de nouveau, justement ces jours-là, en relisant—chacun pour la troisième fois—*Sapho* et *l'Immortel.* Ça m'est une véritable joie de vous voir trouver au sortir (il y paraît bien), de vos sombres années, ce beau et riche roman, où la vie se joue si largement et librement, où l'observation et la poésie s'étreignent et se confondent. J'avais soif du timbre si spécial de votre voix de couleur—de votre monde et vous, tel que vous nous le donnez—et m'en voilà tout rafraîchi. Je tiens à croire que c'est une reprise entière de vos moyens, de vos grandes aises—à croire, c'est à dire, que vous allez bien de mieux en mieux. J'y mettrai plus de foi encore en vous voyant, au mois de mai ou de juin, débarquer sur cette côte hospitalière—qui ne l'aura jamais été pour personne (pas même pour Vallès ou pour Rochefort!)[1] plus que—et de moins entendus!—que moi-même. J'en ai traversé une considérable l'autre jour pour vous—en présidant à la conférence que ce digne et terne M. Huguemet a consacré à University College, à quelques-uns de vos romans. La salle était comble, on y était entassé et debout; je constatais un appétit, une curiosité du sujet qui m'a fait bien regretter que la pauvre conférencier se doutât si peu de ce qu'il y avait à en tirer. J'étais tout tenté de lui arracher la parole—mais j'ai dû me borner, en proposant un vote de remerciements, à le qualifier d'intéressant et d'entraînant et à annoncer à l'auditoire que je vous ferais connaître le plaisir que nous avions eu à passer une heure avec vous—ce qui m'a valu de longs applaudissements. Je viens d'en passer encore une en vous infligeant ces trop nombreuses pages de reconnaissance, de bon espoir et de mauvais français. Trouvez-y, mon cher Daudet, pour tous les vôtres comme pour vous-même l'affectueuse pensée de

Henry James

1. Daudet had informed HJ of his plan to visit London in May. James alludes to Jules Vallès (1835–1885), exiled to England in 1871 for his part in the Commune, and Henri de Rochefort (1830–1913), who had fled France in 1868 for Belgium and England after his journalistic attacks on Napoleon III.

To Mrs. Edward Compton

Ms Texas

The Castle, Dublin
March 15*th* [1895]

Dear Mrs. Compton.

Your letter followed me three days ago to this place, where I am paying a short visit; and in ordinary circumstances I should have answered it immediately. But the day after I got here I was seized with a violent attack of lumbago, which, until today, has made my existence, in very trying and awkward conditions, a burden to me, and keeping me bent almost double, made it impossible I should write. I can't do more today than at least acknowledge your letter—tomorrow or next day I shall write to you more fully, though, after all, there is little "fulness" in what I have to communicate. I have no good news for you—for there has been since the New Year, none but the very worst possible for myself. The utter and complete failure of my play at the St. James's has completely sickened me with the theatre and made me feel, at any rate for the present, like washing my hands of it forever. *Guy Domville* was an unmitigated disaster—hooted at, as I was hooted at myself, by a brutal mob, and fruitless of any of the consequences for which I have striven. It brought me neither profit nor encouragement of any sort—and it represented infinite labour, effort and ingenuity. It had every advantage of production that I could have hoped for and yet proved simply the most horrible experience of my life. As I walked home, alone, after that first night, I swore to myself an oath never again to have anything to do with a business which lets one into such traps, abysses and heart-break. "Never" is a long word, but I don't see beyond it yet. I can't moreover, in the situation in which *Guy Domville* has landed me, *afford* to write another play. I have written six in all, and have made no money to speak of by any. I must do immediate work that pays. These are the wretched, tragic facts. Please communicate them to Compton, with my liveliest regrets. If *G.D.* had succeeded I should have willingly gone on with the subject I sketched to him. But the whole situation is altered now. What the St. James's couldn't do for me nothing can—I have practically renounced my deluded dreams. Such at any rate is the only way in which I can consider the matter now. This is after all the essence of my response to your kind letter. I can't even, alas, *talk* of the thing I talked of to Compton. I wish I could say to you something more gratifying.[1] But I can only thank you both for your friendly confidence in me even after the hideous episode of the St. James's. Believe me, dear Mrs. Compton, yours most truly

Henry James

1. It will be recalled that HJ originally offered *Guy Domville* to the Comptons and that they argued its lack of appeal to British audiences (see letter to Compton, 2 May 1893). Compton now hoped HJ would write a play for him.

Appendix
Four Letters from Constance Fenimore Woolson to Henry James

Constance Fenimore Woolson (1840–1894) and Henry James met in Florence during the spring of 1880. The forty-year-old spinster, a writer of regional stories, was an attractive gentlewoman with shy manners and firm opinions; and she was a fervent admirer of James's works. Miss Woolson had brought with her a letter of introduction from one of James's Temple cousins, and James, in deference to this and with his customary courtesies, was an attentive and kindly companion. He expounded on the paintings and the sculptures, and after an intensive period of sightseeing and pleasant encounters, the new friends parted. He was homeward bound, after an absence from the United States of six years. She had come to Europe for a long stay. They did not meet again for three years, but they carried on a correspondence. It is to this period that the letters printed here belong. Much of the time Miss Woolson spent in Florence, Rome, and Venice, and during the hot months of the year she went to Switzerland. Her existence was lonely. After her day at her desk she would go out for a brisk evening walk or, when she was in Venice, a soothing gondola ride; she cheered herself with mountain views, inspiring paintings, and the relics of antiquity. In the autumn of 1883 she left the warm south to spend three years in England, years in which she was never far from James's rooms in Bolton Street. James was leading a very busy literary life, and they met occasionally.

In 1886 Miss Woolson resumed her continental wanderings, consoling herself on her departure with a promise from James that he would visit her in Italy every year. He kept his word during a number of years, even occupying an apartment during the spring of 1887, in her villa Brichieri residence on Bellosguardo in Florence and traveling to Geneva for a rendezvous (in separate hotels) in 1888. Fenimore, as he called her, varied her travels with an 1889 tour of Greece and Egypt and with another sojourn, this time of two years, in England. Then she went back once again to Venice. She passed a depressed 1893 Christmas by her fireside and during lonely sightseeing took notes on cemeteries, lagoon craft, and sunken Venetian islands. Then she fell ill with influenza. On 24 January 1894 she jumped or fell out of an upper window of the Casa Semitecolo, which she had rented for the winter. Henry James, and most of her friends, believed that she had committed suicide. James went to Venice during the spring of 1894 to help her sister wind up Fenimore's affairs.

The four letters that follow are believed to be all that remain of the fourteen-year correspondence between James and Miss Woolson. According to the late Clare Benedict, Miss Woolson's niece, the two destroyed each other's letters by mutual agreement, with Henry James reclaiming such letters as remained in her rooms in the Semitecolo. These four letters survived through the circumstance that three were sent to James in America and the fourth he apparently carried with him from London, having received it shortly before sailing. Once in America, the letters became mingled with the James family papers. When the editor of this volume found them, they were catalogued with the William James correspondence.

For a full account of the friendship between Henry James and Constance Fenimore Woolson, see Leon Edel, *The Conquest of London, 1870–1881* (1962) and *The Middle Years, 1882–1895* (1962), the second and third volumes of *The Life of Henry James.* Clare Benedict, Miss Woolson's niece, edited three volumes of family documents entitled *Five Generations, 1785–1923,* which were privately printed in London (1929–1930) and distributed by Miss Benedict to many libraries. The second volume, entirely devoted to Miss Woolson, contains letters, excerpts from diaries, notebooks, and laudatory comment. HJ's essay on Miss Woolson appeared in *Partial Portraits* (1888). Van Wyck Brooks dealt with her work in *The Times of Melville and Whitman* (1947). See also Rayburn S. Moore, *Constance Fenimore Woolson* (1963), a study of her career and work. There is a substantial entry on Miss Woolson's life and work in *Notable American Women, 1607–1950* (1971), III, 670–672.

To Henry James
Ms Harvard

Hotel Bristol
Sorrento
Feb. 12*th* [1882]

Dear Mr. James.

I *was* much mystified by those two letters of yours. The solution, which slowly presented itself—that you had forgotten on the 21st that you had written me two weeks earlier—was rather mortifying. But I know how full your life is of all sorts of things—engagements, enjoyments, society, duties, traveling, "people," the plans for, and, more than all, the constant accomplishment of work like yours—it is a marvel to me how you can carry them all on together as you do. "If we will take the good we find, asking no questions, we shall have heaping measure"—you know; so I took my "good," and made it as "heaping" as possible. Two letters and a photograph heap quite well.

But the real truth is—I simply forgave you. It does'nt make much difference what you do as an individual—one has to forgive the author of *Hawthorne* and the *Portrait.*[1] In the same way you might have said the most horrible things in Florence and Rome, and I am afraid I should have forgiven them on account of the voice. I have always been critical about voices (of late years there is of course a second reason),[2] and when I find one to my mind, my temper becomes beatific.—If you didn't say any very horrible things in Florence and Rome, you are mentioning a few from Washington—when you tell me my letter was full of "amiable elements"! I don't think a letter could be described in a more depressing way.

The motive of that second letter of yours, I have of course divined. When you wrote on the 6th you had been only a week at home,[3] and had not been seized by homesickness (that anomaly of words is your fault, not mine); but on the 21st you were full in its deadly clutches, and you wrote, I have no doubt, to every foreign friend you have in the world, so that the long snowy winter of exile might be broken by the arrival of the answers, one by one. I presume the very postage-stamps have been like Old Masters to you. The head of Victoria is dearest probably. Then, the mythological figures of Paris. The moustache of Umberto is, I hope, third on the list, because you ought not to care for people who are so thick-skinned as to spend winters in Switzerland and Germany. But I fancy that first homesickness has abated, somewhat. And you are Americanized already—oh yes, you are; you address this last letter with my first and last name and a middle initial!

Your being in Washington interests me.[4] I should have said that you would have preferred Boston or New York. Washington society is more national; it is not the limited (your word) circle of Cambridge-Harvard and Westchester county tradition and antecedents. *I* do not say that limited is your word; but the Boston ladies do, it seems. In Florence I heard a part of a Boston lady's letter read aloud, and in it was this: "I am afraid she *is* awfully limited'—to use Harry James' word."—Day before yesterday, by the way, I heard a portion of a Washington letter read aloud (a young lady's letter), and in it was this: "It has been extremely quiet here—more quiet than it has been for years. But we *have* got Henry James—who has just arrived." I wanted to say—"And now of course it will immediately become hilarious—he is such a turbulently gay, eager, excitable person." But I hope you are finding something to like over there. I note that tepid little line in your letter—about seeing "plenty of people" in New York—but "no one in particular." But there are a number of very particular people indeed in Boston—so I have always been given to understand—and perhaps they have branches in Washington. Perhaps too that New York line was a "subterfuge." I might go on and say that I shall always be looking out for subterfuges after this. But it would'nt be true, and I could never live up to it. So I had better not pretend. I am not clever—as you must have seen for yourself before this—and I have given up trying to learn the manner of it. It was of no use.

Washington is very pretty in the Spring. They have wonderful flowering trees there, like no others I ever saw. Arlington too at that season is something to remember. But you won't remember it. In this connection let me say that I did not fully express myself about that southern beach and "inspirational" headland—to which you refer. I said that you would not believe in them. But what I meant was—not that you would not, or did not, believe in their existence, or even in their beauty—for you have shown in your writings that you appreciate both. But that you did not believe that they could ever be more to you than so much horizontal sand, well smoothed, and so much perpendicular limestone, well set up; whereas *I* believe that, if you could see them under the right conditions, they would be more. I did not fully express myself, but cut off my thread—as I have done before—for fear you would think it "unimportant"—that terrible word of yours! I do'nt deny, you know, that generally it *is* unimportant.

No—you do not love your native land. It is plainly evident. One of Cherbuliez' cleverest divinations—perhaps you remember it?—is, "Quand les femmes aiment quelque chose, cherchez bien, vous trouverez que sous la chose qu'elles aiment, il y a *quelqu'un*"[5] and it has occurred to me that this may not be an exclusively feminine trait, and, that under your dislike for America, there may be—*quelqu'un*. Or perhaps it is the converse. But, do you know, though I am an American of the interior of New Hampshire (my birthplace),[6] an American of the Western Reserve of Ohio, I quite understand why you feel as you do. It is owing to personal characteristics more than to the accident of the sort of life you have led—although the latter has of course intensified the former. But if you had never left the banks of the Maumee, you would still have been, dumbly, an "alienated American" (I suppose you have no idea where the Maumee is!).[7]

I see the *Century* announces a biographical notice of you, with portrait.[8] A "biographical notice"—if only the biographer of Hawthorne could write it, we should see some fine things! I should be sorry for the biographed! I have often noticed your keen judgment of your own work. I do not always agree with it; it is sometimes too keen. I mean by this that you do not always come down fully into the place of the reader—we will say the best reader, for you would'nt accept the ordinary ones. The portrait will show the pretty American girl of seventeen, whom I met at Engelberg, how correct is her idea of you. She had asked if I knew this and that literary personage, and came after a while to you. "How does he look?" she inquired. "I have always fancied that he was very slender, very fastidious and aristocratic-looking, that he spoke in a very low voice, and had those cool sarcastic eyes, and a lovely straight nose, you know." I told her that was precisely you. You asked about Engelberg; I arrived there July 10th, and remained until September 16th. I did not know of course that you were within a thousand miles.[9] But, even if you were, our missing each other was not remarkable. Our meeting would have been that. I have never had such a sense of being hidden, merged, lost, as in this crowded compact little Europe.

I am wondering if you have seen Mr. G. W. Curtis—the champion who used his graceful lance for you in Harper's so many times, during the Hawthorne tournament.[10] And I am wondering if the rumor of a play you are said to have written for Willie Edouin,[11] is true. And I am resigned in advance to the tidings that you have written one for Lawrence Barrett—that eminently respectable actor whom all our American literary men persist in admiring. I never could understand why. (If you see any subjunctive wrong here or anywhere, please remember how little they cared for subjunctives on the Western Reserve! I have always been awe-struck by your use of them—it is so infallible.) My kind friend Mr. R. H. Dana has passed away.[12] They have made his grave in the beautiful cemetery at Rome. During my last stay in Florence—in October—he was so good as to talk to me quite often in the evenings. He told me of the old Transcendental days;—of Emerson as he was at that time; of Thoreau, whom he ridiculed highly; of Margaret Fuller, whom he called "Mag"! and many others. I had known the times and the people only from books. More than once—while listening to him—I caught myself smiling over a remembrance of your group, gathered round "Flaxman's attenuated outlines".[13]—Your poor serious soul-to-soul enemy, Miss Phelps[14]—I wonder if you saw her. I have recently listened to a rather intimate description of the Miss Howard (*One Summer*)[15] of whom you spoke in Rome as the writer-ess who wished to make your acquaintance; and I am sure you would not like her. However, I had better be careful; you liked that Miss Fletcher![16] But you do not want to know the little literary women. Only the great ones—like George Eliot. I am not barring myself out here, because I do not come in as a literary woman at all, but as a sort of—of admiring aunt. I think that expresses it.

Thanks for the *Portrait*. I have seen quite a number of the criticisms that have appeared, and have been interested in them because of one point.

But first—what a splendid success for a book of that grade—a book of such delicately fine workmanship—to have every journal, from the London dailies down through all the magazines to the newspapers of Ohio, bringing out a notice of it as an important event of the day. No other novelist has this but you. (It is true that you do not appreciate the newspapers of Ohio.) You know what I think of the rank of your work; it entertains me much to watch the careless public advancing towards my opinion.

The point I note is—that, over the *Portrait*, our American critics have come to an entirely new, and this time I think permanent, tone about you. Their first tone was unmitigated praise. I do'nt think you appreciated, over there among the chimney-pots, the laudation your books received in America, as they came out one by one. (We little fish did! We little fish became worn to skeletons owing to the constant admonitions we received to regard the beauty, the grace, the incomparable perfections of all sorts and kinds of the proud salmon of the pond; we ended by hating that salmon.) It was but human, however, that this laudation should not go on forever. In addition—as you were all the time advancing—it began to occur to these critics that you were going by even their encouragement; that possibly too you did not estimate at its true worth the importance of their help and sympathy. They began, in short, to be jealous. Your *Hawthorne* gave them their opportunity; your *Washington Square* did not decrease it. That was their second tone.—The *Portrait* has now brought them to a third. The first—flattering as it was—was never without the accompanying chord that you were a young fellow; your talent, your style, your this and that, were marvelous *in* a young fellow etc. They looked forward "confidently" to your "future." But, after all, they would have preferred to continue looking forward. It gave a pleasant sense of patronage. But—in the *Portrait*—this future is more than suspected to have become the present. They see it and cannot deny it. They do'nt like it. The whole tone is different. With ill humor here and there according to their tempers—with more or less clearness according to their powers of perception, they are virtually acknowledging, one and all, in these criticisms, that you are no longer the coming man, but that (whether for good or for ill) you have "arrived." To acknowledge this has been for some of them like little Rosier's selling his bibelots,[17] or rather as that sacrifice of his struck Isabel—"as if he had had all his teeth drawn." One or two remark, gloomily, that you have founded a new school of novel-writing, and get out of it in that way; because they are free, of course, to not admire the school.—I notice that they have all brought out their very best language for the occasion; there has been a great display of theory and choice of epithet.—I have'nt yet seen the review in parallel—whatever that may mean—of you and Mr. Howells, in the *Atlantic;*[18] it is on the way over. But, as I have never been able to comprehend how anyone could possibly compare you two, I shall probably not care for it when it comes. I like to think that you like Mr. Howells—he has such a warm generous feeling for you. Men, as a general thing, are not nice to each other. I told you that once before, and you laughed it to scorn. But it is true.

And now I am going on. On the subject of your book, I do'nt have my usual remembrance that you will think what I say "unimportant." It is'nt that I think it in the least important, but that I do'nt care whether it is or not; I am amusing myself—if you like. Your books are one of the entertainments of my life, and I cannot give up talking about them just to please the author. But he can always evade hearing what I have to say by not writing to me. And I shall not quarrel with you, if he does so evade. I shall go on amusing myself;—I shall talk them over with someone else.

I have come slowly to the conclusion that the *Portrait is* the finest novel you have written. "Slowly," because I so much like the others, and hate to desert old friends. I did'nt completely yield until I had read the last two chapters. Then I had to. The scene between Goodwood and Isabel at the end is, in my opinion, by far the strongest scene of the kind you have given to the public.[19] It has the naturalness which all you write possesses, but it has in addition a force (which real life does contain, I think)—a force which you have rather held back—at least the expression of it—in your other books; purposely—as I have always supposed. I wanted to see it let out a trifle. And here it is let out. I did'nt want much. But that little I did want. Now, I am satisfied.

Goodwood is a marked figure. It suits him that you have not described him minutely; he has no minuteness to describe. But you have made us feel his strength, his narrow strength, his unwasted concentrated strength. We feel him on the page as we feel the living Goodwoods—we women, I mean. We do'nt always like them, or at first prefer them; but, as we grow older, and the great insincerity of life widens out all round—then we appreciate the Goodwoods. And come back to them. Only—it is generally too late.

Most men are so stupid about some women—if you know what that means! I will restate. Most men, although clear-sighted enough about many women, remain dense about the women of Isabel's temperament. A nice man, a lawyer of more than middle-age, fond of books and society in a quiet way, wrote me not long ago—"I was vexed enough when Isabel refused Warburton. He was of course preeminently the man for her—the man with whom she would have been happy. But James, for his own purposes, preferred—" etc. etc. Now see that for denseness—Warburton! Save that he was a manly man, she might as well have married Rosier.

Warburton, by the way, is capital throughout. Is it possible the English do not see how you show them up?—I know a Warburton or two—without the title and setting—and I am never weary of noticing the narrowness, yet extreme and hopeless depth, of the chasm which separates them from the almost ideally delightful man.

Nothing could be better than the Touchetts, Henrietta and her Bantling, the Countess Gemini—whose face I perfectly see—little Rosier, and those enchanting Misses Molyneux. (Only, did they, *could* they, wear seal-skin jackets in summer? Because if they did, I can never stay long in England, much as I wish to. Life would'nt be to me "a vast old English garden," if that is the weather; nor could I even enjoy pulling "down the stream to Iffley, and to the slanting woods of Nuneham," if seal-skin jackets were required!)—Ralph is very touching. We love Ralph. Pansy is an exquisite little creature from beginning to end. I have plenty more to say about each and all of these people. But, as one envelope wo'nt carry it all, I reserve my space for the things I most wish to mention.

I think you were mistaken in the judgment of the story you gave me, briefly, in Rome—mistaken in two points. One is Madame Merle. You thought that in the beginning she was too much described—that it gave the impression that she was to be more prominent than she really becomes. I do not agree with you. She looms up in the latter part of the story so darkly and powerfully—powerfully although always in a sort of haze—that for the time being she overshadows Isabel, and one cares more for her than for the younger woman. The touch that does it is given when the Countess says—"And the end of it is that he is tired of her. And what is more, today she knows it." Life holds no deeper tragedy than that. I have never believed that bad people suffered any the less because they were bad.—And, beside Osmond, Mme Merle is almost good! Who can help feeling for her when she buries her face in her hands after Osmond's horrible—"You seem to me quite good enough," and—"Good enough to be always charming" (49th chapter). It is tragic. Yet Mme Merle herself is not tragic. The combination marks *your* skill.

The other point is Osmond. You said you saw him distinctly yourself, but that you doubted whether he would be distinct to your readers. Rest easy (only you are always easy!); he is. He is a more finished creation even than Grandcourt (*Daniel Deronda*); as distinct; more finely detestable; and haunting, and suffocating than George Eliot's Englishman, and overtopping him by not being emphasized by a violent death. It is real life in all its unavenging cold monotony that Osmond should go on living; and that point shows by how much you are the finer artist. But George Eliot could'nt stand it; she had to kill off her Englishman. A woman, after all, can never be a complete artist.

Such a character as Osmond's is an entirely new one in literature. Yet one sees at once that he is completely possible. What a combination to be fine, and fastidious, and without heart! I have known one or two persons who were cultivated, and fastidious, and without heart; but they also had a brutal side—which Osmond has not. Save in the thought, which underlies his words. The whole of the 42d chapter is a masterpiece.

I have a good deal to say about Isabel (I wo'nt say it all). With no character of yours have I ever felt myself so much in sympathy. I watched with much curiosity your Christina, Mme de Cintré, the Baroness, Mme de Mauves, and others,—I looked on with interest as Gertrude and Charlotte, Mary Garland, Bessie Alden, Angela, Catherine, poor Daisy[20] and the rest, came and went. But with Isabel it has been quite different. I found myself judging her and thinking of her with a perfect sympathy, and comprehension, and a complete acquaintance as it were; everything she did and said I judged from a personal standpoint. I never said to myself as I did about Christina, for instance—"I do'nt know;—it may be so." I always knew exactly all about Isabel. (Of course I only mean that it has seemed so. Very likely you will say that my fancied knowledge is not correct.)

Poor Isabel! poor idealizing imaginative girls the world over—sure, absolutely sure to be terribly unhappy. And the worst of it is that it cannot be prevented. One would suppose that a father and mother might do something. But, strangely enough, a mother is often the last person to understand her daughter; she understands her as her child, but not as the woman. And the father, if he really loves his child, does not welcome the thought that she may love some one else; he puts it as far from him as possible, and only accepts it, when it must be accepted, as a dose to be swallowed with as good a grace as he can summon. He never wants to talk about it beforehand! And thus the poor Isabels go believingly to their ruin. One gets hopeless enough sometimes (while watching them) to think that a duller mind, a more commonplace character, is the better gift. Simple goodness, and a gentle affectionate unjudging nature, seem the high prizes for a woman to gain in this lottery of life.

The Isabels—your Isabel—are always so sure! She *knows* she is right. She cannot say so openly, because it presupposes the superior fineness of her own comprehension and intelligence over that of her friends and relatives. And this is the fatal pitfall; because, if she could talk it over frankly with someone, she might be saved. But she never can. She sees her Osmond in a certain light; the different light in which others see him, is only their own coarser vision. And being always self-conceited—poor Isabel!—she at heart rather prefers this state of things. And so she moves onward proudly, securely, and often nobly according to her light—to the miserable end.

How you know her! In chapter 14, for instance, where she begins a half-explanation, saying that she can't escape—escape by separating herself—and the rest of it—that is a wonderful and true bit of portraiture. Again in the latter part of the 21st chapter, where she sees that she might even like the limitations of Goodwood, some day far in the future—that they might then be like "a clear and quiet harbor, enclosed by a fine granite breakwater"—that is also a perfect divination. Because that is the peculiarity of such a temperament—there is no end to the visions, the imaginations. It is like the spirit which the fisherman let out of the vial—it grows into a great mist and fills the whole sky.

Poor Isabel!—(I am afraid I shall be beginning every paragraph with that)—what a cameo-like picture of her, and her sure mistake, is that visit with Mme Merle to Osmond's villa on Bellosguardo. His method of beginning to interest her; his assumed half-embarrassment yet desire to please; his asking her how she likes his sister; his leading with him his little daughter, in her short white frock—everything so exquisitely designed and carried out to produce a certain impression—nothing underscored, all so delicately moderate.

And then the impression summed up in chapter 26—page 242—how perfectly one understands the effect—sees what she saw, feels what she felt. It was precisely the sort of picture to win an Isabel. And it almost seemed to me as if you were the only man who has ever divined it.

I have some criticisms to make. Small ones. In the 21st chapter, page 196—from the 8th line to the 20th. I do'nt altogether agree with your portraiture there. It is true that an Isabel has a great capacity for enjoying the present and the future; but it seems to me also true that the past is always safely stored in her memory. The lower floors of her tower are firm and well filled, although she enjoys life in an upper story.

Again, in chapter 27, page 255—I do'nt think she should say—"Poor Lord Warburton!" It seems to me that a girl of her age and of her delicate feeling, would not say it. A woman of the world might; but even a woman of the world would feel it to be dangerous, or at least a false note—unless she intended to yield to him sometimes. Women do'nt pity men (who amount to anything) to their faces! They often do it behind their backs.

(And I must be allowed to put in here my great satisfaction in the enchanting naturalness of Isabel's using the word—"Incommoded," and thinking it "a ridiculous word" even then, but being unable to change it—on page 272, chapter 29. I put it in here so as not to forget it. So long as you give us such morsels, you may behave as badly as you please otherwise. I do'nt know that you do. But you could.)

My last criticism is that you do not let us see, with any distinctness, whether Isabel really loved Osmond. She tells Mrs. Touchett that she does'nt love Lord Warburton; but she does'nt tell her or anybody (if my memory serves me) that she does love Gilbert Osmond. You do'nt let her even tell Osmond himself—at least with the public *entiers*. We are therefore left to a choice between two beliefs. One is that she never really loved Osmond; it is her imagination, not her love, which has been led captive. He fills an ideal. No one else did that. She *thinks* she loves him; but as she does not, the absence of heart-breaking, insupportable, killing griefs in her heart and life, after she finds out what he really is, is explained, and quite natural.

The other hypothesis is that she did love him. But that a distinct expression of it, and of the following agony, is left to the imagination of the reader, as things easily to be supplied;—according to the time-honored method of Mr. Henry James.

Personally, you know, I would rather not have it "left." But I add, with willingness, that probably you know best.

How did you ever dare write a portrait of a lady? Fancy any woman's attempting a portrait of a gentleman! Would'nt there be a storm of ridicule! Every clerk on the Maumee river would know more about it than a George Eliot. For my own part, in my small writings, I never dare put down what men are thinking, but confine myself simply to what they do and say. For, long experience has taught me that whatever I suppose them to be thinking at any especial time, that is sure to be exactly what they are *not* thinking. What they *are* thinking, however, nobody but a ghost could know.

Feb. 23*d*

I have been to Pompeii, Salerno, and Paestum. We drove from Salerno to Paestum on a divinely beautiful day, the air as soft as that of June at home, the sea and sky marvelously blue, and the landscape veiled in that soft haze you know. We had lunch in the cella of the Temple of Neptune. We gathered acanthus leaves. After gazing and gazing and gazing at everything—all so beautiful—I confess that I secretly purchased some very ancient coins, proffered by a very ancient man. If they turn out treasures, I will send you one, and you must pretend to believe it was not made in Naples, and buried by that mariner.

I look over my letter, and it seems very "unimportant!" But what can I do? I am not important, you know, and my letter is naturally like its writer. I shall probably stay here some time longer, although I am homesick for Rome. The violets will soon be out in the Villa Borghese! Of course you find the women over there "sympathetic." They are more sympathetic as well as more intelligent than any other women in all the world. Did you see a Miss Palmer? I do'nt know her in the least, but I am told that several persons have picked her out for you. The one *I* picked out you met in New York; and then you write me "no one in particular"! Remember the crooked-stick proverb.[21]

Later

A letter from Miss Dana, at Rome, mentions that a great sorrow has come to you—that your Mother is dead.[22] At first I thought I would not send this letter at all—but merely a few lines of sympathy. I will, however, let it go, as it will come to you long afterwards. A tie is broken in your life that can never be replaced, and I know you will feel it greatly. I sympathize with you the more, because I have never been my old self since my Father died, but have always felt desolate and oppressed with care without him; and then when, three years ago, my Mother too was taken, there seemed nothing left to live for. A daughter feels it more than a son, of course, because her life is so limited, bounded by home-love; but the son feels it in his own way, and I want you to believe that I am very sorry for your sorrow.—It must be a comfort to you that you were at home; and not far away in London.—Death is not terrible to me; I do'nt know what it is to you—you have never spoken of it, or alluded to it in your writings. To me it is only a release; and if, at any time, you should hear that I had died, always be sure that I was quite willing, and even glad, to go. I do'nt think this is a morbid feeling, because it is accompanied by a very strong belief, that, while we *are* here, we should do our very best, and be as courageous, and work as hard, as we possibly can.—I feel sure there are no uncertainties in your belief—whatever it may be—; you are much too calm for a person who is swayed by uncertainties.

I hope you are well; and I send you my best wishes. Take care of yourself; and be as determinedly good, in all this splendid success, as though you were a "failure." Failures often fall back on their "goodness"; let us see a man of genius who is "good" as well. Always sincerely your friend,

C. F. Woolson

1. HJ's *Hawthorne* appeared in 1879 and *The Portrait of a Lady* was serialized in 1880.

2. Miss Woolson's growing deafness.

3. HJ sailed 20 October 1881, arriving in the United States on 1 November.

4. This was HJ's first visit to Washington.

5. Victor Cherbuliez (1829–1899), a French novelist of Swiss origin who wrote novels of manners admired by HJ.

6. Miss Woolson was borne at Claremont, New Hampshire, 5 March 1840. She was three years older than HJ.

7. The Maumee river runs for 175 miles from Fort Wayne northeast to Lake Erie near Toledo.

8. W. D. Howells, "Henry James, Jr.," *Century*, XXV (November 1882), 25–29. The portrait was a study in pencil by Timothy Cole.

9. HJ had spent a week at Engelberg visiting Mrs. Kemble in the spring but had left for London by the time Miss Woolson arrived.

10. HJ had been savagely attacked by the American press for insisting on the parochialism of New England life in his critical study of Hawthorne. George W. Curtis had been among his defenders.

11. Willie Edouin (1841–1908), a well-known English low comedian.

12. Richard Henry Dana, Jr. (1815–1882), a lawyer and legal writer known principally for his seafaring novel, *Two Years before the Mast* (1840).

13. John Flaxman (1755–1826), an English neoclassical sculptor and draftsman.

14. This may have been Elizabeth Phelps-Ward (1844–1911), a Massachusetts writer of religious fiction.

15. Blanche Willis Howard (1847–1898), American novelist who lived after 1875 in Germany and became the Baroness von Teuffel. She was the author of many exotic romances. *One Summer* was published in 1875.

16. Constance Fletcher (pseud. George Fleming). See p. 459.

17. A reference to Edward Rosier, a young American character in *The Portrait of a Lady*.

18. Horace E. Scudder, "*The Portrait of a Lady* and *Dr. Breen's Practice*," *Atlantic Monthly*, XLIX (January 1882), 126–130.

19. The scene that contains the one kiss in the novel, Caspar Goodwood's passionate embrace of the heroine, Isabel Archer.

20. These HJ characters figure in the following works: Christina and Mary Garland in *Roderick Hudson* (1875); Mme de Cintré in *The American* (1877); the Baroness, Gertrude, and Charlotte in *The Europeans* (1878); Mme de Mauves in "Madame de Mauves" (1874); Bessie Alden in "An International Episode" (1879); Angela in *Confidence* (1879); Catherine in *Washington Square* (1880); Daisy in "Daisy Miller" (1878).

21. The saying she alludes to may have been: "I have an idea that gal will either die a sour old maid or have to take a crooked stick for her husband at last."

22. Mary Walsh James died on 29 January 1882.

To Henry James

Ms Harvard

(Care Knauth, Nachod, and Kühne,
Leipzig, Germany)
Dresden. Aug. 30*th* [1882]

Dear Mr. James.

School is out. And now I am going to amuse myself writing to you. As a beginning let me say that the above Leipzig address will be hereafter *my* general address, while I remain abroad. You may feel that instead of a beginning, it is an ending;—three such names are enough to end any acquaintance. I acknowledge it. But, tired of asking so many favors of Moquay, Hooker, & Co., I have been driven at last to use these Leipzig bankers because, as my Letter of Credit is upon them, I have a right to their services. Why I have a Letter of Credit upon them instead of upon Brown Brothers, or Munroe, would take too long to explain; it dates back to a period before my birth! As I write, I seem to remember, or half remember, that I sent you this Leipzig address in my last. If I did, ascribe the repetition to the curious state of fatigue in which I find myself. In Baden-Baden, for six consecutive weeks, I worked ten hours a day, and for two more (making eight in all), thirteen. I then started immediately for this place, and have not really rested at all save for a sort of serenity that came over my spirit after I had seen the Sistine Madonna and that beautiful little picture of Van Eyck's in the Holbein room—I am sure you remember it? It is the first Van Eyck I have seen, and comes fully up to my high expectations.

Do'nt suppose that I approve of such hard work as that of this summer, or of traveling when one is tired out. I do'nt. You, master of all the situations in which you find yourself, would never have been caught in any such position. But *I* am constantly doing the things I do'nt want to do. The hard work came from a misunderstanding. I had agreed to have ready a little thing for *Harper's Magazine* this autumn; as I supposed, October.[1] But in May I heard that August, not October, was the time. I had then to make a choice between disappointing the magazine people, and throwing their winter arrangements into confusion, or working very hard myself. It seemed best to do the latter. Mind you—no one else, probably, would have taken anything like the time I took for so small a piece of work. That is my own slowness. I always write very slowly, and, when there is any pressure, I write more slowly than ever! It is unfortunate for me. But cannot be helped. The work of those last two weeks—from five in the morning to six at night—was the copying—always with me a painful task. I do'nt hold a pen easily, and my hand soon becomes cramped. The arm often aches to the shoulder. And this brings back to my mind an occasion (which I have no hesitation in describing because of course you have forgotten it; you forget everything) when, seated upon a bench at the end of the pretty little Cascine, surrounded by Italian children, you said, in answer to a remark of mine, "Oh, *I* never copy." And upon a mute gesture from me, you added, "Do you think, then, that my work has the air of having been copied, and perhaps more than once?" I think I made no direct reply, then. But I will now. The gesture was despair,—despair, that, added to your other perfections, was the gift of writing as you do, at the first draft!

I finished my MS. at last, and came here as fast as I could. As you may imagine, my sister has not enjoyed my being shut up in my own rooms, invisible until evening. She wanted me to go with her to various places, among them Bayreuth, to hear *Parsifal.* But I could'nt. So she and Clare had to go without me.[2] We met here, and have still some weeks together, as she does not sail until September 21st. She greatly detests all my MSS, and has already presented me with a new dress and round-hat, so that I shall not look too "literary."

As I believe I told you, I have decided to stay on over here, for a while longer. I came very near going home. To be ill alone in a foreign land is a dreary experience. And it seemed to me as I lay feverish and coughing, that I must go home; go home, get my precious books, and little household gods together, a dog or two, and never stir again. This is the thirteenth year I have spent without a home. After the death of my father, in 1869, I took my mother south for her health, and we led a wandering life, after that, for many years, in search of climates. It was a happy life in one way, for we were together, and one's mother cares for one. But, in other ways, there is nothing like a home. My sister, however, has represented to me that probably I should not be contented (in America) without two homes—one in Florida for the winter, and in Cooperstown or Mackinac for the summers. And that all three localities she hates! In addition, she wishes to bring Clare over, now and then, during her school days, and, if *I* am here,—why, that is an anchor out. Meanwhile, as I regained my strength, I also regained my courage or some of it; and I remembered how beautiful was Italy. So here I am for an indefinite time longer. Indefinite does not necessarily mean long; it means only "indefinite." But I suppose there never was a woman so ill fitted to do without a home as I am. I am constantly trying to make temporary homes out of the impossible rooms at hotels and pensions. I never give up, though I know it cannot be done; I keep on trying. Like a poor old bird shut up in a cage, who tries to make a nest out of two wisps of straw. Or the beaver I saw in the Zoological Gardens here, who had constructed a most pathetic little dam out of a few poor fragments of old boughs. I stood and looked at that beaver a long time. He is an American—as I am! But I suppose *you* know nothing of beavers, but hats. You do'nt know beavers, or prairies; you only know—Mme de Katkoff.[3]

It was good of you to speak so sympathetically of my illness. You say you knew, in former years, what it was to be ill over here alone. I have heard that you were not strong,—that it was your health which kept you living on over here. (I do'nt believe the latter; you stay for your pleasure.) But you are such a picture of blooming composure, that I can never realize, when with you, that you have ever been ill in your life. You see I associate illness with nervousness and bones. My illness was fever, and a bad cough. The English doctor said the two had no connection with each other. I think they had. I think I had the American "lung-fever"—a fever the English have outgrown, with their avoirdupois. I presume the ancient Saxons had it—when they took cold. As I am not strong, the cough pulled me down. But I am well now, or shall be when rested. I sometimes think I was enervated by the densely sweet perfume of the miles of orange-blossoms at Sorrento. I lived in a cloud of it, day and night. It was—the air—so warm, and thick with fragrance, that it was a sort of lethargic intoxication. Or an opiate. It is so hard to leave Italy early. Yet that is what one should do—I suppose.

In your letter you say—alluding to the illness—"Pray do me the *favour* not to recommence." That brought back instantly to my mind poor little Désirée and her hummingbirds, in Daudet's "Fromont"—do you remember the place? Where she has tried to drown herself, and has been rescued, and they tell her (at the police station) that she must promise "not to recommence." She does so, and goes home. Not to recommence. By delightful good luck (once in awhile there *is* some good luck) I fell upon that very copy of the *Atlantic* which contains your article on Daudet,[4] in the reading room of this hotel. I have been anxious to read it ever since I saw it announced, and vexed enough with you because you would not send it to me! Now that I have read it, and know that you like Daudet, I dare mention Désirée. I should not have done so if I had not fallen upon this *Atlantic;* I should have thought, without it, that probably you considered him sensational. He is French; but, in some things, he captivates me, and always has. Désirée, for instance. And I do'nt know when I have enjoyed a little thing more than I did his *Tarascon,* which I chanced upon at Mentone, three years ago. I am now enchanted to know that you like him too. And I am so much obliged to you for writing that article and saying so. Your essay converted me to Tourguénieff;[5] but I had to study him for some time before it was accomplished. Daudet I liked of my own accord. By nature; not by grace. Did I tell you, by the way, that I at last got hold of that *Dominique*[6] you admire so much, and that there I am not yet converted. I suppose however it is only the different point of view.

At Bamberg, where I was wearily waiting for a train (the Crown Prince was there reviewing troops, so that the crowd was dense; and at Nuremburg, where there is a great Exposition, I could'nt get a room, tired as I was), what do you suppose I found among the news-dealer's wares? Your "Eugene Pickering" done into French under the title of *Une Femme Philosophe.*[7] Of course I instantly bought it. Have you seen it? But I should not have asked that question—there's no use. A question of any sort you never answer! If, however, you would make *one* exception and tell me—sometime when you are writing,—there is no hurry—where in London I can get some really delicious tea, its name, and the price I should pay per pound, I should be deeply grateful. I want the address for future use—as I have at present a quantity on hand,—just sent to me from America.

I am writing on in the most inconsequent inartistic way. But you know I never wrote to you half so much for your entertainment as for my own. At present it rests me to write to you. But the letter itself wo'nt be, can't be, good.—If I were clever, I should always bear in mind the fact, that when I have written to you many sheets, I have received a short note in reply, beginning with some such sentence as this: "Dear Miss Woolson. One does'nt answer your letters; one can't. One only reads them and is grateful"; and this followed up by three very small pages (in a very big hand) in which no allusion is made to anything I have said, the "faithfully" of the signature occupying the room of several of my sentences. Then, when I have written you a short note myself, I have received from you a charming letter in reply, eight pages long, and not such a very big hand either, and the "faithfully" even put across the top or side of the first page instead of being relied upon to fill the half of the last! But I am not clever. And then I am always thinking that perhaps you will improve. I hope right in the face of facts. It does'nt do any harm; and it amuses me. My idea is that we shall make a George Washington of you yet.

I sent you back that article written by Mrs. Rollins, because I supposed myself obliged to. You did not say—as you have said other times—"destroy it"; or "you need not return it." So I thought that possibly you might wish to keep it. It was certainly nice enough to keep. I continue to be jealous of her; the very fact that she did not answer your note will make you think her more important—make you like her better. Ah—do'nt suppose I do'nt know that—though I have conducted myself so differently. You see I was enjoying the pleasure of a very real and deep admiration, and, if I had to choose between that and your having, perhaps, a higher idea of me, personally—why, the first was of the most consequence to me. Especially as the second was so doubtful in any case! Mrs. Rollins can take another stand. She has, perhaps, a Greek nose.

I will now tell you that American story. Not that it has any connection with the above; I am too tired to be connected. A young lady, whom I have mentioned to you, wrote it to me just after you had left America. She said that she had met you at a dinner-party at her brother's, in New York, but, after that, she saw no more of you, to her disappointment. (You see I had written to her how nice you were. Evidently you did not take a fancy to her. I suppose because she is not tall and thin, with grey eyes! She is one of the most sympathetic girls I know. If you had cared for her, she would have adored you.) When you came back to Boston, she said to herself, "Now I shall see him." For she knew you were intimate with some intimate friends of hers, and she thought they would be having you to lunch and dinner, and that she would be included. "All of which" (I quote) "came to pass but the last part. They had him, but they did not have me! I did my best; I asked at what hours he generally came, and said frankly that I should like to happen in at the same time. But nothing definite could I get out of them. At last, after he had finally gone, I asked my friend—a most lovely girl—why I had been let so severely alone. 'It was because you were so *horrid* about him in London,' she replied. I, having a perfectly clear conscience, exclaimed at this. 'You said,' said my friend with heat, 'that he would not care for *simple* pleasures. That nothing would induce him to go, for instance, to a simple picnic!'—And all this time she has been treasuring that poor little speech of mine up against me! What do you think of a man capable of inspiring such partisanship as that?"—I wrote back that I was as bad as the Boston friend; that if anyone so much as dared to allude to you in anything less than superlatives of liking, I instantly brought out my biggest guns and blew them into mid-air in a minute. I have done it; several of my friends are floating there still! Do we spoil you, telling you such stories? But I think not. The best part of you is your incorruptible, and dignified, and reasonable modesty; and your perfectly balanced common sense. It is such a comfort that you have them! Besides, there are always, I suppose, people enough who do'nt like you, to keep the scales straight. At least I hope there are.

Baden-Baden was the prettiest little place I have ever seen. I felt so sorry that I could not spend all the time in those pretty forests all about,—forests so queer to me because they are all "preserved," —each tree known and guarded. Still, they are lovely. It is the most restful landscape I have seen. Sometimes I must go back, and walk every day for miles; in all directions. Of course I bought another copy of *Confidence*[8] (my third) to read over on the spot. I fell in love with the little Oos, and was never tired of walking in the Lichtenthaler Allée—all I had time for; though I did walk up to Hohen Baden twice, and get in some sunset hours in the dear old garden of the Schloss. We were in lodgings near the Trinkhalle. They were not "over a confectioner's," however. I could'nt find any confectioner who had rooms to let. It did'nt strike me as in the least a gay place. Plenty of stout common-looking Germans, and English girls in shirred dresses, big boots, and two-button kid gloves. But the music was very good, and I spent every evening listening to it, with closed eyes. I suppose it was gay in the gaming days. At present Newport, Saratoga, and Long Branch far outshine it in dress, carriages, jewels, and that sort of thing.—I thought of you writing *Roderick Hudson* there.[9] Would that I had been there at the same time! I should like to see you when you are actually engaged, for part of the day, upon some piece of work. I want to see if you would be cross. I am very fond of *Roderick Hudson*—as you know. Did you see the notice the *Nation*[10] (N.Y.) had of your *Portrait of a Lady*? In some respects it was very good, and, if by any chance, you have not seen it, you must let me send it to you. I kept it. It spoke of the excellence of *Roderick Hudson,* and the deliberate change you made in your writings, after it.

I am sorry that I said anything to you of my small success in *Anne,*[11] at home. When your answer came, I was vexed that I had. At the time I was writing you, I was in a state of surprise over a letter from the Messrs. Harper voluntarily doubling the sum they had already paid me for the story, and also proposing to give me a liberal percent on the sale in book form,—a thing expressly denied me in the original sale of the MS. This struck me as so remarkable that I mentioned it to you. But of course you understood that what is great success to me, would be nothing to you. All the money that I have received, and shall receive, from my long novel, does not equal probably the half of the sum you received for your first, or shortest. It is quite right that it should be so. And, even if a story of mine should have a large "popular" sale (which I do not expect), that could not alter the fact that the utmost best of my work cannot touch the hem of your first or poorest. My work is coarse beside yours. Of entirely another grade. The two should not be mentioned on the same day. Do pray believe how acutely I know this. If I feel anything in the world with earnestness it is the beauty of your writings, and any little thing I may say about my own comes from entirely another stratum; and is said because I live so alone, as regards to my writing, that sometimes when writing to you, or speaking to you—out it comes before I know it. You see,—I like so few people! Though I pass for a constantly smiling, ever-pleased person! My smile is the basest hypocrisy.

I suppose you did not go to Cooperstown at all. Mrs. Leslie [Pell-Clark][12] told Clara that you declined her invitation to visit her in the snows of winter. You did wisely. But in summer Cooperstown is very pretty, and when I have made my fortune, and built that cottage on the little lake there, you must come and stay with me, bringing with you that sweet young American wife I want you to have—whom you *must* have—even if only (as you horribly write) as "a last resort." And then you must come down to Florida, and I will show you a beautiful swamp.

I have seen the Rhine. And the Cathedral. Beautiful. But Italy is better.—All this while, even in the midst of my hard work at Baden, I have been reading *Daisy,* with the greatest delight. Each time I take it up, I like it better. I should never have believed that you could make an actable play of it, without the positive evidence of the book in my own hand; the conception seemed to me too delicate for the stage. But you have succeeded. I have always thought Daisy a masterpiece. No one but you would have dared select the subject; but some of us can at least appreciate the exquisite quality of the workmanship you have put into it. Not only that, but I have always been so proud that you were capable of the conception! Its beauty is of such a fine quality that it escapes the common observer. It was this that made it seem impossible to me, for a play. But you have arranged that difficulty by bringing out more distinctly Mme de Katkoff. Against *her,* as a background, Daisy shines out in the way the common observer can understand. (Here opens out in my mind a long parenthesis. But I will postpone it until later.) The humor all through is delicious. And the minor characters strike me as excellent for the stage: Mrs. Costello; the camp-stool youth and Miss Durant just "getting" in their proposal and acceptance; Mrs. Walker; and the always incomparable Randolf. The Italian and Eugenio are now much more distinct and strike me as capital for acting purposes. As a whole, it reminds me more of some of the perfect little French comedies I have read, than of anything we have in English. Still, I may be mistaken. I do not know much of plays. The difficulty would be, I think, to find an actress who could play Daisy. I cannot imagine an English woman in the part. A French woman would make an ingenue of it, and Daisy is not that; no American girl is—though they are as innocent as wild flowers in the woods. I hope you will let me keep the book longer.[13] It is under lock and key, and no one has seen it or heard of it; or shall ever see it, or hear of it. I am a very faithful sort of person in such respects. I want to read it more, and when I am not so tired. I will return it to you sometime during the winter. I am so desirous to know whether you are going on in this new field? And everything you are doing.

I now come back to my parenthesis. You do'nt like the "personal note" I know (poor Henrietta!), but, after admiring the play as a whole, I return to what struck me instantly upon the first reading. You may say, or not say, what you choose, but I am sure I know now, beyond a doubt, the sort of woman you care for, or rather the sort that interests you—though one side of you is against her. Probably that has been your trouble—, you could'nt unreservedly admire. Yet you do'nt care for the other kind. You touched upon the same subject in the Baroness (*Europeans*); but you felt it a sort of duty, there, to show her up; and you did it. Here, as Mme de Katkoff is a side-character, you have not felt it so necessary to point a moral. Oh, of course, for the ordinary observer, the moral is there; Daisy conquers, etc. I only mean that you hav'nt put your incomparable skill to work to make us despise her, in spite of her charm; as you make us despise the Baroness before we get through with her. You leave her as she is probably, in real life. You have'nt dissected her as a public warning.

You know I have found fault with you for not making it more evident that your heroes were in love with the heroines; really in love. There is no trouble about that here! Winterbourne is more in love with Mme de Katkoff—or has been—than any of your other men have been in love before. It has *the true ring.*—True,—there is equally no doubt of Goodwood's love for Isabel; but Goodwood was an exceptional fellow and his love is exceptional too; not a type. Winterbourne comes more within the range of one's daily life. He will love Daisy—yes. He will be a good husband. All the same, Mme de Katkoff interested him in a way far beyond Daisy's simple charm.

Do you suppose in the next world you will find a person who combines the two characters? That is what you want.

I must stop; it is late. I hope you are well, and happy. I send you my best wishes.

Always sincerely your friend,
C. F. Woolson

1. Miss Woolson's short novel, *For the Major,* began serialization in *Harper's* in November 1882.

2. Clara Woolson Benedict was Miss Woolson's widowed younger sister; Clare was her niece.

3. The "wicked" European lady in HJ's dramatic version of "Daisy Miller."

4. Alphonse Daudet's two novels were *Fromont jeune et Risler aîné* (1874) and *Tartarin de Tarascon* (1872). HJ reviewed Ernest Daudet's *Mon frère et moi* in the *Atlantic Monthly,* XLIX (June 1882), 846–851.

5. The essay on Turgenev appeared in *French Poets and Novelists* (1878).

6. *Dominique* (1863), the only novel of the painter and art critic Eugène Fromentin (1820–1876), regarded as one of the very few novels of psychological analysis in French literature before 1880.

7. HJ's tale "Eugene Pickering" (1874) translated by Lucien Biart in the *Revue des Deux Mondes,* 1 January 1876, and reprinted in 1876 as *Une Femme Philosophe: Le Premier Amour d'Eugène Pickering* along with stories by Bret Harte and Michel Masson.

8. A large part of *Confidence* (1879) is set in Baden-Baden.

9. HJ had stayed in Baden-Baden for five or six weeks during the summer of 1874 when he was working on *Roderick Hudson.*

10. Anonymous review of HJ's *The Portrait of a Lady, Nation,* XXXIV (2 February 1882), 102–103.

11. Miss Woolson's highly popular novel *Anne* was published in 1882 both in New York and in London.

12. Henrietta Pell-Clark, a sister of Minny Temple, had given Miss Woolson her original letter of introduction to Henry James.

13. HJ had evidently sent Miss Woolson a copy of his dramatization of *Daisy Miller: A Comedy* (1882), printed at his own expense by Macmillan for copyright protection. It was published in 1883.

To Henry James
Ms Harvard

(My general address is always:
"Care Knauth, Nachod, and Kühne,
Leipzig, Germany.")
Venice. May 7*th* [1883]

Dear Mr. James.

I have been wishing to write to you ever since I reached Venice (about two weeks ago), because I know how fond you are of the beautiful old water-city, and I thought that perhaps the sight of a

"Venezia" postmark might please your expatriated[1] eyes. I do'nt know how long I should have held out—against the wish to give you this faint little pleasure; fortunately I am not called upon to solve the question, because, at Blumenthal's, the other day (my gondola waiting at "the wave-washed steps"), I found your letter of April 17th—which had been forwarded from Florence. I was very glad to get it.

You asked for "a picture"—to keep you "going." But it wo'nt be Florentine—or even Bellosguardo—as you imagined. Do you know the Palazzo Gritti-Swift? Probably not—by that name. Well, then, do you know the dilapidated old yellow palace, not quite opposite Santa Maria della Salute—below it—which is decorated with the signs of "Salviati?" I presume you do—because you are so fond of signs. In this old palace—on the top floor (third), are two large low-ceilinged rooms, with round-arched windows, and small—very small—balconies, on the Grand Canal. In addition there are two side-windows, one of which is the treasure of the abode because it faces the east (jutting out beyond the next palace), commanding the harbor, the Riva with its masts, the fresh green of the Public Gardens, and, best of all, San Giorgio Maggiore, its pink campanile tipped with your tall gold angel—the other side-window—by greatest good-fortune—looks directly down into one of the narrowest and darkest emerald-green canals in the city; so narrow that the gondolas can pass only by closely hugging the walls. You may be sure that I immediately demanded cushions of the padrona, for my little balconies (they are so small—the balconies—that you use them as sofas), and that these cushions are freshly covered with red. And that I also have red ledges for my two side-windows. Nothing but red would do.

Now should'nt all this make me happy? If you will only stop treating me as you did about the "Salvini" article,[2] it will.

To my top floor, a very winding stone stairway leads—like a stairway in a lighthouse—though it is'nt by any means a light stairway. And, when at last you reach the top floor, you find the entrance-door guarded by a little loophole, with a grating over it; and through this aperture the handsome Italian maid, Pietra, will inspect you, before she lets you in. And when at last you are in, you can't imagine where to go, so involuted is the hall, with all sorts of inscrutable doors, and curtains, and even steps (though you know you are at the very top of the house) leading out of it.

And, down below, the water-story ("sea-story" of Ruskin) is the lowest and darkest I have seen—empty, save for high-backed seats, with a coat of arms painted on them, fixed against the walls. And then, suddenly, out of this low vast hall, opens an ideal courtyard, with a round well, armorial bearings set on the pink facade, a willow tree, and an *outside* stairway of ancient white marble, which leads up to the second story, at present most happily occupied by no less a personage than Mr. Symonds, the English writer on Italian Art.[3] I do'nt know him; but he leans from his balcony below, as I lean from mine above; and I wonder if he is writing any more of those articles of his,—so rich in some aspect, so fatally defective in others. He little knows that he has an American, who criticizes him, over his head! And he would'nt care if he did know;—which is the advantage of an English temperament. When Miss Poynter comes over from Florence to visit the Symonds, she will be astonished to find me above her. Miss Poynter I met in Florence; and liked. She is a sister of Mr. Poynter,[4] the artist, whom perhaps you know. A writer herself, *very* quiet, and typically "English" in appearance and dress—I thought her at heart more—more appreciative—than some of the English ladies I met at the same time.

Behold me, then, established. Nothing could possibly be more deeply Venetian than my surroundings. How long do I expect to stay? I do'nt know. I am here at last. Here at the perfect season of the year;—and I have no plan or date for departing. I suppose sometime I must go away; if it should become too hot, for instance. Through May and June I shall remain; and possibly July. Then I shall seek the mountains somewhere—on the general principle that a whole summer in Italy is not the best thing for an American woman. Though I do'nt know that it makes much difference now —I am so shamefully well. I am well all the time—every minute. And the back view of me as I depart from you, is like that of a Veronese woman! One of the elderly ones, not very clearly seen.

Do you want to know what I am doing here? I get up very early; look out of the arched windows; have my coffee; look out of the arched windows; see to the flowers (for of course I have ever so many, all in pots, all in bloom); and more looking out of the windows. Then I write, for a good part of the day (diversified by occasional looking), until it gets to be, say, four o'clock. Then—

having had a bowl of bread and milk meanwhile—I put on my straw hat, and go down my lighthouse stairs, and either take a gondola and float luxuriously through all the color until six; or else I go, on foot, to all sorts of enchanting places—like Santa Maria dell' Orto,—over myriad bridges, losing my way all the time and enjoying it, and wondering only now and then how I shall ever be able to get away from Venice; whether the end of the riddle of my existence may not be, after all, to live here, and die here, and be buried on that plateau in the lagoon. This prospect does'nt make me sad at all, and I come home,—having dined on color—to my tangible dinner—first, of course, stopping in at St. Mark's for a few minutes, as a fit close for the beautiful day. Then, immediately after dinner, out I go again in another gondola. And when respectability requires that I should come within at last, I come. And then I sit in my red-cushioned balcony, and watch the lights on the gliding gondolas, and the colored lanterns of the music-barges, and listen for something of the music—and make out Schubert's "Serenade." Is'nt this being as happy as Fate allows us—no, I mean allows *me*—to be?

But what can I say to you—in reality—of all the enchantment,—all the delicious, rich, lovable beauty of this sweet place, when you know it all so well,—when you have written out your feeling about it in those exquisite pages[5] I love so much myself—whose every word I know, almost by heart. The magazine containing them lies on this table as I write—the copy you sent me in Paris. And I care so very much for it that—like the old Indulgences—you may sin a good deal, on the strength of it; let letters lie forever unanswered; not answer them even when you do write; stay continually over there in America; etc. etc. Of course I have all Ruskin, and read it. And of course I go to see Tintorettos. And Carpaccios. And Bellinis. And I stand in front of the "Europa" picture, and fail to "ache with envy";—yet comprehend that you may feel differently about it; though still I think you like a Memling better. I wander everywhere. I shall never come to the end of it. I can't begin to tell you. And why should I try, when you know it all so much better than I do? In the same way; but better. I wonder if you will understand me if I should tell you that this is the deepest charm of your writings to me—; they voice for me—as nothing else ever has—my own feelings; those that are so deep—so a part of me, that I cannot express them, and do not try to; never think of trying to. Once, at a dinner-party in Florence this last winter—a small one—the conversation had turned upon Clarence King[6] (that remarkable man); and, as it veered from the subject again, John Hay, who sat next me, could not let it go without a few words more; so he said to me—under cover of much talking among the others—"When I heard, the other day at Cannes, that King was in Paris again, I felt like taking the next train there! I said to myself—'Ah, where *he* is, there is my true country, my real home.' " I think I have got the words—or very nearly—for they made an impression upon my memory; John Hay was so much in earnest as he said it—though he spoke, too, with a half-laugh. Well—that is my feeling with regard to your writings; they are my true country, my real home. And nothing else ever is fully—try as I may to think so. Do you think this is quite an assumption,—or presumption? But one may be as quiet as possible, yet comprehend. One may be a bad workman one's self, yet appreciate perfect work. One may admire the path (as Mr. Wentworth said to Felix—with variations)[7] which one is at the same time, unable to follow. If you will only bear all this in mind, it will—or should—excuse me to you; for your writings have been to me like a new, and beautiful, and unexpected land.

Do you know, by the way, how much John Hay is your friend? I did not, until one day in the Boboli Gardens, when he said—among other things—(I omit the context): "If anyone speaks against James' writings in my presence, I consign that person to contempt. And if anyone speaks against James himself, I immediately *hate* him" (the speaker). "He cares nothing for me; I have always known it, and it came out again, plainly, in Paris. But I care a great deal for him." You will be glad to know that John Hay is better. I have just had a letter from him, describing with enthusiasm the "carpets of primroses" they had seen, on some of their English excursions. They sail for home, May tenth.

You once remarked to me that Mrs. Hay occasionally expressed herself with a singular lack of cultivation. What, then, do you say of Mrs. Howells? (I have not known her until this past winter.) It seems to me that Mrs. Hay has at least a large, and even noble, nature; that she is above the petty things of life. Small feminine malice, and everlasting little jealousies.—I am afraid I fail to please Mrs. Howells. Yet I have tried—; because she is Mr. Howells' wife;

I have tried a good deal. And failed. I do'nt in the least mean, however, that we have had any difficulty. Far from it. She would probably tell you (at least I *think* she would; I never feel sure what she will do!) that we—she and I—were "great friends." Certainly, I have seen her often.—Ah, well—why should I care? Probably because Mr. Howells is your friend—an especial one, I mean. For herself, she is happy (or should be; though she never seems to be *very* happy about anything), because Mr. Howells is entirely devoted to her, markedly so; and he thinks everything she says, and does, most admirable. I like Mr. Howells. He strikes me as having strong convictions, and even principles (the old-fashioned ones which have rather gone out of fashion); and as standing by them honestly, and as closely as he can. He has never had a millionth part of your experience in the world—the world of society. And he is as unlike you as it is possible to be. Perhaps I do'nt do him justice; I have seen—known—*so* many men of his manner and experience. They were all (no; almost all) I knew, when I lived, in the old days, in Cleveland ("Cleveland, *Ohio*," *you* would say in your amusing foreign way). I have to put in "the old days," because even Cleveland—*Ohio*—has gone ahead, and become cultured; I am told there is now no end to their cultivation, out there.

I might as well say, here, that my regard for Mr. Howells (a regard he cares nothing for)—made me at last consent (it is a long story; I will tell it to you, if we ever meet again on this earth; on the next, I prefer to forget it) to a horrible suggestion for a portrait-medallion, to be made by Mr. Mead, Mrs. Howells' brother.[8] The whole thing was, and is, acutely disagreeable to me. I made a great sacrifice; which they did not in the least—and never will—appreciate. Comfort me a little by appreciating it yourself. I am not a subject for a sculptor; as far as possible from it. In addition, I do not think that because a woman happens to write a little, herself, or her personality in any way, becomes the property of the public. Mr. Mead has done Mr. Howells, and admirably. John Hay,—not so well. He wishes to do you. For a man, that sort of thing is quite in order, and I beg you to consent when next you find yourself in Florence.[9] It is the only thing that can console me, in a measure, for my own sufferings in the matter. You have just the profile for it. And be sure and have the exact profile. I do not like the picture in the *Century,* nor the photograph I have (should you ever feel generous, you would send me another), because they are not exact profiles. I am rather devoted to profiles; it is the profile-view of a face that I notice first; and remember longest.

I have something for you—if you will have it. Two Greek coins. I had them set, by Accorisi of Florence, as scarf-pins. It is quite probable that the settings are not at all right; but they could easily be changed. I have a weakness for old coins, and have bought several—in Paestum, Sorrento, Rome—only to find that they were not "old." Mr. Felton—who belonged to our Florentine walking-parties until he went off to Athens—wore a beauty, and, upon my speaking of it one day, he said, that, if I had a fancy for such things, perhaps I could get one from Mr. Stillman (whom perhaps you know), as he had a few fine ones. It ended in my getting three. One—an owl—I have kept for myself. The others are, first: "Drachm of Thebes.[10] Obverse: head of Bacchus, bearded, crowned with ivy. Reverse: Shield of Boeotia." Second—and much smaller,—"Drachm of Thebes. Obverse: wine-jar. Reverse: Shield of Boeotia." Date of both, 350 B.C. I should say that the coins are not especially beautiful, in themselves. The head of Bacchus was the rarest Mr. Stillman had. Was'nt it Benvolio who wore a Syracusan coin?[11] I asked Mr. Stillman if he had any "Syracusan coins." And he was rather scornful about them; said his Greek ones were better. Such as they are, they await you here, in a little satin case—if you will have them. I confess I am going on general principles merely—having seen you wearing six rings on one hand, you know. Perhaps you will say that rings are not scarf-pins, and that scarf-pins you detest, and never wear. In that case you must wait until I can dig up an antique intaglio for you on the Campagna; and then you will have seven.[12] Rings, I mean. If I had not dug it up myself, I should never believe—nor you either—that it was authentic. Nobody knows of my coins—the ones destined for you. So, will you have them, and shall I send them to America, and by whom? Or, will you have them, and shall I keep them, and send them to your London lodgings—should you ever arrive there during this life? or, do you really not care for scarf-pins at all, and, in that case, shall I wear them myself—all in a row—the owl, the head of Bacchus, and the Shield of Boeotia—astonishing newly arrived American ladies, who wear only diamonds, and mosaics? John Hay says (I seem to be all the time quoting him! But wait—I have Julian Hawthorne[13] still in reserve) that you have "extraordinary candor." So be candid now; I only want to do what you like best.

You ask what the winter gave me. Not much—save such advantage as may be derived from constantly seeing a "lot of people," and caring not in the least for it, or them. (Let me put in, though, that I *did* have a great many most delightful walks, over the Tuscan hills in all directions—walks of six and eight miles in length.) Florentine society—as I saw it,—seemed to me like that picture of wraiths and shades being swept round in a great, misty, crowded circle, by some bewildering and never-ceasing wind; I do'nt know whether it is Flaxman's with "attenuated outlines," or Blake's. Have'nt you heard that Mr. Howells was left without a moment to himself, and that his wife could not begin to keep up with their invitations, engagements, and calls? The same fate that befell the great masculine Lion, befell the very little feminine one—though on a *much* smaller scale. We happened to be the only Americans in a crowd of English—I mean American writers. Nobody knew of me, of course, as they knew of him; but because I was there, and an American, and the only one, they sometimes included me, when they were inviting him. The English invitations came, I think, from their usual half-patronising, half interested curiosity. And the Americans, of course—residents and tourists—rallied round their national productives.—I do'nt know how the Howellses liked it. I did not like it at all. And never again, if I can possibly help it, shall I be drawn into anything of the "society" over here. It does'nt amuse me. Nor do I amuse it. Did we see the best, you ask? I doubt it. And here let me whisper to you, in all confidence, that this was the Howells'—I wo'nt say mistake,—for perhaps they did it on purpose; preferred it. One day, you would hear of them, dining with very nice people. The next, they would be at a reception given by persons of whom the first people—those of the dinner—had probably never heard. They made no distinctions. Perhaps they would say they could not.

For my own part, I met a few people I liked; saw hosts I cared nothing for; and a few I greatly disliked. Let me see if I met any one you may perhaps know. Mme Villari[14]—who says she knows Mrs. Kemble; and Mr. Cross. Mme Rahe—who lives in the Via del Mandorlo, and entertains a good deal, and had to visit her a Mr.—Synge or some such name, whom I was given to understand was a

London literary man. But I did not see him. Mrs. Lamont Thompson (I saw a great deal of her), who is clever, but *perchée*—as you said of Mrs. McKaye—on her "family." I saw Miss Greenough often. She was very kind to me—asking me a number of times to come up to the villa and lunch with her. She had a lovely plan, towards the last; nothing less than that I should take Mrs. Bracken's apartment, under her winter one, and spend the summer in Bellosguardo. She made terms with Mrs. Bracken for me, and was so good as to do everything she could in the matter. I hesitated some time over this; it was a temptation; the greatest I have had in Italy. You know how I adore that view,—down the valley of the Arno towards the west. And I should have had that old garden—with the parapet. But I have the conviction that a whole summer in Italy is not the best thing for me (I do'nt in the least mind dying, you know, if one could be sure to die, and have it over; but I have a horror of being ill—ill a long time, over here all alone). In addition, Mrs. Bracken's furniture is all "choice"; each article has been "collected," with affection and care—as I understand it; every table is a "treasure," and every chair "cinque-cento." And I did'nt want to spend the summer thinking of chairs. Also, she wished me to keep her two servants; and thus it would have ended, probably, in my living as *they* wished, because I should not have had the power to discharge them. *Do'nt betray* me, I know Mr. Boott corresponds with Miss G. but I was a little afraid, too, of Miss Greenough herself; the dear old lady had plans for our taking "excursions" together, and "drives"; and all sorts of things. These were delightful in themselves, and I like Miss Greenough much. But I cannot give the time for that sort of life this summer. I am such an absurd individual that, if I know that "at four o'clock" I must go somewhere, with somebody, I cannot write at ten, or at two. If I have not promised to go, beforehand, if there is no engagement, it is very probable that "at four o'clock," I shall find myself delighted to do the very thing. But, I must not know it beforehand. I must have the day serenely free. I go into these details because the villa is yours, you know; Osmond and you have known, perhaps, how I have wished to live on Bellosguardo.—Mrs. Bracken's rooms are a *terrano*, and just a trifle gloomy. Miss Greenough herself has all the best rooms in that house.

I am most sorry to hear that you have had "care, and anxiety." It is difficult for me to think of you with anything of that sort to bear. I have thought of you as a little spoiled; yet have rather enjoyed it—in you. Perhaps a little "care" will be good for you. I hear you are staying on in America to be with your sister, who is now, save for you, left alone. That you are doing this only confirmed my idea of you—that you are, really, the kindest hearted man I know,—though that is not, perhaps, the outside opinion about you.

Oh—such a quantity as I have heard about you, lately! I mean, since I last wrote. Names—dates—or rather times; all sorts of gossip. Nothing against you, though. I would tell you, if I supposed it would amuse you. But you have never responded when I have put in such things. So I leave it out.

You could not possibly have pleased me more than by telling me—as you do in this letter—of your plans for work. I have often thought of the motif you told me about, in Rome; now I shall see it completed. You have undertaken a great deal. But I am very glad you have undertaken it. You will do it all; and superbly. There is no one like you; and pretty much everyone—(who amounts to anything)—knows it now. Tourguénieff is dying, I hear. You are now our Tourguénieff. (I do'nt mean that you are like him; but that you have his importance.) The other day, in New York, my sister dined with the Stedmans, to meet the Julian Hawthornes and Whitelaw Reids.[15] Mr. Hawthorne was assigned to her, and she liked him so much. She writes me that the conversation turned principally upon yourself, and Mr. Howells, and that a great many bright things were said. Then she goes on to add "Mr. Hawthorne, in his slow deliberate way (such a contrast to the quickness of the other two men), said this: "I like, I greatly admire, *every word James ever wrote in his life.*"—Do you smile at my putting these little things in? I do it because they please me so much, myself.

I shall be delighted to get the criticisms in the *Century*, if you will be so good as to send them. That you did not send the "Salvini" (I have it, however) gave me a quite little ache of disappointment. I had not expected you to write; I never want you to do that, until just the right time and mood come to you,—though you should wait months for them; but I did think that perhaps you would send the magazine. When you did not, I drew the conclusion that you were tired of sending. It must come, of course—, I mean that you should be tired. But—stretch it a little longer. When I go home, I cut the thread of everything over here. And then you need send no more. I wonder if you have seen Clara Morris[16] with Salvini, and what you think of her. And I remember that—but I wo'nt go on; it was only about someone who was such an admirer of Salvini.

I speak of going home. It will not be this next winter, probably. I am thinking of trying Algiers. What do you say to that plan for me? I should at least have the climate I like—the climate of Florida. It is all very well to hold out the prospect of "talking it over" (the going home) "against an Italian church-wall." Your letters are better than you are. You are never in Italy, but always in America; just going; or there; or just returned. And as to a "church-wall," there has never been but that one short time (three years ago—in Florence) when you seem disposed for that sort of thing. How many times have I seen you, in the long months that make up three long years? I do'nt complain, for there is no reason in the world why I should expect to see you; only, do'nt put in these decorative sentences about "Italian church-walls."

There is a very nice sofa here, placed at just the angle that commands the beautiful eastern view. And there is a tea-table, with the same sputtering little kettle you saw in my sky-parlor at Rome (I have left my nicer one, packed, at Florence). If you could come in now, and rest a while (till time to go to the next dinner-party), I would make you some of the water-bewitched you consider "tea." And you would find at least the atmosphere of a very perfect kindness. You say you "fall back" upon my "charity," feeling that it is "infinite." You can safely fall back; for infinite it is. Only charity is not precisely the word. Call it, rather, gratitude. This is'nt for you, personally—though of course you have to be included; it is for your books. You may be what you please, so long as you write as you do.

I have scribbled a very long letter. It is because I am in Venice. I do not ask you to answer at present; I give you six months to do it in. I am entirely in earnest when I say this; and I should be glad if, once in a while, you would believe me. I expect to be very busy all summer; and you will be the same. So, send me, as they come out, the *Century* articles;[17] and answer this next year. Oh—I forgot the coins. If you would like them sent to America, you will have to write a line—wo'nt you.

I send my Venetian blessing to you. I am now going to San Georgio Schiavoni, and then, on foot, to the far Fondamente Nuova, for a breezy walk; then home by gondola, on the Grand Canal. If there is anything in the world I can do for you here, command me. The Howellses are at the "Citta di Monaco," and Winifred is better, and enjoys Venice—which makes her father and mother happy.—Your lodgings (at least those belonging to the number I remember) are to let; white papers are pasted on the shutters. I go by, on my way to the Gardens; but I do'nt see the young lady, with one little white button on her black gloves.[18] Good-by. I hope you keep well. Be quite sure that you have added much to the pleasure of my summer by writing as you have; and that I shall often think of you, as I grow fonder and fonder of all this beauty you love so well.

Yours sincerely,
C. F. Woolson.

Mr. Howells seems very much attached to you.

Perhaps you will go to Cooperstown this summer. If you do, please go and see my dear cousins, the Coopers. They are old ladies now. I have plenty of relatives in Cooperstown; but these are the ones I love best. Only, you need'nt say I said so!

1. HJ had returned to the United States in December 1882 for the death of his father.

2. Apparently a reference to HJ's article on the Italian actor in the *Atlantic Monthly,* LI (March 1883), 377–386.

3. John Addington Symonds. See letter of 22 February 1884.

4. Edward John Poynter (1836–1919), a distinguished painter, later knighted and made President of the Royal Academy. See letter of 8 June 1893.

5. HJ's essay on Venice in the *Century,* XXV (November 1882), 3–23, reprinted in *Portraits of Places* (1883) and *Italian Hours* (1909).

6. See Letter to John Hay, 24 December 1886.

7. In *The Europeans* (1878).

8. Larkin G. Mead (1835–1910), an American sculptor and illustrator with a studio in Florence.

9. Mead executed a medallion of HJ, commissioned by John Hay, during 1887.

10. Drachm or drachma, a unit of weight, also an ancient Greek silver coin.

11. In HJ's story "Benvolio," *Galaxy,* XX (August 1875), 209–235, Benvolio wears on occasion "his hat on his ear, a rose in his button-hole, a wonderful intaglio or an antique Syracusan coin, by way of a pin, in his cravat." Later photographs exist showing HJ wearing a tie-pin that fits Miss Woolson's description, apparently her gift to him.

12. An allusion to HJ's early tale "Adina," *Scribner's Monthly,* VIII (May–June 1874), 33–43, 181–191, in which a ring of the Emperor Tiberius is found in the Campagna.

13. See letter to Charles Eliot Norton, 6 December 1886, n. 6. See also *Letters* II, 216–217.

14. See letter to William James, 20 January 1893.

15. Edmund Clarence Stedman (1833–1908), a successful Wall Street broker who was also a poet; Whitelaw Reid (1837–1912), editor of the New York *Tribune.*

16. Clara Morris (1848–1925), an American actress.

17. Two essays published in the *Century:* one on Trollope, XXVI (July 1883), 384–395, and one on Daudet, XXVI (August 1883), 498–509.

18. In his article on Venice in the *Century* (see n. 5) HJ spoke of a Venetian dancer, a niece of his landlady, who "hovered about the premises in a velvet jacket and a pair of black kid gloves with one white little button."

To Henry James
Ms Harvard

Venice. May 24*th* [1883]

Dear Mr. James.

I have been thinking about all this work you have undertaken; and I have wished that I could send you a message across the ocean —a spoken one. I will write it instead; you will believe, I hope, that it is said with the utmost sincerity, though you may not care for it in itself.—In one of the three novels—or if that is impossible, in one of the shorter stories, why not give us a woman for whom we can feel a real love? There are such surely in the world. I am certain you have known some, for you bear the traces—among thicker traces of another sort.—I do not plead that she should be happy; or even fortunate; but let her be distinctly lovable; perhaps, let some one love her very much; but, at any rate, let *her* love, and let us see that she does; do not leave it merely implied. In brief, let us care for her, and even greatly. If you will only care for her yourself as you describe her, the thing is done.

We pitied Mme de Cintré, and we pitied Daisy. One step more and we should have loved them. To my idea, all that was needed—and the same applies to Isabel—was that we should have been sure that they themselves loved—really loved; that Mme de Cintré felt for Newman the first love of a repressed, until then unopened, heart; and, that, fluttering in poor Daisy's primitive soul, was the beginning of a real love for Winterbourne.

If you answer that the reason you did not make a love of this sort clear was simply because it was not clear—was not clear to themselves; that Mme de Cintré's feeling for Newman was a mixture of gratitude, tremulous suspense, and sweet surprise; and that Daisy hardly knew herself whether she loved Winterbourne or not; and that Isabel was led more by her imagination than by simple love—if you say all this, then I reply, take the one further step, and use your perfect art in delineating a real love as it really is. For you will never deny that it exists—though it may be rare.

There was Mary Garland—but I never liked her; and you yourself confessed that you did not like her, either—; that is, not very much; (which of course, *en passant,* is the reason I—representing here the public—did not care for her); and Gertrude is but a sketch; though in the right direction.

You have described some men who really love. Now give us a woman who loves.

Believe me, it is the touchstone to sympathy. Why—I even cared (for a few moments) for Mme Merle, as she sat with her face buried in her hands before the man she had once loved, while he said "Good enough to be always charming." One feels, there, that she *had* loved him. But with Isabel one is not so sure—you do not allow one to be; one is not certain whether, added to her dread and horror, is a tortured love—or not. On the whole, I think I fancied that her love for Osmond (if she ever had really loved him) had died, early in her married life.

This is all commonplace enough no doubt; this desire in the reader to be stirred; to be worked upon; to care. But I only ask you to do it once. You can do, and have shown that you can do, everything else; now do that also. And silence those who say you cannot—when it is simply that you have not chosen to do it.

Last of all forgive me—if you dislike what I have said.

But no, that is not quite last. Quite last is that if your judgment pushes away all these suggestions of mine, I yield. You know best.

The Howells have gone. I am sorry. I went with Mr. H. to a reception on board a steamship here, and met a Mrs. Bronson.[1] The Captain came to me and said a lady wished to be introduced. The introduction was made, and we sat down to talk a while. Of course it was *Anne* (*Anne* is a book I once wrote),[2] and the lady paid me some very pretty compliments. I had no idea who she was (I never have, you know; never get a name right; Mrs. Howells had been carried off to see some English people, so I was vaguely looking on), and I think she may have thought that I received her compliments rather as though they were perfunctory, for she appealed to a friend near. "I want you to tell Miss Woolson how few novels I really like. How I *hate* most of them." The lady appealed to, confirmed this statement, and informed me that the other woman, the first speaker, generally threw all the new novels on the floor, after the first few pages. They then abused Hardy's last,[3] and one or two others; and then the friend began "And as to James"—Here I woke up. "Oh," I said "*of course* you like James. I am sure you like all he has written—as I do." Upon this the lady who had asked to be introduced to me began to look pleased, and—I hardly know what to call it—happier; less indifferent, less cold. "Mr. James is one of my dearest friends," she said. "He is also a friend of mine," I answered. Upon this we both began to smile and be content. She informed me (upon my speaking of that "Venice" article of which I am so fond) that it was *her* balcony where you used to end your Venetian day, with a cigarette.[4] I had'nt anything so nice to tell her in return; but it did quite as well for me to admire her advantage—which I most cordially did. She has asked me to come and see her. I do'nt know that I shall go—because I do not want to be making calls here. Yet perhaps I may go once, as she is sure to be charming if she is such a friend of yours. I mean that I shall be sure to like her if she likes you as much as she appeared to, on the steamer. Yesterday I saw a lovely Cinna in Santo Maria de Cassine; I wonder if you remember it? I have paid two visits to San Giovanni Crisostomo to see your two pictures.[5] Here is a piece of good fortune: they are repairing the Nun's Chapel in San Zaccaria, and the beautiful Bellini is out in the church, in an excellent light, and seeable position. The lagoons, the Piazzetta, and the little still canals all send their love to you. They wish you were here. And so do I. I could go by in a gondola, you know, and see you on Mrs. B.'s balcony. That would—be something. Good-by.

C.F.W.

1. Katherine De Kay Bronson.
2. See Miss Woolson's letter of 7 May 1883, n. 10.
3. This might have been *Two on a Tower* (1882).
4. See Miss Woolson's letter of 7 May 1883, n. 5. Miss Woolson is referring to the last few sentences in the article: "If you are happy, you will find yourself after a June day in Venice (about ten o'clock), on a balcony that overhangs the Grand Canal, with your elbows on the broad ledge, a cigarette in your teeth and

a little good company beside you . . . The serenading (in particular) is overdone; but on such a balcony as I speak of you needn't suffer from it, for in the apartment behind you—an accessible refuge—there is more good company, there are more cigarettes. If you are wise you will step back there presently."

5. The two pictures, dealt with in some detail by HJ in his Venice essay, were Giovanni Bellini's St. Jerome, "a delightful old personage" painted in a red dress; and a smallish canvas of Sebastian del Piombo placed above the high altar of San Giovanni Crisostomo. HJ was particularly drawn to "three figures of Venetian ladies which occupy the foreground." The ladies hold little white caskets. Two are in profile, one is full face and "walks like a goddess . . . It is impossible to conceive a more perfect expression of the aristocratic spirit, either in its pride or in its benignity . . . But for all this, there are depths of possible disorder in her light-coloured eye."

Index